THE CHANGING CONSTITUTION

THE CHANGING CONSTITUTION

Eighth Edition

EDITED BY

JEFFREY JOWELL
DAWN OLIVER
COLM O'CINNEIDE

OXFORD
UNIVERSITY PRESS

OXFORD
UNIVERSITY PRESS

Great Clarendon Street, Oxford, OX2 6DP,
United Kingdom

Oxford University Press is a department of the University of Oxford.
It furthers the University's objective of excellence in research, scholarship,
and education by publishing worldwide. Oxford is a registered trade mark of
Oxford University Press in the UK and in certain other countries

© Oxford University Press 2015

The moral rights of the authors have been asserted

Fifth Edition 2004
Sixth Edition 2007
Seventh Edition 2011

Impression: 1

Public sector information reproduced under Open Government Licence v2.0
(http://www.nationalarchives.gov.uk/doc/open-government-licence/open-government-licence.htm)

Published in the United States of America by Oxford University Press
198 Madison Avenue, New York, NY 10016, United States of America

British Library Cataloguing in Publication Data
Data available

Library of Congress Control Number: 2014959961

ISBN 978–0–19–870982–4

Printed in Great Britain by
Ashford Colour Press Ltd, Gosport, Hampshire

PREFACE TO THE EIGHTH EDITION

In our introductory chapter to this edition, we reflect on the thirty years of constitutional change since this volume first appeared in 1985: the pace of change seems to be ever-quickening. Empirical evidence for that proposition can be found in successive editions of this volume. This edition is no exception. All seven of the authors who contributed to the previous edition have revised and updated their chapters to a greater extent than has been necessary in previous editions. And seven of the chapters are new.

NEW TO THIS EDITION

Having co-edited this book since its first edition in 1985, Jowell and Oliver are delighted that Colm O'Cinneide has joined the editorial team.

Mark Elliott's chapter on parliamentary sovereignty focuses on the multi-layered nature of the UK's constitutional arrangements, their effects on the legal doctrine of parliamentary sovereignty, and in particular the paradox that a law may be valid and yet 'unconstitutional'. Colm O'Cinneide's chapter on human rights analyses the controversial role played by the Human Rights Act 1998 and other legal tools for protecting fundamental rights and liberties within the overall functioning of the UK's constitutional system. Philip Norton's discussion of Parliament focuses on the House of Commons' assertiveness in relations with the government, especially since 2010 and its direct engagement with the public, and on the increasing importance of the House of Lords in the intra-parliamentary scrutiny of bills and draft bills.

The Coalition government of 2010 to 2015 affected the operation of the executive radically: Richard Rawlings analyses the implications for constitutional conventions including individual and collective ministerial responsibility to Parliament. Other reforms to executive arrangements, not all connected with the coalition, include the placing of the civil service on a statutory basis, agencification, and an attempt at a 'bonfire of the quangos'. In the light of the devolution of powers to Scotland, Wales, and Northern Ireland, relationships between the UK/English executive and devolved bodies suggest the development of a 'New Union' mindset.

Changes to the infrastructure of the system of justice—courts and tribunals—are the focus of Andrew Le Sueur's chapter. He notes the potential for conflict between judges as experts and politicians under the new dispensation of the Constitutional Reform Act 2005 and in the light of austerity cuts and suggests that a system in which politics and expertise are blended rather than separated would be more likely to produce good policies.

There have been dramatic changes to arrangements for devolution to Scotland, Wales, and Northern Ireland since the seventh edition, and in the aftermath of the Scottish independence referendum of September 2014 further changes are inevitable. Brice Dickson explores these, including how the exclusion of England from the devolution process might be dealt with, and implications of devolution for the working of the House of Commons.

Dawn Oliver's new chapter explores the process by which powers that have in the past been exercised by ministers have been transferred to arm's-length bodies, and the development of intra-governmental soft law to set the 'rules of the game' and regulate the exercise of political powers that remain in the hands of government.

We are grateful to all the authors for their considerable efforts and to Tom Young and Carol Barber at Oxford University Press for their encouragement and assistance. Thanks to OUP's kindness, it has been possible to include a 'Late News' page outlining certain highly significant new constitutional developments that have taken place since the original text of each of the individual chapters was finalized in late November 2014.

Jeffrey Jowell
Dawn Oliver
Colm O'Cinneide
24 March 2015

LATE NEWS

CHAPTER 9—DEVOLUTION

The UK government published its White Paper, *Scotland in the United Kingdom: An enduring settlement* (Cm 8990), on 22 January 2015 setting out how it intended to implement the recommendations of the Smith Commission on further devolution for Scotland. Annex A to the White Paper contained 44 draft clauses which would form the basis of a Scotland Bill to be introduced before the UK Parliament after the general election in May 2015. They made provision for substantial new powers in the field of taxation and welfare to be devolved to the Scottish Parliament, for the Sewel convention to be put on a statutory footing, and for the Scottish Parliament to be recognized as a permanent part of the UK's constitutional arrangements.

The Wales Act 2014 received Royal Assent on 17 December 2014. Amongst other things, it lengthens from four to five years the lifespan of all future National Assemblies (s 1), renames the Welsh Assembly Government as the Welsh Government (*Llywodraeth Cymru*) (s 4), and enables the Assembly to pass laws in respect of devolved taxes (s 6). Subject to a favourable vote in a future referendum (s 12), the Welsh Assembly will also be able to set the rates of income tax to be paid by Welsh taxpayers (s 8). On 27 February 2015, the UK government subsequently published its White Paper, *Powers for a Purpose: Towards a Lasting Devolution Settlement for Wales* (Cm 9020), setting out how it intended to give effect to the Silk Commission's 2014 recommendations relating to non-fiscal powers. The White Paper proposed the establishment of a 'reserved powers' model of devolution. It also proposed the devolution of a wide range of new powers to the Welsh Assembly, including the power to regulate local government elections and its own procedures and electoral arrangements and to rename itself the Welsh Parliament.

In the case of *Recovery of Medical Costs for Asbestos Diseases (Wales) Bill – Reference by the Counsel General for Wales* [2015] UKSC 3, the Supreme Court held that the Welsh Assembly lacked the legal competence to charge bodies providing compensation to victims of asbestos diseases for the costs incurred by the NHS for their care, as the measure in question a) was not sufficiently related to the powers conferred on the Assembly to make provision for the 'organisation of the funding of the NHS' and b) breached the requirements of Article 1 of the First Protocol ECHR (right to property).

On 23 December 2014 the Stormont House Agreement was reached between the British and Irish governments and five political parties represented in the Northern Ireland Executive (see www.gov.uk/government/uploads/system/uploads/attachment_data/file/390672/Stormont_House_Agreement.pdf). The parties agreed to make adjustments to the Executive's fiscal and welfare policies, in return for securing new funding from the UK government. The parties also agreed to devolve to the Northern Ireland Assembly responsibility for regulating parades and related protests along with the power to set a lower rate of corporation tax, and made provision for the adoption of a range of other measures relating to historical reconciliation and the institutional structure of the Assembly. However, on 9 March 2015 a new political crisis erupted at Stormont when Sinn Féin withdrew its support for the draft Welfare Reform Bill.

CH. 14—FREEDOM OF INFORMATION

On 26 March 2013, the Supreme Court in *R (Evans)* v. *Attorney General* [2015] UKSC 21 dismissed an appeal against the Court of Appeal's ruling that the Attorney General was not entitled to issue a certificate under section 53 of the Freedom of Information Act 2000 overriding a decision by the Upper Tribunal that communications passing between various government departments and the Prince of Wales should be disclosed.

CONTENTS

PART III REGULATION AND THE CONSTITUTION

TABLE OF CASES

EUROPEAN UNION

EUROPEAN COURT OF HUMAN RIGHTS (ECtHR)

TABLE OF LEGISLATION

EUROPEAN LEGISLATION

TREATIES AND CONVENTIONS

INTERNATIONAL LEGISLATION

AUSTRALIA

FRANCE

LIST OF CONTRIBUTORS

Jeffrey Jowell, QC Director of the Bingham Centre for the Rule of Law and Emeritus Professor of Public Law, University College London

Dawn Oliver, QC, FBA Emeritus Professor of Constitutional Law, University College London

Colm O'Cinneide Reader in Law, University College London

Patrick Birkinshaw Professor of Public Law and Director of the Institute of European Public Law, University of Hull

Paul Craig, QC, FBA Professor of English Law, St John's College, Oxford

Brice Dickson Professor of International and Comparative Law, Queen's University Belfast

Mark Elliott Reader in Public Law, University of Cambridge

David Feldman, QC, FBA Rouse Ball Professor of English Law at the University of Cambridge, and Fellow of Downing College, Cambridge

Ian Leigh Professor of Law, University of Durham

Andrew Le Sueur Professor of Constitutional Justice, University of Essex

John McEldowney Professor of Law, University of Warwick

Philip Norton Life Peer, Professor of Government, University of Hull

Tony Prosser, FBA Professor of Public Law, University of Bristol and Visiting Professor, The College of Europe, Bruges

Richard Rawlings Professor of Public Law, University College London

EDITORS' INTRODUCTION

Jeffrey Jowell, Dawn Oliver, and Colm O'Cinneide

MAGNA CARTA AND THE UNITED KINGDOM CONSTITUTION

The first edition of this book was published in 1985, precisely 100 years after the publication of Dicey's *The Law of the Constitution*. The publication of this edition coincides with the 800th anniversary of the sealing of Magna Carta in Runnymede Green on 15 June 1215 between a despotic, bankrupt King John and the great aristocrats of the land, desperate to protect their feudal rights. Magna Carta was a document that did not endorse class, religious, or gender equality. It was in essence a peace treaty which was soon to be annulled by the Pope who called it a 'shameful and demeaning agreement, forced upon the king by violence and fear'. Two years later, however, the agreement was reaffirmed by John's son, Henry III. It was reissued on a few occasions during the thirteenth century and in 1297 Edward I's Magna Carta was given statutory status.

The great significance of this document lies in the 'golden passages', which made it the first legally binding document to limit the power of the king over his subjects. In that sense it was a document of epic importance. Chapters 39 and 40 even today quicken the blood, providing that:

39: No free man shall be seized or imprisoned, or stripped of his rights or possessions, or outlawed or exiled, or deprived of his standing in any other way, nor will we proceed with force against him, or send others to do so, except by lawful judgment of his peers or by the law of the land.

40: To no one will we sell, to no one deny or delay right or justice

Its greatest champion was Sir Edward Coke who, as Chief Justice of England in the seventeenth century, regarded it as 'the principal grounds of the fundamental laws of England'. The first bill of rights, echoing Magna Carta, was adopted in Virginia on 12 June 1776 and then on 4 July of that year the American Declaration of Independence itself echoed Chapter 39 of Magna Carta in Articles 1 and 8, the latter ending with the words that 'no man be deprived of his liberty except by the law of his land and the judgment of his peers'.

One further aspect of Magna Carta is significant for those societies whose constitutions may be packed with rights and promises which have no hope of practical enforcement. Magna Carta, in Chapter 61, has its own built-in enforcement clause under which the barons could, if the King did not comply, seize his 'castles, land and possessions' (although, tolerantly, not his Queen or children, a tolerance also found in other chapters, such as Chapter 21 which provides that earls and barons shall be fined only by their equals, and in proportion to the gravity of their offence).

Today in this country only three clauses of Magna Carta remain on the statute book: those guaranteeing the freedom of the church, the 'ancient liberties' of the City of London, and the famous Chapter 39 which, in its later incarnation, in Edward III's statute in 1354, lays down the idea of *due process of law* (which found its way into the fifth amendment of the US Constitution in 1791).

So in this edition we salute the symbolic impact of the sealing of Magna Carta: in the words of Tom Bingham, it 'changed the constitutional landscape of this country and, over time, the world'. 'There', he said, 'clearly recognizable, was the rule of law in embryo.'[1]

When Jowell and Oliver first chose the title to this book we could not possibly have foreseen how much the constitution would indeed change or how much we would need to add to the book in the 30 years since its first publication. In our Preface to the first edition we noted how:

> Dicey's shadow still dominates British constitutional law and political theory...His satisfaction with an unwritten constitution still influences opposition to entrenched protections of our civil liberties. Dicey's word has in some respects become the only written constitution we have.[2]

And Anthony Lester wrote that:

> 'The Scottish problem'— that is, the problem of how to concede home rule to Scotland without destroying the unity of the Kingdom—may well perplex Whitehall and Westminster...It is therefore still worthwhile to consider the consequences of the absence of enforceable constitutional criteria in this context.[3]

At the time of writing, we are no longer so dependent upon Dicey's view of the constitution. Constitutional discourse has moved on greatly, as commentators and the courts grapple with the opportunities and problems that beset a modern European liberal democracy committed to equality and the rule of law. However, as Anthony Lester predicted, the issue of devolution remains greatly challenging to our previously centralized system and the debate around it is bringing to the fore, as never before, questions about the role of our constitution in both enabling and constraining government.

THE STILL-CHANGING CONSTITUTION

When the first edition of this book appeared in 1985 its title reflected the significant changes that the UK constitutional system was then undergoing. Thirty years and eight editions later, key elements of the British constitution have undergone radical

---

[1] Tom Bingham, *The Rule of Law* (2010), 11.
[2] J. Jowell and D. Oliver *The Changing Constitution* (1985), v.   [3] Ibid., at 282.

transformation. The functioning of Parliament and the networks of political account-ability that bind the legislature, the executive, and local government together have undergone far-reaching reform. Human rights laws and freedom of information legis-lation now play an important role in opening up decisions by public authorities to legal challenge and public debate. Devolution has fundamentally reconfigured the relation-ship between Westminster and Scotland, Wales, and Northern Ireland, while the UK's membership of the EU has added a crucially important new dimension to its system of constitutional governance.

However, despite all these changes, the process of constitutional evolution con-tinues apace. Indeed, the pace of change seems to be ever-quickening. Since the last (the seventh) edition which was published in 2011, significant new developments have taken place in every area covered by the chapters of this book. In particular, the estab-lishment of the first coalition government of the modern constitutional era in May 2010, continuing controversy about UK membership of the EU and the influence of the European Convention on Human Rights (ECHR) on national law, the deepening of devolution, and the fall-out from the Scottish independence referendum in September 2014 have all influenced existing constitutional arrangements in diverse ways.

Furthermore, many of these developments have cast a shroud of uncertainty over key elements of the existing constitutional framework. At the time of writing, political debate continues as to whether to hold a referendum in 2017 on continued UK mem-bership of the EU, while the Conservative Party has committed itself to repealing the Human Rights Act 1998 and replacing it with a new Bill of Rights if it obtains an over-all majority in the 2015 general election. In Scotland, the aftermath of the independ-ence referendum has left key issues about the future of devolution unresolved, which also have implications for Wales and Northern Ireland, and England and the UK as a whole. The political landscape is becoming increasingly fractured, which makes coali-tion or minority governments more likely in the short-to-medium future.

It remains to be seen whether the current climate of political uncertainty will actu-ally lead to far-reaching changes to the British constitution. It is entirely possible that the current set of constitutional arrangements, as uncertain and contested as they are, will prove to have perhaps unexpected durability. However, it is clear that there exists a lack of consensus about certain key elements of the constitution. This makes it likely that the process of change and evolution mapped out across every edition of this book will continue, and that little if anything of the British constitutional order can be viewed as set in stone.

The preparation of this volume was complicated by this background context. All chapters were initially scheduled to be sent to the publisher in early October 2014. However, the timing of the Scottish referendum meant that this timetable had to be adjusted, with the completed volume being sent to OUP in late November 2014. Some updating was done in January 2015. This serves as one more illustration of both the pace of constitutional change and the cloud of uncertainty that hangs over existing arrangements. It also demonstrates the continuing appropriateness of the title of the book: the British constitutional system continues to change and evolve.

THE CHAPTERS

FUNDAMENTAL PRINCIPLES

The chapters in Part I consider some of the fundamental principles that affect and underlie the operation of the British constitution. The first two chapters focus on the rule of law and the doctrine of parliamentary sovereignty, identified together as principles of the UK constitution by Dicey in his *Introduction to the Law of the Constitution* (1885).

The rule of law is, suggests Jowell in chapter 1, a principle of institutional morality that is inherent in any constitutional democracy. That principle vies with parliamentary sovereignty as to which of the two is the 'controlling' principle of constitutional democracy in the UK. Dicey's account of the rule of law and parliamentary sovereignty in 1885, though subjected to much criticism for his rejection of official discretion in the system, continues to provide important insights into the concept, and has influenced developments of it: widespread acceptance that substantive principles of legality, certainty, equality, and access to justice and rights are essential elements in any well-functioning constitutional democracy. They are not however the only such principles.

The current status of the doctrine of the legislative supremacy or sovereignty of the UK Parliament, particularly having regard to the multilayered nature of the UK constitution in the light of devolution with the UK, the European Union and the European Convention on Human Rights, is the subject of chapter 2. Elliott notes that much of the UK constitution is founded on constitutional principles developed by the courts over many years, including legality and the rule of law. In recent cases some judges have made comments, *obiter*, that suggest that the courts might be justified in refusing to give effect to 'unconstitutional' laws. If this were to happen the confrontation between Parliament and government, on the one hand, and the courts, on the other, would give rise to a serious constitutional crisis.

In chapter 3 O'Cinneide develops the subject of human rights, one of the elements of the rule of law discussed by Jowell in chapter 1. UK human rights law has undergone radical transformation over the last few decades, principally as a result of the influence exerted by the ECHR on the UK's legal system and the enactment of the Human Rights Act 1988 (HRA). However, the important role played by the HRA and ECHR in protecting rights remains the subject of considerable political controversy.

In chapter 4 Paul Craig discusses the constitutional implications for the UK of its membership of the European Union. The UK became a member of the European Communities (now the European Union) in 1973. Since 1973 the powers of European institutions have increased substantially, including those of the now directly elected European Parliament. UK courts are also European courts when EU law issues arise. The role of national parliaments in the EU has been enhanced. Thus the UK Parliament is significantly affected by EU membership, including the work of the select committees in both Houses which scrutinize and report on proposals for EU legislation and its implementation.

The EU position is that its laws have direct effect in and prevail over the law of member states; the courts of member states are required to implement EU law. The UK Supreme Court has held that the relationship of EU law with UK law is to be determined by the law of the UK. The European Union Act 2011 imposes a UK referendum lock on increases in the competences of the EU, in addition to the normal requirement that new Treaty provisions should be ratified by Act of Parliament to have domestic effect.

Municipal law is always influenced by foreign developments. This is the subject matter of chapter 5. David Feldman argues that, while it is clear that much international law and many international institutions promote universal goods including human rights, some may legitimate the use or threat of force by bodies that are not subject to effective legal or democratic accountability. After summarizing the influences from international law, Feldman focuses on the filters that protect the national interest and rule of law in the UK and general public law standards from inappropriate foreign and international influences. These include degrees of 'dualism', expansion by the courts of jurisdiction in judicial review, and development of parliamentary scrutiny of government decisions by the House of Lords Delegated Powers and Regulatory Reform Committee, its Constitution Committee, and the Joint Committee on Human Rights.

INSTITUTIONS

The chapters in Part II consider the principal constitutional institutions in the UK. Philip Norton adopts three themes in chapter 6 on the UK Parliament: its essential nature as a reactive, policy-influencing body—reactive to government; the current assertions of independence from government, in reforms to House of Commons' select committees and increased activity in legislative scrutiny and debate in the House of Lords; and increasingly direct relationships with and responsiveness to the public, with televised proceedings, parliamentary debate of e-petitions, online consultations, and parliamentary websites.

In chapter 7 Richard Rawlings focuses on changes to the executive under the Coalition government formed in 2010. Here, as in other aspects of the UK constitution, the use of soft law documents is striking. Many conventions have been affected by the Coalition, including collective ministerial responsibility. The Constitutional Reform and Governance Act 2010 placed the Civil Service, at last, on a largely statutory footing, though still reliant on soft law to smooth its operation. In the light of the Scottish independence referendum of September 2014, the roles of and relations between executives at UK and devolved levels is bound to change. A 'New Union' mindset should develop. Overall the need for cooperative working of a non-hierarchical nature based on comity between the devolved and UK institutions is becoming clear.

Andrew Le Sueur discusses the infrastructure of the system of justice—courts and tribunals—in England and Wales in chapter 8. Changes under the Constitutional

Reform Act 2005 to the roles of Lord Chancellor and Lord Chief Justice, and the establishment of a new Supreme Court and a Judicial Appointments Commission, raise issues as to the roles of and relationships between judges and politicians in running the system, and the scope for parts of the system to be run in partnerships between such bodies. Here, as in other areas, soft law documents are significant, especially the 'concordat' reached between Lord Chief Justice Woolf and Lord Chancellor Falconer about the position of judges under the Constitutional Reform Act 2005. The legal aid system is now run by an agency of the Department of Justice instead of by an arm's length body; government proposals to limit access to judicial review (clearly having implications for the rule of law) were made without prior consultation or evidence gathering, and explicitly for party political reasons. A system in which politics and expertise are blended would be more likely to produce good policies.

In chapter 9 Brice Dickson discusses the implications of devolution within the UK. Since the devolution of powers to Scotland, Wales, and Northern Ireland in 1998 the arrangements for self-government in each of these countries have developed in response to pressures from those countries for more powers and responsibility to be granted to them. Here too resort has been had to soft law, including memorandums of understanding between the UK government and the devolved bodies, and other informal arrangements such as legislative consent motions. In September 2014 the Scots voted narrowly in a referendum to remain in the UK, but on the understanding that further devolution of powers would take place: as of 2015 that process is underway. As yet no devolution has taken place in England, save to London. This aspect of the asymmetry raises issues as to how, if at all, power can or should be devolved *within* England.

As of January 2015 there are no conventions or provisions in the Standing Orders of the House of Commons regarding the participation of MPs sitting for non-English constituencies in England only (or England and Wales only) legislation and debates. These may, however, be likely to develop as devolution to Scotland increases.

Over the last 20 years or so, and particularly in the last decade, major changes have been made to the role and functions of local authorities: this is the subject of chapter 10 by Ian Leigh. Many authorities now work in partnership with other bodies—public, private, and in the voluntary sector—to provide services that were previously provided directly by these authorities. These authorities now have mixed community-based roles, including the promotion of the general well-being of their communities and their citizens, and furtherance of 'localism'. Local authorities now enjoy powers of general competence, thus freeing them from the restrictions of the ultra vires rule. Governance structures have also been reformed in recent years, introducing among other things elected mayors. Forms of direct and deliberative decision-making have been introduced. Regional policy, by contrast, has had a chequered history. In the aftermath of the Scottish referendum vote to remain in the Union, however, the question of decentralization to regional bodies, particularly to major cities, resurfaced.

REGULATION AND THE CONSTITUTION

Part III of this collection surveys the roles of regulation in the UK's constitutional arrangements.

In chapter 11 Dawn Oliver considers the development over the last 30 years or so of systems to regulate the practice of party politics in government. Many policy areas that were previously in the hands of government have been replaced by a layer of national, non-political regulation as formerly state-owned industries have been privatized. Arm's length bodies now exercise powers in relation to formerly political matters such as fixing the minimum lending rate, publication of statistics, and public appointments. In relation to matters which remain with central government, systems of soft law regulation and self-regulation have developed in recent years. Oliver suggests that these rules reflect public opinion and the opinions of opposition parties and their members as to the 'rules of the game' of politics.

Prosser (chapter 12) discusses administrative regulation and its range of rationales (including control of monopoly, consumer protection, and promotion of social solidarity) broadly. The importance of effective regulation was demonstrated by the financial crisis of 2008–9 which was attributable in large part to inadequate regulation and failures of unregulated markets. A feature of recent regulatory reforms has been promotion of independence from government and other bodies. The arrangements for regulation are varied and often confusing, lacking coherence. The fact that important decisions are taken by regulators rather than politicians raises accountability and legitimacy issues: these have been met in part by openness on the part of some regulators about their operations, and open decision-making procedures, and in part through appeals and judicial review. What is lacking is a set of constitutional principles that can govern regulation.

Much has changed in the rules relating to public expenditure and the control of public finance since the seventh edition of this work was published in 2011. These are discussed by John McEldowney in chapter 13. The positions of the Comptroller and Auditor General and the National Audit Office have been reformed, the Office of Budget Responsibility has been established on a statutory footing, and the role of Bank of England has been reformed with increased responsibilities for the economy. In this field, as in many others, self-regulatory soft law is extensively relied upon. The Treasury remains dominant in controlling taxation policy and executive expenditure, especially during the financial crisis. Parliamentary control has weakened in the financial crisis and Treasury power has increased. Nevertheless the House of Commons Committee for Public Accounts and the Treasury Committee exercise important functions *ex post* in seeking to regulate and scrutinize these matters.

In chapter 14 Birkinshaw discusses the law relating to access to official and other forms of information and the protection of personal data. The quantity and quality of such information, and its accessibility on the internet, have produced the need not only to facilitate access but also to restrict it, for instance in the public interest and interests of individual privacy and commercial confidentiality. Here, as in many areas of constitutional law, there have been changes in recent years. Some of these have been justified in the interests of national security in an age of international terrorism: the protection of the rights of suspected terrorists in such cases is difficult to reconcile with public interests. Other changes have been required to deal with the realities of the internet and the abuses it makes possible.

In this field, as in many others, recognition of the need for public bodies to provide their justifications for policy and acts by providing information has been influential. The mere say-so of governments is no longer considered to give authority for actions, whether in relation to identifiable individuals or as matters of general policy. This factor is coupled with the aim of enabling well-qualified and well-informed people to participate in political life. But the development of freedom of information law was hindered for many years by fears that it would undermine the authority of government and thus the very core of representative democracy.

A number of themes recur in these chapters: the relationships between the law and politics in the operation of the UK constitution; the effects of multilayered govern-ance; the extensive reliance on soft law to oil the wheels of the system in the public or general interest; a shift from a culture of authority to one of justification. The one issue we have not discussed, but which lurks obviously beneath the surface, is whether our constitution, and indeed our culture, has now reached the stage where we would be better off with a written constitution. If there is another edition of this book, perhaps that will be a live issue, or indeed already have taken place. If so, it will be interesting to see to what extent codification will slow down the pace of constitutional change reflected in the past 30 years of this book's existence.

PART I

THE CONSTITUTIONAL FRAMEWORK

Editorial note

This book is divided into three parts. The chapters in the first part are concerned with the fundamental principles, theories, and factors that underpin the UK constitution. What Dicey in his *Introduction to the Law of the Constitution* referred to as the 'twin pillars' of the constitution, the rule of law and the sovereignty of the UK Parliament, are dealt with in chapters 1 and 2. The relationships between these two principles are among the issues explored in the following chapters in this part. Chapter 3 deals with human rights, particularly the fundamental civil and political rights which are contained in the European Convention on Human Rights (ECHR) and incorporated into UK law by the Human Rights Act 1998.

The fact that the UK is a member of the European Union affects many aspect of government in the UK. These are discussed in chapter 4. The European Union wields very great power over member states, and this raises issues about accountability arrangements and democracy within the Union as well as the approach of the UK courts to European legislation and the challenges that it poses to parliamentary sovereignty.

Chapter 5 focuses further on international influences on the UK constitution. It shows both filters and defences in our arrangements which protect the legal system from unwanted outside influences, and how common standards and concepts from other legal systems influence domestic constitutional developments.

1

THE RULE OF LAW

Jeffrey Jowell

SUMMARY

Dicey believed that discretionary power offended the rule of law as it would inevitably lead to arbitrary decisions. His critics pointed out that in the modern state discretion is necessary to carry out a variety of welfare and regulatory tasks. The rule of law contains four central features which cohere and overlap: legality, certainty, equality, and access to justice and rights. These are not only formal values but also substantive. The rule of law is a principle of institutional morality inherent in any constitutional democracy. In a country without a written constitution it constrains the way power is exercised. It is enforced and elaborated through judicial review but also serves as a critical focus for public debate. Although the rule of law is not the only requirement of a constitutional democracy, it is of great practical significance in promoting fair decisions, restraining the abuse of power, encouraging investment, and in furthering empowerment and respect for equal human dignity.

INTRODUCTION

In 1885, Professor Albert Venn Dicey wrote that the two principles of our unwritten constitution were the sovereignty of Parliament and the rule of law.[1] Although he regarded parliamentary sovereignty as the primary principle—one that could override the rule of law—he recognized that, ideally, Parliament and all public officials should respect the rule of law as a quality that distinguished a democratic from a despotic constitution.

---

[1] A. V. Dicey, *The Law of the Constitution* (1885) referred to here in its 10th edn, edited by E. C. S. Wade (reprinted 1960). For an account of Dicey's conception, see the articles on 'Dicey and the Constitution' in [1985] *PL* 583–724; I. Harden and N. Lewis, *The Noble Lie* (1986), ch. 2; P. Craig, *Public Law and Democracy in the United Kingdom and the United States of America* (1990), ch. 2; M. Loughlin, *Public Law and Political Theory* (1992); T. R. S. Allan, *Constitutional Justice: A Liberal Theory of the Rule of Law* (2001); A. Hutchinson and P. Monahan (eds.), *The Rule of Law: Ideal or Ideology?* (1987). See also, Lord Bingham of Cornhill, 'Dicey Revisited' [2002] *PL* 39. See also D. Dyzenhaus, *The Constitution of Law* (2006). For a critical view of the rule of law see R. Ekins (ed.), *Modern Challenges to the Rule of Law* (2011).

What is meant by the rule of law and what is its value? Is it any more than a statement that individuals or officials should obey the law as it is? Or does it simply require
positive legal authority for the acts of all public officials? Is it a guide to the justice
of public decision-making—a framework that constrains the abuse of power? Or is
it an assertion that law itself contains inherent moral qualities? Is its proper place
not in the realm of constitutional legality but in the rhetoric of liberal–democratic
values? Is it, as a distinguished legal historian has written, an 'unqualified human
good'[2] or, as alleged by another, a device that 'enables the shrewd, the calculating,
and the wealthy to manipulate its form to their own advantage'?[3] Is it 'an impossible
ideal'?[4]

These days the rule of law is accepted as never before as one of the fundamental
principles of our uncodified democratic constitution. It is frequently invoked by
the courts as a standard by which to judge whether power has been abused. It is
engaged as a yardstick by which to assess the validity of government proposals.
One of the most senior and distinguished British judges recently wrote a book
extolling the virtues of the rule of law and elaborating its content.[5] It has even
received statutory recognition in the Constitutional Reform Act 2005,[6] the first
section of which states that that Act does not adversely affect 'the existing constitutional principle of the rule of law'. Most significantly, some of our judges have
recently suggested that Dicey's hierarchy of principle, with the rule of law playing
second-fiddle to the sovereignty of Parliament, might be changing, and that 'the
rule of law enforced by the courts is the ultimate controlling factor on which our
constitution is based'.[7]

DICEY'S RULE OF LAW: ITS CRITICS
AND SUPPORTERS

In analysing what we mean by the rule of law it is probably best, even today, to start
with Dicey's interpretation, because of the immense authority he has exercised for so
long over the perception of our constitutional arrangements.[8]

---

    [2] E. P. Thompson, *Whigs and Hunters: The Origin of the Black Act* (1975), 266.
    [3] M. Horwitz, book review (1977) 86 *Yale LJ* 561, 566.
    [4] M. Loughlin, *Foundations of Public Law* (2010), 337.
    [5] Lord Bingham, *The Rule of Law* (2010).
    [6] The Act seeks to further the principle of the separation of powers and independence of the judiciary.
In particular, it removes the power of appointment of judges from the Lord Chancellor and places it in the
hands of an independent Judicial Appointments Commission. It also precludes the Lord Chancellor from
any judicial role and establishes a Supreme Court outside the House of Lords.
    [7] e.g. Lord Hope, *obiter*, in *Jackson v. Her Majesty's Attorney General* [2005] UKHL 56, at [107].
    [8] The conception of the rule of law has an older provenance than Dicey but was rarely mentioned as such
before his account. For an account of its origins in the ancient world, see M. Loughlin, *Swords and Scales*
(2000), ch. 5; B. Tamanaha, *On the Rule of Law: History, Politics and Theory* (2004), ch. 1.

For Dicey, the rule of law distinguished the British (or 'English', as he preferred to call it) from all other constitutions. He described how foreign observers of English manners (Voltaire and de Tocqueville in particular) visited England and were struck by the fact that here was a country distinguished above all by the fact of being under the rule of law:

> When Voltaire came to England—and Voltaire represented the feeling of his age—his predominant sentiment clearly was that he had passed out of the realm of despotism to a land where the laws might be harsh, but where men were ruled by law and not by caprice.[9]

That passage encapsulates Dicey's approach to the rule of law. By allowing for 'harsh' laws to coexist with the rule of law it is clear that he does not equate the rule of law with the notion of 'good' law. Nor does he contend that in order to qualify as 'law' a particular rule has to be fair, or reasonable, or just. So what did he mean by the rule of law?

According to Dicey, the rule of law has at least three meanings. The first is that individuals ought not to be subjected to the power of officials wielding wide discretionary powers. He wrote that no one 'is punishable or can be lawfully made to suffer in body or goods except for a distinct breach of law established before the ordinary courts of the land'. Fundamental to the rule of law, therefore, is the notion that all power needs to be authorized. But he took that notion further by contrasting the rule of law with a 'system of government based on the exercise by persons in authority of wide, arbitrary or discretionary powers of constraint'.[10] Here Dicey contends that to confer wide discretion upon officials is equivalent to granting them scope to exercise arbitrary powers, to which no one should be forced to submit. He writes that 'wherever there is discretion there is room for arbitrariness'[11] and therefore excludes discretionary powers from what he later calls 'regular law'.

Dicey's second meaning engages a notion of equality—what he calls the 'equal subjection'—of all classes to one law administered by the ordinary courts. He contrasts here what he saw as special exemptions for officials in continental countries such as France, where he considered that the French *droit administratif* operated a separate form of justice that treated ordinary citizens differently from the way it treated its public officials. 'With us', he wrote, 'every official, from the Prime Minister down to a constable or a collector of taxes, is under the same responsibility for every act done without legal justification as any other citizen.'[12]

Thirdly, Dicey saw the rule of law as expressing the fact that there was in England no separate written constitutional code, and that the constitutional law is 'the result of the judicial decisions determining the rights of private persons in particular cases brought before the courts'.[13] Like Bentham before him, he was against a basic document setting out a catalogue of human rights and saw our law and liberties as arising from decisions in the courts—the common law.

---

[9] Dicey, *Law of the Constitution*, 189.   [10] Ibid., 188.   [11] Ibid.   [12] Ibid., 193.
[13] Ibid., 195.

One of the first attacks on Dicey's meanings of the rule of law came in 1928 when William Robson wrote his celebrated book *Justice and Administrative Law*, in which he roundly criticized Dicey for his misinterpretation of both the English and French systems on the question of whether officials were treated differently from others. He pointed out that there were, in England 'colossal distinctions'[14] between the rights and duties of private individuals and those of the administrative organs of government, even in Dicey's time. Public authorities possessed special rights and special exemptions and immunities, to the extent that the citizen was deprived of a remedy against the state 'in many cases where he most requires it'.[15] Robson also convincingly showed how Dicey had misinterpreted French law, where the *droit administratif* was not intended to exempt public officials from the rigour of private law, but to allow experts in public administration to work out the extent of official liability. Robson also noted the extent of Dicey's misrepresentation that disputes between officials and private individuals in Britain were dealt with by the ordinary courts. He pointed to the growth of special tribunals and inquiries that had grown up to decide these disputes outside the courts, and was in no doubt that a 'vast body of administrative law' existed in England.[16]

The attack on Dicey continued a few years later with Professor W. Ivor Jennings's *The Law and the Constitution*, which appeared in 1933. Repeating many of Robson's criticisms of Dicey's second and third meanings of the rule of law, Jennings also delivered a withering, and almost fatal, attack upon Dicey's first meaning—his claim that wide discretionary power had no place under the rule of law. It should be remembered here that Dicey was a trenchant critic of notions of 'collectivism'. An unreconstructed Whig, he had, throughout his life, believed in a *laissez-faire* economic system and had resisted increasing the regulatory role of the state.[17] He was supported by other constitutional theorists of his time,[18] and had an ally in the 1920s in Lord Hewart, who expressed similar views in his book *The New Despotism*.[19] Robson and Jennings were committed to the expansion of the state's role in providing welfare and other social services. Robson, George Bernard Shaw, Leonard Woolf, John Maynard Keynes, Harold Laski, and others worked together in the 1930s to promote these ideas.[20]

---

[14] W. A. Robson, *Justice and Administrative Law* (1928; 2nd edn, 1947), 343.   [15] Ibid., 345.

[16] Ibid. Robson approved of, and wished to develop, administrative law, but through a separate system outside of the 'ordinary courts'. See his 'Justice and Administrative Law Reconsidered' (1979) 32(1) *Current Legal Problems* 107. For an excellent critique and historic corrective of Dicey, see H. W. Arthurs, 'Rethinking Administrative Law: A Slightly Dicey Business' (1979) 17 *Osgoode Hall LJ*, Part I; and *Without the Law* (1985).

[17] See R. A. Cosgrove, *The Rule of Law: Albert Venn Dicey, Victorian Jurist* (1980), and the review by D. Sugarman (1983) *MLR* 102.

[18] e.g. J. Bryce, *Modern Democracies* (1921).   [19] Published in 1929.

[20] See e.g. Keynes's lecture published by Leonard and Virginia Woolf at The Hogarth Press in 1926, entitled *The End of Laissez-Faire*. See Victoria Glendinning, *Leonard Woolf* (2006).

Jennings felt that the rule of law implicitly promoted Dicey's political views. He equated Dicey's opposition to state regulation with that of the 'manufacturers who formed the backbone of the Whig Party', who:

> wanted nothing which interfered with profits, even if profits involved child labour, wholesale factory accidents, the pollution of rivers, of the air, and of the water supply, jerry-built houses, low wages, and other incidents of nineteenth-century industrialism.[21]

Jennings then turned his attention directly to Dicey, who:

> was more concerned with constitutional relations between Great Britain and Ireland than with relations between poverty and disease on the one hand, and the new industrial system on the other.[22]

Jennings concluded that if the rule of law:

> means that the state exercises only the functions of carrying out external relations and maintaining order, it is not true. If it means that the state ought to exercise these functions only, it is a rule of policy for Whigs (if there are any left).[23]

There were not too many Whigs or unreconstructed Diceyists left by the 1930s, when further legitimacy for the growth of official power was provided by the Donoughmore Committee, inquiring in 1932 into the question whether the growth of subordinate legislation (promulgated at the discretion of the executive) violated the rule of law.[24] Donoughmore found that it was inevitable, in an increasingly complex society, that Parliament delegate powers to ministers to act in the public interest. The Second World War then provided further compelling reasons to centralize power, an opportunity built upon by the Labour government of 1945. As Robson wrote in the second edition of his book in 1947, increasingly Parliament had given powers to resolve disputes between the citizen and the state not to the courts—to Dicey's 'ordinary law'—but to specialized organs of adjudication such as administrative tribunals and inquiries. This was not 'due to a fit of absentmindedness' but because these bodies would be speedier and cheaper, and would possess greater technical knowledge and have 'fewer prejudices against government' than the courts.[25] Here he may have been echoing the words of Aneurin Bevan, Minister of Health in the 1945 Labour government and architect of the National Health Service, who caused a stir in the House of Commons by establishing tribunals in the Health Service, divorced from 'ordinary courts', because he greatly feared 'judicial sabotage' of socialist legislation.[26]

---

[21] Sir W. Ivor Jennings, *The Law and the Constitution* (1933), 309–10.   [22] Ibid., 311.
[23] Ibid.   [24] Report of the Committee on Ministers' Powers (1932) Cmd 4060.
[25] Robson, *Justice and Administrative Law*, 347.
[26] Hansard, HC, col. 1983 (23 July 1946). See modern criticisms of the rule of law in Ekins (ed.), *Modern Challenges to the Rule of Law*.

Despite this onslaught on Dicey's version of the rule of law, its epitaph refused to be written. In 1938, the American jurist Felix Frankfurter (later a Supreme Court Justice) wrote that:

> the persistence of the misdirection that Dicey has given to the development of admin-istrative law strikingly proves . . . that many a theory survives long after its brains are knocked out.[27]

Two particularly strong supporters wrote in favour of the rule of law in the 1940s. F. A. Hayek's *The Road to Serfdom* in 1943 graphically described that road as being paved with governmental regulation and unconstrained discretionary power. C. K. Allen, with less ideological fervour, pleaded for the legal control of executive action, as a nec-essary quality of the rule of law.[28] Not much heed was paid to these pleas until the late 1950s when the Franks Committee[29] revived interest in Diceyan notions by proposing that procedural safeguards be introduced to safeguard the powers of the multiplying tribunals and inquiries of the growing state. It was in the 1960s, however, that dispa-rate groups once again started arguing in favour of legal values. Some of these groups were themselves committed to a strong governmental role in providing social welfare, but objected to the manner in which public services were carried out. Recipients of discretionary state benefit, known as 'supplementary benefit', for example, objected to the fact that benefits were administered by officials in accordance with a secret code (known as the 'A Code') and asked instead for publication of a set of welfare 'rights'.[30] They also objected to the wide discretion allowed their case-workers to determine the level of their benefits. The heirs of Jennings and his followers, such as Professor Richard Titmuss, opposed this challenge to the free exercise of official discretion and objected strongly to a 'pathology of legalism' developing in this area.[31]

Another plea for the rule of law came at about the same time from individuals who were being displaced from their homes by programmes of urban redevelopment. While not asking for a catalogue of 'rights', their claim was for participation in decisions by which they were affected.[32] Their plea did not primarily concern the substance of the law. Just as the welfare recipients were not simply arguing for higher benefits, but for prede-termined rules and fair procedures to determine the benefits, citizens' groups directed their demands for the rule of law less at the content of the decisions ultimately taken than at the procedures by which they were reached. They were by no means adopting the

---

[27] F. Frankfurter, Foreword to 'Discussion of Current Developments in Administrative Law' (1938) 47 *Yale LJ* 515, 517. The reference to administrative law is in response to Dicey's view that there should be no separate system of law in relation to the exercise of power by public officials.

[28] See C. K. Allen, *Law and Orders* (1945). See also F. A. Hayek, *The Constitution of Liberty* (1960), and *Law, legislation and liberty* (2 vols., 1976).

[29] Report of the Committee on Administrative Tribunals and Inquiries (1957) Cmnd 218.

[30] See e.g. T. Lynes, *Welfare Rights* (1969); and in the USA: C. Reich, 'The New Property' (1964) 73 *Yale CJ* 733.

[31] R. Titmuss, 'Law and Discretion' (1971) 42 *Pol Q* 113.

[32] N. A. Roberts, *The Reform of Planning Law* (1976); P. McAuslan, *The Ideologies of Planning Law* (1980), esp. chs. 1 and 2.

undiluted Diceyan view that all discretionary power is bad. Nevertheless, they asked not to be condemned (in those cases, evicted from their communities) unheard.

After the two world wars, as people became less deferential to government and expected it to be more accountable, the rule of law has frequently been employed as a yardstick by which to challenge proposals, such as to reduce legal aid, or to limit the opportunity to challenge government decisions by way of judicial review. It has also formed the basis of opposition to secret trials, detention without trial, the unconstrained powers of tax or immigration officials, and other issues mentioned later.

WHAT DOES THE RULE OF LAW REQUIRE?

Dicey's rule of law has been criticized, as we have seen, for the fact that it tendentiously seeks to promote an individualistic political theory and because of its inaccurate descriptions of the then-existing systems of governance—both in France and England. Yet it remains a compelling idea, despite being thought of by some leading thinkers as an 'essentially contested concept',[33] and therefore has been interpreted in different ways.[34] Some see the rule of law as embodying formal qualities in law (such as clarity, prospectivity, stability, openness, and access to an impartial judiciary).[35] Others criticize that view, called by Ronald Dworkin the 'rule-book conception' of the rule of law and prefer the 'rights conception', under which legal rules contain inherent moral content.[36] Dworkin's view must be seen in the context of his and others' opposition to the view of the positivist thinkers who contend that even extremely harsh and unjust laws, such as the discriminatory laws of Nazi Germany, must be regarded as law, despite their moral repugnance.[37] Dicey and Dworkin are aiming at different targets. Dworkin is seeking a general theory of law, focusing more on the nature of 'law' under the concept of the rule of law,[38] whereas Dicey seeks a principle of how power should be deployed under a system of government under law. Nevertheless, Dworkin raises the question as to whether the rule of law is a merely formal or procedural concept (the 'thin' version of the rule of law), or whether it embodies certain fundamental rights (the 'thick' version of the rule of law).[39]

---

[33] J. Waldron, 'Is the Rule of Law an Essentially Contested Concept (in Florida)?' (2002) 21 *Law and Philosophy* 137.

[34] See P. Craig, 'Formal and Substantive Conceptions of the Rule of Law: An Analytical Framework' [1997] *PL* 467; N. Barber, 'Must Legalistic Conceptions of the Rule of Law Have a Social Dimension?' (2004) 17(4) *Ratio Juris* 474.

[35] J. Raz, 'The Rule of Law and its Virtue' (1977) 93 *LQR* 195, and *The Authority of Law* (1979). Compare Lon Fuller's requirements of 'legality': generality, clarity, public promulgation, stability, consistency, fidelity to purpose, and prohibition of the impossible. L. Fuller, *The Morality of Law* (1964), 153. See also R. Summers, 'The Principles of the Rule of Law' (1999) 74 *Notre Dame LR* 1691.

[36] R. Dworkin, *A Matter of Principle* (1985), ch. 1, 11ff.

[37] See generally, H. L. A. Hart, *The Concept of Law* (1961).

[38] See J. Waldron, 'The Concept and the Rule of Law' (2008) 43 *Georgia L Rev* 1.

[39] See J. Waldron, 'The Rule of Law and the Importance of Procedure', New York University Public Law and Legal Theory Working Papers 234 (2010).

In a recent book on the rule of law which has received much attention, the great British judge Tom Bingham defines the rule of law as follows:

> all persons and authorities within the state, whether public or private, should be bound by and entitled to the benefit of laws publicly made, taking effect (generally) in the future and publicly administered in the courts.[40]

This definition may at first reading sound rather too economical, but it encapsulates a number of features of a state grounded in the rule of law. It also seems at first sight to fall into the procedural, or thin version of the rule of law, but Bingham expands that definition with eight features, or 'ingredients' of the rule of law, including that the law must give protection to human rights.[41]

One of the key problems in explaining the rule of law is that it consists of four really rather distinct and separate aspects which are contained within the Bingham definition and the eight ingredients, but which are not specifically articulated (I exclude for these purposes the international aspects of the rule of law).[42] It is the lack of appreciation of the fact that the sum of the rule of law requires attention to all four parts, which are some-what distinct, but nevertheless cohere and indeed overlap, that accounts for some of the lack of understanding of the rule of law's really rather clear meaning and significance.

Legality

At its most fundamental, the rule of law requires everyone to comply with the law. Legality is distinct from anarchy, on the one hand, and tyranny on the other. Legality contains two features. First, the law must be followed (Bingham's requirement that all persons must be 'bound by the law'). This requirement of the rule of law is often asserted by those who call for 'law and order' in the face of lax enforcement of the law. It speaks both to the public (who are expected to obey the law) and to law-enforcement officials (who are expected reasonably to implement the law).

Secondly, in so far as legality addresses the actions of public officials, it requires that they act within the powers that have been conferred upon them. All decisions and acts of public officials should generally therefore be legally authorized. The modern view, as we shall shortly discuss, is that discretionary power is not wholly inimical to the notion of legality, but that discretion must also be exercised within the scope of

---

[40] Bingham, *The Rule of Law*, 8. Compare the definition of the former Secretary General of the United Nations, Kofi Annan that the rule of law is a 'Principle of governance in which all persons, institutions and entities, public and private, including the State itself, are accountable to laws that are publicly promulgated, equally enforced and independently adjudicated, and which are consistent with international human rights norms and standards. It requires, as well, measures to ensure adherence to the principles of supremacy of law, equality before the law, accountability to law, fairness in the application of law, separation of pow-ers, participation in decision-making, legal certainty, avoidance of arbitrariness and procedural and legal transparency'. *The Rule of Law and Transitional Justice in Conflict and Post Conflict Societies*, Report of the Secretary General, Doc. S/2004/616 23 August 2004, para. 6.

[41] Bingham's eight features are: accessibility of the law; law not discretion; equality before the law; the exercise of power; human rights; dispute resolution; a fair trial; and the rule of law in the international order.

[42] See ch. 5.

legality—in accordance with the purpose and objects of the power conferred on the decision-maker, and not in a way that is capricious or arbitrary.

Certainty

The essence of Dicey's rule of law is that law should be certain and predictable. His later followers, Hewart and Hayek, extolled the virtue of defined rules to govern the exercise of public power.

There is of course great virtue in the notion of law which is prospective and not retrospectively applied. Fair warning is an important requirement of the rule of law. However, we have seen that Dicey was less concerned that laws were 'harsh' than that they be known. Certainty, rather than substantive fairness, was the key value. Maitland wrote that 'Known general laws, however bad, interfere less with freedom than decisions based on no previously known rule.'[43] Hayek said:

> [I]t does not matter whether we all drive on the left or the right-hand side of the roads so long as we all do the same. The important thing is that the rule enables us to predict other people's behaviour correctly, and this requires that it should apply in all cases—even if in a particular instance we feel it to be unjust.[44]

The need for legal certainty was another reason why Dicey mistrusted official discretion.

Rules permit fair warning. They allow affected persons to know what they are required to do—or not do—in advance of any sanction for breach of the rule. Certainty in that sense has an instrumental value in that it allows decisions to be planned in advance and people to know clearly where they stand. However, the value of legal certainty is also grounded in *substantive fairness*. It is unfair to penalize someone for an action that was lawful when it was carried out and it is unfair to punish someone for the breach of a law which they were not able to discover. And, as we shall see, when a person is encouraged by the decision-maker to believe that a particular course of action will take place, certainty will dictate that his 'legitimate expectation' shall not be disappointed.

The notion of legal certainty does of course not mean that the law cannot be changed. But change should be carried out in a way that is transparent so that any amendments, repeals, or new laws should be accessible.

Equality

We have seen that Dicey considered that the rule of law required all officials, from the Prime Minister down to a constable or a collector of taxes, to be subject to the same responsibility for every act done without legal justification as any other citizen.[45] Dicey is here claiming for the rule of law formal equality, by which he meant that no person is exempt from the enforcement of the law; rich and poor, revenue official and

---

[43] *Collected Papers*, vol. I (1911), 81. Maitland equated arbitrary power with power that was 'uncertain' or 'incalculable': ibid., 80.

[44] F. A. Hayek, *The Road to Serfdom* (1943), 60.   [45] See Dicey, *Law of the Constitution*, 193.

individual taxpayer, powerful and marginalized are all within the equal reach of law's implementation.

This type of equality, although sometimes derided,[46] is important. It is inherent in the very notion of law, and in the integrity of law's application that like cases be treated alike. And it forbids vices such as corruption, which allow the benefits of law to be denied to those who do not offer bribes, and allow law to be sold to the highest bidder.

An interesting question is whether this notion of equality within the rule of law refers not to the content of the law but to its *enforcement* and *application* alone. So long as laws are applied equally—that is, consistently without irrational bias or distinction—then formal equality is complied with. Formal equality does not however prohibit *unequal laws*. It forbids, say, racially biased enforcement of the law, but does not forbid racially discriminatory laws from being enacted. For Dicey, the rule of law embraced only formal equality. This is because for him the role of equality in the rule of law was instrumental; to buttress the central value of legal certainty. It was not espoused as a virtue for its own sake. We have seen how Dicey's supporters freely acknowledged that it is more important that the law be certain than it be not 'harsh', 'bad', or 'unjust'.[47] Discriminatory or arbitrary enforcement of the law would violate legal certainty, but laws themselves that discriminated against certain groups or classes, but were uniformly enforced within the groups or class, would not violate legal certainty, or therefore Dicey's rule of law.

There are two opposing views as to whether substantive equality qualifies as a feature of the rule of law.[48] Those who believe that discriminatory laws are not 'law' would of course not permit them to qualify as complying with the rule of law.[49] On the other hand, as Lord Hoffmann has said, equality is in itself 'one of the building blocks of democracy'.[50] And Lady Hale has said that 'democracy values everyone equally, even if the majority does not'.[51] It is therefore not necessary to subsume substantive equality within the rule of law in order to demonstrate that discriminatory laws violate one of the fundamental requirements of democratic constitutionalism.[52]

Access to justice and rights

The fourth feature of the rule of law requires access to courts or equivalent institutions for the enforcement of rights. As early as 1215, Chapter 39 of Magna Carta provided that no person should be condemned 'except by lawful judgment of his peers or by the law

---

[46] J. D. Heydon, 'Are Bills of Rights Necessary in a Common Law System?' (2014) 130 *LQR* 392, at 411.

[47] See Maitland, *Collected Papers*, vol. I (1911), 8, and Hayek, *Road to Serfdom*.

[48] Raz, 'The Rule of Law and its Virtue', thinks not. Bingham, *The Rule of Law*, thinks it does.

[49] See Dworkin, *A Matter of Principle*.

[50] *Matadeen* v. *Pointu and Minister of Education and Science* [1999] AC 98 (PC). See also *Ghaidan* v. *Godin Mendoza* [2004] 2 AC 557 (same-sex partner entitled to same inheritance rights as different sex partner): '[Unequal treatment] is the reverse of rational behaviour . . . Power must not be exercised arbitrarily' (*per* Lady Hale).

[51] *Chester* v. *Secretary of State for Justice* [2013] UKSC 63, at [88].

[52] I have expanded on this point in 'Is Equality a Constitutional Principle?' (1994) 47 *Current Legal Problems* (Part 2) 1. See also R. Singh, 'Equality: The Neglected Virtue' [2004] *EHRLR* 141. For a view that equality (both formal and substantive) is part of the rule of law, see T. Allan, *Constitutional Justice* (2011).

of the land'. The requirement of 'due process' or 'natural justice' (these days called 'procedural propriety' or 'procedural fairness') furthers Bingham's requirement that people should be entitled to the 'benefit' of laws, and to ensure this by being able to enforce its application or to challenge its mis-application. In order to do this, the claimant will need access to the courts or equivalent institutions. Access to justice is therefore a further key element of the rule of law. It is a feature very different in kind from the notions of certainty and equality: it brings life to the rule of law by permitting its practical application.

Whatever degree of legality, certainty, or equality there may be, if a person is not able to challenge the government to assert his rights, including human rights, the rule of law cannot be said to pertain. In fact it could be said that the most important feature of a rule of law state is that it allows a person to challenge a decision of the government of the day with a reasonable prospect of success in an appropriate case.

Access to justice, however, requires more than a system of courts to which an individual may apply. Once the claimant reaches the court, a further aspect of the rule of law is engaged, namely the requirement that the decision-maker be unbiased—that is, both independent (in the sense of free of external pressure) and impartial (not apparently interested in the outcome of the case in favour of any one of the participants). Even if perfect impartiality on the part of the adjudicator is an unattainable goal (because we all have unconscious predilections and biases), the system should not give the appearance of bias. Justice must both be done and seen to be done. And the independence must extend not only to the judges but also to the legal profession, who must be able to provide advocacy services without fear or favour.

And once the person reaches a court, there must be a fair trial, with the opportunity to submit arguments and facts. Viewed in that light, access to justice is not a merely formal virtue. Its substantive dimension emerges when we consider that it endorses the notion that every person is entitled to be treated with due regard to the proper merits of their cause. Failure to provide that treatment diminishes a person's sense of individual worth and impairs their dignity.[53] The right to due process goes further than forbidding actual punishment without a trial. It extends to a concern that individuals should not have decisions made about their vital interests without an opportunity to influence the outcome of those decisions. And it requires restrictions on rights, liberties, and interests to be properly *justified*. The culture of justification, rather than the culture of authority,[54] is another mark of the difference between democracy and despotism. Due process therefore provides 'formal and institutional expression to the influence of reasoned argument in human affairs'.[55] Overt reference to irrational or

---

[53] For a full account of the variety of justifications of procedural protections, see D. J. Galligan, *Due Process and Fair Procedures* (1996), and see G. Richardson, 'The Legal Regulation of Process' in G. Richardson and H. Genn (eds.), *Administrative Law and Government Actions* (1994). The aspect of natural justice that requires the decision-maker to be unbiased also incorporates an aspect of the principle of separation of powers into the rule of law.

[54] E. Mureinik, 'A Bridge to Where? Introducing the Bill of Rights' (1994) 10 *SAJHR* 31.

[55] L. Fuller, 'Collective Bargaining and the Arbitrator' (1963) 1 *Wisconsin L Rev* 3. See also Rawls's view of natural justice as an element of the rule of law, in his *A Theory of Justice* (1972), 241–2.

particularistic factors (such as the defendant's class, gender, or race) may therefore be difficult to sustain. Because procedural fairness promotes full and fair consideration of the issues and evidence, as Lord Steyn has said, it plays 'an instrumental role in promoting just decisions'.[56]

Although Dicey favoured adjudication through the regular courts of law, different kinds of dispute-resolution provide procedural checks on discretion in order to comply with the rule of law. Some are provided through appeals—for example, in planning, from local to central government by means of written representations or a public inquiry; or in immigration and asylum matters, from an adjudicator to an appeal tribunal.

Some decisions decide not only rights between the individual and the public organization, but also questions of policy, such as whether a motorway should be built over a stretch of land. In those situations the decision may be structured by means of an inquiry or tribunal hearing, or may simply be made by an official within a government department. There has been a demand for public participation in those decisions. Even though those seeking participation have mere interests (rather than vested rights) in the decision's outcome, they ask for the right to participate in the process of making that decision. Neighbours want to be consulted about an application for planning permission on a local site, and people want to be consulted about the closure of hospitals, local railway lines, or coal pits.[57] If the rule of law is concerned to protect individuals from being deprived of their rights without an opportunity to defend themselves, the concern is only narrowly stretched to protect group interests from being overridden without the opportunity to express views on the matter to be decided.[58] For example, a challenge to a government review which reversed the 'high policy' against nuclear power was struck down by the Administrative Court on the ground that the review was so deficient in content and form that its process was 'manifestly unfair'.[59]

THE RULE OF LAW AS AN IDEAL

The rule of law contains, as we have seen, the requirements of legality, certainty, equality, and access to justice, which promote both formal and substantive goals. However, they are not unqualified; they constitute ideals which may permit of some exceptions.

In relation to legality, not all law can be enforced. Sometimes the prosecuting agency will lack the resources to prosecute offences. This happened when the police withdrew full enforcement of the law against unlawful protesters against the shipping of live

---

[56] *Raji* v. *General Medical Council* [2003] UKPC 24.

[57] R v. *British Coal Corpn and Secretary of State for Trade and Industry, ex parte Vardy and others* [1993] ICR 720 (CA).

[58] For an account of 'the ideology of public participation', see P. McAuslan, *The Ideologies of Planning Law* (1980); J. Habermas, *Towards a Rational Society* (1971).

[59] R (*Greenpeace Ltd*) v. *Secretary of State for Trade and Industry* [2007] EWHC 311 (Admin).

animals across the channel. The House of Lords accepted that the action was justified because it was stretching the chief constable's resources to the detriment of policing elsewhere in the county.[60] Full enforcement may also distort the purpose of the
rule and require, for example, the prosecution of a doctor who narrowly exceeded the
speed limit on a deserted street late at night while rushing to the scene of an accident.
That prosecution makes no sense in furthering the goal of preventing unsafe driving.

In December 2006 the Director of the Serious Fraud Office (the Director) decided to
abandon an investigation into allegations of bribery and corruption by BAE Systems
Ltd (BAE), in relation to contracts for Al-Yamamah military aircraft with the Kingdom
of Saudi Arabia. Threats had been made by Saudi officials that if the investigation
were to continue the Saudi government would cancel a proposed order for Eurofighter
Typhoon aircraft and withdraw security and intelligence cooperation with the UK.

Despite internal political pressure to drop the investigation, and just at the point
when the trail of investigation was extended to Swiss bank accounts, the Director was
persuaded to drop the case on the advice particularly of the British Ambassador to
Saudi Arabia that national security ('British lives on British streets') would be imper-
illed if the threat were carried out. The Director's decision was challenged through
judicial review and the Divisional Court held that the Director had not paid sufficient
regard to the danger to the rule of law in submitting to the threat.[61] However, the
House of Lords disagreed and held that the Director's decision was lawful and that
courts should be 'very slow to interfere' in prosecutorial decisions outside of 'exceptional cases'.[62] This was because, first, respect should be accorded to the independence
of the prosecutor. Secondly, it was said that prosecutorial decisions are not susceptible to judicial review because it is within neither the constitutional function nor the
practical competence of the courts to assess matters concerning the public interest,
especially when national security is in issue, as it was in this case.

On the other hand, it could be argued that the House of Lords gave too little weight
to the fact that the Director caved in to threats to our system of justice, and thus to the
rule of law. Had the threats been made by a British citizen, he would be liable at least to
prosecution for perverting the course of justice.

In relation to legal certainty, the benefits of rules—their objective, even-handed
features—may be opposed to other administrative benefits, especially those of individual treatment, and responsiveness. The virtue of rules to the administrator (routine
treatment and efficiency) and to the general public (predictability and the opportunity
to plan) may be a defect to the claimant with a special case (such as the brilliant applicant for a university place who failed to obtain the required grades because of a family
upset or illness just before the examination). Officials themselves may consider that a

---

[60] R v. *Chief Constable of Sussex, ex parte International Traders' Ferry Ltd* [1999] 2 AC 418. But see also
R v. *Coventry City Council, ex parte Phoenix Aviation* [1995] 3 All ER 37, where it was held that substantial
non-enforcement of the law was in breach of the rule of law.

[61] R *(on the application of Corner House)* v. *Director of the Serious Fraud Office* [2007] EWHC 311 (Admin).

[62] [2008] UKHL 6.

task requires flexibility, or genuinely want to help a particular client, but feel unable to do so. Hence the classic bureaucratic response: 'I'd like to help you—but this is the rule.'

Our administrative law itself recognizes the limits of rule-governed conduct through the principle against the 'fettering' of discretion. Where an official has wide discretion—for example, to provide grants to industry or to students or to regulate safety standards for taxi drivers—a rule will often be introduced both to assist in the articulation of the standard and its even-handed application, and also to announce the standard to affected persons. Driving safety rules, for example, may require passengers to wear seat belts, and regular vehicle maintenance inspections. A policy of promoting safe driving could be legalized by a rule specifying speeds of no more than 20 miles per hour on certain streets. The courts do not object to the use of a rule in itself, but they do sometimes object to its rigid application without giving a person with something new or special to say about his case the opportunity to put his argument to the decision-maker. The principle against the 'fettering of discretion' acknowledges how the rigid application of rules can militate against good and fair public administration.[63]

This balance of rule and discretion can be found etched into particular areas of public administration. In town planning, for example, permission is needed for development of land. By what criteria is that permission granted or refused? Some countries have adopted a system of zoning, by which the local map clearly marks out what can be done in each area. A would-be developer knows from the colour coding whether he can build a factory or change a shop to an office on a given site. In Britain this approach, whereby the zoning map in effect creates a series of rules about what can be done on the land, is greatly softened. Officials will take into account the formal plan for the area, but account may also be taken of 'other material considerations'.[64] So rule and discretion are mixed together, in an attempt to gain the benefits of each. Thus, an applicant for a craft centre in an area zoned as residential on the plan may nevertheless be granted permission because the centre fits in with the area, does not adversely affect its amenity, and generates local employment. These 'other material considerations' provide the flexibility to mitigate the rigours of a rule-bound plan.

Access to justice may also be subject to limitations. Litigation will not be within the reach of everyone's pocket, and legal aid depends upon national resources. Nor is adjudication an appropriate way to resolve all disputes. In the nineteenth century, writers such as Bentham[65] and his disciple Chadwick voiced strong opposition to the judicialization of administration which 'would lead to mindless disputes upon such simple questions as to whether a cask of biscuits was good or bad'.[66] Due process may impede speed and despatch. Could we really allow a hearing as to whether the

---

[63] See D. Galligan, 'The Nature and Function of Policies within Discretionary Power' [1976] *PL* 332 and *Discretionary Powers* (1986); C. Hilson, 'Judicial Review, Politics and the Fettering of Discretion' [2002] *PL* 111. See Woolf, Jowell, Le Sueur, et al., *de Smith's Judicial Review* (7th edn, 2013), ch. 9.

[64] Town and Country Planning Act 1990, s. 54A.

[65] L. J. Hume, *Bentham and Bureaucracy* (1981), 82.

[66] H. Parris, *Constitutional Bureaucracy* (1969), 82.

firefighters should douse a burning house with water? Or a pavement hearing before a police officer is able to tow away an illegally parked car? Should there be an appeal from a university lecturer's examination grade? Or from a decision to reject admission to a university? Sometimes parties who have to live with each other after the dispute prefer techniques of mediation to negotiate a compromise that is acceptable to both sides.[67] These forms of resolving disputes differ from adjudication where the final decision is taken by the independent 'judge' and is imposed rather than agreed.

THE PRACTICAL IMPLEMENTATION OF THE RULE OF LAW

The rule of law is a principle of institutional morality. As such it guides all forms both of law enforcement and of law-making. In particular, it suggests that legal certainty, equality, and access to justice are fundamental requirements of democratic constitutionalism. Nor, as we have seen are all its virtues simply formal. It promotes accountability, but also fairness and respect for human dignity.

In a country like the UK that does not have a codified constitution, the rule of law serves as a principle that constrains governmental power. We return now to Dicey's contention that the rule of law stands together with parliamentary sovereignty as a constitutional principle. Although many of Dicey's notions may have delayed the development in this country of a coherent public law, his genius was to recognize that our constitution does contain implied principles. The principle of parliamentary sovereignty, together with what he called conventions, *enables* powers to be exercised by government and specifies how it is to be exercised. The rule of law however *disables* government from abusing its power.

In countries with written constitutions the text itself provides the enabling features (such as who may vote and the composition of the executive and legislature). It also normally provides the disabling features through a Bill of Rights that constrains government, even elected Parliaments, from interfering with certain fundamental rights and freedoms (such as freedom of expression and association) which are considered necessary and integral to democracy.[68] In Britain, the rule of law as an unwritten principle performs a similar disabling function, in the area where its values apply.

How does the rule of law operate in practice in the UK? Let us first note that our courts have not yet, outside directly effective European Union law, felt themselves able to disapply primary legislation that offends the rule of law. However, since 1998 the Human Rights Act incorporates into domestic law most of the provisions of the ECHR, some of which contain values that inhere in the rule of law (such as the prohibition against retroactive laws, the prohibition of torture, the right to liberty, and the requirement of a fair trial). All decisions of public officials, including the courts,

---

[67] See V. Aubert, 'Competition and Dissensus: Two Types of Conflict and Conflict Resolution' (1963) 7(1) *J Conflict Res* 26.

[68] Although in some cases the state has a positive obligation to secure or enforce certain rights.

must now conform with Convention rights. Parliament's statutes may be reviewed by the courts for compatibility with Convention rights, but the courts may not, under the Act, strike down statutes that offend the ECHR; it may only declare them incompatible with Convention rights.[69]

However, the absence of judicial authority to disapply primary legislation that is contrary to the rule of law does not mean that the rule of law has no influence on the content of legislation. As a constitutional principle, the rule of law serves, as has already been noted, as a basis for the evaluation of all laws and provides a critical focus for public debate. There have been a number of occasions in recent years where proposals to evade the rule of law (for example, by prohibiting judicial review of decisions about asylum or immigration) were abandoned, in the face of strong opposition on the ground that the proposals offended the rule of law's moral strictures.[70]

Even before the Human Rights Act 1998 came into force, the courts would seek to reconcile the principles of parliamentary sovereignty and the rule of law where possible. For example, in the case of *Pierson*,[71] it was held that, despite the fact that the Home Secretary had very broad discretionary power to set a prisoner's tariff (the minimum sentence prior to parole), the decision to increase the tariff retrospectively—contrary to an earlier indication that the lesser sentence would be imposed—offended the rule of law in its substantive sense. Lord Steyn in that case said:

> Parliament does not legislate in a vacuum. Parliament legislates for a European liberal democracy based upon the traditions of the common law . . . and . . . unless there is the clearest provision to the contrary, Parliament must be presumed not to legislate contrary to the Rule of Law.[72]

This presumption in favour of the rule of law (and other fundamental constitutional principles, such as freedom of expression) was referred to as 'principle of legality', described by Lord Hoffmann in a later case as follows:

> Parliamentary sovereignty means that Parliament can, if it chooses, legislate contrary to fundamental principles of human rights . . . But the principle of legality means that Parliament must squarely confront what it is doing and accept the political cost. Fundamental rights cannot be overridden by general or ambiguous words. This is because there is too great a risk that the full implications of their unqualified meaning may have passed unnoticed in the democratic process. In the absence of express language or necessary implication to the contrary, the courts therefore presume that even the most general words were intended to be subject to the basic rights of the individual. In this way the courts of the United Kingdom, though acknowledging the sovereignty of

---

[69] See ch. 3.

[70] See the account by R. Rawlings, 'Review. Revenge and Retreat' [2005] *MLR* 378; A. Le Sueur, 'Three Strikes and You're Out? The UK Government's Strategy to Oust Judicial Review from Immigration and Asylum' [2004] *PL* 225; and Joint Committee on Human Rights, *The Implications for Access to Justice of the Government's Proposals to Reform Judicial Review* (2013–14, HL 174, HC 868).

[71] *R v. Secretary of State for the Home Department, ex parte Pierson* [1998] AC 539.

[72] Ibid., 575.

Parliament, apply principles of constitutionality little different from those which exist in countries where the power of the legislature is expressly limited by a constitutional document.[73]

JUDICIAL REVIEW OF THE EXERCISE OF PUBLIC POWER

In addition to the rule of law being recognized as what is called a 'common law constitutional right', the practical implementation of the rule of law has taken place primarily through judicial review of the actions of public officials. During the first half of the twentieth century, a time of reaction to Dicey's rule of law, the courts rarely interfered with the exercise of discretionary powers.[74] From that time on, however, they began to require that power be exercised in accordance with three 'grounds' of judicial review, each of them resting in large part on the rule of law.

The first ground, 'legality', requires officials to act within the scope of their lawful powers. The courts ensure that the official decisions do not stray beyond the 'four corners' of a statute by failing to take into account 'relevant' considerations (that is, considerations that the law requires), or by taking into account 'irrelevant' considerations (that is, considerations outside the object and purpose that Parliament intended the statute to pursue).[75] This exercise is, as we have discussed, a clear instance of the implementation of the rule of law, whereby the courts act as guardians of Parliament's intent and purpose. The definition of the purpose of a given statute is no mere mechanical exercise, and is often complicated by the fact that the statute confers very wide discretionary powers on the decision-maker, for example to act 'as he sees fit'. For instance, where a statute conferred broad powers upon a local authority to sell its own dwellings to their inhabitants, and where some local councillors decided to sell those dwellings for the cynical purpose of securing electoral advantage for their party, the courts had to grapple with the question whether the councillors were entitled, as elected politicians, to assist their party to win the next election. The House of Lords held that statutory powers are conferred on trust, and not absolutely, and that the motive of the councillors—party gain—was extraneous to the purpose for which the powers were conferred.[76]

Although there are a number of administrative tasks that cannot be predetermined by any rule, the courts have reconciled Dicey's fear of any discretion with a view that no discretion is wholly unfettered. As was said in a leading case on the issue of 'legality', even if a discretion were expressly defined as 'unfettered':

> The use of that adjective . . . can do nothing to unfetter the control which the judiciary have over the executive, namely that in exercising their powers the latter must

---

[73] *R* v. *Secretary of State for the Home Department, ex parte Simms* [2003] 2 AC 115, 131.

[74] For an account of this history, see J. Jowell, 'Administrative Law', and R. Stevens, 'Government and the Judiciary' in V. Bogdanor (ed.), *The British Constitution in the Twentieth Century* (2003).

[75] e.g. *Padfield* v. *Minister of Agriculture, Fisheries and Food* [1968] AC 997.

[76] *Magill* v. *Porter* [2001] UKHL 67.

act lawfully and that is a matter to be determined by looking at the Act and its scope and object in conferring a discretion upon the Minister rather than by the use of adjectives.[77]

The second ground of review, that of 'procedural propriety', requires decision-makers to be unbiased and to grant a fair hearing to claimants before depriving them of a right or significant interest (such as an interest in livelihood or reputation). We have seen that the right of due process—the right not to be condemned unheard—is a central value of the rule of law, which the courts presume Parliament to respect. The courts have affirmed the principle of procedural fairness, even where the statute conferring the power to decide was silent on the matter. In the nineteenth century the courts were not slow to allow the 'justice of the common law' to supplement the legislature's omission, looking back to the Garden of Eden as an example of a fair hearing being granted before Adam and Eve were deported from their green and pleasant land.[78] In the first half of the twentieth century the courts became reluctant to grant hearings, restricting them to matters where rights were in issue (rather than privileges). The case of *Ridge* v. *Baldwin*[79] then extended the hearing to the protections of more important interests, such as reputation or livelihood.

This kind of procedural protection, whether established by statute or the common law, is a concrete expression of the rule of law. Its content is variable, depending on the issue. However, as was said:

> The Rule of Law rightly requires that certain decisions, of which the paradigm examples are findings of breaches of the criminal law and adjudication as to private rights, should be entrusted to the judicial branch of government.[80]

Over the past few years, the courts have extended the requirement of a fair hearing even where the claimant does not possess a threatened right or even an important interest. A hearing will be required where a 'legitimate expectation' has been induced by the decision-maker.[81] In such a case the claimant has, expressly or impliedly, been promised either a hearing or the continuation of a benefit. The courts will not sanction the disappointment of such an expectation unless the claimant is permitted to make representations on the matter. The notion of the legitimate expectation is itself rooted in that aspect of the rule of law which requires legal certainty.

The third ground of judicial review, 'irrationality' or 'unreasonableness', also applies aspects of the rule of law. Suppose the police charge only bearded drivers, or drivers of a particular race, with traffic offences? Suppose an education authority chose to dismiss all teachers with red hair? Suppose a prison officer refused to

---

[77] *Per* Lord Upjohn in *Padfield* v. *Minister of Agriculture, Fisheries and Food* [1968] AC 997.

[78] *Cooper* v. *Wandsworth Board of Works* (1863) 14 CB (NS) 180.   [79] [1964] AC 40.

[80] *Alconbury Developments Ltd* v. *Secretary of State for the Environment, Transport and the Regions* [2001] UKHL 23, at [42], *per* Lord Hoffmann. See also *Runa Begum* v. *Tower Hamlets LBC* [2003] UKHL 5, at [4].

[81] Endorsed in the House of Lords in *Council of Civil Service Unions* v. *Minister of the Civil Service* [1985] AC 374.

permit a prisoner to communicate with his lawyer? Suppose a minister raised the minimum sentence of a prisoner, having earlier told him that the sentence would be set at a lower level? Would these decisions offend the rule of law? If so, the rule of law becomes a substantive doctrine and not merely formal or procedural. Our courts, through judicial review, tread warily in this area, interfering only if the decision was beyond the range of reasonable responses.[82] However, where the rule of law or other constitutional principles or fundamental rights are in issue, the courts scrutinize the decision with greater care[83] and also adopt the 'principle of legality' that we have seen earlier,[84] which presumes that Parliament intends the rule of law to prevail.

In practice, many of the decisions held unreasonable are so held because they offend the values of the rule of law discussed earlier. The concept of 'unreasonableness', or 'irrationality', in itself imputes the arbitrariness that Dicey considered was the antithesis of the rule of law. Decisions based upon insufficient evidentiary basis,[85] or which are inconsistent,[86] fall foul of the rule of law's values. Where bye-laws are not sufficiently clear they have been held unlawful for 'uncertainty'.[87] Dicey's abhorrence of arbitrary decisions is also endorsed when a decision is struck down because it is simply unreasonably harsh or oppressive.[88]

The practical implementation of the rule of law over the years makes it clear that its substantive aims underlie and endorse the striking down of a number of decisions, albeit often without mentioning its name. A local authority which withdrew the licence of a rugby club whose members had visited South Africa during the apartheid regime fell foul of the rule of law on the ground that there should be no punishment where there was no law (since sporting contacts with South Africa were not then prohibited).[89] A minister's rules allowing a prison governor to prevent a prisoner corresponding with his lawyer, even when no litigation was contemplated, was held to violate the prisoner's 'constitutional right' of access to justice.[90] As we have seen, common law constitutional rights include the rule of law in its different manifestations. Thus access to justice was held to be a 'higher order' right which was violated by the Lord Chancellor's imposition of substantial court fees which an impecunious litigant was unable to afford.[91] The inability of the remaining white farmers in Zimbabwe to challenge the proposed taking of their land, following a constitutional amendment, was held to violate the rule of law as a foundational

---

[82] *Associated Provincial Picture Houses* v. *Wednesbury Corporation* [1948] 1 KB 223.

[83] Under the Human Rights Act 1998, applying the ECHR, the courts will adopt even stricter scrutiny under the test of 'proportionality'. See ch. 3.

[84] See n. 75.   [85] *E* v. *Secretary of State for the Home Department* [2004] EWCA Civ 49.

[86] See R. Clayton, 'Legitimate Expectations, Policy and the Principle of Consistency' [2003] *Camb LJ* 93. See *R (Rashid)* v. *Secretary of State for the Home Department* [2005] EWCA Civ 744.

[87] *Percy* v. *Hall* [1997] QB 924. And see *R (L)* v. *Secretary of State for the Home Department* [2003] EWCA Civ 25 ('Legal certainty is an aspect of the rule of law', at [25]).

[88] See e.g. *Wheeler* v. *Leicester City Council* [1985] AC 1054 (HL).   [89] Ibid.

[90] *R* v. *Secretary of State for the Home Department, ex parte Leech* (No. 2) [1994] QB 198.

[91] *R* v. *Lord Chancellor, ex parte Witham* [1997] 1 WLR 104.

principle of the Southern African Development Community (SADC).[92] And an order seeking to freeze the assets of known terrorists such as Usama Bin-Laden on a consolidated list was held by the Supreme Court to violate the rule of law because the person whose name is on the list had no right to challenge the listing before a court.[93] Immigration Rules were held unlawful because they were changed by the minister after having been laid before Parliament.[94] Sedley LJ held that the practice abandoned a 'constitutional principle which for four centuries has stood as a pillar of the separation of powers in what is today a democracy under the rule of law'. He held that rules which differed from those approved by Parliament violated 'the certainty which rules must have if they are to function as law'. Similarly, the Supreme Court pronounced in a case where the release date of a prisoner was not accurately calculated by the Home Office (due to a morass of legislation and further amending legislation) that 'it is simply unacceptable in a society governed by the rule of law for it to be well nigh impossible to discern from statutory provisions what a sentence means in practice'.[95]

The remarkable elasticity of the rule of law, and the richness of its underlying values, was demonstrated in a case that concerned the legal effect of a decision that had not been communicated to the person affected. The relevant legislation permitted asylum seekers' right to income support to be terminated once their application for asylum had been refused by a 'determination' of the Home Secretary. The refusal in this case was recorded only in an internal file note in the Home Office and communicated to the Benefits Agency, which promptly denied the appellant future income support. The determination was not, however, communicated to the appellant.[96]

The appellant in this case could not easily invoke the normal requirements of the rule of law in her favour. The decision did not take effect retrospectively; ignorance of the law does not normally excuse its application. Nevertheless, the House of Lords, by majority, held that the decision violated 'the constitutional principle requiring the Rule of Law to be observed'.[97] Lord Steyn, with whom the majority of their Lordships concurred, based his argument both upon legal certainty ('surprise is the enemy of justice') and upon accountability: the individual must be informed of the outcome of her case so 'she can decide what to do' and 'be in a position to challenge the decision in the courts' (this being an aspect of the principle of the right of access to justice).[98] The House of Lords had no truck with the notion that the Home Secretary's determination had formally and strictly been made. This was 'legalism and conceptualism run riot', which is reminiscent of the state described by Kafka 'where the rights of an individual

---

[92] *Campbell et al.* v. *The Republic of Zimbabwe* [2007] SADC (T) Case no. 2.

[93] *Her Majesty's Treasury* v. *Ahmed and others* [2010] UKSC 2. See more recently *Bank Mellat* v. *H.M. Treasury* [2013] UKSC 39.

[94] *R (PaninkaPankina)* v. *Secretary of State for the Home Department* [2010] EWCA Civ 719. See also *Her Majesty's Treasury* v. *Ahmed and others* [2010] UKSC 2, discussed above, n. 93.

[95] *R (Noone)* v. *The Governor of HMP Drake Hall* [2010] UKSC 30.

[96] *R (on the application of Anufrijeva)* v. *Secretary of State for the Home Department* [2003] 3 WLR 252.

[97] Ibid., at [28], *per* Lord Steyn.   [98] Ibid., at [26] and [31], *per* Lord Steyn.

are overridden by hole in the corner decisions or knocks on the doors in the early hours'.[99]

The rule of law does, therefore, possess substantive content.[100] The protection of a legitimate expectation, which began by grounding a procedural right to a fair hearing,[101] has since been extended to a substantive doctrine, upholding not merely a fair hearing but the promised benefit itself. For example, a local authority which promised the claimant a 'home for life' in an institution for the chronically ill was not permitted to disappoint the resultant legitimate expectation.[102]

These various aspects of the practical implementation of the rule of law show that its requirements of legality, certainty, equality, and access to justice do not merely, as Jennings would have it, further the aims of free trade and the market economy. They certainly do encourage investment as they signal a society based on stability and fairness. However, they also enhance accountability and promote respect for the dignity of the individual.[103] As Tom Bingham said, rejecting Raz's view of the 'thin' concept of the rule of law, in which Raz holds that slavery is compatible with the rule of law:

> A state which savagely represses or persecutes sections of its people cannot in my view be regarded as observing the rule of law, even if the transport of the persecuted minority to the concentration camp or the compulsory exposure of female children on the mountainside is the subject of detailed laws duly enacted and scrupulously observed.[104]

THE RULE OF LAW AND PARLIAMENTARY SOVEREIGNTY

What about the rule of law's status in relation to the sovereignty of Parliament? In the UK the principle of parliamentary sovereignty has always been able to override the rule of law; not on the authority of any written constitution, but on the authority of commentators such as Dicey and repeated assertions by the courts over time. In the absence of any formal constitutional source, is it theoretically open to the rule of law to replace the sovereignty of Parliament as our primary constitutional principle? This issue was raised in a most unlikely case involving a challenge to the Hunting Act 2004, which banned the hunting of most wild mammals with dogs.[105] The central issue in the case was the validity of the Parliament Acts 1911 and 1949, which were

---

[99] Ibid., at [32] and [28], *per* Lord Steyn. See also *FP (Iran)* v. *Secretary of State for the Home Department* [2007] EWCA Civ 13, where Arden LJ invoked the rule of law to safeguard access to a tribunal—a right which 'cannot be taken away before it has been communicated to the person entitled to it', at [61].

[100] This passage was cited with approval by Lord Steyn in *R* v. *Secretary of State for the Home Department, ex parte Pierson* [1998] AC 539 (HL).

[101] See n. 81.

[102] *R* v. *North and East Devon Health Authority, ex parte Coughlan* [2001] QB 213.

[103] See Rawls, *A Theory of Justice*, 235–43, and cf. Joseph Raz's view of the rule of law as a negative value in 'The Rule of Law and its Virtue' (1977) 93 *LQR* 195–211. See also J. Raz, *Ethics in the Public Domain* (1994), ch. 16. See P. Joseph, 'The Rule of Law: Foundational Norm' in Ekins (ed.), *Modern Challenges to the Rule of Law*, 47, and other chapters there on this issue.

[104] Bingham, *The Rule of Law*, 67.

[105] *Jackson* v. *Her Majesty's Attorney General* [2005] UKHL 56.

invoked to ensure the passage of the bill without the approval of the House of Lords. The Parliament Acts were upheld, as was the Hunting Act 2004, but three significant *obiter dicta* questioned the relation of parliamentary sovereignty to the rule of law as had never been done before. Lord Steyn said that:

> in exceptional circumstances involving an attempt to abolish judicial review or the authority of the courts, [the courts] may have to consider whether this is a constitutional fundamental which even a complaisant House of Commons cannot abolish.

Lady Hale said:

> The Courts will treat with particular suspicion (and might even reject) any attempt to subvert the rule of law by removing governmental action affecting the rights of the individual from all judicial powers.

And Lord Hope, even more forthrightly, said that 'it is no longer right to say that [Parliament's] freedom to legislate admits of no qualification' and that 'the rule of law enforced by the courts is the controlling principle upon which our constitution is based'.[106]

It may take some time, provocative legislation, and considerable judicial courage for the courts to assert the primacy of the rule of law over parliamentary sovereignty, but it is no longer self-evident that a legislature in a modern democracy should be able with impunity to violate the strictures of the rule of law.[107]

IS THE RULE OF LAW A UNIVERSAL CONCEPT?

Finally, we must ask whether the rule of law is a construct that is the preserve of advanced democracies alone. This view is strongly denied by the distinguished jurist and former Attorney General of India, Soli Sorabjee, who has recently said:

> It needs to be emphasised that there is nothing western or eastern or northern or southern about the underlying principle of the rule of law. It has a global reach and dimension. The rule of law symbolizes the quest . . . to combine that degree of liberty without which the law is tyranny with that degree of law without which liberty becomes licence. In the words of the great Justice Vivien Bose of [the Indian] Supreme Court, the rule of law 'is the heritage of all mankind because its underlying rationale is belief in . . . the human dignity of all individuals anywhere in the world'.[108]

In 2011 the Council of Europe's Venice Commission (the Commission for Democracy Through Law—formed in 1990 to assist the countries of the former Soviet Union with constitutional advice) agreed on a document on the rule of law which accepted Tom Bingham's definition and eight ingredients.[109] This was remarkable in a body

---

[106] Ibid., at [104]–[107], Lord Hope repeated this view in *AXA General Insurance Ltd and others v Lord Advocate and others* [2011] UKSC 46, at [51].

[107] See J. Jowell, 'Parliamentary Sovereignty under the New Constitutional Hypothesis' [2006] *PL* 562.

[108] 'The Rule of Law: A Moral Imperative for the Civilised World' [2014] *Supreme Court Cases* 59, at 61.

[109] European Commission for Democracy Through Law, *Report on the Rule of Law*, CDL-AD (2011)

representing 47 countries with very different traditions, from common law to codified systems and from the German 'Rechsstaat' to the French 'Etat de droit' and onwards. That approach and definition has recently been adopted by a consultation paper on the rule of law issued by the Commission of the European Union.[110]

It must of course be acknowledged that there may be different ways of achieving the rule of law in countries with very different traditions, history, and institutions. That does not, however, lead to the conclusion that the rule of law is an entirely relative and shifting concept and therefore may be readily excused by the standard of national convenience. As we have seen, the rule of law has a core meaning and a profound purpose in a world where the value of human dignity is too often compromised by oppression and a desire to rule not by law but by ideology—by raw power and by extreme dogma.

It is surely patronizing to say that the rule of law is for some parts of the world only. Turn the four features of the rule of law on their heads and, as each of its core elements falls to the ground the unmistakable features of tyranny come ominously into view: laws which are uncertain and retrospective; corruption and favoritism in the implementation of law; no access to courts; unfair trials before judges who routinely decide in favour of the government of the day or other powerful elites. Can we really say that any of those are suitable for any country? Or that the features of the rule of law are strictly the preserve of any country or group of countries?

One must also add the instrumental benefits of the rule of law. Legal certainty and equal application of the law are central ingredients to accountability and the possibility of legal challenge. This is clearly a necessary ingredient of investment and therefore growth. Investment will shirk countries which do not honour contracts or property rights, or which tax retrospectively or discriminate or intimidate selected firms or individuals without any hope of recourse.[111]

But the rule of law is not only for the investor or the entrepreneur. It is an instrument of empowerment. We have seen that the ability to challenge public decisions is a key feature of the rule of law. An example from South Africa illustrates this starkly: rule of law was incorporated as a founding principle of the post-apartheid South African constitution and South Africa was the first constitution in the world to establish a constitutional right to just administrative action—the right to challenge public officials for breach of legal, fair, or unreasonable acts.[112] It was the utilization of this provision that permitted access to be provided to retroviral drugs to HIV-ridden women and children in South Africa—a decision that has probably done more for the well-being of women and children in Africa than any other.[113] Without the rule of law power and

---

[110] EU Commission, *Communication from the Commission to the European Parliament and the Council, a New EU Framework to Strengthen the Rule of Law*, COM 2014 158 final/2.

[111] See the critical discussion about law and development in D. Marshall (ed.), *The International Rule of Law Movement* (2014). The defence of the rule of law in that work is put by J. Goldston, 'New Rules for the Rule of Law', at 1.

[112] Section 33 of the Constitution of South Africa, 1994.

[113] See *Minister of Health* v. *Treatment Action Campaign* (TAC) 2002 (5) SA 721 (CC).

resources tend to fall into—or remain in—the hands of the powerful to the exclusion of the poor and the marginalized.

CONCLUSION

Dicey's rule of law has indeed been damaged over the years by those who attacked it for failing to recognize that official discretion is necessary to perform the welfare and regulatory functions of modern government. Writing about American law from 1780 to 1860, Morton Horwitz describes the growth of legal power to bring about economic redistribution in favour of powerful groups who carefully disguised under a neutral façade the class bias inherent in the law.[114] Robert Unger distinguishes the rule of law which exists in societies governed by formal rules and procedures from one in which communal bonds and shared values leave no need for this formal legality.[115] Writing in 2010, Martin Loughlin still considers the rule of law's limitations to be evident:

> not least because, founded on eighteenth-century political convictions concerning lim-
> ited government, it has little bearing on the contemporary world. Like rule by law, the
> doctrine of the rule of law presents itself as an impossible ideal.[116]

And we have seen other recent contemporary attacks on the rule of law, in domestic and international contexts.[117] In his book *Whigs and Hunters*[118] on the origins of the Black Act of 1723, which led to a 'flood-tide of eighteenth-century retributive justice',[119] E. P. Thompson, the Marxist historian, concludes that 'the Rule of Law itself, the imposing of effective inhibitions upon power and the defence of the citizen from power's all-intrusive claims, seems to me to be an unqualified human good'.[120] In a critical review, Horwitz disagreed:

> I do not see how a man of the left can describe the Rule of Law as an 'unqualified human
> good'! It undoubtedly restrains power, but it also prevents power's benevolent exercise.
> It creates formal equality—a not inconsiderable virtue—but it *promotes* substantive
> inequality by creating a consciousness that radically separates law from politics, means
> from ends, processes from outcomes. By promoting procedural justice it enables the
> shrewd, the calculating, the wealthy to manipulate its forms to their own advantage. And
> it ratifies and legitimates an adversarial, competitive, and atomistic conception of human
> relations.[121]

---

[114] M. Horwitz, *The Transformation of American Law 1780–1860* (1977).

[115] R. Unger, *Law in Modern Society* (1976).

[116] M. Loughlin, *Foundations of Public Law* (2010) 337.

[117] See e.g. the recent books by Ekins (*Modern Challenges to the Rule of Law*) and Marshall (*The International Rule of Law Movement*).

[118] Thompson, *Whigs and Hunters*.   [119] Ibid., 23.   [120] Ibid., 266.

[121] M. Horwitz (1977) 86 *Yale LJ* 561. Like Horwitz, Unger, in *Law in Modern Society*, sees general rules as crystallizing and legitimizing the power of the ruling class, yet giving a false appearance of neutrality.

Horwitz's view of the rule of law is misleading. Law can, of course, be oppressive, but we must be careful about equating the rule of law with the substance of particular rules or with the substantive quality of the legal system. To claim that unjust laws and their rigorous enforcement demonstrate that the rule of law is an instrument of oppression is as misleading as the claim (often made in totalitarian countries) that the world described in Kafka's *The Trial*, with its maze of legal procedures, consistently yet heartlessly enforced, represents a state of perfect legality. Legality must be distinguished from legalism; rule *by* law is different from the rule of law.[122]

Thompson is right that the rule of law does impose 'effective inhibitions upon power' and the defence of the citizen from power's 'all-intrusive claims'. As a general principle it asserts important moral claims for legality, certainty, equality, and access to justice. These requirements do not suffer from vagueness, as the rule of law's opponents often claim. They are universal ideals which seek a set of practical constraints upon officials who step outside their conferred powers or who act arbitrarily or unfairly. By permitting challenge to the abuse of power it promotes individual empowerment and respect for equal human dignity that is too often ignored or neglected by even the most compassionate governments.

FURTHER READING

ALLAN, T. R. S., *Constitutional Justice: A Liberal Theory of the Rule of Law* (2001).

BINGHAM, T., *The Rule of Law* (2010)

CRAIG, P., 'Formal and Substantive Conceptions of the Rule of Law: An Analytical Framework' [1997] *PL* 447

DWORKIN, R., 'Political Judges and the Rule of Law', in his *A Matter of Principle* (1985), ch. 1

EKINS, R. (ed.), *Modern Challenges to the Rule of Law* (2011)

EUROPEAN COMMISSION FOR DEMOCRACY THROUGH LAW (The Venice Commission), *Report on the Rule of Law* (CDL_AD (2011)003-e-March 2011)

MARSHALL, D. (ed.), *The International Rule of Law Movement* (2014)

RAZ, J., 'The Rule of Law and its Virtue' (1977) 93 *LQR* 195

---

[122] This has been interpreted as the current Chinese government's understanding of the rule of law, as requiring strict enforcement of the law as determined by the Party, irrespective of the content of the law. See B. Tamanaha, *On the Rule of Law: History, Politics, Theory* (2004) 92.

2

THE PRINCIPLE OF PARLIAMENTARY SOVEREIGNTY IN LEGAL, CONSTITUTIONAL, AND POLITICAL PERSPECTIVE

*Mark Elliott**

SUMMARY

Parliamentary sovereignty has long been regarded—by most, at least—as an axiomatic feature of the United Kingdom's constitutional arrangements. The orthodox view holds that the UK Parliament has authority that is unlimited in domestic law, meaning that it is legally free to enact any legislation it wishes. However, precisely what parliamentary sovereignty means—and, ultimately, whether it accurately describes the reality of Parliament's relationship with other institutions—is a less cut-and-dried matter than orthodox accounts may suggest. This chapter examines the sovereignty of Parliament by reference to phenomena that may be considered to sit uncomfortably with it. In particular, devolution, British membership of the European Union, the UK's being a party to the European Convention on Human Rights and common law constitutional principles are addressed. The implications for parliamentary sovereignty of these matters are examined not only in legal, but also constitutional and political, perspective. The conclusion is reached that different pictures are revealed when legal and other lenses are applied, and that whether—and, if so, to what extent—political and constitutional forms of constraint may sound in the legal realm is inherently uncertain. Such uncertainty concerning the extent of Parliament's legislative authority reflects a necessary tension between the judicial and political branches, the unresolved nature of that tension evidencing a form of institutional comity that is imperative to the functioning of an unwritten constitutional system.

* Reader in Public Law, Faculty of Law, University of Cambridge; Fellow, St Catharine's College, Cambridge.

INTRODUCTION

The claim lying at the core of the doctrine of parliamentary sovereignty is—on the face of it—as simple as it is extravagant. In the well-known words of Dicey, it means that the United Kingdom Parliament has 'the right to make or unmake any law whatever' and that 'no person or body is recognised by the law of England as having a right to override or set aside the legislation of Parliament'.[1] Well over 100 years since Dicey wrote in those terms, the UK constitution has changed significantly—and, in some respects, almost beyond recognition. While the Union remains—albeit in a geographically diminished form following the departure, contrary to Dicey's strongly held views, of what became the Republic of Ireland—the UK has been transformed through the development of a multilayered constitution. Through devolution on the one hand and the UK's membership of pan-European institutions on the other, the notion of a sovereign Westminster Parliament may remain, but it subsists today within a constitutional setting that is radically different. It would be mistaken and simplistic to assert that parliamentary sovereignty has been caught and killed by a pincer movement effected by new tiers of sub- and supranational governance. At the same time, however, it would be naïve to suggest that those phenomena sit entirely comfortably with an unreconstructed Diceyan version of the sovereignty doctrine.

This chapter situates parliamentary sovereignty in its wider constitutional setting by examining it from three perspectives. It examines, first, the implications of devolution and, secondly, the implications of the UK's membership of the European Union (EU) and its being a party to the European Convention on Human Rights (ECHR). Thirdly, the viability of the sovereignty doctrine from the perspective of its *own* constitutional plane—namely, the plane of domestic constitutional law—is addressed. In particular, the role of the common law, and the nature of its interaction with statute law, are considered.

From each of these vantage points, the notion of sovereignty is explored and tested by reference to two key questions. The first asks whether, at any of the three constitutional levels with which this chapter is concerned, we encounter a competitor institution in the form of law or a law-maker that may viably claim to be the legal superior, or at least equal, of the Westminster Parliament or of its legislative outputs. The second question asks whether there exist benchmarks against which the constitutionality of legislation enacted by the Westminster Parliament may plausibly be tested.

The two questions are related but distinct. They amount to the examination of Parliament's legislative authority through two different lenses that are concerned respectively with purely legal and broader constitutional criteria. The first question has an all-or-nothing quality to it. Which institution—whose law—prevails in the event of conflict? The second question, far from being binary, is granular in nature. It

---

[1] A. V. Dicey, *The Law of the Constitution*, ed. E. C. S. Wade (10th edn, 1959), 40–1.

is concerned not with crisp questions of hierarchical priority, but with the existence of constitutional norms that may amount to standards by reference to which the constitutionality of legislation may be evaluated. The use of these two different lenses implies that the legal validity of legislation and its constitutionality may be distinguishable phenomena. The nature and plausibility of that claim will be examined during the course of the chapter.

DEVOLUTION

In a lecture she gave in 2012, Lady Hale said: 'The United Kingdom has . . . become a federal state with a Constitution regulating the relationships between the federal centre and the component parts.'[2] This is a striking claim about how, in constitutional terms, we ought to characterize devolution.[3] It is certainly the case that the UK system today *resembles* a federal one to a greater extent than ever before. However, for all that it might appear to have some of the trappings of a federal state, the UK constitution clearly deviates from that paradigm. The asymmetric nature of the system—such that different geographical parts of the UK have different amounts of devolved authority from one another—is an obvious example of such deviation.[4] So, too, is the fact a significant part of the UK—England—is presently excluded from the devolution settlement, making it, as Rawlings put it, 'the "spectre at the feast"'.[5]

Lady Hale's claim concerning federalization carries a further implication that is particularly pertinent to our inquiry. If she is right—if the UK is indeed a federal system—then the UK Parliament must no longer be sovereign. Parliamentary sovereignty is flatly incompatible with any conventional understanding of the federal model, since one of its cardinal features is the existence of a constitutionally entrenched balance of power between governing institutions at the national and subnational levels. This means that no single institution at either level may have the capacity unilaterally to alter the balance of power. If the position were otherwise, the balance of power would not be constitutionally guaranteed, and the system would not be a federal one in any meaningful sense.

This analysis may seem to hammer a further nail into the coffin of Lady Hale's federalization claim. One of the hallmarks of devolution is that the national legislature, far from *transferring* legislative competence, merely *shares* such competence with devolved institutions. A further hallmark of devolution is that such sharing of authority occurs only for as long as the national legislature so provides, and on whatever terms it sets out. The UK legislation that forms the constitutional bedrock of the devolution

---

[2] Lady Hale, 'The Supreme Court in the UK Constitution' (Legal Wales Lecture, 12 October 2012), available at http://www.supremecourt.uk/docs/speech-121012.pdf.

[3] See ch. 9 for discussion of devolution.

[4] See e.g. R. Brazier, 'The Constitution of the United Kingdom' [1999] *Camb LJ* 96.

[5] R. Rawlings, 'Concordats of the Constitution' (2000) 116 *LQR* 257, 266.

settlements clearly adheres to these standard aspects of the devolution model. Indeed, the legislation explicitly repudiates any suggestion that the empowerment of devolved institutions to enact legislation might effect a commensurate—or any—diminution in the authority of the UK Parliament. For instance, s. 28 of the Scotland Act 1998, which is the root of the Scottish Parliament's legal authority to legislate, is explicitly caveated in the following terms: 'This section does not affect the power of the Parliament of the United Kingdom to make laws for Scotland.'[6] The Government of Wales Act 2006 and the Northern Ireland Act 1998 are similarly caveated.[7] On the face of it, provisions such as these slam the door in the face of any argument that devolution amounts to a form of creeping federalization that would call into question the ongoing sovereignty of the UK Parliament. The position may be somewhat different if a proposal to enact UK legislation providing that the Scottish Parliament and government are 'permanent' institutions is implemented.[8] If such legislation were enacted, this might be taken to suggest that the UK Parliament would be legally disabled from abolishing the Scottish Parliament and government. The orthodox view, however, is that the Westminster Parliament cannot legally relinquish its sovereign authority,[9] meaning that any statement in UK legislation as to the 'permanence' of the Scottish Parliament would be likely to have political rather than legal effects.

In any event, the position is not as straightforward as bald interpretation of the existing legislation might suggest. This point can best be made by returning to, and posing, the two questions set out at the beginning of this chapter. Those questions, it will be recalled, are respectively concerned with the existence of competitor institutions representing a threat to the UK Parliament's sovereign claim of legal superiority, and with the existence of normative benchmarks by reference to which the constitutionality of the UK Parliament's legislative outputs might be assessed. We will see that, in the devolution context, those questions yield divergent answers—a divergence that underscores the necessity of approaching questions about sovereignty not only through the binary lens supplied by the first question, but also via the more subtle, analytical tools provided by the second.

What, then, of the first question? Are the devolved legislatures the legal superiors of the UK Parliament? Can legislation enacted by the devolved legislatures assert any plausible claim to legal superiority over UK legislation? It is certainly possible for devolved legislation to override UK legislation to the extent that UK legislation impinges upon devolved competence. As the Northern Ireland Act 1998 makes clear, 'an Act of the [Northern Ireland] Assembly may modify any provision made by or under an Act of [the UK] Parliament in so far as it is part of the law of Northern Ireland'.[10]

---

[6] Scotland Act 1998, s. 28(7).
[7] Government of Wales Act 2006, s. 107(5); Northern Ireland Act 1998, s. 5(6).
[8] *Report of the Smith Commission for Further Devolution of Powers to the Scottish Parliament* (2014), 13.
[9] See e.g. *Thoburn v. Sunderland City Council* [2002] EWHC 195 (Admin), [2003] QB 151, para. 59, *per* Laws LJ: 'Being sovereign, [Parliament] cannot abandon its sovereignty.'
[10] Northern Ireland Act 1998, s. 5(6).

Equivalent propositions hold true in relation to Acts of the Scottish Parliament and Acts of the Welsh Assembly: they can modify, repeal, or replace UK legislation in so far as it affects matters upon which those devolved bodies are competent to legislate.

It does not, however, follow that the devolved legislatures, or their legislation, enjoy hierarchical superiority over the UK Parliament, or its legislation, in a presently relevant sense. The devolved legislatures are able to enact legislation capable of modifying or otherwise asserting priority over UK legislation only because the UK Parliament has, in the first place, authorized the devolved legislatures—through the inclusion in the devolution legislation of so-called Henry VIII powers[11]—to do so. Any authority the devolved legislatures have to deviate from UK legislation is therefore nothing more than a reflection of the authority of the UK Parliament itself as the author of the those legislatures' powers.

So far, so straightforward: the UK Parliament's claim to ongoing sovereignty is not threatened by the existence of the devolution schemes because those schemes do not give life to competitor institutions that can make any plausible claim to being Westminster's legal superior or equal. What, however, of our second question? Clearly, it would be *politically* difficult for Westminster to intervene unilaterally in relation to devolved affairs, but do the devolution schemes amount to, give rise to, or contain benchmarks by reference to which the *constitutionality* of UK legislation might be assessed—and, therefore, found to be wanting? It might appear that our conclusion in relation to the first question makes the second question redundant. If the devolution schemes have not generated institutions that represent a hierarchical challenge to the UK Parliament, it surely follows that Parliament's capacity to do as it pleases—to make or unmake any law—remains undiminished. If the UK Parliament can do no legal wrong, the possibility of its acting unconstitutionally appears counterintuitive.

'This' analysis presupposes that legality and constitutionality are synonymous with one another—yet the constitutional position wrought by the UK devolution programme arguably demonstrates the falsity of that supposition, and instead suggests that to equate lawfulness and constitutionality is to conflate two distinguishable notions. As a matter of strict law, devolution, as noted earlier, does not effect a permanent division—but merely a potentially transitory sharing—of authority. If, therefore, the UK Parliament wanted to diminish the powers of the devolved legislatures, or to enact legislation overriding laws passed by the devolved legislatures, or even to abolish those legislatures, nothing in *law* prevents it from doing so. However, the binary analysis yielded by this sort of exclusively legal analysis must be supplemented by considering the matter in broader constitutional terms. When such a perspective is adopted, it becomes clear that the devolution schemes both acknowledge and conjure into life a constitutional principle—that of devolved autonomy—whose

---

[11] 'Henry VIII' powers enable constitutional actors other than the UK Parliament to amend or repeal provisions contained in an Act of Parliament. For discussion of their constitutional implications, see N. Barber and A. Young, 'The Rise of Prospective Henry VIII Clauses and their Implications for Sovereignty' [2003] *PL* 112.

fundamentality is increasingly difficult to dispute. This demands, among other things, that the authority of devolved institutions be respected, and implies the general impropriety of UK legislation impinging upon self-government within the devolved nations.

The principle of devolved autonomy is closely related to a further fundamental principle—namely, democracy. That principle is engaged by both the democratic background to the implementation of the devolution schemes—including, most significantly, the referendums that preceded their introduction—and the democratic nature of the institutional arrangements to which they give effect. It may seem odd to postulate democracy as a constitutional principle capable of casting doubt upon UK legislation, given that such legislation necessarily enjoys (some form of) a democratic mandate. However, the introduction of devolution suggests that democratic concerns are not exhausted by ensuring adherence to the legislation enacted by the UK Parliament. Devolution creates other sites of democratic law-making authority within the polity: as a result, the democratic credentials of UK legislation that cuts across the constitutional remit of devolved legislatures cannot be taken for granted.

Viewed in this light, the statutory regimes contained in the devolution legislation acquire a constitutional significance that outstrips their status as a matter of strict law. In particular, the distinction between the sharing and the transfer of competence which is central to the way in which devolution operates at a technical level is deprived, at least to some extent, of its significance. This point is institutionalized by means of the Sewel convention, according to which the UK Parliament will not normally legislate in relation to devolved matters without the consent of the relevant devolved legislature.[12] It has been proposed that the Sewel convention should be 'put on a statutory footing'.[13] However, as noted earlier, the orthodox understanding of the doctrine of parliamentary sovereignty holds that the UK Parliament cannot limit its own authority; as such, while a statutory version of the rule currently enshrined in the Sewel convention would constitute a powerful political statement as to the need for Westminster to avoid uninvited involvement in Scottish devolved affairs, it is unlikely that it would be considered to be a binding legal restriction upon Westminster's legislative power.

The existence of such a political constraint can be conceived of in terms that place constitutional law and politics in tension with one another, the realities of political life being factors that impinge upon exercises by the UK Parliament of its sovereign legislative competence. An obvious example is supplied by legislation that granted independence to Dominions and overseas territories as part of the dismantling of the British Empire. As a matter of technical law, such legislation could be repealed—meaning, again as a matter of technical, UK law, that independence would be revoked. However, as Lord Denning MR observed in *Blackburn* v. *Attorney General*, 'Freedom once given

---

[12] The convention is recorded in the Memorandum of Understanding and Supplementary Agreements entered into by the UK and devolved administrations (available at https://www.gov.uk/government/publications/devolution-memorandum-of-understanding-and-supplementary-agreement). In practice, under the convention, the UK Parliament does not legislate in relation to devolved matters unless the relevant devolved legislature has signalled its agreement by adopting a 'legislative consent motion'.

[13] *Report of the Smith Commission*, 13.

cannot be taken away. Legal theory must give way to practical politics.'[14] A similar point might be made in relation to devolution, its technical legal reversibility being eclipsed by the political difficulty—and 'perhaps even' impossibility—of putting the devolution genie back in the bottle.

However, while an analysis that casts political reality as a constraining influence upon legislative freedom is correct as far as it goes, it arguably diminishes the constitutional significance of what is going on here. The difficulty which would attend any attempt by the UK Parliament unilaterally to intervene in devolved affairs—or, for that matter, unilaterally to adjust, curtail, or rescind the devolution settlements—is of a type which is more than merely political. The *political* difficulties that any such legislative adventure would attract are attributable to deeper *constitutional* problems that it would raise, in that unilateral UK intervention in devolved affairs would be an affront to what are now recognized, at least in the devolved bodies, as fundamental constitutional principles. That such principles are not enshrined in a written constitution does not detract from the appropriateness of regarding them as constitutional—indeed, as constitutionally fundamental—in character. Understood thus, the devolution schemes may not effect a *legal* division of authority between the UK legislature and its devolved counterparts, but this is not incompatible with the view that the devolution schemes effect a *constitutional* division of authority. This point will only be emphasized if, as has been proposed, the Sewel convention is placed on a statutory footing and UK legislation provides that the Scottish Parliament is a permanent institution. The fact that such statutory provisions may not amount to technical legal restraints upon the sovereign Westminster Parliament is likely to prove far less significant than the potency of the political commitment that such legislative provisions would disclose. In this way, the distinction between legal and political restraint begins to dissolve, and the form of restraint that is in play takes on a character that is neither fully one thing nor the other, but which, instead, is constitutional in nature. The devolved competences set out in the devolution legislation can thus properly be regarded as benchmarks by reference to which the constitutionality—as distinct from the legal validity—of UK legislation may be assessed.

That official, including legislative, action might be lawful yet unconstitutional is an ostensibly paradoxical notion, but it is hardly novel. Indeed, it is a notion that finds ready expression when the relationship between law and convention[15] is considered, the latter institutionalizing constitutional values that might serve to undermine the legitimacy, as distinct from the legality, of incompatible laws.[16] A good (if exotic)

---

[14] [1971] 1 WLR 1037, 1040.   [15] See discussion of conventions and 'soft law' in ch. 11.

[16] Whether constitutional conventions, or the values that animate them, may acquire legal effect and/or prevail over inconsistent laws is an aspect of a much broader question about the relationship between the considerations of legality and constitutionality that are raised by our two key questions. This matter is considered in the final section of the chapter. For discussion of the relationship between law and convention, compare T. R. S. Allan, *The Sovereignty of Law: Freedom, Constitution and Common Law* (2013), ch. 2; D. Feldman, 'Constitutional Conventions' in M. Qvorup (ed.), *The British Constitution: Continuity, Change and the Influence of Europe—A Festschrift for Vernon Bogdanor* (2013).

example of the phenomenon is supplied by the decision of the Canadian Supreme Court concerning the policy of the Canadian federal government to seek to press ahead with significant constitutional changes in the face of opposition from the majority of the Canadian provinces.[17] The Court concluded that while nothing in law stood in the federal government's way, its conduct conflicted with the constitutional principle of federalism—and with a related constitutional practice institutionalized by means of a convention—such that it was 'unconstitutional'.[18] Although not underpinned by any legal sanction, the importance of such a conclusion should not be underestimated. Indeed, while it would be easy to dismiss as irrelevant a finding of lawful-but-unconstitutional official conduct, such condemnation is merely indicative of a mindset that inappropriately treats legality as exhaustive of constitutionalism. That, however, is not the nature of the UK constitution. It has been said that the UK has a 'political' rather than a 'legal' constitution.[19] This does not connote that the UK's constitution is wholly non-legal in nature; it does, however, imply that what is lawful and what is constitutional are not necessarily coextensive categories. We should therefore be far from surprised if we find—as in the devolution context—that an evaluation of a measure's lawfulness is not inevitably decisive as to its constitutionality.

The conclusion that particular legislation is, or would be, suspect in constitutional (as distinct from legal) terms sounds in the political realm, in that it contributes to—indeed, generates—the political difficulty that would attend an attempt to legislate in breach of fundamental constitutional values. This is apparent, for example, from the work of the House of Lords Constitution Committee which (among other things) examines bills that are before Parliament from a constitutional perspective, drawing the attention of the House to any aspects of bills that are constitutionally suspect.[20] It is possible to infer from the Committee's many reports a suite of constitutional values that serve as benchmarks against which draft bills fall to be assessed.[21] However, it would be mistaken to suppose that the incapacity of those values to deprive Parliament of the authority to legislate contrary to them necessarily renders them legally irrelevant. The relationship between the legal, political, and constitutional realms is too porous to permit any such conclusion: the implications of fundamental constitutional values resonate throughout the constitutional system—in both its legal and political guises. As a result, although constitutional values such as devolved autonomy and democracy

---

[17] *Re Resolution to amend the Constitution* [1981] 1 SCR 753.   [18] Ibid., 909.

[19] J. A. G. Griffith, 'The Political Constitution' (1979) 42 *MLR* 1. For a more recent elaboration of the notion of a political constitution, see A. Tomkins, *Our Republican Constitution* (2005). More generally, for discussion of the idea of political constitutionalism see G. Gee and G. C. N. Webber, 'What Is a Political Constitution?' (2010) 30 *OJLS* 273.

[20] See generally A. Le Sueur and J. Simson Caird, 'The House of Lords Select Committee on the Constitution' in A. Horne, G. Drewry, and D. Oliver (eds.), *Parliament and the Law* (2013).

[21] J. Simson Caird, R. Hazell, and D. Oliver, *The Constitutional Standards of the House of Lords Constitution Committee* (2014).

may not enjoy a legal status that ultimately circumscribes the UK Parliament's legislative authority, they may nevertheless find legal expression in other, more modest, ways, including as norms which influence the interpretation of legislation. In this way, fundamental constitutional values can and do both shape the *meaning* of statute law and serve to determine its *constitutionality*, even if, according to the orthodox theory of parliamentary sovereignty, they are ultimately incapable of determining primary legislation's *validity*. Devolution thus serves as a case study in the importance of contextualizing the notion of sovereignty. Accepted on its own terms, the doctrine concedes unfettered legal authority to the UK Parliament: but that concession does not imply an absence of constitutional standards that may operate both as benchmarks of constitutionality and as powerful interpretative constructs.[22]

THE EUROPEAN UNION AND THE EUROPEAN CONVENTION ON HUMAN RIGHTS

The law and institutional machinery associated with the UK's being a party to the ECHR and a member of the EU can justifiably be characterized as a distinct layer within the UK's contemporary constitutional architecture. The transnational nature of the institutional arrangements from which EU and European human-rights law flow instinctively prompts us to think of those arrangements as somehow sitting 'above' the merely domestic constitutional tier. In one sense, this reaction is misplaced; the international law character of the EU and the ECHR does not render them legally *superior* to, but *different* from, domestic law. International law does not, from a domestic legal perspective, enjoy automatic priority over national law. Rather, the nature and extent (if any) of the domestic legal status of any given international law measure is a function of domestic law itself. The picture changes, however, when the relationship between international law regimes and domestic law is considered from a different vantage point. From an international law perspective, the ECHR and EU law are legally binding upon the UK as a state.[23] In this sense, *national* sovereignty is compromised by participation in arrangements that are binding upon the UK in international law. What, however, about *parliamentary* sovereignty? Is this also curtailed, such that, for as long as the UK is a party to the ECHR and/or a member of the EU, Parliament cannot be said to be sovereign? Our inquiry in this area will proceed according to the same two key questions that we asked in the previous section concerning devolution.

---

[22] The role of judicial interpretation in upholding fundamental constitutional values is developed later, in the section entitled 'Common law'.

[23] See ch. 5.

THE EUROPEAN UNION: LEGALITY

The first of those questions, it will be recalled, concerns the matter of hierarchical priority. It is convenient to address this 'issue' first in relation to EU law;[24] the position regarding the ECHR is considered later. According to the doctrine of supremacy of EU law, directly effective EU law takes priority over any incompatible provisions of national law.[25] This goes further than merely asserting the binding force, upon the UK as a state, of its international obligations under the EU Treaties. Rather, the Court of Justice of the European Union (CJEU) has held that the EU 'constitutes a new legal order . . . the subjects of which comprise not only Member States but also their nationals'.[26] As a result, EU law is a body of law which regards itself as binding not only upon member states as states in the international law sense, but as binding also upon governing institutions *within* member states. It is for this reason that it is considered, as a matter of EU law, to be *unlawful* for a national legislature to enact law that breaches EU law, with the attendant possibility, in certain circumstances, of financial liability being incurred as a result of such legally wrongful action.[27]

Whether the sovereignty of Parliament can be squared with the primacy of EU law depends upon the perspective from which the matter is viewed. From an EU perspective, the doctrine of parliamentary sovereignty must yield in the face of the overriding force of EU law. However, the position may be different viewed from a domestic law perspective. Admittedly, there are writers—most notably Sir William Wade[28]—who argue that the sovereignty of Parliament has been not merely suspended but terminated by EU membership. Wade pointed in this regard to the seminal decision of the House of Lords in *Factortame (No. 2)*,[29] in which EU law was accorded priority over an incompatible Act of Parliament. The UK legislation in question—which conflicted with a right conferred by what is now Art. 49 of the Treaty on the Functioning of the European Union—was thus 'disapplied': the operation of relevant parts of the Act was suspended and the government ordered not to enforce them. This, argued Wade, evidenced a fundamental shift of judicial fidelity from Westminster to the EU. However, this explanation does not sit easily with the way in which UK courts themselves rationalize the status enjoyed by EU law within the national legal system. Absent detailed judicial discussion of that matter in *Factortame (No. 2)* itself, we must look to other, more recent, decisions that have—albeit only by means of *obiter dicta*—addressed the point. In this regard, the cases of *Thoburn*[30] and *HS2 Action Alliance*[31] are particularly germane.[32]

---

[24] See ch. 4.   [25] Case 6/64, *Costa* v. *Enel* [1964] CMLR 425, 455.

[26] Case 26/62, *Van Gend en Loos* [1963] ECR 1, 12.

[27] See e.g. Cases C-6/90 and 9/90, *Francovich* v. *Italy* [1991] ECR I-5357.

[28] H. W. R. Wade, 'Sovereignty: Revolution or Evolution?' (1996) 112 *LQR* 568.

[29] *R* v. *Secretary of State for Transport, ex parte Factortame Ltd (No. 2)* [1991] 1 AC 603.

[30] *Thoburn* v. *Sunderland City Council* [2002] EWHC 195 (Admin), [2003] QB 151.

[31] *R (HS2 Action Alliance Ltd)* v. *Secretary of State for Transport* [2014] UKSC 3, [2014] 1 WLR 324. For more detailed discussion of this case, see P. Craig, 'Constitutionalising Constitutional Law: HS2' [2014] *PL* 373; M. Elliott, 'Constitutional Legislation, European Union Law and the Nature of the United Kingdom's Contemporary Constitution' (2014) 10 *European Constitutional L Rev* 379.

[32] See also discussion of these cases in ch. 4.

In the latter case, a question arose concerning the extent to, and the basis upon, which EU law could assume priority over fundamental principles of domestic constitutional law. In particular, the Supreme Court considered whether a UK court would have to give effect to a provision of EU law even if doing so would contravene the principle, reflected in Art. 9 of the Bill of Rights 1689, that parliamentary proceedings 'ought not to be impeached or questioned in any court'.[33] The Supreme Court thought not. In arriving at that view, it proceeded on the basis that the matter could not, as Lord Reed put it, be 'resolved simply by applying the doctrine developed by the Court of Justice of the supremacy of EU law, since the application of that doctrine in our law itself depends upon the 1972 Act'.[34] It followed, said Lord Reed, that, 'If there is a conflict between a constitutional principle, such as that embodied in article 9 of the Bill of Rights, and EU law, that conflict has to be resolved by our courts as an issue arising under the constitutional law of the United Kingdom.'[35] On this view—which is consistent with the detailed examination of this subject in the earlier judgment of Laws LJ in *Thoburn*—the extent to, and terms upon, which EU law takes priority over UK law, including over Acts of the Westminster Parliament, is a question that falls to be determined by reference to UK law.[36] Thus, whether EU law could override a fundamental constitutional principle turned upon interpretation of the 1972 Act, that being the statute which determines the domestic effect of EU law. And, in the absence of clear textual provision to such effect, it was not to be readily assumed that Parliament had intended, when enacting the 1972 Act, to confer upon EU law priority over fundamental constitutional principles.

However, this analysis only gets us so far. It is one thing to say that EU law has acquired primacy over UK law by virtue of, and to the extent that, domestic legislation provides. But this leaves unanswered the question whether the primacy thereby accorded to EU law can be rationalized in a way that is compatible with the view that the UK Parliament remains sovereign. Did Parliament, by enacting the 1972 Act, sign the death warrant of its own sovereign authority? As noted earlier, Wade took the view that this is precisely the outcome Parliament secured, whether or not intentionally, thanks to the fact that—as Wade saw it—the judiciary shifted its allegiance in *Factortame* from the Westminster Parliament to the EU, recognizing the latter as having supreme law-making power.[37] However, in *HS2*, the *Factortame* judgment is presented in far less stark terms. In a joint judgment, Lords Neuberger and Mance

---

[33] In fact, the Supreme Court concluded that the provision of EU law in question did not require anything to be done that would conflict with the principle referred to in Art. 9 of the Bill of Rights. However, the question of principle that arose was nevertheless addressed.

[34] *R (HS2 Action Alliance Ltd)* v. *Secretary of State for Transport*, para. 79, *per* Lord Reed.

[35] Ibid.

[36] This view is also of a piece with s. 18 of the European Union Act 2011, which provides that directly effective EU law 'falls to be recognised and available in law in the United Kingdom only by virtue of [the European Communities Act 1972] or where it is required to be recognised and available in law by virtue of any other Act'.

[37] Wade, 'Sovereignty: Revolution or Evolution?' (1996).

characterize *Factortame* as a 'significant development',[38] but not one which evidenced the kind of shift—implying the termination of parliamentary sovereignty—identified by Wade. Rather, said Lords Neuberger and Mance, *Factortame* demonstrated the 'special status of the 1972 Act and of European law'.[39] Later in their judgment, they referred to the analysis of Laws LJ in *Thoburn*,[40] according to which the European Communities Act 1972 is a 'constitutional statute', signifying that it is, on Laws LJ's view, immune from the doctrine of implied repeal.[41] Laws LJ thus distinguished between constitutional legislation and ordinary legislation: the latter must give way to any subsequent legislation that is inconsistent with it, even if the later Act does not acknowledge the inconsistency; in contrast, said Laws LJ, constitutional legislation prevails over ordinary legislation unless the latter *explicitly* overrides the former. On this analysis, ordinary Acts of Parliament that are incompatible with directly effective EU law but which do not specifically seek to countermand the priority accorded to EU law by the 1972 Act fall to be disapplied: the 1972 Act, as a constitutional statute, takes priority—and, as such, continues to ascribe priority to EU law—over a merely implicitly inconsistent ordinary statute. The implication is that if the UK Parliament were *explicitly* to derogate from directly effective EU law, national courts would apply the domestic provision notwithstanding its incompatibility with EU law. And this, in turn, suggests that Parliament remains ultimately capable of securing—as a matter of domestic law—the primacy of Acts of Parliament in the face of conflicting provisions of EU law.

Where, then, does this leave us? Does the UK legislature encounter, in its EU counterpart, a competitor institution whose laws claim legal superiority over domestic legislation? EU law explicitly asserts primacy over all national law—and, *as a matter of EU law*, enjoys precisely such primacy. In this respect, the EU presents a challenge to parliamentary sovereignty quite different in type from any entailed by the devolution settlements. Yet this does not entitle us to go as far as to say that EU membership—whether temporary or permanent—has extinguished the sovereignty of the Westminster Parliament. As a matter of domestic constitutional law, the primacy enjoyed by EU law is a function of, rather than a challenge to, the sovereignty of Parliament, since its effect—and the extent of its priority over domestic legislation—is in the first place attributable to an Act of Parliament.

THE EUROPEAN UNION: CONSTITUTIONALITY

Viewed through an exclusively domestic legal lens, parliamentary sovereignty is thus capable of accommodating the implications of EU membership. However, as with devolution, an analysis based only upon questions of technical legality risks incompleteness if our objective is to understand the place of parliamentary sovereignty in

---

[38] *R (HS2 Action Alliance Ltd)* v. *Secretary of State for Transport*, para. 206.
[39] Ibid., para. 206.   [40] See n. 30.   [41] Ibid., paras. 60–7.

more holistic constitutional terms. It is necessary, therefore, to address the implications of EU membership by reference to the second of our two questions, concerning the existence of constitutional benchmarks that might render constitutionally
improper an exercise of the legal sovereignty which the UK Parliament arguably
retains, EU membership notwithstanding.

The practical opportunity that Parliament has to flex its muscles by asserting its
sovereignty in the face of EU law is heavily circumscribed, not least by the political
opprobrium that any deliberate and unauthorized derogation from EU law would
likely attract at the EU level. It would be going too far to assert that such derogation
would inevitably result in the UK's ejection from the EU, but it is clear, at the very
least, that substantial—and potentially insuperable—political and diplomatic difficulties would arise. One source of such difficulties is that derogation would result in a
breach by the UK of obligations that are binding upon it in international law[42]—a
consequence that would inevitably frame political responses to derogation, both internally and externally. However, this leaves open the question whether, from a *domestic*
(as distinct from international) perspective, it would be constitutionally illegitimate
for the UK Parliament to legislate in breach of EU law. Subject to a caveat that will be
entered later, it is strongly arguable that such legislative action *would* be constitutionally improper—and that, in this sense, the terms of the UK's membership of the EU
represent a benchmark of constitutionality by reference to which the legislative conduct of the Westminster Parliament falls to be assessed.

The notion of government according to law is a fundamental aspect of the rule of
law.[43] It reflects both the Diceyan notion of equality before the law[44]—such that those
who wield official authority should not for that reason be exempt from the general
obligation that binds everybody else to obey the law—and the need for those who
are entrusted with state power to be subject to particular obligations to exercise that
power fairly, reasonably and for the public good. The requirement of government
according to law extends not only to national but also to international law. As Lord
Bingham put it:

> although international law comprises a distinct and recognizable body of law with its own
> rules and institutions, it is a body of law complementary to the national laws of individual
> states, and in no way antagonistic to them; it is not a thing apart; it rests on similar prin-
> ciples and pursues similar ends; and observance of the rule of law is quite as important on
> the international plane as on the national, perhaps even more so . . . The rule of the jungle
> is no more tolerable in a big jungle.[45]

Lord Bingham thus argues that the rule of law requires 'compliance by the state with
its obligations in international as in national law'.[46] For the purpose of the present
argument, the effect of this fundamental constitutional principle is to render suspect,

---

[42] See ch. 5.   [43] See generally Lord Bingham, *The Rule of Law* (2010).
[44] Dicey, *The Law of the Constitution*, ch. IV.   [45] Bingham, *The Rule of Law*, 110–12.
[46] Ibid., 110.

as a matter of domestic constitutionalism, any derogation by the UK from its international, including EU, law obligations.

Although it does not follow that UK legislation derogating from such obligations would be invalid in domestic law, nor does it follow that the rule-of-law requirement that demands adherence to such obligations is without legal effect. To the contrary, the principle that international law obligations should be respected functions—like other aspects of the rule of law—as a potentially potent interpretative construct which may shape the meaning given to UK legislation. As Lord Diplock put it, it is a 'well established' principle of construction that 'the words of a statute passed after [a] Treaty has been signed' are, if 'reasonably capable of bearing such a meaning', to be interpreted compatibly with the relevant treaty obligation.[47] This principle of construction, said Lord Diplock, applies with particular force where the treaty obligation relates to EU law.[48]

The rule-of-law requirement identified by Lord Bingham thus sounds in the legal realm in the sense that it is capable of influencing the meaning given to—but not the validity of—domestic legislation. More generally, the requirement is capable of operating as a benchmark that informs assessments of the constitutional legitimacy of legislation that may breach EU law. All other things being equal, such legislation discloses a significant departure from an important standard of constitutional behaviour and, as such, is constitutionally suspect. Such a conclusion would not sound in domestic legal terms—it is tolerably clear that legislation that explicitly derogates from EU law would be upheld by UK courts[49]—but would inevitably and rightly inform political-constitutional discourse as to the legitimacy of derogation from the UK's international law obligations.

A caveat, however, ought to be entered. It would be an oversimplification to suggest that any derogation from EU law would necessarily be constitutionally improper. This point is highlighted by the *HS2* case,[50] referred to earlier, in which the possibility was canvassed of EU law itself conflicting with constitutional values considered to be fundamental at the domestic level. Such circumstances are unlikely to arise, not least because EU law can assert a claim to legal primacy only to the extent that it is valid—a condition that is unlikely to be satisfied if the EU measure in question infringes individual rights or other values considered to be fundamental.[51] However, if circumstances were to come about in which valid EU law conflicted with a fundamental domestic value, it would not necessarily be appropriate to characterize as unconstitutional derogating measures taken by the UK Parliament.[52] In such a scenario, the

---

[47] *Garland* v. *British Rail Engineering Ltd* [1983] 2 AC 751, 771.   [48] Ibid., 771.

[49] See e.g. *Macarthys Ltd v Smith* [1979] 3 All ER 325, 329, *per* Lord Denning MR; *Thoburn v. Sunderland City Council*, para. 63.

[50] See n. 31.

[51] See G. de Búrca, 'The Evolution of EU Human Rights Law' in P. Craig and G. de Búrca (eds.), *The Evolution of EU Law* (2nd edn, 2011).

[52] On one reading of the *HS2* case, such derogating measures may not be required: Lords Neuberger and Mance suggest in their joint judgment that, properly interpreted, the European Communities Act 1972 may

constitutional fundamentality of the value jeopardized by EU law would have to be weighed against the fundamentality of the rule-of-law requirement to abide by international law obligations.

EUROPEAN CONVENTION ON HUMAN RIGHTS

Many of the points already made in relation to EU law apply—with some adaptation—to the ECHR. Like EU law, the Convention gives rise to obligations that bind the UK in international law.[53] States that are parties to the Convention have agreed to 'secure to everyone within their jurisdiction the rights and freedoms defined in Section I of [the] Convention'[54] and to 'abide by the final judgment of the [European] Court [of Human Rights] in any case to which they are parties'.[55] The ECHR, like EU law, thus forms a body of international law that is binding upon the UK as a state.

There are, however, important differences between the ECHR and EU legal regimes. Thanks to the principle of direct effect, many provisions of EU law are automatically applicable and judicially enforceable within member states: that is, they take effect without any need for national implementing measures.[56] In contrast, the rights set out in the ECHR do not have direct effect. It is for this reason that, until the Human Rights Act 1998 (HRA) entered into force, the Convention rights were not straightforwardly enforceable in UK courts.[57] Moreover, to the extent that the ECHR asserts any kind of primacy over domestic law, including over Acts of the UK Parliament that are incompatible with Convention rights, the form of primacy in play is only that which is associated with international law generally. In other words, as a matter of international law, the UK as a state acts unlawfully if a state organ, including the UK Parliament, acts in breach of the ECHR by, for example, enacting or retaining legislation that is incompatible with it. However, the ECHR, as a body of law, does not specifically assert primacy over domestic law in the way that EU law does. While, therefore, legislative (or other) infractions of the Convention trigger the UK's international law liability, the Convention regime—unlike its EU counterpart—lays no claim to the invalidation of incompatible domestic legislation.

Viewed thus, the ECHR regime does not sit in tension with the notion of parliamentary sovereignty in the way that EU law does. The latter claims priority over domestic law in a way that is, viewed from an EU law perspective, incompatible with the sovereignty doctrine (albeit that, as we have seen, that claim can be reconciled with the sovereignty of Parliament when the matter is viewed through a domestic law lens). The ECHR regime, however, makes no such claim. As a result, any argument that

---

not accord domestic legal force to EU law that itself conflicts conflicting with fundamental constitutional values.

  [53] See also chs. 3 and 5.   [54] ECHR, Art. 1.   [55] ECHR, Art. 46(1).
  [56] See e.g. Case 26/62, *Van Gend En Loos* [1963] ECR 1.
  [57] This does not, however, mean that Convention rights were irrelevant in domestic legal proceedings. On the pre-HRA position, see M. Hunt, *Using Human Rights Law in English Courts* (1997).

the Convention regime represents a competitor institution that places the legal sovereignty of the Westminster Parliament in question would be difficult to sustain.

However, the contrast between the EU and ECHR systems is less stark when the matter is approached through our second question. That question is concerned not with whether the ECHR qualifies Parliament's sovereign capacity lawfully to legislate as it chooses, but with the broader question whether the ECHR may be characterized as a constitutional benchmark by reference to which UK legislation may fall to be measured. That the Convention can be so characterized is an argument that can be sustained relatively straightforwardly. Like EU law, the Convention is a body of international law by which the UK has agreed to be bound. As a result, any failure by the UK to discharge its international law obligations under the Convention has the same dubious quality, viewed in rule-of-law terms, as domestic action at odds with EU-related obligations. It follows that there are good grounds for doubting the constitutionality—as distinct from the legality—of UK legislation that breaches Convention rights.

Further such grounds are supplied by the fact that some Convention rights mirror or at least intersect with values that are also recognized through the doctrine of common law constitutional rights.[58] The nature of such rights—and the broader notion that the common law constitution acknowledges certain values to enjoy a fundamental status—is addressed in the next part of this chapter. For the time being it suffices to say that the breach of at least some Convention rights will imply a breach of a parallel common law constitutional right. The constitutional dubiousness of ECHR-incompatible legislation is thus attributable both to its repudiation of the rule-of-law requirement to abide by international obligations and (at least sometimes) to the simultaneous infraction of common law constitutional rights.

The remedy of declaration of incompatibility (a declaration that a provision in an Act of Parliament is incompatible with the ECHR, but not invalid in UK law) made available to certain courts by the HRA can be understood as a means of signalling the dual lawful-but-unconstitutional character of ECHR-incompatible legislation.[59] The HRA makes it very clear that the issue of a declaration of incompatibility leaves intact the legislative provision concerned: a declaration 'does not affect the validity, continuing operation or enforcement of the provision in respect of which it is given'.[60] Declarations of incompatibility thus explicitly acknowledge that Convention rights, from a domestic law perspective, do not narrow Parliament's legislative authority. At the same time, however, issuing a declaration of incompatibility sends a clear and powerful signal that the UK is acting in breach of its international law obligations—and, therefore, inconsistently with the domestic rule-of-law obligation to adhere to commitments that bind the UK as a state in international law. In this way, declarations of incompatibility bring into play on the national stage breaches by the UK of international law,

---

[58] See e.g. *R (Osborn)* v. *Parole Board* [2013] UKSC 61, [2013] 3 WLR 1020.
[59] HRA, s. 4. See discussion in ch. 3.   [60] Ibid., s. 4(6)(a).

thus serving to problematize such infractions in domestic terms and ensuring that they are understood as something other—and more—than a failure to adhere to exotic norms that lack purchase in the municipal constitutional sphere.

A second aspect of the way in which Convention rights are domesticated via the HRA deserves mention too. As well as authorizing courts to declare that legislation is incompatible with Convention rights, the Act requires courts to interpret legislation compatibly with such rights when possible.[61] This underlines the fact that while the Convention rights lack decisive legal bite at the domestic level, in that they do not operate to circumscribe Parliament's sovereign capacity to legislate, they are far from being without domestic legal impact. To the contrary, the Convention rights operate as a powerful influence upon the judicial-interpretative process, often finding legal expression through successful attempts to read domestic legislation compatibly. In this way, the Convention rights, as international law constructs that also operate as benchmarks of domestic constitutionality, enjoy substantial domestic legal impact, albeit that they stop short of curtailing the legal authority of the UK Parliament. This is of a piece with the view, advanced in the section on devolution earlier, that while constitutional values may not ultimately diminish Parliament's sovereign freedom to legislate, this does not rob them of all legal significance.

COMMON LAW

On one analysis, sub- and supranational strata within the multilayered constitution might be thought to stand in tension with—even if they do not amount to an outright challenge to—the sovereignty of Parliament. However, the discussion so far in this chapter has shown that any such tension in fact has its foundations in the domestic constitutional order—the national stratum, as it were. This is so because UK legislation that cuts across the authority of devolved legislatures or that is inconsistent with international obligations engages domestic values, including democracy, devolved autonomy, and the rule of law,[62] that find expression in what is often referred to as the common law constitution. The idea of a common law constitution is reflective of the fact that, in the absence of a sovereign constitutional text, many aspects of the constitution are attributable to judicial development of the common law. On one view, for instance, it is in the common law that we find the numerous principles applied by courts when assessing the lawfulness of exercises of executive power;[63] and, as we shall see, it is in the common law that we find constitutional values that shape the interpretation of legislation. It follows that our analysis of the contemporary nature of parliamentary sovereignty must address not only the further extremities of the multilayered constitution, but also its common law core. This is important both for its own

---

[61] Ibid., s. 3(1)   [62] See discussion in ch. 1.
[63] For discussion, see C. F. Forsyth (ed.), *Judicial Review and the Constitution* (2000).

sake—the common law constitution forms the overarching context within which the doctrine of parliamentary sovereignty falls to be understood—and because, for the reason just given, it informs our understanding of the implications for sovereignty of multi-layered constitutionalism.

The analysis in this section will proceed by reference to the two key questions, respectively concerning legal authority and constitutionality, deployed in earlier parts of the chapter in relation to devolution and Europe. As far as the first question is concerned, the answer may seem so obvious as to negate the need to ask the question. An inevitable implication of any orthodox account of parliamentary sovereignty is that the common law is hierarchically inferior to statute law: Acts of Parliament supersede the common law to the extent of any inconsistency. This suggests that there can be no question of the common law amounting to a competitor institution that places in doubt Parliament's superior claim to legal authority. However, this invites the question whether the orthodox account accurately captures the relationship between common law and statute law—whether, in particular, the common law should inevitably be regarded as something that gives way in the face of incompatible legislation. That matter will be addressed, but it is desirable to return to it only once the second of our two key questions has been considered.

COMMON-LAW PRINCIPLES AS CONSTITUTIONAL BENCHMARKS

That question asks whether the legal regime in question—here, the common law—can be regarded as a benchmark by reference to which the constitutionality of Acts of Parliament may be measured, as distinct from a constraint that circumscribes the legal capacity of the UK Parliament to legislate as it wishes. The answer to that question is affirmative in the sense that the common law can readily be characterized as (among other things) a repository of constitutional values. That those values are legal in nature is clear from the fact that they receive substantial protection through the mechanism of statutory construction. As Lord Steyn put it in *Pierson*:

> Parliament does not legislate in a vacuum. Parliament legislates for a European liberal democracy founded on the principles and traditions of the common law. And the courts may approach legislation on this initial assumption. But this assumption only has prima facie force. It can be displaced by a clear and specific provision to the contrary.[64]

Understood thus, the 'principles and traditions of the common law'—a category that must overlap considerably with, if it is not merely a synonym for, the rule of law—form a crucial part of the backdrop against which legislation is interpreted. What those principles are is a question whose detailed exploration lies beyond the scope of this chapter, but which is considered in depth elsewhere in this volume.[65] Our focus, rather, must be on the legal and constitutional implications of such principles.

---

[64] *R v. Secretary of State for the Home Department, ex parte Pierson* [1998] AC 539, 587.
[65] See ch. 1.

In many contexts, common law constitutional principles operate so as to deny authority to constitutional actors, such as Ministers of the Crown, executive agencies, local authorities, and even devolved legislatures.[66] They do so through the application of the principle of legality, according to which legislation conferring legal authority upon such constitutional actors falls to be interpreted in the way described earlier by Lord Steyn. Unless the legislation provides in crystal-clear terms to the contrary, the effect of the principle of legality is to yield an interpretation of the statute that withholds from the constitutional actor any authority to act incompatibly with common law constitutional principles. This, in turn, renders unlawful any such action that cuts across those principles.

A good illustration of this phenomenon is the *Witham* case, in which the executive government enacted secondary legislation raising court fees and removing an exemption in favour of individuals on low incomes.[67] It was held that such secondary legislation had the effect of limiting the 'constitutional right of access to the courts',[68] and that it would be invalid unless clearly authorized by primary legislation. Since the relevant provision in the Act of Parliament concerned contained no clear indication that the power it created could be used to limit or abrogate the right in question, the court concluded that the right-infringing secondary legislation was unauthorized by the Act, and was therefore unlawful. In arriving at this view, Laws J, giving the only reasoned judgment, said this about the notion of constitutional rights:

> In the unwritten legal order of the British state, at a time when the common law continues to accord a legislative supremacy to Parliament, the notion of a constitutional right can in my judgment inhere only in this proposition, that the right in question cannot be abrogated by the state save by specific provision in an Act of Parliament, or by regulations whose vires in main legislation specifically confers the power to abrogate. General words will not suffice, and any such rights will be creatures of the common law, since their existence would not be the consequence of the democratic political process but would be logically prior to it.[69]

On this analysis, common law constitutional rights are independent of any exercise of legislative authority: they owe their existence to common law, not to statute. Laws J's related claim that common law constitutional rights are 'logically prior to' the 'democratic political process' might be taken to mean that such rights are in some sense hierarchically superior to the products of that process, such that legislation that was incompatible with such rights would be invalid. Such a reading of Laws J's *dictum* is somewhat undermined by his earlier concession that the right in question can be 'abrogated . . . by specific provision' in primary legislation, although, significantly, that statement is caveated by his characterization of legislative sovereignty as something that exists *for the time being* and which is accorded to Parliament *by the common*

---

[66] On the position in relation to devolved legislatures, see *AXA General Insurance Ltd* v. *HM Advocate* [2011] UKSC 46, [2012] 1 AC 868.
[67] *R* v. *Lord Chancellor, ex parte Witham* [1998] QB 575.   [68] Ibid., 580.   [69] Ibid., 581.

law. These two caveats are pregnant with possibilities—one of which is that at some point in the future, the common law might cease to accord legislative supremacy to Parliament. The implication is that common law constitutional principles might shift from being interpretative constructs that generally operate to ensure that Acts of Parliament are consistent with them (and that other constitutional actors are thereby denied the authority to breach them) to being factors that delimit the legislative authority of Parliament itself.

However, even if we leave these possibilities to one side for now, the notion of common law constitutional principles is not without significance for our understanding of the contemporary nature of parliamentary sovereignty. Such principles may not restrict the UK Parliament's authority, but they undoubtedly form highly significant benchmarks against which the constitutionality of legislation can be assessed. As a result, common law constitutional principles serve to ensure that the all-powerful legislature bequeathed by the doctrine of parliamentary sovereignty does not inhabit a normatively barren constitutional landscape that is empty but for exercises of its will. To the contrary, the existence of common law constitutional principles tells of a richer constitutional landscape within which exercises of legislative authority fall to be evaluated and interpreted by reference to fundamental constitutional values. Once the constitution is understood in such terms, no contradiction would arise were a provision in an Act of Parliament to be characterized as legally valid but constitutionally unsound. Indeed, for as long as the system acknowledges constitutional principles whose fundamentality is qualified by the doctrine of parliamentary sovereignty, a disjunction between technical questions of legality and broader questions of constitutionality remains inevitable.

COMMON LAW PRINCIPLES AS CONSTRAINTS UPON PARLIAMENT?

The notion of such a disjunction raises both normative and empirical questions. On a normative level, is it desirable or justifiable? And, in empirical terms, does such a disjunction remain a feature of the UK constitution or are common law constitutional principles to be regarded as legal constraints upon Parliament's legislative authority? These two questions are in fact both facets of the first of the two key questions which we have used to shape our analysis in this chapter: are common law constitutional principles, and should they be, treated as something that competes with and places in doubt Parliament's sovereign law-making capacity? In other words, are they matters that impinge upon the *legal* authority of Parliament as opposed to influencing our sense of legislation's constitutional—as distinct from legal—legitimacy?

For some writers, like Allan, the answers to both elements of the question are 'yes' because (on this view) the distinction between questions of legality and constitutionality is an ultimately unhelpful and unsustainable one. He does not doubt that common law principles can and should shape the interpretation of legislation, but he contends that they can and should go further by, where appropriate, determining its validity.

He argues, for instance, that an Act authorizing 'draconian restrictions on personal liberty may be capable of salvage, for example, by implying (or imposing) appropriately rigorous requirements of due process or procedural fairness'.[70] For Allan, however, this possibility is without prejudice to the further possibility that a court unable interpretatively to finesse unconstitutionality away would be fully entitled to refuse to enforce the legal provision in question on the ground that an unconstitutional law is not a valid law.[71] Thus, although he says that '[t]here is almost always scope, in practice, for reasonable accommodation between statutory purpose and legal principle', Allan argues that 'even when the scope for accommodation diminishes, or entirely disappears, the court must adhere resolutely to the rule of law'.[72]

This view is clearly in tension with the Diceyan conception of parliamentary sovereignty outlined at the start of this chapter. The latter reflects an ultimately positivist view, according to which the validity of an Act of Parliament is decisively determined by virtue of its having been enacted by Parliament, validity being an entirely separate matter from the merits or otherwise of the law in question. Such a view is consistent with the idea, noted in this chapter, that questions of legality and questions of constitutionality are distinguishable and may have different answers. Allan, however, criticizes this perspective, arguing that 'legality [must be] annexed to legitimacy',[73] and that, as a result, it is 'impossible to reconcile . . . the rule of law with the unlimited sovereignty of Parliament'.[74]

Other writers dispute Allan's view.[75] Oliver, for instance, writes that the notion of parliamentary sovereignty is sustained by 'a pragmatic recognition by politicians and the courts that the functioning of the British system imposes responsibility for the Constitution and the rule of law on every organ of state rather than placing that responsibility solely or primarily in the hands of a Supreme or Constitutional Court'.[76] On this view, the rule of law operates as a constraining force, but not as one which judges are ultimately equipped to impose upon other constitutional branches. Goldsworthy also argues that, properly understood, the rule of law does not require legal-judicial restriction of legislative authority[77] and goes on to point out that there is a 'mountain of evidence' demonstrating that parliamentary sovereignty is the 'current orthodoxy'.[78]

There is certainly a great number of *dicta* evidencing judicial recognition of parliamentary sovereignty; and there are no examples, outwith the EU context, of UK

---

[70] Allan, *The Sovereignty of Law*, 142.   [71] Ibid., 142–3.

[72] T. R. S. Allan, 'Parliament's Will and the Justice of the Common Law: The Human Rights Act in Constitutional Perspective' (2006) 59 *Current Legal Problems* 27, 50.

[73] Allan, *The Sovereignty of Law*, 142.

[74] T. R. S. Allan, *Law, Liberty, and Justice: The Legal Foundations of British Constitutionalism* (1994), 16.

[75] See e.g. Bingham, *The Rule of Law*, ch. 12.

[76] D. Oliver, 'Parliament and the Courts: A Pragmatic (or Principled) Defence of the Sovereignty of Parliament' in A. Horne, G. Drewry, and D. Oliver (eds.), *Parliament and the Law* (2013), 310.

[77] J. Goldsworthy, *Parliamentary Sovereignty: Contemporary Debates* (2010), ch. 3.

[78] Ibid., 97.

courts declining to apply Acts of Parliament on the ground that they are incompatible with the rule of law. However, we should be careful before allowing ourselves to be convinced by Goldsworthy's 'mountain of evidence'. It is possible to argue—although the argument is not without difficulty—that although courts *profess* fidelity to parliamentary sovereignty, they do not invariably *exhibit* such fidelity. Many writers have cited the *Anisminic* case as an example of this phenomenon.[79] Faced with an ouster clause directing that determinations made by the defendant decision-maker 'shall not be called in question in any court of law',[80] the Appellate Committee of the House of Lords held that this did not in fact prevent courts from striking down determinations lying outside the decision-maker's jurisdiction. Even commentators who generally take an orthodox line in relation to matters concerning parliamentary sovereignty have argued that *Anisminic* is hard to reconcile with it. Wade and Forsyth, for example, state that *Anisminic* evidences a judicial conviction that 'administrative agencies . . . must *at all costs* be prevented from being sole judges of the validity of their own acts',[81] since otherwise ' "the rule of law would be at an end" '.[82] The judges, say Wade and Forsyth, were thus forced 'to rebel against Parliament'.[83]

There are, however, two difficulties with this analysis. First, the House of Lords insisted that it was merely construing the statute in *Anisminic*—and, the radical interpretative surgery performed upon the ouster clause notwithstanding, this characterization of the decision enjoys at least some credence. Lord Wilberforce, for instance, pointed out that Parliament had conferred only limited authority upon the decision-maker, and that such limits would be meaningless if there were no way of enforcing them.[84] On this view, the propriety of some form of judicial control of an agency is implicit in the fact that Parliament has in the first place sought to limit the agency's authority. A second problem with Wade and Forsyth's argument is that it is built upon the assertion that the *Anisminic* judgment rendered the ouster clause 'totally ineffective'.[85] Developments in administrative law doctrine since *Anisminic* mean that Wade and Forsyth's point is true now, but it is not an accurate description of the effect of the case upon the ouster clause *at the time the case was decided*.[86] This sits uncomfortably with the assertion that judges exhibited disobedience to the statute by denying the ouster clause any effect whatever.

If, therefore, *Anisminic* was the best that critics of parliamentary sovereignty could offer in response to Goldsworthy's 'mountain of evidence' in its favour, the empirical

---

[79] *Anisminic Ltd* v. *Foreign Compensation Commission* [1969] 2 AC 147.

[80] Foreign Compensation Act 1950, s. 4(4).

[81] H. W. R. Wade and C. F. Forsyth, *Administrative Law* (11th edn, 2014), 614 (emphasis added).

[82] Ibid., quoting Denning LJ in *R* v. *Medical Appeal Tribunal, ex parte Gilmore* [1957] 1 QB 574, 586.

[83] Wade and Forsyth, *Administrative Law*, 614.   [84] See n. 79, 208.

[85] Wade and Forsyth, *Administrative Law*, 614.

[86] At that time, certain matters—non-jurisdictional errors—that would otherwise have been reviewable were immunized by the ouster clause as interpreted by the House of Lords. The category of errors that are non-jurisdictional but reviewable has fallen away since *Anisminic*; it is this that means that, from a modern perspective, an ouster clause subjected to an *Anisminic*-style interpretation would be 'totally ineffective'.

case against sovereignty would look rather weak. However, that case has arguably received a shot in the arm in recent years thanks to several *dicta* by senior judges openly questioning the idea of parliamentary sovereignty. The *Jackson* case is perhaps the leading example. It concerned a challenge to the validity of the Hunting Act 2004.[87] It had been enacted without the House of Lords' consent using the special procedure laid down in the Parliament Act 1911.[88] The particular procedure used was one that derived from amendments made to the Parliament Act 1911 by the Parliament Act 1949, which amendments, the claimants contended, had been invalidly made. This, argued the claimants, called into question the validity of the procedure under which the Hunting Act had been enacted, hence placing in doubt the validity of that Act itself. No part of this argument—which was rejected by the House of Lords—turned upon the suggestion that Parliament's authority to legislate may be limited by rule-of-law values. Nevertheless, in the course of reaching their decision, three of the Law Lords considered (*obiter*) whether sovereignty might be limited by such values.

They did so against the backdrop of a bruising constitutional confrontation a year or so earlier. The executive had promoted a bill containing an ouster clause that went considerably further than that which was at stake in *Anisminic*, and which would probably have defied the sort of interpretative solution adopted in that case. With that doubtless firmly in mind, Lord Steyn said that the 'pure and absolute' notion of sovereignty was 'out of place in the modern United Kingdom', albeit that it is 'still the *general* principle of our constitution'.[89] Lord Steyn went on to say that the Supreme Court ought at least to consider refusing to apply legislation at odds with a 'constitutional fundamental'.[90] Lord Hope[91] and Lady Hale[92] expressed comparable sentiments. Lord Hope returned to this theme in the later case of *AXA*, saying that 'whether the principle of the sovereignty of the United Kingdom Parliament is absolute or may be subject to limitation in exceptional circumstances is still under discussion'.[93] In the *Cart* case, meanwhile, Lord Phillips said that the proposition that Parliament could not exclude judicial review was 'controversial'—thereby declining to reject the proposition as constitutionally heterodox—but said that it would '[h]opefully remain academic'.[94]

These comments contrast sharply with earlier judicial statements of orthodoxy, such as Lord Reid's rejoinder in *Pickin* in that the suggestion that courts may disregard 'a provision in an Act of Parliament on any ground must seem strange and startling to anyone with any knowledge of the history and law of our constitution'.[95] Do *dicta* such as those found in *Jackson*,[96] *AXA*,[97] and *Cart*[98] therefore signify a profound shift in judicial attitudes? Faced with legislation that might be characterized as

---

[87] *R (Jackson)* v. *Attorney General* [2005] UKHL 56, [2006] 1 AC 262.

[88] The effect of the Parliament Act 1911 is that, in certain circumstances, bills can become Acts of Parliament without being passed by the House of Lords.

[89] See n. 87, para. 102 (original emphasis).   [90] Ibid., para. 102.   [91] Ibid., para. 104.

[92] Ibid., para. 159.   [93] See n. 66, para. 50.

[94] *R (Cart)* v. *Upper Tribunal* [2011] UKSC 28, [2012] 1 AC 663, para. 73.

[95] *British Railways Board* v. *Pickin* [1974] AC 765, 782.   [96] See n. 87.   [97] See n. 66.

[98] See n. 94.

unconstitutional—for example, legislation purporting to abolish all judicial review,[99] suspend or abolish general elections,[100] or preclude courts from determining the meaning of legislation[101]—would a court really adopt the nuclear option and decline to recognize it as a valid law? And, if a court were to take such a step, would *it* be acting in an unconstitutional—or, as Wade put it, revolutionary[102]—way? Such conundrums place in sharp relief the relationship between the two key questions with which we have been concerned in this chapter, ultimately reducing to the issue whether there exist constitutional principles that enjoy a fundamentality so great as to limit the authority of Parliament as a matter of law. It is to this matter that we must now turn by way of conclusion.

CONCLUSIONS: THE RELATIONSHIP BETWEEN LEGALITY AND CONSTITUTIONALITY

Lord Hope's aspiration, mentioned earlier, that the question whether Parliament is truly sovereign will 'remain academic' is telling.[103] That aspiration derives from the fact that if the question ever arose in a concrete form, it would imply the eruption of an unprecedented constitutional crisis. From the courts' perspective, precipitating such a crisis by declining to uphold a provision in an Act of Parliament would be profoundly unappealing, not least because it cannot be taken for granted that such an adventure would end well for the courts. Oliver argues that it is entirely possible that courts would lose the confrontation with Parliament and the executive that would inevitably ensue: if they did, 'untold damage' would be done to the courts' constitutional position and '[t]he rule of law itself would . . . [be] weakened'.[104] At the same time, there is also reluctance on the political branches' part to test such deep and unknown constitutional waters; it is hardly in politicians' interests to risk a bruising encounter with the courts whose outcome cannot be known with certainty. Indeed, political capitulation in relation to the ouster clause that was the elephant in the room in *Jackson* is evidence of precisely this phenomenon.[105] When the bill containing the ouster clause was published, judges dropped strong hints that the consequences might be severe if Parliament and the government pressed on;[106] against that background, politicians stepped back from the constitutional brink and the clause was withdrawn.

---

[99] Lord Woolf, '*Droit Public*—English style' [1995] *PL* 57, 67–9.

[100] J. Jowell, 'Parliamentary Sovereignty under the New Constitutional Hypothesis' [2006] *PL* 562, 573.

[101] *R (Cart)* v. *Upper Tribunal* [2009] EWHC 3052 (Admin), [2010] PTSR 824, paras. 36–8, *per* Laws LJ.

[102] Wade, 'Sovereignty: Revolution or Evolution?'; and H. W. R. Wade, 'The Basis of Legal Sovereignty' [1955] *Camb LJ* 172.

[103] *Cart* (see n. 94), para. 50.   [104] Oliver, 'Parliament and the Courts', 320.   [105] See n. 87.

[106] See e.g. Lord Woolf, 'The Rule of Law and a Change in the Constitution' [2004] *Camb LJ* 317, 329.

This suggests that we should be cautious about ascribing too much weight either to Goldsworthy's 'mountain of evidence' in favour of untrammelled legislative authority or to contrary judicial *dicta* found in cases like *Jackson* and *AXA*. The reality of the UK's constitutional framework is that what-if questions about the periphery, if any, of Parliament's legislative capacity and about how courts would react were Parliament to transgress any such periphery defy abstract resolution. We cannot know for certain how a direct confrontation between Parliament and the courts would play out because, in the absence of a written constitution, we have no roadmap that provides for such exceptional circumstances. As a result, while it is perfectly possible to make cogent normative arguments about whether or not courts *should* enforce legislation considered to be constitutionally excessive, it is impossible to predict with certainty what *would* happen in such circumstances.

This does not, however, mean that no predictions whatever can be ventured. Understood by reference to the two key questions that have shaped our analysis throughout this chapter, the issue at hand is whether there is some point at which the dubiousness of legislation viewed through a *constitutional* lens is so great as to undermine its validity when the matter is examined through a *legal* lens. In other words, at what point—if any—does legislation become so profoundly offensive to fundamental constitutional values as to render it unlawful? While we cannot be confident about whether—and, if so, where—such a point arises, we can be more confident in our assessment if the matter is conceived of not as a binary question but as one of degree. The *more important* the value and the *greater the extent* of its disturbance by the legislation in question, the *less certain* we can be that a court would straightforwardly enforce the legislation.

We can envisage, therefore, a continuum that tracks the relationship between the legality and constitutionality of legislation. At one end of the continuum, the images yielded by the legal and constitutional lenses clearly diverge: even if a given statutory provision impinges upon, and is therefore to a degree suspect from the vantage point of, a given constitutional value, this raises no serious prospect of the provision's being deprived of legality. This may be because the constitutional value in question is insufficiently fundamental to call the legality of inconsistent legislation into question, or because the legislation in question does not represent an attack upon the essence (as distinct from a more-peripheral aspect) of the value. However, as we move along the continuum, the images yielded by the legal and constitutional lenses are likely to become less distinctive. This reflects the fact that as the constitutional offensiveness of the legislation increases—because the value it engages is peculiarly fundamental and/or the statutory provision cuts across the very core of the value—the positivist claim that the legislation should be treated as law merely because it was enacted by Parliament is likely to be regarded as having less purchase. As such, a point may arise at which the images yielded by the constitutional and legal lenses begin to converge, signifying that the constitutional offensiveness of a statutory provision might jeopardize its recognition by courts as a valid law. However, even if, as we move along the continuum, we can predict with greater confidence that a court which refused to uphold legislation would be judged to have acted constitutionally, it remains impossible to say for certain whether, and if so where on the continuum, such a point arises. This is because at what point (if any) it becomes constitutional for judges to refuse to enforce legislation is a matter that would become apparent only *after* the event, in the light of reactions to it.

This highlights a key difference between the UK's constitution and systems based upon a written text. Such texts are predicated upon the possibility of unconstitutional behaviour by constitutional actors: they both define what amounts to unconstitutional legislative action and stipulate the legal consequences of such conduct. In this way, they supply an *ex ante* framework: one that seeks to determine, in advance, how unconstitutional behaviour should be managed. The UK's constitution provides no such framework. It supplies neither a decisive statement of the periphery of what is constitutionally legitimate nor a roadmap for determining what should happen in the event of the transgression of any such boundary. It follows that whether a point arises at which constitutional offensiveness collapses into illegality is a question that could be answered in the UK only on an *ex post* basis. Any judicial refusal to uphold legislation could be no more than the opening salvo in a debate about whether the legislation was so constitutionally offensive as to have caused Parliament to exceed a legal limit upon its authority and (the flip-side of the same coin) justified the courts' refusal to acknowledge its legality. The conclusion of that debate might be that the judges were right; if so, the outcome would be the recognition of a circumstance in which considerations of legality and constitutionality converge so as to constrain Parliament's legislative competence. However, the conclusion might equally well be that the court itself had constitutionally overreached itself by refusing to uphold duly enacted legislation; such a conclusion would not decisively establish that there is *no* point at which the legality–constitutionality distinction dissolves, but would certainly establish that the legislation in question did not lie at such a point. The essential matter, then, is that fundamental questions of this nature can be decisively resolved only with the benefit of hindsight. In the absence of explicitly stipulated *ex ante* constitutional ground rules, the existence and content of such rules would fall to be inferred from the aftermath of a constitutional crisis in which judges and politicians sought to test the limits of one another's constitutional authority.

Conceding that matters of this nature must, in the absence of a clarifying constitutional crisis, remain shrouded in uncertainty is perhaps unsatisfying, in that it may appear to be an obstacle to understanding the form that the inner workings of the constitution takes. However, it is arguable that uncertainty of this nature, rather than obscuring some deeper but unknown constitutional truth, itself represents a fundamental aspect of the constitution's workings. Indeed, uncertainty about the relationship between questions of legality and constitutionality—and, hence, about the hierarchical ordering of the rule of law and the authority of Parliament—may be regarded as essential to the effective functioning of the system.

The burden of this argument lies in the capacity of such uncertainty to place in doubt which institution—Parliament or court—has the final word in relation to fundamental constitutional values, thereby giving rise to a constructive form of institutional tension-cum-comity. This argument will be briefly elaborated by way of conclusion.

Traditional Diceyan analysis of the UK constitution holds that Parliament's untrammelled legal authority is circumscribed by nothing more than whatever restraint is invited by democratic politics. The notion of 'constitutional'—as distinct from 'political'—restraints upon Parliament's authority might therefore appear inapt within this tradition: such restraints as exist are, on this view, transient artefacts of political expediency rather than embedded features of the constitutional system. The better view, it has been argued in this chapter, is that Parliament's legislative freedom is restrained—even if it is not unambiguously restricted—by values that are genuinely constitutional in nature. That is to say, the values—or at least some of the values—that operate as restraining influences reflect deep-rooted commitments to fundamental principles, including the rule of law, the separation of powers, and the autonomy of devolved institutions.

For the most part—and perhaps invariably—such values find expression other than as hard constraints upon Parliament's legislative authority. As we have seen, they constitute, among other things, principles of interpretation that shape the meaning ascribed by the courts to legislation, and they serve to disincentivize the enactment of legislation that is insensitive to them. However, for the reasons explored in this chapter, the possibility cannot be discounted that fundamental constitutional values may have an irreducible core whose infraction would test the courts' commitment to the notion of parliamentary sovereignty. Nor can the possibility be discounted that a court would be judged, in the aftermath of the inevitable constitutional crisis, to have acted properly if it were to uphold the very essence of a truly fundamental constitutional value in the face of a legislative attack upon it. The existence of these possibilities—we can put it no higher than that—serves to underpin the notion that Parliament's legislative authority subsists within a constitutional order that supplies more than merely political restraint. Although, absent hard-to-conceive-of legislative excess, it is impossible to determine whether basic constitutional values may ultimately form hard legal constraints, the possibility of their operating in such a way *in extremis* places the operation of such values in more prosaic circumstances in a different light. At the very least, it serves as a reminder that the depth of their constitutional fundamentality is uncertain, and that they should not readily be dismissed as nothing more than 'political' constructs that are wholly fragile in the face of a bare parliamentary majority.

What this boils down to is that the absence of textual or otherwise clearly articulated constitutional ground rules should not necessarily be taken to imply that none exists. Nor should it be taken for granted that the *ex ante* unavailability of such ground rules necessarily precludes the possibility of their *ex post* emergence in the aftermath of a constitutional crisis. This is not to suggest that the opposite propositions should blithely be assumed to be correct. The point, rather, is that uncertainty about the legal status of fundamental constitutional values yields a form of necessary institutional tension between the courts and Parliament. Each is understandably loath to test the limits of the other's authority, and, as a result, each generally observes a self-denying ordinance that avoids the infraction of such constitutional ground rules as might exist. If courts were to contemplate the rejection of unconstitutional legislation or Parliament its enactment, each would stare into a constitutional abyss. What lies at the bottom of that abyss is unknown, since the depth—if any—of the constitutional bedrock that must be reached before the possibility arises of unconstitutionality transmogrifying into illegality is uncertain. Crucially, however, the existence of that abyss and its uncertain content exert a significant, if generally unarticulated, effect upon our constitutional life. They provide, at the very least, a strong disincentive to legislative (and judicial) excess, and invest constitutional values with a status that transcends the merely 'political'.

So, is Parliament sovereign? For the reasons explored in this chapter, no definitive answer can be given to that question. However, intellectually frustrating though that might be, it is in fact relatively unimportant. What is more important is that to view the authority of Parliament through an exclusively legal lens inevitably yields an incomplete and misleading constitutional picture. The reality of the contemporary UK constitution is that Parliament's legislative authority falls to be exercised against the backdrop of a normatively rich constitutional order and in the light of the restraining influences of multilayered and common law constitutionalism. The possibility that the constitutional values associated with those influences may possess irreducible cores that sit in tension with the notion of absolute legislative authority can neither be taken for granted nor rejected out of hand. It is to be expected, and hoped, that these matters will remain 'academic', as Lord Hope put it, and thus shrouded in mystery—for the absence of any definitive resolution of such questions is evidence of the mutual respect which (for the most part) the courts and Parliament exhibit in relation to one another, and without which the UK's unwritten constitution could not function. It is a constitution that is predicated not upon prescribing the consequences that would ensue were the worst to happen, but upon the premise that the worst will not happen in the first place. That system is built upon and presupposes a form of institutional respect that would already have disintegrated if we were ever to be in a position to resolve decisively the fundamental questions of constitutional authority examined in this chapter. In answer to the question with which this paragraph began, Parliament might or might not be sovereign, but that is largely beside the point—for the constitutional system demands and expects that Parliament will desist from exercising the full width of the extravagant powers which it would possess if it were sovereign.

FURTHER READING

ALLAN, T. R. S., *The Sovereignty of Law: Freedom, Constitution and Common Law* (2013)

GOLDSWORTHY, J., *Parliamentary Sovereignty: Contemporary Debates* (2010)

LAWS, SIR JOHN, 'Law and Democracy' [1995] *PL* 72

OLIVER, D., 'Parliament and the Courts: A Pragmatic (or Principled) Defence of the Sovereignty of Parliament' in A. Horne, G. Drewry and D. Oliver (eds.), *Parliament and the Law* (2013)

WADE, H. W. R., 'The Basis of Legal Sovereignty' [1955] *Camb LJ* 172

3

HUMAN RIGHTS AND
THE UK CONSTITUTION

Colm O'Cinneide

SUMMARY

UK human rights law has undergone radical transformation over the last few decades, in part because of the influence exerted by the European Convention on Human Rights (ECHR) on British law. The Human Rights Act 1998 (HRA) is now central to the UK's system of legal rights protection. The HRA incorporates the civil and political rights protected by the ECHR into national law and makes them enforceable by British courts. It is designed to deepen and extend legal protection for human rights, while still giving the Parliament the final say on all disputed issues of individual liberty and fundamental rights. However, this system of legal rights protection is controversial: politicians regularly subject the HRA to criticism, and bemoan the influence exerted by the ECHR over UK law. The place of both the HRA and ECHR within the UK's legal system thus remains open to debate: no consensus yet exists as to how human rights should best be protected within the framework of the British constitution.

INTRODUCTION

Liberal democratic states like the UK are now expected to respect a range of fundamental human rights, extending from freedom from torture to the right to fair trial and freedom from discrimination, which are set out in international human rights treaties such as the ECHR. Furthermore, it is generally recognized that the functioning of any genuine democracy must be based on respect for these rights, without which individuals cannot participate freely or effectively in the political process.[1]

---

[1] See J. Habermas, 'Constitutional Democracy: A Paradoxical Union of Contradictory Principles?' (2001) 29 *Pol Theory* 766–9; R. Dworkin, *Taking Rights Seriously* (1978).

Human rights are nevertheless contested concepts, which are capable of being interpreted and understood in different ways. Deep disagreement often exists as to what exactly constitutes a breach of a fundamental right. In the UK constitutional system, it is generally assumed that the political branches of government should play a leading role in resolving disputes about the scope and substance of individual rights. However, the courts have become increasingly involved in adjudicating human rights issues over the last few decades; the protection of individual rights is now usually viewed as forming part of the 'mission statement' of the judicial branch of government, and human rights cases now form a considerable element of the caseload of the UK's superior courts.[2]

This trend is not just confined to Britain: it has become a feature of constitutional systems across the democratic world.[3] The enhanced role that courts have come to play in this regard makes it easier for public authorities to be held legally accountable for interference with fundamental rights, and it provides individuals and groups who lack political power with a forum to challenge unjust laws.[4] It also can help to create what Feldman has described as a culture of 'politico-legal justification', whereby governments can be required to justify the impact their actions have on the individual rights and liberties of persons subject to their jurisdiction.[5]

However, different views exist as to when and how the courts should intervene to protect individual rights, and who should enjoy the final say when it comes to giving shape and substance to abstract human rights guarantees. In many states, such as the USA, Germany and South Africa, courts have been given wide-ranging constitutional powers to overturn decisions of elected legislatures if they are deemed to violate basic rights. However, the UK has not followed this approach. Instead, over the few decades, it has developed its own unique system of legal rights protection, which gives judges the authority to overturn acts of public bodies which violate basic rights while ensuring that the ultimate law-making authority remains in the hands of the Westminster Parliament.

The HRA is central to this system of rights protection: the common law and other statutes such as the Equality Act 2010 also feature, albeit in more minor supporting roles. The HRA incorporates the civil and political rights protected by the ECHR into national law and makes them enforceable by British courts. It is designed to deepen and extend legal protection for human rights, while still giving the Parliament the final say on all disputed issues of liberty and rights. The ECHR provides an additional safety net: individuals who have been unsuccessful in obtaining a remedy for alleged rights violations in national law can bring a case to the European Court of Human Rights (ECtHR) in Strasbourg and seek a finding that the UK has breached its obligations

---

[2] B. Dickson, *Human Rights and the UK Supreme Court* (2013).
[3] B. Ackerman, 'The Rise of World Constitutionalism' (1997) 83 *Virginia Law Review* 771.
[4] See J. Jowell, 'Beyond the Rule of Law: Towards Constitutional Judicial Review' [2000] *PL* 671–83.
[5] D. Feldman, ' "Which In Your Case You Have Not Got": Constitutionalism at Home and Abroad' (2011) 64(1) *Current Legal Problems* 117–49.

under the Convention. However, this system of legal rights protection is controversial: politicians regularly subject the HRA to criticism, and bemoan the influence exerted by the jurisprudence of the ECtHR over UK law. The place of both the HRA and ECHR within the UK's legal system thus remains open to debate: no consensus yet exists as to how human rights should best be protected within the framework of the British constitution.

THE HISTORICAL BACKGROUND AND CONTEXT: RESPECT FOR CIVIL LIBERTIES AND THE SLOW DEFLATION OF DICEYAN COMPLACENCY

A respect for civil liberties—that is, for personal freedoms which allow individuals to participate in public life[6]—is often assumed to be a characteristic feature of the British constitution. Views differ as to whether this image corresponds to reality. However, the normative expectation that the various organs of state *should* respect civil liberties has become embedded within British constitutional culture as a result of an extended process of political struggle, legal evolution, and constitutional transformation.

The beginning of this process in English law is usually traced back to the issuing of Magna Carta in 1215.[7] This affirmed that limits existed to the arbitrary power of the sovereign monarch. Sometimes anachronistically described as the foundational text for modern understandings of liberty and rights, in reality Magna Carta is best viewed as an assertion of baronial prerogatives.[8] Nevertheless, it acquired considerable symbolic status over time, as the document came to embody the idea that the exercise of sovereign power should both respect established liberties and conform to the law of the land.[9]

Royal disregard of this concept of bounded sovereign power lent fuel to the parliamentary revolt against the Crown in the early seventeenth century. This culminated in the 'Glorious Revolution' of 1688 and the passing of the Bill of Rights 1689, which affirmed parliamentary control over taxation, limited the power of the Crown, and presented personal liberty and representative governance as marching hand in hand. Over time, this opened the way for the evolution of the modern doctrine of parliamentary sovereignty, with Parliament becoming the supreme law-making body.[10] Initially

---

[6] C. Gearty, *Civil Liberties* (2007), 1.

[7] The history of human rights law in Scotland differs in several important respects from that of England: see A. Boyle, 'Introduction' in A. Boyle (ed.) *Human Rights and Scots Law* (2002), 1–8, 1.

[8] See in general J. C. Holt, *Magna Carta* (2nd edn, 1992).

[9] See further the Introduction to this volume.

[10] As Anthony Lester put it in the previous edition of this book, '[t]he alliance of Parliament and the common lawyers ensured that the supremacy of the law would mean the supremacy of Parliament: more realistically, it came to mean, between elections, the supremacy of the government in Parliament': A. Lester,

a vehicle for oligarchic control, the gradual expansion of the franchise in the nineteenth and early twentieth centuries meant that Parliament also became the principal
locus for the expression of the popular will and the exercise of democratic rights.

The symbolic legacy of Magna Carta also exerted a significant influence over the
development of the common law. In the early seventeenth century, jurists such as
Edward Coke argued that the common law imposed limits on monarchical power,
invoking the liberties set out in Magna Carta in support of their reasoning.[11] Over
the course of the next two centuries, the basic ingredients of the rule of law gradually became embedded within the British legal system. In cases such as *Entick*
v. *Carrington*,[12] the common law courts set out the principle of legality—namely that
executive power may do nothing but that which is expressly authorized by law, meaning that public authorities must have a clear legal basis for any action that they may
take which infringes upon individual freedom.[13] The corollary of this principle also
emerged—the presumption of liberty, whereby individuals were free to do anything
not clearly prohibited by law. This in turn gave rise to the canon of statutory interpretation that the scope of criminal law and police powers should be given a restrictive
interpretation in the interests of protecting individual liberty.[14] The evolution of the
criminal trial process, along with the law of tort and other elements of statute and
common law,[15] also reflected this emphasis on protecting individual autonomy and
limiting the discretionary power of the state.

A bias in favour of personal liberty was thus gradually incorporated into the DNA
of the common law. By the late eighteenth century, it was established that infringe-
ments of personal freedom had to be clearly authorized by statute or common law. This
did not in itself prevent the enactment of oppressive laws.[16] However, as the century
proceeded, popular mobilization in support of political radicals such as John Wilkes
and Brass Crosby played a key role in enlarging the scope of civil liberty.[17]

After the repression that accompanied the Napoleonic Wars and the birth pangs
of the Industrial Revolution, the gradual democratization of the UK political system
over the course of the nineteenth and early twentieth centuries laid the foundations
for a developed system of electoral democracy. This was based upon a broadly-based
political consensus as to the need to respect core civil liberties. The expectation was
established that Parliament should exercise its sovereign law-making powers in
a manner that respected both the rule of law and basic liberties such as freedom of
religion, freedom of speech, and freedom of association. These political constraints,

---

'Human Rights and the British Constitution' in D. Oliver and J. Jowell (eds.) *The Changing Constitution*
(7th edn, 2011), 72.

[11] See e.g. *Bonham's Case* (1610) 8 Coke's Reports 114.   [12] (1765) 19 St Tr 1029.
[13] See further ch. 1 of this volume.
[14] For a recent example of the application of this presumption, see *R* v. *Zafar* [2008] EWCA Crim 184.
[15] See e.g. *Somerset* v. *Stewart* (1772) 98 ER 499.
[16] See E. P. Thompson, *Whigs and Hunters: The Origins of the Black Act* (1975).
[17] For a general overview of the development of 'political liberty' during this time period, see L. Ward,
The Politics of Liberty in England and Revolutionary America (2004).

taken together with the presumption in favour of personal liberty built into the common law, helped to give rise to a culture of individual freedom that was comparatively well-developed for its era.[18]

Writing near the end of the nineteenth century, Dicey argued that the respect for rule of law engrained in British political culture and the common law prevented public authorities exercising arbitrary power over the lives of private individuals, and thereby provided strong protection for civil liberties. He compared this state of affairs favourably with the protection afforded to fundamental rights by written constitutions in countries such as France and the United States. In his view, such constitutional bills of rights set out abstract guarantees which often failed to give rise to substantive, enforceable legal entitlements—or alternatively gave judges excessive leeway to determine their content at the expense of the elected legislature.[19]

Dicey's views were regarded as constitutional orthodoxy for many decades. However, as the twentieth century progressed, his complacent view that 'the securities for personal freedom are in England as complete as the laws can make them'[20] gradually began to be called into question, as gaps opened up between constitutional image and reality.

As Anthony Lester commented in a previous edition of this book, 'the prevailing British constitutional ideology . . . treated British subjects as "subjects of the Crown" without the benefit of fundamental constitutional rights'.[21] The liberties of the subject were 'residual and negative in their nature': the individual was free to do anything that the law had not forbidden, but enjoyed no embedded positive entitlements that could not be altered by new legislation. Respect for rights and freedoms in the UK thus depended on Parliament showing restraint when it legislated on matters that affected civil liberties.

However, that restraint was not always evident when legislation was enacted in the midst of populist panics or concerns about national security, or where the interests of marginalized social groups were at stake. For example, repressive legislation authorized wide-ranging use of special arrest and detention powers in Ireland and across much of the British Empire, while the enactment of the Official Secrets Act 1911, the Defence of the Realm Act 1914, Emergency Powers Act 1920, and other national security and public order laws eroded speech, movement, and association rights and granted the police new powers of search, seizure, and arrest.[22] Immigration control

---

[18] As the former Attorney General, Dominic Grieve QC, recently commented: 'how well [these] liberties were in practice maintained through the centuries . . . is very questionable . . . But they are part of an entirely distinctive national narrative [which] has been so powerful that it has acted as an almost mythic restraint on successive British governments trying to curb freedoms.' See D. Grieve, 'Why Human Rights Should Matter to Conservatives', UCL Judicial Institute, 3 December 2014, available at https://www.ucl.ac.uk/constitution-unit/research/judicial-independence/CU_JIP_DOMINIC_GRIEVE_SPEECH_3_DEC.pdf.

[19] A. V. Dicey, *Introduction to the Study of the Law of the Constitution* (1st edn, 1885; 10th edn, 1959), in particular at 144.

[20] Ibid., at 220.   [21] Lester, 'Human Rights and the British Constitution', 71.

[22] This tendency has continued to the present time, with the impact in particular of anti-terrorism legislation on civil liberties continuing to generate controversy.

legislation has often been marred by a similar tendency to play fast and loose with fundamental rights—for example, Parliament passed the Commonwealth Immigrants Act 1968 which to appease racist sentiment denied entry to the UK to a large number of British Overseas Passport holders, after a rushed three-day parliamentary debate.[23]

Of course, Parliament has often enacted legislation which has extended the rights and freedoms of minorities and other disadvantaged groups, such as the Sexual Offences Act 1967 which decriminalized homosexuality and the Race Relations Act 1976 which prohibited race discrimination. However, in general, its track record has been sufficiently mixed so as to call into question Dicey's belief that the deliberative nature of the parliamentary process served as a secure guarantee of personal liberty.

This reflects a structural feature of representative democratic institutions, namely their inevitable majoritarian bias: the perspectives of minorities who possess limited social capital and/or political power are often neglected in favour of the views of popular majorities, or more powerful interest groups who can exert greater influence over the electoral process. Furthermore, the control generally exerted by the government over a majority of the House of Commons, taken in tandem with the discipline of modern party political structures, means that the executive usually exerts a dominant influence over legislative decision-making. As Lester puts it, the concept of parliamentary sovereignty 'has come to mean, between general elections, the supremacy of the government in Parliament'.[24] As a result, concerns about civil liberty and fundamental rights can often struggle to gain a legislative foothold when they run counter to government policy.

The changing nature of public governance in the modern world also served to undermine Diceyan assumptions about how best to protect civil liberty within the framework of the UK constitutional order. As the role of the state expanded in the wake of the two world wars and the Great Depression, enabling legislation conferred wide-ranging new discretionary powers on public authorities. This prompted fears of the birth of a 'new despotism', based on concern that the enlarged powers of the administrative state would lead to the erosion of individual liberty.[25]

All of these factors generated calls for courts to play a more active role in protecting individual rights. However, the capacity of British courts to discharge this role was limited. Under the established rule-of-law framework, their function was confined to ensuring that public authorities had a legal basis for exercising their powers and applying the presumption of liberty when interpreting legislation or developing the common law. They had no power to review the conduct of public authorities and determine whether they had complied with fundamental rights. Furthermore, the primary constitutional task of the courts was to give effect to the will of Parliament: this meant that, when interpreting legislation, the presumption of liberty would only come into

---

[23] A. Lester, 'Thirty Years On: The East African Case Revisited' [2002] *PL* 52–72.

[24] Lester, 'Human Rights and the British Constitution', 72.

[25] Lord Hewart, *The New Despotism* (1929). See also R. H. S. Crossman, *Socialism and the New Despotism* (1956); Lord Hailsham, *The Dilemma of Democracy: Diagnosis and Prescription* (1978).

play if it was not incompatible with the presumed intention of Parliament in passing the statute in question. In cases such as *Liversidge* v. *Anderson*,[26] *Malone*,[27] and *ex p. Hosenball*,[28] this meant that enabling legislation was interpreted as conferring wide discretionary powers on the executive to interfere with individual rights in a manner that was exempt from any meaningful judicial scrutiny.

Over time, the courts began to subject the use of discretionary and prerogative powers to closer scrutiny.[29] The development of modern administrative law established that public authorities had to have a clear legal basis for their actions, respect the requirements of fair procedure and act in a 'rational' manner.[30] However, the lack of any form of 'rights review' meant that the role of the courts in protecting fundamental rights remained very limited.

This state of affairs came under increasing criticism from civil society organizations campaigning in the field of law reform, such as Justice, Charter 88, and the National Council for Civil Liberties (subsequently renamed Liberty), and prompted calls for a new British Bill of Rights.[31] Developments in other legal systems also helped to lend weight to these calls for reform. In the United States, the civil rights jurisprudence of the US Supreme Court demonstrated that courts could play a role in protecting minority rights against majoritarian prejudice. In the aftermath of the Second World War, most Western European states also gave their constitutional courts the power to review acts of both the legislature and the executive for compatibility with fundamental rights. In 1982, the Canadian Charter of Rights and Freedoms gave the Canadian courts the authority to strike down both acts of the executive and legislative enactments, subject to a 'notwithstanding' clause which gave the federal and provincial legislatures the power to override a Charter judgment for a five-year renewable time period. In 1990, New Zealand introduced a Bill of Rights, which gave its courts a more limited power to review acts of the executive for compatibility with core civil and political rights. These developments in other liberal democratic states made the lack of legal protection in UK law appear to be more and more of an anomaly.

From the late 1960s on, two additional sets of factors also came to play a key role in shifting attitudes in this regard—one political, one legal. Taken together, they dealt serious blows to any lingering complacency about rights protection within the UK constitutional system, and lent irresistible new momentum to calls for reform.

The first set of factors related to the gradual breakdown of political consensus about civil liberties and rights which took place from the late 1960s on, which reflected the

---

[26] [1942] AC 206.

[27] *Malone* v. *Metropolitan Police Commissioner* [1979] Ch 344. Contrast the subsequent judgment of the ECtHR in *Malone* v. *UK* (1984) 7 EHRR 14.

[28] *R* v. *Secretary of State for the Home Department, ex parte Hosenball* [1977] 1 WLR 766.

[29] See further ch. 1 of this volume.

[30] *Council of Civil Service Unions* v. *Minister for the Civil Service* [1984] 3 All ER 935.

[31] See e.g. A. Lester, *Democracy and Individual Rights* (1969); Sir Leslie Scarman, *English Law: The New Dimension*, The Hamlyn Lectures Twenty-sixth Series (1974); A. Lester et al., *A British Bill of Rights* (1990); R. Dworkin, *A Bill of Rights for Britain* (1990).

emergence of wider political divides in UK society.[32] In Northern Ireland, which had been largely self-governing since 1922, the Protestant/Unionist majority had used its control over the Stormont legislature to discriminate against the Catholic/Nationalist minority in housing, employment, and the electoral process. The civil rights movement which begun to campaign against these inequalities in the 1960s was subject to sectarian violence and state harassment, which in turn led to the eruption of large-scale inter-communal conflict in 1969 and the introduction of direct rule from Westminster in 1972. During the ensuing 28 years of the 'Troubles', the use by the state of coercive interrogation methods, internment, and a range of special anti-terrorism powers proved to be politically divisive, while allegations of the existence of 'shoot to kill' policies and state collusion with paramilitary groups continued to be made for the duration of the conflict.[33] In mainland Britain, the use of police stop-and-search powers to target ethnic minorities also proved to be highly controversial, with it playing a role in triggering race riots in the early 1980s in Brixton, Toxteth, and elsewhere. The use of police powers during the coal miners' strike of 1984–5 also proved to be divisive, while attempts to use the Official Secrets Act to suppress the leaking of state secrets led to the fiasco of the Ponting[34] and Spycatcher[35] trials. The combined impact of these controversies fuelled calls for greater protection for rights and liberties to be built into British law.[36] By 1997, when the Labour Party returned to power after 18 years of being in opposition, the political climate was ripe for reform—which cleared the way for Parliament to enact the HRA in 1998.

The political momentum in favour of reform was also influenced by a second set of factors, namely the development of international and European human rights law since 1945. Beginning with the ECHR in 1951, the UK has ratified a variety of UN and Council of Europe treaty instruments which set out a range of human rights standards which states are expected to respect, protect, and fulfil. In particular, the civil and political rights set out in the ECHR and the interpretation given to these rights by the ECtHR in Strasbourg has become a key reference point for all European legal systems. From the early 1970s on, judgments of the Strasburg Court exposed the existence of human rights 'blind spots' in UK law.[37] This contributed to the growing disenchantment with the Diceyan constitutional orthodoxy, and played a role in encouraging the UK courts gradually to expand the protection afforded by common law to individual rights (see later). It also drew attention to the lack of a domestic counterpart to the ECHR, and the absence of any legal mechanism in British law which could perform the rights protective function being played by the Strasbourg

---

[32] See ch. 11 of this volume.

[33] See in general C. Campbell and I. Connolly, 'Making War on Terror? Global Lessons from Northern Ireland' (2006) 69 *MLR* 935–57, 945–55.

[34] *R* v. *Ponting* [1985] *Criminal LR* 318.

[35] *Attorney General* v. *Guardian Newspapers No. 2* [1988] 3 All ER 545.

[36] In general, see K. Ewing and C. Gearty, *Freedom under Thatcher: Civil Liberties in Modern Britain* (1990).

[37] See Lester, 'Human Rights and the British Constitution', 75–6.

Court. This gap became the focus of reform efforts in the 1990s, culminating in the enactment of the HRA.[38]

THE RELATIONSHIP BETWEEN THE UK LEGAL SYSTEM AND INTERNATIONAL HUMAN RIGHTS LAW

International human rights law, and the ECHR in particular, has thus played a key role in shaping how human rights are currently protected within the UK constitutional order. It is therefore necessary to outline in a little more detail the international and European dimension to current human rights law in the UK, before turning to examine in detail the existing state of the law.

THE UN SYSTEM OF RIGHTS PROTECTION

The international human rights movement emerged in the wake of the horrors of the Second World War. It drew inspiration from natural law and Enlightenment philosophy—including the ideas of British thinkers such as Locke, Paine, and Mill—and sought to define the fundamental rights that all individuals should enjoy by virtue of their inherent dignity as human beings.[39]

The UN General Assembly in December 1948 adopted the Universal Declaration of Human Rights (UDHR), which gave authoritative expression to these ideas. Subsequently, two legally binding treaty instruments concluded within the UN framework, the International Covenants on Civil and Political Rights and Economic, Social and Cultural Rights, were opened for signature in 1966. States which signed and ratified these instruments, including the UK, entered into a binding commitment under international law to respect and give effect to the rights set out in their text.

The provisions of the two Covenants have subsequently been supplemented and reinforced by a number of other UN human rights conventions. The UK has signed and ratified the most prominent of these treaty instruments—namely, the Convention on the Elimination of Racial Discrimination (CERD), the Convention on the Elimination of Discrimination against Women (CEDAW), the Convention against Torture (CAT), the Convention on the Rights of the Child (CRC), and the Convention on the Rights of Persons with Disabilities (CPRD).

The UK's compliance with these UN human rights treaty instruments is regularly reviewed by the expert monitoring committees established within the framework of each of these treaty instruments, through a national reporting procedure. It has

---

[38] For further analysis of the shift away from Diceyan orthodoxy, see F. Klug, *Values for a Godless Age: The Story of the UK's New Bill of Rights* (2000).
[39] See ibid.

also ratified the Optional Protocols to two of these instruments, namely CEDAW and the CPRD—this makes it possible for individuals to bring complaints to the relevant expert committees for both treaties alleging a violation of their rights.[40] However, thus far, successive UK governments have been unwilling to sign up to the individual complaint mechanisms that exist for the other treaties.

The UK's compliance with international human rights norms is also monitored through its involvement in the Universal Periodic Review (UPR) process conducted by the UN Human Rights Council, and it participates actively in shaping UN human rights standards. However, the UN human rights framework has little impact within UK domestic law. The UK is a dualist legal system, which means that international treaty commitments have no binding legal force unless their provisions have been incorporated into domestic law. None of the UN treaties have been incorporated: courts periodically refer to their provisions in interpreting statute law or developing the common law, but they do not create any enforceable legal obligations.[41] The UN human rights treaties and the conclusions of the various UN review processes as to the UK's record of compliance with their provisions are taken into account by the Joint Committee on Human Rights of the Westminster Parliament in discharging its scrutiny functions (see further later). They are also invoked in political debate and civil society activism, and have played an important role in shaping human rights discourse within the UK. However, they remain marginal to the functioning of the UK's constitutional system.

THE ECHR SYSTEM OF RIGHTS PROTECTION

The same is not true for the ECHR. The Convention was drawn up in 1950 within the framework of the Council of Europe.[42] Inspired by the UDHR, the drafters of the Convention hoped that it would provide a safeguard against any relapse into 1930s-style totalitarianism, and set a standard of rights protection that would stand in stark contrast to that applying east of the Iron Curtain. The Convention was intended to create a binding code of human rights protection, covering core civil and political rights such as the right to life, freedom of expression, and the right to a fair trial. It was also intended to provide effective safeguards for individuals whose rights were violated by contracting states, reflecting the post-1945 idea that state sovereignty was not absolute and that contracting states should be held accountable for rights abuses committed within their own borders.

---

[40] At the time of writing, three individual communications have been transmitted under the Optional Protocol to the CEDAW, and one under the Optional Protocol to the CPRD; none have been declared to be admissible by the relevant expert committees.

[41] See in general M. Hunt, *Using Human Rights Law in English Courts* (1997).

[42] The Council of Europe was established in 1949 to promote respect for rights, democracy, and the rule of law across the continent. It should be distinguished from the European Union (EU): all EU states are members of the Council of Europe, but so too are non-EU states such as Norway, Switzerland, Serbia, Russia, and Turkey.

As such, the Convention made provision for the establishment of what was at the time a unique judicial body: the European Court of Human Rights, made up of judges from each of the contracting states, which was given the authority to interpret the text of the Convention and determine whether states are acting in conformity with its requirements.[43] The establishment of the ECtHR was significant, as for the first time it made it possible for individuals to seek a remedy for violations of their rights before an international tribunal.[44] Contracting states were not initially required to accept the jurisdiction of the Court. However, states which did sign up to its jurisdiction were by virtue of Art. 53 of the original text of the Convention (now Art. 46) required to comply with its judgments, with the Committee of Ministers of the Council of Europe assuming responsibility for monitoring how states are giving effect to their obligations in this regard.

In general, the ECtHR has come to exert considerable influence over how rights are protected across Europe. The Convention has established a floor of minimum standards which all European states are expected to respect. Article 6(3) of the Treaty on European Union (TEU) provides that '[f]undamental rights, as guaranteed by the European Convention for the Protection of Human Rights and Fundamental Freedoms and as they result from the constitutional traditions common to the member states, shall constitute general principles of the Union's law'. The 'Copenhagen criteria' for EU membership applied to Central and Eastern European candidate countries from 1993 on required them to have ratified the Convention and to comply in general with its provisions as interpreted by the ECtHR.[45] All member states of the Council of Europe, including non-EU members such as Switzerland, Norway, Serbia, and Russia, have now ratified the Convention, accepted the jurisdiction of the Court and incorporated Convention rights into their national law (as the UK has done via the HRA, as discussed further later).

Furthermore, the extensive case law of the Court is regularly cited and applied by national courts, and has exerted a considerable influence over how rights are protected across Europe. It has become perhaps the most successful and effective international legal mechanism for protecting fundamental rights in the world: European states are subject to strong diplomatic pressure to respect the authority of the Court, and in general feel compelled to demonstrate their commitment to the rule of law and European democratic values by complying with its judgments.

British lawyers played a key role in drafting the Convention.[46] The UK was also the first country to ratify it in 1951, albeit not without reservations on the part of

---

[43] The ECtHR should be distinguished from the European Court of Justice, which sits in Luxembourg and interprets EU law: the ECtHR is an international adjudicatory body and has no link with the EU as such.

[44] The Court can hear complaints brought by one state against another alleging a breach of Convention rights, and also complaints brought by individuals who satisfied certain restrictive admissibility criteria.

[45] V. Miller, 'Is Adherence to the European Convention on Human Rights a Condition of European Union Membership?', House of Commons Library Note, SN/IA/6577, 25 March 2014, 2.

[46] E. Bates, The Evolution of the European Convention on Human Rights (2010); G. Marston, 'The United Kingdom's Part in the Preparation of the ECHR, 1950' (1993) 42(4) ICLQ 796–826.

the Attlee government who were concerned that it might open up the exercise of executive power to external judicial review.[47] Subsequently, the Wilson government in December 1965 decided to accept the right of individual petition to the Court.[48] This decision, taken without much debate either in government or Parliament, was momentous. It opened the way for individuals to seek redress in Strasbourg for alleged violations of their human rights, and opened up the UK legal system to external scrutiny.

The vast majority of cases that have been brought against the UK since it accepted the Court's jurisdiction have been dismissed.[49] However, there have been almost 300 judgments of the ECtHR which have found the UK to have been in breach of the Convention. Some of these decisions have been politically controversial.[50] Many more have identified gaps in rights protection in UK law which have been quickly and uncontroversially remedied by legislation, executive action, or judicial development of the common law.[51] Unlike EU law, there is no requirement under the ECHR to ensure that judgments of the Strasbourg Court are given direct effect in national law; as a result, the sovereignty of Parliament is unaffected by ratification of the ECHR, and national authorities are not required to comply with decisions of the ECtHR as a matter of *domestic* law. Successive UK governments have nevertheless chosen to comply with their *international* law obligations under the Convention by giving effect to the Court's judgments, even those they publicly criticized. As a consequence, the Court's jurisprudence has played an important role in enhancing protection for human rights in the UK, for example in the areas of freedom of expression,[52] privacy,[53] freedom from discrimination,[54] freedom from inhuman and degrading treatment,[55] and the right to fair trial.

[47] See A. W. B. Simpson, *Human Rights and the End of Empire* (2001); A. Lester, 'Fundamental Rights: The United Kingdom Isolated?' [1984] *PL* 46; A. Lester, 'UK Acceptance of the Strasbourg Jurisdiction: What Went on in Whitehall in 1965?' [1998] *PL* 237.

[48] The UK accepted the jurisdiction of the Court in respect of petitions by individuals on a periodically renewable basis with effect from 1966: see Lester, 'UK Acceptance of the Strasbourg Jurisdiction'. With effect from November 1998, Protocol No. 11 (ratified by all the contracting states, including the UK) amended the Convention to require that all state parties accept the compulsory jurisdiction of the Court.

[49] From 1966 to 2010, approximately 14,460 individual applications to the Court related to the UK, of which the vast majority were declared inadmissible. During this time period, only 1.3% of cases brought against the UK resulted in a finding of a violation. See A. Donald, J. Gordon, and P. Leach, *The UK and the European Court of Human Rights*, Equality and Human Rights Commission Research Report No. 83 (2012), 30–43.

[50] See e.g. the criticisms expressed of the judgment of *McCann* v. *UK* (1995) 21 EHRR 97 by Jacques Arnold MP, reported at *HC Deb.*, 6th March 1996, vol. 273, cc. 308–16.

[51] See Donald, Gordon, and Leach, *The UK and the European Court of Human Rights*, 44–86.

[52] See e.g. *Tolstoy* v. *UK* (1995) 20 EHRR 442 (excessive damages in libel actions).

[53] See e.g. *Malone* v. *United Kingdom* (1984) (No. 282), 4 EHRR 330 (privacy of telephone communications); *S and Marper* v. *UK* (2009) 48 EHRR 50 (DNA evidence).

[54] *Dudgeon* v. *UK* (1981) 4 EHRR 149.

[55] *Price* v. *UK* (2002) 34 EHRR 1285 (treatment of a disabled person in prison).

COMMON LAW RIGHTS

The Strasbourg case law thus served to expose the existence of human rights 'blind spots' in UK law. In so doing, it also served to highlight the lack of an equivalent domestic 'rights review' mechanism, and the limited extent to which British law protected fundamental rights and freedoms. As Anthony Lester has argued in previous editions of this book, this had a 'profound impact upon senior British judges', causing them to take account of the Strasbourg jurisprudence even though the ECHR was not incorporated into UK law.[56] In particular, they began to have regard to the ECtHR's case law in developing what become known as the 'common law rights' jurisprudence of the British courts.[57]

Beginning in the early 1990s, the courts began to identify the existence of certain fundamental constitutional rights which were recognized by the common law, including the right to freedom of expression, the right of access to the courts and lawyers, and the right to equal treatment without discrimination. In so doing, they also started to apply a more intense standard of review where public authorities interfered with these rights in the course of exercising their discretionary powers: the standard, light-touch *Wednesbury* 'rationality' standard gave way to a more pressing 'reasonableness' review.[58] Furthermore, the courts also began to interpret legislation as subject to a presumption that Parliament did not intend to permit public authorities to violate these common law rights, unless the statutory text contained express or clearly implied provisions to that effect.[59]

In the leading case of *Simms*,[60] Lord Hoffmann made it clear that this jurisprudence was based around a substantive understanding of the rule of law:

[T]he principle of legality means that Parliament must squarely confront what it is doing and accept the political cost. Fundamental rights cannot be overridden by general or ambiguous words. This is because there is too great a risk that the full implications of their unqualified meaning may have passed unnoticed in the democratic process. In the absence of express language or necessary implication to the contrary, the courts therefore presume that even the most general words were intended to be subject to the basic rights of the individual.[61]

The development of the concept of common law rights also served as a response to the Strasbourg jurisprudence. In declaring the existence of these common law rights, the courts began to cite the case law of the ECtHR in support of their common

---

[56] Lester, 'Human Rights and the British Constitution', 76.

[57] See further ch. 1 of this volume.

[58] See e.g. *R v. Ministry of Defence, ex parte Smith* [1996] QB 517, [1996] 1 All ER 257; *R v. Lord Saville of Newdigate, ex parte A* [1999] 4 All ER 860.

[59] See e.g. *Raymond v. Honey* [1983] 1 AC 1; *Secretary of State for the Home Department, ex parte Leech* [1994] QB 198; *R v. Secretary of State for Social Security, ex parte JCWI* [1996] 4 All ER 385.

[60] *R v. Home Secretary, ex parte Simms* [2000] 2 AC 115.   [61] [2000] 2 AC 115, 131.

law reasoning, thereby emphasizing the shared values that underpinned them both. Thus, in *Attorney General* v. *Guardian Newspapers Ltd (No. 2)*, Lord Goff of Chieveley expressed the view that there was in principle no difference between English law on freedom of speech and the provisions of Art. 10 of the Convention,[62] while the Strasbourg jurisprudence was regularly cited in many of the cases that followed in order both to support the rights-based reasoning of the British courts and also to affirm the commonality of approach that united both the ECHR and the common law case law.[63]

Despite the subsequent enactment of the HRA, this common law rights jurisprudence remains an important element of the British framework of legal rights protection. It can play a particularly significant role in the context of freedom of expression and access to justice, where the case law is most developed.[64] In *Osborn* v. *Parole Board*,[65] the Supreme Court overturned a refusal by the Parole Board to grant prisoners an oral hearing in respect of their application for release or transfer to open conditions: the Court ruled that the common law duty of procedural fairness, an aspect of the right of access to justice, required that such a hearing be provided in the circumstances at issue. In delivering the judgment of the Court, Lord Reed stated that the enactment of the HRA did not 'supersede the protection of human rights under the common law or statute' and emphasized in particular 'the importance of the continuing development of the common law' in this context.[66]

However, the scope of protection afforded by these common law rights remains unclear. Some judges have adopted a 'common law constitutionalist' perspective, and suggested that the courts might even have the authority to refuse to give effect to parliamentary legislation which nullified the right of access to the courts or otherwise failed to respect 'constitutional fundamentals'.[67] Others have expressed grave reservations about 'judicial law-making' and argued that courts engaged in the protection of common law rights should be very slow to convert 'political questions' into justiciable legal issues.[68]

---

[62] [1990] 1 AC 109, at 283–4.

[63] See e.g. the comments of Lord Keith of Kinkel in *Derbyshire County Council* v. *Times Newspapers Ltd* [1993] AC 534, at 550H–551A; Lord Cooke in *R (Daly)* v. *Secretary of State for the Home Department* [2001] UKHL 26, [30]. The Scottish courts were slower to make reference to the ECHR, but see Lord President Hope's *obiter* comments in *T, a Petitioner* [1997] SLT 724.

[64] See e.g. *R (West)* v. *Parole Board* [2005] UKHL 1; *A* v. *BBC* [2014] UKSC 25; *R (on the application of Laporte)* v. *Chief Constable of Gloucestershire* [2006] UKHL 55.

[65] *Osborn* v. *The Parole Board* [2013] UKSC 61.

[66] Ibid., [54]–[63]. Note however Lord Rodger's more sceptical view on this point in *Watkins* v. *Home Office* [2006] UKHL 17, [64].

[67] See e.g. Lord Steyn's comments in *Jackson* v. *Attorney General* [2005] UKHL 56, [102].

[68] See J. Sumption (as he was then), 'Judicial and Political Decision-Making: The Uncertain Boundary', F. A. Mann Lecture 2011, text available at http://www.legalweek.com/digital_assets/3704/MANNLECTURE_final.pdf.

There also exists no fixed list of common law rights: the case law defining their scope and content is still at an early stage of development.[69] In *Watkins* v. *Home Office*, Lord Rodger expressed doubts about whether it was possible to identify with precision what constituted a 'constitutional right' within the framework of the common law, in the absence of a written constitution.[70] The scope and substance of common law rights is also often lacking in clear definition, and it is unclear what standard of review should be applied by the courts in assessing whether public authorities are justified in interfering with their enjoyment.[71]

THE HUMAN RIGHTS ACT 1998—PURPOSE AND DESIGN

In contrast to the situation under the common law, the ECHR sets out a clearly defined list of rights which contracting parties have agreed to respect, which is more comprehensive than the narrow scope of protection afforded under the common law.[72] The case law of the Strasbourg Court is also much more developed than the common law rights jurisprudence of the English courts, due in part to the sheer volume of cases received by the ECtHR. Also, in applying the proportionality test to determine whether state interference with 'qualified rights' such as freedom of expression and freedom of association complied with the Convention, the Strasbourg Court uses a more structured and demanding mode of review than the 'reasonableness' or 'anxious scrutiny' standard usually applied by the British courts in similar situations.[73]

As a consequence, even as the common law rights jurisprudence emerged in the 1990s, litigants continued to trek to Strasbourg looking for redress. This was a slow process, as they had to exhaust domestic remedies first. However, the House of Lords concluded in *Brind* that public authorities were not required to act in accordance with the terms of an unincorporated treaty such as the ECHR.[74] This meant that the Convention remained unincorporated, and a disparity persisted between the UK's international law obligations and the limited and uncertain protection afforded to human rights in national law.

---

[69] e.g. it is not clear whether there exists a common law right not to be discriminated against: see *Association of British Civilian Internees (Far Eastern Region)* v. *Secretary of State for Defence* [2003] EWCA Civ 473, especially paras. 85–6. See also the discussion of whether a common law right to vote exists in *Moohan* v. *Lord Advocate* [2014] UKSC 67.

[70] [2006] UKHL 17, [58]–[64].

[71] See e.g. the different views expressed by different members of the Supreme Court in *Kennedy* v. *Charity Commissioners* [2014] UKSC 20 as to the scope of the common law principle of access to justice and the standard of review to be applied in cases where it was engaged.

[72] In particular, the common law has not recognized the existence of a right to privacy, in contrast to Art. 8 ECHR: see *Wainwright* v. *Home Office* [2003] UKHL 53.

[73] Compare the different standards of review applied by the Court of Appeal in *R* v. *Ministry of Defence, ex parte Smith* [1996] QB 517, [1996] 1 All ER 257 to that applied by the ECtHR in *Smith and Grady* v. *UK* (2000) 29 EHRR 493.

[74] *R* v. *Secretary of State for Home Department, ex parte Brind* [1991] 1 AC 696.

As political momentum in favour of reform built in the 1990s, this gap in domestic human rights protection increasingly became viewed as a problem in need of a solution. Before the 1997 general election, the Labour Party entered into a manifesto commitment to incorporate the Convention into domestic law.[75] After winning the election, the new Labour government proceeded to give effect to this commitment by publishing in October 1997 a White Paper, *Rights Brought Home*, which made the case for incorporation on the basis that it would make it easier for individuals to 'argue for their rights in the British courts' without incurring the delay and cost of a trip to Strasbourg.[76] The White Paper also argued that incorporation would ensure that 'rights will be brought much more fully into the jurisprudence of the courts throughout the United Kingdom, and their interpretation will thus be far more subtly and powerfully woven into our law'. It would also enable British judges 'to make a distinctively British contribution to the development of the jurisprudence of human rights in Europe'.

The White Paper's proposals were subsequently translated into law in the form of the HRA and associated provisions in the devolution statutes of the same year. The Act incorporates the key rights set out in the ECHR into UK law; these 'Convention rights', as defined in Schedule 1 of the Act, are made legally enforceable before the UK courts. The Act thus introduces for the first time a comprehensive form of 'rights review' into the British constitutional system. It leaves the general contours of the system intact, but adds an important new dimension to its functioning. It has been described as a 'constitutional instrument',[77] and has become an integral element of the UK's unwritten constitution.

The Act sets out to strike a delicate constitutional balance: it leaves parliamentary sovereignty intact, while modifying the legal framework that governs how British courts interpret and give effect to primary legislation.[78] The courts are not given the power to set aside parliamentary legislation, unlike the case with directly effective EU law under the European Communities Act 1972 or the national constitutions of many democratic states like the USA, Germany, South Africa, and Canada. However, the British courts are required to interpret primary and secondary legislation under s. 3 HRA 'as far as possible' so as to maintain conformity with Convention rights. Where that is not possible, specified higher courts are given the power under s. 4 to issue a non-binding 'declaration of incompatibility', stating that the legislation in question was incompatible with the Convention. The grant of such a declaration does not affect

---

[75] Labour also entered into the Cook-Maclennan Agreement on Constitutional Reform of 1997 with the Liberal Democrats, committing both parties to supporting ECHR incorporation as part of a wider package of measures designed to reshape the British constitution.

[76] *Rights Brought Home: The Human Rights Bill*, Cm 3782, October 1997.

[77] *R (HS2 Action Alliance Ltd.) v. Secretary of State for Transport* [2014] UKSC 3, [207], *per* Lords Neuberger and Mance.

[78] See in general F. Klug, 'The Human Rights Act: Origins and Intentions' in N. Kang-Riou, J. Milner, and S. Nayak (eds.), *Confronting the Human Rights Act: Contemporary Themes and Perspectives* (2012); C. Gearty, *Principles of Human Rights Adjudication* (2004); T. Hickman, *Public Law after the Human Rights Act* (2010).

the legal validity of the legislation, and Parliament is under no obligation to respond to a declaration of incompatibility. However, this does not prevent a litigant taking a claim to Strasbourg and seeking a determination by the ECtHR that the UK is in breach of the Convention.

Furthermore, the Act was intended to be a 'constitutionally holistic' measure, in the words of Anthony Lester, in the sense that 'each branch of government—the legislative and executive, as well as the judiciary—[was] called upon to use its public powers compatibly with Convention rights'.[79] Section 6(1) HRA thus imposes a duty on all public authorities aside from Parliament[80] to act compatibly with Convention rights (unless required to do otherwise by primary legislation).[81] This in essence creates a new constitutional tort: if a public authority acts or proposes to act in a manner contrary to s. 6(1), the courts are able to grant any victim[82] of this breach of duty such relief or remedy as it considers just and appropriate within the scope of its powers.[83] Courts fall within this definition of 'public authority' and are therefore subject to the duty to exercise their powers in conformity with Convention rights—including when they develop the common law and construe legislation in the course of deciding cases between private parties.[84] As a consequence, this means that the HRA 'weaves Convention rights into the warp and woof of the common law and statute law',[85] by requiring the courts to ensure that the development of tort law, contract law, and other areas of private and public law respect the requirements of the ECHR.

While Convention rights do not bind Parliament, as noted earlier the power given to courts under s. 4 HRA to issue declarations of incompatibility is intended to ensure that Parliament engages with issues of potential legislative non-conformity with the Convention rights. Furthermore, s. 10 and Schedule 2 of the Act make it possible for legislation subject to a declaration of incompatibility to be amended via a

---

[79] Lester, 'Human Rights and the British Constitution', 79.

[80] The broad definition of 'public authority' set out in s. 6(3) HRA does not include either of the Houses of Parliament or 'a person exercising functions in connection with proceedings in Parliament'.

[81] See the provisions of s. 6(2) HRA, which link back to the provisions of ss. 3 and 4 of the Act.

[82] s. 7 HRA.

[83] Section 8(1) of the HRA establishes a discretionary jurisdiction by which English courts can award damages for breaches of incorporated ECHR rights. Section 8(3)(b) provides that damages will be awarded only where 'the court is satisfied that the award is necessary to afford just satisfaction' and s. 8(4) provides that approach of the ECtHR in awarding monetary compensation under Art. 41 of the Convention must be taken into account in awarding damages and setting quantum. In applying this provision, the UK courts have elected to mirror the approach of the ECtHR in deciding whether to award damages and setting levels of compensation, rather than adopting an approach based on domestic tort law: see *R (Greenfield)* v. *Secretary of State for the Home Department* [2005] 1 WLR 673; *R (on the application of Faulkner)* v. *Secretary of State for Justice* [2013] UKSC 23. For critical commentary on this approach, see R. Clayton, 'Damage Limitation: The Courts and the Human Rights Act Damages' [2005] *PL* 429–39; J. Varuhas in 'A Tort-based Approach to Damages under the Human Rights Act 1998' (2009) 72(5) *MLR* 750–82; J. Steele, 'Damages in Tort and Under the Human Rights Act: Remedial or Functional Separation?' (2008) 67 *Camb LJ* 606–34.

[84] See e.g. *X* v. *Y* (2004) ICR 1634; *Pay* v. *Lancashire Probation Service* [2004] IRLR 129; *Turner* v. *East Midlands Trains Ltd* [2012] EWCA Civ 1470.

[85] Lester, 'Human Rights and the British Constitution', 91.

fast-track parliamentary procedure. Taken together, these provisions make it possible for Parliament to react quickly to a declaration of incompatibility. Similarly, the provisions of s. 19 of the Act, which requires the minister in charge of a bill before Parliament to make a 'statement of compatibility' before its Second Reading stating whether or not in her opinion its provisions comply with the Convention, are intended to focus parliamentary attention on any issues of potential incompatibility, and to encourage the executive to engage actively with the rights implications of a legislative proposal.

As the HRA was coming into effect in 2000, Parliament also established a Joint Committee on Human Rights (JCHR), composed of members from both the Commons and the Lords. The JCHR was given the task of scrutinizing the human rights impact of legislative proposals and existing law, and of identifying any issues of inconsistency between domestic law and policy and the international human rights treaties ratified by the UK. Since its establishment, the Joint Committee has ensured that human rights concerns are consistently fed into parliamentary debates. In particular, the Committee plays a key role in drawing Parliament's attention to the UK's human rights commitments and helps to head off possible clashes between draft legislation and Convention rights. The JCHR should therefore be regarded as an important element of the HRA scheme of rights protection, even though it is a creation of Parliament rather than of the Act itself.[86]

The 'constitutionally holistic' ambitions of the HRA scheme of rights protection are also reflected in the legislation establishing the devolved legislatures in Northern Ireland, Scotland, and Wales. All devolved authorities, including the Northern Irish and Welsh Assemblies and the Scottish Parliament, are required to comply with Convention rights by virtue of specific provisions set out in the devolution statutes.[87] This means that courts can strike down devolved legislation on the grounds of non-conformity with the Convention; only primary legislation enacted by the Westminster Parliament is immune from the supervisory authority of the UK courts in this respect. This limit on the powers of the devolved authorities reflects the assumption underlying the HRA that Convention rights constitute a floor of legal rights protection which all public authorities should respect; it also demonstrates the extent to which rights protection has been woven into the fabric of the UK constitution in the wake of Labour's constitutional reform agenda of the late 1990s.

---

[86] D. Feldman, 'Parliamentary Scrutiny of Legislation and Human Rights' [2002] *PL* 323–48.

[87] ss. 6(2)(c) and 24(1)(a) of the Northern Ireland Act 1998; ss. 29(2)(d) and 57(2) of the Scotland Act 1998; ss. 81(1) and 94(6)(c) of the Government of Wales Act 2006. Devolved authorities can take measures to give further effect to the UK's international human rights obligations when acting within the scope of their powers, including but not confined to those that arise under the ECHR: see Sched. 2(3)(c) of the Northern Ireland Act 1998; Sched. 5(7)(2) of the Scotland Act 1998; and in general Sched. 5 of the Government of Wales Act 2006.

THE FUNCTIONING OF THE HRA

In general, the HRA scheme of rights protection is designed to work with the grain of Britain's constitutional traditions, rather than against it. It preserves parliamentary sovereignty while attempting to ensure that Convention rights will nevertheless 'exert a magnetic force over the entire political and legal system'.[88]

Since coming into force in 2000, the machinery of the Act has by and large functioned according to its purpose.[89] Its provisions have helped to ensure that the various branches of government have become more aware of the need to respect Convention rights. They have also made it easier for individuals to challenge national laws and practice which infringe their rights. Decisions by the UK courts applying Convention rights in line with the HRA framework have, for example, reformed defamation law by extending protection for freedom of speech,[90] enhanced the rights of patients undergoing mental health treatment,[91] granted new rights to unmarried would-be adopters in Northern Ireland,[92] and clarified the rights of persons with serious disabilities.[93]

Furthermore, the HRA case law has helped to inform the work of the Joint Committee on Human Rights and other parliamentary committees. Certain major legislative reforms, including the Mental Health Act 2007, the Coroners and Justice Act 2009, and the Protection of Freedoms Act 2012 were passed partially in response to HRA judgments which identified problems with the justice and fairness of existing law.[94] Successive governments have engaged with the s. 19 statement of compatibility procedure, while the courts have been prepared to give Convention rights 'horizontal effect' through the interpretation of statutes and the development of the common law by, for example, recognizing the existence of a breach of privacy action.[95]

Not all public authorities have engaged with the values underlying the legal provisions of the HRA, as the JCHR noted with concern in 2003.[96] The Equality and Human

---

[88] A. Lester, 'Human Rights and the British Constitution' in D. Oliver and J. Jowell (eds.) *The Changing Constitution* (4th edn, 2000), 89–110, at 109. The subtle design of the Act helped to smooth its passage through Parliament in 1998. Lord Kingsland, the opposition spokesman during the bill's passage through the House of Lords, described it as a 'masterly exhibition' of the art of the parliamentary draftsman: *HL Deb.*, 3 November 1997, col. 1234.

[89] See for a general overview A. Kavanagh, *Constitutional Review under the Human Rights Act* (2009); T. Hickman, *Public Law after the Human Rights Act* (2010); S. Gardbaum, 'How Successful and Distinctive is the Human Rights Act? An Expatriate Comparatist's Assessment' (2011) 74 *MLR* 195–215.

[90] *Jameel* v. *Wall Street Journal* [2006] 4 All ER 1279.

[91] See e.g. *HL* v. *UK* (2005) 40 EHRR 32.

[92] *Re G (Adoption: Unmarried Couple)* [2008] UKHL 38.

[93] *A* v. *East Sussex County Council* [2003] EWCA Admin 167.

[94] For analysis of how Parliament could play a more active role in protecting and developing human rights, see M. Hunt, H. Hooper, and P. Yowell, *Parliaments and Human Rights: Addressing the Democratic Deficit* (2012), available at http://www.ahrc.ac.uk/News-and-Events/Publications/Documents/Parliaments-and-Human-Rights.pdf.

[95] *Campbell* v. *MGN* [2004] 2 AC 457. See also G. Phillipson and A. Williams, 'Horizontal Effect and the Constitutional Constraint' (2011) 74(6) *MLR* 878–910.

[96] JCHR, *The Case for a Human Rights Commission*, 6th Report of the 2002–3 Session, HL 67/HC 489.

Rights Commission (EHRC) was established in 2006 with a mandate to promote compliance with human rights, but has enjoyed at best mixed success in attempting to inculcate a 'human rights culture'.[97]

Legal issues have arisen in respect of the definition of public authorities set out in s. 6 HRA, which covers two different categories of public bodies: 'core' and 'hybrid'. Core public bodies are legal entities which are inherently 'public' in character and must act compatibly with Convention rights in discharging all their functions, even those which could be performed by a private body.[98] Hybrid bodies are legal entities 'some of whose functions are of a public nature'.[99] Section 6(5) HRA provides that these bodies are only bound to respect Convention rights when performing these public functions, as distinct from acts of a private nature. The inclusion of both 'core' and 'hybrid' bodies within the definition of public authorities in s. 6 HRA was an attempt to ensure that private bodies providing public services as a result of privatization, contracting-out, and the establishment of other forms of public/private partnership would be obliged to respect Convention rights when providing these services. However, defining when a legal entity comes within the definition of a public authority for the purposes of s. 6 has proved to be a difficult matter. The public/private line is increasingly blurred and indistinct in practice.[100] Furthermore, the case law of the UK courts has struggled to provide clear guidance as to when private bodies will be deemed to be performing public functions.[101]

In the case of *Weaver*, the Court of Appeal summarized the factors taken into account by the courts in assessing when a legal entity came within the scope of s. 6, which include whether a body is publicly funded in carrying out the relevant functions in question, whether it is exercising statutory powers or 'taking the place' of central government or local authorities, providing a public service, or performing acts of a distinctively private character.[102] The Court then proceeded to apply an integrated approach taking account of all these factors. This judgment has brought some degree of clarity to what had been a very uncertain area of case law. However, this aspect of the HRA jurisprudence continues to attract some criticism on the basis that it has

---

[97] JCHR, *The Equality and Human Rights Commission*, 13th Report of the 2009/10 Session, HL 72/HC 183; C. O'Cinneide and N. Crowther, 'Bridging the Divide? Integrating the Functions of National Equality Bodies and National Human Rights Institutions in the European Union' in C. Gooding, A. Lawson, and B. Niven (eds.), *Equality Bodies in Europe: Impact and Effectiveness* (forthcoming).

[98] Lord Nicholls in *Parochial Church Council of the Parish of Aston Cantlow and Wilmcote with Billesley, Warwickshire v. Wallbank* [2004] 1 AC 546 (hereafter *Aston Cantlow*), [7], listed government departments, local authorities, the police and armed forces as examples of core public authorities.

[99] *Aston Cantlow*, [35], *per* Lord Hope.

[100] To complicate the situation, if a legal entity is classified as a core public authority, it may be unable to qualify as a 'victim' of a Convention breach according to the case law of the ECtHR. See Lord Nicholls in *Aston Cantlow*, at [8].

[101] See *Poplar Housing and Regeneration Community Association Ltd v. Donoghue* [2001] EWCA Civ 595, [2001] 3 WLR 183; *R (on the application of Heather) v. Leonard Cheshire Foundation* [2002] EWCA Civ 366; *YL v. Birmingham CC* [2007] UKHL 27; *Aston Cantlow*.

[102] *R (Weaver) v. London & Quadrant Housing Trust* [2009] EWCA Civ 587.

generally adopted a relatively restrictive approach to the definition of public authorities.[103] Section 145 of the Health and Social Care Act 2008 now provides that the provision of nursing care and accommodation in a care home which is paid for by a public authority will qualify as a public function, which reserves the immediate effect of the controversial Supreme Court decision in the *YL* case which had adopted a narrower interpretation of the scope of s. 6 HRA.

THE CONSTITUTIONAL DIMENSION OF THE HRA—ISSUES AND UNCERTAINTIES

Legal issues have also arisen as to how the HRA's provisions should be interpreted and applied within the general constitutional framework of UK law. Some of these issues have mainly concerned the relationship between the UK courts and the ECtHR, on the one hand, and the relationship between the courts and Parliament, on the other. Questions have also arisen as to when the courts should defer to decisions of other branches of government when determining whether Convention rights have been breached. What links these different issues is that they reflect a degree of uncertainty about the HRA's place within the UK constitutional system and how its interlocking provisions should be interpreted and applied by national courts.

THE MIRROR PRINCIPLE

The first set of issues relates to the relationship between UK courts and the ECtHR in Strasbourg, and in particular the nature of the requirement set out in s. 2 HRA that British courts should 'take into account' Strasbourg jurisprudence. This wording makes it clear that UK courts are not bound to treat ECtHR judgments as binding precedents when interpreting and applying Convention rights. However, in the early case of *Alconbury*, the House of Lords indicated that, while the ECtHR's case law was not binding in a strict sense, the courts should, in the absence of some special circumstances, follow any clear and constant jurisprudence of the Strasbourg court.[104] In the subsequent case of *Ullah* in 2004, Lord Bingham expanded on this approach:

> the Convention is an international instrument, the correct interpretation of which can be authoritatively expounded only by the Strasbourg court . . . it follows that a national court subject to a duty such as that imposed by section 2 should not without strong reason dilute or weaken the effect of the Strasbourg case law . . . It is of course open to member states to provide for rights more generous than those guaranteed by the Convention, but

---

[103] See e.g. JCHR, *The Meaning of Public Authority under the HRA*, 9th Report of Session 2006/07, HL Paper 77/HC 410; C. Donnelly, 'Leonard Cheshire Again' [2005] *PL* 785; J. Landau, 'Functional Public Authorities after *YL*' [2007] *PL* 630.

[104] *R (Alconbury Developments Ltd)* v. *Secretary of State for the Environment, Transport and the Regions* [2001] UKHL 23, [26], *per* Lord Slynn.

such provision should not be the product of interpretation of the Convention by national courts, since the meaning of the Convention should be uniform throughout the states party to it. The duty of national courts is to keep pace with the Strasbourg jurisprudence as it evolves over time: no more, but certainly no less.[105]

This 'mirror principle', whereby the UK courts should faithfully reflect the approach of the Strasbourg court in defining the scope and content of Convention rights, has exerted a considerable degree of influence over the subsequent development of the HRA case law. The British courts have thus 'kept pace' with Strasbourg when it came to defining the floor of protection afforded by Convention rights,[106] but shown reluctance to extend protection beyond that on offer from the ECtHR.[107]

However, the 'mirror principle' has been subject to academic and judicial criticism, on the basis that it prevented British judges developing their own 'native' approach to the interpretation of Convention rights.[108] Lord Kerr has suggested that British judges are under a duty to develop their own interpretation of Convention rights, rather than acting as a 'modest underworker of Strasbourg'. He also suggested that this would better enable the UK courts to develop a meaningful judicial dialogue with Strasbourg as to how Convention rights should be interpreted and applied in the context of UK law, which could benefit both national jurisprudence and the case law of the ECtHR.[109]

These criticisms of the mirror principle appear to have resonated with the British courts. Masterman has identified a number of circumstances where the courts have shown a willingness to depart from the Strasbourg case law,[110] including the following:

(i) when the application of the mirror principle would compel a conclusion which would be 'fundamentally at odds' with the UK's constitutional system of separation of powers or some other fundamental procedural or substantive aspect of UK law[111]

---

[105] *R v. Special Adjudicator, ex parte Ullah* [2004] UKHL 26, [20].

[106] See e.g. *Secretary of State for the Home Department v. AF (No. 3)* [2009] UKHL 28, where Lord Rodger commented at [98] as follows: '[e]ven though we are dealing with rights under a United Kingdom statute, in reality we have no choice. *Argentoratum locutum, iudicium finitum*—Strasbourg has spoken, the case is closed'.

[107] See e.g. *Ambrose v. Harris (Procurator Fiscal, Oban) (Scotland)* [2011] UKSC 43, where Lord Hope commented at [20]: '[i]t is not for this court to expand the scope of the Convention rights further than the jurisprudence of the Strasbourg court justifies'.

[108] See e.g. J. Lewis, 'The European Ceiling on Human Rights' [2007] *PL* 720; Lord Irving, 'A British Interpretation of Convention Rights' [2012] *PL* 237. For a contrary view, see P. Sales, 'Strasbourg Jurisprudence and the Human Rights Act: A Response to Lord Irvine' [2012] *PL* 253–67.

[109] Lord Kerr, 'The UK Supreme Court: The Modest Underworker of Strasbourg?', Clifford Chance Lecture, 25 January 2012, text available at https://www.supremecourt.uk/docs/speech_120125.pdf. See also his dissent in *Ambrose*, at [126]; Lady Hale, '*Argentoratum Locutum*: Is Strasbourg or the Supreme Court Supreme?' (2012) 12(1) *Human Rights Law Review* 65–78.

[110] R. Masterman, 'The Mirror Crack'd', *UK Constitutional Law Blog*, 13 February 2013, available at http://ukconstitutionallaw.org/2013/02/13/roger-masterman-the-mirror-crackd/.

[111] *Manchester City Council v. Pinnock* [2010] UKSC 45, [48], *per* Lord Neuberger.

(ii) when it is 'reasonably foreseeable' that the Strasbourg Court would now come to a different conclusion than in the available authorities[112]

(iii) when the UK courts wish to enter into a 'dialogue' with the European Court of Human Rights, on the basis that existing Strasbourg case law may be defective or difficult to apply in the context of the UK legal system—as demonstrated in the case of *R v. Horncastle*[113] when the Supreme Court refused to follow a judgment of a Chamber of the ECtHR on the admissibility of hearsay evidence

(iv) when the Strasbourg Court views an issue as coming within the 'margin of appreciation' left to signatory states, i.e. as involving an issue of rights interpretation that should be left to be resolved by national authorities in the absence of a general pan-European consensus on the relevant values to be taken into account in defining the scope and substance of the right at issue—in such a situation, the UK courts will interpret the relevant Convention rights in a manner that is appropriate in light of the specifics of the UK's constitutional system, as held by the Supreme Court in the cases of *In re G (Adoption: Unmarried Couple)*[114] and *Nicklinson*[115]

(v) when 'special circumstances' or a 'good reason' otherwise exist for departing from the Strasbourg jurisprudence.[116]

As the width of these exceptions suggest, it is clear that the UK courts now regard themselves as being at best loosely bound by the mirror principle. It is perhaps better to say that a strong presumption exists that a clear and consistent line of settled Strasbourg jurisprudence will be followed,[117] but British courts are not bound to adhere rigidly to this rule. In response, the Strasbourg Court has shown a willingness to look again at its previous judgments and to engage with alternative interpretations of Convention rights put forward by the UK courts.[118] British courts have also shown some readiness to develop their own interpretation of Convention rights in situations where the Strasbourg jurisprudence is underdeveloped, especially where a particular conclusion could be said to 'flow naturally' from the existing ECtHR case law.[119]

---

[112] *R (Quila) v. Secretary of State for the Home Department*, at [43], *per* Lord Wilson.

[113] [2009] UKSC14.   [114] [2008] UKHL 38.   [115] *R (Nicklinson) v. DPP* [2014] UKSC 38.

[116] *R (Alconbury Developments Ltd) v. Secretary of State for the Environment, Transport and the Regions* [2001] UKHL 23, [26], per Lord Slynn.

[117] See e.g. *Manchester City Council v. Pinnock* [2010] UKSC 45.

[118] See e.g. *Al-Khawaja and Tahery v. UK*, Application Nos. 26766/05 and 22228/06 [GC], Judgment of 15 December 2011 (responding to the judgment in *R v. Horncastle*). See also N. Bratza, 'The Relationship between the UK Courts and Strasbourg' [2011] *European Human Rights Law Review* 505–12; M. Amos, 'The Dialogue between United Kingdom Courts and the European Court of Human Rights' (2012) 61(3) *ICLQ* 557–84.

[119] As noted by Lord Brown in *Rabone v. Pennine Care NHS Foundation* [2012] UKSC 2, [112], citing the judgments of *R (Limbuela) v. Secretary of State for the Home Department* [2006] 1 AC 396, *In re G (Adoption: Unmarried Couple)* [2009] AC 173 and *EM (Lebanon) v. Secretary of State for the Home Department* [2009] AC 1198. See also Lord Wilson's dissenting judgment in *Moohan v. Lord Advocate* [2014] UKSC 67, [92]–[106].

This shift away from a rigid application of the mirror principle may reflect a more fundamental change in how the courts view the purpose and function of the HRA. In *Ullah*, Lord Bingham made it clear that he regarded the HRA as an instrument designed to ensure more effective compliance by the UK with its international law obligations under the ECHR.[120] In contrast, many critics of the mirror principle tend to view the HRA as a functional equivalent of a domestic bill of rights, which was intended to allow the UK judges to develop their own approach to interpreting and applying human rights standards—by drawing on common law standards and comparative jurisprudence from other Commonwealth states and the USA, as well as the Strasbourg case law. There are arguments to be made in favour of both approaches. However, at present, judicial and academic opinion appears to be favouring the second approach, as reflected in the recent dilution of the *Ullah* doctrine.

THE RELATIONSHIP BETWEEN SECTIONS 3 AND 4 HRA

The relationship between the interpretation obligation set out in s. 3 HRA and the power conferred on courts to grant a declaration of incompatibility under s. 4 HRA has also generated a degree of controversy. Many judges and academic commentators have discussed the potential of 'democratic dialogue' between the courts, government, and Parliament, which would involve the different branches of government interacting in a constructive manner to resolve issues of non-conformity with Convention rights.[121] However, how this dialogue should be structured through the interaction of ss. 3 and 4 of the Act remains a matter of debate.

As discussed earlier, s. 3 requires the courts to interpret legislation 'as far as possible' so as to comply with Convention rights. This requires the courts to recalibrate their standard approach to interpreting statutes, which is primarily focused on giving effect to the intent or purpose of Parliament, and to give legislation a rights-friendly interpretation where 'possible'. Furthermore, s. 3(2)(a) HRA provides that this duty applies to all primary and subordinate legislation 'whenever enacted'. This means that the doctrine of implied repeal, whereby any inconsistency between statutes are resolved in favour of the later statute, will not apply: the provisions of the HRA will govern the interpretation of subsequently enacted primary legislation, unless Parliament expressly repeals it or suspends its effect.[122] However, s. 3 provides no real guidance as to how far the courts

---

[120] For useful analysis on this point, see A. Young, 'Whose Convention Rights Are They Anyway?', *UK Constitutional Law Blog*, 12 February 2012, http://ukconstitutionallaw.org/2012/02/12/alison-l-young-whose-convention-rights-are-they-anyway/.

[121] See e.g. R. Clayton, 'Judicial Deference and "Democratic Dialogue": The Legitimacy of Judicial Intervention under the Human Rights Act 1998' [2004] *PL* 33; T. Hickman, 'Constitutional Dialogue, Constitutional Theories and the Human Rights Act 1998' [2005] *PL* 306; A. Young, *Parliamentary Sovereignty and the Human Rights Act* (2008).

[122] See in contrast s. 4 of the New Zealand Bill of Rights 1990. In *R (HS2 Action Alliance Ltd) v. Secretary of State for Transport* [2014] UKSC 3, the Supreme Court appeared to take the view that the doctrine of implied repeal did not apply in respect of 'constitutional instruments' such as the European Communities Act 1972 and the HRA, but this did not mean that other fundamental constitutional principles could be abrogated as a result. See also *Thoburn v. Sunderland City Council* [2002] EWHC 195.

can stretch the meaning of legislative text so as to achieve a rights-compliant interpretation. An excessively cautious approach in this respect risks unduly narrowing the scope of legal rights protection on offer under the HRA. But if judges go too far in rewriting legislation they risk trespassing on the domain of elected legislators.[123]

Some leading academic commentators have argued that s. 3 should be read as giving judges wide interpretative latitude. For example, Aileen Kavanagh has suggested that it is only if an innovative, rights-compliant interpretation is 'so radical and wide-ranging, so beyond the typical expertise of the judicial body, that it deserves the label of "legislation"'.[124] Others have argued for a more restrained approach to the use of the s. 3 interpretative power.[125] Such proponents of restraint often caution against an excessive reliance on s. 3 to 'solve' problems of legislative incompatibility with Convention rights at the expense of the s. 4 power to issue a declaration of incompatibility; in their view, Parliament is often better placed than the courts to decide how to respond to potential rights violations.[126]

The courts have by and large adopted an expansive interpretative approach under s. 3 HRA. However, they have also recognized that this interpretative power is limited, and that it does not permit a radical rewriting of statutory text.

In the early case of *R* v. *A (No. 2)*,[127] the House of Lords read words into s. 41 of the Youth Justice and Criminal Evidence Act 1999 so as to make it possible for evidence to be introduced as to the previous sexual history between the defendant and the victim in sexual offence trials where necessary to ensure compliance with the accused's right to a fair trial under Art. 6 ECHR. Lord Steyn argued that 'the interpretative obligation under s. 3 of the 1998 Act is a strong one. It applies even if there is no ambiguity in the language in the sense of the language being capable of two different meanings.' He further noted that it may be necessary under s. 3 to 'adopt an interpretation which linguistically may appear strained' and that a declaration of incompatability was a 'measure of last resort'.[128]

In the subsequent case of *In re S (Minors)*,[129] the House of Lords overturned a far-reaching Court of Appeal judgment which had applied s. 3 HRA in interpreting certain provisions of the Children Act 1989 as requiring local authorities to follow

---

[123] I. Leigh and R. Masterman, *Making Rights Real: The Human Rights Act in its First Decade* (2008), ch. 5.

[124] A. Kavanagh, 'The Elusive Divide between Interpretation and Legislation under the Human Rights Act 1998' (2004) 24(2) *OJLS* 259–85, 285. See also the suggested approach to the interpretation of ss. 3 and 4 based around the concept of 'democratic dialogue' set out by Alison Young: see A. L. Young, *Parliamentary Sovereignty and the Human Rights Act* (2009), chs. 5, 6, and 8.

[125] See e.g. P. Sales and R. Ekins, 'Rights-consistent Interpretation and the Human Rights Act 1998' (2011) 127 *LQR* 217–38. Sales and Ekins also argue that the interpretative obligation set out in s. 3 has not displaced the central purpose of statutory interpretation, namely to give effect to the intention of Parliament in enacting legislation. In their eyes, s. 3 'requires continued judicial attention to the legislative intent in enacting [the particular statute at issue]'.

[126] R. Bellamy, 'Political Constitutionalism and the Human Rights Act' (2011) 9(1) *Int J Const Law* 86–111; D. Nicol, 'Law and Politics after the Human Rights Act' [2006] *PL* 722.

[127] [2001] UKHL 25.   [128] Ibid., [12]–[13].

[129] *In Re S (Minors) (Care Order: Implementation of Care Plan)* [2002] UKHL 10.

certain procedures in discharging their care plans for vulnerable children. Lord Nicholls stated that the reach of s. 3 was not unlimited: '[i]nterpretation of statutes is a matter for the courts; the enactment of statutes, and the amendment of statutes, are matters for Parliament'.[130] He went on to say that 'a meaning which departs substantially from a fundamental feature of an Act of Parliament is likely to have crossed the boundary between interpretation and amendment. This is especially so where the departure has important practical repercussions which the court is not equipped to evaluate.'

Subsequently, in the key case of *Ghaidan* v. *Godin-Mendoza*, the House of Lords interpreted the word 'spouse' in the Rent Act 1977 to include unmarried homosexual partners. Lord Steyn emphasized that s. 3 required the courts to adopt a 'broad approach concentrating, amongst other things, in a purposive way on the importance of the fundamental right involved'.[131] Lord Nicholls was a little more restrained in his analysis of the scope of s. 3:

> [T]he mere fact the language under consideration is inconsistent with a Convention-compliant meaning does not of itself make a Convention-compliant interpretation under s. 3 impossible. Section 3 enables language to be interpreted restrictively or expansively. But section 3 goes further than this. It is also apt to require a court to read in words which change the meaning of the enacted legislation, so as to make it Convention-compliant . . . [However] the meaning imported by application of section 3 must be compatible with the underlying thrust of the legislation being construed. Words implied must, in the phrase of my noble and learned friend Lord Rodger of Earlsferry, 'go with the grain of the legislation'. Nor can Parliament have intended that section 3 should require courts to make decisions for which they are not equipped.[132]

Subsequently, Lord Bingham in *Sheldrake* v. *Director of Public Prosecutions* took the view that s. 3 should not be used to read legislation in a manner which 'would be incompatible with the underlying thrust of the legislation, or would not go with the grain of it, or would call for legislative deliberation, or would change the substance of a provision completely, or would remove its pith and substance, or would violate a cardinal principle of the legislation'.[133] However, as confirmed by the majority of the Supreme Court in *GC* v. *The Commissioner of Police of the Metropolis*[134] if a rights-friendly s. 3 interpretation of legislation was not incompatible with the presumed intention of Parliament in enacting the relevant statute or its text, then only 'exceptionally cogent' factors would justify a refusal to apply such an interpretation.[135]

If legislation cannot be given a rights-compliant interpretation under s. 3, then the courts may grant a declaration of incompatibility under s. 4. The House of Lords issued such a declaration in the case of *Bellinger* v. *Bellinger*, where legislation which prevented transsexuals marrying was deemed to be incompatible with Convention rights; the Lords considered that remedying this situation of incompatibility would

---

[130] Ibid., [39].   [131] *Ghaidan* v. *Mendoza* [2004] UKHL 30, [41].   [132] Ibid., [32]–[33].
[133] [2004] UKHL 43, [28].   [134] [2011] UKSC 21.   [135] Ibid., [56], *per* Lord Phillips.

involve the creation of a detailed new statutory scheme and require the legislature to choose between different policy options, and as such was not suitable for the exercise of the s. 3 power of interpretation.[136] In two recent high-profile cases, *Chester* and *Nicklinson*, the Supreme Court has emphasized the discretionary nature of the s. 4 power to grant a declaration of incompatibility. In *Chester*, the Court did not grant a declaration to an individual whose own rights had not been violated, other than by being subject to a law which might violate the rights of others.[137] In *Nicklinson*, the majority of the Court elected not to grant a declaration of incompatibility on the basis that the legal issue in question—assisted suicide—was a particularly difficult, controversial, and sensitive issue to which Parliament was giving active consideration. Lady Hale and Lord Kerr dissented strongly on this point.[138]

In general, the interaction between courts and Parliament as regulated by the provisions of ss. 3 and 4 HRA has so far functioned relatively smoothly, despite the potential for tension to arise between the different branches of government. Parliament has responded positively to all but one of the declarations of incompatibility issued by British courts under s. 4 HRA by amending the relevant statutory provisions. (The single exception has been the declaration issued in 2007 by the Scottish Registration Appeal Court in *Smith* v. *Scott*[139] following the 2005 decision of the Strasbourg Court in *Hirst* v. *UK (No. 2)*[140] that the blanket legislative ban on prisoners voting was disproportionate.) The government has sometimes been critical of particular judgments which have resulted in the grant of a declaration of incompatibility, but has nevertheless taken action to remedy the issue of potential non-compliance.[141] Issues of incompatibility have usually been resolved through the enactment of new primary legislation, rather than the use of the special fast-track remedial option.[142] The issue of prisoner voting for now remains the one unresolved issue of incompatibility. The reluctance of successive British governments and parliaments to remedy British law in respond to the *Hirst* judgment remains an open sore in the relationship between the UK and the ECHR system of rights protection, as it risks causing the UK to be in breach of its treaty obligations under the ECHR.[143]

---

[136] [2003] 2 AC 467.   [137] *R (Chester)* v. *Secretary of State for Justice* [2013] UKSC 63.

[138] See n. 115.   [139] [2007] CSIH 9.   [140] (2006) 42 EHRR 41.

[141] Lady Hale has noted that the prime minister, David Cameron MP, was critical of the Supreme Court's decision to grant a declaration of incompatibility in *R (F and Thompson)* v. *Secretary of State for the Home Department* [2010] UKSC 17, but nevertheless introduced the Sexual Offences Act 2003 (Remedial) Order 2012 to remedy the perceived incompatibility while making 'no mention of the fact that the Government could have chosen to do nothing about it': see Lady Hale, 'What is the Point of Human Rights?', Warwick Law Lecture 2013, 28 November 2013, text available at http://adam1cor.files.wordpress.com/2013/12/speech-131128.pdf. See also G. Phillipson, 'The Human Rights Act, Dialogue and Constitutional Principles' in R. Masterman and I. Leigh (eds.), *The United Kingdom's Statutory Bill of Rights: Constitutional and Comparative Perspectives* (2013).

[142] Lady Hale has noted that the fast-track s. 10 procedure had only been used to respond to 3 out of 19 'final' declarations of incompatibility by November 2013: ibid.

[143] See the conclusions of the Parliamentary Joint Committee on the Draft Voting Eligibility (Prisoners) Bill, *Report: Draft Voting Eligibility (Prisoners) Bill*, 16 December 2013, available at http://www.publications.parliament.uk/pa/jt201314/jtselect/jtdraftvoting/103/10302.htm.

DEFERENCE, RESPECT, AND PROPORTIONALITY

The question of how courts should interact with the executive and legislative branches again arises in relation to the interpretation and application of Convention rights, and in particular when courts are called upon to determine whether government inter- ference with 'qualified rights' such as freedom of expression and association can be objectively justified.[144] Space prevents a detailed analysis of the HRA and ECtHR case law in this respect. However, similar issues arise in this context as in respect of the relationship between ss. 3 and 4 HRA—namely, how the courts should discharge the constitutional responsibility conferred upon them by the HRA to protect individual rights while avoiding trespassing into the appropriate sphere of legislative action.

State interference with a qualified Convention right will only be objectively justified if it is prescribed by law and 'necessary in a democratic society'—that is, if it satisfies the proportionality test set out in general terms by the Strasbourg Court and devel- oped in further detail by the HRA case law of the UK courts.[145] Lord Neuberger sum- marized this test in *Nicklinson*:[146]

(a) Is the legislative objective sufficiently important to justify limiting a fundamental right?

(b) Are the measures which have been designed to meet it rationally connected to it?

(c) Are they no more than are necessary to accomplish it?

(d) Do they strike a fair balance between the rights of the individual and the inter- ests of the community?

In determining whether this test is satisfied, the British courts have emphasized the need to respect the democratic legitimacy of Parliament and the overall structure of the constitutional system of separation of powers, as well as the expertise of other branches of government.[147] In respecting separation of powers, the courts should give due weight to the determination of the relevant issues adopted by the primary decision-maker.[148] The courts should also respect the institutional limits of their expertise.[149]

---

[144] Interference with 'absolute rights', such as right to life or freedom from torture, cannot be justified under the ECHR system of rights protection: see *Chalal* v. *UK* (1999) 23 EHRR 413.

[145] Lord Reed in his minority judgment in *Bank Mellat* v. *Her Majesty's Treasury (No. 2)* [2013] UKSC 39, [71]–[74] indicated that the UK courts would not necessarily mirror the approach of the ECtHR in applying the proportionality test in each and every case, due to the different institutional roles played by national courts. He went on to suggest that the approach to proportionality analysis set out by Dickson CJ in the lead- ing Canadian case of *R* v. *Oakes* [1986] 1 SCR 103 provided the 'clearest and most influential judicial analysis of proportionality within the common law tradition'.

[146] *Nicklinson*, [80].

[147] *R (Animal Defenders International)* v. *Secretary of State for Culture, Media and Sport* [2008] UKHL 15.

[148] [2014] UKSC 38, [296], *per* Lord Reed.

[149] See in general the majority opinions in *R (Carlile)* v. *Secretary of State for the Home Department* [2014] UKSC 60; however, note by way of contrast Lord Kerr's dissenting judgment in the same case.

However, in the words of Lord Neuberger, 'the court has a duty to decide for itself whether the decision strikes a fair balance between the rights of an individual or individuals and the interests of the community as a whole'.[150] Lord Bingham in his leading judgment in the seminal case of *A v. Secretary of State for the Home Department* (the 'Belmarsh' case)[151] affirmed that the HRA had conferred a distinct constitutional role on the courts, including the responsibility of delineating the scope of legal protection afforded to Convention rights. He also rejected the argument that the courts should apply a general doctrine of deference in relation to the other branches of government, including Parliament:

> It is of course true that the judges in this country are not elected and are not answerable to Parliament. It is also of course true . . . that Parliament, the executive and the courts have different functions. But the function of independent judges charged to interpret and apply the law is universally recognised as a cardinal feature of the modern democratic state, a cornerstone of the rule of law itself. The Attorney General is fully entitled to insist on the proper limits of judicial authority, but he is wrong to stigmatise judicial decision-making as in some way undemocratic. It is particularly inappropriate in a case such as the present in which Parliament has expressly . . . required courts, so far as possible, to give effect to Convention rights . . . The effect is not, of course, to override the sovereign legislative authority of the Queen in Parliament, since if primary legislation is declared to be incompatible the validity of the legislation is unaffected (s. 4(6) HRA) and the remedy lies with the appropriate minister (s. 10 HRA), who is answerable to Parliament. The 1998 Act gives the courts a very specific, wholly democratic, mandate. As Professor Jowell has put it 'The courts are charged by Parliament with delineating the boundaries of a rights-based democracy' ('Judicial Deference: Servility, civility or institutional capacity?' [2003] PL 592, 597).[152]

In *Nicklinson*, Lord Neuberger acknowledged that 'it is not easy to identify in any sort of precise way the location of the boundary between the area where it is legitimate for the courts to step in and rule that a statutory provision . . . infringes the Convention and the area where it is not'.[153] He emphasized that factors such as relative institutional competence, the 'familiarity and confidence' of judges with the subject matter of the case, and the extent of the interference with the right in question would play a key role in marking out the areas where the courts would be prepared to subject the decisions of other branches of government to close and exacting scrutiny.[154] In his minority judgment in *Bank Mellat*, Lord Reed similarly emphasized the importance of context, the nature of the right at stake, and the context in which the interference occurs.[155] Some judges have suggested that the courts should adopt a broadly deferential approach in HRA cases towards legislative decisions relating to controversial

---

[150] Ibid., [57]. See also *Nicklinson*, [100].
[151] *A v. Secretary of State for the Home Department* [2004] UKHL 56.   [152] Ibid., [37]–[42].
[153] [2014] UKSC 38, [101].   [154] Ibid., [106]. See also Lord Mance at [166].
[155] *Bank Mellat* v. HM Treasury (No. 2) [2013] UKSC 39, [68]–[76].

and contested areas of law and policy.[156] However, the majority of the Supreme Court in cases such as *Nicklinson* and *Carlile* have been reluctant to endorse this argument.

In general, the constitutional issues that arise in relation to the interpretation of Convention rights must be consistently negotiated on an ongoing basis. However, Lord Bingham's seminal judgment in *A* is significant, as it affirms that the HRA makes the judges responsible for determining the scope and substance of rights protection within UK law, subject to the ultimate sovereign law-making authority of Parliament.[157]

THE CHANGING CONTEXT: DEMANDS FOR REFORM OF UK HUMAN RIGHTS LAW

Other statutes, such as the Freedom of Information Act 2000 and the Equality Act 2010 also play an important role in protecting rights; in particular, the 2010 Act prohibits public authorities from discriminating on the basis of race, gender, disability, and a range of other grounds and requires all public authorities to give due regard in the performance of their functions to the need to eliminate discrimination and promote equality of opportunity.[158] As discussed earlier, the common law also provides some protection for certain individual freedoms, even though the scope of this protection is uncertain. However, the HRA is now central to the UK's system of legal rights protection. Vernon Bogdanor has described it as forming the 'cornerstone' of a new UK constitutional order, whereby the untrammelled exercise of political power is subject to new constraints linked to the concept of rule of law.[159]

However, Bogdanor has also noted that the enactment of the HRA reflected the belief that a wide political consensus existed about the importance of respecting human rights and adhering to the UK's international law obligations under the ECHR, which has proved to be a questionable assumption.[160] The Act has also been subject to sustained criticism from certain quarters. A media narrative has developed which portrays human rights adjudication as being excessively concerned with the rights of minorities at the expense of the public interest.[161] The *Hirst (No. 2)* decision of the European Court on prisoner voting rights has attracted considerable political

---

[156] See in particular the judgment of Lord Sumption in *Nicklinson*, [232].

[157] For a sample of the voluminous academic commentary on the issue of 'deference', see e.g. J. Jowell, 'Judicial Deference: Servility, Civility, or Institutional Capacity?' [2003] *PL* 592–601; T. R. S. Allan, 'Human Rights and Judicial Review: A Critique of "Due Deference"' (2006) 65(3) *Camb LJ* 671–95; A Kavanagh, 'Defending Deference in Public Law and Constitutional Theory' (2010) 126 *LQR* 222–50; J. King, 'Proportionality: A Halfway House' (2010) *New Zealand Law Review* 327–36; T. Hickman, *Public Law after the Human Rights Act* (2010), 128–72; A. Brady, *Proportionality and Deference under the UK Human Rights Act: An Institutionally Sensitive Approach* (2012); A. Young, 'Will You, Won't You, Will You Join the Deference Dance?'(2014) 34(2) *OJLS* 375–94.

[158] s. 149 of the Equality Act 2010.

[159] V. Bogdanor, *The New British Constitution* (2009), esp. 53–88.   [160] Ibid.

[161] Some of this media commentary has been criticized for its lack of accuracy and balance: see in general Donald, Gordon, and Leach, *The UK and the European Court of Human Rights*.

hostility,[162] as have judgments by both the ECtHR and UK courts which have imposed constraints on the power of ministers to deport non-nationals.[163] Sharp criticism of the existing status quo has also come from former judges, certain politicians (including both Tony Blair MP and David Cameron MP during their terms as prime minister), and commentators linked to centre-right think-tanks. Calls have been made for a fundamental rethink of the UK's relationship with the Strasbourg Court, and for the HRA to be replaced by a new 'Bill of Rights'.[164]

Critics of the ECHR and HRA have focused in particular on specific institutional and structural aspects of human rights law which they consider to be seriously defective. In particular, they have attacked how the Strasbourg Court interprets Convention rights and discharges its functions under the ECHR. For example, Lord Hoffmann in 2009 suggested that an international court like Strasbourg lacked the 'constitutional legitimacy' to impose its interpretation of the abstract rights set out in the text of the Convention on national parliaments and courts, and attacked what he saw as expansionist tendencies within the jurisprudence of the Court.[165] Similar criticisms were aired in a parliamentary debate on a motion tabled in the House of Commons on 11 February 2011, which was intended to demonstrate the extent of cross-party opposition to the Strasbourg Court's decision in the *Hirst* prisoner voting rights case.[166] Labour MP Jack Straw, the minister responsible for introducing the HRA, joined with many Conservative MPs in asserting that the Strasbourg Court lacked the legitimacy to intervene in matters in respect of which 'member states . . . have not surrendered their sovereign powers' and criticized the 'living instrument' approach adopted by the Court in interpreting Convention rights.[167] The argument was also made that the original drafters of the ECHR saw it as a minimalist instrument intended to guard against totalitarianism, not as a treaty which would be reinterpreted over time to extend rights protection in healthy democracies.

Criticism has also been directed against the HRA, on the basis that the 'mirror principle' has linked UK law too closely to the Strasbourg case law and stunted the development of a 'home-grown' domestic rights jurisprudence.[168] The HRA has also been attacked for striking a less than optimum balance between individual rights and

---

[162] *Hirst (No. 2)* v. *UK* (2006) 42 EHRR 41.

[163] See e.g. BBC News Online, 'Theresa May Under Fire Over Deportation Cat Claim', 4 October 2011, available at http://www.bbc.co.uk/news/uk-politics-15160326.

[164] See e.g. M. Pinto-Duschinsky, *Bring Rights Back Home: Making Human Rights Compatible with Parliamentary Democracy in the UK* (2011).

[165] Lord Hoffmann, 'The Universality of Human Rights' (2009) 125 *LQR* 416.

[166] *HC Deb.* 10 Feb 2011, cols. 493–586. The wording of the motion asserted that the question of prisoner voting rights was a 'legislative decision . . . which should be a matter for democratically-elected law makers' and it was ultimately carried by 234 votes to 22. No legal consequences flowed from the passing of the motion.

[167] *HC Deb.* 10 Feb 2011, cols. 502–4.

[168] See the nuanced analysis presented by D. Grieve MP, 'It's the Interpretation of the HRA that's the Problem—Not the ECHR Itself', available at http://conservativehome.blogs.com/platform/2009/04/dominic-grieve-2.html.

democratic rule, and for being out of synch with British traditions of governance. Others view the legislation as being both under-inclusive and over-inclusive: it fails to protect rights which have been in the past regarded as fundamental within the UK constitutional tradition, such as the right to jury trial, but grants excessive protection to individuals when it comes to the Art. 8 right to family life and other areas of human rights law.[169]

Some of these arguments are less than convincing. For example, the suggestion that the Strasbourg Court has exceeded its mandate through adopting a 'living instrument' approach is very debatable. The ECtHR's interpretative approach to the Convention allows the Court to maintain the integrity of its case law by reflecting modern moral and social standards, and ensures that its jurisprudence remains relevant and effective rather than being marooned in the early 1950s.[170] It is very similar to the approach adopted by other international courts,[171] and by the Privy Council, Commonwealth courts, and Continental European courts in interpreting the fundamental rights provisions of their national constitutions.[172] In any case, it should be noted that the relationship between Strasbourg and the UK is not a one-way street: in decisions such as Z v. UK[173] and Al-Khawaja v. UK,[174] the Strasbourg Court has shown a willingness to adjust its case law in response to reasoned and well-developed criticisms of its previous decisions emanating from national authorities.

The argument that it is inherently objectionable in principle for an international court to exert such wide-ranging influence over UK law is also open to question. States often limit their own sovereign authority and defer to external decision-makers when entering into international agreements: the UK voluntarily ratified the Convention and accepted the jurisdiction of the Court, as well as encouraging other states to do likewise.[175] Richard Bellamy, a prominent academic critic of granting excessive power to the judiciary, considers that the Strasbourg jurisprudence helps to enrich

[169] Society of Conservative Lawyers, *Response to the Commission on a Bill of Rights Consultation*, written by Lord Faulks, Andrew Warnock, and Simon Murray, 21 October 2011.

[170] See G. Letsas, 'The ECHR as a Living Instrument: Its Meaning and Legitimacy' in G. Ulfstein, A. Follesdal, and B. Peters (eds.), *Constituting Europe: The European Court of Human Rights in a National, European and Global Context* (2013), 106–41. It is also highly debatable whether the Court is in fact applying an approach that is contrary to the clear intentions of the original framers of the Convention: see D. Nicol, 'Original Intent and the European Convention on Human Rights' [2005] *PL* 152–72.

[171] See e.g. *Effect of Reservations on the Entry into Force of the American Convention on Human Rights (Arts. 74 and 75)*, Advisory Opinion OC-2/82, 24 September 1982, Inter-Am Ct HR (Ser. A) No. 2 (1982), (1983) 22 ILM 37.

[172] See e.g. the judgment of Lord Wilberforce in the Privy Council case of *Minister of Home Affairs (Bermuda) v. Fisher* [1980] AC 319 (PC), 328–9; Dickson J. in the Canadian case of *R v. Big M Drug Mart Ltd* (1985)18 DLR (4th) 321, 395–6; Kentridge AJ in the South African case of *S v. Zuma and others* 1995 (4) BCLR 401 (CC), 1995 (2) SA 642 (CC), [13]–[18]. Common law adjudication in the English courts has adopted a similar approach: see e.g. *R v. R* [1991] UKHL 12.

[173] [2001] 2 FCR 246

[174] *Al-Khawaja and Tahery v. UK*, Application Nos. 26766/05 and 22228/06 [GC], Judgment of 15 December 2011.

[175] As Jeremy Waldron has commented, '[p]art of the point of being a sovereign is that you take on obligations': Oral Evidence, Joint Committee on Human Rights, 15 March 2011, Q 57, 22.

democratic debate by bringing an international legal perspective to bear on domestic law and practice.[176]

In addition, even though the UK is required under the Convention as a matter of *international law* to give effect to judgments of the Strasbourg Court, Parliament and the UK government are under no formal constitutional obligation in *national law* to give effect to a Strasbourg judgment. As Lord Mackay of Clashfern has argued, a refusal to abide by a judgment of the Court could be viewed as an abrogation of rule-of-law principles.[177] Furthermore, a failure by a leading democratic state like the UK to comply with its obligations under the ECHR could weaken the entire Convention system and potentially undermine human rights protection and the development of democracy across the continent.[178] It could expose the UK to diplomatic sanctions, and cause irreparable damage to its international standing. However, Parliament retains the final say: it can always elect to disregard judgments of the Strasbourg Court, or even to renounce the Convention and withdraw from the ECHR system of rights protection, if it decides the price is worth paying.[179]

Similarly, it is difficult to identify patent flaws in the functioning of the HRA, or clear defects in the case law of the UK courts. As discussed earlier, the courts have recognized exceptions to the mirror principle, while thus far serious conflict between the different branches of government has not been triggered by the interplay of ss. 3, 4, and 6 HRA or the application of the proportionality test in respect of qualified Convention rights.

In general, it is by no means apparent that the existing state of UK human rights law is incompatible with fundamental constitutional principles, including the principle of democratic self-governance as reflected in the doctrine of parliamentary sovereignty. However, critics of the HRA continue to argue that radical reform is needed. Some argue that Convention rights should be de-incorporated and that the UK should revert back to relying solely on the common law to protect rights.[180] Others would prefer that Convention rights be removed from UK law and replaced with new 'home-grown' standards set out in a Bill of Rights, and/or that the UK courts be freed from any obligation to take the case law of the Strasbourg Court into account when deciding human rights cases. Other critics are critical of how the HRA has failed to capture the public imagination. In their view, an instrument designed to protect rights should be

---

[176] R. Bellamy, 'ECHR—Bringing Home the Facts', UCL European Institute, 21 February 2011, available at http://www.ucl.ac.uk/european-institute/comment_analysis/commentary/ecthr/rbellamy. See also Donald, Gordon, and Leach, *The UK and the European Court of Human Rights*, 164–77.

[177] Oral evidence to the House of Commons Political and Constitutional Reform Committee, 1 February 2011, Q. 13.

[178] Loose talk of a UK withdrawal may already have caused damage to the status and standing of the Court and the Convention in Eastern Europe: see Donald, Gordon, and Leach, *The UK and the European Court of Human Rights*, 145–8, 174–7.

[179] See E. Bates, 'British Sovereignty and the European Court of Human Rights' (2012) 128 *LQR* 382–411.

[180] Society of Conservative Lawyers, *Response to the Commission on a Bill of Rights Consultation*, written by Lord Faulks, Andrew Warnock, and Simon Murray, 21 October 2011.

couched in more accessible and less abstract terms, which will better resonate with the public.[181]

Any attempt to amend or repeal the HRA, and in particular to de-incorporate the Convention rights from UK law, will give rise to serious legal and political complications. To start with, as discussed earlier, the Northern Ireland Act 1998, the Scotland Act 1998, and the Government of Wales Act 1998 all require the devolved legislatures to comply with Convention rights. As a result, any amendment or repeal of the HRA would either have to leave this requirement intact, or involve a revision of the devolved settlement which could generate a degree of constitutional turmoil.[182] In addition, the Court of Justice of the EU has held that Convention rights form part of the 'general principles' of EU law, which member states are obliged to respect whether or not they give effect to EU legislation.[183] Therefore, even if the HRA was repealed or amended so as to de-incorporate Convention rights, they would still be potentially applicable by UK courts whenever EU law was in play.[184] Furthermore, given that almost all existing UK human rights law, including the case law on common law rights, is heavily influenced by the Strasbourg jurisprudence, any de-incorporation of Convention rights would generate considerable legal uncertainty: the status of all of these precedents would be called into question, which might open the door to fresh waves of litigation.

It is also difficult to identify how a 'home-grown' jurisprudence would differ in substance from what has emerged from the ECHR and HRA case law. British concepts of liberty have cross-bred with the universal language of human rights, while UK law has been influenced by the Strasbourg jurisprudence for decades now. As a result, it is unlikely that UK courts would interpret rights such as freedom of expression or freedom of privacy in a radically different way than they do at present under the HRA, unless a new Bill of Rights were to restrict current levels of rights protection or limit the categories of people who can avail of its protection.[185] A new Bill of Rights could grant individuals a higher degree of legal protection, especially if it incorporated new rights such as socio-economic entitlements or children's rights into UK law: however, such an extension of rights protection is likely to be opposed by many of those currently campaigning for the HRA to be replaced by a new instrument.

---

[181] Some concern has also been expressed that the HRA does not make it clear that individuals have responsibilities as well as rights. See the Green Paper produced by the previous Labour government in 2009 seeking views on whether the HRA should be supplemented by a parallel Bill of Rights and Responsibilities: Ministry of Justice, *Rights and Responsibilities: Developing our Constitutional Framework*, Cm 7577, March 2009.

[182] C. O'Cinneide, 'Human Rights, Devolution and the Constrained Authority of the Westminster Parliament', *UK Constitutional Law Blog*, http://ukconstitutionallaw.org/2013/03/04/colm-ocinneide-human-rights-devolution-and-the-constrained-authority-of-the-westminster-parliament/.

[183] Case 4/73, *Nold v. Commission* [1974] ECR 491 [13]; Case C-260/89, *ERT* [1991] ECR I-2925, [41].

[184] See now Arts. 52(3) and 53 of the EU Charter of Fundamental Rights.

[185] See in general M. Amos, 'Problems with the Human Rights Act and How to Remedy Them: Is a Bill of Rights the Answer?' (2009) 72 *MLR* 883–908; H. Fenwick, 'The Human Rights Act or a British Bill of Rights: Creating a Down-grading Recalibration of Rights against the Counter-terror Backdrop?' [2012] *PL* 468–90.

However, the political debate about the HRA goes on. The Commission on a Bill of Rights established by the Coalition government to discuss reform of UK human rights law reported in December 2012.[186] Seven of the nine commissioners took the view that there were 'strong arguments in favour of a UK Bill of Rights', on the basis that it would represent a 'fresh beginning' and provide a way of side-stepping the 'highly polarised debate' that now surrounds the HRA. In their view, such a Bill of Rights should provide 'no less protection than is contained in the Human Rights Act', and be 'written in language which reflected the distinctive history and heritage of the countries within the United Kingdom' in order to attract 'greater public ownership' and popular legitimacy than the HRA currently enjoys.[187] However, two commissioners, Baroness Kennedy QC and Philippe Sands QC, disagreed: in their view, the majority have failed to identify any real shortcomings in the functioning of the HRA and the case for introducing a new Bill of Rights has not been made.

Subsequently, in October 2014, the Conservative Party published a policy document calling for the HRA to be repealed and replaced by a new British Bill of Rights and Responsibilities, which would 'clarify the Convention rights, to reflect a proper balance between rights and responsibilities', narrow the scope of protection afforded to non-nationals in the context of immigration and national security cases, limit the reach of human rights law and confine its application to the 'most serious cases', prevent legislation from being 'effectively rewritten' through judicial interpretation by requiring courts to 'interpret legislation based upon its normal meaning and the clear intention of Parliament', and ensure that UK courts will no longer 'be required to take into account rulings from the Court in Strasbourg'.[188] The Conservative proposal thus envisages scrapping the s. 3 interpretative duty currently set out in the HRA, and the s. 2 duty to 'take into account' ECtHR judgments. It also proposes altering the status of Strasbourg judgments so that they are purely 'advisory': if this proves to be irreconcilable with the requirements of the ECHR, the policy paper states that 'the UK would be left with no alternative but to withdraw' from the Convention.

These proposals have been subject to heavy academic criticism, not least because key elements are lacking in detail—in particular the question of how ECtHR judgments could be made 'advisory' within the existing framework of the Convention.[189] Dominic Grieve MP, the former Conservative Attorney General, has also been very critical of the proposals, in part because of their potential impact on the integrity

---

[186] Commission on a Bill of Rights, *A UK Bill of Rights? The Choice Before Us*, December 2012, available at http://www.justice.gov.uk/about/cbr

[187] See also M. Amos, 'Transplanting Human Rights Norms: The Case of the UK's Human Rights Act' (2013) 35(2) *Human Rights Quarterly* 386–407.

[188] Conservative Party, *Protecting Human Rights in the UK*, October 2014, available at https://www.conservatives.com/~/media/Files/Downloadable%20Files/HUMAN_RIGHTS.pdf.

[189] For commentary, see Mark Elliott's views at http://publiclawforeveryone.com/2014/10/03/my-analysis-of-the-conservative-partys-proposals-for-a-british-bill-of-rights, and Alison Young's analysis at http://ukconstitutionallaw.org/2014/10/07/alison-young-hra-howlers-the-conservative-party-and-reform-of-the-human-rights-act-1998.

and functioning of the ECHR system of rights protection.[190] If enacted, they would substantially restrict rights protection in the UK, especially as regards the rights of non-nationals. They would also call into question the UK's continued status as a state party to the ECHR, and perhaps to the Council of Europe and EU as well. At the time of writing, the Conservative policy paper reads like a wish-list of political outcomes rather than a substantive legislative proposal. However, the extent to which these proposals involve a radical departure from the existing state of UK human rights law demonstrates the lack of political agreement that currently exists about constitutional fundamentals in this context.

CONCLUSION

The manner in which fundamental rights are protected within the UK constitutional framework has changed dramatically over the last few decades. The influence of the ECHR, taken together with other legal and political factors, has transformed British law. There appears to be no going back to Diceyan orthodoxy; even the Conservative proposals for a new Bill of Rights envisage courts playing an active role in enforcing compliance with basic rights. The HRA was carefully tailored to provide strong rights protection while leaving the fundamentals of the UK constitutional system unaltered. In many ways, it has achieved its intended objectives. However, the Act, and the relationship between UK law and the ECHR, remain politically controversial. The place of human rights within British constitutional culture remains uncertain and contested.

FURTHER READING

AMOS, M., *Human Rights Law* (2nd edn, 2014)

BATES, E., *The Evolution of the European Convention on Human Rights* (2010)

DICKSON, B., *Human Rights and the UK Supreme Court* (2013)

FENWICK, H, *Civil Liberties and Human Rights* (5th edn, 2015)

GEARTY, C., *Principles of Human Rights Adjudication* (2004)

HICKMAN, T., *Public Law after the Human Rights Act* (2010)

KAVANAGH, A., *Constitutional Review under the Human Rights Act* (2009)

KLUG, F., *Values for a Godless Age: The Story of the UK's New Bill of Rights* (2000).

LESTER, A., PANNICK, D., and HERBERG, J. (eds.), *Human Rights Law and Practice* (3rd edn, 2009)

MASTERMAN, R. and LEIGH, I. (eds.), *The United Kingdom's Statutory Bill of Rights: Constitutional and Comparative Perspectives* (2013)

SIMPSON, A. W. B., *Human Rights and the End of Empire* (2001)

YOUNG, A. L., *Parliamentary Sovereignty and the Human Rights Act* (2009)

---

[190] See Grieve, 'Why Human Rights Should Matter to Conservatives'.

USEFUL WEBSITES

Council of Europe: **http://www.coe.int/**
Equality and Human Rights Commission: **http://www.equalityhumanrights.com/**
European Court of Human Rights: **http://www.echr.coe.int/**
Office of the UN High Commissioner for Human Rights: **http://www.ohchr.org/**
Public Law for Everyone blog: **http://publiclawforeveryone.com/**
UK Constitutional Law blog: **http://ukconstitutionallaw.org/**
UK Human Rights Law blog: **http://ukhumanrightsblog.com/**
UN Human Rights Law: **http://www.un.org/en/law/**

4

BRITAIN IN THE EUROPEAN UNION

Paul Craig

SUMMARY

Membership of the European Union raises a number of important issues in domestic constitutional law. In political terms, the fact that an increasing amount of legislation emanates from the European Union means that we should be concerned about the method by which this legislation is made at EU level, and the way in which it is scrutinized in Parliament. In legal terms, EU law raises issues about sovereignty and how our membership of the European Union has affected traditional conceptions of parliamentary supremacy. Treaty articles and norms made thereunder often give rise to rights which individuals can use in their own name in national courts. The EU Charter of Rights is binding and has legal implications for national law. Membership of the European Union has also had important constitutional implications for the judiciary, since national courts also function as EU courts.

INTRODUCTION

All aspects of national law have been affected to varying degrees by membership of the European Union (EU). Constitutional law is no exception. Indeed it is arguable that the effects of EU law on constitutional law have been particularly far-reaching. This chapter describes and evaluates this impact. The discussion begins by considering the effect of the European Union on the political order. There will be analysis of the European Union's legislative process, and the ways in which the Westminster Parliament has sought to accommodate this legislation. The focus will then shift to the effect of the European Union on the constitutional legal order. There will be discussion of sovereignty, the constitutional importance of direct effect, the relevance of EU concepts of fundamental rights, and the changed role of national courts.

THE EUROPEAN UNION AND
THE NATION STATE

The idea of national identity played a powerful part in forging modern nation states out of principalities in both Germany and Italy in the second half of the nineteenth century. The nation state was lauded in literature, philosophy, and music. The horrors of the Second World War were however believed by many to be the result of excessive nationalism. It was felt that the states within Europe should be organized so as to reduce the likelihood of further conflict.[1] This practical ideal lay behind the European Coal and Steel Community (ECSC) which was signed in 1951. Coal and steel were the primary materials used in warfare. If production and distribution could be controlled by a centralized authority it would be less possible for any country to develop a war machine which could be used against its neighbours. The success of the ECSC led pro-Europeanists to believe that more complete economic and political integration was feasible. Plans were drawn up for a European Defence Community (EDC). This was felt to require some form of wider European Political Community (EPC), which would coordinate foreign policy, as well as provide for economic and political integration.[2] Germany would be allowed a limited rearmament within the framework of the EDC. These plans proved to be too ambitious. The French left and right wings both objected, albeit for different reasons, to the idea of German rearmament, even within the EDC. The collapse of the EDC led also to the abandonment of ideas for the EPC.

This setback convinced advocates of European integration that a less overtly political step would be more likely to gain agreement. This was the rationale behind the European Economic Community (EEC) in 1957, created by the Treaty of Rome. The focus was primarily on economic integration, bringing down trade barriers and ensuring free movement of economic factors of production. The architects of the original Treaty were however fully aware of the relationship between economics and politics. They realized that closer economic integration would bring closer coordination on social policy, as well as matters which had a more direct political impact.

There were important amendments to the Treaty of Rome. The Single European Act 1986 had the principal objective of facilitating the completion of the single market. The Treaty on European Union, the Maastricht Treaty, which entered into force in 1993, was more far-reaching. It introduced the three-pillar structure. The First Pillar embraced the Community Treaties, and was supranational in nature. A number of important institutional and substantive changes were made, including an increase in

---

[1] J. Pinder, *European Community: The Building of a Union* (3rd edn, 1998); D. Urwin, *The Community of Europe: A History of European Integration since 1945* (2nd edn, 1995); M. Holland, *European Integration from Community to Union* (1993).

[2] The proposal for an EDC was made by France in 1950 and the EDC Treaty was signed, but not ratified, in 1952 by the six states of the ECSC. The French National Assembly refused to ratify the EDC Treaty. Plans for both defence and political union were then shelved.

the powers of the European Parliament, and the setting of a detailed timetable for eco-nomic and monetary union. The Second Pillar was concerned with Common Foreign and Security Policy, and the Third Pillar with Justice and Home Affairs. What dis-tinguished the Second and Third Pillars was that decision-making remained much more intergovernmental in nature, as compared to that which operates in the First Pillar. The member states dominated decision-making under the Second and Third Pillars, largely to the exclusion of the Commission and the European Parliament, with the European Court of Justice excluded from the Second Pillar and given only a lim-ited role under the Third Pillar. Notwithstanding this fact, it should not be forgot-ten that the Maastricht Treaty overall increased the powers of the European Union and the European Community. Decision-making under the Second and Third Pillars may well have been more intergovernmental than under the First Pillar, but the real-ity was nonetheless that the sphere over which the European Union had competence increased, and there was now an institutionalized forum within which to discuss important matters such as foreign policy, asylum, cross-border crime, and the like. The Treaty of Amsterdam, which entered into force in 1999, brought further changes. The line between decision-making within the Second and Third Pillars, and that within the First Pillar, was blurred. While the former remained intergovernmental in nature, they were infused with more supranational tenor than hitherto, and some of the subject matter previously dealt with under the Third Pillar was transferred to the First Pillar. The Treaty of Nice 2000 dealt primarily with the institutional con-sequences of enlargement. The Treaty provisions dealing with institutional issues had remained largely unchanged since the inception of the EEC. The expansion of the European Community to include 15 member states, with the prospect of further significant enlargement eastwards, was the catalyst for addressing some of the basic issues concerning institutional structure, such as the size of the European Parliament, the voting rules in the Council, and whether each member state should continue to have one Commissioner.

The new millennium saw attempts at more comprehensive treaty reform, the origins of which are to be found in the Nice Treaty, which left open four issues for future deliberation: the 'delimitation of powers' between the European Union and the member states, the status of the Charter of Fundamental Rights, simplification of the Treaties, and the role of the national parliaments. The Laeken European Council in 2001 issued a Declaration that considerably broadened the range of matters that should be discussed concerning the future of Europe. No longer were there four 'dis-crete' issues. The Laeken Declaration placed just about every issue of importance con-cerning the future of Europe on the agenda for discussion, including major issues concerning the inter-institutional disposition of power within the European Union. It led to the establishment of the Convention on the Future of Europe, headed by the ex-French President, Giscard d'Estaing. It was not preordained that it would pro-duce a Constitutional Treaty, but it did so.[3] The Constitutional Treaty was, after some

---

[3] Treaty Establishing a Constitution for Europe [2004] OJ C310/1.

hesitation and amendment, accepted by the member states. It then had to be accepted by all of the member states in accord with their constitutional traditions for Treaty ratification. After the negative votes in the French and Dutch referenda the ratification process was however put on hold.

The process of treaty reform was revived in 2007, and this led to the Treaty of Lisbon,[4] which was finally ratified by all member states in 2009.[5] The Treaty of Lisbon amends the previous treaties. The European Union is henceforth to be founded on the Treaty on European Union (TEU), and the Treaty on the Functioning of the European Union (TFEU), and the two Treaties have the same legal value.[6] The European Union replaces and succeeds to the European Community.[7] The TEU contains some but not all of the constitutional principles that govern the European Union. The TFEU contains the provisions as amended that were previously to be found in the EC Treaty. The Treaty of Lisbon has removed the formal three-pillar structure. The provisions of the Third Pillar have been incorporated into the TFEU and are subject to the ordinary Treaty regime. There are however still distinct rules relating to the Common Foreign and Security Policy that are found in the TEU. In terms of overall content the Treaty of Lisbon drew heavily on the Constitutional Treaty.

There are now seven formal EU institutions.[8] The Assembly was originally an indirectly elected body representing the people. It is now called the European Parliament and is composed of directly elected representatives from the member states. The European Council consists of the heads of state, the President of the European Council, and the President of the Commission. The Council of Ministers is composed of representatives from the member states. The members of the Commission are appointed from the states, but they are independent of their own country and represent the EU interest. The fifth official EU institution is the Court of Justice of the European Union, known prior to the Lisbon Treaty as the European Court of Justice, ECJ, and the remaining two are the European Central Bank and the Court of Auditors. The powers accorded to the different institutions, and the way in which they interact, have changed markedly over time.

THE LEGISLATIVE AND DECISION-MAKING PROCESS

For the first 30 years of the Community's existence decision-making was dominated by the Council and Commission. The Assembly, had limited formal powers in the EEC Treaty. Its role in the legislative process was restricted: it only had a right to be consulted where a specific Treaty article stipulated that this should be so. The confined nature of the Assembly's powers was explicable in part because few if any

---

[4] P. Craig, *The Lisbon Treaty: Law, Politics and Treaty Reform* (2010).
[5] Consolidated Versions of the Treaty on European Union and the Treaty on the Functioning of the European Union [2010] OJ C83/1.
[6] TEU, Art. 1, para. 3.   [7] Ibid., Art. 1 para. 3.   [8] Ibid., Art. 13.

international organizations had any democratically elected legislature with real power at the international level. The explanation was also in part a reflection of the view of the Community held by its prime architects. Monnet, one of the principal founders, adopted a strategy of what has been termed elite-led gradualism.[9] It was hoped that popular consent would follow this lead, but the need to engage powerful business and labour organizations was accorded a much higher priority than the 'direct involvement of as yet uninformed publics'.[10] While Monnet was broadly in favour of a democratic Community 'he saw the emergence of loyalties to the Community institutions developing as a *consequence* of elite agreements for the functional organization of Europe, not as an essential *prerequisite* to that organization'.[11] Moreover, the legitimacy of the Community was to be secured through outcomes: peace and prosperity.

It was the Commission and the Council that dominated decision-making during this 30-year period. The Commission was given a plethora of powers of a legislative, administrative, executive, and judicial nature.[12] Its legislative powers were of particular importance. The Commission has the right of legislative initiative, which means that it has a major influence over the development of the Community's legislative agenda. This, and its other powers, served to place the Commission at the heart of the Community.

Notwithstanding this array of formal powers, the Council exerted increasing control over the Commission during this period. This was largely through institutional developments that were initially outside the strict letter of the Treaty, which increased the Council's influence over Community legislation. The Luxembourg Accords ensured that decisions that affected important interests of a particular member state would not be taken unless that state agreed, even where the Treaty stipulated that voting was to be by qualified majority. Decision-making was thus carried forward under the 'shadow of the veto' even when it was not formally invoked. The Committee of Permanent Representatives, the organ providing institutional support for the Council, developed its own working parties which enabled it to engage in a dialogue with the Commission over the details of legislative proposals. Management and regulatory committees emerged as the vehicle through which member state input could be ensured when decision-making had been delegated to the Commission. Finally, the European Council, meetings of the heads of state, became an institutionalized forum through which member states could influence the overall direction of the Community at the highest level.

The Assembly, formally renamed the European Parliament (EP) by the Maastricht Treaty, pressed for greater powers in the legislative process, bolstered by the fact that it had been directly elected since 1979. In the early 1980s it put forward radical proposals

---

[9] W. Wallace and J. Smith, 'Democracy or Technocracy? European Integration and the Problem of Popular Consent', in J. Hayward (ed.), *The Crisis of Representation in Europe* (1995), 140.

[10] Ibid., 140.

[11] Holland, *European Integration from Community to Union*, 16. Original emphasis.

[12] P. Craig and G. de Búrca, *EU Law, Text, Cases and Materials* (6th edn, 2015), ch. 2.

for a revision of the Treaty, which would have placed it in the centre of the legislative process. These proposals fell largely on stony ground. However, the Single European Act 1986 did afford the EP a real role in the legislative process for the first time. The cooperation procedure gave the EP power in the enactment of legislation, and made it necessary for the Commission, when drafting legislation, to take account of the EP's views.[13] The years since 1986 saw the powers of the EP increase still further. The Maastricht Treaty[14] introduced the co-decision procedure, which gave more power to the EP than the cooperation procedure. The Treaty of Amsterdam[15] further strengthened the EP's position under the co-decision procedure and extended its sphere of application. The Treaty of Lisbon has continued this development. The co-decision procedure has been relabelled the ordinary legislative procedure and its sphere of application has been further extended with the consequence that the Council and EP are said to exercise legislative functions jointly.[16]

The details of the procedure are complex.[17] A proposal is sent by the Commission to the Council and the EP. The EP can if it wishes propose amendments at its first reading of the measure. If the Council approves these then the proposed act can be adopted at that stage. The Council may however not agree with the EP's amendments, in which case the Council adopts its position, which is communicated to the EP. The EP then has three months to respond. It can at this Second Reading of the measure agree to the Council's position, or not take a decision. The act will then be deemed to have been adopted in accordance with the Council's position. The EP may alternatively reject the Council's position in which case the act will not be adopted. It may however suggest further amendments. It is open to the Council to accept the EP's Second Reading amendments, in which case the act becomes law in the form of the Council's position as amended. If the Council does not approve of all the amendments then a meeting of the Conciliation Committee is convened. The Conciliation Committee has an equal number of representatives from the Council and the EP. Its task is to reach agreement on a joint text. If it is able to do so, then this must be approved by the EP and the Council.

Although the ordinary legislative procedure is complex it accommodates the differing institutional interests of those concerned with the passage of EU legislation. The Commission will consult with the EP and the Council about the overall legislative programme for the coming year. It will also consult with the Council, or more accurately the Committee of Permanent Representatives, and the EP, or the relevant committee thereof, about a draft measure before it begins to go through the TFEU, Art. 294 procedure. The formal powers given to the EP by Art. 294 enable it to propose changes at an early stage which, if accepted by the Council, can then be embodied in the measure which becomes law at that stage. The EP is then given further power if the Council

---

[13] M. Westlake, *The Commission and the Parliament: Partners and Rivals in the European Policy-Making Process* (1994), and *A Modern Guide to the European Parliament* (1994).

[14] The Maastricht Treaty entered into force in 1993.   [15] The Treaty entered into force in 1999.

[16] Treaty of Lisbon, TEU, Arts. 14(1) and 16(1).   [17] Ibid., TFEU, Art. 294.

does not accept all the EP's first reading suggestions. The EP can accept, reject, or propose further amendments to the Council's position at the Second Reading stage. The bottom line is that an act will not be passed unless both the EP and the Council agree.

THE NATURE OF THE EUROPEAN UNION

It is important not to view the European Union as if it were a nation state, nor should one necessarily expect the form of institutional ordering to conform to that commonly found at the domestic level. Conceptions of the separation of powers, which play a marked role in the allocation of functions within domestic constitutions, do not have the same centrality within the European Union. The legislative process is divided between the Council, the EP, and the Commission. This has a real impact on the relationship between the EP and the Council. The latter, for all its power, cannot dominate the former in the way that the executive dominates the legislature at Westminster. The EP will be run by the largest party, or a coalition, which will have its own agenda, albeit being mindful of what will be acceptable to the Council and the Commission. Responsibilities of an executive nature are exercised by the Commission, the Council, and the European Council. Administrative responsibility for the implementation of EU policy lies principally with the Commission, but it will often work through and with national bureaucracies. The EP does moreover have oversight powers through which it can call the Commission to account for the way in which EU policy is administered. It was the exercise of these powers that led to the appointment of the Committee of Independent Experts, whose report prompted the resignation of the Santer Commission in 1999.

Judicial power resides principally with the Court of Justice of the European Union (CJEU) and the General Court (GC), which is the new name for the Court of First Instance (CFI). The Commission also has powers of a judicial nature. It will be the body that brings member states to court under TFEU, Art. 258 if they are in breach of the Treaty. The Commission will give the initial judicial decision on important issues such as competition law and state aids. The CJEU and the GC have far-reaching powers of judicial review, which can be used to ensure that EU institutions do not exceed their power. The CJEU will adjudicate on important inter-institutional disputes between the principal EU organs. The CJEU has read into the Treaty general principles of law which are used to judge the legality of EU action. These principles include proportionality, legitimate expectations, procedural legality, and fundamental rights. It is the CJEU which will also adjudicate on disputes concerning subsidiarity, whereby member states will challenge the competence of the European Union to act, arguing that the subject matter should have been left for resolution at state level.[18]

---

[18] Case C-84/94, *United Kingdom v. Council* [1996] ECR I-5755; Case C-233/94, *Germany v. European Parliament and the Council* [1997] ECR I-2405.

The theme which appears repeatedly in papers emanating from the European Union is that of institutional balance, rather than separation of powers.[19] This refers to the desirability of preserving a proper balance of power between the Council, as representing the interests of the member states, the EP as representing the people, and the Commission as guardian of the overall aims of the treaty. While classical ideas of the separation of powers are not therefore central to the institutional ordering within the European Union, another constitutional principle, the rule of law, is of prime importance. TEU, Art. 2 declares that the European Union is founded on the respect for human dignity, freedom, democracy, equality, human rights, and the rule of law. Respect for these principles is made a condition of membership of the EU.[20]

THE UK PARLIAMENT AND LEGISLATIVE SCRUTINY

EU membership has significant implications for the Westminster Parliament, and also for the Welsh Assembly and the Scottish Parliament. We shall begin by considering the machinery introduced to deal with EU legislation, and then consider the subsidiarity controls that reside with national parliaments.

In terms of machinery,[21] Committees of the House of Commons have been established to consider whether legislation is necessary to implement, for example, an EU directive, and also to scrutinize proposals that emerge from the European Union, in order to provide Parliament with information about impending European legislation. The system works in the following way. The European Scrutiny Committee examines EU documents, such as draft proposals for legislation, and reports on the 'legal and political importance' of each document. The scrutiny is conducted in the light of the Explanatory Memorandum produced by the relevant government department on the EU documents. The Committee considers approximately 1,100 documents each year, half of which are deemed to be of legal or political importance, such that the Scrutiny Committee reports substantively on them. It recommends approximately 40 such documents per year for further consideration by one of the European Standing Committees, and approximately three per year for debate on the floor of the House. The latter only occurs if the House decides that they should be considered in this way. There are three European Standing Committees[22] and the

---

[19] P. Craig, 'Democracy and Rulemaking within the EC: An Empirical and Normative Assessment' (1997) 3 *ELJ* 105.

[20] Treaty of Lisbon, TEU, Art. 49.

[21] T. St J. N. Bates, 'European Community Legislation before the House of Commons' (1991) 12 *Stat LR* 109; E. Denza, 'Parliamentary Scrutiny of Community Legislation' (1993) 14 *Stat LR* 56; *European Scrutiny System in the House of Commons* (2012), http://www.parliament.uk/business/committees/committees-a-z/commons-select/european-scrutiny-committee/guides/.

[22] Committee A: Energy and Climate Change; Environment, Food and Rural Affairs; Transport; Communities and Local Government; Forestry Commission. Committee B: HM Treasury; Work and

relevant committee will consider the merits of the issues. The reports of the European Scrutiny Committee are clearly and succinctly presented.[23] They show an awareness of the legal and political importance of issues that are often complex. The committee's evaluation will sometimes support that of the relevant government minister, and will sometimes take a differing line. The very fact that there is a body within the UK looking at such issues, other than the relevant department of state, is undoubtedly beneficial. The European Scrutiny Committee will also liaise where necessary with departmental select committees. The new regime has undoubtedly had a positive impact.[24] It has been enhanced by the scrutiny reserve resolution, which means that, subject to certain exceptions, a UK minister will not vote in the Council on matters that have not been cleared by the ESC.

It has in the past been hampered by the brevity of time left for discussion before the EU legislation is considered by the Council. The Treaty of Lisbon is designed to alleviate this problem. Documents such as green and white papers are sent to national Parliaments as soon as they are published, and draft legislative acts are transmitted to them at the same time as they are sent to the Council and Commission.[25] The general rule is that an eight-week period must elapse between transmission of a draft legislative act to national Parliaments, and its being placed on a provisional agenda for the Council for its adoption or for adoption of a position under a legislative procedure.[26] The national Parliaments also receive the agendas and outcomes of Council meetings at the same time as national governments.[27]

There is in addition a House of Lords' Select Committee on the European Union. It is chaired by a salaried officer of the House[28] and considers any EU proposal that it believes should be drawn to the attention of the House. The Committee functions through a number of subcommittees which are subject matter-based.[29] These subcommittees will co-opt other members of the House of Lords for the investigation of particular issues. The House of Lords' Select Committee is therefore different from that in the House of Commons. The latter will sift through EU legislation and refer matters on to the standing committee where this is warranted.

Pensions; Foreign and Commonwealth Office; International Development; Home Office; Justice; and matters not otherwise allocated. Committee C: Business, Innovation and Skills; Children, Schools and Families; Innovation, Culture, Media, and Sport; and Health.

[23] See e.g. Fourteenth Report of the European Union Scrutiny Committee, *Aspects of the EU's Constitutional Treaty*, HC 38-xiv-1 (2005); Fourteenth Report of the European Union Scrutiny Committee, 2008–9, *Free Movement of Workers in the EU*, HC 324 (2009); Eleventh Report of the European Scrutiny Committee, *Ukraine and Russia: EU Restrictive Measures*, HC 219-xi (2014)

[24] *The European Scrutiny System in the House* (see n. 21).

[25] TEU, Art. 12; Protocol (No. 1) On the Role of National Parliaments in the European Union, Art. 1.

[26] Protocol (No. 1), Art. 4.   [27] Ibid., Art. 5.

[28] The chairman will decide which issues are of sufficient importance to warrant scrutiny by one of the subcommittees.

[29] There are six such subcommittees which deal with: economic and financial affairs; internal market, infrastructure and employment; external affairs; agriculture, fisheries, environment and energy; justice, institutions and consumer protection; home affairs, health and education.

The House of Lords' committee will produce its own valuable, detailed reports on particular issues.[30]

The role of national parliaments in the scrutiny of draft EU legislation has been strengthened by the Treaty of Lisbon provisions on subsidiarity. The basic idea behind subsidiarity is that action should only be undertaken at EU level where because of the scale or effects of the action it can be better achieved through EU action rather than national action.[31] The detailed scheme is contained in the Protocol on the Application of the Principles of Subsidiarity and Proportionality.[32] It imposes an obligation to consult widely before proposing legislative acts.[33] The Commission must provide a detailed statement concerning proposed legislation so that compliance with subsidiarity can be appraised.[34] The Commission must submit an annual report on the application of subsidiarity to the European Council, the EP, the Council, and to national parliaments.[35] The CJEU has jurisdiction to consider infringement of subsidiarity under TFEU, Art. 263, brought by the member state, or 'notified by them in accordance with their legal order on behalf of their national Parliament or a chamber of it'.[36]

The most important innovation in the Protocol on Subsidiarity is the enhanced role accorded to national parliaments.[37] The Commission must send all legislative proposals to the national parliaments at the same time as to the EU institutions.[38] A national parliament or chamber thereof, may, within eight weeks, send the Presidents of the Commission, EP, and Council a reasoned opinion as to why it considers that the proposal does not comply with subsidiarity.[39] The EP, Council, and Commission must take this opinion into account.[40] Each national parliament has two votes[41] and where non-compliance with subsidiarity is expressed by national parliaments that represent one-third of all the votes allocated to them, the Commission must review its proposal.[42] The Commission, after such review, may decide to maintain, amend, or withdraw the proposal, giving reasons for the decision.[43] Where a measure is made in accord with the ordinary legislative procedure, and at least a simple majority of votes given to national parliaments signal non-compliance with subsidiarity, then the proposal must once again be reviewed and although the Commission can decide not

---

[30] See e.g. Third Report of the Select Committee on the European Communities, HL 23 (1999), dealing with reforms to Comitology procedures; Tenth Report of the European Union Committee, *The Future Regulation of Derivatives Markets: Is the EU on the Right Track?*, HL 93 (2010); Second Report of the European Union Committee, *EU Data Protection Law: 'A Right to be Forgotten?'* HL 40 (2014)

[31] TEU, Art. 5(3).

[32] Protocol (No. 2), On the Application of the Principles of Subsidiarity and Proportionality.

[33] Ibid., Art. 2.   [34] Ibid., Art. 5.   [35] Ibid., Art. 9.   [36] Ibid., Art. 8.

[37] J.-V. Louis, 'National Parliaments and the Principle of Subsidiarity: Legal Options and Practical Limits' in I. Pernice and E. Tanchev (eds.), *Ceci n'est pas une Constitution—Constitutionalization without a Constitution?* (2009), 131–54; G. Bermann, 'National Parliaments and Subsidiarity: An Outsider's View', ibid., 155–61; J. Peters, 'National Parliaments and Subsidiarity: Think Twice' (2005) *European Constitutional L Rev* 68.

[38] Protocol (No. 2), On the Application of the Principles of Subsidiarity and Proportionality, Art. 4.

[39] Ibid., Art. 6.   [40] Ibid., Art. 7(1).   [41] Ibid.

[42] Ibid., Art. 7(2). This threshold is lowered to one-quarter in certain cases concerning the area of freedom, justice, and security.

[43] Protocol (No. 2), On the Application of the Principles of Subsidiarity and Proportionality, Art. 7(2).

to amend it, the Commission must provide a reasoned opinion on the matter and this can, in effect, be overridden by the EP or the Council.[44]

It is clear that there will continue to be many areas in which the comparative efficiency calculus in TFEU, Art. 5(3) favours EU action, more especially in an enlarged European Union. Much will depend on the willingness of national Parliaments to devote the requisite time and energy to the matter. The national Parliament has to submit a reasoned opinion as to why it believes that the measure infringes subsidiarity. It will have to present reasoned argument as to why the Commission's comparative efficiency calculus is defective. This may not be easy. It will be even more difficult for the requisite number of national parliaments to present reasoned opinions in relation to the same EU measure so as to compel the Commission to review the proposal.[45] The Commission is nonetheless likely to take seriously any such reasoned opinion, particularly if it emanates from the parliament of a larger member state.

SOVEREIGNTY

THE TRADITIONAL DEBATE

A detailed analysis of parliamentary sovereignty is provided by Mark Elliott in this volume.[46] The present discussion will focus on sovereignty and the European Union. It is however necessary to mention, albeit briefly, some of the background to the general sovereignty debate.

The debate over sovereignty has been characterized as a contest between the traditionalists, represented by Dicey and Wade,[47] and upholders of the New View, represented by Jennings,[48] Heuston,[49] and Marshall.[50] The form of argument used by Sir William Wade is in fact different from that advanced by Dicey, and therefore it is the views of Wade that will be considered here. No attempt will be made to consider the detail of the debate between Wade and the advocates of the New View.[51] The view of sovereignty advanced by Sir William Wade is captured in the following quotation:[52]

> An orthodox English lawyer, brought up consciously or unconsciously on the doctrine of parliamentary sovereignty stated by Coke and Blackstone, and enlarged on by Dicey,

---

[44] Ibid., Art. 7(3).

[45] P. Kiiver, *The Early Warning System for the Principle of Subsidiarity: Constitutional Theory and Empirical Reality* (2012); A Cygan, 'The Parliamentarisation of EU Decision-making? The Impact of the Treaty of Lisbon on National Parliaments' (2011) 36 *ELRev* 48.

[46] Ch. 2 in this volume.

[47] A. Dicey, *An Introduction to the Study of the Law of the Constitution* (10th edn, 1967); H. W. R. Wade, 'The Basis of Legal Sovereignty' [1955] *Camb LJ* 172.

[48] Sir I. Jennings, *The Law and the Constitution* (5th edn, 1959), ch. 4.

[49] R. F. V. Heuston, *Essays in Constitutional Law* (2nd edn, 1964), ch. 1.

[50] G. Marshall, *Constitutional Theory* (1971), ch. 3.

[51] P. Craig, 'Parliamentary Sovereignty of the United Kingdom Parliament after *Factortame*' (1991) 11 *YBEL* 221.

[52] Wade, 'The Basis of Legal Sovereignty', 174.

could explain it in simple terms. He would say that it meant merely that no Act of the sovereign legislature (composed of the Queen, Lords and Commons) could be invalid in the eyes of the courts; that it was always open to the legislature, so constituted, to repeal any previous legislation whatever; that therefore no Parliament could bind its successors . . . He would probably add that it is an invariable rule that in case of conflict between two Acts of Parliament, the later repeals the earlier. If he were then asked whether it would be possible for the United Kingdom to 'entrench' legislation—for example, if it should wish to adopt a Bill of Rights which would be repealable only by some specially safeguarded process—he would answer that under English law this is a legal impossibility: it is easy enough to pass such legislation, but since that legislation, like all other legislation, would be repealable by any ordinary Act of Parliament the special safeguards would be legally futile. This is merely an illustration of the rule that one Parliament cannot bind its successors. It follows therefore that there is one, and only one, limit to Parliament's legal power: it cannot detract from its own continuing sovereignty.

This thesis has been vigorously challenged by the proponents of the New View, who argued that 'manner and form' provisions enacted in a particular statute would be binding, in the sense that a later statute dealing with the same subject matter could only alter the earlier statute if passed in accordance with the provisions of that earlier statute.[53]

THE JUDICIAL RESPONSE PRIOR TO *FACTORTAME*

On the traditional view of sovereignty as represented by Sir William Wade the latest will of Parliament must predominate. If there is a clash between a later and an earlier norm, then the former impliedly repeals the latter. This view of sovereignty meant that there could be tensions between UK and EU law. The primacy of EU law over national law[54] was asserted by the ECJ early in its developing jurisprudence,[55] and extended by later case law.[56]

Prior to *Factortame* there were three differing strands within the UK jurisprudence. In some cases courts spoke in terms of the traditional orthodoxy on sovereignty.[57] The second, and dominant, line of cases sought to blunt the edge of any conflict between the two systems by using strong principles of construction: UK law would, whenever possible, be read so as to be compatible with EU law.[58] In the third type of case the courts accepted, in principle, the idea of purposive construction, but felt unable to read the UK legislation to be in conformity with the relevant EU norm.[59]

---

[53] See nn. 48, 49, and 50.   [54] Craig and de Búrca, *EU Law: Text, Cases and Materials*, ch. 10.
[55] Case 6/64, *Costa* v. *ENEL* [1964] ECR 585, 593.
[56] Case 106/77, *Amministrazione delle Finanze dello Stato* v. *Simmenthal Spa* [1978] ECR 629.
[57] *Felixstowe Docks Railway Co.* v. *British Transport Docks Board* [1976] 2 CMLR 655, 664.
[58] *Litster* v. *Forth Dry Dock* [1990] 1 AC 546.   [59] *Duke* v. *GEC Reliance* [1988] AC 618.

FACTORTAME, EOC, THOBURN AND HS2

The leading decision is now *R* v. *Secretary of State for Transport, ex parte Factortame Ltd*.[60] The applicants were companies incorporated under UK law, but the majority of the directors and shareholders were Spanish. The companies were in the business of sea fishing and their vessels were registered as British under the Merchant Shipping Act 1894. The statutory regime governing sea fishing was altered by the Merchant Shipping Act 1988. Vessels that had been registered under the 1894 Act had to register under the new legislation. Ninety-five vessels failed to meet the new criteria and the applicants argued that the relevant parts of the 1988 Act were incompatible with the EC Treaty, Arts. 52, 58, and 221.[61]

Whether the 1988 statute was in breach of EC law was a contentious question, and therefore a reference was made to the ECJ under EC Treaty, Art. 177 (now TFEU, Art. 267). The issue in the first *Factortame* case concerned the status of the 1988 Act pending the ECJ's decision on the substance of the case. If the applicants could not fish in this intervening period they might well go out of business. Their Lordships held that, as a matter of domestic law, interim relief against the Crown was not available,[62] and therefore the applicants could not be given financial protection pending the outcome of the case. The House of Lords then sought a preliminary ruling as to whether the absence of any interim relief against the Crown was itself a violation of EC law.

The ECJ decided in favour of the applicants.[63] It reasoned from the *Simmenthal* case[64] where it had held that provisions of EC law rendered 'automatically inapplicable' any conflicting provision of national law. The *Simmenthal* decision gave a broad construction to the idea of a 'conflicting provision' of national law, interpreting it to cover any legislative, administrative, or judicial practice that might impair the effectiveness of EC law.[65] With this foundation the ECJ in the *Factortame* case concluded that the full effectiveness of EC law could be impaired by the absence of interim relief.[66]

The case then returned to the House of Lords to be reconsidered in the light of the preliminary ruling given by the ECJ, *R* v. *Secretary of State for Transport, ex parte Factortame Ltd (No. 2)*.[67] Their Lordships accepted that, at least in the area covered by EC law, such relief would be available against the Crown. *Factortame (No. 2)* also contains *dicta* by their Lordships on the more general issue of sovereignty. The final decision on the substance of the case involved a clash between articles of the EC Treaty, and a later Act of the UK Parliament, the Merchant Shipping Act 1988. The traditional idea of sovereignty in the UK is, as we have seen, that if there is a clash between a later statute and an earlier legal provision the later statute takes precedence. The ECJ has repeatedly held that EC law must take precedence in the event of a clash with national law. Moreover, the conflict in this instance was between national law and articles of

---

[60] [1990] 2 AC 85.   [61] TFEU, Arts. 49, 54, and 55, after the Treaty of Lisbon.
[62] Such relief is now available: *M* v. *Home Office* [1994] 1 AC 377.
[63] Case C-213/89, *R* v. *Secretary of State for Transport, ex parte Factortame Ltd* [1990] ECR I-2433.
[64] See n. 56.   [65] See n. 56, paras. 22 and 23.   [66] See n. 63, para. 21.
[67] [1991] 1 AC 603.

the Treaty itself. The ECJ has made it clear that in the event of such a clash EC law trumps national law. The dicta of the House of Lords in *Factortame (No. 2)* are therefore clearly of importance. Lord Bridge had this to say:[68]

> Some public comments on the decision of the Court of Justice, affirming the jurisdiction of the courts of the member states to override national legislation if necessary to enable interim relief to be granted in protection of rights under Community law, have suggested that this was a novel and dangerous invasion by a Community institution of the sovereignty of the United Kingdom Parliament. But such comments are based on a misconception. If the supremacy within the European Community of Community law over the national law of member states was not always inherent in the EEC Treaty it was certainly well established in the jurisprudence of the Court of Justice long before the United Kingdom joined the Community. Thus, whatever limitation of its sovereignty Parliament accepted when it enacted the European Communities Act 1972 was entirely voluntary. Under the terms of the 1972 Act it has always been clear that it was the duty of a United Kingdom court, when delivering final judgment, to override any rule of national law found to be in conflict with any directly enforceable rule of Community law. Similarly, when decisions of the Court of Justice have exposed areas of United Kingdom statute law which failed to implement Council directives, Parliament has always loyally accepted the obligation to make appropriate and prompt amendments. Thus there is nothing in any way novel in according supremacy to rules of Community law in areas to which they apply and to insist that, in the protection of rights under Community law, national courts must not be prohibited by rules of national law from granting interim relief in appropriate cases is no more than a logical recognition of that supremacy.

Three aspects of this reasoning should be distinguished. One was essentially *contractarian*: the UK knew when it joined the European Community that priority should be accorded to EC law, and it must be taken to have contracted on those terms. If, therefore, 'blame' was to be cast for a loss of sovereignty then this should be laid at the door of Parliament and not the courts. The second facet of Lord Bridge's reasoning was *a priori* and *functional*: it was always inherent in a regime such as the European Community that it could only function adequately if EC law could take precedence in the event of a clash with domestic legal norms. The third factor at play was the existence of the European Communities Act 1972 (ECA 1972), which was said to impose a duty on national courts to override national law in the event of a clash with directly enforceable EC law.

The impact of *Factortame* was made clear in the *Equal Opportunities Commission* case,[69] which was concerned with the compatibility of UK legislation on unfair dismissal and redundancy pay with EC law. Under UK law[70] entitlement to these protections and benefits operated differentially depending upon whether the person was in full-time or part-time employment. Full-time workers were eligible after two years;

---

[68] Ibid., 658–9.
[69] *R v. Secretary of State for Employment, ex parte Equal Opportunities Commission* [1995] 1 AC 1.
[70] Employment Protection (Consolidation) Act 1978.

part-time workers only after five. The majority of part-time workers were women and the Equal Opportunities Commission (EOC) took the view that the legislation discriminated against them, contrary to Art. 119.[71] The EOC sought a declaration that the relevant provisions of the UK legislation were in breach of EC law. The House of Lords held that the national legislation was in breach of Art. 119 and the directives. The *Factortame* case was regarded as authority for the proposition that it was open to a national court to declare provisions of a primary statute to be incompatible with norms of EC law.[72] The House of Lords also made it clear that this power to review primary legislation resided in all national *courts*, not just the UK's top court.

The impact of the European Union on traditional concepts of sovereignty was also considered in *Thoburn*.[73] Certain street traders were prosecuted for continuing to use imperial measures, rather than metric, when selling their goods. The obligation to use metric measures as the primary form of measurement derived from EC directives, and the UK government had complied with this obligation through the enactment of a series of regulations, some of which were based on ECA 1972, s. 2(2). The defendants argued that in this context the power to make such regulations through s. 2(2) had been impliedly repealed by provisions contained in the Weights and Measures Act 1985. Laws LJ held that there was no inconsistency between ECA 1972, s. 2(2) and the Weights and Measures Act 1985, and therefore that no issue of implied repeal arose in the case. He held more generally that the constitutional relationship between the UK and the European Union was not to be decided by the ECJ's jurisprudence: that case law could not itself entrench EU law within national law.[74] The constitutional relationship between the European Union and the UK, including the impact of membership of the European Union on sovereignty, was to be decided by the common law in the light of any statutes that Parliament had enacted.[75] The common law had, said Laws LJ, modified the traditional concept of sovereignty, in the sense that it had created exceptions to the doctrine of implied repeal. Ordinary statutes were subject to the doctrine of implied repeal. What Laws LJ referred to as 'constitutional statutes', which conditioned the legal relationship between citizen and state in some overarching manner, or which dealt with fundamental constitutional rights, were not subject to the doctrine of implied repeal.[76] The repeal of such a statute, or its disapplication in a particular instance, could only occur if there were some 'express words in the later statute, or by words so specific that the inference of an actual determination to effect the result contended for was irresistible'.[77] The ECA 1972 was regarded as just such a constitutional statute. It contained provisions that ensured the supremacy of substantive EU law in the event of a clash with national law, and was not subject to implied repeal.

The reasoning in *Thoburn* has been endorsed by the Supreme Court in the *HS2* case.[78] The case is important in two respects. First, the Supreme Court affirmed that the

---

[71] Now TFEU Art. 157.   [72] [1995] 1 AC 1, 27.
[73] *Thoburn v. Sunderland City Council* [2003] QB 151.   [74] Ibid., paras. 57–8.
[75] Ibid., para. 59.   [76] Ibid., para. 62.   [77] Ibid., para. 63.
[78] *R (HS2 Action Alliance Ltd) v. Secretary of State for Transport* [2014] UKSC 3; P. Craig, 'Constitutionalizing Constitutional Law: HS2' [2014] *PL* 373.

constitutional relationship between the UK and European Union was to be decided by the UK courts in accord with UK constitutional principle. Thus Lord Reed made it clear that the supremacy of EU law only took effect within the UK through the European Communities Act 1972, and that any conflict between EU law and UK law would be resolved by UK courts as a matter of UK constitutional law.[79] Secondly, the Supreme Court reaffirmed the idea that there was a separate category of constitutional statutes in the UK constitutional order, with the consequence in this context that it could not be assumed that when Parliament enacted the ECA 1972 that it impliedly authorized the limitation or abrogation of such principles by EU law. In the instant case the relevant principle was derived from Art. 9 of the Bill of Rights 1689, which precluded the impeaching or questioning in any court of debates or proceedings in Parliament. Lord Mance and Lord Neuberger put the matter as follows:[80]

> The United Kingdom has no written constitution, but we have a number of constitutional instruments. They include Magna Carta, the Petition of Right 1628, the Bill of Rights and (in Scotland) the Claim of Rights Act 1689, the Act of Settlement 1701 and the Act of Union 1707. The European Communities Act 1972, the Human Rights Act 1998 and the Constitutional Reform Act 2005 may now be added to this list. The common law itself also recognises certain principles as fundamental to the rule of law. It is, putting the point at its lowest, certainly arguable (and it is for United Kingdom law and courts to determine) that there may be fundamental principles, whether contained in other constitutional instruments or recognised at common law, of which Parliament when it enacted the European Communities Act 1972 did not either contemplate or authorise the abrogation.

SUPREMACY AFTER *FACTORTAME, EOC, THOBURN* AND *HS2*: THE SUBSTANTIVE IMPACT OF THE DECISIONS

The decisions considered earlier generated much academic comment.[81] Space precludes a detailed analysis of the differing views. It is nonetheless clear that there are two issues of central importance: the substantive impact of these decisions on the previous orthodoxy concerning sovereignty; and the best way of conceptualizing what has occurred. The former will be considered here, the latter in the section that follows. The substantive impact of the cases set out earlier may be described as follows.

First, the relationship between EU law and national law in terms of supremacy is to be decided by the UK courts as a matter of UK constitutional law, taking account of any statutes enacted by Parliament.

Secondly, in doctrinal terms the effect of the case law is that the concept of *implied repeal*, or *implied disapplication*, under which inconsistencies between later and

---

[79] *HS2*, para. 79. The superior courts of most member states adopt the same conceptual approach in this respect, as exemplified by the case law of the German Federal Constitutional Court.

[80] Ibid., at para. 207.

[81] Craig, 'Parliamentary Sovereignty of the United Kingdom Parliament after Factortame'; Sir William Wade, 'Sovereignty: Revolution or Evolution?' (1996) 112 *LQR* 568; T. R. S. Allan, 'Parliamentary Sovereignty: Law, Politics and Revolution' (1997) 113 *LQR* 443.

earlier norms were resolved in favour of the later norms, will, subject to what is said later, no longer apply to clashes concerning EU and national law. This proposition is sound in terms of principle, whether viewed simply in terms of membership of the European Union, or as part of a broader category of constitutional statutes that are not subject to implied repeal. There are good normative arguments for requiring the legislature to state expressly its intent to repeal or derogate from statutes of constitutional importance,[82] or for this to be unequivocally clear in some other manner, and this is so notwithstanding the fact that there may be room for disagreement as to which statutes come within this category.

Thirdly, if Parliament wishes to derogate from its EU obligations then it should do so *expressly and unequivocally*. The reaction of our national courts to such an unlikely eventuality remains to be seen. In principle, two options would be open to the national judiciary. Either they could follow the latest will of Parliament, thereby preserving some remnant of traditional orthodoxy on sovereignty. Or they could argue that it is not open to our legislature to pick and choose which obligations to subscribe to while still remaining within the European Union. Which of these options our courts would choose will be dependent, in part, on the issues addressed in the next section.

Fourthly, the supremacy of EU law over national law *operates in areas where EU law is applicable*, as is made clear from the dictum of Lord Bridge set out earlier. This may well be a statement of the obvious, but the point is more complex than might initially have been thought.[83] The problem addressed here is often referred to as *Kompetenz-Kompetenz*: who has the ultimate authority to decide whether a matter is within the competence of the European Union? The ECJ may well believe that it is the ultimate decider of this issue. However, national courts may not always be content with this arrogation of authority. This is particularly so given that the ECJ has, as is well known, often reasoned 'teleologically'[84] and expanded the boundaries of EU competence in a manner which has caused disquiet in some national legal systems. The German Federal Constitutional Court held that it will not inevitably accept EU decisions, including those of the ECJ, which it regards as crossing the line between legitimate Treaty interpretation and de facto Treaty amendment.[85] The general tenor of Laws LJ's judgment in *Thoburn* is also inclined to the conclusion that the ultimate competence to decide on the scope of EU competence resides with the national court. This is reinforced by his statement that if the European Union were to enact a measure repugnant to a constitutional right guaranteed by UK law, it would be for the national

---

[82] Craig, 'Constitutionalizing Constitutional Law: *HS2*'.

[83] P. Craig, 'Report on the United Kingdom' in A.-M. Slaughter, A. Stone Sweet, and J. Weiler (eds.), *The European Courts and National Courts, Doctrine and Jurisprudence* (1998), ch. 7.

[84] Teleological judicial reasoning connotes the idea that a court will reason in order to attain the end which it believes that the particular Treaty article was intended to serve.

[85] *Brunner* v. *The European Union Treaty* [1994] 1 CMLR 57, paras. 49 and 99; *Treaty of Lisbon Constitutionality Case*, BVerfG, 2 BvE 2/08, 30 June 2009, available at http://www.bverfg.de/entscheidungen/es20090630_2bve000208.html; English translation available at http://www.bundesverfassungsgericht.de/entscheidungen/es20090630_2bve000208en.html.

courts to decide whether the general words of the ECA 1972 were sufficient to give it overriding effect in domestic law.[86] It is moreover clear from the *HS2* decision that it will not be assumed that the European Union has authority to limit or abrogate UK constitutional statutes or principles.[87]

SUPREMACY AFTER *FACTORTAME, EOC, THOBURN*, AND *HS2*: THE CONCEPTUAL BASIS OF THE DECISIONS

Commentators have been divided as to how best to conceptualize the impact of the courts' jurisprudence.[88] The issues here are complex, but the main features of the debate can be presented as follows.

The construction approach

It is possible to rationalize what the courts have done as a species of *statutory construction*. If a statute can be reconciled with an EU norm through construing the statutory words without unduly distorting them then this should be done, more especially when the statute was passed to effectuate a directive. However the species of statutory construction being considered here is more far-reaching. On this view accommodation between national law and EU law is attained through a rule of construction to the effect that inconsistencies *will* be resolved in favour of EU law *unless* Parliament has indicated clearly and unambiguously that it intends to derogate from EU law. The degree of linguistic inconsistency between the statute and the EU norm is not the essential point of the inquiry. Provided that there is no unequivocal derogation from EU law then it will apply, rather than any conflicting domestic statute.

Counsel for the applicants framed their argument in this manner in the first *Factortame* case.[89] This view was posited by Lord Bridge in the same case where he stated that the effect of ECA 1972, s. 2(4) was that the Merchant Shipping Act 1988 should take effect as if a section were incorporated that its provisions would be without prejudice to directly enforceable Community rights.[90] We have already seen that Lord Bridge relied on ECA 1972 in his argument in the second *Factortame* case.[91] A similar argument has been made judicially by Laws LJ in *Thoburn*.[92] Laws LJ voiced the same views extrajudicially,[93] as did Lord Hoffmann.[94]

The construction view is said to leave the essential core of the traditional view of legal sovereignty intact, in the sense that it is always open to a later Parliament to make it unequivocally clear that it wishes to derogate from EU law. In the absence of

---

[86] *Thoburn*, para. 69.   [87] *HS2*, para. 207.

[88] Limits of space preclude coverage of all views on this issue. The sophisticated argument presented by Neil MacCormick can be found in *Questioning Sovereignty: Law, State and Nation in the European Commonwealth* (1999), ch. 6.

[89] [1990] 2 AC 85, 96.   [90] Ibid., 140.   [91] [1991] 1 AC 603, 658–9.   [92] See n. 73.

[93] 'Law and Democracy' [1995] *PL* 72, 89.

[94] Lord Hoffmann, 'Europe and the Question of Sovereignty', the Second Lord Neill Lecture, 15 October 1999.

this, s. 2(4) serves to render EU law dominant in the event of a conflict with national law. The attractions of this approach are self-evident. Clashes between EU law and national law can be reconciled while preserving the formal veneer of legal sovereignty. There are nonetheless two points to note about the construction approach.

First, the wording of s. 2(4) is notoriously difficult to disentangle. The section is framed in terms of 'any enactment passed or to be passed . . . shall be construed and have effect' subject to Community rights. The very word 'construed' conveys the sense that the later statute must be capable of being read so as to be compatible with EU law without thereby unduly distorting its meaning or rewriting it. This may well not be possible. A statute might be seriously at odds with EU law, even where Parliament has not, through any express wording, manifested its intent to derogate from the EU norm. It is doubtful whether s. 2(4) was intended to cure all such absences of fit.

Secondly, Sir William Wade has argued forcefully that Lord Bridge's reasoning entails more than an exercise of construction as we normally understand that phrase. He contends that putatively incorporating s. 2(4) of the 1972 Act into a later statute, such as that of 1988, 'is merely another way of saying that the Parliament of 1972 has imposed a restriction upon the Parliament of 1988', which is what 'the classical doctrine of sovereignty will not permit'.[95] Nor can this be countered simply by saying that the later Parliament could defeat the exercise of construction by expressly providing that the later statute is to prevail over any conflicting EU law. It is by no means clear that an express provision of the kind being postulated here would work, *given* the very reasoning of Lord Bridge. Such a statutory provision would itself be held to be contrary to EU law by the ECJ. This holding would be part of the 'Community law to which by the Act of 1972 the Act of 1988 is held to be subject'.[96] In order to overcome this argument the later statute would have to contain an express provision that it was to prevail over any conflicting EU law and also a provision rendering the relevant provisions of the ECA 1972 inapplicable to the subject matter covered by the later statute.

Technical legal revolution

A second way to conceptualize what the courts have done is to regard it as a *technical legal revolution*. This is the preferred explanation of Sir William Wade who sees the courts' decisions as modifying the ultimate legal principle or rule of recognition on which the legal system is based.[97] On this view the 'rule of recognition is itself a political fact which the judges themselves are able to change when they are confronted with a new situation which so demands'.[98] Such choices are made by the judiciary at the point where the law 'stops'.[99]

---

[95] Wade, 'Sovereignty: Revolution or Evolution?', 570.
[96] Wade, 'Sovereignty: Revolution or Evolution?'
[97] H. L. A. Hart, *The Concept of Law* (1961), ch. 6.
[98] Wade, 'Sovereignty: Revolution or Evolution?', 574.
[99] Wade, 'The Basis of Legal Sovereignty', 191–2.

Principled legal evolution

There is however a third way in which to regard the courts' jurisprudence. This is to regard decisions about supremacy as being based on *arguments of legal principle the content of which can and will vary across time*. This is my own preferred view[100] and a similar argument has been advanced by Allan.[101] On this view there is no *a priori* inexorable reason why Parliament, merely because of its very existence, must be regarded as legally omnipotent. The existence of such power, like all power, must be justified by arguments of principle that are normatively convincing. Possible constraints on parliamentary omnipotence must similarly be reasoned through and defended on normative grounds. This approach fits with the reasoning of Lord Bridge in the second *Factortame* case. His Lordship did not approach the matter as if the courts were making an unconstrained political choice at the point where the law stopped. His reasoning is more accurately represented as being based on *principle*, in the sense of working through the principled consequences of the UK's membership of the European Union. The contractarian and functional arguments used by Lord Bridge exemplify this style of judicial discourse. They provide sound normative arguments as to why the UK should be bound by EU law while it remains within the European Union. These arguments would moreover be convincing and have force even if s. 2(4) had never been included in the 1972 Act.

SUPREMACY AFTER THE TREATY OF LISBON

The Constitutional Treaty contained a supremacy clause in Art. I-6, which provided that the 'Constitution, and law adopted by the Union's institutions in exercising competences conferred on it, shall have primacy over the law of the member states'. There were, however, problems surrounding the interpretation of this provision. It was, for example, unclear whether it was intended to assert the supremacy of EU law over all national law, including national constitutions. If this was indeed the case then it was doubtful whether it would have proven to be constitutionally acceptable to the member states.[102] The Treaty of Lisbon dropped the primacy clause, and replaced it with Declaration 17 which states that the 'Conference recalls that, in accordance with well settled case law of the Court of Justice of the European Union, the Treaties and the law adopted by the Union on the basis of the Treaties have primacy over the law of Member States, under the conditions laid down by the said case law'. This Declaration suffers from the same ambiguity as the primacy clause in the Constitutional Treaty, and it is very unlikely that national courts will be persuaded to forget their previous concerns,

---

[100] P. Craig, in articles cited earlier—'Parliamentary Sovereignty of the United Kingdom Parliament after *Factortame*', 'Report on the United Kingdom'—and also in 'Public Law, Political Theory and Legal Theory' [2000] *PL* 211.

[101] Allan, 'Parliamentary Sovereignty: Law, Politics and Revolution'.

[102] Craig, *The Lisbon Treaty: Law, Politics and Treaty Reform*, ch. 4.

and accept that EU law prevails over national constitutions, based on a Declaration appended to the Treaties.[103]

SUPREMACY AND THE EUROPEAN UNION ACT 2011

The discussion thus far has focused on the impact of EU membership on traditional concepts of UK sovereignty as determined by the case law of the UK courts and the ECJ. The UK legislature has however also made an important contribution in this respect through the enactment of the European Union Act 2011.[104] The statute is complex, and imposes a regime of parliamentary and referendum 'locks' on Treaty amendments and a range of other EU decisions.

Prior to the 2011 Act the general position under UK law was that any amendment to the EC Treaty required ratification by the UK through an Act of Parliament. This was the standard approach for ratification of any Treaty by the UK. The 2011 Act now requires that there must also, subject to limited exceptions, be a positive vote in a referendum, whenever new competence is to be granted to the EU, when an existing competence is to be extended, or when certain powers are to be accorded to the EU. The 2011 Act is not entrenched, and thus Parliament could choose to disapply it, but subject to this the obligation to secure a positive vote in a referendum as well as in Parliament is binding.

DIRECT EFFECT

The doctrine of the supremacy of EU law has been a cornerstone in the building of an EU legal order. The ECJ's other principal contribution has been the doctrine of direct effect. Detailed analysis can be found elsewhere.[105] It is nonetheless important to understand the basic tenets of direct effect in order that its constitutional significance can be appreciated.

DIRECT EFFECT: AN OUTLINE

The meaning of direct effect is not free from ambiguity. It most commonly connotes the idea that individuals can bring actions in national courts in order to vindicate rights secured to them by the Treaty, or legislation made thereunder. It is in this sense a species of private enforcement of EU law. The Treaty makes explicit provision for public enforcement of EU law in TFEU, Art. 258: the Commission can bring an action before the CJEU if member states fail to comply with the Treaty or EU legislation.[106]

---

[103] See n. 85, the *Treaty of Lisbon Constitutionality Case.*

[104] P. Craig, 'The European Union Act 2011: Locks, Limits and Legality' (2011) 48 *CMLRev* 1881.

[105] Craig and de Búrca, *EU Law, Text, Cases and Materials*, ch. 7.

[106] It is also possible for a member state to initiate an action against another member state under TFEU, Art. 259, but this rarely happens.

Whether the framers of the original Treaty intended for there to be direct effect is doubtful. It is, however, clear that private enforcement through direct effect provided a welcome supplement to public enforcement through the Commission, enabling EU law to be applied on a scale and in a manner that would not otherwise have been possible.[107] Moreover, the fact that individuals were given rights that they could enforce in their own name transformed the very nature of the Treaty. It could no longer be viewed solely as the business of nation states in the manner of many other international treaties. It was to be a form of social ordering in which individuals were involved in their own capacity. They were no longer to be passive receptors, who had to await action taken on their behalf by others. They were now accorded rights that they could enforce in their own name.

The seminal case in the development of direct effect was *Van Gend en Loos*.[108] Dutch importers challenged the rate of duty imposed on a chemical imported from Germany. They argued that a reclassification of the product under a different heading of the Dutch tariff legislation had led to an increase in the duty and that this was prohibited under EEC Treaty, Art. 12 (now TFEU, Art. 30), which prohibits the imposition of any new customs duties on imports and also precludes any increase in existing rates. The Dutch court asked the ECJ whether Art. 12 gave rise to rights that could be invoked by individuals before their national courts. The member states argued that the Treaty was simply a compact between states, to be policed in the manner dictated by the Treaty, through public enforcement at the hands of the Commission. They believed that direct effect would alter the nature of the obligations accepted by the signatories.

The ECJ disagreed. It held that the EEC Treaty was not simply to be viewed as a compact between nations. The 'interested parties' included the people. This was affirmed by the preamble and by the existence of institutions charged with the duty of making provisions for those individuals. It was this crucial conceptual starting point which laid the foundation for the now famous passage from the judgment, depicting the European Community as a new legal order for the benefit of which states have limited their sovereign rights, with the consequence that individuals have rights and can be regarded as subjects of the Community. The ECJ emphasized that Art. 12 was a natural candidate for enforcement by individuals through national courts. It stressed the negative nature of the obligation, the fact that it was unconditional, and that its implementation was not dependent on any further measures before being effective under national law.

The years immediately following *Van Gend en Loos* witnessed the application of the concept to a growing range of Treaty articles. The Court was keen to expand the concept given the advantages it possessed. In applying direct effect to other treaty articles the ECJ relaxed the conditions for its application. Direct effect was applied in circumstances where it could not be said that the Treaty article in question created a

---

[107] J. Weiler, 'The Community System: The Dual Character of Supranationalism' (1981) 1 *YBEL* 267; P. Craig, 'Once Upon a Time in the West: Direct Effect and the Federalization of EEC Law' (1992) 12 *OJLS* 453.
[108] Case 26/62, *Van Gend en Loos* v. *Nederlandse Administratie der Belastingen* [1963] ECR 1.

negative obligation which was legally perfect, in the sense that no further action was required by the Community or the member states, and no real residue of discretion existed. The concept was applied to articles of the Treaty dealing with broad areas of regulatory policy, which were as much social as economic.[109] The general test now is that a Treaty article will have direct effect provided that it is intended to confer rights on individuals and that it is sufficiently clear, precise, and unconditional.

It was inevitable that the ECJ should be asked whether EC legislation passed pursuant to the Treaty could also have direct effect. There are various types of such legislation. Regulations are defined in TFEU, Art. 288 as having general application. They are binding in their entirety and directly applicable in all member states. The ECJ had no reluctance in concluding that regulations were capable of having direct effect, provided that they were sufficiently certain and precise, which was normally the case.[110]

There has been more difficulty over directives. These are, according to TFEU, Art. 288, binding as to the result to be achieved while leaving the choice of form and methods to the states to which they are addressed. Moreover, while regulations are binding on all states, directives are only binding on the specific states to which they are addressed. Directives have proved to be a particularly useful device for legislating in an enlarged European Union. Many areas of EU policy concern complex topics ranging from product liability to the environment, and from the harmonization of company law to the free movement of capital. If legislation could only be enacted in the form of regulations then it might be difficult to draft a measure with sufficient precision that it could be immediately applicable within the territories of all the member states. The directive enables the European Union to specify the ends to be attained, often in great detail, while leaving a choice of form and methods of implementation to the individual member states.

However, the very nature of directives seemed to indicate that they could not have direct effect: they clearly require further action on the part of the member states, and they leave them with discretion as to methods of implementation. The ECJ nonetheless concluded that directives are capable of having direct effect. It held that it would be inconsistent with the binding effect of directives to exclude the possibility that they can confer rights.[111] The ECJ also drew on TFEU, Art. 267, which allows questions concerning the interpretation and validity of EU law to be referred by national courts to the ECJ. From the generality of this provision the Court concluded that questions relating to directives can be raised by individuals before national courts.[112] A further reason for according direct effect to directives is the estoppel argument: a member state that has not implemented the directive 'may not rely, as against individuals, on its own failure to perform the obligations which the directive entails'.[113] Provided,

---

[109] Case 2/74, *Reyners* v. *Belgian State* [1974] ECR 631; Case 43/75, *Defrenne* v. *Sabena* [1976] ECR 455.
[110] Case 93/71, *Leonosio* v. *Italian Ministry of Agriculture and Forestry* [1973] CMLR 343; Case 50/76, *Amsterdam Bulb* v. *Produktschap voor Siergewassen* [1977] ECR 137.
[111] Case 41/74, *Van Duyn* v. *Home Office* [1974] ECR 1337, para. 12.   [112] Ibid., para. 12.
[113] Case 148/78, *Pubblico Ministero* v. *Ratti* [1979] ECR 1629, para. 22.

therefore, that the directive is sufficiently precise, that the basic obligation is unconditional, and that the period for implementation has passed, an individual can derive
enforceable rights from a directive.

While the ECJ has been willing to give direct effect to directives it has, however, also
held that they only have vertical as opposed to horizontal direct effect. Treaty articles
and regulations give individuals rights that can be used both against the state, vertical
direct effect, and against private parties, horizontal direct effect. Directives only have
vertical direct effect. Thus, in the *Marshall* case[114] the ECJ held that Directive (EEC)
76/207 on equal treatment could not impose obligations on individuals, but only on
the state, either *qua* state or *qua* employer. The reason proffered by the court for this
limitation was the wording of Art. 288: the binding nature of the directive existed only
in relation to 'each Member State to which it is addressed'. The correctness of this ruling and the rationale for this limitation of direct effect are by no means self-evident.[115]
The existence of this limitation has however generated a very complex case law.

This is in part because the ruling that directives only have vertical and not horizontal direct effect requires some definition of the state for these purposes.[116] The
complexity of the case law in this area is in part the result of the doctrine of indirect
effect. The doctrine is associated with the decision in *Von Colson*.[117] The applicants
relied upon the provision of a directive in order to argue that the quantum of relief
provided by German law in cases of discrimination was too small. The ECJ held that
the provisions were not sufficiently precise to have direct effect. It held, however, that
national courts had an obligation to interpret national law to be in conformity with the
directive. The purpose of the directive was to provide an effective remedy in cases of
discrimination, and if states chose to fulfil this aim through the provision of compensation then this should be adequate in relation to the damage suffered. National courts
should, therefore, construe their own national law with this in mind. In *Marleasing*[118]
the ECJ held that in applying national law, whether passed before or after the directive,
a national court was required to interpret national law in every way possible so as to be
in conformity with the directive.

While therefore an individual cannot, in a literal sense, derive rights from a
directive in an action against another individual, it is possible to plead the directive in such an action. Once the directive has been placed before the national court,
then the obligation to interpret national law in conformity with the directive where

---

[114] Case 152/84, *Marshall* v. *Southampton & South West Hampshire Area Health Authority (Teaching)*
[1986] ECR 723; Case C-91/92, *Faccini Dori* v. *Recreb Srl* [1994] ECR I-3325.
[115] W. van Gerven, 'The Horizontal Direct Effect of Directive Provisions Revisited: The Reality of
Catchwords' in T. Heukels and D. Curtin (eds), *Institutional Dynamics of European Integration, Liber
Amicorum for Henry Schermers* (1994); P. Craig, 'The Legal Effect of Directives: Policy, Rules and Exceptions'
(2009) 34 *ELRev* 349.
[116] Case C-188/89, *Foster* v. *British Gas* [1990] ECR I-3133; D. Curtin, 'The Province of
Government: Delimiting the Direct Effect of Directives in the Common Law Context' (1990) 15 *ELRev* 195.
[117] Case 14/83, *Von Colson and Kamann* v. *Land Nordrhein-Westfalen* [1984] ECR 1891.
[118] Case C-106/89, *Marleasing SA* v. *La Commercial International De Alimentacion SA* [1990] ECR 4135.

possible comes into operation. Where the directive encapsulates precise obligations, and where the national court is minded to interpret national law in the
required fashion, this 'indirect' species of enforcement of a directive as between
individuals will have much the same results as if the directive had been accorded
horizontal direct effect.

The interpretative obligation does however create problems for courts and litigants
alike.[119] It places national courts in some difficulty in deciding how far they can go in
reconciling national legislation with directives while still remaining within the realm
of interpreting, as opposed to rewriting or overruling, national norms. It places litigants in a difficult position since they will have to guess how far their national courts
might feel able to go in reconciling national law with differently worded EU legislation. If directives had horizontal direct effect then at least the individual would know
that in the event of any inconsistency between the two norms EU law would trump
national law.

The jurisprudence in this area has become even more complex as a result of case law
in which the ECJ has been willing to accord some measure of 'incidental horizontal
direct effect' to a directive in actions between private individuals,[120] and because the
ECJ has held that general principles of EU law can have horizontal direct effect, even
where they cover the same terrain as a directive which would not have such effect
between private parties.[121]

DIRECT EFFECT: CONSTITUTIONAL IMPLICATIONS

There are two ways in which direct effect is of constitutional relevance, one of which
is obvious, the other less so.

First, direct effect enables individuals to derive rights that are enforceable in
their own national courts from an international treaty and legislation made thereunder. The general position in public international law is that individuals do not
derive such rights.[122] There are instances where individuals have been held to have
such rights, but they are exceptional and there has been nothing on the scale of the
direct effect doctrine as developed by the ECJ. Indeed this was one of the reasons
why the ECJ sought to distance EC law from general public international law in the
Van Gend case. It wished to buttress the argument that because the EEC Treaty was

---

[119] G. de Búrca, 'Giving Effect to European Community Directives' (1992) 55 *MLR* 215.

[120] Case C-194/94, *CIA Security International SA* v. *Signalson SA and Securitel SPRL* [1996] ECR I-2201;
Case C-129/94, *Criminal Proceedings against Rafael Ruiz Bernaldez* [1996] ECR I-1829; Case C-441/93,
Panagis Pafitis v. *Trapeza Kentrikis Ellados AE* [1996] ECR I-1347; Case C-443/98, *Unilever Italia SpA*
v. *Central Foods SpA* [2000] ECR I-7535. For discussion, J. Coppel, 'Horizontal Direct Effect of Directives'
(1997) 28 *ILJ* 69; S. Weatherill, 'Breach of Directives and Breach of Contract' (2001) 26 *ELRev* 177;
M. Dougan, 'The Disguised Vertical Direct effect of Directives' [2000] *Camb LJ* 586; Craig, 'The Legal Effect
of Directives: Policy, Rules and Exceptions'.

[121] Case C-144/04, *Mangold v Helm* [2005] ECR I-9981.

[122] Brownlie's *Principles of Public International Law* (8th edn, 2012, James Crawford), ch. 16.

distinct from other international treaties, therefore it should not be thought strange that an individual derived rights from the former, even though he normally did not do so from the latter. There was clearly an element of circularity in this argument. The very decision as to whether direct effect did or did not exist was of crucial importance in deciding whether the EEC Treaty really could be regarded as distinct from other international treaties. Major constitutional developments are not infrequently characterized by such reasoning. Be that as it may, direct effect is a central feature of EU law, and recognized as such by all the member states. In terms of national constitutional significance this means that law derived from sources other than Parliament and the common law will avail individuals before their own national courts in a way which has not been so on this scale hitherto.

The second reason why direct effect is of constitutional significance resides in the connection between this concept and the supremacy of EU law. The essence of this connection is that direct effect allows the supremacy doctrine to be applied at national level, and thereby makes it far more potent than it would otherwise have been. It would in theory be perfectly possible for the ECJ to have developed its supremacy doctrine even if it had never created direct effect. EU law would have been held to be supreme, and judicially enforceable through actions brought by the Commission under Art. 258. The supremacy doctrine applies to such actions. Direct effect however enables the supremacy of EU law to be enforced by individuals through their own national courts. This renders such supremacy more effective for a number of reasons. Member states might be more inclined to listen to their own national courts than to the ECJ. The national courts become EU courts in their own right, being able to pass judgment on national primary legislation in the context of an action brought by an individual. Direct effect spreads the workload of enforcing EU law, and its supremacy, across all the individuals and the national courts of the European Union.

FUNDAMENTAL RIGHTS

There is little doubt that most claims to protect rights will now be brought under the Human Rights Act 1998 (HRA 1998).[123] It is however open to claimants to use rights-based arguments derived from EU law.

The European Union promulgated a Charter of Fundamental Rights in 2000. The ECJ had, however, developed a fundamental rights' jurisprudence prior to this. The original EEC Treaty contained no list of traditional fundamental rights. The catalyst for the creation of such rights was the threat of revolt by some national courts. Individuals who were dissatisfied with an EC regulation argued before their national court that it was inconsistent with rights in their national constitutions. The ECJ denied that EC norms could be challenged in this manner. However, in order to stem

---

[123] See ch. 3 in this volume.

any national rebellion it also declared that fundamental rights were part of the general principles of EC law, and that the compatibility of an EC norm with such rights would be tested by the ECJ.[124] It became clear that national norms could also be challenged for compliance with fundamental rights. This was so where member states were applying provisions of EC law based on the protection of human rights;[125] where they were enforcing EC rules on behalf of the European Community or interpreting EC rules;[126] or where member states were seeking to derogate from a requirement of EC law.[127] The supremacy doctrine applied with the consequence that national norms, including primary legislation, which were inconsistent with EC law could be declared inapplicable in the instant case. This is by way of contrast with the HRA 1998 where the courts are limited, in cases involving primary legislation, to making a declaration of incompatibility under s. 4.

The EU Charter of Fundamental Rights of the European Union was promulgated in 2000.[128] The direct catalyst for this development came from the European Council. In June 1999 the Cologne European Council[129] decided that there should be a Charter of Fundamental Rights to consolidate the fundamental rights applicable at EU level and to make their importance and relevance more visible to the citizens of the European Union. It was made clear that the document should include economic and social rights, as well as traditional civil and political rights. A Convention was established to produce the Charter, which consisted of representatives of the member states, a member of the Commission, members of the EP, and representatives from national Parliaments. The Charter was accepted by the member states, but its legal status was left undecided by the Nice Treaty.

This issue has now been addressed by the Treaty of Lisbon. The Charter is legally binding and has the same legal value as the TEU and the TFEU.[130] The Charter itself is not therefore incorporated in the Treaty of Lisbon, but it is accorded the same legal value as the Treaties. The Treaty of Lisbon is premised on the version of the Charter as amended in 2004, and this version has been reissued in the *Official Journal*.[131] The Treaty of Lisbon also stipulates that the European Union shall accede to the European Convention on Human Rights.[132] The member states are bound by the Charter only when they are implementing EU law.[133] This has been interpreted by the ECJ to mean

---

[124] Case 11/70, *Internationale Handelsgesellschaft* v. *Einfuhr- und Vorratstelle für Getreide und Futtermittel* [1970] ECR 1125, 1134.

[125] Case 222/84, *Johnston* v. *Chief Constable of the Royal Ulster Constabulary* [1986] ECR 1651.

[126] Case 5/88, *Wachauf* v. *Germany* [1989] ECR 2609; Case 63/83, *R* v. *Kent Kirk* [1984] ECR 2689.

[127] Case C-260/89, *Elliniki Radiophonia Tileorassi AE* v. *Dimotki Etairia Pliroforissis and Sotirios Kouvelas* [1991] ECR I-2925; Case C-159/90, *Society for the Protection of Unborn Children Ireland Ltd* v. *Grogan* [1991] ECR I-4685.

[128] Charter of Fundamental Rights of the European Union [2000] OJ C364/1.

[129] 3–4 June 1999.   [130] TEU, Art. 6(1).

[131] Charter of Fundamental Rights of the European Union [2007] OJ C303/1; Explanations Relating to the Charter of Fundamental Rights [2007] OJ C303/17. The Charter has been reissued with the Treaty of Lisbon [2010] OJ C83/2.

[132] TEU Art. 6(2).   [133] Charter, Art. 51(1).

that they are bound whenever they act within the scope of EU law, which coheres with the interpretation in the explanatory memorandum that accompanied the Charter,[134] which must be given due regard when interpreting Charter rights.[135] The UK and Poland negotiated a Protocol designed to limit the application of the Charter in certain respects.[136] Space precludes detailed interpretation of this Protocol here. Suffice it to say for the present that it does not wholly exclude the application of the Charter in the UK, but merely limits the application of certain Charter provisions.[137]

NATIONAL COURTS AS EU COURTS

Those who are not familiar with EU law are accustomed to think that there are only two EU courts: the CJEU and the GC. This belies reality. National courts have general jurisdiction over matters of EU law. This is a matter worthy of constitutional note. The explanation for this role played by national courts is to be found in a conjunction of two factors.

The first is the very concept of direct effect considered earlier. The fact that individuals are able to enforce their EU rights through national courts means that it will be the national judiciaries that frequently apply EU law doctrine.

This first factor has been reinforced by a second. The ECJ made it clear that national courts should apply existing case law of the ECJ and the GC. They should therefore only refer a case to the ECJ pursuant to TFEU, Art. 267 where the question before the national court had not already been adequately answered in a previous ruling given by the ECJ. This became clear from the seminal decision in the *Da Costa* case.[138] The facts in the case were materially identical to those in *Van Gend en Loos*,[139] as were the questions posed by the national court. The ECJ acknowledged that a national court of final resort was bound to refer a question to the ECJ, but then qualified this by stating that 'the authority of an interpretation under Article 177 already given by the Court may deprive the obligation of its purpose and thus empty it of its substance'.[140] This would especially be the case where the question raised was 'materially identical with a question which has already been the subject of a preliminary ruling in a similar case'.[141] The ECJ made it clear that the national court could refer the issue again if it had new questions to ask. It made it equally clear that if this was not so, then it would simply repeat the ruling given in the original case from which the legal point arose.

---

[134] Case C-617/10, *Åklagaren* v. *Hans Åkerberg Fransson*, 26 February 2013.

[135] TEU, Art. 6(1).

[136] Protocol (No. 30) on the Application of the Charter of Fundamental Rights of the European Union to Poland and to the United Kingdom.

[137] Cases C-411 and 493/10, *NS* v. *Secretary of State*, 21 December 2011.

[138] Cases 28–30/62, *Da Costa en Schaake NV, Jacob Meijer NV and Hoechst-Holland NV* v. *Nederlandse Belastingadministratie* [1963] ECR 31.

[139] See n. 108.   [140] See n. 138, 38.   [141] See n. 138.

The *Da Costa* case, therefore, initiated what is in effect a system of precedent, whereby national courts would apply the prior rulings of the ECJ.

The ECJ extended this idea in *CILFIT*[142] where it held that the obligation to refer contained in Art. 267(3) could also be qualified 'where previous decisions of the Court have already dealt with the point of law in question, irrespective of the nature of the proceedings which led to those decisions, even though the questions at issue are not strictly identical'. Provided that the point of law had already been determined by the ECJ, this should be relied on by a national court in a later case, thereby obviating the need for a reference. The application of precedent by national courts has enhanced the enforcement of EU law, and eased the workload on the ECJ and the GC. The EU system of adjudication could not have functioned as it has if the national courts had not been accorded this role.

The *Equal Opportunities Commission* case[143] considered earlier provides a good example of this process at work. Not only did the House of Lords make a declaration that provisions of a statute were incompatible with EU law, but it did so without making a reference to the ECJ, having satisfied itself that the existing ECJ precedents meant that the national statute was indirectly discriminatory.

CONCLUSION

The EEC has, since its inception, had an impact on national constitutional law. The significance of this impact has become greater over time, in part through the ECJ's jurisprudence and in part through subsequent Treaty amendments. The Treaty of Lisbon has brought further changes that are relevant legally and politically in the ways explicated in this chapter. It should moreover be recognized that the impact of the EU over national law, including constitutional law, can be affected by major economic 'shocks' such as the financial crisis, which has led to increased centralization of control over national budgetary decisions.

FURTHER READING

ANTHONY, G., *UK Public Law & European Law: The Dynamics of Legal Integration* (2002)

BIRKINSHAW, P., *European Public Law: The Achievement and the Challenge* (2nd edn, 2014)

CRAIG, P., *The Lisbon Treaty: Law, Politics and Treaty Reform* (2010)

CRAIG, P. and BÚRCA, G. DE, *EU Law, Text, Cases and Materials* (6th edn, 2015)

LADEUR, K.-H. (ed.), *Europeanisation of Administrative Law: Transforming National Decision-making Procedures* (2001)

MACCORMICK, N., *Questioning Sovereignty* (1999)

---

[142] Case 283/81, *Srl CILFIT and Lanificio di Gavardo SpA v. Ministry of Health* [1982] ECR 3415, para. 14.
[143] See n. 69.

NICOL, D., *EC Membership and the Judicialization of British Politics* (2001)

PINDER, J., *The Building of the European Union* (3rd edn, 1998)

SLAUGHTER, A.-M., STONE SWEET, A. and WEILER, J. H. H. (eds.), *The European Court of Justice and National Courts: Doctrine and Jurisprudence* (1998)

URWIN, D., *The Community of Europe: A History of European Integration since 1945* (2nd edn, 1995)

WITTE, B. DE, 'Direct Effect, Primacy and the Nature of the Legal Order' in Craig, P. and de Búrca, G. (eds.), *The Evolution of EU Law* (2nd edn, 2011), ch. 12

USEFUL WEBSITE

European Union: **http://europa.eu**

5

THE INTERNATIONALIZATION OF PUBLIC LAW AND ITS IMPACT ON THE UK

David Feldman*

SUMMARY

Municipal public law is always influenced by foreign developments. The existence of a state depends at least partly on its recognition by other states. Political theories and legal ideas have always flowed across and between regions of the world. Yet any state has good reasons for controlling the introduction of foreign legal and constitutional norms to its own legal order. National interests and a commitment to the rule of law, human rights, and democratic accountability demand national controls over foreign influences. This chapter considers the nature and legitimacy of the channels and filters, particularly as they apply in the UK, in the light of general public law standards.

INTRODUCTION

'Internationalization of public law' refers to several phenomena. They include: the influence of public international law, and (related but distinct) of international institutions such as the UN, on municipal systems of public law; development of general principles of public law and their adoption by municipal systems; adoption of rules of

* I am grateful to the Rev'd Professor John Bell, His Honour Ian Campbell, Professor Constance Grewe, Professor Jeffrey Jowell, Professor Didier Maus, Professor Nicolas Maziau, Professor Dawn Oliver, Judge Tudor Pantiru, Professor Cheryl Saunders, Anna-Lena Sjolund, Christian Steiner, and Dr Rebecca Williams for valuable discussions of the subject matter of this chapter and helpful comments on drafts. Remaining errors and idiosyncrasies are, of course, entirely my responsibility.

municipal law which require officials, including judges, to apply municipal rules of public law to events outside the state's territory or to apply rules developed outside the state; and acceptance as principles of international law and the internal law of international institutions of principles derived from the constitutional and administrative laws of states. This chapter focuses on the first three of those phenomena, but we should note that advocates of the use of public-law principles to regulate international law and institutions recognize that such principles help to legitimate the use or threat of force, which may be important for systems and institutions with no democratic accountability.[1]

In its municipal manifestations, internationalization of public law has an obvious but complex relationship to multilayered governance and the expansion of judicial review, two of the themes of this book. The problems in relation to multilevel governance are that international law does not fit straightforwardly into the hierarchy of legal norms operating within states. Different states assign different levels of authority to international law, and sometimes (as in the UK) the status of different bits of international law differ. Some international influences, such as judgments of courts in other states, have no legal status, and operate outside any hierarchy of norms. In respect of judicial review, when judges are given jurisdiction to determine issues arising outside the state's territory (for example, by virtue of the need to apply human rights law) they may be required to deal with matters which have never before been within their remit, such as the behaviour of UK armed forces operating overseas. This presents novel problems of both law and judicial competence.

Only extremely isolated states can avoid direct limits by other states on their domestic and external policies. When states seek each other's cooperation and enter into treaties, they agree to restrict the range of options open to them in exchange for the benefits of pursuing objectives unattainable without coordination. International organizations can help to maintain peace, bolster social or economic stability, and foster free trade and open markets. The UK as we know it is partly a result of an extreme form of such an agreement. In 1706–7, the Treaty of Union between England and Scotland led to the foundation of the United Kingdom of Great Britain. It was an instrument of international law, negotiated between the representatives of two sovereign nations and given effect in national law by a combination of Acts of their respective Parliaments and action taken by the monarch of each state (who happened by coincidence to be the same person).[2]

Events on the international plane continue in the twenty-first century to help shape the UK's constitution through international human rights and other treaties,

---

[1] See e.g. Philip Allott, *Eunomia: New Order for a New World* (2001), esp. chs. 12 and 13, on constitutionalizing international law; Spyridon Flogaitis, 'I principi generali del diritto nella giurisprudenza del Tribunale Amministrativo delle Nazione Unite' in Marco D'Alberti (ed.), *Le Nuove Mete del Diritto Amministrativo* (2010), 93–114, on developing general principles of administrative law in the UN's Administrative Tribunal.

[2] For discussion of the implications of this, see Elizabeth Wicks, 'A New Constitution for a New State? The 1707 Union of England and Scotland' (2001) 117 *LQR* 109–26, and Elizabeth Wicks, *The Evolution of a Constitution: Eight Key Moments in British Constitutional History* (2006), ch. 2.

and participation in international organizations such as the United Nations, the Council of Europe, NATO, and the European Union (EU). For example, the devolution legislation prevents the devolved legislatures and ministries from acting in a manner incompatible with the UK's obligations under the European Convention on Human Rights (ECHR) (so far as they have been made part of municipal law in the UK by the Human Rights Act 1998) or EU law.[3] International law is woven into the fabric of public law.

At the same time, cooperation has significant costs for states. They must take account of internationally agreed objectives and values in their internal decision-making. Sometimes they must subordinate their own interests to those of other states. This may compromise systems of accountability for the exercise of public power which are traditionally based on the political and legal processes operating within states. Traditional criteria for the legitimacy of state action, such as democracy, compliance with rule-of-law standards, or respect for fundamental rights, may be hard to apply when decision-making processes are shaped by international agreements or institutions which do not contain equivalent systems for control and accountability of the exercise of power. This leads some people to argue that a 'democratic deficit' in the European Union leads to a crisis of legitimacy which the Treaty of Lisbon has only partly addressed.[4]

This has consequences for UK public law. The structures of important state institutions are potentially challenged by such organizations as the Group of States against Corruption (GRECO), operating under the aegis of the Council of Europe,[5] and the European Charter of Local Self-Government,[6] which the UK ratified with effect from 1 August 1998, and its Additional Protocol on the right to participate in the affairs of a local authority (which the UK signed in 2009 but has not yet ratified). This chapter

---

[3] Northern Ireland Act 1998, ss. 6, 14(5), and 26; Scotland Act 1998, ss. 29(2), 35(1), and 58; Government of Wales Act 2006, ss. 80–82.

[4] See ch. 4 in this volume.

[5] GRECO, *First Evaluation Report on the United Kingdom* (2001), criticized the UK Parliament's handling of complaints against members, because (e.g.) the Parliamentary Commissioner for Standards, who dealt with the House of Commons, had not been put on a statutory basis, and there was no independent system for dealing with complaints against members of the House of Lords. See A. Doig, 'Sleaze Fatigue: An Inauspicious Year for Democracy' (2002) *Parliamentary Affairs* 389; GRECO RC-I (2003) 8E, *Compliance Report on the United Kingdom*, 7–11 July 2003, paras. 27–31; GRECO RC-I (2003) 8E Addendum, 1 July 2005, paras. 9–13. The position changed in 2009 after it was revealed that some members of both Houses had made highly questionable use of their entitlement to claim reimbursement of expenses. The House of Commons is now subject to the statutory Independent Parliamentary Standards Authority: see Parliamentary Standards Act 2009, as amended by the Constitutional Reform and Governance Act 2010. The House of Lords is still self-regulating, but since 2010 peers and their staff are required to comply with Codes of Conduct: see *Code of Conduct for Members of the House of Lords; Guide to the Code of Conduct; Code of Conduct for Staff of Members of the House of Lords*, 3rd edn, HL Paper 5 of 2013–14 (2014). Complaints are investigated by an independent House of Lords Commissioner for Standards (http://www.parliament. uk/mps-lords-and-offices/standards-and-interests/the-commissioner-for-standards/), who reports to the Lords' Conduct Sub-Committee of the Committee on Privileges and Conduct. Members may appeal to the Committee against a recommendation of the Commissioner or Sub-Committee.

[6] European Treaty Series No. 122 (1985).

attempts to draw out three characteristics of the relationship between national systems of public law and international developments. The first is the importance of international influence over the very existence and fundamental structures of states. No state is an island (although some islands are states). Secondly, the channels between national and international planes normally permit influence to be exerted in both directions, and are usually subject to filters allowing states to preserve an element of autonomy, although the nature and effectiveness of the filters depends on national traditions and interests. Thirdly, the mechanisms by which states allow foreign influences to affect their systems of public law reflect their constitutional traditions and patterns of social interaction, and their legitimacy depends at least in part on their compatibility with those traditions and patterns.

FOREIGN INFLUENCES ON THE FOUNDATIONS OF PUBLIC LAW

THE EXISTENCE OF A STATE AND ITS CONSTITUTION

An entity or group of entities may seek the status of statehood in a variety of circumstances: for example, following the break-up of an existing state, the attempted secession of part of a state, a merger of existing states, or an exercise of foreign control over a state. In such situations, the reaction of other states is of great consequence when deciding whether the entity has the necessary characteristics of statehood. International lawyers agree that recognition by other states is important, although they disagree about its strictly legal significance. Whether recognition by other states is legally constitutive of the new state in international law or not is important only as evidence that the new state already has that status in international law (and the balance of opinion currently tends towards the latter, 'declaratory' theory),[7] lack of recognition is at least persuasive evidence that an entity is not a state,[8] and international recognition may be crucial, as when the United Nations agreed to the establishment of the state of Israel in 1948. Sometimes other states or international institutions may intervene in the process of developing or renewing statehood, and control the form and content of the new state's constitution. If the international community uses armed force to end a conflict and secure a state's continued existence, it may impose a new constitution designed to protect the interests of the various parties to the conflict in order to give effect to the agreement which brings it to a close, as in Bosnia and Herzegovina in 1995,[9]

---

[7] See the discussions in James Crawford, *The Creation of States in International Law* (2nd edn, 2006), ch. 1, esp. 26–8; Ian Brownlie, *Principles of International Law* (6th edn, 2003), 86–8; Malcolm Shaw, *International Law* (6th edn, 2008), 197–208.

[8] Shaw, *International Law*, 207–8.

[9] For an illuminating analysis of the kinds and consequences of international intervention in the formation of states and their constitutions, see Nicolas Maziau, 'L'internationalisation du pouvoir constituant' (2002) 3 *Revue Générale de Droit International Public* 549–79.

or effectively dictate the terms of a defeated state's constitution as an aspect of the peace settlement, as in Japan and West Germany following the Second World War.[10]

But there are no internationally accepted criteria for recognition. Individual states must decide on what grounds to recognize other entities as states. Most states look for an organized governmental authority exercising effective control over a permanent population and a defined territory, together with an ability to carry on external relations independently of other states and give effect to international obligations.[11] Other relevant factors may include: respect for the UN Charter, human rights, and established international frontiers; a commitment to peaceful resolution of international disputes; and respect for the rights of minorities.[12] None of these factors is necessarily decisive. For example, when the constituent parts of the former Yugoslavia broke up from 1992, the government of one of the republics claiming the status of a new state, Bosnia and Herzegovina, controlled only about half its territory when it was recognized by (among others) the UK. The remainder was under the control of anti-secessionist military groups. The integrity of the new state was secured only when military action by the North Atlantic Treaty Organization (NATO) ended three years of war, and the Dayton–Paris Accord of 1995 imposed a General Framework Agreement for Peace (GFAP) on the warring parties. Among other things, this set in stone an internationally agreed constitution, and put in place continuing international control through an international Peace Implementation Council and a High Representative with extensive powers. It has been argued that this external control makes it hard to accept that Bosnia and Herzegovina is an independent sovereign state.[13]

POLITICAL AND CONSTITUTIONAL IDEAS

It is some time since the UK has faced that level of external intervention in its affairs, but ideas from abroad have shaped its structure for centuries. Medieval feudalism was imported from Western Europe,[14] and overlay the pre-Norman structures to produce a system of government which made possible the growing central authority of the

[10] On Japan, see Ray A. Moore and Donald L. Robinson, *Partners for Democracy: Crafting the New Japanese State under MacArthur* (2002). On West Germany and Italy, see Chris Thornhill, *A Sociology of Constitutions: Constitutions and State Legitimacy in Historical-Sociological Perspective* (2011), 327–41.

[11] See e.g. Montevideo Convention on the Rights and Duties of States 1933, Art. 1; American Law Institute, *Restatement of the Foreign Relations Law of the United States* (3rd edn, 1987), § 201.

[12] See Shaw, *International Law*, 374–5.

[13] For an analysis of efforts to end the war and the Dayton Agreement, see Christine Bell, *Peace Agreements and Human Rights* (2000), esp. pp. 91–117. On whether post-Dayton Bosnia and Herzegovina is a state, see Gerald Knaus and Felix Martin, 'Lessons from Bosnia and Herzegovina: Travails of the European Raj' (2003) 14(3) *Journal of Democracy* 60–74; Crawford, *The Creation of States in International Law*, 398–401; Shaw, *International Law*, 201.

[14] See R. C. van Caenegem, *An Historical Introduction to Western Constitutional Law* (1995), ch. 4.

monarchy and the standardization of law across the country. Similarly, between the tenth and twelfth centuries, Scotland:

> was regulated by a complex patchwork combining a typically western European feudal framework with Celtic custom, which can be traced in many of its details to Irish law tracts of the seventh or eighth centuries. The result was what has been called a 'hybrid kingdom', and one of its marks was the emergence of a composite common law of Scotland by the end of the twelfth century.[15]

Public law and political theory in England and Scotland were essentially modelled on those of Western Europe at that period. In the thirteenth century, the model was extended to Wales by military conquest. As elsewhere in Europe, there was a tension between the gradual centralization of law and bureaucracy and the vigorous desire of the nobility and a developing class of free men for an increased role in decision-making.[16] The tension remained, but the structures of the constitution developed so as to accommodate both central and local authority and recognize the interests of a wider variety of free people than previously within the 'community of the realm',[17] encapsulated in such instruments as Magna Carta (1215) and the Statute of Marlborough (1267), which provided that writs should be issued freely against those who were alleged to have committed breaches of Magna Carta, putting it (or at least those parts of it which were capable of judicial enforcement) on the same footing as a statute.

By the sixteenth century, British public lawyers and administrators travelling to Avignon, Paris, Pavia, and other European universities to study Roman law and Greco-Roman political theory at the fountainhead of the Renaissance brought their learning home.[18] In the seventeenth century, the English state was effectively re-founded three times (in 1649 after the Civil War and the execution of King Charles I, at the end of the Protectorate in 1660, and after the flight of King James II in December 1688). The royalists in the lead-up to the Civil War relied on ideas derived from the law of nations (*ius gentium*) or natural law to bolster their claim to the divine right of kings,[19] and political philosophers, including Thomas Hobbes on the side of absolute monarchy and John Locke for constitutional monarchy, were part of major Western European philosophical traditions.[20]

---

[15] Michael Lynch, *Scotland: A New History* (1992) 53 (footnotes omitted).

[16] van Caenegem, *An Historical Introduction to Western Constitutional Law*, ch. 5.

[17] See Sir Maurice Powicke, *The Thirteenth Century 1216–1307* (2nd edn, 1962), 131–50, 216–18.

[18] W. Gordon Zeefeld, *Foundations of Tudor Policy* (1969), chs. I–VI, esp. 20–2, 50–1, 79–80, 129–31; David Ibbetson and Andrew Lewis, 'The Roman Law Tradition' in A. D. E. Lewis and D. J. Ibbetson (eds.), *The Roman Law Tradition* (1994), 1–14.

[19] See e.g. J. W. Gough, *Fundamental Law in English Constitutional History* (1955), 12–174. The parliamentarians looked more to the pre-Norman period of English constitutional history: see Christopher Hill, 'Sir Edward Coke: Myth-Maker' in Christopher Hill, *Intellectual Origins of the English Revolution* (1972), 225–65.

[20] On the Western European roots of the idea of public law as developed in the UK, see Martin Loughlin, *Foundations of Public Law* (2010), Introduction and Pt I; John Allison, *The English Historical Constitution: Continuity, Change and European Effects* (2007).

INTERNATIONALIZATION AND PROTECTION FOR NATIONAL INTERESTS: INFLUENCES, CONTROLS, AND FILTERS

PROTECTION AGAINST INTERNATIONAL LAW: FILTERS AND CHANNELS

As foreign influences can derail national arrangements, national authorities do not usually allow ideas from elsewhere to permeate national institutions unless two conditions are met. First, the state must have something to gain from accepting the ideas, either in terms of rationalizing or guaranteeing its own organization and security (as in the case of Bosnia and Herzegovina in 1995) or because of a promise of reciprocal benefits from other states. Secondly, unless the state faces irresistible armed force or economic sanctions it will insist on being able to influence the development and application of the ideas which it agrees to accept. Internationalization is thus a two-way street. Benefits must flow inwards to the nation, and the state must have the benefit of being able to influence or export as well as import ideas.

International law reflects this in that a treaty does not bind a state unless it has accepted the obligations arising under it. Internally, state constitutions usually impose filters to ensure that the state's legislative organs maintain control of the impact on municipal law of international treaties (binding agreements between two or more states), customary international law (those state practices internationally accepted as obligatory by most states),[21] and general principles of law.[22] Constitutions usually adopt a position lying on a continuum between two poles, commonly known as 'monism' and 'dualism'. A 'monist' approach draws no clear division between national and international law, allowing both customary international law and treaties[23] to produce effects in national law without the need for national legislation to give effect to them. In civil law systems, the influence of classical Roman law ensured that *ius gentium*, which by the time of Justinian had come to be seen as founded on human reason assumed to be common to Roman citizens and foreigners alike,[24] encouraged the adoption of constitutions which made at least some international obligations directly part of municipal law, treating national and international law as parts of a single, continuous fabric of law, rather than two entirely separate systems. This makes it easier to allow standards of civilized behaviour which form part of international law, including respect for human rights and prohibitions on genocide, torture, and other crimes against humanity, to take effect within states without the need for legislation, and to some extent to control inconsistent national laws.[25] Furthermore, if

---

[21] Shaw, *International Law*, 68–88.   [22] Ibid., 92–103.   [23] Ibid., 88–92.

[24] See Barry Nicholas, *An Introduction to Roman Law* (1962), 54–9; Wolfgang Kunkel, *An Introduction to Roman Legal and Constitutional History*, trans. J. M. Kelly (2nd edn, 1973), 100.

[25] See e.g. Hersh Lauterpacht, 'International Law: The General Part' in Hersh Lauterpacht, *International Law: Collected Papers*, ed. Elihu Lauterpacht, 5 vols. (1970), I, 153ff.

the existence of a state and its legal system depend on that state being recognized as meeting criteria for statehood set by international law (the 'constitutive theory' mentioned earlier), there can logically be no separation between national and international law.[26] Constitutions in civil law countries, and some common law countries like the USA which rebelled against British control, usually adopt some form of monism.

But there are sound reasons for having filters at national level to control the way in which the obligations affect national law- and policy-making. The principled reason is the desire to uphold constitutional guarantees, including the rule of law, and keep in the hands of the nations the democratic control of and accountability for national law and policy, in order to maintain the legitimacy of politics and public law in the state. The pragmatic reason is that international obligations may be contrary to the national interest and may derail important national objectives. 'Dualism' provides such a filter by treating national and international law as two separate systems. This prevents international law from directly affecting national law. The UK has traditionally adopted a broadly dualist approach.

However, there is no sharp distinction between monist and dualist approaches. The principled and pragmatic considerations mentioned earlier ensure that few monist states are without controls over the incorporation of international law, while in dualist states the separation between municipal and international law has never been total. Monist states typically maintain essential national interests in the face of international pressure by providing that treaty obligations become enforceable through national law without national legislation only under strict conditions: they must be reciprocal obligations, binding on all the states parties to the treaty; and they must be compatible with the national constitution, which remains hierarchically superior to treaties as a matter of national constitutional law. For example, Art. 25 of the *Grundgesetz* (Basic Law) of the Federal Republic of Germany makes the 'general rules of public international law' integral to federal law, creating rights and duties directly for inhabitants of the federal territory and taking precedence over national laws. This is an understandable reaction to the disregard, during the Third Reich, of the norms of public international law. On the other hand, under Art. 59.2 treaties which regulate the political relations of the Federation or relate to matters of federal legislation must have the consent or participation, in the form of a federal statute, of the bodies which are competent to make such federal legislation, and treaties affecting federal administration must have the consent or participation of the competent bodies for federal administration. Even then the treaty has the status of a federal statute; it is of no effect if it is incompatible with a provision of the Basic Law, including those protecting state sovereignty, democracy, and fundamental rights.[27]

[26] Hans Kelsen, *General Theory of Law and State* (1946), 363–80; Hans Kelsen, *The Pure Theory of Law*, trans. Max Knight (1967), 328–47.

[27] *Internationale Handelsgesellschaft mbH* v. *Einfuhr- und Vorratstelle für Getreide und Futtermittel* [1974] 2 CMLR 540 (BvfG); *Re the Application of Wünsche Handelsgesellschaft* [1987] 3 CMLR 225 (BvfG); *Unification Treaty Constitutionality Case* (1991) 94 ILR 42 (BvfG); *Lisbon Treaty Constitutionality Case*, BVerfG, 2 BvE 2/08, 30 June 2009, available at http://www.bverfg.de/entscheidungen/

Furthermore, the constitutional structures of monist states normally allow the legislature to control the exercise of treaty-making power by state institutions authorized by the constitution to exercise that power. For example, the US Constitution provides that treaty obligations, together with the Constitution and federal laws made in pursuance of it, are the supreme law of the land,[28] but the President may make treaties only with the concurrence of two-thirds of the members of the Senate who are present.[29] The legislative arm has a veto—at least in theory—over the USA's treaty obligations, and so over the state of federal law, although executive agreements, such as those recognizing foreign states, do not require Congressional approval, and may allow federal authorities to enforce obligations arising from them despite the Tenth Amendment, which reserves to the states all powers not conferred by the Constitution on federal authorities.[30] In France, Constitution of the Fifth Republic (1958), Art. 52 provides that the President of the Republic negotiates and usually also ratifies treaties, and under Art. 55 once ratified or approved they prevail over legislation if the other state party reciprocally gives similar effect to the treaty obligations in its own law. But Art. 53 preserves parliamentary control by providing that certain kinds of treaties may be ratified or approved only under an enactment, and take effect only after ratification or enactment.[31] What is more, no cession, exchange, or annexation of territory is valid without the consent of the population of the territory.[32]

THE UK'S PARTIAL DUALISM AND THE FEEDBACK LOOP BETWEEN MUNICIPAL AND INTERNATIONAL LAW

In the UK, too, dualism is only partial. Courts have long accepted that 'customary international law', the part of international law consisting of standards accepted by states by common consent without the need for multinational treaties or resolutions of international organizations, forms part of municipal law automatically, by incorporation, without the need for legislation, if sufficiently clear.[33] However, this is subject to the operation of certain filters.

---

es20090630_2bve000208.html; English translation available at http://www.bundesverfassungsgericht.de/entscheidungen/es20090630_2bve000208en.html. On which see Jo Erik Khushal Murkens, '"We want Our Constitution Back" – The Revival of National Sovereignty in the German Federal Constitutional Court's Decision on the Lisbon Treaty' [2010] PL 530–50.

[28] US Constitution, Art. VI bis.   [29] Ibid., Art. II.2 bis.

[30] See United States v. Belmont, 301 US 324 (1937) on the recognition by the USA of the USSR. See also Breard v. Commonwealth 248 Va 68, 445 SE 2d 670 (1994), cert. denied 513 US 971 (1994).

[31] The types of Treaty are: 'peace treaties, trade treaties, treaties or agreements concerning international organizations, those which commit national resources, those which modify provisions of a legislative character, those concerning personal status, and those involving the cession, exchange, or annexation or territory', Art. 53, trans. in S. E. Finer, Vernon Bogdanor, and Bernard Rudden, Comparing Constitutions (1995), 229.

[32] For further examples, see Shaw, International Law, 151–62.

[33] See Shaw, International Law, 141–8; Trendtex Banking Corporation v. Central Bank of Nigeria [1977] QB 529 (CA); J. H. Rayner (Mincing Lane) Ltd v. Department of Trade and Industry [1990] 2 AC 418 (HL).

First, customary international law is incorporated only so far as it is compatible with national statutes and binding case law. But, since customary international law responds to state practice, the influence works in both directions. For example, in *Al-Adsani* v. *Government of Kuwait* the Court of Appeal held that torture was contrary to customary international law, but that the plaintiff, who claimed to have been tortured by Kuwaiti officials in Kuwait, could not sue the Government of Kuwait in English courts because by clear words the State Immunity Act 1978 established that the defendant could still rely on state immunity notwithstanding any violation of customary international law.[34] This is an example of statute giving one principle of international law—state immunity—priority over another—the prohibition of torture in customary law—and, partly because state practice is a source of customary international law, international law currently has the same priority rule. In both municipal and international law, state immunity is not (yet) subject to any exception even in respect of alleged violation of *jus cogens*, and even protects individual torturers against civil liability if they acted in an official capacity.[35] The immunity has been restricted by the Convention against Torture and other Cruel, Inhuman or Degrading Treatment or Punishment 1984 (CAT) to allow criminal proceedings against state agents, but it has not been limited so as to allow civil proceedings against representatives of states for torture.

Secondly, crimes in customary international law do not automatically become crimes justiciable before domestic courts in England and Wales. The common law is no longer capable of generating new crimes, and there are good constitutional reasons for requiring parliamentary authorization for new crimes and extensions to the criminal jurisdiction of domestic courts.[36] The requirement preserves parliamentary sovereignty and the integrity of municipal common law, and protects people against uncontrolled creation of criminal liabilities. The value of filters protecting a state's constitution and law from being changed without national authorization explains the decision in *R* v. *Jones (Margaret)*[37] that the crime of aggression in international law was not part of English criminal law, so people who used force to try to prevent the UK's preparations for the attack on Iraq in 2003 could not rely on the defence under Criminal Law Act 1967, s. 3 of having used reasonable force to prevent an unlawful act. Nevertheless, it points up the moral argument for a more monistic approach in order to uphold international criminal law.

---

[34]   (1996) 107 ILR 536 (CA). This was held not to violate the right to be free of torture or the right to a fair hearing under ECHR, Arts. 3 and 6.1: Application no. 35763/97, *Al-Adsani* v. *United Kingdom*, judgment of 21 November 2001, RJD 2001-XI, 34 EHRR 273.

[35]   *Jones* v. *Ministry of the Interior of the Kingdom of Saudi Arabia and another (Secretary of State for Constitutional Affairs and others intervening)* [2006] UKHL 26, [2007] 1 AC 270 (HL); *Jones* v. *United Kingdom*, Application No. 34356/06, judgment of 14 January 2014, 59 EHRR 1, applying *Al-Adsani* v. *United Kingdom*, and *Germany* v. *Italy*, ICJ Reports 2012, 99, paras. 81–97; Shaw, *International Law*, 715–8,

[36]   Roger O'Keefe, 'Customary International Crimes in English Courts' [2001] *BYIL* 293, 335.

[37]   [2006] UKHL 16, [2007] 1 AC 136 (HL).

The interplay of customary international law, international treaty obligations, and UK statute is illustrated by *R* v. *Bow Street Metropolitan Stipendiary Magistrate and others, ex parte Pinochet Ugarte (No. 3).*[38] The applicant was a former President of Chile who was alleged to have authorized acts of torture and murder during his period in power, including some against Spanish citizens. A Spanish judge had issued an international arrest warrant seeking his extradition to Spain to face trial. The applicant had been arrested in England while on a visit to receive medical treatment. The question was whether he could be extradited. An exceptional seven-judge appellate committee of the House of Lords decided a number of issues.

(a) They held unanimously that a head of state would normally be entitled to claim immunity from legal process in the UK by virtue of a combination of customary international law and UK statutes dealing with state immunity and diplomatic immunity.[39]

(b) By a majority of four to three,[40] they held that torture (unlike murder) is an international crime against humanity by virtue of customary international law, and a peremptory norm of general international law (sometimes called *jus cogens*), defined in Vienna Convention on the Law of Treaties 1969, Art. 53 as 'a norm accepted and recognized by the international community of States as a whole as a norm from which no derogation is permitted and which can be modified only by a subsequent norm of general international law having the same character', so that it overrides incompatible rules in customary international law or treaties.

(c) Unanimously they held that the Extradition Act 1989 in the UK prevented extradition for a crime which was not a crime in the UK (as well as in the state which has requested extradition of the suspect) at the time when it was committed (known as the 'double criminality rule').

(d) By a majority of four to three,[41] they held that torture committed outside the UK did not become a criminal offence in the UK until two conditions were met. First, there had to be legislation to make it a criminal offence. This was done by the Criminal Justice Act 1988, which came into force on 29 September 1988. Secondly, all the relevant states (Spain, Chile, and the UK) had to have

---

[38] [2000] 1 AC 147 (HL).

[39] See State Immunity Act 1978, s. 20(1) read together with Diplomatic Privileges Act 1964, Sched. 1, para. 39 (giving effect to the Vienna Convention on Diplomatic Relations).

[40] Lords Browne-Wilkinson, Hope of Craighead, Hutton, and Saville of Newdigate. Lords Millett and Phillips of Worth Matravers dissented on the ground that conspiracy to murder in Spain was also an international crime for which no immunity would be available. Lord Goff dissented on the ground that the statutory immunity applied even in relation to torture.

[41] Lords Browne-Wilkinson, Goff, Hope of Craighead, and Saville of Newdigate. Lord Hutton argued that it became an offence in the UK from the 29 September 1988 when Criminal Justice Act 1988, s. 134 came into force. Lords Millett and Phillips of Worth Matravers argued that it had been an international crime under customary international law before that, so there could be no immunity.

ratified the CAT, which required states to recognize and provide in their own law for universal jurisdiction over offences of torture. In other words, every state party to the CAT was then obliged in international law both to accept jurisdiction over such cases in its own courts (wherever the torture was alleged to have been committed) and to recognize that other states' courts had similar jurisdiction. That happened on 8 December 1988.

(e) By a majority of six to one, it was held that after 8 December 1988 torture committed abroad was a criminal offence in the UK and so was an extradition crime.

This makes three constitutional principles clear. First, the UK operates a dualist filter not only in respect of treaties, but even in respect of a peremptory norm of general international law which establishes a crime against humanity. Only a legislature can authorize courts in the UK to impose criminal liability. Secondly, even when legislation is in place, English law[42] may recognize a treaty binding on the states involved in a case as an additional necessary step in establishing that there is international jurisdiction. In other words, English courts do not give effect to treaties as such, but may require a treaty before accepting that there is jurisdiction to extradite someone for an international crime against humanity, even when that crime has been shown to exist under statute and customary international law. Thirdly, so far as UK statutes dealing with state and diplomatic immunity are designed to give effect to international treaties, they will be interpreted in the light of those treaties, which themselves may be subject to a peremptory norm of general international law.

TERRITORIALITY AND INTERNATIONAL LAW

A further constitutional filter is the territorial principle. The scope of UK legislation is generally limited to the territory of the UK, even when giving effect to international obligations, although the legislation will be read in the light of those obligations, which may require courts to give limited extraterritorial effect to the legislation. For example, the Human Rights Act 1998 gives domestic effect to rights under ECHR, Art. 1 of which requires the high contracting parties to secure the rights to everyone within their jurisdictions. The European Court of Human Rights has interpreted this as imposing obligations towards people in areas outside a state's territory if the state has actual control there or, perhaps, exercises factual or *de jure* authority over the victim of the alleged violation.[43] The House of Lords and the Supreme Court held that it should follow the Strasbourg Court's recognition

---

[42] This is probably also the position in Northern Ireland. Nothing is said here about the applicability of the *Pinochet Ugarte (No. 3)* decision in Scotland.

[43] See e.g. *Banković v. Belgium*, Application No. 52207/99, judgment of 12 December 2001 (GC); *Ilascu v. Moldova and Russia*, Application No. 48787/99, judgment of 8 July 2004 (GC); Marko Milanovic, *Extraterritorial Application of Human Rights Treaties: Law, Principles, Policy* (2011), esp. chs. 2 and 4.

of extraterritorial effect for the ECHR, but only so far as a clear line of case law in the Strasbourg Court requires. At first, a majority of the Supreme Court regarded the Strasbourg jurisprudence on this matter as extending jurisdiction only to areas directly and effectively controlled by the UK's armed forces.[44] The Grand Chamber of the Strasbourg Court decided, however, that the notion of jurisdiction is more elastic, including cases where a state's agents have effective, extraterritorial control over persons or premises. As a result, civil liability may arise under the Human Rights Act 1998, although there may also be cases which give rise to issues in private, rather than public, international law.[45]

COUNTERVAILING OBLIGATIONS IN INTERNATIONAL LAW

Where international law operates as a source of domestic law, the courts have regard to the whole of public international law when establishing the scope of any right or obligation that is to have effect in domestic law. Elements cannot be examined in isolation. We have already seen one example of this: tort liability for torture is limited by the international as well as national law of state immunity.[46] Other international law rules capable of limiting human rights obligations in international and domestic law include those concerning diplomatic immunity[47] and the capacity of UN Security Council Resolutions made under Chapter VII of the UN Charter, protecting international peace and security, to authorize states to act inconsistently with their international human-rights obligations, if the authorization is sufficiently explicit.[48]

Thus dualism operates in the UK, but the division between municipal and public international law should be seen as a semi-permeable membrane, which allows rules to pass through it in different directions for different purposes. The matter is further complicated by two decisions going in different directions. In one, the Strasbourg Court held that acts of a country's armed forces operating abroad under the authority of a UN Security Council resolution made under UN Charter, Chapter VII were attributable to the United Nations rather than the state concerned, which was accordingly not liable for any violation of the ECHR, but the Grand Chamber has since made it clear, following the International Law Commission and the House of Lords, that this depends on the UN Security Council having effective control over (or at the very

---

[44] *R (Al-Skeini)* v. *Secretary of State for Defence (The Redress Trust and another intervening)* [2007] UKHL 26, [2008] AC 153 (HL); *R (Smith)* v. *Oxfordshire Assistant Deputy Coroner (Equality and Human Rights Commission intervening)* [2010] UKSC 29, [2010] 3 WLR 223 (SC).

[45] *Al-Skeini* v. *United Kingdom*, Application No. 55721/07, judgment of 7 July 2011, 53 EHRR 589, (GC); *Smith* v. *Ministry of Defence (JUSTICE intervening)* [2013] UKSC 41, [2014] AC 52 (SC); cf. *Al-Jedda* v. *Secretary of State for Defence* [2010] EWCA Civ 758, [2011] QB 773 (CA).

[46] *Jones* v. *Ministry of the Interior of the Kingdom of Saudi Arabia and another (Secretary of State for Constitutional Affairs and others intervening)* [2006] UKHL 26, [2007] 1 AC 270 (HL).

[47] *R (B.)* v. *Secretary of State for Foreign and Commonwealth Affairs* [2004] EWCA Civ 1344, [2005] QB 643 (CA).

[48] *Al-Jedda* v. *United Kingdom*, Application No. 27120/08, judgment of 7 July 2011, 53 EHRR 789 (GC).

least ultimate authority for) the conduct of forces.[49] In the other, the European Court of Justice held that the European Union is an autonomous legal order independent of international law, so that its fundamental rights are not affected by developments such as UN Security Council Chapter VII resolutions.[50] This will have effect in the UK in relation to EU norms and acts, including those carried out by UK authorities on behalf of the European Union's organs.

DUALISM, TREATIES, AND INTERNATIONAL ORGANIZATIONS

The UK's dualist filter has been most fully applied in respect of treaties and action of international organizations established under treaties. Usually, rights and obligations arising under treaties do not take effect in municipal legal systems with a dualist principle unless legislation has been passed to give effect to them. For example, rights under the ECHR, as a multilateral treaty, could not be directly litigated before courts in the UK until the Human Rights Act 1998 had made them effective in municipal law.[51] This has two effects. First, it prevents the Crown (in reality the government of the day, which conducts foreign affairs under the royal prerogative) from exercising its treaty-making prerogative in ways which change the law in the UK without parliamentary approval. In the absence of a statutory requirement, there is no need to obtain parliamentary approval before negotiating, signing, or ratifying a treaty.[52] The main statutory exceptions relate to EU Treaties. Under the European Union Act 2011, ss. 2–4 and 6, a minister may not ratify a treaty or confirm approval of (or, in some cases, vote in favour of) a European Council decision increasing the competences of the EU in specified respects without an Act of Parliament or, in certain cases, holding a referendum.

In other cases, to compensate for the loss of democratic control, dualism prevents the treaty-making prerogative being used to extend the power of the executive, and protects the legislative supremacy of Parliament against attrition. It also protects both the government and Parliament against the direct imposition of the will of other states, contrary to the UK's national interests, through international treaties and the resolutions of international organizations. The UK Parliament can refuse to give effect to treaty obligations in municipal law. It, and the government of the day, can also refuse to accept that a treaty imposes any binding obligation. For example, the

---

[49] *Behrami* v. *France*, Application no. 71412/01, admissibility decision of 2 May 2007 (GC); *R (Al-Jedda)* v. *Secretary of State for Defence* [2007] UKHL 23, [2004] 1 AC 185 (HL); *Al-Jedda* v. *United Kingdom*, Application No. 27021, judgment of 7 July 2011 (GC), para. 84.

[50] Joined Cases C-402/05P and C-415/05P, *Kadi* v. *Council of the European Union* [2008] ECR I-6351, [2009] AC 1225 (CJEC). See also *A.* v. *HM Treasury* [2010] UKSC 2, [2010] 2 WLR 378 (SC).

[51] See e.g. *Malone* v. *Metropolitan Police Commissioner (No. 2)* [1979] Ch 344; *R* v. *Secretary of State for the Home Department, ex parte Brind* [1991] 1 AC 696 (HL); *R* v. *Ministry of Defence, ex parte Smith* [1996] QB 517 (CA).

[52] See *JH Rayner (Mincing Lane) Ltd* v. *Department of Trade and Industry* [1990] 2 AC 418 (HL), 500, *per* Lord Oliver of Aylmerton. Statutory requirements for parliamentary approval are rare.

previous (Labour) government's view of economic and social rights arising under the International Covenant on Economic, Social and Cultural Rights and the Convention on the Rights of the Child was that the obligations were aspirational rather than immediate, and did not require the state to guarantee an ascertainable level of protection at any one time.[53] Refusing to recognize or comply with treaty obligations might lead to sanctions for breach of international law if any are available, but it leaves the UK's legislatures ultimately in control of their own legal systems.[54]

This protection for state autonomy can be attenuated. The European Communities Act 1972 provides for some EU rights and obligations to be enforced directly in courts and tribunals in the UK.[55] This allows ministers to change the law in the UK by agreement in Brussels without parliamentary approval. There are some safeguards for national interests. When the supremacy of EC law was established by the Court of Justice of the European Communities (CJEC), the Council needed to agree unanimously in order to legislate. This has since changed. The range of decisions requiring unanimity has steadily narrowed, most recently in the Treaty of Lisbon, and there is no legal protection for parliamentary sovereignty, although some procedural safeguards have been put in place. These include the 'scrutiny reserve' which usually prevents the UK government from agreeing to measures being adopted in Brussels until they have been scrutinized by the Houses of Parliament, a task performed with distinction by committees in both Houses.[56]

In relation to treaties which do not directly alter municipal law, Parliament's position is weak, despite (or because of) dualism. At present, the two Houses normally have no right to be consulted before the text of a treaty is concluded, much less a veto over its signing or ratification. The government makes treaties, and is usually accountable to Parliament only afterwards. There used to be a constitutional convention (the 'Ponsonby rule', dating from 1924) that treaties would not be ratified until they had been laid before both Houses of Parliament for 21 days. This did not apply to treaties which did not require ratification and were merely technical;[57] but the government

[53] For the government's position on the Convention on the Rights of the Child and criticism of it, see Joint Committee on Human Rights, Tenth Report of 2002–3, *The UN Convention on the Rights of the Child*, HL 117/HC 81 (2003), paras. 21–3.

[54] This fundamental point has been lost in the heated exchanges concerning cases in which the European Court of Human Rights has held that the UK's blanket prohibition on convicted prisoners' voting in elections violates the right to vote under ECHR Protocol 1, Art. 3. See David Feldman, 'Sovereignties in Strasbourg' in Richard Rawlings, Peter Leyland, and Alison L. Young (eds.), *Sovereignty and the Law: Domestic, European, and International Perspectives* (2013), ch. 12, esp. 223–4.

[55] European Communities Act 1972, s. 2, discussed further later.

[56] See the resolutions of the two Houses at Hansard, HC, cols. 778ff. (17 November 1998), and Hansard, HL, cols. 1019ff. (6 December 1999); K. M. Newman, 'The Impact of National Parliaments on the Development of Community Law' in F. Capotorti (ed.), *Du Droit International au Droit de l'Integration: Liber Amicorum Pierre Pescatore* (1987), 481–97; T. St. John Bates, 'European Community Legislation before the House of Commons' (1991) 12 *Stat LR* 109–24.

[57] 'Technical' is not a technical term. It is capable of covering treaties establishing procedures for giving effect to already existing substantive obligations, and perhaps treaties concerned with the way states deal with fields in which their jurisdictions overlap, for instance in relation to double-taxation agreements.

would 'inform the House of all agreements, commitments and undertakings which may in any way bind the nation to specific action in certain circumstances'.[58] The rule, with certain adjustments to limit its impact on governmental freedom, was put on a statutory footing by the Constitutional Reform and Governance Act 2010, ss. 20–5. However, this gives Parliament no more than a right to receive information about the government's treaty-making activities.

Treaties by which the UK becomes a member of supranational or international organizations whose institutions have law-making powers especially call for filters to protect the municipal legal systems against adverse effects, but also make it more difficult to secure that protection. The value of filters in such a system depends on the power of the state to influence the content of obligations imposed on it by treaty bodies. When the UK became part of the European Economic Community (EEC) in 1973 it was an association of a small group of Western European nations designed to remove national barriers to economic development and to turn the member states into a single market (the 'Common Market') in goods and services. At that stage, national interests were strongly protected by equal state representation on the main law-making body and (as noted earlier) a requirement for unanimity to make law. The veto power of each member state gave reasonable protection for the UK's national interests, making possible the UK's acceptance of the direct effect of some Community legislation and of the doctrine of the supremacy of Community law. Over time, however, the number of member states and the diversity of their interests increased, and the law-making activities of the institution grew in range and complexity. The EEC turned into the European Community and later the European Union, dedicated to harmonizing a growing range of economic and social policies, including the regulation of police and judicial cooperation and other fields of common concern. As qualified majority voting was introduced, the safeguards for vital national interests, which had originally justified relaxing the national filters by accepting the direct effect of EC law, became progressively weaker, and the Treaty of Lisbon in 2007 (which came into force on 1 December 2009) continued that trend. Parliament's attempt in the European Union Act 2011 to restrict the government's power to agree to EU measures is in part a response to it.

Some international organizations never demand unanimity in decision-making. From its establishment in 1946, the United Nations had such a large membership that unanimity was never a practical option. Each member state has a seat in the General Assembly, but that body's recommendations do not bind states in public international law except in relation to the internal governance of the United Nations[59] (although resolutions may be evidence of the emergence of binding rules of customary international law if they reflect state practice). The main power to impose obligations binding states in international law is conferred on the Security Council, which forms the executive group of the United Nations with special responsibility for preserving international

---

[58] Hansard, HC (5th series), vol. 171, col. 2001 (1 April 1924).   [59] UN Charter, Art. 17.

peace and security.[60] Decisions of the Council (but not mere recommendations) bind all member states.[61] Only 15 states are members of the Security Council. Five of them, the 'great powers' of the period following the Second World War (China, France, Russia, the UK, and the USA), are permanent members. The other ten members are elected for a period of two years from among the remaining members of the General Assembly, as laid down by UN Charter, Art. 23(2) Security Council Resolutions must be approved by an affirmative vote of at least nine members, but any of the permanent members may veto any proposed resolution, except in relation to procedural matters (such as the agenda for sessions, or the states which should be given the opportunity to address the Council in matters affecting them), where there is no veto.[62] This offers asymmetric protection to national interests. Those of the five permanent members are well protected by their veto. Those of the non-permanent members can be subordinated to the interests of nine concurring members, although they may benefit from overlapping the vital interests of one of the permanent members. States without a seat on the Security Council are even less well protected. As members of the United Nations they can use diplomatic techniques in defence of their interests, but their success will depend significantly on the balance of power and the interests of the 'great powers'.

For historical reasons, the UK is a permanent member of the UN Security Council, so it has a measure of control over the most important decisions. In other international organizations, it has influence rather than control, and the extent of its influence depends on the arguments and pressure it can apply. By contrast, the USA, the former USSR, and today China, as world superpowers in terms of their military or economic might, can exercise great influence by offers of aid with strings attached, or by explicit or implicit threats of trade sanctions, withdrawal of aid, or in extreme cases invasion. Such influence does not depend on the quality of the superpower's arguments or the morality of its stance. It extends beyond organizations of which the superpowers are members, although even a superpower must sometimes take account of other states' points of view, as the aftermath of the second Gulf War in 2003 has shown.

MECHANISMS FOR INTERNATIONALIZATION, CONSTITUTIONAL STRUCTURES, AND LEGITIMACY

Those international influences to which states are inevitably subject must be channelled into municipal law and made to fit within the state's constitutional law and traditions. How is this done?[63]

---

[60] Ibid., Arts. 23, 24, 25, and 28.   [61] Ibid., Art. 25.   [62] Ibid., Art. 27.
[63] David Feldman, 'Modalities of Internationalisation in International Law' (2006) 18 *ERPL* 131.

INCORPORATION OR DIRECT APPLICATION OF INTERNATIONAL OR SUPRANATIONAL LEGAL RULES

The most direct form of international (or at least supranational) influence arises when rules made by another state or states, or accepted at inter-state level, are automatically incorporated into the municipal legal system, without the need for any prior or subsequent legislative action. In the UK, the most straightforward example of this is the automatic incorporation of rules of customary international law (subject to inconsistent legislation or earlier judicial decisions), as mentioned in the previous section.

Marginally less direct, but more powerful, is the process whereby certain rules of EU law become part of the municipal legal system. The European Communities Act 1972, s 2(1) creates what is, in effect, a statutory rule of automatic incorporation of what it calls 'enforceable Community rights'. Because of the doctrine of the supremacy of EC law over national law, this form of incorporation has a greater impact than the incorporation of customary international law. Enforceable Community rights need not be compatible with previous or subsequent parliamentary legislation. Instead, inconsistent parliamentary legislation must be disapplied to the extent that it is inconsistent with enforceable Community rights.[64]

In addition, s. 2(2) of the Act allows Her Majesty in Council or designated ministers and departments to give effect to or implement other EC obligations or rights (including those arising under directives which do not have direct effect) in municipal law by way of statutory instruments, a form of subordinate legislation. These are usually subject only to the negative resolution procedure: they take effect unless either House passes a resolution annulling them.[65] Statutory instruments under s. 2(2) can make any provision that could be made by Act of Parliament. They can even amend or repeal Acts of Parliament; and any provision of primary legislation is to be construed and to have effect subject to the provisions of the statutory instrument.[66] A subsequent Act of Parliament could revoke the statutory instrument, as long as that would not be incompatible with the enforcement of enforceable Community rights. Nevertheless, the filters protecting parliamentary control over the implementation of EU law are limited: the negative resolution procedure is hardly a strong form of scrutiny or protection, and the best filter is the pre-adoption scrutiny of EU measures by the House of Commons EU Scrutiny Committee and the House of Lords EU Select Committee and its subcommittees.[67] What is more, in some fields the member states have delegated power to the European Commission to negotiate treaties on their behalf with non-member states, including agreements on tariffs and trade and arrangements for extradition. The impact of such agreements on the rights and obligations of member states is as yet uncertain.[68]

---

[64] See ch. 4 in this volume.   [65] European Communities Act 1972, Sched. 2, para. 2(2).
[66] Ibid., s. 2(4).   [67] See discussion in ch. 4 in this volume.
[68] See Vienna Convention on the Law of Treaties between States and International Organisations and between International Organisations 1986; Shaw, *International Law*, 953–5.

Following the establishment of the United Nations in 1946, Parliament conferred power on the government to implement certain decisions of the UN Security Council by way of subordinate legislation, with limited or non-existent parliamentary oversight. When the Security Council, acting to preserve international peace and security under UN Charter, Chapter VII, calls on the government to apply any measures to give effect to any decision of the Council under UN Charter, Art. 41 (that is, decisions not involving the use of armed force), United Nations Act 1946, s. 1(1) allows Her Majesty by Order in Council to make 'such provision as appears to Her to be necessary or expedient for enabling the measures to be effectively applied'. The Order must be laid before Parliament forthwith after it is made, and, if it relates to a matter within the legislative competence of the Scottish Parliament, before that Parliament as well,[69] but neither Parliament can annul the Order save by means of an Act. Still less do such Orders require the approval of either House. The only control available is through judicial review. An Order can be quashed if it is outside the scope of the power conferred by the Act or is incompatible with a Community right (such as the right to be free of quantitative restrictions on free movement of goods)[70] or a Convention right under the Human Rights Act 1998. But if it acts compatibly with EC law and Convention rights the government has a very wide discretion as to the terms of the Order and the Treasury has a very wide discretion as to the manner of its implementation.[71]

The scope of the power is enormous, and Orders can directly affect individuals. For example, after the terrorist attack on the World Trade Center on 9 September 2001 the UN Security Council passed Resolution 1373 of 28 September 2001, calling on the governments of member states to apply measures to give effect to decisions of the Council to combat terrorist activities. It required steps to be taken to freeze terrorist assets. In the UK, the government implemented this by Orders in Council making it a criminal offence to make funds or financial services available to or for the benefit of people participating in acts of terrorism or to fail to report suspicions that people are intending to use funds for such a purpose, and allowing the Treasury to freeze the funds of such people whom the Treasury has reasonable grounds for suspecting may be holding funds for the purpose of committing, facilitating, or participating in acts of terrorism.[72] These Orders were subject to no parliamentary control or scrutiny either before or after they were made. In reliance on them, the Treasury froze the assets of several dozen people, and announced its action in press releases.[73] The Security Council resolution thus authorized a direct attack by the British government

---

[69] European Communities Act 1972, s. 1(4), as amended by the Scotland Act 1998.

[70] See R v. HM Treasury, ex parte Centro-Com Srl [1997] QB 863 (CJEC).

[71] See R v. HM Treasury, ex parte Centro-Com Srl, The Independent, 3 June 1994 (CA), affirming (in relation to municipal law) [1994] 1 CMLR 109. On the implications of EC law, see the decision of the Court of Justice on the reference from the Court of Appeal: [1997] QB 683 (CJEC).

[72] Terrorism (United Nations Measures) (Channel Islands) Order 2001 (SI 2001/3363); Terrorism (United Nations Measures) (Isle of Man) Order 2001 (SI 2001/3364); Terrorism (United Nations Measures) Order 2001 (SI 2001/3365).

[73] See e.g. Treasury Press Release 110/01, 12 October 2001, which includes a list of names.

on individuals' property, with very limited safeguards and filters within the jurisdiction for rule-of-law requirements and the democratic process.

However, the Supreme Court reasserted respect for fundamental rights, holding that several of these orders were ultra vires the United Nations Act 1946, s. 1. This was partly because they infringed fundamental rights without a fair hearing and subordinate legislation could not validly do that unless an Act of Parliament had expressly conferred a power to do so, and partly because the orders were drafted more broadly than was justified by the Security Council resolutions. The government introduced an emergency bill to preserve the orders until new legislation was passed to define the asset-freezing power more closely and provide for appeal to or review by courts of Treasury decisions.[74]

Today, a provision in a bill allowing the government to introduce international obligations to municipal law by delegated legislation would be likely to face more intensive parliamentary scrutiny than in 1946. In particular, the House of Lords Select Committee on Delegated Powers and Regulatory Reform, which scrutinizes all provisions in bills before Parliament which confer power to make delegated legislation, would seek to insist on including sufficient safeguards in the bill by way of a requirement for adequate parliamentary scrutiny of proposed subordinate legislation to protect the rule of law and human rights. Where the proposed power could affect human rights or constitutional principles, the Joint Select Committee on Human Rights and the House of Lords Select Committee on the Constitution provide additional pressure. It is noteworthy that the powers included in the Anti-terrorism, Crime and Security Act 2001 to permit EU initiatives on police and judicial cooperation in criminal matters to be given effect in the UK by way of subordinate legislation included far more safeguards than are found in the United Nations Act 1946.[75] Even then the government agreed that legislation to implement the Framework Decision on the European Arrest Warrant would be introduced by way of a bill (now Extradition Act 2003, Pt 1) rather than by using the power to make subordinate legislation under the 2001 Act.[76]

Similar caution about authorizing subordinate legislation can be seen in the Human Rights Act 1998 and the devolution legislation to making rights under the ECHR ('the Convention rights') effective in municipal law in the UK.[77] The Human Rights Act 1998, s. 1, applied in the devolution legislation,[78] appears to import the rights bodily

---

[74] *Ahmed and others v. HM Treasury (JUSTICE intervening) (Nos. 1 and 2)* [2010] UKSC 2, [2010] 2 WLR 378 (SC); Terrorist Asset-Freezing (Temporary Provisions) Act 2010; Terrorist Asset-Freezing etc. Act 2010, Pt 1.

[75] See Anti-terrorism, Crime and Security Act 2001, ss. 111 and 112. For further primary legislation on cross-border cooperation, see Crime (International Co-operation) Act 2003. The same point was made by Lord Hope of Craighead DPSC in *Ahmed v. HM Treasury* [2010] UKSC 2, [2010] 2 WLR 378 (SC), at [48]–[53], arguing that the government should have used either primary legislation or the procedure under the 2001 Act to give effect to the Security Council resolutions.

[76] See Joint Committee on Human Rights, Second Report, 2001–2, *Anti-terrorism, Crime and Security Bill*, HL 37/HC 372, para. 13.

[77] See chs. 4 and 9 in this volume.

[78] See Scotland Act 1998, ss. 29(2), 54(2) and 126(1); Northern Ireland Act 1998, ss. 6(2), 24(1) and 98(1); Government of Wales Act 2006, ss. 81(5) and 158(1).

from international law (the ECHR) to national law. However, the transplant is complicated by two factors. First, the rights in international law bind states, whereas in municipal law they bind public authorities within the state. This necessitated adjustments designed, among other things, to adapt the rights for municipal application and maintain consistency with constitutional principles such as parliamentary sovereignty and parliamentary privilege.[79] Secondly, there is a difference between formulating a right and understanding what it means when applied in practice. Both the scope of the Convention rights and the circumstances (if any) in which it is justifiable to interfere with them in international law depend on the extensive case law of the European Commission and the European Court of Human Rights. Parts of it, such as the notion of the 'margin of appreciation', arise from the position of international tribunals vis-à-vis national authorities and cannot be transferred to municipal law. Even if a particular line of case law can be transferred to the municipal sphere, there may be good reasons for limiting its impact. The Human Rights Act 1998, s. 2 therefore provides that courts and tribunals in the UK must take into account the case law of the Strasbourg organs when interpreting the Convention rights, but does not make it binding. Courts in the UK have on occasions declined to follow judgments of the European Court of Human Rights.[80] For example, the House of Lords has held that normal rules of precedent generally require a lower court in England and Wales to follow an earlier decision of a higher domestic court on the application of Convention rights in preference to a later, inconsistent decision of the European Court of Human Rights, unless it is clear that the policy justification for the earlier English decision no longer applies.[81] This introduces a filter into the channel by which the Convention rights enter municipal law: courts and tribunals in the UK are not required to follow decisions of international tribunals if they seem inappropriate to the structure of the domestic legal order or plainly wrong.

The Act also empowers ministers to make statutory instruments for various purposes, providing further channels for bringing municipal law into line with the ECHR. With relatively few preconditions or procedural filters a Secretary of State can make a statutory instrument adding an extra right to the list of Convention rights which became part of municipal law by virtue of s. 1 of the Act. With equally little formal constraint, a Secretary of State can add a reservation to the newly recognized right to the list of reservations in s. 1 of, and Pt 1 of Sched. 3 to, the Act, or add a derogation

---

[79] See e.g. the partial delimitation of the term 'public authority' in the Human Rights Act 1998, s. 6.

[80] On the circumstances in which courts in the UK should follow Strasbourg judgments, see e.g. *R (Alconbury Developments Ltd)* v. *Secretary of State for the Environment, Transport and the Regions* [2001] UKHL 23, [2003] 2 AC 295 (HL), at [26], *per* Lord Slynn of Hadley; *R (Ullah)* v. *Special Adjudicator* [2004] UKHL 26, [2004] 2 AC 323, at [20], *per* Lord Bingham of Cornhill; *R* v. *Horncastle* [2009] UKSC 14, [2010] 2 WLR 47 (SC); *Manchester City Council* v. *Pinnock* [2010] SC 45, at [48]–[49]; *Rabone* v. *Pennine Care NHS Foundation Trust* [2012] UKSC 2, [2012] 2 AC 72, SC; *R (Chester)* v. *Secretary of State for Justice* [2013] UKSC 63, [2014] AC 271, at [27, *per* Lord Mance; *R (Haney and others)* v. *Secretary of State for Justice* [2014] UKSC 66, at [18]–[40].

[81] *Kay* v. *Lambeth LBC; Leeds City Council* v. *Price* [2006] UKHL 10, [2006] 2 AC 465 (HL) (not overruled on this point in *Manchester City Council* v. *Pinnock*, and reaffirmed in *R (Haney)* (see n. 80).

from a Convention right to those recognized in s. 1 of, and Pt 2 of Sched. 3 to, the Act. Any UK court or tribunal interpreting a Convention right must then read it subject to the reservation or derogation in question. There have been two changes to the deroga- tions recognized in the Act, both in relation to terrorism: the original derogation was repealed, and later a new one was inserted;[82] but the derogation order adding the new derogation was subsequently held to be ultra vires because the measures concerned were not strictly required by the exigencies of the terrorist threat and consistent with the UK's other international obligations so as to meet the requirements of Art. 15 of the ECHR, so at present (as of November 2014) there is no designated derogation.[83]

   If the Strasbourg Court or a UK court decides that UK legislation is incompatible with a Convention right, the Human Rights Act 1998, s. 10 empowers the appropriate Secretary of State to make an Order in Council amending or repealing the incompat- ible provision, which is usually in an Act of Parliament. When the Human Rights Bill was before the House of Lords in 1997, the Select Committee on Delegated Powers and Deregulation[84] recommended that this 'Henry VIII' power should be hedged about with preconditions and procedural requirements, now contained in s. 10 of, and Sched. 2 to, the Act, even though the purpose is to protect and extend, rather than to interfere with, human rights. This has the odd result that it is easier to make a statutory instrument which restricts rights by requiring courts in the UK to interpret Convention rights in the light of a reservation or new derogation than to extend rights by way of a statutory instrument (a remedial order) amending previously incompatible legislation.

INFORMAL INFLUENCE OF INTERNATIONAL LEGAL RULES

Even where there is no express legislative authority for allowing international stand- ards and treaties to influence municipal law, both treaties and the judgments of international and foreign tribunals can influence parliamentary and judicial decision- making in the UK. Parliament and government departments are increasingly aware

---

   [82] Human Rights Act 1998 (Amendment) Order 2001, SI 2001/1216 and Human Rights Act 1998 (Designated Derogation) Order 2001, SI 2001/3641 respectively.

   [83] See Human Rights Act 1998 (Amendment) Order 2001 (SI 2001/1216), removing a derogation made to remove the derogation from ECHR, Art. 5 in relation to detaining terrorist suspects without charge for up to seven days before being brought before a judicial officer; Human Rights Act 1998 (Designated Derogation) Order 2001 (SI 2001/3644), introducing a new derogation from Art. 5 to allow indefinite detention without trial of suspected international terrorists who were not UK nationals if they could not be removed abroad for legal or practical reasons under the Anti-terrorism, Crime and Security Act 2001; Human Rights Act 1998 (Amendment) Order 2004 (SI 2004/1574), replacing Protocol 6 with Protocol 13 in the list of Convention rights; and Human Rights Act 1998 (Amendment) Order 2005 (SI 2005/1071), removing the derogation from Art. 5 after the House of Lords had held it to be invalid in *A v. Secretary of State for the Home Department* [2004] UKHL 56, [2005] 2 AC 68 (HL). Lord Scott of Foscote expressed doubt as to the applicability of Art. 15, as it was not one of the provisions made part of the legal systems of the UK by the Human Rights Act 1998, s. 1, but the Home Secretary had conceded its relevance.

   [84] The forerunner of the Select Committee on Delegated Powers and Regulatory Reform.

of the UK's obligations as a result of the work of the government's legal advisers, and select committees and individual members in Parliament. This is affecting both the content of legislation and the way in which scrutiny of government is conducted.[85] If it cannot yet be said that the influence is pervasive, it is at least significant and growing. The main constraint is the government's unwillingness to accept that economic, social, and cultural rights can impose immediate, binding, and justiciable obligations on the UK,[86] but this may change over time. This use of international standards is fully consistent with parliamentary democracy. When used within Parliament, the standards merely help to inform debate rather than foreclose it. When judges look to international standards as guides to the implementation of legislation, they do so on the assumption that legislation is to be given effect compatibly with the UK's international obligations (in the absence of a clear indication to the contrary). Neither this nor any effect on the common law can limit or extend either the UK's international obligations or the freedom of the Queen in Parliament to legislate inconsistently with those obligations for the purpose of municipal law.[87]

JUDGES AS COMPARATISTS AND INTERNATIONALISTS

The judiciary too is a channel for allowing foreign influences into national public law systems. Judges in many countries round the world have a keen interest in foreign and international public law standards, including—but not limited to—human rights. In many common law jurisdictions they consider and draw illumination from public law judgments of courts elsewhere in the world. Judges do not simply adopt solutions or interpretations which have found favour elsewhere. The differences between constitutional and political structures in different countries make that undesirable: there may be no certainty that the solutions would fit a local context. Instead, they find it helpful to see how courts in different constitutional traditions have conceptualized and analysed the conflicting interests relevant to public law problems. This can help to crystallize issues and suggest approaches without dictating an outcome. Courts in the UK regularly use comparative law as a source of ideas for developing the common law and interpreting human rights.[88] Senior British judges have long been familiar with different constitutional and human rights arrangements through sitting regularly as members of the Judicial Committee of the Privy Council on public law appeals.

---

[85] See e.g. Lord Lester of Herne Hill, QC, 'Parliamentary Scrutiny of Legislation under the Human Rights Act 1998' [2002] *EHRLRev* 432; David Feldman, 'The Impact of Human Rights on the Legislative Process' (2004) 25 *Stat L Rev.* 91; Janet Hiebert, 'Parliamentary Review of Terrorism Measures' (2005) 58 *MLR* 676; Janet Hiebert, 'Interpreting a Bill of Rights: The Importance of Legislative Rights Review' [2005] *BJPS* 235; Carolyn Evans and Simon Evans, 'Legislative Scrutiny Committees and Parliamentary Conceptions of Human Rights' [2006] *PL* 785.

[86] See n. 54.   [87] See Feldman, 'Sovereignties in Strasbourg'.

[88] For a critical analysis of the uses made of comparative law, see Mads Andenas and Duncan Fairgrieve, '"There Is a World Elsewhere" – Lord Bingham and Comparative Law' in Mads Andenas and Duncan Fairgrieve (eds.), *Tom Bingham and the Transformation of the Law: A Liber Amicorum* (2009), 831–66.

Interaction with academics also encourages judges to take an interest in comparative law. Judges regularly participate in academic seminars and conferences concerning international and comparative public law. The Judicial College increasingly involves academics in judicial discussions and seminars. A growing number of senior judges had previous experience as legal academics.

Senior judges in different jurisdictions communicate extensively with each other, building up personal friendships and professional links through judicial colloquia and email. The internet offers access to a huge archive of legal materials from many jurisdictions.[89] The Law Commission and other bodies entrusted with the task of law reform now routinely undertake comparative research on the areas of law under review. English judges have also become far readier than before to make use of international legal materials in their judgments, including opinions, recommendations, and resolutions of experts and international bodies that do not bind states in public international law. This 'soft law' influences outcomes by establishing a normative framework which tends to favour one outcome of the 'hard law' dispute over another. In England and Wales, judges sometimes assume that its appropriateness is self-evident, but may in many cases be able to justify it on the ground that it represents customary international law. Where that is so, it is tenable to argue that treaty obligations should be interpreted in the light of the matrix of international obligations within which they operate, and 'if, and to the extent that, development of the common law is called for, such development should ordinarily be in harmony with the UK's international obligations and not antithetical to them'.[90] This open intellectual atmosphere, influenced by judges' growing familiarity with international and comparative methods through their work with the Human Rights Act 1998, various commercial law conventions, and other sources, is likely to grow stronger. Judges will be keen to compare techniques of constitutional reasoning and hear how courts elsewhere approach such matters as the interpretation of legislation so as to make it compatible with human rights.

This approach offers benefits, but it can be taken too far if, without constitutional authority, one makes comparative legal methods a judicial duty rather than an optional aid. For example, in *Lange* v. *Atkinson and Australian Consolidated Press NZ Ltd*[91] David Lange, a former prime minister of New Zealand, sued for libel in both New Zealand and Australia in respect of a magazine article criticizing his performance as a politician and suggesting that he suffered from selective memory loss. The defendants pleaded, among other defences, that the article was 'political expression' and, as such, entitled to privilege against liability. They also pleaded qualified privilege (which protects people from liability for libel if they act pursuant to a duty to bring the

---

[89] See A.-M. Slaughter, 'A Global Community of Courts' (2003) 44 *Harvard International Law Journal* 191.

[90] *A* v. *Secretary of State for the Home Department (No. 2)* [2005] UKHL 71, [2006] 2 AC 221 (HL), at [27], *per* Lord Bingham of Cornhill; see also [28]–[29]. See further e.g. cases on the implications for law in the UK of allegations of torture abroad: *Jones* v. *Ministry of the Interior of the Kingdom of Saudi Arabia (Secretary of State for Constitutional Affairs and others intervening)* [2006] UKHL 26, [2007] 1 AC 270 (HL).

[91] [2000] 1 NZLR 257 (PC).

matters to the attention of the intended recipients, and do not act maliciously). In the Australian proceedings, the High Court of Australia decided that common law qualified privilege protected communications to the public of information, opinions, and arguments relating to governmental and political matters, as long as the publishers proved that they had acted reasonably.[92] In the New Zealand proceedings, however, the Court of Appeal held that the publications attracted qualified privilege, but, unlike the High Court of Australia, held that at common law in New Zealand, only malice could deprive the publishers of the privilege, so the reasonableness of the publishers' conduct was irrelevant.[93]

Mr Lange appealed to the Privy Council against the decision of the Court of Appeal. Before the Privy Council could deliver its judgment, the House of Lords ruled on the same issue in *Reynolds* v. *Times Newspapers Ltd*, an unrelated but similar libel action. The House held that at common law in England and Wales a publication was not privileged merely because it was about governmental or political matters. The publisher had to show that there was a duty to publish the material to its intended recipients (or, to put it another way, that publication was in the public interest).[94]

Giving judgment subsequently on Mr Lange's appeal, the Privy Council noted the differences between the Australian, New Zealand, and English approaches, and accepted that 'striking a balance between freedom of expression and protection of reputation calls for a value judgment which depends upon local political and social conditions'. Furthermore, 'there is a high content of judicial policy in the solution of the issue raised by this appeal; . . . different solutions may be reached in different jurisdictions without any faulty reasoning or misconception . . .; and . . . within a particular jurisdiction the necessary value judgment may best be made by the local courts'. Nevertheless, the Privy Council sent the case back for a further hearing in New Zealand because the Court of Appeal had not had the opportunity to consider the Law Lords' decision in *Reynolds* before making its decision.[95]

This comes close to imposing a duty on top common law courts to have regard to (though not to follow) each other's leading decisions. Yet the decision does not explain the legitimate basis for having regard to foreign authorities as guides to developing one's own public law, let alone justify allowing an appeal in order to force another court to do so.

On constitutional grounds, the decision is hard to justify. Unstructured picking and choosing between sources can undermine or evade the filters which, for good constitutional reasons, constrain foreign influences on domestic legal systems. There has been heated disagreement in the USA about the propriety of taking account of

---

[92] *Lange* v. *Australian Broadcasting Corporation* (1997) 189 CLR 520 (HC of Australia).

[93] *Lange* v. *Atkinson and Australian Consolidated Press NZ Ltd* [1998] 3 NZLR 424 (CA of New Zealand).

[94] [2001] 2 AC 127 (HL). On the meaning of a duty to publish, see now *Jameel (Mohammed)* v. *Wall Street Journal Europe Sprl* [2006] UKHL 44, [2007] 1 AC 359 (HL).

[95] *Lange* v. *Atkinson and Australian Consolidated Press NZ Ltd* [2000] 1 NZLR 257 (PC). For the further proceedings in the Court of Appeal of New Zealand, see [2000] 3 NZLR 385.

either international law standards which do not form part of municipal law in the USA or decisions of courts in other common law countries. American judges are comfortable with comparative law techniques, as federal law must take account of dozens of state legal systems and constitutions, but some have challenged the legitimacy of relying on international developments when taking US constitutional jurisprudence in a new direction. In *Atkins* v. *Virginia*[96] the US Supreme Court, in a footnote to the majority judgment of Stevens J, adverted in passing to the fact that 'within the world community, the imposition of the death penalty for crimes committed by mentally retarded offenders is overwhelmingly disapproved' as evidence for an evolving standard of decency making such punishment cruel and unusual, and so contrary to the Eighth Amendment to the US Constitution.[97] The dissent by Rehnquist CJ (in which Scalia and Thomas JJ joined) argued that only standards within the USA, evidenced by federal and state legislation and decisions of juries, were relevant when deciding whether a punishment is cruel and unusual for constitutional purposes. It would be illegitimate to decide US constitutional law by reference to foreign standards.

This does not mean that the dissentients are unaware of developments elsewhere. In *Lawrence* v. *Texas*,[98] the majority of the US Supreme Court held that there was no rational basis for a state law criminalizing homosexual sodomy. Scalia J's dissent (in which Rehnquist CJ and Thomas J joined) referred to a Canadian decision[99] as part of a 'slippery slope' argument, suggesting that judicially striking down laws which discriminate against homosexuals could lead to the judicial imposition on the legislature of homosexual marriage, which would be unacceptable under the US Constitution. Where the national constitution does not authorize courts to draw on foreign decisions, it may (as Rehnquist CJ pointed out in *Atkins* v. *Virginia*) be difficult to justify being guided from elsewhere in interpreting one's own constitution. As aids to articulating issues and becoming aware of possible approaches, not to mention a state's international obligations, comparative and international studies are hard to better, but in the USA, unlike most other jurisdictions, the matter is being approached as one of constitutional principle.[100]

It is rare for a codified constitution either to authorize or to prohibit courts taking account of international legal standards or judgments of foreign or international tribunals when deciding municipal public law cases, but the 1996 Constitution of the Republic of South Africa is an exception. The Constitution is an outward-looking

---

[96]   536 US 304 (2002).

[97]   Ibid., n. 21 of the judgment, referring to the Brief for the European Union as *Amicus Curiae* in *McCarver* v. *North Carolina*, O.T. 2001, No. 00–1727, 4.

[98]   539 US 558 (2003), overruling *Bowers* v. *Hardwick* 478 US 186 (1986).

[99]   *Halpern* v. *Toronto*, 2003 WL 34950 (Ontario CA).

[100]   See e.g. *Printz* v. *United States*, 521 US 898 (1997); *Foster* v. *Florida*, 537 US 990 (2002); *Roper* v. *Simmons*, 125 S Ct 1183 (2005); Norman Dawson, 'The Relevance of Foreign Legal Materials in US Constitutional Cases: A Conversation between Justice Antonin Scalia and Justice Stephen Breyer' (2005) 3 *Int J Const Law* 519, available at http://www.wcl.american.edu; Ruth Bader Ginsburg, '"A Decent Respect to the Opinions of [Human] Kind": The Value of a Comparative Perspective in Constitutional Adjudication' (2005) 64 *Camb LJ* 575.

document. The formulation of the Constitution's Bill of Rights was heavily influenced by the examples of Canada, Ireland, India, and Nigeria, but the formulation of the rights and their constitutional status was a response to the particular needs of post-apartheid society. Section 39(1) of the 1996 Constitution provides that a court, tribunal, or forum, when interpreting the Bill of Rights:

a. must promote the values that underlie an open and democratic society based on human dignity, equality and freedom;
b. must consider international law; and
c. may consider foreign law.

As a result, the judgments of the Constitutional Court of South Africa are a valuable repository of learning on international and comparative human rights law, and their constitutional legitimacy is beyond question.

Courts in the UK are not required to be as systematic as those in South Africa in their use of international and foreign law, but UK judges have regularly used both international and comparative law.[101] Treaties can be used to interpret legislation, on the assumption that Parliament does not intend to violate the UK's international obligations unless an intention to do so appears clearly.[102] Where a statute is designed to give effect to international obligations, the assumption is that Parliament intended to achieve that and nothing else.[103] A treaty may give rise to a legitimate expectation, enforceable in administrative law, that the government will act in accordance with the UK's international obligations, although this has been criticized as a 'constitutional solecism' amounting 'to a means of incorporating the substance of obligations undertaken on the international plane into our domestic law without the authority of Parliament'.[104] Treaties may provide a guide to the requirements of public policy,[105] and can guide courts when exercising discretion in relation to such matters as levels of damages.[106] Where an administrative act or decision infringes a human right

---

[101] Historically, Roman law (including the notion of *ius gentium*) had an influence on parts of the common law: see Andrew Lewis, '"What Marcellus Says Is Against You": Roman Law and Common Law' in A. D. E. Lewis and D. J. Ibbetson (eds.), *The Roman Law Tradition* (1994), ch. 12; Daan Asser, '*Audi et Alteram Partem*: A Limit to Judicial Activity', ibid., ch. 13. Courts have also had regard to treaties, although only relatively recently in Scotland: see *T., Petitioner* 1997 SLT 734 (Court of Session (Inner House)), and see this chapter under heading 'Territoriality and International Law'.

[102] See e.g. *Waddington v. Miah* [1974] 1 WLR 683 (HL).

[103] See e.g. *R (on the application of Mullen) v. Secretary of State for the Home Department* [2004] UKHL 14, [2005] 1 AC 1 (HL), where the problem was to decide how the international treaty should be interpreted.

[104] For the origin of the application of the doctrine to human rights treaties, see *Minister for Immigration and Ethnic Affairs v. Teoh* (1995) 183 CLR 273 (HC of Australia); *R v. Secretary of State for the Home Department, ex parte Ahmed and Patel* [1998] INLR 570; *R v. Uxbridge Magistrates' Court, ex parte Adimi* [2001] QB 667 (DC), esp. at 686, *per* Simon Brown LJ. For the criticism, see *Behluli v. Secretary of State for the Home Department* [1998] Imm AR 407, 415, *per* Beldam LJ; *R (European Roma Rights Centre) v. Immigration Officer at Prague Airport (United Nations High Commissioner for Refugees intervening)* [2003] EWCA Civ 666, [2004] QB 211 (CA), at [99] and [101], *per* Laws LJ (the source of the quotation in the text), and see also Simon Brown LJ, at [51]. On appeal in the *Roma Rights* case, the House of Lords did not consider the issue.

[105] See e.g. *Blathwayt v. Baron Cawley* [1976] AC 397 (HL).

[106] See e.g. *John v. MGN Ltd* [1997] QB 586 (CA).

in international law, courts will anxiously scrutinize it, giving more attention than usual to the evidence, though not necessarily applying a higher than usual intensity of review, when deciding whether it is 'unreasonable'.[107]

However, UK courts maintain a certain reserve in the face of treaties. Unless a treaty has been transformed into municipal law by legislation, like parts of the ECHR, they do not usually consider that they are under any obligation to take account of them:[108] for the UK lawyer, the dualism of the constitution means that treaties generally still exist as part of a different system of law. In cases reported in 11 leading series of law reports for England and Wales in 2001 and 2002, only two international conventions apart from the ECHR were considered, in a total of six public law cases: the Convention and Protocol relating to the Status of Refugees, and the Convention on International Trade in Endangered Species of Wild Fauna and Flora.[109] UK courts clearly felt no obligation to delve into a wide range of treaties such as is imposed on the South African judiciary in cases on constitutional rights. In the first seven months of 2010, a broadly similar pattern emerged: apart from the ECHR, the Refugee Convention and its Protocol were considered in three cases, and in one of them the court also considered the Statute of the International Criminal Court.[110]

Direct application of foreign judgments in public law cases is also limited, though they may have persuasive authority. One must leave aside decisions which have to be considered as a matter of law, such as foreign judgments in certain cases in the Privy Council, decisions of the Court of Justice of the European Communities and the Court of First Instance, and those of the European Court of Human Rights. Studying *The Law Reports 2013 Cumulative Index*[111] reveals that no more than four foreign, public law judgments received, in the opinion of the editors of *The Law Reports*, significant consideration in just two cases in the courts of England and Wales reported in the main series of law reports in 2013. Both the domestic cases arose in private law. One concerned pleas of sovereign and diplomatic immunity in a claim concerning employment rights;[112] the other, direct and indirect discrimination on the ground of sexual orientation.[113] This is a significant drop since 2001, when an equivalent study revealed the very modest total of 13 foreign public law cases (12 decided by the Privy Council) receiving substantial consideration in 17 English public law cases. The decline may

---

[107] See e.g. *Bugdaycay* v. *Secretary of State for the Home Department* [1987] AC 514 (HL), and Paul Craig, 'Judicial Review and Anxious Scrutiny: Foundation, Evolution and Application' [2015] *PL* 60–78.

[108] See e.g. *R.* v. *Secretary of State for the Home Department, ex part Brind* [1991] 1 AC 696 (HL).

[109] *The Consolidated Index 2001–2002 to Leading Law Reports* (2002). 347.

[110] *Law Reports Cumulative Index August 2010* (2010), 144.

[111] Incorporated Council of Law Reporting for England and Wales, *The Law Reports Cumulative Index 2013* (2013), 162–225.

[112] *Wokuri* v. *Kassam* [2012] EWHC 105 (Ch), [2013] Ch 80, Newey J, at [13]–[26], discussing *Tabion* v. *Mufti* (1996) 73 F 3d 535, US CA, 4th Circuit, *Baoanan* v. *Baja* (2009) 627 F Supp 2d 155, US DC Southern District of New York, and *Swarna* v. *Al-Awadi* (2010) 622 F 3d 123, US CA, 2nd Circuit.

[113] *Black* v. *Wilkinson* [2013] EWCA Civ 820, [2013] 1 WLR 2490 (CA), at [22]–[23], *per* Lord Dyson MR, discussing *Rodriguez* v. *Minister of Housing of Government of Gibraltar* [2009] UKPC 52, [2010] UKHRR 144 (PC).

result from the increased dominance of the ECHR and EU in our public law, leaving little room for seeking guidance from the courts of Canada, Australia, New Zealand, and elsewhere in the Commonwealth.

That is not to say that foreign decisions have a minimal impact. Many more have been cited to and by courts, and might have influenced their thinking, without being expressly analysed, followed, or distinguished in judgments. Some public law principles have been shaped, at least partly, by foreign influences. The rule against anyone being a judge in his own cause derives from Roman law,[114] as does much else in the common law. Coercive interim remedies against the Crown entered English law after they came to be available to protect Community rights in EU law.[115] The principle of proportionality is significant in national law because of its importance in EU and ECHR law, and there has been some support for applying it in preference to *Wednesbury* unreasonableness, even in cases not involving EU law or Convention rights.[116] Whilst it is hard to see what role it could have except as a tool for evaluating a purported justification for interfering with a vested right, it offers another example of the capacity of the common law to develop eclectically and its taste for the exotic.

CONCLUSION

The internationalization of public law in the UK is a process of long standing and is continuing. It has benefits, but there are also risks. These are, first, that a borrowed solution will not be workable in a constitution with the special balance of power and democratic accountability found within the state, and, secondly, that reasoning relying on foreign thinking will not be regarded as a legitimate way of deciding public law cases under the constitution. The latter concern is evident in the Chief Justice's dissenting opinion in the US Supreme Court in *Atkins* v. *Virginia*, mentioned earlier. Where in the UK's constitutional rules are judges authorized to look for emerging standards abroad to guide UK public law? Statutes can authorize or require courts to look abroad, as the European Communities Act 1972 and the Human Rights Act 1998 show. But in the absence of such express provisions, there is a danger to the perceived constitutional legitimacy of judicial decisions if courts resort to foreign guidance without a legal basis in national law.

For these reasons, international influences must be treated with caution in developing the structures of an established state and constitutional arrangements. Filters

---

[114] See Asser, 'Audi et Alteram Partem'.

[115] *R* v. *Secretary of State for Trade and Industry, ex parte Factortame (No. 2)* (Case C-213/89) [1991] 1 AC 603 (CJEC and HL); see now e.g. *R* v. *Secretary of State for Health, ex parte Imperial Tobacco Ltd* [2002] QB 161 (CA).

[116] See e.g. *R (Daly)* v. *Secretary of State for the Home Department* [2001] 2 AC 532, 548–9, *per* Lord Cooke of Thorndon; *R (Alconbury Developments Ltd)* v. *Secretary of State for the Environment, Transport and the Regions* [2001] UKHL 23, [2003] 2 AC 295, at [51], *per* Lord Slynn of Hadley; *R (Association of British Civilian Internees: Far East Region)* v. *Secretary of State for Defence* [2002] EWCA Civ 473, [2003] QB 1397, at [34]–[37].

are needed. If the relationship between national and international legal planes is not defined in a constitutional document (such as South Africa's 1996 Constitution) or statute, a case-by-case approach can lead to distinct oddities. We can conclude with two questions about the UK to illustrate this. First, how well are the fundamental values of representative democracy, executive accountability to Parliament, and parliamentary sovereignty protected against the inappropriate introduction to municipal law (either by the executive or by judges) of obligations derived from international law or EU law? Secondly, why do UK judges seem more receptive to foreign judicial developments than to international treaties? One could argue that treaty obligations binding the UK in international law impose standards which should be respected by all organs of the state, including courts, and that there can be no justification in terms of UK constitutional law for having regard to judgments of foreign courts in jurisdictions which have no current constitutional link to the UK. This distinction is recognized by the Constitution of South Africa: there is a duty to consider treaties, but no duty to consider foreign judgments, in cases on constitutional rights. It will be interesting to see whether the influence of the ECHR and the European Court of Human Rights under the Human Rights Act 1998, ss. 1 and 2, bringing with it other treaties which the European Court of Human Rights uses to interpret the ECHR, will gradually lead UK courts to give greater weight to a range of treaties than they presently feel able to do. It will also be interesting to see whether political furore surrounding a small number of Strasbourg decisions of which some politicians disapprove, notably concerning whether prisoners should be allowed to vote and whether the UK should be allowed to remove suspected terrorists to countries where they face the prospect of torture and other violations of their rights, will lead to political action to remove the UK from the authority of Strasbourg and other international human rights bodies. It needs to be reiterated, however, that international institutions like the Strasbourg Court exercise authority over the UK because the UK has repeatedly bound itself by treaty to accept their rulings (an exercise of, rather than interference with, national sovereignty), and that has nothing to do with the legislative sovereignty of the Queen in Parliament or the political sovereignty of the UK's electorate, which rely on municipal, particularly constitutional, law and cannot be reduced by international law.[117]

FURTHER READING

ALLISON, JOHN W. F., 'Transplantation and Cross-fertilisation in European Public Law' in Jack Beatson and Takis Tridimas (eds.), *New Directions in European Public Law* (1998), ch. 12

BELL, J., 'Mechanisms for Cross-fertilisation of Administrative Law in Europe' in Jack Beatson and Takis Tridimas (eds.), *New Directions in European Public Law* (1998), ch. 11

BREWER-CARRÍAS, A. R., 'Constitutional Implications of Regional Economic Integration' in John Bridge (ed.), *Comparative Law facing the 21st Century* (2001), 675–752, on the way in

---

[117] See Feldman, 'Sovereignties in Strasbourg'.

which integration of markets between states depends on and in turn influences national constitutional structures and rules.

CHIGARA, B., 'Pinochet and the Administration of International Criminal Justice' in Diana Woodhouse (ed.), *The Pinochet Case: A Legal and Constitutional Analysis* (2000), ch. 7, on the interaction of Treaties, peremptory norms of customary international law, and the criminal law.

DUPRÉ, C., *Importing the Law in Post-Communist Transitions: The Hungarian Constitutional Court and the Right to Human Dignity* (2003), esp. ch. 2 on the importation by nascent or re-nascent states of constitutional law and constitutional values from other systems.

ELLIS, E. (ed.), *The Principle of Proportionality in the Laws of Europe* (1999), for essays on the use of a single public law principle in a variety of legal systems.

EUROPEAN REVIEW OF PUBLIC LAW (2006) 18(1) (Spring) 25–653 contains papers derived from a valuable colloquium of the European Group of Public Law in 2005 on the internationalization of public law, including general surveys and studies of particular European jurisdictions.

FATIMA, S., *Using International Law in Domestic Courts* (2005), for full consideration of the various ways in which municipal legal systems can take account of different kinds of public international law.

FELDMAN, D., 'The Role of Constitutional Principles in Protecting International Peace and Security through International, Supranational and National Legal Institutions' in Claudia Geiringer and Dean R. Knight (eds.), *Seeing the World Whole: Essays in Honour of Sir Kenneth Keith* (2008), 17–47, examines the relationship between UN Security Council resolutions under UN Charter, Chapter VII and national constitutional law. (A slightly earlier version can be found at (2008) 6(1) *New Zealand Journal of Public International Law* 1–33.)

FELDMAN, D., 'Sovereignties in Strasbourg' in Richard Rawlings, Peter Leyland, and Alison L. Young (eds.), *Sovereignty and the Law: Domestic, European, and International Perspectives* (2013), ch. 12, on the relationship between human rights treaty bodies in international law and legislative and democratic sovereignty in municipal politics and law.

HENKIN, L., ET AL., *International Law: Cases and Materials* (3rd edn, 1993), ch. 3, on the relationship between public international law and municipal law.

SMITH, E., 'Give and Take: Cross-fertilisation of Concepts in Constitutional Law' in Jack Beatson and Takis Tridimas (eds.), *New Directions in European Public Law* (1998), ch. 8.

ZINES, L., *Constitutional Change in the Commonwealth* (1991), ch. 1, on the development of the constitutional orders of Australia, Canada, and New Zealand towards autonomy from the UK.

USEFUL WEBSITES

Foreign and Commonwealth Office: **http://www.fco.gov.uk**
The website of the Foreign and Commonwealth Office includes a link to an Official Documents page, which allows further links to useful information, including an explanation of UK treaty practice and procedure, a Treaty Enquiry Service giving access to a searchable database of treaties to which the UK is a party, and the texts of the treaties.

United Nations: **http://www.un.org**

The United Nations website provides (among much other information and material) the text of the UN Charter, information about the working of the institutions of the United Nations including the General Assembly and the Security Council, the texts of many international treaties, and information about international tribunals.

Venice Commission: **http://www.venice.coe.int**

This website, maintained by the European Commission for Democracy through Law (the 'Venice Commission') under the auspices of the Council of Europe, offers a wealth of material, including reports, recommendations, and amicus curiae opinions, together with summaries of significant decisions of, and links to, constitutional courts and other courts with similar jurisdictions in Europe and elsewhere.

Virtual Institute of the Max Planck Institute for Comparative Public Law and International Law: **http://www.mpil.de/ww/en/pub/news.cfm**

This website offers both valuable documentation and links to many other useful sources.

World Legal Information Institute: **http://www.worldlii.org**

The website of the World Legal Information Institute provides links to web-based sources on international and national law throughout the world. It includes decisions of international tribunals as well as constitutional texts and decisions of national courts.

Yale University Law School's Comparative Administrative Law Blog: **http://blogs.law.yale. edu/blogs/compadlaw**

This is an interesting website with information about developments in many jurisdictions.

PART II

THE INSTITUTIONAL CONTEXT

Editorial note

The chapters in this part of the book are concerned with institutional matters.

Chapters 6, 7, and 8 focus on institutional reform at UK level. Parliament itself has been going through a period of reform, particularly of the procedures and working practices of the House of Commons. Since 2010 the powers of backbenchers in the House of Commons in relation to their party whips and to the government have been increased by reforms to the arrangements relating to select committees and control of the agenda for backbench business. Norton shows how that House is becoming more assertive in its relations with the government.

The committee structure in the House of Lords has also been going through changes. In particular the Constitution Committee is enhancing its role in the scrutiny of bills and draft bills. It has however proved difficult to achieve consensus in Parliament for reform of the membership, save to make retirement possible and to provide for the expulsion of members convicted of criminal offences.

The conduct of government has been altered in many significant ways under the coalition agreement that was entered into after the general election in 2010, and in response to the devolution of powers to Scotland, Wales, and Northern Ireland. These are among the foci of Rawlings' discussion in chapter 7. In effect a 'New Union' mindset needs to develop to take account of the devolved aspect of the UK constitution.

The system of justice has been changed in significant ways since the Constitutional Reform Act 2005 and under the Coalition government. These are the themes of chapter 8. The role of the Lord Chancellor has become controversial in the light of cuts in legal aid and proposals to change the rules for access to judicial review to reduce the jurisdiction of the courts. Le Sueur suggests that a 'blended' approach to the relations between the judges and politicians would be likely to produce better policy outcomes.

Chapter 9 considers devolution and it effects both at devolved and at UK level. These are widespread and complex particularly in the light of the Scottish independence referendum of September 2014 and the 'vow' of UK party leaders to devolve more powers to Scotland in the event of a 'no' vote. This is currently being put in place. In consequence issues as to decentralization in England and the representation of England in the legislative and governmental processes have risen up the political agenda and are currently under consideration.

Finally in this part, chapter 10 focuses on local government, which has historically lacked formal constitutional recognition or strong autonomy from central government. As Leigh notes in this chapter, successive governments over the last twenty years have attempted to reform and reinvigorate local democracy after decades of decline, with mixed results. The Coalition government's policy of localism is the latest such reform initiative, while the aftermath of the Scottish referendum has triggered a debate about regionalism and the need to decentralize powers. It remains to be seen how the position of local government with the UK's constitutional system continues to evolve in the years ahead.

6

PARLIAMENT: A NEW ASSERTIVENESS?

Philip Norton (Lord Norton of Louth)

SUMMARY

Parliament fulfils functions that are long-standing, but its relationship to government has changed over time. It has been criticized for weakness in scrutinizing legislation, holding government to account, and voicing the concerns of the people. Despite changes in both Houses in the twentieth century, the criticisms have persisted and in some areas Parliament has seen a constriction in its scope for decision-making. The twenty-first century has seen significant steps that have strengthened both Houses in carrying out its functions, the House of Commons in particular acquiring new powers. Members of both Houses have proved willing to challenge government. Parliament has seen a greater openness in contact with citizens. It remains a policy-influencing legislature, but a stronger one than in the preceding century.

Parliament has its origins in the thirteenth century. It has developed over the centuries, though its core functions developed within the first two centuries of its existence. Knights and burgesses were summoned in order to approve the King's request for additional taxation. Granting supply, that is, money, was core to its existence. However, Parliament used its power of supply to ensure that petitions were accepted by the King. These were presented by the King's subject for a redress of grievances and Parliament began to make voting supply conditional on petitions being granted. The first known instance of this was early in the fourteenth century.[1] The petitions developed into statutes. These required the approval of the Commons, Lords, and monarch, and were separate from ordinances, which were orders promulgated solely by the monarch. Statutes soon came to dominate and in the fifteenth century the task of writing them passed from the King's scribes to Parliament.

---

[1] Albert B. White, *The Making of the English Constitution 449–1485* (1908), 369.

There were various clashes between monarch and Parliament, not least in the sixteenth and seventeenth centuries, resulting in a civil war and later the Glorious Revolution of 1688–9, when the King was forbidden by the Bill of Rights 1689 from making law without the consent of Parliament. Parliament was thus central to the law-making process, but nonetheless continued to look to the monarch to come forward with proposals for approval. The onus for determining matters of state remained with the Crown.

From this, various generalizations can be drawn that remain germane to understanding Parliament in the twenty-first century. The key characteristic is that it is a reactive legislature. For most of its history, it has looked to the executive—initially the monarch, but, from the eighteenth century onwards, the King's ministers—to bring forward measures of public policy for it to consider.

Law *making*, in the sense of initiating and drafting measures of public policy, has thus not been the defining function of Parliament. Rather, as with other legislatures, its defining function has been that of assenting to measures of public policy.[2] However, before giving (or withholding) its assent, it has debated those measures. It has also given voice to the grievances of the monarch's subjects. These functions have provided the basis of parliamentary activity over the centuries. They have developed or been refined, but they have remained at the heart of the political system.

Although the functions have largely endured, the nature of the relationship between Parliament and the executive has changed. Leadership by the monarch has given way to leadership by ministers heading a major political party. The dominance of political parties has been facilitated by the achievement of a universal suffrage. Virtual representation has given way to a representative democracy, MPs being elected by citizens aged 18 and over.[3] The nineteenth century saw not only the widening of the franchise, but also the outlawing of electoral malpractices. The twentieth century saw a significant change in the nature of membership, partly a product of the payment of MPs and also the emergence of a working-class party in the form of the Labour Party.[4]

Parliament has often been perceived as a subordinate and at times ineffectual body. It was often seen in the twentieth century as having declined in power, the growth of mass-membership political parties acting as conduits for the transfer of decision-making power from Parliament to the executive. This perception was not confined to the United Kingdom. It was seen as part of an international phenomenon. The perception was also arguably overstated. It was not clear that there had been any significant shift of power from Parliament to the executive. Rather, the shift had been from monarch to the King's ministers assembled in Cabinet. That was the most significant effect of the growth of the franchise and mass-membership parties. Before the nineteenth century, royal patronage and bribery had usually ensured Parliament acceded to the King's wishes. From the nineteenth century onwards, it was political parties that delivered cohesive voting and ensured the ministry got its measures through Parliament.

---

[2] Philip Norton, 'General Introduction' in Philip Norton (ed.), *Legislatures* (1990), 1.
[3] See David Judge, *Representation: Theory and Practice in Britain* (1999).
[4] See Michael Rush, *The Role of the Member of Parliament Since 1868: From Gentlemen to Players* (2001).

Perceptions, however, persisted and the two Houses were the subject of criticisms and proposed reforms throughout the twentieth century. Both Houses were chamber-oriented bodies, often sitting for only a part of each year, with members frequently being part-time and with the executive getting its business without undue difficulty. The reputation of Parliament was enhanced during the Second World War, when both Houses continued to meet and to scrutinize the wartime government, but this was the exception and not the rule.[5] The growth of government and the welfare state led to a growth in the volume of legislation. The growth of the state also increased the burden on individual MPs, constituents having greater contact than before with public bodies. Collectively and individually, the burden on MPs increased, but was not matched by a capacity to cope with the demands. The negative perception was encapsulated in the 1964 book by the pseudonymous authors, Hill and Whichelow, *What's Wrong with Parliament?*[6] The view was not confined to observers. 'Well, it's dead', declared one MP in 1963, 'power has now by-passed the House of Commons'.[7] This view, that there was something wrong with Parliament, was an enduring feature of the century.

It endured despite changes within Parliament. The House of Lords underwent major reform, primarily but not exclusively in 1958 and 1999. The Life Peerages Act 1958 introduced the concept of life peerages, enabling individuals to be ennobled solely for their own lifetime. This facilitated bringing into the House people who otherwise would not have accepted peerages. Life peerages helped contribute to a reawakening of the House.[8] The House of Lords Act 1999 removed over 500 hereditary peers from membership, retaining only 92 in the House, of whom 90 were elected by the House or the political groupings in the House. The two Acts transformed the House, which become a much more active, and assertive chamber, engaging in detailed scrutiny of legislation and—like the Commons—becoming a more specialized body through the use of investigative committees.

The House of Commons saw not only improvements in the resources made available to MPs, but also in its own structures and procedures. The most significant reform of the latter half of the century was the introduction of departmental select committees in 1979.[9] These provided the House with the means for more detailed and consistent

---

[5] Philip Norton, 'Winning the War, But Losing the Peace: The British House of Commons during the Second World War'(1998) 4(3) *The Journal of Legislative Studies* 33–51.

[6] Andrew Hill and Anthony Whichelow, *What's Wrong with Parliament?* (1964). See, for other literature, Philip Norton, *The Commons in Perspective* (1981), 201–4.

[7] Quoted in Ronald Butt, *The Power of Parliament* (1967), 10.

[8] Nicholas Baldwin, 'The House of Lords: Behavioural Changes' in Philip Norton (ed.), *Parliament in the 1980s* (1985), 107–8.

[9] See e.g. Gavin Drewry (ed.), *The New Select Committees* (revised edn, 1989); Derek Hawes, *Power on the Back Benches? The Growth of Select Committee Influence* (1993); Michael Jogerst, *Reform in the House of Commons* (1993); David Natzler and Mark Hutton, 'Select Committees: Scrutiny à la Carte' in Philip Giddings (ed.), *The Future of Parliament: Issues for a New Century* (2005); and Andrew Hindmoor, Philip Larkin, and Andrew Kennon, 'Assessing the Influence of Select Committees in the UK: The Education and Skills Committee, 1997–2005' (2009) 15 *The Journal of Legislative Studies* 71–89.

scrutiny of government departments. It enabled not only greater specialization by the House, but also by its members. It provided a new agenda-setting capacity—the committees determined their own agenda—and a means of informing the House independent of government. They contributed to destroying the government's near monopoly as a supplier of information to Parliament.

Structural changes were accompanied by changes in behaviour. MPs became more independent in their voting behaviour. The high point of party loyalty was the 1950s. The period from the 1970s onwards saw MPs willing to vote against their own side more often, in greater numbers, and with greater effect than before.[10] This independence resulted on occasion in government being defeated in the division lobbies. Defeat in the division lobbies also became a feature of the House of Lords. A Tory-dominated hereditary House was not afraid to frequently defeat a Labour government, but the Tory government of Margaret Thatcher regularly suffered defeats at the hands of their lordships.[11] The frequency of defeat was less than under a Labour government, but nonetheless more extensive than that seen in the Commons.

Both Houses also became better resourced and more visible. Each voted to admit the television cameras. Televising proceedings began in the Lords in 1985 and in the Commons in 1989. People could now watch parliamentarians in action.

However, despite these changes, the perception of Parliament appeared not to improve. Indeed, the televising of proceedings in the Commons may have contributed to the negative perception. The disproportionate coverage accorded prime minister's question time reinforced public perceptions of adversarial politics and what amounted to almost yobbish behaviour by MPs.[12] If the collective behaviour of MPs contributed to a poor public perception, then so too did the behaviour of individual MPs. In the 1990s, media stories of MPs accepting money for tabling parliamentary questions—the 'cash for questions' scandal—enhanced public perceptions that MPs were in politics for personal gain rather than public service. In the wake of the scandal, surveys showed that most people questioned thought that MPs were in politics for personal gain. A 1994 MORI poll found that 64 per cent of those questioned thought that 'most' MPs made lots of money by using public office improperly (up from 46 per cent in 1985) and 77 per cent agreed that 'most MPs care more about special interests than they care about people like you'. New rules were introduced, a code of conduct instigated, and a Parliamentary Commissioner for Standards appointed.

In the event, any good work done by the reforms of the 1990s were swept away in 2009 by media revelations of the expenses claimed by MPs.[13] Some members were

---

[10] Philip Norton, *Dissension in the House of Commons 1945–74* (1975); Philip Norton, *Conservative Dissidents* (1978); Philip Norton, *Dissension in the House of Commons 1974–1979* (1980); Philip Norton, 'The House of Commons: Behavioural Changes' in Norton (ed.), *Parliament in the 1980s*, 212–47.

[11] Philip Norton, 'Introduction' in Norton (ed.), *Parliament in the 1980s*, 14.

[12] See Hansard Society, *Audit of Political Engagement 11: The 2014 Report* (2014), 62–73.

[13] Robert Winnett and Gordon Rayner, *No Expenses Spared* (2009).

found to have been utilizing expenses—that is, public money—for inappropriate purposes and, in some cases, to be making claims that were illegal. Some were subsequently jailed. Inappropriate claims by peers also became the subject of press scrutiny, leading to two peers being jailed. Both Houses also variously used their power of suspension (the Lords having resuscitated the power, not previously employed since the seventeenth century) in respect of members who contravened the rules of conduct.

These events affected Parliament's reputation. Wider constitutional changes also appeared to diminish Parliament's capacity to legislate and to protect the rights of the citizen.[14] Membership of the European Communities (now the European Union) limited its capacity to determine public policy that was to apply throughout the United Kingdom. By virtue of membership, European regulations had binding applicability in the United Kingdom. With devolution, law-making powers in areas other than those reserved to Westminster were vested in the Scottish Parliament, Northern Ireland Assembly, and, later, under the Government of Wales Act 2006, the National Assembly for Wales. Not only was the power to determine laws devolved, but the capacity to discuss matters affecting the devolved parts of the United Kingdom was limited in both Houses. A consequence of devolution was that the responsibilities of the Secretaries of State for Scotland, Wales, and Northern Ireland were limited and in 1999 the Commons adopted what *Erskine May* dubbed a 'self-denying ordinance'.[15] By standing order, the House provided that questions could not be tabled on matters for which responsibility had been devolved, unless they covered information which the UK government was empowered to seek from a devolved executive or related to legislative proposals, concordats between the UK government and devolved administrations, or matters in which UK ministers had taken an official interest. The formal remit of Parliament was thus restricted. It also had practical implications for the work of MPs returned from constituencies in Scotland, Wales, and Northern Ireland.

The enactment of the Human Rights Act 1998 was also perceived as Parliament passing the capacity to determine rights of the citizens to the courts. Although the senior courts were not empowered to strike down legislative provisions deemed incompatible with articles of the European Convention on Human Rights, they could issue declarations of incompatibility.[16] Though Parliament was not formally obliged to change the law to bring it into line with the judgments of the courts, it has done so on every occasion other than in respect of prisoner voting rights.[17]

---

[14] Philip Norton, *Parliament in British Politics* (2nd edn, 2013), 151–95.

[15] *Erskine May's Treatise on The Law, Privileges, Proceedings and Usage of Parliament* (24th edn, 2011), 190.

[16] Norton, *Parliament in British Politics*, 184–7.

[17] A declaration of incompatibility was made in *Smith* v. *Scott*, 2007 SLT 137 in respect of the blanket ban on prisoners having the right to vote, but ministers and MPs resisted acting on it. A draft Voting Eligibility (Prisoners) Bill was published in 2013 and considered by a joint committee of both Houses. The committee's report, recommending prisoners serving up to 12 months in prison be entitled to vote, was published in 2014, but by the end of the year had not been acted upon. Joint Committee on the Draft Voting Eligibility (Prisoners) Bill, *Report,* Session 2013–14, HC 103, HL Paper 924.

The use of referendums was also seen as a means of limiting Parliament through giving the final say on an issue to the people. Previously unknown to the constitution, referendums were utilized in the 1970s in different parts of the United Kingdom on the issue of devolution (and Northern Ireland remaining part of the United Kingdom) and throughout the UK on continued membership of the European Communities. They were again variously utilized after 1997 again on devolution and in the new century on a new electoral system for parliamentary elections—the second UK-wide referendum, but on this occasion a binding one[18]—and in Scotland on whether it should become an independent nation. Though some argued they complemented representative democracy, others contended that their use undermined the concept of parliamentary democracy.[19]

By the beginning of the twenty-first century, one could see the continuing relevance of the question posed by Hill and Whichelow. Constitutional changes were diminishing its capacity to legislate on the behalf of the people. Even where it retained the power to legislate, the perception was of an institution still too responsive to the wishes of the executive—what the government wanted, the government got—and with a membership more geared to its own interests, and the interests of party, than to the interests of the public. Though MPs individually were generally viewed in a positive light by their constituents, MPs collectively were not.[20] In surveys of professions that people would trust to tell the truth, MPs fared poorly.

Against this, there is an argument that Parliament is demonstrating a new assertiveness in its relationship to the executive and, indeed, developing its relationship with the public. Parliament remains at the nexus between government and the people. The distinguished parliamentarian, Enoch Powell, observed that Parliament was the body through which the people, through their representatives, spoke to the government and through which the government spoke to the people.[21] The institution is developing the means for listening to the people and ensuring that they are being heard.

Parliament has witnessed significant changes in the twenty-first century. The most notable in terms of the relationship between Parliament and the executive have been in respect of war-making, treaty-making, confidence, scrutinizing the executive, examining legislation, and in the work of the House of Lords. There have also been some notable developments in the relationship between Parliament and the public, with the institution becoming more open and outward-looking.

---

[18] The Parliamentary Voting System and Constituencies Act 2011 provided that the decision in the referendum was not to be advisory and in the event of a 'yes' vote the Alternative Vote was to be introduced for elections to the House of Commons.

[19] See Constitution Committee, House of Lords, Referendums in the *United Kingdom*, 12th Report, Session 2009–10, HL Paper 99.

[20] See Norton, *Parliament in British Politics*, 234–5.

[21] Enoch Powell, 'Parliament and the Question of Reform' (1982) 11(2) *Teaching Politics* 169.

PARLIAMENT–GOVERNMENT RELATIONS

When power passed from monarch to ministers, the use of prerogative power passed in effect to the prime minister. Prerogative powers were exercised formally by the Crown, but on the advice of the monarch's first minister. Prerogative powers are those powers which traditionally have been exercised by the monarch and have not been displaced by statute. They have given significant scope for the government to act independent of Parliament. These have encompassed the power to declare war, to ratify treaties, and to determine the dates of general elections within a maximum period stipulated by statute. All three have been affected fundamentally by statute or by parliamentary action.

The prerogative power to commit armed forces abroad remains, but its exercise has been constrained by the executive seeking parliamentary approval for such action, approval that in 2013 was not forthcoming. The power to ratify treaties has passed from the Crown to Parliament. The prime minister no longer determines when Parliament will be dissolved. Though the government continues to rest on the confidence of the House of Commons for its continuance in office, the means by which confidence is expressed has been modified by statute.

WAR-MAKING POWERS

One of the most important prerogative powers throughout history has been the war-making power. The Crown can commit armed forces to action abroad. This may encompass a declaration of war, as with the two world wars, or limited military engagement. Parliament has been informed usually of such action and been able to debate it, but the control, in so far as it exists, is retrospective and parliamentarians are reluctant usually to criticize military engagement when British troops are in action. Some engagement has been highly controversial, as with the invasion of the Suez Canal in 1956, but Parliament has not been in a position to prevent the prime minister taking such action as he or she thought necessary. Towards the end of the century, military action had been debated prior to the engagement of troops, most notably in respect of action to retake the Falkland Islands in 1982 and of UK involvement in the first Gulf War in 1991. In the latter case, military action had been discussed on a motion for the adjournment. Opponents of action forced it to a vote, losing by 534 votes to 54.[22] As MPs opposed to action had complained on the previous day, it was not a substantive motion—the House was being invited to discuss, but not to endorse, action—and could not be amended.

A major change was proposed during the premiership of Gordon Brown. He was keen to transfer a number of prerogative powers to Parliament. These formed part of his *Governance of Britain* agenda[23] and encompassed the war-making power.

---

[22] House of Commons Debates (Hansard), 15 January 1991, cols. 821–5.
[23] See Ministry of Justice, *The Governance of Britain*, Cm 7170, July 2007.

On 3 July 2007, he told the House of Commons that the government 'will now consult on a resolution to guarantee that on the grave issue of peace and war it is ultimately the House of Commons that will make the decision'.[24] However, as the Government White Paper on *War Powers and Treaties* declared:

> In seeking to give Parliament the final say in decisions to commit UK troops to armed conflict overseas, it is nevertheless essential that we do not undermine the ability of the executive to carry out its proper functions. The responsibility to execute such operations with minimum loss of British lives has to remain with the executive.[25]

The statement encapsulated the conundrum that faced those responsible for finding a form of words giving Parliament the capacity to say yes or no to engagement by British forces abroad, but leaving government with the flexibility deemed necessary to respond quickly to defend British interests and lives. The White Paper canvassed various options, including legislation, but in the event, no agreement was reached and no motion or bill brought before Parliament.

Rather, the practice has developed of the House of Commons being consulted, and if necessary voting, on government proposals to commit forces in action abroad. This is in line with the resolution of the House on 15 May 2007, supported by the government, 'That This House welcomes the precedents set by the Government in 2002 and 2003 in seeking and obtaining the approval of the House for its decisions in respect of military action against Iraq; is of the view that it is inconceivable that any Government would in practice depart from this precedent.'[26]

The precedents in 2002 and 2003 were in respect of war in Iraq. The Foreign Secretary, Jack Straw, believed that any decision to go to war should be approved by the House of Commons and, along with the Leader of the House of Commons (and former Foreign Secretary), Robin Cook, he persuaded Prime Minister Tony Blair that he should seek parliamentary approval before committing forces to action in Iraq.[27] The principal debate took place on 18 March 2003 and the motion supporting the government was carried by 412 votes to 149. The vote saw the largest rebellion by Labour MPs in post-war history, the motion being carried with the support of the Opposition. The key point, though, was that, as Tony Blair recorded, 'It was the only military action expressly agreed in advance by the House of Commons.'[28]

This set the basis for any future military engagement, at least where such engagement was contemplated and could be a matter of public debate. In 2013 the presumed use of chemical weapons against its citizens by the Assad regime in Syria generated calls for military action by the UK government. Parliament was recalled on 29 August 2013 to debate the use of force in Syria. A combination of a switch in the opposition's stance—expected initially to support the use of force—and opposition from a sizeable

---

[24] House of Commons Debates (Hansard), 3 July 2007, col. 816.
[25] Ministry of Justice, *War powers and treaties: Limiting executive powers*, Consultation Paper CP26/07, CM 7239, October 2007.
[26] House of Commons Debates (Hansard), 15 May 2007, col. 492.
[27] Jack Straw, *Last Man Standing* (2012), 375.   [28] Tony Blair, *A Journey* (2010), 428.

number of Tory MPs resulted in a government defeat. The House rejected an opposition amendment, but then proceeded to defeat the government motion supporting action by 285 votes to 272. Prime Minister David Cameron immediately accepted the outcome. 'It is very clear tonight that, while the House has not passed a motion, the British Parliament, reflecting the views of the British people, does not want to see British military action. I get that, and the Government will act accordingly.'[29]

The vote was important not only politically, but also constitutionally. The House of Commons had prevented Her Majesty's Government from engaging in military action. It was the most important defeat of the government on a matter of military involvement since the mid-nineteenth century, in other words since the emergence of party government in the United Kingdom. It also confirmed in the eyes of some commentators that it was now a convention that no government could embark on military action without first getting the endorsement of the House of Commons,[30] though such a status was not endorsed by Downing Street. In 2014, Prime Minister Cameron indicated he may be willing to authorize some military action in Iraq against Islamic State (IS) militants, 'if the UK were judged to be at risk', and seek retrospective, rather than prospective, approval from Parliament.[31]

TREATY-MAKING

Before 2010, treaties were negotiated by government and ratified by the Crown. In practice, most treaties were laid before Parliament under the 'Ponsonby Rule', dating from a statement in 1924 by junior Foreign Affairs minister, Arthur Ponsonby, and followed consistently by government since 1929. Under the rule, treaties were published and laid before Parliament as Command Papers and then 21 sitting days elapsed before ratification took place. Should a request be made to debate a treaty within the 21 days, the government acceded to the request. Both Houses also got to debate legislation that was necessary to give effect in UK law to treaty obligations. Parliament did not ratify the Treaty of Accession to the European Communities, for example, but it was necessary to enact the European Communities Act 1972 in order to give effect to obligations arising under the treaty. The same applied to subsequent European treaties. Such legislation was normally enacted prior to ratification to avoid any possibility of the UK being in breach of its international obligations.

Some parliamentary committees recommended that treaties, especially treaties with significant financial, legal, or territorial implications, should be subject to parliamentary

---

[29] House of Commons Debates (Hansard), 29 August 2013, cols. 1555–6.

[30] James Strong, 'Why Parliament Now Decides on War: Tracing the Growth of the Parliamentary Prerogative through Syria, Libya and Iraq', *The British Journal of Politics and International Relations*, forthcoming; Constitution Committee, House of Lords, *Constitutional Arrangements for the Use of Armed Force*, 2nd Report, Session 2013–14, HL 46.

[31] Sam Coates, 'We Can Bomb Jihadists without Asking MPs, Says Cameron', *The Times*, 2 September 2014, 1.

debate and approval.[32] The Brown government responded positively to such proposals and consulted on them as part of the *Governance of Britain* agenda. The result was
the displacement of the prerogative by statute through the Constitutional Reform and
Governance Act 2010. Part 2 of the Act provides that treaties shall be ratified if within
21 sitting days neither House has resolved that the treaty shall not be ratified. Provision
was made for exceptional cases, though ratification was prohibited if either House had
already resolved that the treaty should not be ratified. The government also accepted a
backbench amendment that a treaty had to be accompanied by an explanatory memorandum explaining the provisions of the treaty and the reasons for seeking ratification.[33] It
had become the practice to supply such memoranda, but this put it in on a statutory basis.

The change was formally more definitive than the change to the war-making power.
The Constitutional Reform and Governance Act transferred a convention to statute,
whereas parliamentary approval for committing forces in action acquired or was close
to acquiring the status of a convention. However, the latter was politically more significant. Putting the Ponsonby Rule in statute meant that about 30–35 treaties each year
fell within the purview of the law, but few treaties are of major political significance
and, under the Ponsonby Rule, a debate could have been triggered and, if both Houses
objected, it was unlikely ratification would have taken place. Either House could also
have refused to enact the legislation necessary to give effect in UK law to a treaty's provisions. The change in 2010 was nonetheless important in conferring on Parliament a
significant constitutional power.

CONFIDENCE

Her Majesty's Government rests on the confidence of the House of Commons for its
continuance in office. Until 2011, it was a convention of the constitution that if a government was defeated on a vote of confidence the prime minister either tendered the
resignation of the government or requested the dissolution of Parliament. The precedent was set in 1841 and was maintained thereafter. Three types of confidence vote
existed.[34] One was explicitly worded motions expressing confidence, or lack of it,
in the government. A second was on motions designated as confidence votes by the
prime minister. In the Second Reading debate on the European Communities Bill
in February 1972, for example, Prime Minister Edward Heath made clear that confidence attached to the vote. He informed the House that 'if this House will not agree to
the Second Reading of the Bill ... my colleagues and I are unanimous that in these circumstances this Parliament cannot sensibly continue'.[35] The third category comprised

---

[32] See e.g. Public Administration Select Committee, House of Commons, *Taming the Prerogative: Strengthening Ministerial Accountability to Parliament*, Fourth Report, Session 2003–4, HC 422.

[33] The author declares an interest as he was the peer responsible for the amendment.

[34] Philip Norton, 'Government Defeats in the House of Commons: Myth and Reality' [1978] *PL* 362–70.

[35] House of Commons: Official Report (Hansard), 17 February 1972, col. 752.

issues of such significance that they were regarded as implicit votes of confidence, such as the Queen's Speech and the Budget.

The government could suffer defeats on motions that were not matters of confidence and these did not engage the convention.[36] Between 1972 and 1979, the government suffered an exceptional 65 defeats in the division lobbies of the House of Commons,[37] but only the last of these—on 28 March 1979, when the House carried a motion of no confidence—triggered a general election.

As part of the negotiations between the Conservatives and the Liberal Democrats following the 2010 general election, a bill providing for fixed-term Parliaments was conceded by the Conservatives and included in the coalition agreement. A Fixed-term Parliaments Bill was subsequently introduced, although deviating somewhat from the terms of the coalition agreement. The bill provided for an early election if two-thirds of all members voted for it. It also stipulated that an early election was to take place if the government was defeated on a vote of confidence and if within 14 days of the defeat a new government could not be formed and gain the confidence on the House. The reference to losing a vote of confidence was ambiguous. There was no definition as to what constituted a vote of confidence. The bill was amended during its passage in the House of Lords to provide that the motion 'That this House has no confidence in Her Majesty's Government' had to be carried in order to engage the provision.[38]

The Fixed-term Parliaments Act 2011 took effect upon Royal Assent in September 2011. The effect was twofold in relation to the power of the prime minister. The first and intended effect was to deny the prime minister the power to determine the date of a general election at a time of his choosing, usually four or the full five years after the previous election. The second largely overlooked consequence was to remove the power to ensure the outcome of a particular vote by making it one of confidence. A prime minister could still announce a vote was one of confidence, but it would have no effect in terms of triggering an election if the vote was lost. The only sanction open to the prime minister would be to offer the resignation of the government. What would happen in those circumstances is unclear. The provisions of the Fixed-term Parliaments Act in respect of an early election would not be satisfied.

The effect of the Fixed-term Parliaments Act is thus to limit the powers of the prime minister, including in his relationship to the House of Commons. The government could only engineer an early election if it persuaded an MP to move a motion of no confidence in it and invite its own supporters to back it, a move considered not impossible but highly unlikely. It could facilitate an early election in a passive sense if it failed to vote against a motion of no confidence tabled by the Leader of the Opposition.

---

[36] Norton, 'Government Defeats in the House of Commons: Myth and Reality', 360–78.

[37] There were six in the 1970–4 Parliament, 17 in the Parliament of Feb.–Oct. 1974, and 42 in the Parliament of 1974–9. On those in the 1974 and 1974–9 Parliaments, see Norton, *Dissension in the House of Commons 1974–1979*, 491–3.

[38] See Philip Norton, 'From Flexible to Semi-fixed: The Fixed-term Parliaments Act 2011' (2014) 1(2) *Journal of International and Comparative Law* 203–20.

Again, the conditions in which a government would do so are difficult to contemplate: if the opposition was pursuing a motion of no confidence, the presumption is that it would do so where its prospects of winning a general election looked promising.

The Fixed-term Parliaments Act 2011 has thus affected substantially the relationship between the government and the House of Commons, though the full effects have yet to be fully realized. The most obvious area of uncertainty is in the unlikely, though not unprecedented, event of a government resigning without being defeated on a vote of confidence.[39]

SCRUTINIZING THE EXECUTIVE

The 2010 Parliament saw notable changes in how the House of Commons scrutinizes the executive. These encompassed both Select Committees and debates on the floor of the House. A number of MPs had been pressing for some time for a further strengthening of the House in its ability to scrutinize the executive. Various reform manifestos had been published, both by bodies outside and inside the House. However, the most notable changes occurred as a result of the expenses scandal of 2009.

The start of the twenty-first century had seen some expansion of scrutiny by select committees. A Joint Committee on Human Rights was established in 2001 and proved to be an active, and productive, body. It appears to have contributed to a greater rights culture on the part of both Houses.[40] References by MPs and peers to committee reports were notable in the 2005–10 Parliament, in the context of a marked increase of references to human rights in both Houses, but especially in the House of Lords.[41] The House of Lords also expanded its committee work, creating in 2001 a Constitution Committee and an Economic Affairs Committee, the former proving especially active in scrutinizing bills of constitutional significance as well as producing reports on a range of constitutional issues. It was especially influential in the 2010–15 Parliament in shaping debate on a number of key pieces of government legislation, including the Public Bodies Bill and the Fixed-term Parliaments Bill.

However, the most important changes occurred at the start of the 2010 Parliament. The genesis for reform has its roots in the expenses scandal. Prime Minister Gordon Brown described it as 'the biggest parliamentary scandal for two centuries'.[42] It reinforced the public's negative perceptions of politicians, dented MPs' morale and fed the belief that something had to be done to restore public trust. A Select Committee on Reform of the House of Commons was appointed, under Labour MP Tony Wright, and it quickly produced a report entitled *Rebuilding the House*.[43] Among its

---

[39] Arthur Balfour tendered his government's resignation in December 1905, the government having run out of steam and hoping to wrong-foot the Liberal opposition. See R. J. Q. Adams, *Balfour: The Last Grandee* (2007), 227; and A. K. Russell, *Liberal Landslide: The General Election of 1906* (1973), 34–5.

[40] Philip Norton, 'A Democratic Dialogue? Parliament and Human Rights in the United Kingdom' (2013) 21(2) *Asia Pacific Law Review* 141–66.

[41] Murray Hunt, Hayley Cooper, and Paul Yowell, *Parliaments and Human Rights* (2012), 25–6.

[42] Winnett and Rayner, *No Expenses Spared*, 349.

[43] Select Committee on Reform of the House of Commons, Rebuilding the House, *First Report*, Session 2008–9, HC 1117.

recommendations were that select committees should be strengthened and that the chairs should be elected by the House, and members by their respective parliamentary parties. It also proposed the creation of a House business committee to allocate business in government time and a backbench business committee to allocate backbench business, until then within the gift of the government.

The recommendations on select committees were approved by the House and then implemented at the beginning of the 2010 Parliament. Some committee chairs were hotly contested, including that of the Treasury Committee. The elections were by the Alternative Vote (AV), though in practice all chairs that were elected in contested elections triumphed in the first round. (As in previous Parliaments, parties agreed as to which parties should hold the chairs, divided proportionate to party strength in the House.) The elections had implications not only for the committees, but also for the patronage powers of the whips. Election meant that those wanting to chair committees now needed the support of fellow MPs, indeed MPs on both sides of the House, in order to secure election and not the endorsement of the whips. Previously, the whips had been able in effect to offer the chairs of select committees as rewards for good service or consolation prizes for those who had missed out on ministerial office. Now they had lost a significant patronage tool. Power shifted from the whips to backbench MPs. The same applied to membership of the committees. Those wanting to serve on a particular committee no longer needed to gain the endorsement of their party whips, but their fellow backbenchers. The focus of attention thus shifted paradigmatically. MPs collectively were in control.

The elections also served to give the committees a higher profile, both in the House and in the media. Those elected to chair committees enjoyed the kudos of election and the concomitant attribute of independence. They were not seen as party appointees. Some committees, and especially their chairs, gained a notable media profile. These included the Treasury Committee under Conservative MP Andrew Tyrie, the Home Affairs Committee under Labour MP Keith Vaz, and the Culture, Media and Sport Committee under Conservative MP John Whittingdale. Some committees undertook high-profile inquiries, summoning major public figures as witnesses. A number of the hearings attracted widespread media coverage, though not all were as successful as the committees may have wished.[44] Media magnate Rupert Murdoch had shaving foam pushed in his face by a member of the public when appearing before the Culture, Media and Sport Committee.

The profile of scrutiny by committee was also enhanced by the appointment in 2012 of a Parliamentary Commission on Banking Standards to consider professional standards and culture in the UK banking sector, lessons to be learned about corporate governance, transparency and conflicts of interest, and to make recommendations for legislative action. This was established as a ten-member joint committee, had a substantial support staff, and was empowered to work through panels, which could

---

[44] See Norton, *Parliament in British Politics*, 277–8.

comprise only one or two members. The 11 panels covered topics such as corporate governance, HBOS, mis-selling and cross-selling, and Financial Exclusion and Basic Bank Accounts. The commission was chaired by Andrew Tyrie, chair of the Treasury Committee, and it achieved an increased public profile when one of its members, Justin Welby, the Bishop of Durham, became the Archbishop of Canterbury. It proved highly productive, producing reports on banking reform, proprietary trading, and the collapse of HBOS, before publishing its final report, *Changing Banking for Good*, in 2013. Its work formed the basis of regulatory reform and banking legislation. As the government acknowledged in response to the Commission's final report, it 'strongly endorses the principal findings of the report and intends to implement its main recommendations'.[45]

There were also advances in post-legislative scrutiny. Post-legislative review of Acts began in 2008, which entailed government departments assessing whether Acts of Parliament, three to five years after enactment, achieved what they were intended to do.[46] The reviews were published and sent to the relevant Departmental Select Committee in the Commons, but the committees had little or no time to consider them. The House of Lords, however, began utilizing ad hoc committees to review Acts in particular areas. It set up committees to review adoption legislation, the Inquiries Act 2005, the Mental Health Capacity Act 2005, and extradition legislation.

The combined effect of these changes was to develop further the specialization of both Houses and to enhance, both qualitatively and quantitatively, the scrutiny of government. The committees engaged with government, affected interests, and achieved in some cases notable media coverage.

DEBATE

The work of both Houses was not only to subject the actions and proposals of government to scrutiny, but also to raise concerns of citizens and at times to fulfil an agenda-setting role, raising issues that had never before or not recently been on the political agenda. The established means of debate in both Houses was through debate in the chamber. In the Lords, peers could raise issues through Questions for Short Debate (previously known as Unstarred Questions) and balloted debates. Though the Government Whips' Office played a facilitating role in business, the House, as a self-regulating chamber, retained ultimate responsibility. The timetable was not wholly within the gift of government. Unlike in the Commons, there was formally no distinction between government and private members' time, though in practice most days were normally given over to government business. In response to pressure from peers, a Working Group on the Practices of the House was established and it recommended a range of changes. Responding to demands for greater control by backbenchers over

---

[45] *The Government's Response to the Parliamentary Commission on Banking Standards*, Cm 8661, July 2013, 5.
[46] Norton, *Parliament in British Politics*, 100–1.

business, the Leader of the House in 2013 arranged for more Questions for Short Debate to be taken in grand committee and also for greater use to be made of ad hoc committees, especially for post-legislative scrutiny.

However, the most notable reforms took place in the House of Commons. In 1999, the House had approved the creation of a parallel chamber, housed in the Grand Committee Room off Westminster Hall, but styled as sittings in Westminster Hall. Sittings in Westminster Hall can be held while the chamber is in session and any member can attend. They are employed to debate topics raised by private members—similar to the half-hour adjournment debates at the end of daily sittings (though the first debates are normally of 90 minutes in duration)—and select committee reports. Meetings are held on Tuesdays, Wednesdays, and Thursdays, and may also be held on some Mondays, and provide notable additional time to that available in the chamber for MPs to raise issues of concern. Though meetings are not usually well attended, they serve a useful purpose in enabling MPs to put matters on the public record and to ensure that there is a ministerial response.

The other major reform occurred in 2010 as a consequence of the recommendations of the Select Committee on Reform of the House of Commons. The House approved the recommendation for the creation of a Backbench Business Committee. The membership of the committee, like other select committees, is elected, though—unlike other committees—the election is sessional. The committee allocates backbench business on 35 days each session, 27 of them on the floor of the House and the rest in Westminster Hall. The committee proceeds by inviting MPs to put forward proposals for debate, taking into account the extent to which a proposal is supported, on a cross-party basis, by other MPs. It also has responsibility for considering whether to schedule for debate topics that have achieved 100,000 signatures through e-petitions. It has scheduled for debate subjects that the government may not have chosen and which may cause some embarrassment to it. Among topics selected in the first long session of 2010–12 was the conflict in Afghanistan, providing, for the first time, the opportunity for MPs to vote on the issue. It also scheduled debates, among other topics, on prisoner voting rights (proposed for debate to the committee by a senior Labour MP, Jack Straw, and a senior Conservative, David Davis), immigration, the Big Society, the future of pubs, banking reform, and holding a referendum on EU membership. Although the government decides on which days the debates will be held, removing from government the decision as to topics for debate represents a substantial shift of decision-making from government to the House. Some of the debates have been well attended, attracting more attention from backbenchers than the normal run of government business.

LEGISLATIVE SCRUTINY

Legislative scrutiny by the Commons has been identified by some commentators, and by members, as a weak, if not the weakest, part of parliamentary scrutiny.[47] 'Parliament

---

[47] See especially *Making the Law: The Report of the Hansard Society Commission on the Legislative Process* (1993).

is at its weakest', declared the Commission to Strengthen Parliament in 2000, 'in scru-tinising legislation. It needs new tools.'[48] Time in the Commons for considering bills is limited and has been constrained by the use of guillotine motions, imposing a time-table for the remaining consideration of a bill, and since 1997 by the use of timetable motions, time-tabling bills following Second Reading. Committee stage was seen as unproductive, government supporters being encouraged to be silent and anecdotally reported to use the occasion to get on with correspondence.

There were proposals to scrutinize bills in draft (pre-legislative scrutiny) and for the use of evidence-taking committees. Experiments with special standing committees (SSCs), which were empowered to receive evidence, had been seen as productive.[49] Pre-legislative scrutiny developed after 1997, with various government bills being published in draft and being sent to a select committee, or a joint committee, for pre-legislative scrutiny. The experience was seen as improving the quality of legis-lation, the government being more willing to listen to proposals for change prior to the formal introduction of the bill. Between 1997 and 2010, 76 bills were pub-lished in draft, though not all received pre-legislative scrutiny (either because they were published too late or because the relevant select committee was too busy). The Joint Committee on the Communications Bill in 2002 was indicative of what could be achieved: of 148 recommendations made in its report, 120 were accepted by the government. Though pre-legislative scrutiny creates additional pressure on parlia-mentary resources, and can create major time pressures if a bill is published late in a session, it is recognized as a valuable means of parliamentary scrutiny. There have been recommendations for it to be used routinely, rather than leaving it to the discre-tion of government.[50] However, the number has shown no underlying increase in the twenty-first century, though in the long session of 2010–12, the Coalition govern-ment published twelve bills in draft.

Another notable reform was achieved in 2006, when the House voted for the intro-duction of public bill committees, essentially to replace standing committees. Public bill committees are empowered, other than in certain circumstances (for example, when a bill comes from the Lords) to take written and oral evidence, before consid-ering amendments to the bill. The change represented a notable advance on the old standing committees.[51] Problems remain in that committees remain appointed afresh for each bill, witnesses tend to be selected because of the stance they are expected to take, and the time between taking evidence and reverting to the traditional format of considering amendments is constricted, limiting the opportunity to digest and uti-lize evidence effectively.[52] The government still manages to get its bills through, with

---

[48] *Strengthening Parliament: The Report of the Commission to Strengthen Parliament* (2000), 22.

[49] See *Making the Law: The Report of the Hansard Society Commission on the Legislative Process*, 75.

[50] Constitution Committee, House of Lords, *Parliament and the Legislative Process*, 14th Report, Session 2003-04, HL Paper 173-I.

[51] See Norton, *Parliament in British Politics*, 92.

[52] See Jessica Levy, 'Public Bill Committees: An Assessment. Scrutiny Sought; Scrutiny Gained' (2010) 63 *Parliamentary Affairs* 534–44.

amendments approved normally being government amendments. The committees, as Louise Thompson has shown, tend to be working harder, though with less obvious material gain. Nonetheless, as she notes, 'A much greater number of amendments are introduced by the government at the report stage in response to bill committees.'[53]

One other proposed change to the legislative process achieved particular visibility following the referendum on Scottish independence in September 2014. As a response to the West Lothian Question, the Conservative Party had previously pursued the possibility of 'English votes for English laws'—that is, measures that were exclusive to England (or England and Wales) being voted on in the House of Commons solely by MPs from English (or English and Welsh) constituencies, either at some or all stage of a bill's passage. The Coalition government established a Commission (the McKay Commission) to examine ways of achieving this. The Commission reported in 2013,[54] but no legislation or changes to Standing Orders were forthcoming. However, as discussed in chapter 9, the commitment by the principal parties to devolve more powers to Scotland spurred Prime Minister David Cameron, on the day after the referendum, to make an early morning statement supporting the proposal to make provision for 'English votes for English laws' and to establish a Cabinet Committee chaired by William Hague MP, Leader of the House, to examine how to proceed. The Committee reported in December 2014, outlining different options.

HOUSE OF LORDS

ACTIVITY

The House of Lords continued to become a more specialized body, making greater use, as we have seen, of select committees. It was notable also for its role in legislative scrutiny. This continued to occupy most of the time of the floor of the House and, increasingly, of grand committee. To facilitate its detailed scrutiny of bills, the House moved from taking the committee stage of most bills on the floor of the House to sending the less politically contentious bills to grand committee. The grand committee (similar to sittings in Westminster Hall) is a form of parallel chamber. The grand committee can meet while the chamber is in session. Any peer can attend and participate. This enables those peers interested only in particular parts of a bill to attend for discussion of those matters of concern to them. Sittings normally take place in the Moses Room, a dedicated committee room close to the chamber, though occasionally it meets in a normal committee room. No votes are taken in grand committee. As a result, only amendments that are not opposed are made at this stage. Any amendments to which

---

[53] Louise Thompson, 'More of the Same or a Period of Change? The Impact of Bill Committees in the Twenty-first Century House of Commons' (2013) 66(3) *Parliamentary Affairs* 477.

[54] McKay Commission, *Report of the Commission on the Consequences of Devolution for the House of Commons* (2013).

Table 1 Membership of the House of Lords, August 2014

Conservative	219
Labour	216
Cross-bench	180
Liberal Democrats	99
Bishops	26
Other parties	14
Non-affiliated	20
TOTAL	774

objections are made have to be held over until report stage. The use of grand committee has effectively created more time for the House to devote to scrutinizing legislation.

The House can claim to be effective in fulfilling its scrutiny function. More amendments are usually secured to bills in the Lords than they are in the Commons. Each session, anything between a few hundred to a few thousand amendments are secured to government bills. In the 2012–13 session, for example, 1,114 amendments were made. A record number of 4,761 amendments were achieved in the 1999–2000 session.

The capacity to influence legislation to this extent has been ascribed to the nature of the membership of the House and to the extent to which the House is prepared to carry amendments against the wishes of the government. The House has been characterized as a House of experience and expertise, members being appointed because of holding senior office in a wide range of sectors (government, the arts, industry, trade unions) or because they are leading experts in their field.[55] The political composition is also significant. The House of Lords Act 1999 removed the Conservative bias of the membership. Since 1999, no party has enjoyed an overall majority in the House. As can be seen from Table 1, the cross-bench peers—those with no party political affiliation—constitute more than 20 per cent of the membership.

Between 1999 and 2010, it was the Liberal Democrat peers who were the swing voters, given that they were more likely to turn out in force, and to vote more cohesively, than cross-bench peers.[56] After the creation of a Coalition government in 2010, with the Liberal Democrats forming part of the Coalition, the cross-bench peers assumed a new significance as holding the balance of power. They demonstrated a willingness on occasion to turn out in large numbers and, if they divided disproportionately against the government, voting with the opposition, the government went down to defeat. Between May 2010 and the summer of 2014, the government suffered 88 defeats in the House, almost all attributable to how the cross-benchers voted. The independence of the House in its voting behaviour is a result of how the different political groupings

[55] See Meg Russell and Meghan Benton, *Analysis of Existing Data on the Breadth of Expertise and Experience in the House of Lords: Report to the House of Lords Appointments Commission* (2010).

[56] See Meg Russell and Maria Sciara, 'Why Does the Government Get Defeated in the House of Lords? The Lords, the Party System and British Politics' (2007) 2 *British Politics* 571–89.

in the House come together, rather than as a consequence of dissenting behaviour by party members.[57]

The activity of the House was facilitated by a growth in numbers. Prior to the 1999 Act, the House had over 1,200 members. In the wake of the Act, it had 666. This number grew as creations outnumbered deaths. The Labour government under Tony Blair was keen to bolster Labour ranks in the House. When the Conservative–Liberal Democrat coalition was formed in 2010, more Conservative and Liberal Democrat peers were created. Tony Blair and David Cameron created a record number of peers. By the end of August 2014, there were 774 members. (If those members on leave of absence or not eligible to sit—because of serving, for example, on the Supreme Court—are included, the number rises to 828.) This growth in numbers has affected the average daily attendance, which has continued to rise decade by decade, and in the 2012–13 session was 484, up from 475 the previous session and 388 in the 2009–10 session. The number attending has put pressure on facilities, including on the chamber. During Question Time in the House, and major debates, there is not enough space in the chamber for all peers wishing to attend. Seats that are below the bar of the House, and previously used for visitors, are now occupied by peers, while others stand by the bar or, at the other end of the chamber, by the throne. Various commentators and peers have made the case for a reduction in numbers,[58] either by having a moratorium on new appointments or by having a cap on the total membership.

REFORM

The functions of the House of Lords are generally accepted as appropriate to an appointed second chamber and well fulfilled. Criticism has, however, regularly been levelled at the composition. Lords reform has been an enduring feature of political debate for more than a century. The Labour Party when returned to office in 1997 implemented its manifesto pledge to reform the House, resulting in the removal of all bar 92 of the hereditary peers. This was deemed the first stage of its reform process. It appointed a Royal Commission on Reform of the House of Lords (the Wakeham Commission) to make recommendations for the second stage. However, the Commission's recommendations[59]—for a partially elected House—attracted widespread criticism and were not implemented. The government advanced other proposals, initially for a 20 per cent elected element and then 50 per cent, before agreeing, following votes in the Commons in 2007 on various options for reform (in which a majority had voted for an 80 per cent and 100 per cent elected membership), to accept the case for a largely elected House.[60] No legislation, however, was brought forward.

---

[57] Party cohesion in divisions is a feature of the House. See Philip Norton, 'Cohesion without Discipline: Party Voting in the House of Lords' (2003) 9(4) *The Journal of Legislative Studies* 57–72.

[58] See e.g. Meg Russell, supported by Lord Adonis et al., *House Full* (2011).

[59] Royal Commission on Reform of the House of Lords, *A House for the Future*, Cm 4534, 2000.

[60] Norton, *Parliament in British Politics*, 287.

The measures agreed by the Conservatives and Liberal Democrats in 2010 as part of their negotiations to form a coalition included one to create a largely elected second chamber. The government in May 2011, as part of a White Paper on Lords Reform, published a draft House of Lords Reform Bill, providing for 80 per cent of members of the second chamber to be elected. The bill was sent to a joint committee set up for the purposes of pre-legislative scrutiny. It reported in March 2012 and recommended that the proposal be subject to a referendum.[61] Almost half the members of the committee, including a majority of the Conservative members, published an alternative report opposing election.[62] The government introduced the bill three months later. It was expected to have a difficult passage through the Lords, but in the event faced immediate criticism in the Commons. It was opposed by a number of Conservative MPs, who ran a well-organized campaign against it.[63] In the vote on Second Reading, 91 Conservatives voted against the bill and a further 19 abstained from voting. The opposition voted in favour, but made clear that it would not support a programme motion to limit debate on the bill. Given that a combination of the opposition and Conservative rebels was sufficient to defeat the motion, the government decided not to move it. This opened the prospect for endless debate on the bill, similar to that experienced during an earlier attempt in 1968–9 to reform the Lords, when MPs from both sides, led by Enoch Powell on the Tory benches and Michael Foot on the Labour, had effectively talked out the bill.[64] On 6 August, Deputy Prime Minister Nick Clegg announced the government would not be proceeding with the bill.

Although the government's House of Lords Reform Bill did not make it to the statute book, a private member's bill did. Introduced by Conservative MP Dan Byles, the bill emanated from a cross-party and cross-chamber group (the Campaign for an Effective Second Chamber) formed in 2003 to oppose an elected second chamber, but to support reform of the existing House. The bill was not opposed by government and made it to the statute book.

The House of Lords Reform Act 2014 took effect in August 2014 and enables peers to resign, removes non-attending peers (those who have not attended for a session) from membership, and provides for the expulsion of peers convicted and sentenced to 12 months or more in prison. The Act was expected to have a modest effect on the numbers in the House. Campaigners continued to press for measures designed to reduce the size of the House.

---

[61] Joint Committee on the Draft House of Lords Reform Bill, *Draft House of Lords Reform Bill: Report*, Session 2010–12, HL Paper 284-I, HC 1313-I, 92–6.

[62] *House of Lords Reform: An Alternative Way Forward* (2012).

[63] See Philip Norton, 'The Coalition and the Conservatives' in Anthony Seldon and Mike Finn (eds.), *The Coalition Effect, 2010–2015* (2015).

[64] Janet Morgan, *The House of Lords and the Labour Government 1964–1970* (1975), 208–22.

PARLIAMENT–PUBLIC RELATIONS

There have also been significant advances in the relationship between Parliament and the public. Both Houses have expended considerable resources in ensuring that what they do is made more accessible to the public and that members of the public have greater opportunities to make their views known to members, committees, or the House.

A dedicated BBC television channel, *BBC Parliament*, allows viewers to watch live proceedings in the Commons' chamber and to watch recorded proceedings in the Lords. It also broadcasts lectures and programmes about Parliament. In 2010, the channel had a monthly viewing audience of 1.9 million. This is now complemented by a website, *BBC Democracy Live*, that provides live feeds from both chambers (as well as the European Parliament and the devolved legislatures). This, though, is just one aspect of how the internet is being employed to make Parliament and its proceedings more accessible.

Those wanting copies of *Hansard*, the record of daily proceedings, can access the material online for free rather than having to pay for paper copies. Parliamentary papers are accessible online and both Houses have invested considerable resources not only in creating a Parliament website, but also enhancing it over time, moving the emphasis from structure and process and more to issues that are likely to interest people. Committee meetings are televised on a selective basis, but all chamber and committee proceedings are now webcast. Webcasting was begun on an experimental basis in 2002 and made permanent the following year.

Both Houses have not only been more willing in recent years to provide more access to broadcasters, including filming from Central Lobby, but also sought to engage more with interest groups and members of the public. As we have seen, public bill committees are empowered to receive written and oral evidence, thus mirroring the power of select committees. However, some committees have gone further and utilized online consultations. These have covered topics as diverse as family tax credit, electronic democracy, the Constitutional Reform Bill, the draft Communications Bill, hate crimes in Northern Ireland, and the role of prison officers. Online consultations have also been employed by the Parliamentary Office of Science and Technology (POST) and by some all-party groups. In utilizing such consultation, the UK Parliament was, according to Professor Stephen Coleman, ahead of other parliaments.[65] Some committees also utilized Twitter to invite comments.

Input from members of the public has also been facilitated by the use of e-petitions. A government site previously used for petitioning government has been utilized to enable citizens to petition Parliament. The Coalition government announced in 2010

---

[65] Modernisation Committee, House of Commons, *Connecting Parliament with the Public*, First Report, Session 2003–4, HC 368, 20–1.

that petitions that reached 100,000 signatures would be sent to the Backbench Business Committee to consider for debate. Many, including journalists, assumed this meant a debate would be triggered automatically. Although not guaranteed, the Committee has nonetheless normally scheduled the subjects for debate, though has also entertained proposals supported by e-petitions with fewer than 100,000 signatures. The facility of e-petitions has encouraged people to submit petitions, with the prospect of influencing the holding of a debate in the House of Commons.

The work of the House and its committees has been complemented by members individually seeking, or being willing, to engage with members of the public. Demands on MPs by constituents have grown decade by decade. In 2011, MPs newly elected in 2010 estimated that they spent 59 per cent of their time when the House was sitting on constituency business.[66] (This compares with 49 per cent for MPs newly elected in 2005 and surveyed in 2006.) Email correspondence has increased as ordinary mail to MPs has decreased.[67] Apart from utilizing email to correspond with constituents, most MPs have also been proactive through the use of social media, notably Facebook, Twitter, and the use of blogs. By 2009, 92 per cent of MPs used email and 83 per cent had websites.[68] By 2011, over 40 per cent were using Twitter.[69] MPs are far less detached in their contact with people outside the House than ever before.

CONCLUSION

Parliament in the United Kingdom continues to fulfil functions that it acquired early in its history, though expanded in recent centuries, especially as it developed as the legislature at the heart of a representative democracy. It remains, as it has been normally throughout history, a reactive body, waiting for the executive to come forward with proposals of public policy. It has been the subject of criticism for most of its history, and attacked for more than a century for the extent to which it is dominated by political parties, facilitating the party in government getting its programme enacted, often without much effective scrutiny. What effective scrutiny there has been in recent decades has been attributed more to the House of Lords than the people's elected representatives in the House of Commons. There have been frequent calls for reform, though these have frequently lacked any overall coherence. Calls for 'parliamentary reform' have rarely focused on Parliament as Parliament. Rather, calls for reform of the Commons have focused on structures and procedures, while reform of the Lords has concentrated on composition.[70]

---

[66] Hansard Society, *A Year in the Life: From Members of Public to Members of Parliament* (2011), 6.
[67] Norton, *Parliament in British Politics*, 223.
[68] Andy Williamson, *MPs Online: Connecting with Constituents* (2009), 8.
[69] David Harrison, 'OMG! MPs Spend 1,000 Hours a Year on Twitter', *Sunday Telegraph*, 31 July 2011.
[70] Philip Norton, *Parliament in British Politics*, ch. 14.

However, the tweny-first century has seen some significant changes to the power of Parliament in relation to the executive as well as structural and procedural changes in both Houses. Members have proved willing to exploit such changes in order to enhance scrutiny of the executive and to influence changes in public policy. There is also greater engagement with the public, allied to a growing awareness of the importance of such contact. There has been no fundamental change in the basic relationship of Parliament to the executive. It remains what has been termed a reactive, or policy-influencing legislature, rather than a policy-making legislature,[71] but as a policy-influencing legislature it has been strengthened in recent years. The bottle of parliamentary scrutiny is far from full, but it may at least be half-full or better.

FURTHER READING

KELSO, A., *Parliamentary Reform at Westminster* (2009)
NORTON, P., *Parliament in British Politics* (2nd edn, 2013)
RIDDELL, P., *In Defence of Politicians* (2011)
ROGERS, R. and WALTERS, R., *How Parliament Works* (7th edn, 2015)
RUSSELL, M., *The Contemporary House of Lords* (2014).

USEFUL WEBSITES

Constitution Unit, University College London: **http://www.ucl.ac.uk/constitution-unit/research/parliament**
Parliament: **http://www.parliament.uk**
Hansard Society for Parliamentary Government: **http://www.hansard-society.org.uk**

---

[71] See ibid., 69–70.

7

A COALITION GOVERNMENT IN WESTMINSTER

Richard Rawlings

SUMMARY

Constitutional change under the first UK coalition government for many years has exhibited a full range of characteristics: from skilful adaptation of governing arrangements in a famously flexible constitution to ill-conceived reforms inside Whitehall, and on to panic in the face of a remarkable exercise in popular sovereignty. The chapter elaborates on this by looking in turn at three main aspects, beginning with the constitutional footprint produced by the fact of the Cameron–Clegg administration. Developments relating to the office of prime minister (and deputy prime minister), and especially to the need to sustain coalition government through restrictions on termination and via the convention of collective ministerial responsibility, are key features. As regards the second main aspect, the constitutional position of the Civil Service and the relations of ministers with agencies and officials, the Cameron–Clegg government is seen generating more heat than light. The overarching demand for austerity has naturally been a chief driver of reform, but, set in terms of some important historical benchmarks, several significant initiatives appear poorly thought through. The territorial distribution of public power in the UK especially in the light of the Scottish independence referendum is—of course—the third main aspect. With an eye to a looser Union (state), the chapter highlights the demand to rework traditional—centralized—conceptualizations of the 'executive', a basic territorial duality of the Whitehall machine, and the special demands placed on Whitehall if the Union is to survive and prosper. Descriptively telling and suitably provocative, the conceptual label 'UK (English) government' is introduced into the lexicon of the changing constitution.

TWEAKING AND FIXING, REVERTING: TWO PARTY GOVERNMENT

VENTURING THE UNFAMILIAR

Truly a case of the novel and challenging, May 2010 witnessed the establishment of the first peacetime coalition government at Westminster since the 1930s. Successful in becoming the largest party, but failing to secure a majority in the House of Commons at the UK general election, the Conservatives led by new Prime Minister David Cameron had struck deals on policy and process with the third party, the Liberal Democrats, led by new Deputy Prime Minister Nick Clegg. Eschewing other possible outcomes from an inconclusive exercise in popular will, for example minority government with an agreement to provide 'confidence and supply', it was time they explained in suitably uplifting fashion for 'partnership government...inspired by the values of freedom, fairness and responsibility'.[1] In creating a majority administration jointly maintained by some 56 per cent of MPs, the demand for stability and firm action on the public finances in the wake of the global financial crisis was naturally uppermost.[2]

From the constitutional standpoint, the Cameron–Clegg experiment commands attention precisely because many conventions and elements of constitutional practice relating to the Westminster model of parliamentary government developed under single party (commonly majority) rule,[3] a previously dominant set of political conditions effectively buttressed by the non-proportional electoral system misleadingly called 'first past the post'. Conversely, the advent of coalition government at Westminster in part reflects long-term trends in voting behaviour: a decline in major party allegiances and increased representation for a variety of smaller parties.[4] Nor does the dynamic show much sign of slackening: quite the reverse! The auguries for single-party majority rule, in other words, are decidedly mixed.

There obviously was a wealth of comparative material on coalition government to draw upon: close to home in the context of devolution, particularly from Commonwealth countries like New Zealand, and also from other EU member states.[5] Then Cabinet Secretary Gus O'Donnell was notably assiduous in preparing the ground by taking on board comparative experience and helping to facilitate the intense political negotiations leading to government formation.[6] The change-over was duly underwritten in what would be grandly called 'the Coalition documentation'. Ranging widely across the policy piece, the 30-page *Programme for Government* would in turn provide an official benchmark of life under the Cameron–Clegg administration.[7]

---

[1] HM Government, *The Coalition: Our Programme for Government* (20 May 2010), foreword. This document built on an initial set of policy determinations: Conservatives and Liberal Democrats, *Agreements Reached* (11 May 2010).

[2] For more or less racy accounts of the creation, see David Laws, *22 Days in May: The Birth of the Lib Dem–Conservative Coalition* (2010); and (giving a Labour perspective), Andrew Adonis, *5 Days in May: The Coalition and Beyond* (2013).

[3] See to this effect, House of Lords Constitution Committee, *Constitutional Implications of Coalition Government*, HL 130 (2013–14).

[4] For details, see House of Commons Library, *UK Election Statistics 1918–2012* (2012).

[5] As exemplified by K. Strøm et al., *Cabinets and Coalition Bargaining: The Democratic Life Cycle in Western Europe* (2008).

[6] See UK Cabinet Office, *Civil Service Support to Coalition Negotiations* (2010).

[7] HM Government, *The Coalition: Together in the National Interest—Mid-term Review* (2013); and *Programme for Government Update* (2013).

For present purposes, the four-page *Agreement for Stability and Reform* on how the parties envisaged their coalition government operating is especially noteworthy.[8] As a major example of 'soft law'—in broad terms the use of rules and/or agreements which, better to preserve political space and/or administrative flexibility, are not intended to be directly legally enforceable—it signalled some thoughtful tweaking in a famously flexible uncodified constitution, indeed one in which hard law is strikingly absent in matters like the office of prime minister.[9] If strictly conceived there was 'no constitutional difference' between coalition and single-party government, 'working practices need[ed] to adapt'. As for the lovey-dovey stuff, the Coalition parties would 'work together effectively to deliver our programme, on the basis of goodwill, mutual trust and agreed procedures which foster collective decision-making and responsibility while respecting each party's identity'.[10]

It was one thing to exchange vows, another to make them stick. A most practical exercise in political self-preservation, if optimistically on the part of Liberal Democrats otherwise vulnerable to the prime minister's use of prerogative power to go to the country when it suited the Conservatives, longevity was the first item in the parties' agreement. It declared their intention not only to see out the maximum five-year term, but also to bring forward legislation, now the Fixed-term Parliaments Act 2011,[11] to change the constitutional rules of the political game.[12] 'The scaffolding for the coalition building' is an apt—insider's—description.[13]

The new dispensation had been signalled in the Liberal Democrats' election manifesto but not in the Conservatives' one. So it could be said not to enjoy the protection against House of Lords interference under the classic Salisbury–Addison convention.[14] The title of the Act is of course a misnomer since, in establishing the default position of a five-year term, the legislation provides for early dissolution through either a two-thirds vote of MPs or, express space for wheeling and dealing, a successful motion of no confidence and then no successful motion of confidence within 14 days. On the one hand, in reducing the prime minister's room for manoeuvre, with putative knock-on effects in terms of political leverage and party management, the Act naturally colours the calculations over government formation in a future 'hung' Parliament.[15] On the other hand, the legislation stands for twin alterations in democratic accountability: fewer expressions of popular will through the ballot

---

[8] *Coalition Agreement for Stability and Reform* (May 2010).

[9] R. Rawlings, 'Soft Law Never Dies' in D. Feldman and M. Elliott (eds.), *Cambridge Handbook of Public Law* (2015).

[10] *Coalition Agreement for Stability and Reform*, 1.

[11] See House of Lords Constitution Committee, *Fixed-term Parliaments Bill*, HL 69 (2010–11).

[12] *Coalition Agreement for Stability and Reform*, 1.

[13] *Constitutional Implications of Coalition Government*, para. 13. See further, V. Bogdanor, *The Coalition and the Constitution* (2011), ch. 6.

[14] For discussion of this convention in the conditions of coalition government, see *Constitutional Implications of Coalition Government*, paras. 93–100.

[15] For backbench musings as the 2015 UK general election approached, see Hansard, HC, cols. 1069–113 (23 October 2014).

box and limited capacity to break a political logjam by appeal to the people. In fact, the *Programme for Government* envisaged a trigger of 55 per cent of MPs, a figure also just above the then proportion of all non-Conservative Members; only in the light of opposition complaints of gerrymandering was the threshold raised.[16] It all adds up to a telling cocktail of formal statute and opaque and fraught workings of a famously termed 'political constitution'.[17]

ON HIGH

The second item in the *Agreement* concerned distribution of the spoils. At the heart of this was a self-declared 'principle of balance', boldly portrayed as underpinning 'all aspects of the conduct of the Government's business, including the allocation of responsibilities, the Government's policy and legislative programme...and the resolution of disputes'. Underlining the importance of political patronage, it was immediately given tangible expression through a 'share of Cabinet, Ministerial and Whip appointments...approximately in proportion to the size of the two Parliamentary parties'.[18]

A quick look round the UK Cabinet table is revealing.[19] The Conservatives as the much larger party take an iron grip on, first, the historic 'great offices of State' (Chancellor of the Exchequer, Home Secretary, Foreign Secretary); and, secondly, the big-spending departments (Work and Pensions, Health, Defence, etc.) Meanwhile, naturally concerned as the smaller party to guard the *Programme for Government*, the Liberal Democrats opt for width over concentration, with representation in most, though not all, government departments. As Deputy Prime Minster Clegg later explained, being 'held responsible for everything the government do but having no say in what they do across the piece' represented for the party 'the worst of all worlds'.[20] Very much a story of 'one-out, one-in', the basic pattern of ministerial representation would endure throughout the life of the administration, as indeed the *Agreement* had envisaged.

From the constitutional standpoint, attention naturally focuses on the position of the prime minister. After all, a pre-existing historical process of increased prime ministerial functions, even elements of a presidential-type role, is amply attested in the literature.[21] 'A guide to laws, conventions and rules on the operation of

---

[16] *Programme for Government*, 26; Hansard, HC, cols. 628–9 (13 September 2010).

[17] J. Griffith, 'The Political Constitution' (1979) 42 *MLR* 1.

[18] *Coalition Agreement for Stability and Reform*, 1.

[19] For further details, see M. Debus, 'Portfolio Allocation and Policy Compromises: How and Why the Conservatives Formed a Coalition Government' (2011) 82 *Pol Q* 293; and T. Heppell, 'Ministerial Selection and Portfolio Allocation in the Cameron Government' (2014) 67 *Parliamentary Affairs* 64.

[20] House of Lords Constitution Committee, *Annual Oral Evidence Session with the Deputy Prime Minister* (9 April 2014), 12.

[21] P. Hennessy, *The Prime Minister: The Office and its Holders since 1945* (2000); A. Blick and G. Jones, *Premiership: The Development, Nature and Power of the Office of the British Prime Minister* (2010).

government' and first fully published in 2011, the UK *Cabinet Manual* is today the obvious reference point. Reflecting and reinforcing the orthodox understanding, the *Manual* solemnly explains that the prime minister has 'certain prerogatives', for example 'recommending the appointment of ministers' and 'determining the membership of Cabinet and Cabinet committees'; 'however, in some circumstances the Prime Minister may agree to consult others before exercising those prerogatives'.[22] Yet as the *Agreement* had already made evident, this is apt to be economical with the truth in the conditions of coalition. Constitutional nicety recorded: 'the Prime Minister, following consultation with the Deputy Prime Minister, will make nominations for the appointment of Ministers'. Constitutional practice reworked: 'the Prime Minister will nominate Conservative Party Ministers', 'the Deputy Prime Minister will nominate Liberal Democrat Ministers', they 'will agree the nomination of the Law Officers'.[23] Confused and confusing yes, but nonetheless some important precedent was being set, to the effect of blurring a hitherto clear line of constitutional responsibility.

Political scientists have had a field day debating the shifting balances of power (or not) inside the Cameron–Clegg administration. Given that forming a coalition government involves compromise, broader questions are raised about intra-executive political leverage,[24] as well as institutional resources,[25] and in particular about how far the prime minister is constrained by, and more likely constrains, the deputy prime minister. After all, our constitutional actors had again to venture into the unfamiliar. Although the role of deputy prime minister became increasingly familiar in the past half-century, the wartime Churchill–Atlee administration provided the only previous example in coalition government, hardly equivalent. In the event, testimony to the innate sensitivities of coalition politics, the *Agreement* was notably fulsome in buttressing the deputy prime minister's otherwise vulnerable constitutional position. For example, 'close consultation' between the prime minister and deputy prime minister would help found 'the Coalition's success'. More concretely, the establishment and terms of reference of all Cabinet committees would now require the agreement of the deputy prime minister, who would also serve, or nominate anther (Liberal Democrat) minister to serve, on each Cabinet committee and subcommittee. As against a presidential-style model of concentrated informational and agenda-setting powers, a second 'general principle' was established of the prime minister and deputy prime minister both having a full and contemporaneous overview of the business of government, with each having the power to commission papers from the Cabinet

[22] UK Cabinet Office, *Cabinet Manual* (2011), para. 3.3.

[23] *Coalition Agreement for Stability and Reform*, 1.

[24] For this genre, see M. Bennister and R. Heffernan, 'Cameron as Prime Minister: The Intra-Executive Politics of Britain's Coalition Government' (2012) 65 *Parliamentary Affairs* 778.

[25] See House of Lords Constitution Committee, *The Cabinet Office and the Centre of Government*, HL 30 (2009–10); also, Institute for Government, *Centre Forward, Effective Support for the Prime Minister at the Centre of Government* (2014).

secretariat.[26] Reverting to the UK *Cabinet Manual*, a single bland paragraph on the deputy prime minister has again obscured a richer tapestry.[27] Perhaps not surprisingly, Mr Clegg would continue to portray his position as 'quite different' in function, content, and powers from previous holders of the title in single-party government.[28] On the basis of a lengthy inquiry into the office of prime minister,[29] the Commons Political and Constitutional Reform Committee has though reached similar conclusions. Naturally enough, with the powers of the prime minister somewhat constrained, coalition government 'made a more collegiate style of government necessary'.[30]

HANGING TOGETHER

The principle of collective responsibility, which of course provides the basis of Cabinet government, was the other main item in the parties' *Agreement*. As the Lords' Constitution Committee later observed in a wide-ranging report on the constitutional implications of coalition government, this would be the convention most affected.[31] There was though a modicum of constitutional practice to go on in the shape of 'agreements to disagree' on particular issues. Tariff reform is the famous example from the National government in 1931–2, with the other two occasions, also involving agreements made collectively by the Cabinet, being under Labour in the 1970s (the referendum on EEC membership and direct elections to the European Parliament). For the new coalition partners, it was then a case, first, of underscoring the importance of day-to-day routines of collective ministerial responsibility; and, secondly, by building on constitutional precedent, of reflecting the political reality that a coalition cannot be expected to agree on every issue.

Picking up on the twin input and output functions of the convention, collective development of policy with a view to better decisions, and public presentation of, and responsibility to Parliament of the whole government for, agreed policies, the *Agreement* carefully rehearsed the disciplines. The language is familiar from the UK *Ministerial Code* and *Cabinet Manual*:[32] 'an appropriate degree' of consultation and discussion among ministers to allow them 'to express their views frankly as decisions are reached'; 'opinions expressed...within Government to remain private'; and 'decisions of the Cabinet to be binding on and supported by all Minsters'—save, that is, where the convention 'is explicitly set aside'.[33] The *Programme for Government* duly specified five matters on which the parties could

---

[26] *Coalition Agreement for Stability and Reform*, 2.   [27] *Cabinet Manual*, para. 3.11.
[28] 'Annual Oral Evidence Session with the Deputy Prime Minister', 13. Mr Clegg had also been appointed Lord President of the Council, with ministerial responsibility for political and constitutional reform.
[29] Political and Constitutional Reform Committee, *Role and Powers of the Prime Minister*, HC 351 (2014–15).
[30] Ibid, 20.   [31] *Constitutional Implications of Coalition Government*, 4.
[32] UK *Ministerial Code*, paras. 2.1–2.4; UK *Cabinet Manual*, paras. 4.1–4.4.
[33] *Coalition Agreement for Stability and Reform*, 2. The standard exceptions to consultation, such as the Chancellor's Budget judgements, were naturally catered for.

disagree, among them renewal of the UK's nuclear deterrent and the (ill-fated) referendum on electing the House of Commons by Alternative Vote. Thus far, it may
be said, suitably transparent and constitutionally rigorous. The Coalition government could now secure a requisite element of legitimacy through the vote on the
Queen's Speech.[34]

But of course not all eventualities could be anticipated. The architects of the
Agreement were rightly concerned to establish standing machinery to oversee the
functioning of the government and implementation of the *Programme*; and, more
especially, for the resolution of disputes between the parties. Provision was thus made
for a 'Coalition Committee' co-chaired by the prime minister and deputy prime minister and with equal numbers of Conservative and Liberal Democrat ministers.[35]
Perhaps not surprisingly however, this body was rapidly superseded by more stream-
lined machinery in the form of the so-called 'Quad': regular meetings between the
prime minister and Chancellor of the Exchequer, and the deputy prime minister
and (a second Liberal Democrat) the Chief Secretary to the Treasury.[36] Putting this
in constitutional perspective, the fact of the Quad, a kind of equally balanced 'inner
Cabinet', underwrote the constraint on prime ministerial authority. The considerable
space for informal or highly contextual political arrangements at the heart of government is further highlighted.

The rosy days of May 2010 would soon give way to a burst of backbench
Conservative rebellion, which in fluctuating fashion then proceeded to dog the
life of the government.[37] So too, the convention of collective responsibility would
come under increased strain, reflected in some extraordinary acts of constitutional
and political theatre. These include the prime minister and deputy prime minister
making separate statements to the House in response to the Leveson report on
media regulation,[38] and a free vote for Conservative MPs on an amendment regret-
ting the absence of an EU referendum bill in the 2013 Queen's Speech.[39] The most
politically contentious however was the decision by the Liberal Democrats to agree
with a Lords amendment[40] postponing the review of constituency boundaries until
after the 2015 UK general election, in practice to the Conservatives' disadvantage.
According to Deputy Prime Minister Clegg, this setting aside of collective responsibility outside the terms of the *Agreement* was justified because of opposition
among Conservatives to the (ill-fated) House of Lords Reform bill, bogged-down

---

[34] See *Constitutional Implications of Coalition Government*, ch. 3.

[35] *Coalition Agreement for Stability and Reform*, 3.

[36] See further, R. Hazell, 'How the Coalition Works at the Centre' in R. Hazell and B. Yong, *The Politics of Coalition* (2012).

[37] House of Commons Library, *Coalitions at Westminster* (2014), provides references. For critical per-spectives on the competing ideologies, see M. Beech and S. Lee, *The Cameron–Clegg Government: Coalition Politics in an Age of Austerity* (2011).

[38] Hansard, HC, cols. 446–82 (29 November 2012). See also, Hansard, HC, cols. 282–304WH (13 February 2013).

[39] Hansard, HC, cols. 669, 749 (15 May 2013).

[40] To the Electoral Registration and Administration Bill; see Hansard, HC, cols. 806–40 (29 January 2013).

in the House of Commons. A key part of what he was pleased to call 'the coalition's contract' had been broken.[41] Not so said the then Conservative Leader of the House of Lords, Lord Strathclyde, declaring the Liberal Democrats guilty of 'a dirty trick'; the boundary review had as political consideration the AV referendum.[42] Be this as it may, the recriminations would persist through the lifetime of the government.[43]

Civilized partnership, uneasy cohabitation and divorce constitute a simple but neat way of visualizing the life-cycle of the Coalition.[44] Most obviously with a view to exploring possible policy lines and to projecting distinct identities, it would be strange indeed if ministers in both parties had not increasingly expressed differing views as the 2015 UK general election loomed ever larger. For which read, in the party conference season, welfare reform, immigration, and always Europe,[45] to name but a few. Constitutionally speaking, the touchstone of this reversion in favour of single-party politics is the Conservative Party's policy document *Protecting Human Rights in the UK* published in October 2014.[46] In making proposals that involved replacing the Human Rights Act 1998 with a British Bill of Rights and Responsibilities, this was a controversial document, to put it mildly. Correctly, however, it did not appear under an official government imprimatur, being produced instead in-house. Though one cannot help but feel that had the document been subject to the usual governmental processes of legal as well as political scrutiny, it would have been, at the very least, more tightly drafted.[47]

Published in February 2014, the Constitution Committee's report on the constitutional implications of coalition government made some useful recommendations, chief among them on collective responsibility. As one would expect, these senior Parliamentarians stood firmly on the constitutional importance of the convention; setting aside 'should be rare, and only ever a last resort'. Effectively supplying a missing piece in the jigsaw of the parties' *Agreement*, the Committee made the case for a standing process to govern such exigencies in this and any other future coalition government. A clear nod in the direction of collegiality, the Cabinet as a whole should agree a specific exception preferably for a specified period of time; 'rules' should be set out governing how ministers may express their differing views.[48] Properly timed as a prompt to ministers, the report also concentrated on matters relating to the end of the Parliament, for example legislative practice (the 'wash-up') and access to papers of a

---

[41] 'Nick Clegg: Lords Reform to Be Abandoned', *BBC News* (6 August 2012).

[42] *Constitutional Implications of Coalition Government*, para. 71.

[43] See Hansard, HL, cols. 1812–58 (13 May 2014).

[44] See in this vein, R. Hayton, 'Conservative Party Statecraft and the Politics of Coalition' (2014) 67 *Parliamentary Affairs* 6.

[45] E. Goes, 'The Coalition and Europe: A Tale of Reckless Drivers, Steady Navigators and Imperfect Roadmaps' (2014) 67 *Parliamentary Affairs* 45.

[46] Conservative Party, *Protecting Human Rights in the UK: The Conservatives' Proposals for Changing Britain's Human Rights Laws* (2014).

[47] See further, Colm O'Cinneide's chapter in this volume (ch. 3).

[48] *Constitutional Implications of Coalition Government*, paras. 78–9.

previous administration.[49] However, in flagrant disregard of the conventional under-standing of a reply within two months, important for effective parliamentary over-sight of government, the minister was still prevaricating another six months later,[50] a consequence presumably of disagreement between the Coalition parties. Eventually published in November 2014, the response was short and bland, even insulting.[51] It was 'for the government of the day to decide on any process for setting aside collective responsibility': full stop.[52]

THRASHING ABOUT: MINISTERS, AGENCIES, AND OFFICIALS

BENCHMARKS

Some 150 years ago, as Britain experienced an industrial revolution and approached the zenith of empire, the basis of today's Civil Service was being laid. As state interven-tion flowered in fields like public health, education, and the factories, so at home as well in the colonies there was an inexorable demand for a more capable bureaucracy. Opposing patronage and the buying of office, the justly famous Northcote–Trevelyan review[53] grounded a system of entry and promotion on merit via open competition. Viewed in constitutional perspective, this reflected and reinforced the concept of a per-manent and politically disinterested Civil Service; and, more particularly, core values of objectivity, impartiality, and integrity. As today's UK *Cabinet Manual* puts it, first and foremost 'the Civil Service supports the Government of the day in developing and implementing its policies, and in delivering public services'.[54] However, a significant feature in an uncodified constitution centred round parliamentary sovereignty, and it is also implicit that the Civil Service 'does not exist solely to serve the Government of the day, but also future governments'. Put slightly differently, it is 'one of the great institutions of state, critical to the continuation and stability of government'.[55]

Some 100 years ago, against the backdrop of the Great War and also the beginnings of what would become known as the welfare state, much thought was being given to the organization and effective exercise of central government responsibilities. On from more ad hoc and piecemeal arrangements, the Haldane report established a deter-minedly functional approach to the machinery of government premised on individual departments, whereby the 'field of activity in the case of each department' should be

---

[49] Ibid., ch. 5. See also Political and Constitutional Reform Committee, *Fixed-term Parliaments: The Final Year of a Parliament*, HC 976 (2013–14); Institute for Government, *Year Five: Whitehall and the Parties in the Final Year of Coalition* (2014).

[50] Hansard, HL, col. 154W (29 October 2014).

[51] *Government response to the House of Lords Constitution Committee Report: Constitutional Implications of Coalition Government* (2014).

[52] Ibid, 3.   [53] *Report on the Organisation of the Permanent Civil Service*, 1854, q/JN 426 NOR.

[54] *Cabinet Manual* (1st edn, 2011), para. 7.1. But see later, Constitutional Reform and Governance Act 2010, s. 7.

[55] Public Administration Select Committee, *Truth to Power: How Civil Service Reform Can Succeed*, HC 74 (2013–14), para. 1.

'the particular service which it renders to the community as a whole'.[56] Expanding on Northcote–Trevelyan, which had spoken of a professional body of officials advising a minister with direct responsibility to Parliament, Haldane underwrote another key principle in the Westminster model of parliamentary government: the indivisible relationship of ministers and officials. For which read the mathematical-style formula of the great constitutional convention of individual ministerial responsibility: in the first, internal limb that civil servants are fully accountable to ministers; in the second, external limb that ministers are fully accountable to Parliament for all their and their department's actions and omissions. Today the principle is given due prominence in both the Civil Service Code and the UK *Cabinet Manual*; to quote the Cameron–Clegg administration's Civil Service Reform Plan, it is 'well-established and underpins the effective working of Government'.[57] Not forgetting a long-standing and important exception, the role of accounting officer, whereby, bound up with the historic constitutional functions of the House of Commons in providing for and overseeing government expenditure, Parliament holds designated senior civil servants directly to account for their stewardship of public funds.[58]

Some 50 years ago, in the twin contexts, first, of an expanded administrative apparatus associated with 'cradle to grave' welfare provision and substantial public ownership in a mixed economy, and, secondly, of a country struggling to come to terms with relative economic decline and retreat from Empire, the Fulton Committee[59] was tasked with considering issues of recruitment, management, and training with a view to ensuring that the Civil Service was properly equipped for its role in the modern state. Trumpeting a lack of skilled management, and also the limitations of a (public school) cult of the generalist in an increasingly technological age, Fulton's mix of recommendations included a less rigid hierarchy (far fewer classes of civil servant), more responsibilities for specialists including scientists, and increased interchange with the private and voluntary sectors. The inquiry would be heavily criticized, in part for avoiding basic constitutional questions about the design of the Whitehall machinery, and in part for an evident failure of implementation in the face of resistance from the higher Civil Service.[60] Yet in the long view, much in Fulton foreshadows the radical transformation of government, and particularly of administrative culture, pursued by the Conservatives under Margaret Thatcher from 1979.[61]

It is worth pausing to consider how a student of the not-so changing constitution of the 1970s[62] might have visualized the situation. Representing the model of (by now) big Whitehall departments constructed on the basis of strong bureaucratic hierarchy,

[56] Ministry of Reconstruction, *Report of the Machinery of Government Committee*, Cm 9230 (1918), 8.
[57] HM Government, *The Civil Service Reform Plan* (June 2012), 20.
[58] HM Treasury, *Managing Public Money* (updated version, July 2013), ch. 3.
[59] *The Civil Service, Report of the [Fulton] Committee 1966–68*, vol. 1, Cm 3638 (1968).
[60] P. Kellner and N. Crowther-Hunt, *The Civil Servants: An Inquiry into Britain's Ruling Class* (1980).
[61] R. Lowe, *The Official History of the British Civil Service: Reforming the Civil Service*, I: *The Fulton Years, 1966–81* (2011), provides a top-down perspective.
[62] For a suitably provocative account, see N. Johnson, *In Search of the Constitution* (1977).

a series of towering institutional pyramids dominates the scene.[63] Individual departments are governed from on high through a (variable) mix of political direction from
the Secretary of State and junior ministers and the administrative judgement of the
Permanent Secretary and other 'mandarins'; perhaps hopefully, the internal lines of
managerial direction and accountability reach down through the middle ranks to the
very many junior officials applying rules and rendering individual decisions. From
the legal standpoint,[64] two particular pieces of engineering help to sustain this set
of structures. First, there is the time-hallowed method of statutory empowerment,
whereby Parliament delegates public power to 'the Secretary of State'. At one and
the same time, the constitutional and administrative model of individual ministerial responsibility is reflected and reinforced, and, since the statutory phrase also is a
generic one, flexibility is preserved through an ongoing executive capacity to transfer
functions.[65] Secondly, giving tangible expression to the notion of indivisibility, there
is the dose of judicial common-sense constituted in the *Carltona* principle;[66] namely
that, such are the multifarious functions of modern government, responsible officials
may generally exercise them in the name of ministers.

  Our student is also well-versed in the constitutional learning associated with the
famous episode of 'Crichel Down' (1954), in which a minister resigned ostensibly
over serious errors by officials.[67] This is the flipside or shielding aspect of individual
ministerial responsibility, whereby, helping to keep the Civil Service out of the political arena, the minister is expected to protect officials carrying out orders or properly implementing a policy, and not to subject them to public criticism for minor
mistakes.[68] Already however questions are raised about the practical workings in view
of the growth in the size and complexity of the state and a propensity among ministers to distance themselves from government blunders.[69] Much, however, remains
shrouded in mystery, and designedly so, by reason of the draconian Official Secrets
Act 1911.[70] According to the classic routines, the MP may inquire of the minister who,
suitably briefed, will give an answer to the question, but generally no more than that.
Only in 1967 was the Parliamentary Ombudsman created as a supplementary means
of chasing down maladministration through a dose of investigative technique.[71]
Meanwhile, testimony to the strength of the conventional paradigm, direct engage-
ment between parliamentarians and civil servants remains sporadic and peripheral.
Only in 1979 would a properly planned select committee system be established in the

---

[63] C. Harlow and R. Rawlings, *Law and Administration* (1st edn, 1984).
[64] For classic accounts, see R. Brazier *Ministers of the Crown* (1997); and T. Daintith and A. Page, *The Executive in the Constitution* (1999).
[65] See Ministers of the Crown Act 1975.
[66] *Carltona Ltd* v. *Works Commissioners* [1943] 2 All ER 560.
[67] But see I. Nicholson, *The Mystery of Crichel Down* (1986).
[68] Hansard, HC, cols. 1285–7 (20 July 1954) (Home Secretary David Maxwell Fyfe).
[69] A. Birch, *Representative and Responsible Government* (1964).
[70] For a useful overview, see C. Moran, *Classified: Secrecy and the State in Modern Britain* (2012).
[71] Parliamentary Commissioner Act 1967.

House of Commons with a view to securing cross-the-board scrutiny of departmental policy and administration.[72]

AGE OF MANAGERIALISM

Previous editions of this book posed the question: 'The Executive: Towards Accountable Government and Effective Governance?' Behind this seemingly unending quest lay a well-known narrative: the shift toward more market-oriented, performance driven, and 'business-like' modes of public service delivery beginning in earnest with Prime Minister Thatcher.[73] Much would be heard of the functional values of 'economy, efficiency, and effectiveness' and, associated with a rule-bound methodology of targeted goals, standard-setting, performance indicators, measurement and control, and 'value for money' (VFM) audit, something called 'New Public Management' (NPM).[74] In terms of accountability for performance, considerable confidence was reposed in transparency via detailed specification, as with advanced forms of contracting-out of public services, and in pseudo-market forces, as with citizens as consumers and 'league tables' of public bodies.

Attention is drawn to the fashion for 'agencification'; in constitutional terms, more autonomous decision-making by so-called arm's-length public bodies operating outside the classic lines of ministerial hierarchical control hitherto associated with centralist practices of parliamentarianism. To this effect, demands for sharp issue focus and specialist expertise locked up with the prevailing market ideology and, an even stronger driver today,[75] burgeoning European demands for 'independent' regulation in the Single Market. Testifying to the strength of the broad development, the ugly term 'distributed public governance' would soon be used to underscore the sense of greater institutional complexity; and, further, of the old top-down British view of 'the executive' being reworked so as to incorporate broader and more flexible elements of decision-making founded on myriad policy communities and networks.[76] Meanwhile, the related metaphor of 'hollowing out of the state' suitably highlighted the passage of central government functions sideways to agencies and (via privatization, etc.) to business, as well as upwards to Brussels.[77]

Arm's-length bodies would exhibit many forms, ranging through executive agencies tasked with day-to-day implementation of policies, powerful non-ministerial

---

[72] G. Drewry (ed.), *The New Select Committees* (1985).

[73] C. Harlow and R. Rawlings, *Law and Administration* (2nd edn, 1997). For another flavour of the times, see P. Hennessy, *Whitehall* (1989).

[74] As illustrated by G. Hammerschmid et al., *Public Administration Reform in Europe* (2013), the precise contours of NPM remain contested.

[75] C. Harlow and R. Rawlings, *Process and Procedure in EU Administration* (2014).

[76] M. Flinders, *Delegated Governance and the British State* (2008). For the government/governance distinction, see R. Rhodes, 'The New Governance: Governing without Government' (1996) 44 *Political Studies* 652.

[77] R. Rhodes, 'The Hollowing Out of the State: The Changing Nature of the Public Service in Britain' (1994) 65 *Pol Q* 138.

departments such as HM Revenue & Customs, and all those so-called 'quangos': non-departmental public bodies (NDPBs) with their own legal personality but subject to greater or lesser forms of 'steering' by ministers through strategic direction and guidance, funding, etc.[78] Privatization also meant new regulatory agencies armed (if weakly) with statutory powers across broad swathes of the functioning economy. For present purposes, the rise of executive agencies—referred to in the Thatcher years as 'next steps agencies'[79]—further serves to illustrate the important role of 'soft law' techniques in the internal organization and workings of the executive. Cut out of monolithic central departments, bodies like the Prison Service or the Highways Agency would thus remain paper creations, operating according to published framework documents agreed by ministers. By the early 1990s, our model student would have been visualizing the situation in terms of 'hub-and-spoke': not so much institutional pyramids but policy-oriented departmental cores flanked by, or working in partnership with, multiple executive agencies. To which would promptly be added the unsurprising 'core executive thesis' of a small number of powerful institutions like the Treasury doing much by way of policy-setting, business coordination, and oversight above the level of departments.[80]

Concern was naturally expressed about the effects on classic forms of political accountability. The touchstone is the adoption in 1997 of resolutions in both Houses changing the doctrine of individual ministerial responsibility from an unwritten constitutional convention into the express parliamentary rule that 'ministers have a duty to Parliament to account, and be held to account, for the policies, decisions and actions of their departments and executive agencies'.[81] This followed a well-known imbroglio over operational failures in the Prison Service, which saw the minister demand the chief executive's resignation and the chief executive allege that the minister interfered in operational matters while seeking to avoid responsibility for failures in respect of which—shades of Haldane—he was accountable to Parliament.[82] Predictably, the general issue has rumbled on, with senior parliamentarians holding to the line of no constitutional difference between the terms responsibility and accountability in the face of restrictive executive views of ministerial obligation.[83] The proper functioning of the Westminster model of parliamentary government, it may be said, demands nothing less.

The election of Tony Blair's New Labour government famously heralded much by way of constitutional change, some of which bears directly on the position of the Civil

---

[78] For this (simple) threefold classification, see House of Lords Select Committee on the Constitution, *The Accountability of Civil Servants*, HL 61 (2012–13), ch. 5.

[79] UK Cabinet Office, *Improving Management in Government: The Next Steps* (1988).

[80] M. Smith, *The Core Executive in Britain* (1999).

[81] Hansard, HC, cols. 1046–7 (19 March 1997); HL, cols. 1055–62 (20 March 1977).

[82] A. Barker, 'Political Responsibility for UK Prison Security: Ministers Escape Again' (1998) 76 *Public Administration* 1.

[83] *Government Response to the Lords Constitution Committee's Report on the Accountability of Civil Servants* (February 2013).

Service. One thinks immediately of the Freedom of Information Act 2000, which for all its many exceptions has clearly changed much in the day-to-day working assumptions.[84] However, to anticipate the argument in the next section, 'devolution' constituted the more profound change. Another product of a tortuous history, Northern Ireland already had a separately organized Civil Service. But the (re-)birth of parliamentary and governmental institutions in Scotland and Wales also required mirroring inside the home Civil Service. Officials in Edinburgh and Cardiff would now owe their day-to-day loyalty not to London but to their own ministers (a constitutional position subsequently formalized in the Constitutional Reform and Governance Act 2010[85]).

Rather than reverse the paradigm shift denoted by 'the Thatcher revolution'—rolling back the extended administrative state and imposing competitive disciplines—the Blair government aimed to soften some of the effects.[86] In supplementing hard-edged functional values with responsive nostrums of public service, a 1999 White Paper set the tone: linking citizen choice to improved service standards and delivery, it spoke bravely of forward-looking, inclusive, and fair policies.[87] From computerized front-line decision-making to new opportunities for citizen participation or at least consultation, stress was rightly laid on the potentials for 'e-governance' in light of the revolution in ICT. Naturally, however, the looming prospect of a surveillance society,[88] and, latterly underscored in the so-called 'war against terror', the expanding capacities of the security state, were glossed over.

Risk regulation would be a leitmotif of UK public administration under New Labour.[89] Behind this lay the (worldwide) search for 'better' and/or 'smart' regulation founded on principles of proportionality, consistency and targeting, and transparency and accountability.[90] Demonstrating the way in which some Conservative approaches were taken to new heights, this helped to fuel the rise of super-agencies such as OFCOM, the telecommunications regulator, and the Financial Services Authority (later abolished in the wake of the 2007–8 global financial crisis). It was then a time of regulatory commissions, extended regulatory objectives, and enhanced enforcement powers, as well as heightened process requirements.[91] Distributed public governance writ large, this determinedly sprawling development represented the apotheosis in the UK of a familiar if contested concept in law and political science: the regulatory state.[92]

---

[84] See further, Patrick Birkinshaw's chapter 14 in this volume.

[85] Constitutional Reform and Governance Act 2010, s. 7.

[86] C. Harlow and R. Rawlings, *Law and Administration* (3rd edn, 2009).

[87] *Modernising Government*, Cm 4130 (1999).

[88] See especially House of Lords Constitution Committee, *Surveillance: Citizens and the State*, HL 18 (2008–9).

[89] E. Fisher, *Risk Regulation and Administrative Constitutionalism* (2007).

[90] R. Baldwin, M. Cave, and M. Lodge, *Understanding Regulation* (2nd edn, 2011).

[91] See e.g. House of Lords Constitution Committee, *The Regulatory State: Ensuring its Accountability*, HL 68 (2003–4).

[92] M. Moran, *The British Regulatory State* (2003); D. Oliver, T. Prosser, and R. Rawlings (eds.), *The Regulatory State: Constitutional Implications* (2010).

To Prime Minister Gordon Brown goes the accolade of finally delivering one of Northcote–Trevelyan's main recommendations: a clear statutory basis for the Civil Service and hence at least partial release from the arcane mysteries of prerogative power.[93] If by comparison with some other common law jurisdictions[94] the provision in the Constitutional Reform and Governance (CRAG) Act 2010 is limited, nonetheless some of it is appropriately described as constitutionally fundamental. The development also shows the scope for close interplay between hard and soft law techniques, with the statute effectively underpinning, and promoting the further elaboration of, pre-existing requirements in the Civil Service Code. In trumpeting the core values, s. 7 of the Act thus provides that 'the code must require civil servants to carry out their duties…with integrity and honesty…and with objectivity and impartiality'. An updated version of the Code then explains that objectivity for example includes not ignoring inconvenient facts or relevant considerations when providing advice or making decisions (a formulation which the judicial review practitioner would immediately recognize).[95] Meanwhile, corresponding provisions in the *Ministerial Code* state that 'Ministers must uphold the political impartiality of the Civil Service and not ask civil servants to act in any way which would conflict with the Civil Service Code.'[96] Other key legislative statements in CRAG include the merit principle ('a person's selection must be on merit on the basis of fair and open competition' (s. 10)) and separate legal status for the Civil Service Commission, the arm's-length body which oversees recruitment competitions for senior officials (s. 2). The development, it is rightly said, hardly amounts to a revolution in UK public administration; the imposition of formal legal norms should not distract from the overarching importance of organizational culture.[97] The constitutional significance is nonetheless worth emphasizing. Through this assertion by Parliament of its primary authority on the regulation of the Civil Service,[98] there is some further defence against unwarranted political interference. Doings under the Cameron–Clegg government will be seen later highlighting this aspect.

RAGBAG

Ad hoc and piecemeal, naturally politically driven, it is a commonplace that changes in the UK's constitutional arrangements happen on the hoof.[99] Yet viewed against this backdrop, the Coalition's dealings with the machinery of government appear

---

[93] On which see *Council of Civil Service Unions* v. *Minister for the Civil Service* [1985] AC 374 (the famous 'GCHQ case').

[94] For a comparative perspective, see IPPR, *Accountability and Responsiveness in the Senior Civil Service: Lessons from Overseas* (2013).

[95] UK Civil Service Code (2010 version), para. 10.   [96] UK *Ministerial Code*, para. 5.1.

[97] Drewry (ed.), *The New Select Committees*, 209, 212.

[98] See in this vein, A. Tomkins, *The Constitution After Scott* (1998).

[99] D. Oliver, 'Politics, Law and Constitutional Moments in the UK' in D. Feldman (ed.), *Law in Politics, Politics in Law* (2013).

more than usually disjointed. On the one hand, the evident need to tackle a huge budget deficit in the wake of the global economic crisis was a powerful factor: a more stringent approach to the public sector at large was only to be expected. On the other hand, careful and joined-up thinking about important matters of institutional—and hence constitutional—design proved hostage to the particular exigencies of the moment.

A Conservative-led government seeking to roll back the boundaries of agencification: the irony will not be lost on the reader. The policy was one of the key constitutional initiatives of the Coalition's early years and had in theory much to commend it. A seeming bonfire of the quangos, the Minister for the Cabinet Office spoke of restoring political accountability for decisions affecting people's lives and the way taxpayers' money is spent; individual NDPBs should only be retained where there was a demonstrable need for performance of a technical function, or for political impartiality, or for acting independently to establish facts.[100] But the bill which eventually became the Public Bodies Act 2011 was the business manager's nightmare; living up to its unkind nickname of 'quango of the quangos', the House of Lords duly deliberated at great length on the great virtues of executive bodies on which sit the great and good. Ministers reckoned to pre-empt much in the public debate by using so-called 'Henry VIII clause' powers on an industrial scale to abolish, merge, and transfer functions; happily, however, from the standpoint of constitutional—democratic—principle, this too raised the ire of senior parliamentarians.[101] In the event, the government could point to some major savings in the costs of running public bodies (some £900 million per year).[102] Nonetheless, the reform proved something of a damp squib, certainly if an official UK government list of some 500 NDPBs (grouped round 24 ministerial departments or offices) is anything to go by.[103] For confirmation, one need only refer to a 2014 review by the Public Administration Select Committee (PASC), which speaks of 'inconsistency, overlaps, confusion and clutter'.[104] There also were some unfortunate casualties, for example the Administrative Justice and Tribunals Council, a harmless little body which was doing good work in promoting principled guidance, training and research concerning citizen grievance.[105]

Highlighting some complaints by ministers of deliberate obstruction of policy decisions, and also their concerns about institutional constraints in terms of competence and culture, media reports of a 'Whitehall at war' abounded under the Cameron–Clegg

---

[100] Francis Maude MP, UK Cabinet Office statement, 14 October 2010; see further, Institute for Government, *Read before Burning: Arm's Length Government for a New Administration* (2010).

[101] House of Lords Constitution Committee, *Public Bodies Bill*, HL 51(2010–11).

[102] UK Cabinet Office, *Progress on Public Bodies Reform* (2013).

[103] UK Cabinet Office, *Public Bodies* (2013).

[104] Public Administration Select Committee, *Who's Accountable? Relationships between Government and Arm's Length Bodies*, HC 110 (2014–15), para. 78. See further, K. Dommett et al., 'Did they "Read Before Burning"? The Coalition and Quangos' (2014) 85 *Pol Q* 133.

[105] AJTC, *Putting it Right* (2012).

administration. Members of select committees were naturally interested to get to the bottom of this, yet, faced by ministers' failure to improve on anecdote with a firm evidence base, they struggled to do so. In PASC's weary words, 'the Government has not…identified any fundamental problem with the Civil Service'.[106] Equally however, PASC was scathing about the government's initial failure to produce any sort of Civil Service reform plan: for change not to be defeated by inertia, ministers needed to set clear goals and pursue implementation through close timetabling.[107]

Ministers eventually published a Plan in 2012.[108] Predictably in this age of austerity, the chief demand was for a much smaller Civil Service. Connecting with the rise of e-governance (a 'digital by default' approach to the delivery of services), but also sitting comfortably with Conservative ideology, cuts of roughly 25 per cent in staff numbers were envisaged. In the event, staffing would fall from some 480,000 at the Spending Review in 2010 to some 410,000 by mid-2014.[109] Flanking initiatives in the Plan included more outsourcing, to the extent of 'think-tanks' bidding to provide policy advice, and, with a view to tackling a familiar source of government blunders,[110] attempts to improve the handling of major projects. Especially noteworthy from the constitutional standpoint was the demand by Coalition ministers for a greater say in senior appointments in order to reflect their own accountability to Parliament for a department's performance[111]—for which read downplaying Civil Service independence from political masters in favour of (still greater) responsiveness to the government of the day.[112]

An official evaluation in 2013 confirmed that the government was 'slow to mobilise'; indeed, implementation of the Plan had been 'held back by some of the very things that it was designed to address'—'weaknesses in capability', 'lack of clear accountability', and failings in (something called) 'delivery discipline'.[113] Lamenting the many difficulties of driving forward bureaucratic reform across largely autonomous and sprawling departmental structures, an external evaluation in early 2014 further pointed up 'weak and confused' leadership at the centre.[114] Even so, at the same time as having to provide effective support for radical ministerial agendas in various policy domains, the Civil Service at large was already making unprecedented costs-savings. A second official evaluation in late 2014 put a braver face on matters, to the effect of a reform programme gradually picking up speed.[115] It spoke of 'real progress towards

---

[106] PASC, *Truth to Power*, 3.

[107] Public Administration Select Committee, *Change in Government: The Agenda for Leadership*, HC 714 (2010–12).

[108] HM Government, *The Civil Service Reform Plan*.

[109] For the number-crunching, see Institute for Government, *Whitehall Monitor* (Annual Report, 2014).

[110] For chapter and verse, see A. King and I. Crewe, *The Blunders of our Governments* (2013).

[111] HM Government, *The Civil Service Reform Plan*, 21.

[112] On the further, vexed, issue of special advisers, see B. Yong and R. Hazell, *Special Advisers: Who They Are, What They Do and Why They Matter* (2014).

[113] UK Cabinet Office, *Civil Service Reform Plan: One Year On* (2013), 5.

[114] Institute for Government, *Leading Change in the Civil Service* (2014), 9.

[115] UK Cabinet Office, *Civil Service Reform: Progress Report* (2014).

the government's vision of a service that is more skilled, less bureaucratic and hierarchical, and more unified'.[116] Time will tell.

Meanwhile, the scene had been set for a fine establishment imbroglio over the position of permanent secretaries. With the declared aim of strengthening their individual accountability, ministers announced an immediate move to fixed tenure (five-year contracts) for all new appointments at this exalted level.[117] However, praying in aid Northcote–Trevelyan and the concerns about personal favouritism and patronage, the Civil Service Commission stoutly resisted the further idea of substituting direct ministerial choice for the (rarely exercised) prime ministerial power to veto the independently selected candidate. At this point the CRAG Act bit home, with Coalition ministers effectively being dared to amend the provisions enshrining the merit principle and the role of the Commission. By the end of 2012 an uneasy compromise had resulted, with revised Commission guidance allowing for multiple consultations with the relevant Secretary of State.[118] In the face however of renewed party political pressure, the Commission evidently felt obliged to cede more ground. As from late 2014, the prime minister is allowed to interview and choose the top-most civil servants in Whitehall, those heading the main departments and directly accountable to a Cabinet Minister.[119] Yes, the merit principle remains in place, buttressed by the safeguard of an independent panel dealing with the shortlist, but the development naturally reinforces concerns about politicization of the Civil Service. Perhaps hopefully, an important constitutional principle has been dented and not fractured.

Happenings at the very centre of government highlight the propensity for ill-thought-out reform. When chief civil servant Gus O'Donnell retired in 2011, his role was divided three ways: Cabinet Secretary; Head of the Home Civil Service; and Permanent Secretary, Cabinet Office. But as PASC was quick to observe, this was a recipe not only for weakened leadership or domestic tension, but also for blurred lines of responsibility in the heart of Whitehall.[120] Hardly testimony to success, the chairs were then rearranged in the government's final year: first, by (re-)combining the titles of Cabinet Secretary and Head of the Home Civil Service; and, secondly, by conjuring up the title 'Civil Service Chief Executive'. To compound matters, the latter title is misleading. The new office-holder, it is envisaged, will not run much, but instead focus on issues of efficiency and effectiveness, reporting in turn to various ministers including the Chief Secretary to the Treasury, as well as to the Cabinet Secretary.[121] More higgledy-piggledy beckons.

[116] Ibid., foreword.

[117] *Civil Service Reform Plan: One Year On*, 31.

[118] Civil Service Commission, *Recruiting Permanent Secretaries: Ministerial Involvement* (December 2012).

[119] Civil Service Commission, press notice 15 October 2014. Within the Scottish and Welsh governments, it will be the First Minister's decision.

[120] Public Administration Select Committee, *Leadership of Change: New Arrangements for the Roles of the Head of the Civil Service and the Cabinet Secretary*, HC 1582 (2010–12).

[121] UK Cabinet Office, *Chief Executive Job Description* (July 2014). See further, House of Commons Public Accounts Committee, *The Centre of Government*, HC 107 (2014–15).

As regards the broader constitutional issue of ministerial and/or Civil Service accountability, matters plumbed the depths with the collapse in 2012 of the tendering process for the West Coast Main Line.[122] Triggered by a claim for judicial review, this expensive and embarrassing debacle for the government produced a blame game both inside and outside the department. The affair sheds light on the complex web of organizational factors likely to be involved when things go wrong. Yes, there were major errors by front-line officials, but there also were insufficient specialist staff, little by way of institutional memory, serious failings in line management, and so on. Individual shortcomings, long experience teaches, should not be allowed to obscure wider defects in systems, skills, and culture for which others are responsible.

In the light of broader moves towards Westminster asserting its authority over Whitehall, and more particularly the evident ambition of certain parliamentary committees,[123] there would be more calls to open up the accountability of civil servants to MPs.[124] Yet as the Constitution Committee[125] was soon reminding its readers, the convention of individual ministerial responsibility effectively contains the principal mechanism of Civil Service accountability, while also grounding much of the day-to-day conduct of government business and associated scrutiny in the Westminster system. So although it might be supplemented by other accountability mechanisms, these should not dilute ministers' constitutional responsibility to Parliament. Indeed, in the case of thoroughgoing institutional reform of the NHS in England, the Constitution Committee had effectively demanded a statutory guarantee of continuing ministerial responsibility for provision of the service, a constitutional 'first' at Westminster.[126]

A chief touchstone is the so-called 'Osmotherly Rules', the government's (and not Parliament's) guidance to officials appearing before committees in both Houses. Originally couched in highly restrictive language, but liberalized somewhat over the years, this classic soft law document continues to underwrite important classical understandings. Eventually published in October 2014, the current version emphasizes that civil servants giving evidence do so, 'not in a personal capacity, but as representatives of their Ministers'.[127] This, it is (tortuously) explained, 'does not mean that officials may not be called upon to give a full account of government policies, or the justification, objectives and effects of these policies'. Rightly however the purpose in doing so is 'to contribute to the process of ministerial accountability'; likewise, better to avoid undermining their political impartiality, it is 'not to offer personal views or judgements on matters of government policy'. In particular, officials 'should as far as possible avoid being drawn into discussion of the merits of alternative policies, including their advice to Ministers'.[128]

---

[122] *Report of the Laidlaw Inquiry*, HC 809 (2012–13); House of Commons Transport Committee, *Cancellation of the InterCity West Coast Franchise Competition*, HC 537 (2012–13).

[123] See Philip Norton's chapter in this volume (ch. 6).

[124] Institute for Government, *Civil Service Accountability to Parliament* (2013).

[125] House of Lords Select Committee on the Constitution, *The Accountability of Civil Servants*.

[126] House of Lords Constitution Committee, *Health and Social Care Bill*, HL 197 (2010–12); and *Health and Social Care Bill: Follow-up*, HL 240 (2010–12); Health and Social Care Act 2012, s. 1.

[127] UK Cabinet Office, *Giving Evidence to Select Committees: Evidence to Select Committees* (2014), para. 5.

[128] Ibid., paras. 6, 33.

The new guidance contributes two useful tweaks. First, underpinning a constitutionally important piece of machinery, former Accounting Officers can now expect to be called in to give evidence about their previous responsibilities. Secondly, reflecting the contemporary realities of government management, the lead officials ('Senior Responsible Owners') on major projects will now be directly accountable at Westminster for implementation.

Looking forward, PASC makes a powerful case for the establishment of a parliamentary commission into the Civil Service.[129] This would concentrate on the strategic long-term vision or basic issues of role and structure, while facilitating proper—public—debate of the different constitutional implications. As well as the internal relationship between the centre and departments, it would be important to consider changing patterns of Civil Service structures and responsibilities in the context of a loosening Union state—a point missed by PASC. Fifty years on from Fulton, questions of skills and culture also need revisiting, not least because of the immediate and incessant demands of transparency and public scrutiny that so characterize our digital age. Sitting comfortably with the assertion of legislative power in the CRAG Act, an explicitly parliamentary dimension has much to commend it.

SHOCK WAVES: UK (ENGLISH) GOVERNMENT

THE EXECUTIVE(S) IN THE UNION

The Cameron–Clegg administration will go down in history as the government which nearly lost the Union. The sight of a complacent and then panicked Westminster elite vowing[130] major constitutional reform—'devo-more' or 'faster, safer and better change'—in the face of an exercise in (Scottish) popular sovereignty[131] will live long in folk memory. Looking forward, the shock waves generated by the hard-fought campaign and close 'no' vote in the Scottish independence referendum will continue to reverberate, effectively heralding a looser form of Union (state). If the precise contours currently defy prediction, old unitary-style understandings of what is denoted by the 'Executive' (and 'Parliament') will need revisiting. Reflecting the fact of several governments or the sharing (out) of executive power among the Union 'family' of countries, using the conceptual label 'UK (English) government' with reference to an imperiously titled 'Her Majesty's Government' is a fair start.

Viewed through the lens of individual ministerial responsibility, another look round the UK Cabinet table is revealing. The prime minister, the deputy prime minister and the Chancellor of the Exchequer obviously straddle the UK and English

---

[129] PASC, *Truth to Power*; see further, Hansard, HL, cols. 354–93 (16 January 2014).

[130] *Daily Record*, 16 September 2014.

[131] As facilitated by the (Edinburgh) *Agreement between the United Kingdom Government and the Scottish Government on an Independence Referendum for Scotland* (October 2012). See A. Tomkins, 'Scotland's Choice, Britain's Future' (2014) 130 *LQR* 215.

dimensions of policy. Determinedly pan-Union elements are exemplified by the Secretaries of State for Defence and Foreign and Commonwealth Affairs. Conversely, high-spend departments led by the Secretaries of State for Education, Health, and Communities and Local Government, stand for a distinctively English territorial or spatial component[132]—to the extent, it might be said mischievously, that the (histori-cally hallowed) designation is misleading: 'State', what 'English State'? Meanwhile, voices for the 'others', but today largely stripped of day-to-day decision-making responsibilities, the Secretaries of State for Scotland, Wales, and Northern Ireland bring up the rear.

More product of convoluted histories, there are of course other functional motifs: 'Great Britain', as mostly with the Department for Work and Pensions in standing for a 'social union', and more particularly 'England and Wales', as with Home Office and Ministry of Justice responsibilities for policing and criminal justice, and courts and prisons, respectively.[133] In a polity as large and complex as the UK, over-lapping and interlocking responsibilities are common, a point further underscored in the administrative procedural context of EU membership.[134] Collective respon-sibility and efforts at joined-up policies, key elements of commonality in the Home Civil Service,[135] and, yes, a sense of 'Britishness', necessarily contribute to the broader Whitehall mix. Nonetheless, the basic duality of UK (English) government, as also the propensity with a loosening Union further to accentuate the English dimension, shines through. As one of the Coalition's last policy papers shows, even the historical 'England and Wales' paradigm is under increased pressure.[136]

Today, the 'devolution mindset' which starts with the assumption that the UK is fundamentally a centralized state (if never a wholly unitary one[137]) is itself chal-lenged. Representing a determinedly more advanced form of constitutional think-ing, most obviously in terms of greater institutional pluralism and diversity, a 'new Union' mindset[138] speaks directly to a state boasting several systems of parliamentary government grounded in popular sovereignty and cooperating for mutual benefit. 'Devolution', it may be said, is not only about how each country is separately governed, but also the whole governance of the UK, the starting point being four administrations

---

[132] On the argument for tidying away the few exceptions through Transfer of Functions Orders, see Society of Conservative Lawyers, *Our Quasi-Federal Kingdom* (2014).

[133] See further on this chameleon-like quality, R. Hazell and R. Rawlings (eds.), *Devolution, Law Making and the Constitution* (2005).

[134] Harlow and Rawlings, *Process and Procedure in EU Administration*.

[135] See further, Institute for Government, *The Civil Service in Territorial Perspective* (2014). Interestingly, the Scottish government's submission to the Smith Commission (see later) did not make an issue of this.

[136] HM Government, *Powers for a Purpose: Towards a Lasting Devolution Settlement for Wales*, Cm 9020 (2015). For the prior debate, see (Silk) Commission on Devolution in Wales, *Empowerment and Responsibility: Legislative Powers to Strengthen Wales* (2014), especially ch. 10.

[137] See latterly, L. Colley, *Acts of Union, Acts of Disunion* (2013).

[138] As elaborated in particular by Welsh First Minister Carwyn Jones, speech on 'A new Union' (16 October 2014), at: http://wales.gov.uk/newsroom/articles/firstminister/141016fmwales/?lang=en.

which are, in the words of a Welsh government notably committed to the Union, 'in a relationship which is not hierarchical'.[139] In this perspective, the fact of 'national devolution'[140] to Scotland and Wales, with all the political and symbolic capital which this implies, and of course the huge sensitivities associated with the peace process in Northern Ireland,[141] should never be forgotten. Set in these terms, conflating 'Whitehall' with 'the Executive' is highly misleading. Perhaps hopefully, the behaviour of what in the old lexicon is 'central government' will be moulded accordingly.

Public discussion of the legal architecture of human rights protection serves to point up the practical connotations. Evidencing a severe lack of joined-up thinking in public law, the general accounts at first focused almost exclusively on the Human Rights Act 1998, so passing over the doubled protection in three of the four countries of the Union by virtue of the direct incorporation of provisions of the European Convention on Human Rights into the 1998 devolution statutes.[142] As late as 2012, members of the independent Commission on a Bill of Rights were apparently surprised to learn that the Celtic polities might have their own human rights commitments to nurture and defend.[143] At the time of writing, it is the Conservatives' plan to replace the Human Rights Act with a British Bill of Rights and Responsibilities which commands attention. In the words of the policy document, 'we will work with the devolved administrations and legislatures as necessary to make sure there is an effective new settlement across the UK'.[144] Of course behind this lies Dicey's (English) doctrine of Parliamentary Sovereignty, reserved powers, and all that. But while the Whitehall–Westminster axis is dominant in so many ways, countervailing dynamics of constrained authority ranging across the creative legislative power of the 'other' systems, the political discipline of the Sewel Convention,[145] and the overarching sense of a fragile Union, are brought sharply into focus here. If they ever materialize, the projected encounters should be lively.

The wide range of submissions made to the Smith Commission, hastily assembled to facilitate talks in the light of the three pro-Union parties' 'vow',[146] illuminates the competing demands for recalibration—further hollowing-out—of Whitehall capacities as part of the move to a looser Union. The Scottish government (SNP) paper naturally propounded the (slippery) concept of 'devo-max', for which read minimizing (at

[139] Welsh Government, *Evidence to the Commission on Devolution in Wales* (February 2013), para. 5.

[140] R. Rawlings, *Delineating Wales: Constitutional, Legal and Administrative Aspects of National Devolution* (2003).

[141] See Brice Dickson's chapter in this volume (ch. 9).

[142] See R. Rawlings, 'Taking Wales Seriously' in T. Campbell, K. Ewing, and A. Tomkins (eds.), *Sceptical Essays on Human Rights* (2001).

[143] Commission on a Bill of Rights, *A UK Bill of Rights? The Choice Before Us* (2 vols. 2012).

[144] Conservative Party, *Protecting Human Rights in the UK*, 6.

[145] Hansard, HL, col. 791 (21 July 1998). For the subsequent proposal to place the convention on a statutory footing, see HM Government, *Scotland in the United Kingdom: An Enduring Settlement*, Cm 8990 (2015), 16.

[146] See the prime minister's press statement, 'Scottish Independence Referendum' (19 September 2014). The three parties' proposals rehashed their existing policy offers: see Scottish Office, *The Parties' Published Proposals for Further Devolution to Scotland*, Cm 8946 (2014); Hansard, HC, cols. 168–271 (14 October 2014).

least in respect of Scotland) the UK component of UK (English) government.[147] This is the stuff, on the one hand, of full fiscal autonomy, and, on the other hand, of a very basic core (monetary policy; foreign policy, defence, and security; citizenship). At the other end of the spectrum, Labour envisaged some limited expansion of tax devolution[148] as well as some further devolution of specific welfare benefits. The profound nature of the constitutional challenge for a political party historically associated with large-scale and creative uses of the power of *dominium* or deployment of wealth by the (central) state is made apparent.[149] The intermediate position propounded by the Conservatives is especially noteworthy: a major party with a long track record of opposing devolution now envisaging the general passage of income tax powers. Nor is it entirely surprising to find the Smith Commission, tasked with producing a deal between the political parties in Scotland, publishing heads of agreement along similar lines.[150] Projecting forwards into the new UK Parliament, the resulting legislation will see HM Government losing some more pan-Union policy space.[151]

ENGLAND, THEIR ENGLAND

England has been the spectre at the devolution feast. But events in Scotland have predictably served to (re)focus attention on the so-called 'English question', the well-known collection of problems about how England should be governed in a looser Union, particular twists like devolution finance and the dreaded 'West Lothian question',[152] and, ultimately, social and cultural issues of (national) identity or sense of belonging.[153] As for the field of choice, some reform options appear more constitutionally challenging than others not least because of the implications for UK (English) government.

Suggestions for new structures of English localism abound, blending in turn into bigger projects for so-called 'city-states' and, despite having been unsuccessfully trialled under New Labour, regional assemblies. The signing in November 2014 of a 'devolution plan' for Greater Manchester, centred on an elected mayor with powers over transport, planning, housing, and policing, is a milestone in this regard.[154] Much in the general argument is commendable, especially with a view to democratic renewal[155] and in light of the exceeding economic and political dominance of London,

---

[147] Scottish Government, *More Powers for the Scottish Parliament* (2014); building on the White Paper, *Your Scotland, Your Voice* (2009).

[148] Building in turn on the taxing and expenditure powers contained in the Scotland Act 2012. The Wales Act 2014 contains more limited financial powers.

[149] See Gordon Brown, *My Scotland, Our Britain* (2014).

[150] *Report of the Smith Commission for further devolution of powers to the Scottish Parliament* (November 2014).

[151] Following on the draft Scotland clauses published in January 2015: HM Government, *Scotland in the United Kingdom: An Enduring Settlement*, Annex A.

[152] R. Hazell (ed.), *The English Question* (Manchester University Press, 2005); also, IPPR, *Answering the English Question: a new policy agenda for England* (2008).

[153] M. Kenny, *The Politics of English Nationhood* (2014).

[154] HM Treasury, *Greater Manchester Agreement* (2014). See further, Ian Leigh's chapter.

[155] IPPR, *Decentralisation decade: A plan for economic prosperity, public service transformation and democratic renewal in England* (2014).

constitutionally underscored these days by a Greater London Authority made up of the directly elected Mayor and Assembly.[156] From a 'new Union' perspective, there would also be some worthwhile diluting of England in Whitehall, most obviously in terms of budgets. Looking forward, the Commons' Communities and Local Government Committee recently made a compelling case for what it termed 'devolution in England' with special reference to fiscal devolution.[157] After all, the historical legacy of developing Whitehall dominium underwritten by, but also predating, the Thatcher government, there is 'by international standards...a highly centralised system of taxation and expenditure'.[158]

Then there is EVEL, the constitutional mantra of 'English votes for English laws', or more broadly EVEI, 'English votes for English issues'. Confirming the strong sense of dissatisfaction with how England is currently governed, the leading attitudinal survey indicates substantial and increased support for this type of approach.[159] Add in the particular challenge for a Labour Party historically strong in Scotland and Wales, and more immediately the evident populist appeal of UKIP, and the political conditions were ripe for the prime minister immediately to link the Scottish 'vow' and 'no' vote to requiring a 'decisive answer' on EVEL.[160] The idea is hardly new. Indeed, much in the constitutional discussion is tediously familiar: on the one hand, claims about lack of fairness and/or accommodation of Englishness; on the other, concerns about knock-on effects and different classes of MPs (and hence the long-term viability of the Union), as well as technical issues of procedure and definition. However the basic duality of UK (English) government is very pertinent. Adopted in strong form, broad veto powers perhaps on the command of law or exercise of *imperium*, EVEL could conjure risks for governability, and indeed for collective responsibility, precisely because of the element of division. A product of the Coalition's *Programme for Government*, the independent Mackay Commission on the consequences of devolution for the House of Commons was understandably cautious in recommending a greater voice for English MPs subject to the whole House retaining the final say.[161] A combustible product from a dying government, the later command paper on various options was predictably shot through with different party political calculations.[162]

But what, it may be asked, of the suggestion of an 'English Parliament'?[163] In notably paradoxical fashion, the sheer size of the country—some 85 per cent of the UK population—has been seen to present an insuperable difficulty (assuming, that is, the continued existence of the Union).[164] Multiple potentials for problems of governability or stand-offs with the UK Parliament present a grim spectre; indeed, the currency

[156] Greater London Authority Act 1999, as amended.

[157] House of Commons, Communities and Local Government Committee, *Devolution in England: The Case for Local Government*, HC 503 (2014/15).

[158] Ibid, para. 5.

[159] C. Jeffery et al. (eds.), *Taking England Seriously: The New English Politics* (2014).

[160] Via referral to a UK Cabinet Committee: 'Scottish Independence Referendum' (19 September 2014).

[161] *Report of the (Mackay) Commission on the Consequences of Devolution for the House of Commons* (2013).

[162] HM Government, *The Implications of Devolution for England*, Cm 8969 (2014).

[163] Campaign for an English Parliament, at http://thecep.org.uk/.

[164] Hence part of the argument against a formal federal solution: *Report of the Royal Commission on the Constitution, the Kilbrandon Commission* (1973).

markets could have a field day. But our discerning student will happily press the matter. Constitutional responsibility according to the Westminster model: does not an 'English Parliament' in practice mean an 'English government' (first minister, treasury minister, departments and all)? So where, goes the not so gentle inquiry, is the great popular clamour for a bigger governing class? Or is the duality of UK (English) government somehow to be catered for via a practice of representative doubling-up? Prime minister's garb on Mondays and Tuesdays perhaps, first minister's attire later in the week: such would be a constitutional theatre of the absurd.

BEYOND CONSTITUTIONAL PATRIARCHY

'Asymmetrical quasi-federalism' is not a phrase to set the pulses racing. But it suggests a constitutional way of life which Whitehall will be increasingly challenged to adopt.[165] Referencing 'new Union'-style thinking in suitably flexible fashion, their chief institutions are thus said to embody democratic accountability in the four constituent countries, with more or less pooling of powers and resources in the light of particular historic, demographic, and economic considerations. Simply put, the routine workings of Dicey's doctrine of Parliamentary Sovereignty may be fine for the English but not for everybody else. In this determinedly rich perspective, the limited appeal of formal federal structures does not negate the case for a strong dose of federal thinking in the UK constitution: quite the reverse. Typically then, the talk is of enabling unity while guaranteeing diversity through a process of balancing power in a more differentiated political order.[166]

Some encouraging noises are made in the concordats, the myriad soft law documentation on principles, structures, and processes first agreed by the four governments in 1999 with a view to constructive, efficient, and effective forms of intergovernmental relations.[167] As well as providing for political machinery in the guise(s) of the Joint Ministerial Committee, the principal Memorandum of Understanding (MoU) thus highlights cooperation and consultation, as well as coordination, as basic desiderata.[168] Looking forward, Whitehall will have heightened responsibility for upholding such precepts in a looser form of Union characterized by more exclusive territorial authority and much shared interest. To this effect, the political and administrative demands are not new but have still greater significance amid the shock waves now rippling through the UK constitution.

---

[165] See further, Institute for Government, *Governing after the Referendum: Future Constitutional Scenarios for the UK* (2014).

[166] See further in this regard the Council of Europe Parliamentary Assembly's report, *Towards a Better European Democracy: Facing the Challenges of a Federal Europe* (2014).

[167] R. Rawlings, 'Concordats of the Constitution' (2000) 116 *LQR* 257.

[168] *Memorandum of Understanding and Supplementary Agreements between the United Kingdom Government, the Scottish Ministers, the Welsh Ministers, and the Northern Ireland Executive Committee* (2013 version).

In fact, whirring away in the background, the bureaucratic modalities of intergovernmental relations have not received the attention they deserve in discussion of the changing constitution. Notably, much of the traffic involves matters of bilateral relations between Whitehall and one of the other governments. Ranging across the spectrum from open and friendly dealings to poor awareness and failure to engage, the performance of Whitehall departments and policy teams appears decidedly mixed; the Welsh government, for example, speaks of 'professional, business-like, constructive, numerous, complex and sometimes frustrating' working relationships.[169] Despite periodic review and fine-tuning of the multilateral machinery, a lack of transparency and organizational skews in favour of Whitehall (as through permanent chairing of the JMC's disputes panel) have remained matters of concern.[170] Perhaps hopefully, prompted in part by the Smith Commission, the machinery will now be taken more seriously.

In grounding a distinctive set of constitutional priorities, 'new Union'-style thinking also provides a litmus test of future constitutional development and, in particular, of the behaviour of UK (English) government—most obviously in terms of pathology or push-back. Towards the fag-end of the Cameron–Clegg government, a small but significant imbroglio broke out over the state of the NHS in Wales. Aided and abetted by powerful media interests, the prime minister and the Secretary of State for Health went out of their way to criticize performance levels, to the extent of complaining about cross-border flows of patients into England.[171] Meanwhile, the Labour administration in Wales struggled to make its voice heard in rebuttal.[172] Inside Whitehall, the affair was no doubt considered clever politics ahead of a looming UK general election. Yet, not simply a case of robust debate, it can also be viewed as a very public bullying of one member of the Union 'family' by the most powerful one. Attention is drawn to the corrosive potentials for respect and trust, key constitutional qualities on which the Union at large ultimately depends. Reverting to concordatry, it has been said that locked in the chief MoU and waiting to escape is the fundamental constitutional principle of comity.[173] It is time it did.

CONCLUSION

The historical fact of the Cameron–Clegg administration enduring was hardly a given in May 2010. Constitutionally speaking, the obvious product is a Fixed-term Parliaments Act which itself works to shape future political calculation. But there also was some skilful adaptation of governing arrangements, very much in the evolutionary

---

[169] Welsh Government, Written Statement, 18 June 2013.

[170] House of Lords Constitution Committee, *Inter-governmental relations in the United Kingdom*, HL 146 (2014-15); Institute for Government, *Governing in an Ever Looser Union* (2015).

[171] Hansard, HC, cols. 753–4 (21 October 2014) and cols. 890–3 (22 October 2014).

[172] *Record of Proceedings*, National Assembly for Wales, 21 October 2014.

[173] Rawlings, 'Concordats of the Constitution', 267. The reference is to constitutional practice in advanced federal systems like Germany ('Bundestreue').

tradition of the UK's uncodified arrangements. The creative use of soft law technique going with the grain of, and elaborating on, essential conventional understandings is of the essence of this. Time will tell about the scale of the resulting constitutional footprint, though it will surely be more substantial than at first appears. Yes, the Cameron–Clegg experiment is only one possible form of response to the political arithmetic of no overall majority for a single party, but it would be most odd if future constitutional actors did not factor in the seeming strengths and limitations. The fact of political and institutional learning involved in novel processes of government formation and operation is itself significant; the later criticism of insufficient procedural provision for departures from collective ministerial responsibility is also out there. An old truth perhaps, but constitutional effect must be measured not simply by reference to what subsequently happens but also what does not.

Tensions between ministers and officials are hardly new, but they were a particular feature of life under the Cameron–Clegg government. Punctuated with outbursts of negativity, a slew of ad hoc and piecemeal developments also demonstrate the lack of a clear sense of direction when dealing with machinery of government issues: the more so, when measured against the likes of Northcote–Trevelyan and Haldane and even, dare one say it, the Thatcher years. The bonfire or not of quangos, or more accurately the scattered burnings, speaks volumes in this regard. Put another way, individual initiatives may or may not have had merit, but the belated fact of a Civil Service Reform Plan cannot obscure the shortcomings—in the context of a loosening Union, one is tempted to say myopia—in terms of strategic vision. So too, with reference to other developments taking place under the Cameron–Clegg administration, one need not be a devoted follower of the mandarinate to insist on the importance of both sides of the convention of individual ministerial responsibility; and, in particular, of the constitutional value of protecting a professional bureaucracy from political patronage. Viewed in the round, it is a poor way of undertaking the task of machinery of government reform.

Future historians will surely consider September 2014 and all its works a key constitutional moment in the life of this Atlantic archipelago. Indeed, in so far as the Cameron-Clegg coalition is remembered, this will be remembered as happening on their watch. Today, the direction of travel is firmly in favour of a looser Union, with, speak it loudly, profound implications for the structures, powers, and practices of the post-imperial Whitehall machine. This highlights, at one level, the expanding distribution of executive responsibilities to other democratically elected governments and with it the challenge to old (English) conceptions of constitutional hierarchy; at another level, through the concept of UK (English) government, the twin dynamics of hollowing the Union component and reworking the largest territorial one; and at another level again, the extended premium placed on intergovernmental relations. The third part of the chapter has set about bettering predominantly Anglo-centric and Metropolitan views of the changing constitution. Looking forwards, much constitutional and political wisdom will be required, most obviously on the part of ministers in London, if—and it is a big if—the Union is to survive and prosper.

FURTHER READING

First Minister of Wales Carwyn Jones, *A new Union* (2014).

House of Lords Constitution Committee, *Constitutional Implications of Coalition Government*, HL 130 (2013–14)

House of Commons Political and Constitutional Reform Committee, *Role and Powers of the Prime Minister*, HC 351 (2014–15)

House of Lords Constitution Committee, *The Accountability of Civil Servants*, HL 61 (2012–13)

Kenny, M., *The Politics of English Nationhood* (2014)

Public Administration Select Committee, *Truth to Power: How Civil Service Reform Can Succeed*, HC 74 (2013–14)

8

THE FOUNDATIONS OF JUSTICE

Andrew Le Sueur

SUMMARY

Everybody agrees that the constitutional principle of judicial independence is important. In relation to the core judicial functions of hearing cases and writing judgments, the meaning and application of the principle is fairly straightforward: politicians, parliamentarians, and officials must refrain from interfering with judicial decision-making in individual cases. But hearing and judgments do not 'just happen'; they have to be facilitated by a wide array of institutions and processes (the justice infrastructure), covering matters as diverse as court buildings, litigation procedures, judicial careers, and legal aid. The day-to-day running of this infrastructure, along with its periodic reshaping, presents numerous and complex challenges for a legal system intent on respecting judicial independence and facilitating access to justice.

THE JUSTICE INFRASTRUCTURE

'All rise.' Every day, with words like this, thousands of court and tribunal sittings start across the United Kingdom.[1] In the minutes, hours, or days that follow, judges adjudicate on disputes of fact, decide what the common law is, and interpret and apply legislation to the situations before them. In the higher courts and some tribunals, writing judgments is also part of this core judicial function. Judges, and the courts and tribunals they sit in, are the embodiment of the state's judicial power, authorized to impose criminal sanctions, order compensation and other remedies, and adjudicate on the legality of governmental action. These core functions are constitutionally important

---

[1] There are separate justice infrastructures in England and Wales, in Scotland, and in Northern Ireland; each is a distinct legal system; and, under the devolution settlement, justice is a policy field devolved to governments and legislatures in Scotland and Northern Ireland. This chapter focuses on England and Wales.

activities that give practical implementation of the rule of law. In most countries round the world, there is a strong consensus that judges must be insulated from instructions or influences from government or other illegitimate pressures on the outcome of the particular case. Sometimes this understanding is presented as an aspect of the rule of law; sometimes as a strand of the concept of separation of powers; and sometimes as a free-standing principle of judicial independence.

Court and tribunal hearings and judgment writing do not, however, 'just happen'. Behind every sitting and judgment there is a complex array of institutions and processes that facilitate the delivery of justice by the legal system's 35,000 judges. To facilitate the delivery of justice, courts and tribunals must be created and funded. Jurisdiction (the legal power to decide types of cases) is created, transferred, modified, and sometimes 'ousted' by the legislature. There need to be rules of procedure guiding the steps to be taken in litigation. Entitlement, if any, to legal aid, must also be defined. Rules on rights of audience before courts, which in turn may depend on rules about regulation of the legal profession, are required. The practical work of listing hearings, allocating cases to judges, and ensuring parties, lawyers, witnesses, and documents are where they are needed is vital (and in many legal systems increasingly dependent on information technology).[2] Buildings for courts and court staff need to be provided and managed. Judges must be selected and appointed (perhaps thousands each year),[3] disciplined (occasionally), dismissed (very rarely), and eventually allowed to retire with a pension. This 'justice infrastructure' is the focus of this chapter.

It is easy to see what an adverse impact a weak justice infrastructure could have on the quality of court sittings and judgments in particular cases. Imagine a system in which politicians make dramatic changes to the structure of courts without consultation, lawyers without adequate professional expertise are appointed as judges, and chronic underfunding delays litigants obtaining judgments and prevents many people from affording access to the courts. Worse, a justice infrastructure could be affected by endemic corruption. As Lord Phillips of Worth Matravers (Lord Chief Justice of England and Wales) said, repeating the sentiments of Lord Browne-Wilkinson (a former Senior Law Lord): 'Judicial independence cannot exist on its own—judges must have the loyal staff, buildings and equipment to support the exercise of the independent judicial function.'[4]

The justice infrastructure in England and Wales has in recent years been buffeted by some poorly considered reform attempts and (like almost every other part of the public sector) has been reeling from financial cuts introduced by government in the wake of the 2008 financial crisis. The Ministry of Justice (the government department

---

[2] In England and Wales, a £375 million investment programme started in 2014, designed to use information technology, online services, and video links to reduce delays and costs.

[3] e.g. in 2013–14, more than 800 individual judicial appointments had to be made in England and Wales, which involved processing over 5,000 applications.

[4] House of Commons Select Constitutional Affairs Committee, *The Creation of the Ministry of Justice*, 6th Report of 2006–7, HC 466, Ev 27.

responsible for the courts and judiciary) had an 'extremely challenging' settlement in the 2010 Comprehensive Spending Review, requiring it to reduce expenditure by over £2 billion a year during the four-year period 2011–15; and it was required to find a further 10 per cent savings in 2015–16. Pay freezes, job cuts, and court closures are affecting the morale of judges and court staff. Many judges and practitioners are deeply concerned about recent radical changes to the legal aid system.[5]

This chapter explores the justice infrastructure in England and Wales, which has undergone significant reforms in recent years. It does this on two levels—'running' and 'shaping'. The first level (running) is the routine operation of the system, where decisions are taken within the framework of the existing infrastructure. This encompasses day-to-day matters (for example, listing of cases for hearing, making individual judicial appointments, granting or refusing legal aid) and annual planning cycles (such as the allocation of resources to HM Courts and Tribunals Service, the organization that runs many aspects of the infrastructure). The second level (shaping) is strategic, concerned with changing the infrastructure, which typically involves the addition or abolition of a major new process or institution or significant new rules. Recent examples of shaping are the institutional changes introduced by the Constitutional Reform Act 2005 (reforming the office of Lord Chancellor, creating the UK Supreme Court, and a new process for appointing judges in England and Wales).

Both levels of the infrastructure—running and shaping—are of constitutional significance. They generate direct and indirect risks of damaging or enriching judicial independence for the core functions of hearing cases and writing judgments.[6] It may be tempting to think that a neat solution would be to hand over the running and shaping of the justice infrastructure—lock, stock, and barrel—to the judiciary. But, as we will see, a solution along these lines needs to be rejected as being too difficult to square with other constitutional values, especially accountability and the need to reflect the broad public interest.[7] Running and shaping of the justice infrastructure also has direct and indirect implications for the constitutional principle of access to justice.

THE BLUEPRINT FOR THE INFRASTRUCTURE

Where do we find the blueprint—the instruction manual—for the justice infrastructure? In countries with codified written constitutions, the constitution is a source. In the United Kingdom, primary and secondary legislation and specific pieces of 'soft law' provide the detailed rules and requirements that keep the system ticking over.

---

[5] F. Wilmot-Smith, 'Necessity or Ideology?' (2014) 36(21) *London Review of Books* 15.

[6] For a detailed statement of the specific norms grouped under the umbrella term 'judicial independence', see *The Mount Scopus Approved Revised International Standards of Judicial Independence* (2008, as amended) http://www.jwp.org.

[7] On accountability, see further A. Le Sueur, 'Parliamentary Accountability and the Justice System' in N. Bamforth and P. Leyland (eds.), *Accountability in the Contemporary Constitution* (2013).

CONSTITUTIONS

In countries with codified constitutions, the major elements of their justice infra-structure are laid down in part of the constitutional code.[8] It should not surprise us to find that the justice infrastructure contrasts across different constitutional, polit-ical, and legal cultures. What is normal in one system (for example, selecting judges through highly politicized elections in some states of the USA) is anathema in oth-ers (where professional merit is the criterion for appointment). There is, however, broad consensus about some general abstract principles that in the mid-twentieth century came to be included in international human rights treaties. The judicial infrastructure must enable hearings that are 'independent and impartial', in pub-lic (unless there is an overriding public interest in closed hearings), and within a reasonable time.[9]

LEGISLATION

As we muddle through without a codified constitution in the United Kingdom, it is Acts of Parliament that do the work of creating the institutions, rules, procedures, and conferring executive power for the most important elements of the national judicial infrastructure.[10] The Acts are amended quite frequently through the normal parlia-mentary legislative process in the House of Commons and the House of Lords.

Beneath these Acts of Parliament lies a conglomeration of delegated legislation. As with delegated legislation on other topics, most of this comes into force with little parliamentary scrutiny or public controversy. It fills in detail. Occasionally, however, changes sought to be made in this way do receive high-profile scrutiny, such as when the blandly named Civil Legal Aid (Remuneration) (Amendment) (No. 3) Regulations 2014 prompted an outcry, with Lord Pannick leading a 'motion of regret' debate in the House of Lords critical of government proposals to restrict legal aid in judicial review claims.[11] Only one member of the House of Lords—the junior minister representing

---

[8] See e.g. the Australian Constitution, Part III (Judicature); Spanish Constitution, Part VI (Judicial Power); Constitution of Ireland, Arts. 34–7; and so on.

[9] Universal Declaration of Human Rights, Art. 10 ('Everyone is entitled in full equality to a fair and public hearing by an independent and impartial tribunal, in the determination of his rights and obligations and of any criminal charge against him'); European Convention on Human Rights, Art. 6.

[10] These include: the Courts Act 1971 (creating the Crown Court); the Magistrates' Courts Act 1980; the Senior Courts Act 1981 (regulating the High Court and Court of Appeal); the County Courts Act 1984; the Legal Aid Act 1988 (replaced by the Access to Justice Act 1999 and subsequently by the Legal Aid, Sentencing and Punishment of Offenders Act 2012); the Courts Act 2003 (creating HM Courts Service, the agency to administer courts, expanded in 2007 to include tribunals); the Constitutional Reform Act 2005 (reform-ing the office of Lord Chancellor, setting up the UK Supreme Court, and creating a new judicial appoint-ments system); the Legal Services Act 2007 (regulating the legal profession, in conjunction with the Courts and Legal Services Act 1990); and the Tribunals, Courts and Enforcement Act 2007 (creating the First-tier Tribunal and Upper Tribunal in place of the previous maze of separate tribunals).

[11] BBC, 'Grayling Accused of Not Understanding the Legal System', http://www.bbc.co.uk/democracylive/house-of-lords-27319557.

the government's views—defended the new rules; he assured the House that he 'would take back the observations that were made during the course of the debate' to the Ministry of Justice.[12] Lord Pannick did not press the debate to a vote and the new rules came into force.

THE CONCORDAT

Beyond the statute book is a variety of 'soft law' documents, one of which is of special general significance. 'The Concordat' reflects the outcome of an intense period of negotiations in the second half of 2003 between Lord Woolf (the then Lord Chief Justice) and Lord Falconer (the minister in Tony Blair's Labour government responsible for judiciary-related matters).[13] The impetus for the negotiations was the unexpected announcement made by the prime minister's office in June 2003 of several far-reaching changes to the justice infrastructure, including abolition of the ancient office of Lord Chancellor, a new top-level court of the United Kingdom (by creating a UK Supreme Court to replace the Law Lords sitting as the Appellate Committee of the House of Lords), a new judicial appointments system for England and Wales, and disqualification of all senior judges from membership of Parliament. This was dramatic stuff and prompted political opposition in Parliament (primarily from the Conservatives) and criticism from some senior members of the judiciary (though others supported the gist of the proposals).[14] A negotiating team was formed by Lord Woolf to discuss with the government how responsibility for running the infrastructure would be divided between the proposed new Secretary of State (who would, under the Blair plan, have replaced the Lord Chancellor) and the judiciary. In January 2004, after six months of behind-closed-doors brokering, the Concordat was published: it was a relatively short document of 47 paragraphs setting out the principles that would govern the transfer of functions in England and Wales and providing details of the application of those principles to the proposed arrangements.[15] Lord Woolf told the House of Lords: 'In agreeing the proposals, the judiciary has regarded as its primary responsibility, not the protection of its own interests but the protection of the independence of the justice system for the benefit of the public.'[16] Major elements of the Concordat were incorporated into the Constitutional Reform Act 2005 (CRA 2005); but one central aspect was not. Following sustained opposition from Conservative MPs and peers (and some others) in Parliament, the office of Lord Chancellor was retained though

---

[12] Hansard, HL, vol. 753, col. 1567 (7 May 2014), Lord Faulks.

[13] *Constitutional Reform: The Lord Chancellor's Judiciary-related Functions: Proposals, Since Referred to as 'the Agreement' and also 'the Concordat'* http://webarchive.nationalarchives.gov.uk/+/http:/www.dca. gov.uk/consult/lcoffice/judiciary.htm.

[14] For a detailed analysis, see A. Le Sueur, 'From Appellate Committee to Supreme Court: a Narrative' in L. Blom-Cooper, G. Drewry, and B. Dickson (eds.), *The Judicial House of Lords 1876–2009* (2009).

[15] Hansard, HL, vol. 756, col. 13 (26 January 2004).

[16] Hansard, HL, vol. 756, col. 25 (26 January 2004)

in a much-altered form: the office-holder was a government minister, but no longer the constitutional head of the judiciary nor necessarily in the House of Lords or a professionally qualified lawyer.

After the enactment of the CRA 2005, the question arose as to the continuing status of the Concordat. On one view, the document had done its job: it was a statement of outcome of a negotiation and, once implemented, could be filed away as a mere footnote to the policy-making process. Some, however, take a different view, seeing the Concordat as either 'constitutional convention' or a 'living document', which remains a reference point and in future to be developed. In 2005, Lady Justice Arden, giving evidence on behalf of the Judges' Council (the official non-statutory body set up by the judiciary to develop collective policy) to a House of Lords select committee scrutinizing the bill that became the CRA 2005, called for the bill or the bill's explanatory notes to make express reference to the Concordat, arguing 'there is a role for the Concordat even after the bill has been enacted', adding 'not every iota of the Concordat can be reflected in statutory language. There are some matters which have to, as it were, survive within the Concordat and one way in which the Concordat may be relevant in future is when the court is construing what will then be the Constitutional Reform Act, it may be necessary for it to look at the Concordat.'[17] The committee was not convinced, reporting: 'We do not consider it possible, beyond the provisions made by the bill, to accord the Concordat a quasi-statutory status.'[18] Two years later, a different House of Lords committee carrying out an inquiry into the relations between the judiciary, government, and Parliament heard evidence from one academic (Professor Robert Hazell) describing the Concordat as 'a constitutional convention' and the committee went on to recommend:[19]

> We believe that the Concordat is a document of constitutional importance. We are concerned that the Concordat has not been updated to reflect the new arrangements for Her Majesty's Courts Service, and we call on the Government and the judiciary to establish a practice of amending the Concordat whenever necessary to ensure that it remains a living document reflecting current arrangements rather than being merely a historic document recording the outcome of negotiations in 2005. Consideration should be given to introducing a formal mechanism for laying revised versions of the Concordat before Parliament.

No such formal mechanism for change has been put in place and no revisions have been made to the Concordat since it was agreed in 2003.

---

[17] House of Lords Select Committee on the Constitutional Reform Bill, *Report*, Session 2003–4, HL Paper 125-I, para. 75.

[18] House of Lords Select Committee on the Constitutional Reform Bill, *Report*, Session 2003–4 (HL Paper 125-1), para. 85.

[19] House of Lords Constitution Committee, *Relations between the Executive, the Judiciary and Parliament*, 6th Report of 2006–7 (HL Paper 151), para. 14.

OTHER SOFT LAW

In addition to the Concordat (whatever its status), there are other documents of key importance in the justice infrastructure. Of general importance is HM Court and Tribunals Service Framework Document, which was laid before the UK Parliament in July 2014.[20] The document describes itself as reflecting 'an agreement reached by the Lord Chancellor, the Lord Chief Justice and the Senior President of Tribunals on a partnership between them in relation to the effective governance, financing and operation of HM Courts & Tribunals Service'.

RUNNING THE INFRASTRUCTURE

Running the justice infrastructure covers routine decision-making of various kinds: making decisions about individuals (should applicant W be selected for appointment as a judge; should claimant X receive legal aid), about managing workflow (which judges should form the panel of the Court of Appeal hearing case Y next week; should court building Z be closed to save money; are more circuit judges needed in the South West), about supervision of the system (how effectively is the tribunal system operating), and so on. The general characteristic of 'running' is that it takes place within the existing infrastructure.

Who runs the national infrastructure on a day-to-day basis? Who ought to run it? In trying to answer these descriptive and normative questions, it soon becomes clear that there are no straightforward answers for England and Wales. Mapping out the intricacies of the system is a colossal task; although some of this detail is needed, we concentrate on the broad constitutional questions about the allocation of decision-making power. A standard approach is to use the framework of separation-of-powers theory. An elementary and rather eighteenth-century account of this principle is that there are three types of state power, each of which ought to be wielded by different state institutions: executive power (exercised by government, in other words ministers and civil servants), legislative power (the law-making powers of Parliament), and judicial power (exercised by judges).[21] This framework is, however, too broad-brush to provide solutions as to who should run the justice infrastructure. A better approach is to focus on the four main models in use in the infrastructure of England and Wales that can be discerned: (i) functions run by judges; (ii) functions run by politicians and their officials; (iii) functions which are shared between judges and politicians; and (iv) functions which have been allocated to arm's length bodies, independent of both judges and politicians.

---

[20] HM Court and Tribunals Service Framework Document, Cm 8882.
[21] For a more sophisticated account, see N. Barber, 'Prelude to the Separation of Powers' [2001] *Camb LJ* 59.

FUNCTIONS RUN BY JUDGES

The CRA 2005 made the Lord Chief Justice of England and Wales (LCJ) 'head of the judiciary'. Where infrastructure functions are led by the judiciary, in practice it is the LCJ (or his nominee) who makes decisions. The LCJ is assisted by the Judicial Executive Board (consisting of ten senior members of the judiciary and two senior administrators), which meets monthly. The LCJ has a staff of 186 FTE officials in the Judicial Office, which supports his work, including 'professional trainers, legal advisers, HR and communication experts, policy makers and administrators'.[22] The Judicial Office, which has an annual budget of £18 million, is funded by the Ministry of Justice but staff are answerable to the LCJ—not to government ministers—for their day-to-day work.

The Concordat lists six aspects of the infrastructure as ones to be primarily carried out by judges: oath taking—judges take oaths of office in the presence of the LCJ (not a government minister); deployment—the LCJ is responsible for the posting and roles of individual judges, within a framework set by the government; nomination of judges to fill posts that provide judicial leadership (such as senior presiding judges, the deputy Chief Justice, the Vice-Presidents of the Court of Appeal) 'should fall to the Lord Chief Justice either with the concurrence of or in consultation with' the government; the LCJ determines which individual judges are appointed to various committees, boards, and similar bodies; the LCJ makes 'practice directions', with the concurrence of the government, providing guidance to judges on relative minor procedural matters; judicial training is led by the LCJ, within the resources provided by the government.

After reforms to the judicial appointments process in 2013, the LCJ now has a final say in approving selections of candidates made by the independent Judicial Appointments Commission (JAC) to judicial posts below the High Court in the hierarchy, with a similar role in relation to tribunal judges carried out by the Senior President of Tribunals.[23] Previously this function was carried out by government (through the Lord Chancellor); but in practice, only in a tiny number of cases did the government reject the recommendation made by the JAC.

Another major component of the infrastructure led by judges is the operation of the UK Supreme Court (which as well as England and Wales, serves as the highest level appeal court for civil cases from Scotland and civil and criminal cases from Northern Ireland). Before the CRA 2005, the top court was the Appellate Committee of the House of Lords, consisting of 12 professional judges (colloquially called the Law Lords) who on appointment to the court were granted peerages enabling them to take part in non-judicial as well as judicial work of the upper house of the UK Parliament. Cases were heard in a committee room in Parliament and judgments (or 'speeches') were delivered in the House of Lords chamber at times when politicians were absent. Some of the Law Lords integrated themselves into the political work of the House of

---

[22] See http://www.judiciary.gov.uk.
[23] Crime and Courts Act 2013, Sched. 13, amending the CRA 2005.

Lords, for example by listening and speaking in debates on legislation in the chamber and chairing non-judicial committees (such as one on scrutiny of EU legislation). Other Law Lords sought to distance themselves from non-judicial work as much as possible, uneasy about the blurring of lines between judicial and political roles. The CRA 2005 ended the role of the Appellate Committee, transferring the Law Lords to a new UK Supreme Court physically and institutionally separated from Parliament (though it was not until October 2009 that the new court was ready to start work).

Three infrastructure questions relating to the UK Supreme Court were considered in detail during the debates in 2004–5. The first was who should make the rules of court? Initially, the government proposed that it should have a controlling influence, with power to disallow rules proposed by the President of the court. Responding to criticisms, the government backed down and agreed that the President should have sole rule-making power, with a duty to consult the legal profession and government. The government's only role is to lay the rules before Parliament for formal approval as delegated legislation.

A second issue was how the administration of the court should be organized. Initially, the bill provided: 'The Minister may appoint such officers and staff as he thinks appropriate for the purpose of discharging his general duty in relation to the Supreme Court.' Critics, including the Law Lords, argued that this would give the government too much influence over the court's day-to-day operations. Under pressure, the government agreed to amend the bill so that the CRA 2005 now provides: 'The President of the Supreme Court may appoint officers and staff of the Court' (s. 49). Until 2013, the government remained responsible for appointing the court's chief executive, after consulting the President of the Court; but the Crime and Courts Act 2013 amended the CRA 2005 so that s. 48 now reads: 'It is for the President of the Court to appoint the chief executive.'

A third issue was funding. During the passage of the bill, the government gave the reassurance that 'the Minister will simply be a conduit for the Supreme Court bid and will not be able to alter it before passing it on to the Treasury'. The CRA provides that the government (i.e. the Lord Chancellor) 'must ensure that the Supreme Court is provided' with 'such other resources as the Lord Chancellor thinks are appropriate for the Court to carry on its business'. This arrangement is difficult to square with the reassurance and has caused misunderstanding and some ill-will between the court and the government in the ensuing years. Giving a public lecture in 2011, Lord Phillips (President of the court) told his audience about government pressure to make dramatic cost reductions, a 'peremptory' letter he had received from the minister, and his conclusion:

> that our present funding arrangements do not satisfactorily guarantee our institutional independence. We are, in reality, dependant each year upon what we can persuade the Ministry of Justice of England and Wales to give us by way of 'contribution'. This is not a satisfactory situation for the Supreme Court of the United Kingdom. It is already leading a tendency on the part of the Ministry of Justice to try to gain the Supreme Court as an outlying part of its empire.

The following morning, the government responded in the news media. Kenneth Clarke, the Lord Chancellor, was reported as saying 'judicial independence was at the heart of the country's freedom but that Phillips could not be in the "unique position" of telling the government what its budget should be'.[24]

FUNCTIONS RUN BY GOVERNMENT

Most of government's powers to run the justice infrastructure are legally and constitutionally speaking in the hands of the Lord Chancellor. Before the CRA 2005, prime ministers selected senior, experienced lawyers for the role; the Lord Chancellor and senior judges therefore knew each other professionally and moved in the same social circles. On taking up the post, the office-holder became the constitutional head of the judiciary and with that came the right to sit as the presiding judge in the top-level courts (even though, prior to appointment, many Lord Chancellors had little experience of sitting judicially).

The 2003 Blair government proposal was to abolish the Lord Chancellor and transfer government responsibilities for judiciary and court-related functions to a new post of Secretary of State.[25] Once the announcement had been made, a broad consensus quickly emerged that it was no longer appropriate for a government minister to be the constitutional head of the judiciary or to sit as a judge. But the Conservatives (then in opposition), supported by many cross-bencher peers in the House of Lords, were vehemently opposed to the outright abolition of the office of Lord Chancellor: they wanted the government minister responsible for judiciary-related matters and the courts to retain some of the characteristics of previous Lord Chancellors. The minister should, they argued, continue to be called 'the Lord Chancellor', and should be a professionally qualified lawyer, sit in Parliament in the House of Lords (not in the Commons), and be somebody at the end of their political career (rather than being an ambitious mid-career politician keen to please, and therefore be under the patronage of, the prime minister). The protracted political wrangling was brought to an end by the need for the bill to become the CRA 2005 before the general election that year. The outcome in relation to the Lord Chancellor was that the name was retained, but there would be no requirement for the office-holder to be lawyer, or to sit in the House of Lords. The

---

[24] H. Mulholland, 'Kenneth Clarke Rejects Claim of Threat to Supreme Court Independence', *The Guardian*, 9 February 2011.

[25] In law, all Secretaries of State hold a single office. Acts of Parliament confer powers and impose duties on 'the Secretary of State' without further elaboration as to which minister will in practice exercise those powers or carry out those duties. The Interpretation Act 1978 provides that a reference to 'Secretary of State' is a reference to 'one of Her Majesty's Principal Secretaries of State for the time being'. The previous practice of creating statutory ministerial posts responsible for particular areas of policy (e.g. the Minister of Transport or the Minister of Agriculture, Fisheries and Food) has fallen into disuse. The prime minister has considerable scope for making what are often called 'machinery of government' changes, creating new Secretaries of State and departments, and transferring work between Secretaries of State and departments. These are normally done with little parliamentary scrutiny. Changes are given legal effect by secondary legislation made under the Ministers of the Crown Act 1975.

new 'Lord Chancellor' was in most respects a mainstream government minister. There were, however, some special features of the new ministerial office.

Although the CRA 2005 is completely silent on this, the role of Lord Chancellor is in practice combined with that of Secretary of State, so that one person holds two ministerial posts. Between 2005 and 2006, the Secretary of State was called 'Secretary of State for Constitutional Affairs', heading the Department for Constitutional Affairs (DCA). After May 2006, he became 'Secretary of State for Justice', heading a new department—the Ministry of Justice—that combined some of the DCA's responsibilities with areas previously under the remit of the Home Office. In this conjoined-roles ministerial office, the Lord Chancellor is responsible for judiciary and court-related functions (along with a few other areas, such as the Law Commission)—in other words, the justice infrastructure—and the Secretary of State deals with everything else in the Department. Since the CRA 2005 was enacted, the 'everything else' element of the job has grown significantly, to include now the large and inevitably controversial areas of prisons and offender management (moved to the Ministry of Justice from the Home Office).

The distinctive nature of the office of Lord Chancellor—distinguishing it from that of Secretary of State—is achieved by several different means. First, the CRA 2005 and numerous other statutes confer powers and duties on the Lord Chancellor (rather than the Secretary of State). It is difficult to quantify the precise number of these functions: many predate the CRA 2005; between January 2006 and June 2014, Parliament enacted 73 Acts of Parliament referring to the Lord Chancellor, many of which will contain multiple specific statutory powers and duties. Secondly, CRA 2005, s. 20 prevents many powers of the Lord Chancellor (those listed in Sched. 7 to the CRA 2005) from being transferred by the prime minister to other ministers under the general machinery of government provisions of the Ministers of the Crown Act 1975. These Lord Chancellor powers are, in effect, ring-fenced and require primary legislation to allocate them elsewhere (so giving Parliament the final say on whether such changes are made); but the Lord Chancellor also has statutory functions that are not ring-fenced in this way, for example those under the Legal Services Act 2007 (to do with regulation of the legal profession). Thirdly, the CRA 2005, s. 17 makes the oath of office taken by the Lord Chancellor different from that sworn by a Secretary of State: 'I, [name], do swear that in the office of Lord High Chancellor of Great Britain I will respect the rule of law, defend the independence of the judiciary and discharge my duty to ensure the provision of resources for the efficient and effective support of the courts for which I am responsible. So help me God.' Fourthly, the CRA 2005, s. 2 sets out factors that the prime minister 'may take into account' in selecting a colleague to be Lord Chancellor: '(a) experience as a Minister of the Crown; (b) experience as a member of either House of Parliament; (c) experience as a qualifying practitioner; (d) experience as a teacher of law in a university; (e) other experience that the Prime Minister considers relevant'. In reality, these words—described as 'vacuous' during the debate on the bill—provide almost no political or legal constraints on the prime minister's discretion.

This model of conjoined ministerial offices is complex and probably understood by few people outside the Ministry of Justice and the handful of academics specializing in this backwater of public law. What do Lord Chancellors think about it? In February 2010, Jack Straw MP (Lord Chancellor in the Labour government 2007–10) told the Constitution Committee:[26]

> I am perfectly comfortable about exercising both roles. They are distinct. Many of your Lordships will remember the great debate that took place following the original proposals in the Constitutional Reform Bill, which led to the continuation of the position of Lord Chancellor. I happen to think that was the right decision, for all sorts of reasons. The distinction in practice—I believe in theory but actually in practice—is a very important one, because on the one hand you have the Justice Secretary functions, which in terms of their operation and how they are moderated by other colleagues in Government are no different from any other secretary of state functions. The functions may differ but how they are operated is no different. On the other hand, the functions of Lord Chancellor are principally related to the judiciary and the maintenance of the independence of the judiciary. On those, in turn, I act independently of other colleagues in Government.

Giving evidence to the same committee in September 2014, Chris Grayling MP (Lord Chancellor in the Coalition government from 2012 and not a lawyer) spoke strongly in favour of the conjoined-ministers model:[27]

> I think now, given the constitutional changes that took place a decade ago, the role of the Lord Chancellor would be massively devalued if the roles were separated. It is not something I had fully understood until I took the job. But now I have truly understood in carrying out the role myself, I think it would be just the opposite. The danger would be that you would end up with the Secretary of State for Justice holding the Cabinet position. The Lord Chancellor's role is not what it used to be.

The risk, Mr Grayling said, was that if the roles were split the Lord Chancellor would become a junior minister outside the Cabinet whereas 'You want the Lord Chancellor, in a role that is not what it used to be, to be at the top table heading a substantial department with weight around the Cabinet table. I think it would be a big mistake to move away from that.'

So what parts of the justice infrastructure does the government—through the Lord Chancellor—run? The Courts Act 2003, s. 1 provides: 'The Lord Chancellor is under a duty to ensure that there is an efficient and effective system to support the carrying on of the business of [the courts], and that appropriate services are provided for those courts.' To ensure accountability, the Lord Chancellor must 'prepare and lay before both Houses of Parliament a report as to the way in which he has discharged his general duty in relation to the courts'. A comparable duty in relation to the UK Supreme Court, is created by the CRA 2005: the Lord Chancellor 'must ensure that the

---

[26] http://www.publications.parliament.uk/pa/ld200910/ldselect/ldconst/80/10022402.htm.

[27] http://data.parliament.uk/writtenevidence/committeeevidence.svc/evidencedocument/constitution-committee/the-office-of-lord-chancellor/oral/14379.html.

Supreme Court is provided' with 'such other resources as the Lord Chancellor thinks are appropriate for the Court to carry on its business'. Appearing before a parliamentary committee in 2010, Lord Judge (the then Lord Chief Justice) provided insight into the behind-the-scenes discussions that go on between the judiciary and the government in setting annual budgets for the courts. He said there were three possibilities:[28]

> the first is that when the figures are examined, I come to the conclusion that the arrangement is a reasonable one that I can sign up to–that is called a concordat agreement. The second is that he offers a figure that I do not think is necessarily going to enable me to fulfil my responsibilities, and I write to him and say, 'Well, that's all you've got. I understand the difficulty you're in. I have reservations about it, but let's do the best we can'. I do not sign the concordat agreement, but we all get on as best we can and see what events turn out. The third would be a disaster and a crisis of great magnitude and is that the Lord Chancellor of the day offers the Lord Chief Justice money that the Lord Chief Justice is completely satisfied is derisory for the purposes of running the administration of justice, in which case the option available to the Lord Chief Justice is to bring the concordat to an end.

Lord Judge envisaged that if the third eventuality were ever to come about, a new concordat would have to be negotiated between the judiciary and the government, with the Lord Chancellor 'very anxious to exercise such power as is left to him in the context of the parliamentary process' by involving relevant House of Commons and House of Lords Committees and making a written statement to Parliament under CRA 2005, s. 5.

The Concordat also recognized that the government 'is responsible for the pay, pensions and terms and conditions of the judiciary' (para. 21). A key aspect of judicial independence recognized internationally is that judicial salaries should never be reduced (as this would enable government to place pressure on judges); in the United Kingdom this is secured by the Senior Courts Act 1981, s. 12 ('Any salary payable under this section may be increased, but not reduced'). There is no legal impediment to government imposing pay freezes, which is what happened for three years from 2010, followed by a 1 per cent increase. The LJC (Lord Thomas) recently told the Review Body on Senior Salaries (SSRB), an independent body advisory body, that it was 'deeply regrettable' that SSRB recommendations to government on pay increases and a major review of salaries were not being implemented by government and said 'there was a justifiable sense of real grievance among the judiciary'.[29]

Changes to judicial pensions have, similarly, been a source of tension between judges and government. Announcing the new scheme to the House of Commons in 2013, the Lord Chancellor said:[30]

> The Government recognise that although there is a longstanding practice that the total remuneration package offered to the judiciary, including pension provision, should not

---

[28] House of Lords Constitution Committee, *Meetings with the Lord Chief Justice and the Lord Chancellor*, 9th Report of Session 2010–11, HL Paper 89, Evidence from 15 December 2010, Q9.

[29] Senior Salaries Review Body, *Thirty-sixth Annual Report* (Report No. 84), Cm 8822, para. 5.6.

[30] Chris Grayling MP, Hansard, HC, vol. 592, col. 7WS, 5 February 2013.

be reduced for serving judges, this forms part of a broader constitutional principle that an independent judiciary must be safeguarded. However, in the particular context of difficult economic circumstances and changes to pension provision across the public sector, we do not consider that the proposed reforms infringe the broader constitutional principle of judicial independence. Nonetheless we have listened to the concerns of the judges and we have modified our proposals.

FUNCTIONS SHARED BETWEEN JUDGES AND GOVERNMENT

The major area for joint-working is HM Courts and Tribunals Service (an agency of the Ministry of Justice), which 'uniquely operates as a partnership between the Lord Chancellor, the Lord Chief Justice and the Senior President of Tribunals as set out in our Framework Document'.[31] Leadership is provided by a ten-person board, which includes non-executive directors, Ministry of Justice officials, and three senior judges. Over 20,000 staff working at 650 different locations provide administrative support to courts and tribunals. The aims and objectives of the agency are set by the government (Lord Chancellor) and the judiciary (the LCJ and the Senior President of Tribunals).

Another area of shared functions are the numerous specific responsibilities where, following the agreement reached in the Concordat, the CRA 2005 and other legislation requires there to be 'concurrence' between the judiciary (the LCJ) and the government (the Lord Chancellor). One such area is the system for considering and determining complaints against the personal conduct of the judiciary. A body known as the Judicial Conduct and Investigations Office (JCIO) 'supports the Lord Chancellor and the Lord Chief Justice in their joint responsibility for judicial discipline'.

FUNCTIONS GIVEN TO ARM'S LENGTH INDEPENDENT BODIES

Several aspects of the justice infrastructure have been entrusted to 'arm's length' bodies, independent of both government and the judiciary. These bodies may have an executive function (deciding things) or an advisory function. The degree of independence from government and the judiciary varies according to the body.

A body with a high degree of independence is the Judicial Appointments and Conduct Ombudsman office (a team of eight), the remit of which is to resolve grievances about how complaints about judicial conduct have been handled and complaints about the judicial appointments process. It is 'a Corporation Sole who acts independently of Government, the Ministry of Justice (MoJ) and the Judiciary'.[32]

---

[31] HM Courts and Tribunals Service, http://www.justice.gov.uk/about/hmcts.
[32] Judicial Appointments and Conduct Ombudsman, Annual Report 2013–14, 4.

Another specialist ombudsmen service working in the justice infrastructure is the Legal Ombudsman for England and Wales, set up by the Office for Legal Complaints (the Board) under the Legal Services Act 2007, to deal with grievances against legal practitioners.

The Judicial Appointments Commission for England and Wales, another arm's length body, was set up by the CRA 2005, aiming 'to maintain and strengthen judicial independence by taking responsibility for selecting candidates for judicial office out of the hands of the Lord Chancellor and making the appointments process clearer and more accountable'.[33] The body consists of 15 commissioners, including judges, legal practitioners, and lay people (one of whom is the chair). The JAC runs competitions for appointment to tribunals and courts across England and Wales (except for magistrates or for the UK Supreme Court). A variety of modern human resources processes are used, including application forms, written assessments, and selection days at which applicants role-play. The JAC makes recommendations either to the Lord Chief Justice (for positions below the level of the High Court) or the Lord Chancellor (for the High Court and Court of Appeal): in almost all cases the LCJ or Lord Chancellor accept the recommendation though they have a residual power to ask the JAC to reconsider the recommendation or to reject it.

The routine updating of procedural rules are carried out by the Criminal Procedure Rules Committee, the Civil Procedure Rules Committee, and the Family Procedure Rules Committee established by the Courts Act 2003; these are judge-led expert groups, each described as an 'advisory non-departmental public body, sponsored by the Ministry of Justice'. Their membership categories, defined by statute, are mostly judicial, with legal practitioners and lay members (for example, the Civil Procedure Rules Committee includes 'two persons with experience in and knowledge of the lay advice sector or consumer affairs'). The Rules Committees consult, submit rules to the Lord Chancellor, who 'may allow, disallow or alter rules so made' but 'before alter-ing rules so made the Lord Chancellor must consult the Committee'. The Rules are made law through the statutory instrument procedure in Parliament, which is usually a formality.[34]

Some arm's length bodies have been abolished recently as part of the Coalition government's 'bonfire of the quangos', implemented under the Public Bodies Act 2011, which sought to cut public spending, increase accountability, and 'simplify the quango landscape'. For a body to survive the cull, it needed to be shown that it per-formed a technical function, or that its activities require political impartiality, or that it needed to act independently to establish facts. One important body that did not survive was the Administrative Justice and Tribunals Commission (AJTC) (an advi-sory non-departmental public body or NDPB), created by the Tribunals, Courts and Enforcement Act 2007 and abolished in August 2013, with the government moving

---

[33] Judicial Appointments Commission, http://www.jac.judiciary.gov.uk.
[34] Courts Act 2003, Pt 7, as amended, and other legislation.

some of its functions in-house to the Ministry of Justice. The AJTC's purpose was 'to help make administrative justice and tribunals increasingly accessible, fair and effective by: playing a pivotal role in the development of coherent principles and good practice; promoting understanding, learning and continuous improvement; ensuring that the needs of users are central'. There was strong opposition to the AJTC's demise in Parliament. The chair of the House of Commons Justice Committee argued 'because the administrative justice and tribunal system deals with disputes between the citizen and the executive, moving the process closer to Ministers has serious disadvantages. It is vital that oversight is seen to be independent'.[35] In the House of Lords, peers debating the motion that 'this House regrets the proposed abolition of the AJTC, which will remove independent oversight of the justice and tribunal system at a time when it is undergoing major change' called for the AJTC to be retained but the government narrowly won the vote.[36]

DISCUSSION

The previous sections have illustrated which bodies run the different parts of the justice infrastructure. Working inductively, it is possible to detect some general principles of constitutional design in the current network of institutions and processes.

First, independent, arm's length bodies are favoured where decisions relate to individuals—such as in relation handling of grievances against judges, the JAC, and lawyers, and in relation to individual decisions on appointments to judicial office. One of the reasons that the Legal Aid, Sentencing and Punishment of Offenders Act 2012 (LASPO) was controversial is because it transferred decision-making about individual legal aid applications from a body that had substantial operational independence from government to a body closely integrated into the Ministry of Justice.[37]

Secondly, the more closely intertwined with the core judicial function (hearing cases and writing judgments) a function is, the more control or influence judges should have in the running of that function. It has been recognized for many years that (as Lord Mackay of Clashfern, a Lord Chancellor in Conservative governments in the 1990s put it) 'in order to preserve their independence the judges must have some control or influence over the administrative penumbra immediately surrounding the judicial process', for example the listing of cases.[38]

---

[35] http://www.parliament.uk/business/committees/committees-a-z/commons-select/justice-committee/news/ajtc-report/.

[36] See further, C. Skelcher, 'Reforming the Oversight of Administrative Justice 2010–2014: Does the UK Need a New Leggatt Report?' [2015] PL 214.

[37] Discussed later.

[38] Lord MacKay, lecture 6 March 1991 quoted in Lord Bingham, 'Judicial Independence' (a lecture to the Judicial Studies Board on 5 November 1996) published in T. Bingham, The Business of Judging: Selected Essays and Speeches, 1985–1999 (2011), 55.

Thirdly, the more a function involves decisions about allocation of scarce public resources to the justice infrastructure, the greater the control or influence of government. As John Bell argues:[39]

> when it comes to managing the judicial service and setting its budgets, then we are not dealing with potential interference with individual cases, but with the setting of priorities between categories of legal activity, and this involves giving a direction to society, which is an inherently political activity. The suggestion that the judiciary should be given untrammelled authority in this area is seriously problematic.

Not everybody agrees with this principle. Sir Francis Purchas (a Court of Appeal judge) made the bold argument in 1994 that:[40]

> Constitutional independence [of the judiciary] will not be achieved if the funding of the administration of justice remains subject to the influences of the political market place. Subject to the ultimate supervision of Parliament, the Judiciary should be allowed to advise what is and what is not a necessary expense to ensure that adequate justice is available to the citizen and to protect him from unwarranted intrusion into his liberty by the executive.

Lord Bingham (who during his long judicial career held office as Master of the Rolls, Lord Chief Justice of England and Wales, and Senior Law Lord) recognized that such a call lacked democratic legitimacy. Even the judges, he acknowledged:[41]

> cannot overlook the existence of other pressing claims on finite national resources. We would all recognize the defence of the realm as a vital national priority, but I suspect that we would shrink from giving the chiefs of staff carte blanche to demand all the resources which they judged necessary for that end. We would all, probably, recognize the provision of good educational opportunities at all levels as a pressing social necessity, but might even so hesitate to give educational institutions all the money which they sought. We would all regard the health of the people as a vital national concern, but could scarcely contemplate the demands of health service professionals being met in full, without rigorous democratic control. I do not myself find these choices, even in theory, offensive; but in any event they must surely, in the real world, be inevitable.

SHAPING THE INFRASTRUCTURE

The justice infrastructure is always a work in progress: rarely a fortnight goes by without a reform proposal. This flux can be illustrated, for example, by the changing responsibility for legal aid, which was started by the Labour government in 1949

---

[39] 'Sweden's Contribution to Governance of the Judiciary' in M. Andenas and D. Fairgrieve (eds.), *Tom Bingham and the Transformation of the Law* (2009).

[40] F. Purchas, 'What Is Happening to Judicial Independence?' (1994) 144 *New Law Journal* 1306, 1324.

[41] T. Bingham, 'Judicial Independence' in T. Bingham, *The Business of Judging: Selected Essays and Speeches, 1985–1999* (2011), 57.

introducing a national system for public funding of civil litigation for people unable to afford legal fees; the United Kingdom was the first country in the world to recognize legal aid as a component of a welfare state. At first, the scheme was administered by committees of local lawyers organized by the Law Society (the solicitors' regulatory body), rather than by government or the courts; the government's role (through the Lord Chancellor) was one of general supervision. In 1989, the Law Society was replaced by the Legal Aid Board (a government agency) as the main administrator. The Legal Aid Board was, in turn, replaced by the Legal Services Commission in 2000 (a non-departmental public body working at arm's length from government). The Legal Aid, Sentencing and Punishment of Offenders Act 2012 remodelled the system again, replacing the Legal Services Commission with the Legal Aid Agency (an executive agency tightly integrated within the Ministry of Justice). The current set-up gives government more direct control than at any time since 1949 (though the newly created post of 'director of legal aid casework', and a large team of caseworkers, is not subject to the direction of the Lord Chancellor in relation to individual legal aid applications).

Shaping the justice infrastructure is a constitutionally significant activity. It facilitates—or restricts—access to justice and may affect the independence of the core judicial function (hearing cases and writing judgments). An important question is therefore who controls and influences the process of change and what methods they use for developing ideas about change. As with running the system (discussed in the previous section), shaping is not susceptible to analysis based on a basic separation-of-powers theory. Almost all shaping involves government action, input from the judiciary, and scrutiny and law-making by Parliament. What matters is the balance of influence among these institutions and the techniques they and other participants use to develop and discuss ideas for change. A model of what this looks like can be postulated which emphasizes a spectrum of decision-making environments. Towards one end, the environment is highly politicized ('political environment') and at the opposite end the environment is based on expert knowledge ('expert environment'); in the middle the environment is mixed ('blended environment'). Each environment of change has advantages and disadvantages. The challenge for the constitutional system is to find optimal points at which good-quality decisions are likely to be made; this point may differ according to the area of the infrastructure under review and the types of issues under consideration.

POLITICAL ENVIRONMENT

In this environment, proposals for reforming the justice infrastructure are typically led by government ministers. The House of Commons and House of Lords are the fora in which change is debated. The infrastructure is assumed to be an inherently party political artefact, in which opposing viewpoints rest on different values and conflicts are capable of being resolved through the cut-and-thrust of the political argumentation. The justice system tends to be seen as a public service to be reformed according to party political preferences.[42] In the political environment, judges and lawyers have no guaranteed or preferential status at the formative stages of the process; they are merely consultees. Facts about the infrastructure are often asserted as true rather than being demonstrated to be true through use of empirical research. The government may have limited (or no) appreciation that its proposals have constitutional implications. The style of presentation of the changes may be confrontational and populist.

An example of change through the political mode is the events that eventually resulted in the CRA 2005. The package of reforms (on the office of Lord Chancellor, creating a supreme court, radical changes to how judges were appointed, and disqualifying all serving judges from membership of Parliament) was announced inauspiciously in a press briefing by officials at 10 Downing Street during one of Tony Blair's annual Cabinet reshuffles. These complex policies had not been subject to detailed legal or constitutional analysis. The senior judges had not been consulted before the announcement; many heard about the proposals through the news media. The changes were the subject of protracted, sometimes poor-quality, and often highly partisan debates in Parliament over two years. The end result was shaped by behind-the-scenes party political negotiations in Parliament under pressure of time because of the impending 2005 general election. Tony Blair candidly admitted that 'I think we could have in retrospect—this is entirely my responsibility—done it better.'[43] The Conservatives were implacably opposed to the Lord Chancellor ceasing to be a lawyer yet in 2012 Conservative Prime Minister David Cameron became the first prime minister to select a non-lawyer for the role (Chris Grayling MP, an ambitious mid-career politician of the type held up as a spectre by Conservatives nine years earlier)—evidence, perhaps, that short-termism and hypocrisy are endemic in the political environment.

The government seemed not to learn many lessons from the debacle of the 2003–5 reform saga over the Lord Chancellorship. In 2007, there was new failure to consult the judiciary about developments to the justice infrastructure that had constitutional ramifications. The government decided to create a Ministry of Justice, combining responsibility for judiciary and court-related matters (dealt with by the Department for Constitutional Affairs) with responsibility for the weighty and always politically emotive area of prisons and offender management (previously in the Home Office). The senior judiciary first learnt of these plans through a report in the Sunday newspapers; they were concerned the justice infrastructure would, as part of a new huge department, become devalued as resources and political energy were diverted to prisons; moreover, they saw risks of conflicts of interests within a department that was simultaneously responsible for prisons and defending judicial independence (when many of the most controversial and

---

[42] See D. Oliver, 'Does Treating the System of Justice as a Public Service Have Implications for the Rule of Law and Judicial Independence?', UK Constitutional Law Association Blog, 19 March 2014, www. ukcla.org.

[43] Tony Blair, Minutes of Evidence, Liaison Committee, 3 February 2004 (HC 310-I, 2003–4).

politically unpalatable cases involve prisoners and sentencing). A parliamentary committee lamented that:[44]

> The creation of the Ministry of Justice clearly has important implications for the judiciary. The new dispensation created by the Constitutional Reform Act and the Concordat requires the Government to treat the judiciary as partners, not merely as subjects of change. By omitting to consult the judiciary at a sufficiently early stage, by drawing the parameters of the negotiations too tightly and by proceeding with the creation of the new Ministry before important aspects had been resolved, the Government failed to do this. Furthermore, the subsequent request made by the judiciary for a fundamental review of the position in the light of the creation of the Ministry of Justice was in our view a reasonable one to which the Government should have acceded in a spirit of partnership.

Another illustration of change through the political mode are reforms to the judicial review procedure initiated by the Coalition government in 2012. Judicial review is a process for challenging the legality of decisions taken by public bodies in the Administrative Court (part of the High Court); it is a vital way in which the rule of law is protected. Using the opportunity of a speech to the Confederation of British Industry conference in November 2012, the prime minister described judicial review as 'a massive growth industry in Britain today' and said:[45]

> We urgently needed to get a grip on this. So here's what we're going to do. Reduce the time limit when people can bring cases. Charge more for reviews so people think twice about time-wasting. And instead of giving hopeless cases up to four bites of the cherry to appeal a decision, we will halve that to two.

The Lord Chancellor, Chris Grayling, later wrote an opinion piece in the *Daily Mail* in which he warned that judicial review should not be 'not a promotional tool for countless Left-wing campaigners' and 'Britain cannot afford to allow a culture of Left-wing-dominated, single-issue activism to hold back our country from investing in infrastructure and new sources of energy and from bringing down the cost of our welfare state'.[46] Specific proposals were published piecemeal in two consultations several months apart; academics and practitioners criticized them as unsupported by empirical evidence (the Joint Committee on Human Rights concurred) and damaging to the rule of law.[47] Several elements of the proposals contained in the Criminal Justice and Courts Bill were savaged in parliamentary debates in the House of Lords;[48] at the

---

[44] House of Lords Constitution Committee, Relations between the Executive, Parliament and the Judiciary, 6th Report of 2006–7, HL Paper 151, para. 67.

[45] Available at http://www.gov.uk/government/news/prime-ministers-cbi-speech.

[46] Available at http://www.dailymail.co.uk/news/article-2413135/CHRIS-GRAYLING-Judicial-review-promotional-tool-Left-wing-campaigners.html#ixzz3IUbXriTU.

[47] See e.g. V. Bondy and M. Sunkin, 'Judicial Review Reform: Who Is Afraid of Judicial Review? Debunking the Myths of Growth and Abuse', UK Const. L. Blog, 10 January 2013; M. Fordham et al., 'Streamlining Judicial Review in a Manner Consistent with the Rule of Law' (Bingham Centre Report 2014/01), Bingham Centre for the Rule of Law, BIICL, London, February 2014.

[48] Hansard, HL, vol. 756, col. 952, 27 October 2014.

time of writing, the bill is going back to the Commons where the Lords' amendments may be reversed.

Standing back from these illustrations, what are the advantages and disadvantages of changing the justice infrastructure through a political environment? One advantage is that it can provide real impetus to decisive change: if the government decides to do something, it may be done speedily. It is also well suited to dealing with issues of distributive justice and reaching judgements about how, on a national scale, scarce resources are allocated to different areas of government activity. The political environment may also score highly for its democratic credentials: initiatives are typically led by ministers who are accountable to Parliament, where their proposals can be scrutinized.

The political environment has potential disadvantages. Ideas may be formulated by people without detailed knowledge or broad understanding of the implications of their proposals; the range of knowledge and research drawn on may therefore be limited. Of particular concern, is that inadequate regard is had to constitutional principles—notably judicial independence, access to justice, and the rule of law – in developing reform proposals. Expert views are typically sought only after key preferences have been formed; when experts contribute through a consultation process, this may have little or no influence on a government already determined to carry out its plans. Furthermore, proposals are prone to being announced before sufficient research and policy development work has been undertaken. Some forms of communication (for example, political speeches) do not provide good opportunities for points of detail to be refined or complexities to be explored.

EXPERT ENVIRONMENT

A different way of steering change to the justice infrastructure is in an expert environment. Experts and expertise come in various forms. Research may be commissioned or used by the Ministry of Justice, parliamentary select committees, the Law Commission, and other institutions. Academics specializing in the legal system can make expert contributions, carrying out empirical socio-legal research (through the collection and evaluation of data), analytical and normative studies (for example, of the competing constitutional values in the system), and comparative work. Expertise may also be found in the practical knowledge of people deeply immersed within the justice infrastructure, especially judges and legal practitioners, able to reflect on many years of experience of how the system runs to offer insights into how it could be improved. The style of deliberation in expert mode is generally apolitical and predisposed towards searching for consensus.

An example of an expert environment can be seen in how the Law Commission works. Many of its law reform projects relate to the justice infrastructure. For example, after ten years detailed work and consultation, in 1976 the Law Commission published recommendations that previously disparate High Court procedures be unified into a single 'application for judicial review procedure'; further recommendations were made in 1994, including on which types of applicant should have standing to use the judicial review procedure. Expert working can also take place within the court system. In 1999–2000, a small committee was commissioned by the Lord Chancellor to address the pressures on judicial review thought likely to result from the Human Rights Act; chaired by Sir Jeffery Bowman (an accountant with expertise in managing change), it consisted of civil servants, court administrators, an academic, and the director of a NGO.[49] More recently, a judge-led committee developed proposals for the 'regionalization' of judicial review, making it available at High Court centres outside London.[50]

On a larger scale, a paradigm example of shaping through an expert environment was the complete overhaul of thinking about civil procedure rules that took place between 1994 and 1999.[51] Although the reform process was initiated by government, the development work was left to Lord Woolf (the Master of the Rolls). In a two-stage inquiry, Lord Woolf worked with a team of five 'assessors' (members of the judiciary and the legal profession), an academic consultant, and a consultant on information technology. Several academics were commissioned to undertake original research. The inquiry team visited four overseas jurisdictions for comparative studies. The procedural reforms were implemented by the Civil Procedure Act 1997 and the Civil Procedure Rules, neither of which caused any significant party political controversy in Parliament.

Another notable illustration of large-scale change through an expert environment was the comprehensive restructuring of the tribunal system. In 2000, the government appointed Sir Andrew Leggatt (a Court of Appeal judge) 'to review the delivery of justice through tribunals other than ordinary courts of law'; he worked with a retired civil servant to produce a detailed analysis and far-reaching recommendations on the changes that needed to be made. These included reducing the number of tribunals from over 70 to 2 (the First-tier Tribunal and the Upper Tribunal). The government followed best-practice in publishing a draft bill to implement the recommendations but this had so little political resonance that no parliamentary committee was interested in scrutinizing it. The Tribunals, Courts and Enforcement Act 2007 reached the statute book generating no notable party political controversy.

In some contexts, the power of experts has been criticized and the limits of their role debated. Writing about the dominance of experts (a 'technocracy') in how the European Union develops policy ideas, it has been suggested:[52]

> The technocrat believes that rational analysis and scientific examination of the facts will bring about unanimous consensus on policy solutions. By contrast the technocrat feels

---

[49] See T. Cornford and M. Sunkin, 'The Bowman Report, Access and the Recent Reforms of the Judicial Review Procedure' [2001] PL 11.

[50] S. Nason and M. Sunkin, 'The Regionalisation of Judicial Review: Constitutional Authority, Access to Justice and Legal Services in Public Law' (2013) 76(2) MLR 223.

[51] For a critical account, see J. Sorabji, English Civil Justice after the Woolf and Jackson Reforms: A Critical Analysis (2014).

[52] C. Radaelli, 'The Public Policy of the European Union: Whither Politics of Expertise' (1999) 6(5) Journal of European Public Policy 757.

uneasy under conditions of political conflict, ideological debates, and controversies on distributive issues of social justice.

So, some questions about the shaping of justice infrastructure cannot satisfactorily be solved by experts and expert knowledge alone. These include, for example, whether it would be beneficial for the UK to withdraw from the European Union and European Convention on Human Rights (points of deep political conflict) or what proportion of GDP should be allocated to fund legal aid (a distributive issue). There are other possible limitations and disadvantages of an expert environment. Expert working may be regarded as undemocratic: ideas may emerge from people who are unelected and unaccountable. Moreover, if there is a disconnection between the priorities of government and those of experts, proposals developed through expert working (for example, by the Law Commission) may lie on the shelf, unimplemented. In some situations, it may be difficult to disentangle expertise from self-interest, an accusation levelled at the legal profession when it seeks to influence justice infrastructure reforms. For example, in June 2013 a government minister was reported as saying: ' "Let's not kid ourselves. We are in a wage negotiation," Lord McNally warned lawyers this week at the Bar Council's Legal Aid Question Time event at Westminster. "You have a vested interest in this outcome. To deny that, I think, is absurd".'[53]

BLENDED ENVIRONMENT

The political and expert environments for bringing about reform of the justice infrastructure represent points at the extreme ends of a spectrum of styles of decision-making. Between these points, there are ways of working that blend politicization and expertise.

Blended environments may be located within institutions. The government department responsible for judiciary-related and court matters was, in the past, led by people who were experts in the sense that they had insider-knowledge of law and the legal system. The department was known successively as the 'Lord Chancellor's Department' (1885–2003), 'the Department for Constitutional Affairs' (2003–7), and latterly 'the Ministry of Justice'. A government department is led by a politically neutral civil servant—the permanent secretary—who remains in post even if the political party in government changes after a general election. From the nineteenth century until 1997, it was a requirement that the permanent secretary in the Lord Chancellor's Department was a qualified legal professional. As one commentator wrote in the late nineteenth century:[54]

It probably owes its statutory existence to a wise reform initiated by Lord Selborne, who made the office of Principal Secretary to the Lord Chancellor a permanent one. The obvious

[53] J. Robins, 'Cuts Will "Destroy" Legal Aid System' (2013) 177(26) *Criminal Law and Justice Weekly*, online at http://www.criminallawandjustice.co.uk/.

[54] M. Chalmers, 'County Courts Consolidation Act 1888' (1898) 5 *LQR* 1.

object of this reform was to give some chance of continuity to the legal policy of successive Lord Chancellors, and to create what might be the nucleus of a department of Law and Justice. Any one acquainted with the working of a public office must be aware of the wholesale confusion which would result if the staff was changed with every change of government. The hitherto backward state of all non-contentious law reform in this country has probably been due in no small degree to the absence of any body of permanent officials charged with its supervision.

The end of the lawyer-as-permanent-secretary requirement in 1997 came about in consequence of the growth of the department; legal expertise was no longer regarded as the most important—or even particularly relevant—attribute of the most senior official. Legal advice—and sensitivity to constitutional values closely associated with the legal system—were, it was thought, available from other lawyers within the department. There is a perception that, in recent years, the quality of legal advice and sensitivity in the department has diminished. This view is, however, contested by officials. In evidence to a House of Lords committee in October 2014, Rosemary Davies, Legal Director, Ministry of Justice, said:[55]

> It does slightly worry me that there is a perception that the Lord Chancellor is not getting the quality of legal advice that he used to get and perhaps there is an issue about visibility that we should think about. There are 60 lawyers in the in-house public law advisory team, two legal directors and seven other senior Civil Service lawyers. For example, the lawyer responsible for the team advising on the judiciary and courts is about to retire, but he has been in the department and its predecessors for I think 38 years. Likewise, the lawyer responsible for the judicial review reforms has been in the department for something like 27 years. I am not quite sure where this perception has come from that everybody has gone. Obviously, there are lots of new people and people do move around—and generally that is a good thing—but there is no shortage of continuity.

As discussed earlier, the professional background of Lord Chancellors has also changed. Since the CRA 2005 it has been possible for the prime minister to appoint somebody with no legal background as the minister responsible for judiciary and court-related matters; this possibility was made real with David Cameron's appointment of Chris Grayling MP to the role in September 2012. A history graduate, Grayling worked as a television producer and management consultant before becoming an MP. As an opposition MP, he developed a reputation for strongly confrontational questioning of the government (described by some journalists as 'an attack dog' style). The reason given by the Labour government in 2005 for abandoning the requirement that Lord Chancellors be lawyers was that the nature of the role had changed and enlarged so that skills at political leadership to 'deliver' policies had become much more important than in the past; such skills were not necessarily best found among politicians with legal backgrounds; and the prime minister should therefore have a broad discretion

---

[55] Revised transcript of evidence taken before the Select Committee on the Constitution, Inquiry on the Office of Lord Chancellor, Evidence Session No. 4, Q53, 15 October 2014.

to select the best person for the job. At the time, Conservatives in Parliament argued that a lawyer (preferably a senior one in the House of Lords, rather than the House of Commons) would always be better equipped to carry out the Lord Chancellor's functions as the link-pin between government and the judiciary, to defend judicial independence within government, and to act as a guardian of the rule of law across government. Ten years later, the (Conservative) Lord Chancellor Chris Grayling MP told a parliamentary committee:

> My view is that it is a positive benefit for the Lord Chancellor not to be a lawyer. The reason I say that is, certainly at this moment in time, when we are having to take and would be taking difficult decisions [about reducing public spending] regardless of the situation, if we had a distinguished member of the House of Lords occupying the traditional role of Lord Chancellor overseeing the courts today, there would still be the same financial pressures that my department and my team are currently facing. I think that not being a lawyer gives you the ability to take a dispassionate view: not from one side of the legal profession or the other, not from the perspective of the Bar, not from the perspective of the solicitors' profession and not from the perspective of the legal executives. As long as you take very seriously the duty to uphold the principles I talked about earlier—uphold the independence of the judiciary, uphold the independence of our courts—I think there are benefits in not having a lawyer. It does not mean a lawyer cannot do the job, but it is really important to say I think there are benefits to having a non-lawyer in the job as well.

Whatever the merits of moving from a requirement for both the permanent secretary and the government minister to be lawyers to a situation where neither is a lawyer, it is clear that the government department responsible for the justice infrastructure has become in important respects a less blended environment than previously.

Blending of political and expert environments can, however, be seen to be thriving elsewhere in the system. In Parliament, the House of Lords Constitution Committee has grown into a significant institution connecting politics, law, and the judiciary. The committee has produced several reports on aspects of the justice infrastructure and holds annual meetings with the Lord Chancellor and LCJ. Since its creation in 2001, the committee (whose membership is broadly reflective of the political composition of the House of Lords as a whole) has included retired judges (Lord Woolf), a former Lord Chancellor (Lord Irvine), former Attorney Generals, and senior members of the legal profession. Expertise is also brought into its work through a legal adviser (all have been senior academics), specialist advisers appointed to assist with particular inquiries, and experts who contribute written and oral evidence to the committee's inquiries.[56]

Blended working may also take place more informally outside institutions where there is a predisposition by politicians to involve people with expertise at a formative stage of their thinking. An illustration of this is an initiative of the shadow Lord Chancellor Sadiq Khan MP to invite Sir Geoffrey Bindman (a leading solicitor with

---

[56] See further A. Le Sueur and J. Simson Caird, 'The House of Lords Select Committee on the Constitution' in A. Horne, G. Drewry, and D. Oliver (eds.), *Parliament and the Law* (2013).

expertise in public law) and Karon Monaghan QC (a barrister and author on equality law) to lead a review of how to improve diversity in the judiciary. They were encouraged to consider more radical measures such as positive discrimination and gender quotas; academics contributed to a private seminar on the legality and feasibility of gender quotas.[57]

DISCUSSION

The illustrations outlined earlier show how policies to change the justice infrastructure are developed in a variety of different environments. A blended environment which captures the strengths of political and expert methods of working, and minimizes their weakness, is likely to be the best way of reaching considered, evidence-based consensus (so far as possible) on many types of reform question. A predisposition to blended environments can be encouraged if the Lord Chancellor were required to apply three presumptions when contemplating change.

First, the more directly a proposed infrastructure change affects the constitutional principles of judicial independence and access to justice, the stronger the presumption that detailed analysis of the problem and recommendations are developed by an expert body—an ad hoc one (Woolf, Leggett, Bowman), the Law Commission, or (for truly landmark change) a Royal Commission. A decision to develop policy 'in house' within the Ministry of Justice (such as the recent judicial review reforms) or other part of government (10 Downing Street in relation to decisions that led to the CRA 2005) should be carefully justified. Secondly, there should be a strong presumption that infrastructure change should be based on sound evidence and analysis. Academic and other expert research should be commissioned, evaluated fairly, and used at formative stages of thinking about all significant reform proposals. Thirdly, where reforms require legislative backing to be implemented, the government should publish bills and secondary legislation in draft. This will enable parliamentary and other expert scrutiny of detailed proposals.

CONCLUSIONS

The British constitution provides high levels of judicial independence in relation to the core functions of judges (hearing cases and writing judgments). This chapter has explored the constitutional implications of the 'running' and 'shaping' of the justice infrastructure. It has been argued that both of these activities are constitutionally significant. They create opportunities to enhance or risk undermining the principles of judicial independence, access to the courts, and the rule of law.

---

[57] See N. Watt, 'Labour Prepared to Introduce Judge Quotas to Achieve Balanced Judiciary', *The Guardian*, 21 April 2004, 4; UCL Constitution Unit, Monitor 58, 7.

FURTHER READING

GEE, G. ET AL., *The Politics of Judicial Independence in the UK's Changing Constitution* (2015)

LE SUEUR, A., 'From Appellate Committee to Supreme Court: A Narrative' in L. Blom-Cooper, G. Drewry, and B. Dickson (eds.), *The Judicial House of Lords 1876–2009* (2009)

LE SUEUR, A., 'Parliamentary Accountability and the Justice System' in N. Bamforth and P. Leyland (eds.), *Accountability in the Contemporary Constitution* (2013)

SHETREET, S. and TURENNE, S., *Judges on Trial: The Independence and Accountability of the English Judiciary* (2nd edn, 2013)

USEFUL WEBSITES

Ministry of Justice **http://www.justice.gov.uk**

HM Courts and Tribunals Service: **http://www.justice.gov.uk/about/hmcts**

Courts and Tribunals Judiciary: **http://www.judiciary.gov.uk**

Judicial Appointments Commission: **http://www.jac.judiciary.gov.uk**

Judicial Appointments and Conduct Ombudsman: **http://www.gov.uk/government/organisations/judicial-appointments-and-conduct-ombudsman**

9

DEVOLUTION

Brice Dickson

SUMMARY

This chapter begins by reviewing the experience of devolution in the three separate countries of Scotland, Wales, and Northern Ireland from 1998 to the present. It highlights the controversies that have arisen and suggests what may be the issues that will consume most attention in the years immediately ahead. In Scotland the recommendations of the Calman Commission led directly to the devolution of additional powers through the Scotland Act 2012, and the result of the referendum held in September 2014 is likely to have even more profound implications for the extent and nature of devolved powers, especially around taxation and borrowing. The Scottish government has already adopted various social policies which differ from those preferred in other parts of the United Kingdom and Scotland's judicial system remains almost entirely separate. The Supreme Court, however, has made it clear that the powers of the Scottish Parliament must be limited by the concept of the rule of law. In Wales it is now common to describe the devolution process as having fallen into three phases so far. After an examination of the 1998 settlement by the Richard Commission, further devolution was enabled by the Government of Wales Act 2006. In a further referendum in 2011 the people of Wales voted to give the Welsh Assembly the power to issue its own Acts. That is now happening, although two of the new laws have already been referred to the UK Supreme Court for a review of the Assembly's competence to make them. Efforts are also under way to increase the separateness of the Welsh judicial system, and the UK government has accepted the Silk Commission's recommendations concerning the Assembly's taxing and borrowing powers. In Northern Ireland the devolution process has taken longer to roll out and has not had such a smooth passage. The power-sharing government which was mandated by the Belfast (Good Friday) Agreement in 1998 has not led to as much agreement on aspects of economic and social policy as had been hoped, with the result that large swathes of the population are disillusioned by the current arrangements and demands for more extensive devolution are rarely voiced. The next part of the chapter considers the options for increasing the devolution of powers within England, an idea which has been revived by the Scottish referendum debates. The next few years look set to be dominated by constitutional reforms aimed at ensuring that the English do not feel like second-class citizens within the Union. They will also be beset by arguments over whether the United Kingdom should retain its membership of the European Union and its commitment to the Council of Europe's Convention on Human Rights. Any retrenchment on the Europeanization of the United Kingdom is likely to increase the call from all three of the devolved countries for even greater autonomy.

INTRODUCTION

Whilst the United Kingdom is a unitary rather than a federal state, it still accepts the need for some degree of devolved power. At one level this manifests itself through arrangements made for local government, but in this chapter the focus is on arrangements made for devolution to the 'countries' that make up the United Kingdom. At present these arrangements apply to Scotland, Wales, and Northern Ireland—though in asymmetric ways—but not at all to England. The Scotland Act 1998 transferred to the Scottish Parliament all powers formerly vested in the UK Parliament save for those which were expressly reserved.[1] The reserved matters were set out in Schedule 5 to the Act, which extended to 18 pages.[2] The Government of Wales Act 1998 provided for a Welsh Assembly but conferred on it only the power to make secondary legislation when authorized to do so by the UK Parliament; 18 fields were identified in which such secondary legislation could initially be made once the power to do so was transferred to the Assembly by an Order in Council.[3] The Northern Ireland Act 1998 adopted a mid-way approach by transferring all the powers of the UK Parliament to the Northern Ireland Assembly save for (a) 'excepted matters', which were matters intended always to remain within the exclusive competence of the UK Parliament,[4] and (b) 'reserved matters', which were matters that were seen as transferable to the Assembly in due course.[5] In Northern Ireland,

---

[1] Scotland Act 1998, s. 29(2).

[2] Apart from 'general reservations', which cover the constitution, political parties, foreign affairs, public service, defence, and treason, Sched. 5 refers to reserved matters falling under the following headings: financial and economic matters, home affairs, trade and industry, energy, transport, social security, regulation of the professions, employment, health and medicines, media and culture, and 'miscellaneous'. More particularly, the principal reserved matters include the Crown, the Union of England and Scotland, the UK Parliament, the continued existence of the High Court of Justiciary and the Court of Sessions as courts of first instance and of appeal, the registration and funding of political parties, international relations, the civil service, defence, fiscal, economic and monetary policy, the currency, financial services and markets, misuse of drugs, data protection, elections, firearms, immigration and nationality, national security (including terrorism), betting and gaming, emergency powers, extradition, access to information, insolvency, competition, intellectual property, import and export control, sea fishing, consumer protection, product standards, weights and measures, telecommunications, abortion, broadcasting, judicial salaries, and equal opportunities.

[3] Government of Wales Act 1998, s. 22 and Scheds. 2 and 3. The 18 fields included economic development, education and training, the environment, health and social services, housing, local government, transport, water, and the Welsh language.

[4] Northern Ireland Act 1998, s. 4 and Sched. 2. Sched. 2 lists 22 separate excepted matters, including elections, international relations, defence, immigration, taxes, the appointment of judges, the registration of political parties, coinage, and nuclear energy.

[5] Northern Ireland Act 1998, s. 4 and Sched. 3. Sched. 3 lists 42 separate reserved matters, including navigation, civil aviation, postal services, the criminal law and prosecutions, the maintenance of public order,

therefore, the term 'reserved matters' did not have the same content as it did in Scotland and different processes were devised in those two countries for changing a reserved matter into a transferred matter or vice-versa.[6] The Government of Wales Act 1998 did not talk of 'reserved' or 'excepted' matters at all. As a result, the Welsh model is sometimes described as adopting a 'conferred matters approach' to devolution, while the Scottish and Northern Irish models are described as displaying a 'reserved matters approach'.

In all three countries there have been significant developments concerning devolution since 1998. Overall, devolution can be deemed to have been a success, at least as far as political processes within Scotland and Wales are concerned. In Scotland important alterations were made to the powers of the Scottish Parliament by the Scotland Act 2012 and, although there was a clear victory for the 'No' campaign in the referendum on independence in September 2014 (55.3 per cent voted 'No' to independence and 44.7 per cent voted 'Yes'), the three main UK parties had by then made a 'vow' to devolve greater powers to the Scottish Parliament.[7] According to the Smith Commission, set up immediately after the referendum and reporting just ten weeks later, extensive powers over taxation and welfare will be devolved.[8] There is also an evident appetite for greater devolution in Wales, even though support for complete independence may be at its lowest for decades.[9] By way of contrast, the chances of increased devolution in Northern Ireland are at the moment slim, because the coalition government mandated by the Belfast (Good Friday) Agreement 1998 has demonstrated a general tendency towards procrastination, if not outright sclerosis. Even more unknowable is what kind of devolution, if any, will occur within England. In the immediate aftermath of the Scottish referendum there appeared to be some resentment in England that under the so-called 'Barnett formula' the Scots (as well as the Welsh and Northern Irish) may continue to be funded by the Her Majesty's Treasury at a higher rate per capita than their English compatriots. The 'West Lothian' question also reared its head again: why should MPs from outside England be able to vote at Westminster on issues affecting only England, while English MPs cannot vote on any

---

the establishment of the police, firearms, the courts, the rules of evidence, legal aid, import and export controls, the national minimum wage, financial services, units of measurement, telecommunications, human genetics, research councils, consumer safety, data protection, and oaths and declarations.

[6] Compare the Northern Ireland Act 1998, s. 4(2)–(4) with the Scotland Act 1998, s. 30(2)–(4). In Northern Ireland the transfer of powers has to be pre-approved at the Assembly by a resolution passed with cross-community support.

[7] Pro-union parties collectively agreed to work towards greater devolution for Scotland in a statement issued in June 2014: http://www.bbc.co.uk/news/uk-scotland-scotland-politics-27868030. Just over a week before the referendum the former Labour prime minister, Gordon Brown, set out a timetable for devolving greater powers which the Conservative and Liberal Democrats immediately endorsed; it anticipated options being published in October 2014, further details being published in November, and draft clauses for a new Scotland Bill being published early in 2015: http://www.theguardian.com/politics/2014/sep/08/fgordon-brown-leads-scottish-labour-drive-rescue-no-campaign.

[8] *Report of the Smith Commission for Further Devolution of Powers to the Scottish Parliament*, 27 November 2014.

[9] A poll conducted for the BBC just after the Scottish referendum put support for Welsh independence at just 3%: http://www.bbc.co.uk/news/uk-wales-29331475.

of the issues coming before the devolved legislatures? Even prior to the Scottish referendum the Liberal Democrats had expressed their commitment to devolving greater
powers to large English cities.[10] Further imponderables are the impact on devolution
of the outcome of negotiations concerning the future of the United Kingdom within
the European Union (EU) and the consequences of a possible repeal of the Human
Rights Act 1998 and withdrawal from the European Convention on Human Rights
(ECHR).

SCOTLAND

A referendum on Scottish independence took place on 18 September 2014. It occurred
as a result of the Edinburgh Agreement signed by the prime minister, the Secretary of
State for Scotland, and the First and Deputy First Ministers of Scotland on 15 October
2012. This enabled the Scottish Parliament to legislate for a single-question referendum to be held before the end of 2014.[11] Despite the fact that a victory for the 'Yes' campaign would have had a massive impact on the whole of the United Kingdom, there
was remarkably little interest in the debate south of the border until the last two weeks
of campaigning. The dominant performance by the First Minister of Scotland, Alex
Salmond, in the second of two television debates with the leader of the 'Better Together'
campaign, Alistair Darling, provoked frissons of concern in England and Wales,[12]
and these intensified when what is now seen as a rogue opinion poll put the 'Yes'
campaign ahead, by 2 per cent.[13] To some extent complacency within the pro-Union
camp was understandable, given that only residents in Scotland (provided they were
EU citizens) were entitled to vote in the referendum,[14] but it surely also reflected a fundamental assumption that unravelling the Union was almost unthinkable. At times
it was inspiring to see Scottish nationalism come to the fore during the campaigning,
yet in this era of globalized economics and increased international interdependence

---

[10] On 12 September 2014 Nick Clegg, the Liberal Democrat deputy prime minister, launched a report
published by IPPR North entitled *Decentralisation Decade: A Plan for Economic Prosperity, Public Service
Transformation and Democratic Renewal in England*, by Ed Cox, Graeme Henderson, and Luke Raikes.

[11] The legislation in question became the Scottish Independence Referendum Act 2013. The consti-
tutional implications of the Edinburgh Agreement were considered by the House of Lords' Constitution
Committee: see its 8th Report, 2013–14, *Scottish Independence: Constitutional Implications of the
Referendum* (HL 188). See too its 7th Report, 2012–13 (HL 165, November 2012), which was debated by the
House of Lords on 16 January 2013 (HL Debs, vol. 742, cols. 694–756), and its 24th Report, 2010–12 (HL 263,
February 2012).

[12] This debate took place on 25 August 2014. For typical media reaction see *The Times* of 26 August 2014.

[13] The poll was published on 6 September 2014: http://yougov.co.uk/news/2014/09/06/latest-scottish-
referendum-poll-yes-lead.

[14] Commonwealth citizens resident in Scotland and with leave to remain in the UK or not requiring such
leave were also entitled to vote. 'Resident' means resident in accordance with the laws governing the right to
vote in Scottish local elections, as set out in the Representation of the People Act 1983. Children aged 16 and
17 were also entitled to vote, for the first time in any Scottish election. For details about who could vote see
the Scottish Independence Referendum (Franchise) Act 2013, an Act of the Scottish Parliament.

the prevailing mood within other parts of the United Kingdom seems to have been that a supra-national identity, one which stresses cooperation and harmony between the countries in the Union, is an even more inspirational model. In the United States, a classic federal state within which substantial power is vested in 50 state governments, it is collaboration between those states which gives the country as a whole its resilience and the people of the various states their national pride. While the United Kingdom is not a perfect analogy, since its three devolved areas were originally subjugated through force exerted by a fourth and much larger area, the strength in unity philosophy appears to predominate.

Under the Scotland Act 1998 there exists a Scottish Parliament[15] and a Scottish Administration.[16] The former is sometimes referred to as Holyrood, after the area in Edinburgh in which the parliament building is situated.[17] The latter comprises the Scottish government as well as the Scottish Civil Service. The Scottish government was formerly known as the Scottish executive[18] but the title was officially changed by the Scotland Act 2012.[19] Elections to the Scottish Parliament have been held four times to date, in 1999, 2003, 2007, and 2011. The fifth election will be held on 5 May 2016, the five-year gap being explained by the fact that a national general election is scheduled for May 2015 and it is thought better not to have different elections around the same time, especially if they are conducted under different voting systems: while Westminster elections take place entirely on a first-past-the-post basis,[20] Scottish elections are run on the 'additional members system'. The country has been divided into eight electoral regions and 73 constituencies.[21] One MSP (Member of the Scottish Parliament) is elected for each constituency on a first-past-the-post basis and each region elects seven additional MSPs based on the votes received for party lists presented to the electorate.[22] This means that 129 MSPs are elected in all (73 + (8 x 7)) and ensures that there is a reasonable degree of proportional representation in each region and in Scotland as a whole. At the 2011 election, for the first time, a majority government was elected, with the Scottish National Party winning 69 of the 129 seats.[23] It was this significant victory which gave the SNP the impetus to press ahead with its proposal for a referendum on independence in September 2014. The power to hold such a referendum had not been devolved in 1998 but the UK government, accepting

---

[15] Scotland Act, Pt I (ss. 1–43).   [16] Ibid., Pt II (ss. 44–63).

[17] Not to be confused with the nearby Holyrood Palace (or Palace of Holyroodhouse), which is the official residence of the monarch in Scotland.

[18] Scotland Act 1998, s. 44.   [19] s. 12.

[20] A nationwide referendum asking if people wanted to move to a proportional representation electoral system received an overwhelming 'No' on 5 May 2011: only 42% of the electorate participated in the referendum and 68% voted No. In Scotland, on a turn-out of 51%, 64% voted No.

[21] There are, by contrast, 59 Scottish constituencies for the UK Parliament. In the 2010 general election 41 of the MPs elected were from the Labour Party, 11 from the Liberal Democrats, 6 from the SNP, and 1 from the Conservatives.

[22] The Additional Member System is also used for elections to the Welsh and London Assemblies.

[23] The SNP won the highest number of seats in the 2007 election but not a majority; it therefore formed a minority government.

the mandate of the SNP, facilitated the making of an Order in Council to transfer such a power to Holyrood.[24]

In 2009 Scotland had the benefit of the collective wisdom displayed in the report of the Calman Commission, a body established in 2008 'to review the provisions of the Scotland Act 1998 in the light of experience and to recommend any changes to the present constitutional arrangements that would enable the Scottish Parliament to serve the people of Scotland better, improve the financial accountability of the Scottish Parliament, and continue to secure the position of Scotland within the United Kingdom'. Despite its bias towards a pro-Union position (the Commission was established on the assumption that Scotland would not become independent), the Commission's final report contained a helpful record of what the Scottish Parliament had managed to achieve by 2009 and a useful compendium of recommendations.[25] The latter included the proposals that the Scottish and UK Parliaments should agree to 'the elements of the common social rights that make up the social Union and also the responsibilities that go with them', that the Scottish variable rate of income tax should be replaced by a new Scottish rate of income tax,[26] that the Scottish Parliament should be empowered to collect some other taxes (with a corresponding reduction in the Treasury's block grant), and that more formal arrangements should be made to ensure that the UK and Scottish Parliaments liaise appropriately. Some of these recommendations saw their way into the Scotland Act which was passed at Westminster in 2012. In the words of the deputy prime minister, the effect of that Act is that 'by 2016 … £1 in every £3 of public money [spent in Scotland] will be raised by the Scottish Parliament'.[27] Part 3 of the 2012 Act permits the Scottish Parliament to set a rate of income tax for Scottish taxpayers (for a year at a time) and devolves the power to set the rate of stamp duty and landfill tax. It also increases the powers of the Scottish government to borrow money; it can now do so, for example, in order to meet the differences between forecast and outturn receipts for devolved taxes or from income tax. In accordance with these provisions, the Scottish government has announced that from 2015 a land and buildings transaction tax will replace stamp duty; the new tax will impose a charge of 10 per cent on the purchase price of a home selling for more than £250,000 and 12 per cent on a price exceeding £1 million.

In the 14 years between 2000 and 2013 the Scottish Parliament enacted 205 statutes, an average of 14 or 15 per year. In terms of differentiating itself from the UK

---

[24] The Scotland Act 1998 (Modification of Schedule 5) Order 2013 (SI 242). By the new para. 5A(3) of Sched. 5, the referendum had to be held before 31 December 2014.

[25] *Serving Scotland Better: Scotland and the United Kingdom in the 21st Century.* An earlier report was published at the end of 2008 to explain the progress the Commission was making and to provide a basis for consultation.

[26] Amongst the powers transferred to the Scottish Parliament and Executive in 1998 was the power to vary the rate of income tax (see the Scotland Act 1998, Pt IV (ss. 73–80)), but that power has not been exercised and is to be replaced.

[27] Evidence to the House of Commons Political and Constitutional Reform Committee, 13 December 2012, HC 834-I, answer to Q2. In answer to Q57 he said that he personally believed 'that the momentum is towards ever greater fiscal tax devolution'.

Parliament, the Scottish Parliament passed several innovative pieces of legislation. These include the Ethical Standards in Public Life etc (Scotland) Act 2000, the
Convention Rights (Compliance) (Scotland) Act 2001, the Gaelic Language (Scotland)
Act 2005, the Scottish Commission for Human Rights Act 2006, the Police and Fire
Reform (Scotland) Act 2012, and the Alcohol (Minimum Pricing) (Scotland) Act
2012.[28] Another distinctive policy adopted by the Scottish Parliament is free personal
care for the elderly, whether they are residing in care homes or in their own homes.[29]
This policy is still strongly supported by the Scottish National Party, despite the costs
involved rising sharply from £219 million in 2003–4 to £450 million in 2010–11.[30]
There are also no prescription charges in Scotland. As regards education, Scotland
currently allows Scottish and other non-British EU students to attend universities in
Scotland free of charge, while it charges other British students up to £9,000 per year.
Housing policy has also diverged from that in England and Wales but recent reports
have indicated that the demand for housing continues to far exceed supply and that
the private rented sector is not contributing as much to reform as it needs to.[31] The
Housing (Scotland) Act 2014 will bring to an end in 2016 the right of social tenants to
buy the property they are renting and gives social landlords greater flexibility in how
to allocate their housing stock. It also imposes greater safety duties on private sector
landlords, gives local authorities additional powers to deal with private rented property which has fallen into disrepair, and sets up a new tribunal to deal with disputes in
the private rented sector.

The Scottish legal system remains quite separate from that of other parts of the
United Kingdom and in recent years there has been pressure to cut one of the last
links—the ability to take civil cases on appeal to the UK Supreme Court (it has never
been possible to take Scottish criminal cases to the top UK court). The controversy
was reignited by the decision of the Supreme Court in *Cadder* v. *HM Advocate*,[32] a case
which had been referred to the court under the Scotland Act 1998 because it raised
'a devolution issue', namely whether a man's human rights had been violated when
he was questioned in police custody without first being given access to legal advice.
Seven judges in the Supreme Court held unanimously (with the two Scottish judges
writing the agreed judgments) that his rights had indeed been violated. A year later
the Supreme Court again held that a convicted murderer, Nat Fraser, had not received
a fair trial in Scotland because the prosecution had not fully disclosed to him the
information it was holding in connection with his case.[33] Scotland's Justice Secretary,

---

[28] In line with the Marriage (Same Sex Couple) Act 2013, passed for England and Wales, the Scottish
Parliament enacted the Marriage and Civil Partnership (Scotland) Act 2014.

[29] http://www.heraldscotland.com/politics/political-news/cost-of-caring-for-the-elderly-doubles-in-
seven-years.18712220.

[30] http://www.bbc.co.uk/news/uk-scotland-19398213.

[31] *Housing in Scotland* (Audit Scotland, 2013); *Building a Better Scotland* (Report of the Royal Institution
of Chartered Surveyors' Scottish Housing Commission, 2014).

[32] [2010] UKSC 43, [2010] 1 WLR 2601.

[33] *Fraser* v. *HM Advocate* [2011] UKSC 24, 2011 SC (UKSC) 113.

Kenny MacAskill, reacted to the latter decision by asking civil servants to investigate whether Scotland could withdraw its contribution of almost £500,000 to the annual running costs of the Supreme Court.[34]

A survey of Scottish lawyers at the time showed that 76 per cent did not think that the right of the appeal to Supreme Court threatened the independence of Scots law, and almost as many disapproved of the suggestion by Alex Salmond, the First Minister of Scotland, that human rights issues should go straight to the European Court of Human Rights in Strasbourg rather than first to the Supreme Court. After no fewer than three committees had given their views on what, if anything, needed to be done, the Scottish government succeeded in having new provisions inserted into the Scotland Act 2012.[35] The effect of these is to reduce the jurisdiction of the Supreme Court in Scottish cases by making it explicit that, when a criminal case is referred by or appealed from the High Court of Justiciary in Scotland to the Supreme Court in London because it raises a devolution issue, the latter's powers are exercisable 'only for the purpose of determining the compatibility issue'. Once it has determined that issue, the Supreme Court must remit the proceedings to the High Court of Justiciary.[36] The 2012 Act also changes the meaning of 'devolution issue' in criminal proceedings so that it no longer includes a question relating to the compatibility with a Convention right (or with EU law) of a provision in an Act of the Scottish Parliament or a question relating to a function of, or failure to act by, a member of the Scottish executive.[37] These are significant constraints on the Supreme Court's role in Scottish legal affairs and they complicate even further the already variable geometry formed by the devolution arrangements in the United Kingdom.

Civil appeals from Scotland to the Supreme Court remain unaffected by the Scotland Act 2012. Yet they too can be controversial because, unlike civil appeals from other civil courts in the United Kingdom, they do not require either the court being appealed from or the Supreme Court itself to grant permission to appeal: the appeal is as of right provided only that the appellant secures the signature of two willing lawyers in Scotland. The result of this is that Supreme Court justices are sometimes required to spend their time dealing with appeals that turn on questions of the interpretation of contracts rather than on more significant legal questions. On more than one occasion Supreme Court justices have intimated that the appeal brought before them was not important enough to merit their attention.[38] The number of civil appeals from Scotland has also been significant, and has risen in the past three years. In the legal year 2009–10, 6 of the 57 cases in which the Supreme Court issued judgments involved

---

[34] http://www.heraldscotland.com/news/crime-courts/macaskill-threat-to-end-supreme-court-funding-macaskill-threat-to-end-supreme-court-funding.13900094.

[35] See ss. 34–8.

[36] Criminal Procedure (Scotland) Act 1995, ss. 288AA(2)(a) and (3) and 288ZB(6)(a) and (7), inserted by ss. 36(6) and 35, respectively, of the Scotland Act 2012. These provisions have been in force since 22 April 2013: Scotland Act 2012 (Commencement No. 3) Order 2013 (SI 6).

[37] Scotland Act 1998, Sched. 6, para. 1, as amended by the Scotland Act 2012, s. 36(4).

[38] e.g. G Hamilton (Tullochgribban Mains) Ltd v. The Highland Council [2012] UKSC 31.

a Scottish appeal (10 per cent); since then the figures have been 7 out of 60 cases in 2010–11 (12 per cent), 16 out of 58 in 2011–12 (28 per cent), 15 out of 83 in 2012–13 (18 per cent) and 11 out of 70 in 2013–14 (16 per cent). At present there seems to be no pressure to rectify the anomaly concerning Scottish civil appeals.

In this context it is worth mentioning that a civil appeal from Scotland to the UK Supreme Court has set an important precedent regarding judicial powers to review an Act of a devolved legislature. In *AXA General Insurance Ltd* v. *Lord Advocate* the appellant insurance companies challenged the lawfulness of the Damages (Asbestos-related Conditions) (Scotland) Act 2009, an Act of the Scottish Parliament which provides that asbestos-related pleural plaques and certain other asbestos-related conditions constitute personal injury which is actionable under Scots law. The companies argued that the Act was incompatible with their rights under Art. 1 of Protocol 1 to the ECHR and that it also represented an unreasonable, irrational, or arbitrary exercise of the Scottish Parliament's legislative authority. The Court of Session rejected the first argument on the facts and held that the second set of grounds was not available to judges under the common law in the context of Acts of the Scottish Parliament, even though such Acts are technically subordinate legislation.[39] The Supreme Court agreed. It ruled that the ultimate controlling factor in such situations is the rule of law, not unreasonableness, irrationality, or arbitrariness.[40] As Lord Hope put it:

> the rule of law enforced by the courts is the ultimate controlling factor on which our constitution is based. I would take that to be, for the purposes of this case, the guiding principle…It is not entirely unthinkable that a government…may seek to use [its powers] to abolish judicial review or to diminish the role of the courts in protecting the interests of the individual. Whether this is likely to happen is not the point. It is enough that it might conceivably do so. The rule of law requires that the judges must retain the power to insist that legislation of that extreme kind is not law which the courts will recognise.[41]

In *Scotland's Future*, the White Paper on independence which the Scottish government published in 2013, the SNP confirmed that if Scotland were to become independent all appeals to the UK Supreme Court would come to an end and '[t]he Inner House of the Court of Session and the High Court of Justiciary sitting as the Court of Criminal Appeal will collectively be Scotland's Supreme Court'.[42] This position was confirmed when the SNP published its draft Scottish Independence Bill in June 2014, which was promoted as a draft constitution for an independent Scotland.[43] Even though it lost the referendum, the draft Scottish Independence Bill will presumably remain a reference point for the SNP.[44] Some of the proposed measures are beyond the current competence of the Scottish Parliament (such as the conferment of Scottish citizenship[45]), but others may not be (such as the proposal that Scots law, whether or not made by the

---

[39] [2011] CSIH 31, [87]–[85].   [40] [2011] UKSC 46, [2012] 1 AC 868, [48]–[52], *per* Lord Hope.
[41] Ibid., para. 51. Lord Hope adopted a similar approach in *R (Jackson)* v. *Attorney General* [2005] UKHL 56, [2006] 1 AC 262, at [107].
[42] Ch. 7, 260.   [43] See cl. 14 ('Supreme Court').
[44] http://www.scotland.gov.uk/Resource/0045/00452762.pdf.   [45] cl. 18.

Scottish Parliament or government, is to be of no effect so far as it is incompatible with some articles in the ECHR).[46] No doubt constitutional lawyers advising the Scottish government will be pushing the envelope on some of these proposals as far as they possibly can.

Meanwhile all eyes will be on the three main political parties at Westminster to see how far they are willing to go towards the 'devo-max' position.[47] As mentioned earlier in the Introduction, the former Labour prime minister, Gordon Brown, was allowed to reveal just a few days before the referendum that draft legislation would be published before Burns night in 2015 (25 January).[48] The proposals of three main UK parties were officially published on 13 October 2014[49] and Lord Smith of Kelvin was asked to chair a commission overseeing the process which would take forward the devolution commitments on further powers for the Scottish Parliament.[50] The initial report of that Commission[51] recommends that much greater tax-raising powers should be transferred to Edinburgh and that Scotland be given responsibility for part of the country's expenditure on social security benefits. It also suggests that the continuing existence of the Scottish Parliament and Scottish government will be guaranteed and that the Sewel convention, whereby Westminster does not legislate on a matter that has been transferred to the Scottish Parliament without first obtaining its consent, will be placed on a statutory footing.[52] All in all, the proposals could be said to represent an even larger wave of devolution than that which swept across Scotland in 1998,[53] and to at least one prominent commentator they make the eventual creation of a federal United Kingdom much more likely.[54] Given the threat of a backlash from a range of backbench MPs representing English constituencies, it remains possible that Westminster will not in the end go as far as most Scots anticipated when they cast their vote in the referendum. That would no doubt be portrayed as a breach of the vow which the leaders of the three main UK political parties made two days before the

---

[46] cl. 26(2).

[47] 'Devo-max' is usually taken to mean that Scotland would be allowed to raise much more of its revenue through its own tax regime (rather than receiving most of it through a block grant from Westminster) and in turn would be responsible for most of the public expenditure in Scotland. According to one version, money raised from within Scotland would also be paid to the UK government for services provided on a UK-wide basis, such as defence.

[48] *The Independent*, 8 September 2014: http://www.independent.co.uk/news/uk/scottish-independence/scottish-independence-gordon-brown-reveals-timetable-for-further-devolution-to-holyrood-9719629.html.

[49] *The Parties' Published Proposals on Further Devolution for Scotland*, Cm 8946.

[50] See http://www.smith-commission.scot. For criticism of the speed and process by which constitutional change is being made see S. Tierney, 'Solomon Grundy Does Constitutional Change: The Smith Commission Timetable to Transform the Scottish Parliament' (31 October 2014), http://ukconstitutionallaw.org.

[51] Published on 27 November 2014.

[52] On these last two proposals see M. Elliott, 'A "Permanent" Scottish Parliament and the Sovereignty of the UK Parliament: Four Perspectives' (28 November 2014), http://ukconstitutionallaw.org.

[53] That is the view of Jim Murphy MP, the new leader of the Labour Party in Scotland, who thinks Smith exceeds what was in the 'vow': http://www.politicshome.com/uk/article/109087/login.html.

[54] See e.g. S. Tierney, 'Is a Federal Britain Now Inevitable?', *Int'l J Const L Blog* 27 November 2014, http://www.iconnectblog.com.

referendum.[55] In the months and years ahead a great deal of political negotiation will have to take place.

WALES

Since 1998 devolution has undergone more changes in Wales than it has in Scotland or Northern Ireland. It is now customary to refer to 'three phases' of Welsh devolution: 1998–2006, 2006–11, and the period since 2011.[56] In 1998 a minimalist approach was adopted by the Government of Wales Act but as time has gone on more and more powers have been devolved. The initial caution was partly due to the fact that less than 20 years earlier, in 1979, nearly 80 per cent of the people in Wales who voted in a referendum expressed a clear preference *not* to have powers devolved, and in the referendum held in 1998 there was only a tiny majority in favour of the idea (50.3 per cent). Thus, the Government of Wales Act 1998 provided for a Welsh Assembly but conferred on it only the power to make secondary legislation when authorized to do so by the UK Parliament. Eighteen fields were identified in which functions were to be transferred to the Assembly by an initial Order in Council[57] and provision was then made for the transfer of additional matters in future.[58] The 'Executive Committee' of the Assembly was to be chaired by the 'Assembly First Secretary' and to comprise the other 'Assembly Secretaries'.[59]

As in Scotland, there were elections to the Welsh Assembly in 1999, 2003, 2007, and 2011. Voters elect 60 Assembly Members (AMs), 40 of whom are chosen by a first-past-the-post system in individual constituencies, and 20 of whom are elected by a regional top-up system as in Scotland, which gives voters a second vote relating to one of five regions into which Wales has been divided. Four AMs are elected for each of these five regions. To date all of the elections have been dominated by the Labour Party, which won 28 seats in 1999, 28 in 2003, 26 in 2007, and 30 in 2011. From 1999 to 2003 Labour governed in coalition with the Liberal Democrats, and from 2007 to 2011 it did so with Plaid Cymru, a party which supports Welsh independence, but otherwise it has governed alone. There are also 40 MPs elected from Wales to sit in the UK Parliament at Westminster.[60] For a while the majority of AMs in Cardiff were female, but the percentage today is down to 40 per cent (still much higher than in the

---

[55] 'The Vow' appeared on the front page of the *Daily Record*, a prominent Scottish daily newspaper, on 16 September 2014. It promised that 'extensive new powers for the [Scottish] Parliament will be delivered by the process and to the timetable agreed and announced by our three parties'. For updates on this issue, see *Late News*, p. vii.

[56] See e.g. the potted history supplied by the Supreme Court in *In re Agricultural Sector (Wales) Bill* [2014] UKSC 43, [2014] 1 WLR 2622, [19]–[33]. On this case see the text at n. 70.

[57] See n. 3 and s. 22(2) of, and Sched. 2 to, the Government of Wales Act 1998 as well as the National Assembly for Wales (Transfer of Functions) Order 1999 (SI 1999/672).

[58] See s. 22(5) of, and Sched. 3 to, the Government of Wales Act 1998.

[59] Government of Wales Act 1998, s. 56.

[60] In the 2010 general election 26 of the MPs elected were from the Labour Party, 8 from the Conservatives, 3 from the Liberal Democrats, and 3 from Plaid Cymru.

other devolved legislatures and in the Westminster Parliament). The Welsh government's website proudly proclaims that it is 'one of the few governments in the world that publishes Cabinet minutes and papers'.[61]

The Government of Wales Act 2006 was prompted by dissatisfaction with the limited nature of devolution enjoyed in Wales compared to Scotland and Northern Ireland, which is evidence that there is a competitive edge to the devolution process throughout the United Kingdom. It was preceded by the report of a commission chaired by Lord Richard of Ammanford[62] and by a UK government White Paper, *Better Governance for Wales*.[63] Its main reforms were, first, to separate the Executive Committee from the Assembly and call it a government; secondly, to add two fields to the 18 which were already devolved to the Assembly in 1998; thirdly, to allow Orders in Council to be made delegating power from the UK Parliament to enable the Welsh Assembly to make 'Measures' in any of the 20 fields now devolved; and fourthly, to permit a further referendum to be held asking for the people's approval for the devolution of powers allowing the Assembly to pass Acts, just like the Scottish Parliament and the Northern Ireland Assembly. A referendum was duly held on 3 March 2011. Although the turn-out was low (35.2 per cent), 63.5 per cent of those who voted answered 'Yes' to the question 'Do you want the Assembly now to be able to make laws on *all* matters in the 20 subject areas it has powers for?'

Following this result, the first Act of the National Assembly of Wales was passed in 2012. It regulates the use of the Welsh and English languages in the Assembly itself.[64] Controversy then arose over the second proposed Act, the Local Government Byelaws (Wales) Act 2012. Section 6 of this Act removed the power of the Welsh ministers[65] and the Secretary of State for Wales[66] to confirm specific bye-laws, while s. 9 empowered Welsh ministers to add to the categories of bye-laws which could be enacted without confirmation. The Secretary of State for Wales refused to agree to the latter provision, so the Attorney General for the UK asked the Supreme Court, as he was empowered to do under s. 112 of the Government of Wales Act 2006, to rule whether the Act was within the Welsh Assembly's competence. This was the first time this referral mechanism had been used anywhere in the United Kingdom since the devolution settlement of 1998.[67] The Supreme Court had little difficulty in rejecting the challenge because it found that the removal of the Secretary of State's power to confirm byelaws was 'incidental to, or consequential on' the primary purpose of the Act in question, which was

---

[61] wales.gov.uk/about/?lang=en.

[62] Lord Richard was a former Leader of the House of Lords, a Commissioner at the European Commission, and a UK Ambassador at the United Nations. The Commission started work in September 2002 and published its report in March 2004. For a summary of its work see the Isobel White, House of Commons Library Standard Note SN/PC/3018 (updated 22 April 2004).

[63] Cm 6582.   [64] National Assembly for Wales (Official Languages) Act 2012.

[65] i.e. the ministers in the Welsh government.

[66] i.e. the member of the UK government with responsibility for Wales.

[67] The question of the Scottish Parliament's legislative competence had arisen in some 'devolution issue' references or appeals, but those cases all concerned legislation that had already been enacted. See e.g. *Martin v. Most* [2010] UKSC 10, 2010 SC (UKSC) 40.

to remove the need for confirmation of bye-laws by Welsh ministers, thereby stream-lining the way in which bye-laws are made.[68] The Justices said it would have been per-verse for the Secretary of State to retain a veto if the Welsh ministers' veto was being removed. They said little about the wider devolution context within which the case had arisen, but Lord Hope observed that, even though the 2006 Act was of great con-stitutional significance, that of itself was not a guide to its interpretation. He added:

> The rules to [sic] which the court must apply in order to give effect to it are those laid down by the statute, and the statute must be interpreted like any other statute. But the purpose of the Act has informed the statutory language, and it is proper to have regard to it if help is needed as to what the words mean.[69]

The same approach was adopted a year or so later when a second reference concerning Welsh legislation was made to the Supreme Court by the UK's Attorney General, this time in relation to the Agricultural Sector (Wales) Bill 2013.[70] The main purpose of this bill was to establish a new Agricultural Wages Panel to replace the Agricultural Advisory Panel for Wales which had been abolished by the Enterprise and Regulatory Reform Act 2013. The Welsh government was confident that the Assembly had com-petence because the Government of Wales Act 2006 allowed it to make legislation which 'relates to' agriculture.[71] But the Attorney General's view was that the bill related to employment and industrial relations, fields which have not been devolved to the Welsh Assembly. Again the Supreme Court unanimously found that the bill did fall within the Assembly's competence. Following the principle confirmed in the bye-laws case, the Justices interpreted the bill in the same way as it would any other piece of primary legislation. Thus, where a bill can in principle be reasonably classi-fied as relating either to a devolved matter or to a non-devolved matter, and provided that it fairly and realistically satisfies the test for competence set out in section 108 of the 2006 Act[72] and is not within a specified exception, 'it does not matter whether in principle it might also be capable of being classified as relating to a subject which has not been devolved'.[73]

Alongside the growing enthusiasm for legislative and executive devolution, Wales has witnessed a recent surge in support for greater judicial devolution. While England and Wales have been viewed as a single jurisdiction for centuries (and therefore as one 'country' for the purposes of private international law), the inevitable consequence of Wales being able to develop its own legislation and policies has been a clamour, in some quarters, for separate Welsh courts in which disputes about such legislation

---

[68] *Attorney General* v. *National Assembly for Wales Commission* [2012] UKSC 53, [2013] 1 AC 792.

[69] Ibid., [80]. The four other Justices in the case all agreed with Lord Hope's remarks.

[70] *In re Agricultural Sector (Wales) Bill* [2014] UKSC 43, [2014] 1 WLR 2622.

[71] s. 108 and Sched. 7.

[72] This is the provision which, along with Sched. 7, determines the sorts of fields within which the Welsh Assembly has authority to legislate.

[73] [2014] 1 WLR 2622, [67], *per* Lord Reed and Lord Thomas CJ, with whom Lord Neuberger, Lady Hale, and Lord Kerr agreed.

and policies can be dealt with. The First Minister, Carwyn James, announced in 2011 that there was a need for a public debate on the issue[74] and in the following year the Welsh government launched a consultation paper.[75] The Secretary of State issued an icy response to that paper, referring to it as 'a surprising priority for the Welsh Government' and suggesting there was no need to fix something that was not broken.[76] The Constitutional and Legislative Affairs Committee of the Welsh Assembly published a report on the matter at the end of 2012,[77] recommending that additional legal training be put in place to allow specialisms to develop reflecting the legal traditions of Wales, that the Civil Procedure Rules be amended to ensure that public law cases dealing primarily with Welsh issues are generally commenced in the Administrative Court in Cardiff, that a presumption should be established in favour of hearing in Welsh courts all cases relating to laws made bilingually in English and Welsh, and that a senior judge with experience of Welsh devolution and Welsh law should be appointed to the Supreme Court. The Committee's recommendations have not yet been taken up, but it is worth noting that in the case concerning the Agricultural Sector (Wales) Bill 2013, discussed earlier, the Lord Chief Justice of England and Wales, Lord Thomas of Cwmgiedd, was invited to participate as an ad hoc judge in the Supreme Court because, as a Welshman, he would give the decision greater credibility in Welsh eyes. In June 2013 the President of the Supreme Court announced that, while there was as yet an insufficient body of Welsh law to justify reserving a seat on the Supreme Court for a Welsh Justice, in any future appeal involving Welsh devolution issues, the Supreme Court panel will, if possible, include a judge who has specifically Welsh experience and knowledge. If there is no such full-time member of the Supreme Court, an appropriate Lord Justice of Appeal will be asked to sit.[78]

The current phase of devolution in Wales will not be the last. The Silk Commission, which was set up in 2011 to review the current constitutional arrangements in Wales, reported on fiscal powers in November 2012 and on other powers in March 2014.[79]

---

[74] This was at the Annual Conference of the Standing Committee for Legal Wales (SCLW) in Cardiff: wales. gov.uk/newsroom/firstminister/2012/5868155/?lang=en. For the speech of the Solicitor General for England and Wales, Sir Edward Garnier QC, at the same conference see: http://www.gov.uk/government/speeches/ speech-to-2011-legal-wales-conference. The SCLW provides a forum for the discussion of views on issues affecting the administration of justice, the teaching of law, and the provision of legal services in Wales. In its submission to the consultation paper it was broadly supportive of devolving responsibility for the administration of justice in Wales to the Welsh Assembly: http://commissionondevolutioninwales.independent.gov. uk/files/2013/03/Legal-Wales.pdf.

[75] *A Separate Legal Jurisdiction for Wales* (WG-15109): wales.gov.uk/docs/caecd/consultation/120326 separatelegaljurisdiction.pdf.

[76] See http://www.gov.uk/government/news/welsh-secretary-responds-to-welsh-government-consultat ion-into-a-separate-legal-jurisdiction-for-wales.

[77] *Inquiry into a Separate Welsh Jurisdiction*, available on the Assembly's website.

[78] Lecture entitled 'Judges and Policy: A Delicate Balance' delivered at the Institute for Government, 19 June 2013, para. 20 (available on the website of the Supreme Court). The power to appoint acting judges to the Supreme Court is provided by the Constitutional Reform Act 2005, ss. 38–9.

[79] Reports of the Commission on Devolution in Wales (2012 and (2014), http://commissionondevolu-tioninwales.independent.gov.uk/.

On fiscal powers, the Commission recommended that national funding for Wales should be provided on the same 'block grant' basis as is used for Scotland and Northern Ireland but that Wales should also be able to raise revenue through its own taxes. Amongst the taxes which the Silk Commission thought should be devolved to Wales are business rates, stamp duty, landfill tax, aggregates duty, and some air passenger duty. Corporation tax should be devolved only if this occurs in Scotland and Northern Ireland too. The Commission called for a referendum to be held on whether income tax should be devolved but makes it clear that its own view is that the Welsh government should have responsibility for setting income tax rates in Wales. The Welsh government should also be given greater borrowing powers in order to increase capital investment in Wales. In November 2013 the UK government accepted 30 of the 31 recommendations addressed to it in the first Silk Commission report,[80] and promised to publish a draft Wales Bill which would include provisions devolving tax and borrowing powers to the National Assembly for Wales and Welsh ministers. The resulting Wales Bill is currently making its way through Parliament.[81]

As far as non-fiscal powers are concerned the Silk Commission's report in March 2014 proposed that the Welsh devolution model of 'conferred powers' should be changed so as to reflect the model of 'reserved powers' adopted for Scotland and Northern Ireland. This would mean that all powers would be devolved unless they were specifically reserved, unlike the current system under which all powers are reserved unless they are specifically devolved. More particularly, the Commission recommended that greater powers should be devolved in relation to transport, natural resources, policing, community safety, and the treatment of young offenders. There should be further administrative devolution in the court system and within ten years there should be a review of the case for devolving to the Assembly the legislative responsibility for the court service, sentencing, legal aid, prosecutions, and the judiciary. More generally, a statutory Code of Practice on intergovernmental relations should be provided for in a new Government of Wales Act. As yet the UK government has not issued a full response to this second report by the Silk Commission. For updates on this issue, see *Late News*, p. vii.

In view of the fact that Scotland is likely to obtain a greater degree of devolution in the wake of the referendum decision in September 2014, the pressure for increased devolution in Wales is unlikely to abate. As both countries acquire more experience of self-governance they seem destined to want to broaden it. The picture in Northern Ireland is somewhat different.

---

[80] The UK government did not accept that air passenger duty should be devolved. The response is available at: http://www.gov.uk/government/uploads/system/uploads/attachment_data/file/259359/empowerment_and_responsibility_181113.pdf.

[81] The bill had its third reading in the House of Lords on 24 November 2014. For updates on this issue, see *Late News*, p. vii..

NORTHERN IRELAND

There was devolution in Northern Ireland from 1921 to 1972, but it came to an end when serious civil unrest broke out on account of great dissatisfaction on the part of many nationalists (who favour a united Ireland) with the way in which unionist politicians were running the area. More than 3,500 deaths later, a settlement to reinstall devolution was reached through the Belfast (Good Friday) Agreement of April 1998, the essentials of which were put in place through the Northern Ireland Act 1998.[82] A Northern Ireland Assembly was established at Stormont in East Belfast, comprising 108 MLAs (Members of the Legislative Assembly) elected through proportional representation (six MLAs for each of 18 constituencies), and a power-sharing executive was provided for. In the Assembly elections held in 1998 the two most successful parties were, on the unionist side, the Ulster Unionist Party (UUP) (with 28 seats) and, on the nationalist side, the Social Democratic and Labour Party (SDLP) (24 seats).[83] Between 2002 and 2007 the Assembly was suspended, largely on account of unionist dissatisfaction with the lack of progress being made in the decommissioning of weapons held by illegal paramilitary organizations such as the IRA. Elections were nevertheless held in 2003 and it became clear that voters were becoming more polarized: the winner on the unionist side was the Democratic Unionist Party (30 seats) and on the nationalist side it was Sinn Féin (24 seats).[84] This shift in power was further exaggerated in the elections held four years later in the wake of the St Andrews Agreement,[85] when the DUP won 36 seats and Sinn Féin won 28, and again in 2011, when the DUP won 38 seats and Sinn Féin 29.[86] The latter elections occurred a year after the responsibility for justice and policing had finally been devolved to the Assembly following the Hillsborough Castle Agreement;[87] this was a particularly important development because it meant that confidence in the maturity of the devolution arrangements had grown to the extent that law and order could once again be locally controlled (for the

---

[82] A not dissimilar power-sharing deal had been agreed at the Sunningdale conference in 1973, but the resulting Assembly was brought down by the Ulster Workers' Council's industrial action in May 1974.

[83] The other seats were won by the Democratic Unionist Party (20), Sinn Féin (18), Alliance (6), the UK Unionist Party (5), the Progressive Unionist Party (2), and the Northern Ireland Women's Coalition (2).

[84] The other seats were won by the UUP (27), the SDLP (18), Alliance (6), the UKUP (1), and an independent (1).

[85] This was an Agreement reached on 13 October 2006 by the British and Irish governments and the major political parties in Northern Ireland (including the DUP, which had not been party to the Belfast (Good Friday) Agreement); it provided for the restoration of the Assembly, a commitment by the DUP to share power with Sinn Féin, and a commitment by Sinn Féin to support the Police Service of Northern Ireland.

[86] For an excellent website dealing with elections in Northern Ireland, maintained by Nicholas Whyte, see http://www.ark.ac.uk/elections.

[87] This was reached on 5 February 2010; it set out how the Justice Minister should be chosen, what sort of actions he or she might take to implement agreed policies, and what additional financial help the UK government would provide to help deal with justice issues. See http://www.nidirect.gov.uk/castle_final_agreement15__2_-3.pdf.

first time since 1972).[88] Since the reconvening of the Assembly in 2007, therefore, the executive has been dominated by two of the more extreme parties on each side and the First Minister has been drawn from the DUP while the Deputy First Minister has been a representative of Sinn Féin. These two individuals stand or fall together: if one resigns the other ceases to hold office too.[89] The people of Northern Ireland also elect 18 MPs to Westminster, though those elected for Sinn Féin adopt an abstentionist position—that is, they do not take up their seats.[90]

In the eyes of many commentators, and not a few MLAs from parties other than the DUP and Sinn Féin, the result of the mandatory coalition in place since 2007 has been paralysis. A number of reforms, including to education services, the systems for regulating the display of flags and the holding of parades, and the mechanisms for dealing with wrongs committed during the troubles, have all had to be put on hold because the DUP and Sinn Féin cannot reach a compromise. Talks on the last three issues, under the chairmanship of a former US envoy to Northern Ireland, Dr Richard Haass, failed to reach agreement at the end of 2013.[91] Controversies over the way in which police have reviewed some deaths caused by British soldiers during the troubles[92] and over the operation of an administrative scheme to allow so-called 'on the runs' to return to the United Kingdom without fear of prosecution,[93] have dogged further progress on these matters. The biggest stumbling block may yet prove to be the refusal of nationalist MLAs to implement welfare reforms which have been mandated by the coalition government in London. Social security is a devolved matter in Northern Ireland, unlike in Scotland and Wales, but there is a statutory provision requiring the Secretary of State for Northern Ireland and the Northern Ireland Minister having responsibility for social security to 'from time to time consult one another with a view to securing that, to the extent agreed between them, the legislation to which this section applies provides single systems of social security, child support and pensions for the United Kingdom'.[94] As a result of a failure to reach such agreement, very large deductions are already being

---

[88] But as neither the unionist nor nationalist parties could trust one of their opponents to occupy the role of Minister of Justice they agreed that it should be allocated to an MLA from the non-aligned Alliance Party, David Ford. For details of how justice was devolved see G. Anthony, 'The Devolution of Policing and Criminal Justice' (2011) 17 *Eur Pub Law* 197.

[89] Northern Ireland Act 1998, s. 16B(2), inserted by the Northern Ireland (St Andrews Agreement) Act 2006, s. 8(1).

[90] In the 2010 general election the DUP won eight seats at Westminster, Sinn Féin won five, the SDLP won three, the Alliance party won one, and an independent won one.

[91] A copy of the final draft of the proposals was published by the Northern Ireland Office and is available at http://www.northernireland.gov.uk/haass.pdf.

[92] The flaws were highlighted in a report on the PSNI's Historical Enquiries Team issued by Her Majesty's Inspectorate of Constabulary in July 2013: http://www.hmic.gov.uk/media/inspection-of-the-police-service-of-northern-ireland-historical-enquiries-team-20130703.pdf.

[93] This was the subject of a report prepared by Lady Justice Hallett: *An Independent Review Into the On the Runs Administrative Scheme* (July 2014): http://www.gov.uk/government/uploads/system/uploads/attachment_data/file/335206/41003_Hallett_Web_Accessible.pdf. A report on the same topic by the House of Commons' Northern Ireland Affairs Committee is still awaited.

[94] Northern Ireland Act 1998, s. 87(1).

made from the block grant allocated to Northern Ireland by the UK Treasury, a deduction which in turn requires the executive to make cuts to many other budgets within its control. So serious is the impasse that some believe that responsibility for social security may have to be transferred back to Westminster, at least for a while. On the unionist side there is no desire for further devolution, and they actually fear it happening if greater powers are to be devolved to Scotland.[95] The operation of the 'petition of concern' procedure, whereby 30 MLAs can effectively veto any proposal brought to the floor of the Northern Ireland Assembly, has also slowed progress considerably.[96]

In September 2014 the First Minister of Northern Ireland, Peter Robinson, said that the arrangements for devolved government at Stormont were 'no longer fit for purpose'. This hints that he too is supportive of loosening the requirement in the Northern Ireland Act 1998 that there must be a coalition government drawn from the biggest parties in the Northern Ireland Assembly, without any negotiation between the parties in question. Instead, provision could be made for an official opposition in the Assembly. In the 2014 local government elections in Northern Ireland, while the DUP and Sinn Féin won more council seats than any other parties (235 out of 462), the total percentage of first preference votes cast for those two parties was 47.2 per cent. These figures suggest that if all or most of the other parties in Northern Ireland were able to coalesce they might just be able to win more seats than the DUP and Sinn Féin at an Assembly election and so form a government. But voting patterns at Assembly elections often differ from those at local elections (partly because there are fewer parties competing), and a 'rainbow' coalition would comprise several very unlikely bedfellows, so this possibility may be unrealistic at present. An alternative scenario is that disillusionment with the two big parties may cause votes to seep back to the credible 'second' parties on both sides, the UUP and the SDLP, each of which is more moderate than the 'first' parties. The UK government raised the possibility of providing for a formal opposition in a consultation paper issued in 2012,[97] but chose not to proceed with the idea.[98] In April 2014 the Secretary of State for Northern Ireland, Theresa Villiers, made clear the Conservative Party's position:

> There are inherent weaknesses in a system in which it is very difficult to remove one's rulers by voting and to choose a viable alternative. That's why this Government is clear that

[95] See e.g. the views of Northern Ireland's former Finance Minister, Sammy Wilson, as reported in *The Herald*: http://www.heraldscotland.com/politics/referendum-news/no-vote-will-spell-disaster-for-stormont-power-sharing.25113826. For updates on this issue, see *Late News*, p. vii.

[96] Northern Ireland Act 1998, s. 42. See the paper on this issue presented at a Knowledge Exchange Seminar at the Assembly by Dr Alex Schwartz in March 2014, http://www.niassembly.gov.uk/Documents/RaISe/knowledge_exchange/briefing_papers/series3/schwartz200314.pdf.

[97] *Consultation on Measures to Improve the Operation of the Northern Ireland Assembly*. This, and the responses to the consultation, are available on the website of the Northern Ireland Office. See too Briefing Paper 1, *Opposition, Community Designation and d'Hondt*, issued by the Assembly Research and Information Service (2012).

[98] The matter was raised in the consultation paper which preceded the enactment of the Northern Ireland (Miscellaneous Provisions) Act 2014. The Act was also preceded by a draft bill which was made available for public consultation in February 2013 (Cm 8563, paras. 21–3); the bill was scrutinized by the Northern Ireland Affairs Committee, to which the government responded on 10 May 2013.

we would welcome moves that facilitate a more normal system at Stormont that allows for formal opposition, so long as a way can be found to do this which is consistent with power sharing and inclusivity.

But we also believe that if or how this happens really has to be primarily for parties in the Assembly to take forward. This is because it is firmly within the Assembly's competence to deal with those matters that might characterize an opposition—such as speaking rights, financial assistance and committee chairmanships.[99]

The current UK government is also supportive of the devolution of additional fiscal powers to Northern Ireland, but believes that for the present 'the focus should be on delivery and addressing the social division beneath the conflict, not reopening the debate on institutional changes'.[100] An announcement is due shortly on whether the UK government is prepared to allow the Northern Ireland Assembly to set a different rate of corporation tax from that which applies in the rest of the United Kingdom, thereby making Northern Ireland a more attractive investment opportunity in comparison with the Republic of Ireland.[101]

The consultation launched in 2012 led to other changes being made to the way the Assembly operates. Under the Northern Ireland (Miscellaneous Provisions) Act 2014 no person who is an MP at Westminster or a TD in the Dáil Éireann (the Parliament of the Republic of Ireland) can now also sit as an MLA in the Northern Ireland Assembly, the number of seats in the Assembly has become a 'reserved' rather than an 'excepted' matter[102] (meaning that the Assembly itself can legislate to reduce the number, provided the Secretary of State, and the UK Parliament, consent),[103] the length of each elected Assembly has been extended from four to five years to ensure that elections do not take place in the same year as general elections,[104] and the ways in which the Justice Minister is selected and can be removed from office have been altered to provide the Justice Minister with greater security of tenure but also to ensure that his or

---

[99] http://www.conservativehome.com/platform/2014/04/theresa-villiers-mp-how-northern-ireland-can-take-the-next-steps-forward.html.

[100] *Response to the 4th Report 2008–09 of the Political and Constitutional Reform Committee of the House of Commons*, para. 3.12. The commitment to further fiscal devolution was made as part of the implementation of the 'Building a Prosperous and United Community' agreement (June 2013), 7, http://www.gov.uk/government/uploads/system/uploads/attachment_data/file/206979/Building_a_Prosperous_and_United_Community.pdf.

[101] At present corporation tax is set at 21% in the UK, whereas in the Republic of Ireland it is set at 12.5%. For updates on this issue, see *Late News*, p. vii.

[102] See nn. 4 and 5.

[103] Most of the political parties in Northern Ireland are in favour of a reduction, apparently for reasons of cost. For details see the report on this issue in 2012 by the Northern Ireland Assembly's Assembly and Executive Review Committee, http://www.niassembly.gov.uk/Assembly-Business/Committees/Assembly-and-Executive-Review/Reports/Number-of-Members-of-the-Northern-Ireland-Legislative-Assembly. There is also a 2012 report by that Committee on whether the number of government departments in Northern Ireland should be reduced (at present there are 11).

[104] The Fixed-term Parliaments Act 2011 established five-year terms for the UK Parliament, the Scottish Parliament, and the Welsh National Assembly.

her political party does not have more ministers than would otherwise be allowed to it under the distribution system provided for in the Northern Ireland Act 1998.[105]

ENGLAND

The current devolution arrangements in the United Kingdom leave a black hole—England. There is currently no parliament or government exclusively concerned with English matters, and no regional level of government within England except in London. Furthermore, whereas no MP from an English constituency can vote on any laws put up for consideration by the Scottish Parliament, the Welsh Assembly, or the Northern Ireland Assembly, all the MPs from those regions can vote on all legislation put up for consideration by the UK Parliament even when it is intended to apply only in England—the so-called 'West Lothian question'.[106] Of the 650 MPs at Westminster, only 117 (18 per cent) do not represent constituencies in England. By the same token, all MPs representing English constituencies are allowed to vote on bills which are intended to apply in only one of the devolved regions. Thus, when the bill which became the Scotland Act 2012 was given its second reading in the House of Commons, 259 MPs voted on it.[107]

Proposals to devolve powers to regions of England were included in the manifesto of the Labour Party prior to the general election in 1997: 'In time we will introduce legislation to allow the people, region by region, to decide in a referendum whether they want directly elected regional government. Only where clear popular consent is established will arrangements be made for elected regional assemblies.' A separate commitment was made to hold a referendum on establishing a strategic authority and elected mayor for London. This latter referendum took place in 1998 and there is now an elected mayor together with an elected London Assembly of 25 members which holds the mayor to account.[108] The pledge to hold referendums in other regions was met only in the North East, where in 2004, on a turn-out of 49 per cent, 78 per cent of those who voted rejected the proposal to create a Regional Assembly. This led the Labour government to abandon its plans for similar referendums in the North West and in the Yorkshire and Humber region,[109] and the whole

---

[105] See s. 18, which provides for the application of what is known as the *D'Hondt* system.

[106] So called because it was first raised by the then MP for West Lothian, Tam Dalyell. By way of example, Pt I (ss. 1–55) of the Health and Social Care Act 2012 deals with 'the health service in England', yet on the second reading of the bill which became the Act quite a few of the 556 MPs who voted did not represent English constituencies: HC Debs, vol. 522, cols. 605–703 (31 January 2011).

[107] HC Debs, vol. 522, cols. 467–556 (27 January 2011).

[108] The Greater London Authority is the administrative body which implements the policies of the Mayor and Assembly. Following a referendum held in London in 1998 (when 72% of those who voted approved of the proposal) it was set up in 2000 and operates under the Greater London Authority Acts 1999 and 2007. It deals mainly with transport, policing, economic development, and emergency planning.

[109] Such referendums were provided for in the Regional Assemblies (Preparations) Act 2003, which has since been repealed by the Local Democracy, Economic Development and Construction Act 2009.

project was later allowed to wither. It has not been taken up by the Coalition government in power since 2010. Indeed the *Programme for Government* issued by the Coalition just two weeks after the election barely mentioned devolution: it said the government would implement the recommendations of the Calman Commission in Scotland and, after holding a referendum for further devolution in Wales, would set up a similar Commission there (this manifested itself as the Silk Commission). The Coalition recognized that there were concerns about the way in which the funding of devolution was calculated,[110] but stated that any change to the system would have to wait until the national deficit had been reduced. In November 2013 the UK government admitted that it 'has not continued pursuit of regional devolution because previous efforts have not received popular support'.[111] That is why it abolished Regional Development Agencies and Government Offices for the Regions. It prefers to devolve power to 'the lowest appropriate level', namely local government and communities.[112]

Perhaps the most significant devolution commitment in the 2010 *Programme for Government*[113] was to establish a commission to consider the West Lothian question. The 'Commission on the Consequences of Devolution for the House of Commons', chaired by Sir William McKay, began its work in February 2012 and reported in March 2013.[114] It accepted that people in England felt unhappy with present arrangements[115] but it favoured addressing these grievances not through legislation but through procedural changes within Parliament.[116] It proposed that the House of Commons should be asked to support a resolution saying that decisions which will have a separate and distinct effect for England, or for England and Wales, should *normally* be taken only with the consent of a majority of MPs sitting for constituencies in those countries (but there would be no prohibition on other MPs voting on such decisions if they

---

[110] These were highlighted, in particular, by the Independent Commission on Funding and Finance for Wales, chaired by Gerald Holtham. In its final report (*Fairness and Accountability: A New Funding Settlement for Wales*, 2010) the Commission recommended that the Barnett formula, which has been used since the late 1970s to establish the size of the so-called 'block grant' allocated by the UK government to Scotland, Wales, and Northern Ireland, should be amended to better reflect the needs of the region in question (rather than just the number of people living there). The Commission also supported the devolution of some tax-raising powers to the Welsh Assembly. See http://wales.gov.uk/docs/icffw/report/100705funding settlementfullen.pdf.

[111] Response to *Do We Need a Constitutional Convention for the UK?*, 4th Report, 2012–13, of the House of Commons' Political and Constitutional Reform Committee (HC 371–I), Cm 8947, para. 3.21.

[112] e.g. through the Localism Act 2011.

[113] It did also promise that the coalition would 'promote the radical devolution of power and greater financial autonomy to local government and community groups' (p. 11).

[114] Report of the Commission on the Consequences of Devolution for the House of Commons: http://webarchive.nationalarchives.gov.uk/20130403030652/http:/tmc.independent.gov.uk/wp-content/uploads/2013/03/The-McKay-Commission_Main-Report_25-March-20131.pdf.

[115] As evidence it referred in particular to a report by the Institute for Public Policy Research, *The Dog that Finally Barked: England as an Emerging Political Community* (January 2012) and to another by the National Centre for Social Research, *The English Question: How Is England Responding to Devolution?* (February 2012).

[116] Sir William McKay is a former Clerk of the House of Commons.

so wished). In Committees which examine bills there should at times be majorities reflecting the party balance in England, or England and Wales, and provision could be made for a 'legislative consent motion' allowing MPs from England, or from England and Wales, to agree to a UK bill making provisions relating only to England or to England and Wales. The McKay Commission also proposed that a Select Committee on Devolution should be appointed to allow the House of Commons to hold UK ministers to account for their responsibilities in connection with devolution. The government's official response to this report is still awaited.[117] In 2009 the then government, in response to another report, firmly rejected the notion of 'English votes for English laws'.[118]

In the wake of the Scottish referendum in September 2014 the UK government faces an interesting choice. Does it increase the extent of devolution to Scotland (and perhaps Wales) and hope that that will be enough to allow those regions to feel less dominated, politically and economically, by the government in London? Or does it seek to alter the role of the UK government altogether, promote devolution to England, and move ever closer to a federal United Kingdom? The latter may be an attractive option because it marries the advantages of regional autonomy with those of a strong central authority playing a role on the world stage, as in the United States, but it is unlikely to satisfy those in Scotland who voted for complete independence and it may be seen more generally as a way of facilitating the break-up of the union. The McKay Commission gave substantial consideration to the creation of a federal United Kingdom but rejected it outright: it received little evidence of popular support for the idea, it did not think that Regional Assemblies would adequately deal with the sense of English disadvantage and it was firmly against the creation of an English Parliament, which it characterized as a disproportionate and destabilizing response to 'the English question'. It may be that once further devolution of powers has been devolved to large cities, as it already has for London, the appetite for Regional Assemblies will diminish and the call for an English Parliament will disappear. This might be a more attractive option for English residents if a convention were to be established whereby MPs representing constituencies outside England would not vote at Westminster on clauses in bills intended to apply only within England.

One drawback with the option of devolving power to an English Parliament or Assembly is that this is likely to enhance the competitiveness between the devolved countries and to encourage people in Scotland to try again for independence in a few years' time in order to further differentiate their country from that south of the border.[119]

---

[117] For academic comment see e.g. M. Elliott, 'Devolution, the West Lothian Question, and the Nature of Constitutional Reform in the United Kingdom' *UK Const L Blog* 26 March 2013, http://ukconstitutionallaw.org.

[118] Response to the Justice Committee's Report on *Devolution: A Decade On*, Cm 7687, 22, http://www.gov.uk/government/uploads/system/uploads/attachment_data/file/229033/7687.pdf.

[119] Such a referendum would again require the consent of the UK Parliament, which may be loathe to grant it just a few years after the 2014 referendum.

An even more serious drawback is that if an English Parliament or Assembly were to be created it would be almost as large as the UK Parliament and would vastly reduce the significance of the latter. A federation in which one of the four constituent units is itself more than four times larger than all the other units put together is significantly unbalanced. In any House of Commons in the new UK Parliament, the representatives from England would vastly outnumber those from Scotland, Wales, and Northern Ireland,[120] and if equality of representation were to be insisted upon in a second house of the Parliament in the way that occurs in the Senate of the United States,[121] it would be unfair if this could veto the wishes of the first house. There does not appear to be any political, or popular, appetite to resurrect the Labour Party's proposal to create not one English Parliament or Assembly but up to eight Regional Assemblies,[122] plus the one in London. Such Assemblies would also cost money, despite Labour's odd contention in its 1997 manifesto that their plans would not involve any additional public expenditure overall and not mean adding a new tier of government to the existing English system. In that party's 2010 manifesto there was no mention whatsoever of devolution within England. The manifestos for the 2015 election will doubtless contain further pledges from the three main parties as to how they will deal with the West Lothian question, with the Conservatives probably supporting the call for 'English votes for English issues'.[123] One way of achieving that goal would be to refer all such issues—when they are the subject of proposed legislation—to a new parliamentary standing committee comprising only of MPs drawn from English constituencies.[124] This is the mechanism currently preferred by the Labour Party,[125] which otherwise stands to lose considerable parliamentary influence if its MPs from Scotland and Wales are barred from voting in the House of Commons on legislation applying only in England.[126]

[120] In the United States Congress there are 435 members of the House of Representatives, the largest contingent from any one state being 53 (12%) from California. The next largest contingent is 36 (8%) from Texas. In 2009 the then UK government said: 'History shows that where one country in a federation contains more than 30% of the economic wealth or population, the federation is unstable': Cm 7687, 20.

[121] Each of the 50 states in the US elects two senators, regardless of the population of the state.

[122] Based in the regions identified by the Conservative government in the early 1990s: the North East, the North West, Yorkshire and the Humber, the West Midlands, the East Midlands, East Anglia, the South West, and the South East.

[123] See the evidence of Prime Minister David Cameron to the House of Commons' Liaison Committee on 20 November 2014: http://www.parliament.uk/business/committees/committees-a-z/commons-select/liaison-committee/news/evidence-with-pm-20-11-14-subject.

[124] This has been suggested by Sir Malcom Rifkind, a former Conservative Foreign Secretary.

[125] See the debates in the House of Commons on 14 October 2014 (HC Debs, vol. 586, cols. 139–79) and 16 October 2014 (HC Debs, vol. 586, cols. 555–64). During the latter, the former Labour prime minister insisted that when any bill comes to the floor of the House for its report stage or for a second or third reading all MPs should be allowed to vote (col. 556).

[126] In the 2010 general election 67 of Labour's 191 MPs (35%) were elected for constituencies in Scotland or Wales. The three SDLP MPs from Northern Ireland also support Labour, which itself does not put up candidates for election in Northern Ireland.

HOW DEVOLUTION IS FACILITATED

In May 2009 the Justice Committee of the House of Commons published a report on the first ten years of devolution.[127] While acknowledging that devolution had profoundly affected the way the three regions in question were governed, and that its impact on the UK's constitution had been significant, the report nevertheless concluded that Whitehall had not been ready for devolution in the late 1990s and that it still had some way to go in order to make it work better. The Committee accused some government departments of completely overlooking devolution issues. In relation to the Memorandum of Understanding which had been drawn up to help the central UK government liaise with the devolved governments, the report was rather ambiguous: while noting that not many difficulties had arisen to date, it anticipated that these would arise more frequently in future (when politicians from different parties held majorities in the different legislatures) and that one of the weaknesses in the current arrangements was the lack of any structure which provided an opportunity for 'the expression of legitimate political and territorial differences, negotiation, dialogue and dispute resolution'.[128] The Committee therefore looked forward to the Memorandum being revised.

The UK government issued its response to the Committee's report in July 2009.[129] It recorded progress regarding the revival of the Joint Ministerial Committee (see later) and the revision of the Memorandum but, as noted earlier, it set its face firmly against moving towards a system of 'English votes for English laws'. In 2013 the latest version of the Memorandum of Understanding was made public.[130] It explicitly states that it is 'a statement of political intent' and 'does not create legal obligations between the parties'.[131] It is couched in general terms, emphasizing the need for the various governments to consult, to exchange information, and to respect confidentiality where appropriate. It also includes a separate agreement providing for a Joint Ministerial Committee (JMC), a body whose primary role is to consider non-devolved matters which impinge on devolved responsibilities and devolved matters which impinge on non-devolved responsibilities.[132] The JMC is supposed to have one plenary meeting a year (chaired by the prime minister)[133] but it can meet at other times in various guises, such as the 'Domestic JMC' or the 'European JMC'.[134] There is also a 'Finance

---

[127] *Devolution: A Decade On*, 5th Report of the Justice Committee of the House of Commons, 2008–9 (HC 529-I).

[128] Ibid., para. 105.

[129] Cm 7687, https://www.gov.uk/government/uploads/system/uploads/attachment_data/file/229033/7687. pdf.

[130] This replaces the agreement reached in 2001 (Cm 5240). It is available at http://www.gov.uk/government/uploads/system/uploads/attachment_data/file/316157/MoU_between_the_UK_and_the_Devolved_Administrations.pdf.

[131] Para. 2.   [132] See Part IIA of the Memorandum of Understanding.

[133] In fact it did not meet at all in plenary form between 2002 and 2008.

[134] In fact between 2002 and 2007 the only subcommittee which met was that on Europe.

Ministers Quadrilateral', which usually occurs twice a year. The JMC serves too as a forum within which disputes between devolved administrations and the UK government can be resolved: in 2013, for example, a dispute over the £18 billion capital expenditure commitment to Northern Ireland was dealt with in this way.[135] All meetings of the JMC usually result in the issue of a press communiqué, and brief annual reports are published giving details of the number of meetings held and the topics discussed,[136] but as with Cabinet minutes no further details of the discussions are published, even if requested under the Freedom of Information Act 2000.

The Memorandum of Understanding also allows for three further 'Concordats' to ensure that broadly uniform arrangements exist for the coordination of the implementation of EU policies, the provision of financial assistance to industry, and the international relations affecting responsibilities of the devolved administrations.[137] It acknowledges as well that individual UK government departments need to agree and publish bilateral concordats with their counterparts in the devolved administrations.[138] These should not be confused with the concordats which have at times been agreed between a devolved administration and another sector within the same devolved area.[139]

It would appear that the various documents outlined in the two previous paragraphs have been largely successful in reducing and solving the problems that can arise as a result of devolution. With the exception of funding concerns relating to Northern Ireland, there have been very few public spats. Neither the Calman Commission in Scotland nor the Richard, Williams, and Silk Commissions in Wales identified serious problems with the working relationship between the UK government and the devolved administrations in general or with the Memorandum of Understanding in particular. The Memorandum seems to have provided ground rules for effective collaboration. However, having narrowly escaped the secession of Scotland, the UK government will no doubt want to revisit the arrangements agreed with the Scottish government so that the risk of any discontent with 'devo-max', the now preferred route, can be minimized.

An important mechanism in the current devolution arrangements is the 'legislative consent motion' (LCM). This is the motion which is put to a devolved legislature whenever a bill going through the UK Parliament affects the law relating to a devolved matter. To date there have been few controversies over the use of this mechanism, which reflects the 'Sewel convention' that applied to Scotland even before devolution.[140]

---

[135] *JMC Annual Report 2012–2013*, 3.

[136] For the latest available report, covering 2012–13, see http://www.gov.uk/government/uploads/system/uploads/attachment_data/file/251140/JMC-Annual-Report-2013.pdf.

[137] See Parts IIB, IIC, and IID of the Memorandum of Understanding.

[138] e.g. the concordat reached in 2005 between the Scottish Executive and the Department for Constitutional Affairs, http://www.scotland.gov.uk/Publications/2005/07/sedcaconcord.

[139] e.g. the Scottish Executive had a concordat with local government in Scotland between 2007 and 2011, and the Northern Ireland Executive has a concordat with the voluntary and community sector in Northern Ireland.

[140] By February 2013 the Scottish Parliament had considered about 126 LCMs, the Northern Ireland Assembly 41, and the Welsh Assembly 40: Report of the McKay Commission (see n. 114), para. 85.

In Northern Ireland questions were asked when it transpired that a DUP minister had neglected to consider placing an LCM before the Assembly at the time when the bill which became the Defamation Act 2013 was being debated at Westminster.[141] The McKay Commission, referred to earlier, closely examined the LCM system and noted that it operated in a varied and not very transparent manner across the three devolved regions. It recommended that the procedure be made more formal and uniform, with all LCMs being referred to the proposed Devolution Committee, which the McKay Commission saw as operating in a non-party political manner, comparable to the current Joint Parliamentary Committee on Human Rights.[142]

On top of the general facilitative arrangements derived from the 1998 devolution settlement, specific mechanisms have been put in place as a result of the Belfast (Good Friday) Agreement.[143] The principal mechanism is the British–Irish Council (BIC), which the Agreement foresaw as a way 'to promote the harmonious and mutually beneficial development of the totality of relationships among the peoples of these islands'.[144] Its membership comprises representatives not just from the UK government and the governments of Scotland, Wales, and Northern Ireland, but also from the governments of Ireland, the Isle of Man, and the Channel Islands. Like the JMC, the BIC can meet in sectoral formats, but it congregates 'at summit level' twice a year. It seeks to reach agreement on matters of mutual interest that are within the competence of the devolved administrations. A formal published review of the workings of the BIC is required by the Belfast (Good Friday) Agreement 'at an appropriate time',[145] but this has not yet materialized.[146] Likewise, although the Agreement allows two or more members of the BIC to develop bilateral or multilateral arrangements, operating independently of the BIC, no such arrangements have emerged. There is however a British–Irish Intergovernmental Conference (BIIC), which brings together the British and Irish governments 'to promote bilateral co-operation at all levels on all matters of mutual interest within the competence of both Governments'.[147] This can meet as required, either at prime ministerial or ministerial level and, 'in recognition of the Irish Government's special interest in Northern Ireland...there will

---

[141] See the debate on whether the 2013 Act should be extended to Northern Ireland in the Grand Committee of the House of Lords: HL Debs, vol. 746, cols. GC330-GC346 (27 June 2013).

[142] Report of the McKay Commission (see n. 114), paras. 82–7 and 263–74.

[143] These mechanisms were provided for in a British–Irish Agreement annexed to the multiparty Belfast (Good Friday) Agreement. Strand Two of the Belfast (Good Friday) Agreement also provides for North–South bodies within Ireland as a whole, and in particular a North–South Ministerial Council.

[144] Strand Three of the Belfast (Good Friday) Agreement 1998, 'British–Irish Council', para. 1.

[145] Ibid., para. 12.

[146] Inter-party talks on this matter commenced early in 2004, but no report was ever produced. In 2011 the Oireachtas in the Republic of Ireland has established a Joint (Dáil/Seanad) Committee on the Implementation of the Good Friday Agreement (see http://www.oireachtas.ie/parliament/oireachtasbusiness/committees_list/good-friday-agreement), but this ranges over a wider number of issues than the effectiveness of the Agreement and so far, while it has debated many issues and considered much evidence, it has produced no substantive reports or recommendations.

[147] Strand Three of the Belfast (Good Friday) Agreement 1998, 'British–Irish Intergovernmental Conference', para. 2.

be regular and frequent meetings of the Conference concerned with non-devolved Northern Ireland matters, on which the Irish Government may put forward views and proposals'.[148] In particular the BIIC facilitates cooperation in security matters. There was meant to have been a formal published review of the British–Irish Agreement three years after it came into effect,[149] but this has not occurred. Meanwhile the British–Irish Inter-parliamentary Assembly, which has existed since before the 1998 Agreement, continues to function.[150] Its four committees have produced over 30 reports, many of which have provoked a response from the UK, Northern Ireland, or Scottish governments. They mainly concern cross-border cooperation rather than the nature or effectiveness of the devolution arrangements established under the Northern Ireland Act 1998.

INFLUENTIAL FACTORS IN THE FUTURE

Undoubtedly the factor which is most likely to influence the future development of devolution in the United Kingdom is whether the national government decides to recommend withdrawal from the European Union. The Conservative Party has pledged to allow an 'in–out' referendum on membership of the EU 'by the end of 2017'.[151] The Liberal Democrats have promised an in–out referendum 'in the event of proposals for any further significant transfer of powers from the UK to the EU', but add that in any such referendum (regardless, presumably, of the extent of the proposed transfer of powers) they will campaign strongly for the United Kingdom to remain within the EU.[152] The Labour Party's position is that it would 'legislate for a lock that ensures no future Government can transfer powers to Brussels without the explicit consent of the British people'.[153] Under the European Union Act 2011 the existing law is that a referendum must be held before the United Kingdom can agree to an amendment of the Treaty on European Union or the Treaty on the Functioning of the European Union, or before it can agree to certain decisions already provided for by those treaties, if these would transfer power or competence from the United Kingdom to the EU.[154]

In the event that the government which comes to power after the May 2015 elections decides to hold an in–out referendum on membership of the EU, there is a distinct possibility (if opinion polls are to be believed[155]) that a majority of the voting electorate may opt to leave the EU. But in any such referendum it is most unlikely that a

[148] Ibid., para. 5.   [149] Ibid., para. 9.   [150] See http://www.britishirish.org.
[151] Conservative manifesto for the elections to the European Parliament in 2014, 11.
[152] Liberal Democrat manifesto for the elections to the European Parliament in 2014, 32–3.
[153] Labour manifesto for the elections to the European Parliament in 2014, 25.
[154] European Union Act 2011, ss. 2–4 and 6.
[155] In April 2014 the BBC reported that 35% of people would vote to remain and 32% would vote to leave: http://www.bbc.co.uk/news/uk-politics-26892237. In YouGov polls conducted in November 2012 and January 2013, more would have voted to leave than to remain: http://yougov.co.uk/news/2013/01/21/eu-vote-stay-40-leave-34.

majority of voters in Scotland and Northern Ireland will favour leaving the Union. If a 'Brexit' does occur,[156] it could persuade a sizeable proportion of those who voted 'No' to Scottish independence to change their minds in any future referendum and it might even influence some unionist voters in Northern Ireland to opt for a united Ireland when a referendum is eventually held on that question. Such a referendum is required if at any time (but no sooner than seven years after a previous such poll) it appears likely to the Secretary of State for Northern Ireland 'that a majority of those voting would express a wish that Northern Ireland should cease to be part of the United Kingdom and form part of a united Ireland'.[157] Meanwhile the formal constitutional position is that 'Northern Ireland in its entirety remains part of the United Kingdom and shall not cease to be so without the consent of a majority of the people of Northern Ireland voting in [such] a poll'.[158]

A lesser factor which may influence future devolution arrangements is the UK government's policies relating to the ECHR. The Conservative Party has pledged to repeal the Human Rights Act 1998 if it wins the general election in 2015. It has not yet stated what it would put in its place to protect human rights, though it is in favour of a so-called 'British' Bill of Rights. As human rights are a devolved matter in both Scotland and Northern Ireland it would be possible for the legislatures in those countries to enact legislation which is closer to the existing Human Rights Act as regards the duty on judges to 'take account' of decisions of the European Court of Human Rights and the duty on everyone to read and give effect to all legislation, 'so far as it is possible to do so', in a way which is compatible with the ECHR.[159] As the Human Rights Act tends not to have as many detractors in the devolved jurisdictions as it does in England, there would be particular cause for concern in those jurisdictions if the UK government went even further and decided to denounce the ECHR and perhaps even withdraw from the Council of Europe.[160] As far as the position in Northern Ireland is concerned the picture is complicated by the fact that the Anglo-Irish Treaty which accompanied the Belfast Agreement of 1998 obliges the UK government to 'complete incorporation into Northern Ireland law of the ECHR, with direct access to the courts, and remedies for breach of the Convention'.[161] Any change to that commitment would require a renegotiation of the treaty.

CONCLUSION

Within the next few years there is likely to be no let-up in the pressure for further constitutional reform relating to devolution. In March 2013 the House of Commons'

---

[156] This is the term sometimes used to refer to a 'British exit' from the EU.
[157] Northern Ireland Act 1998, Sched. 1, para. 2 (see too para. 3).   [158] Ibid., s. 1.
[159] Human Rights Act 1998, ss. 2(1) and 3(1).
[160] The ECHR is a product of the Council of Europe, not (as many journalists seem to believe) the EU.
[161] Para. 2 of the section headed 'Rights, Safeguards and Equality of Opportunity'.

Select Committee on Political and Constitutional Reform suggested that the government should seriously consider setting up a 'UK Constitutional Convention', involving members of the public, 'to examine the impact of the constitutional changes that have already taken place and to consider how, in the future, our constitution can best serve the people of the UK'.[162] The government's response to this suggestion was cool: it did not detect any strong current public interest in a Constitutional Convention, it thought it was important to first gauge the effectiveness of work already being done before asking what else can be done, and it preferred to make the state of the economy the priority for both the public and the government.[163] However, in the wake of the Scottish referendum result the idea of a Constitutional Convention has been taken up by the Labour Party. As he arrived at the Party's 2014 Annual Conference the Labour leader Ed Miliband responded to the Scottish referendum by saying:

> This referendum has changed Scotland. But it will also change Britain...We need a response that matches the scale of this moment. That starts with delivering on our promise of further powers to Scotland. But other people in Britain, including England, now deserve the chance to shape their own futures with a dynamic devolution settlement...Labour has already set out plans to reverse a century of centralisation by devolving tens of billions of funding to the regions and local government...In the coming weeks we will set out a process to begin before the next election with every region in the country engaged in a dialogue with the people about how power needs to be dispersed, including in England. That process will culminate next year with a Constitutional Convention to discuss how we are governed. It will look at new ideas for representation including reforms at Westminster and the case for a Senate of the Nations and Regions. This is a Convention for the United Kingdom. It is not a Convention to divide or drive our country apart once more.

Clearly any such Constitutional Convention has the potential to raise a huge number of issues, so a preferred option may be to limit its terms of reference in a way which restricts the options that can be considered.[164] Whatever shape future discussions about the UK's constitution take, it is safe to assume that the nature and extent of the arrangements for devolving power to the regions will be very high on the agenda.

FURTHER READING

BIRRELL, D., *Comparing Devolved Governance* (2012)
BOGDANOR, V., *The New British Constitution* (2009), ch. 2
DEACON, R., *Devolution in the United Kingdom* (2nd edn, 2012)

---

[162] 4th Report, 2012–13 (see n. 111), para. 53.

[163] Cm 8749 (November 2013), paras. 2.1, 3.1, and 4.1.

[164] As has recently occurred with the Constitutional Convention in Ireland: see http://www.constitution.ie.

MITCHELL, J., *Devolution in the United Kingdom* (2009)

TURPIN, C. and TOMKINS, A., *British Government and the Constitution* (7th edn, 2011), ch. 4

USEFUL WEBSITES

The UK government: **http://www.gov.uk/devolution-of-powers-to-scotland-wales-and-northern-ireland**

The Smith Commission: **http://www.smith-commission.scot**

10

THE CHANGING NATURE
OF THE LOCAL STATE

Ian Leigh

SUMMARY

As a directly elected institution with powers derived from Parliament local government enjoys a measure of democratic legitimacy and autonomy, giving it the potential to act as a source of political pluralism in a multilayered constitution. In reality, however, it lacks formal constitutional recognition, it is heavily financially dependent on central government, and for much of the last century its powers have been narrowly interpreted by the courts under the ultra vires doctrine. For nearly 20 years successive governments have been engaged in attempting to reform and reinvigorate local democracy after decades of decline. Under the Coalition's policy of localism important changes have been made to the powers of local authorities, introducing a general competence power, and to their governance. The concept of community rights is the latest step in a longer-term trend away from the direct provision of local services by councils themselves. In the aftermath of the referendum on Scottish independence there is growing interest in decentralizing powers in favour of the major cities. Overall the position of local government in a multilayered constitution continues to evolve but there is a growing recognition that legal reform to protect its constitutional status may now be necessary.

THE NATURE OF LOCAL GOVERNMENT

In the absence of a written constitution in the UK, local government enjoys no formal constitutional status or protection. There is no legal restraint on central government enlisting Parliament to abolish local government altogether, still less reforming its essential characteristics. From an international perspective this is anomalous: references to local government abound in written constitutions the world over.[1] They do so because the idea has been found useful and important.

---

[1] See e.g. Constitution of the Fifth Republic 1958, Art. 72 (France); Basic Law of the Federal Republic of Germany, Art. 28.

This idea is no less important in the UK, although for clues to the constitutional significance of local government one must look to different sources. Two can be cited: a little-noticed Treaty ratified in 1998 and official reports.

The Treaty is the European Charter of Local Self-Government 1985. It defines the constitutional status to be given to local government by the signatory states.[2] The Charter contains some important principles, if broadly expressed. These include 'subsidiarity', a democratic principle stipulating that decisions should be taken at the nearest feasible level to those who are affected by them. For example, Art. 4, paras. 3–5 state:

3. Public responsibilities shall generally be exercised, in preference, by those authorities which are closest to the citizen. Allocation of responsibility to another authority should weigh up the extent and nature of the task and the requirements of economy and efficiency.

4. Powers given to local authorities should normally be full and exclusive. They may not be undermined or limited by another, central or regional, authority except as provided for by the law.

5. Where powers are delegated to them by central or regional authority, local authorities shall, insofar as possible, be allowed discretion in adapting their exercise to local conditions.

In addition, Art. 9 guarantees the freedom to determine expenditure priorities and to raise adequate resources. The UK government's decision to ratify this treaty in 1998 is of greater symbolic than legal significance. The Charter is binding between member states only (local authorities cannot invoke it on the international stage) and is only of tangential domestic legal significance: it is open to a court to refer to it in order to help resolve statutory ambiguity.

The UK's accession to the Charter has, however, prompted a debate about the need for constitutional protection of the position of local government. The main reason why this is seen increasingly as a necessary step is the serious imbalance in central–local relations, characterized by a drift to centralization over several decades. A 2012 report concerned with options for codifying central local relations by the Political and Constitutional Reform Select Committee of the House of Commons found that:

English local government lacks some of the most basic constitutional protections that are available to some of its counterparts in a number of other mature European democracies. It is central government that finalises the shape, size, structure, powers, responsibilities and functions of English local government.[3]

The select committee proposed a code for relations between central and local government, enforced by statute. The draft code was based on the following key principles:

that local government should be independent of central government, able to exercise a range of tax-raising powers suitable to the needs of the local community, and that

---

[2] C. Crawford, 'European Influence on Local Self-Government' (1992) 18(1) *Local Government Studies* 69.

[3] Political and Constitutional Reform Select Committee, *Third Report for 2012–13, Prospects for Codifying the Relationship between Central and Local Government*, HC 656-I (2012–13), para. 43.

government, of all levels, should be appropriately consultative and accountable to its people.[4]

Various aspects of local autonomy are asserted in the draft code: that councils are primarily accountable to local citizens; that councils are independent, and able to determine their own affairs; that boundaries cannot be re-organized without the council's consent; that councils should have the ability to raise loans and operate a balanced budget and (subject to local consent) to raise local taxes, and to choose their own political decision-making systems. Concerning central–local relations, the draft code would establish a consultative working relationship and provide for negotiation on an equal footing to create inspection regimes and service standards. Although the select committee put forward these proposals primarily to initiate a debate about the constitutional position of local government, it also tentatively suggested that the code be backed by statute and incursions on the role of local government could be prevented by a 'lock' process under the Parliament Act 1911.

Several characteristics are usually said to distinguish local government in the United Kingdom: that it is elected, that councils have a measure of statutory discretion and financial autonomy, and that they have multiple local functions. In recent decades each of these features has come under some strain, so much so that at times central government (especially during the Conservative administrations from 1979 to 1997) has been accused of acting unconstitutionally in rebalancing them. It is worth briefly considering these further before moving on to discuss the reforms that have been introduced in recent years in an attempt to reinvigorate local democracy.

Local authorities have been elected since the 1880s, with the introduction under the Local Government Act 1888 of elected county councils (earlier legislation gave a right for householders only to vote). The changes since then have been not so much to the democratic character of local government as a regular process of adjusting its structures. The most prominent examples were reforms in the Local Government Act 1972, establishing a two-tier system of elected counties and districts over much of the country, but with variations in the split of functions between the tiers in the metropolitan areas,[5] and the creation in 1963 of the Greater London Council (abolished in 1986). Since a further reorganization of local government in 1992–6 most of England and all of Scotland, Northern Ireland, and Wales now have a single tier of elected local authorities. In places these are district, borough, or city councils, and in others county councils. In parts of rural England, however, the two tiers of counties and districts introduced in the Local Government Act 1972 survive, with functions divided

---

[4] Ibid., para. 47. The draft code is set out in an appendix to the report. See also the proposal from the Institute for Public Policy Research that the constitutional status of local government be strengthened in legislation 'with a view to enabling genuine culture change in the central–local relationship': IPRR North, *Decentralisation Decade: A Plan for Economic Prosperity, Public Service Transformation and Democratic Renewal in England* (2014).

[5] Metropolitan county councils were subsequently abolished, however, by the Local Government Act 1985.

between them. In London, borough councils exercise most of the functions of unitary councils but a new elected strategic body, the Greater London Authority, came into operation in 2000.

The independent electoral approval that local councillors enjoy underlines the claim that this is local *government*, rather than local administration or agency. The latter would suggest local implementation of centrally determined policies for merely practical reasons. The former implies that locally elected politicians have some degree of democratic legitimacy and discretion and control over how local functions are performed. Without such discretion local elections would be largely meaningless exercises. The elected nature of local authorities inevitably imports into their business party political conflict (although it is still common to find some independent councillors in a council). It also creates the possibility of conflict between the politics of the council and of central government, with each claiming their own electoral mandate.

Significantly, less than a decade after the introduction of popularly elected local authorities the courts could be seen deferring to the new bodies in a case in which a local bye-law was unsuccessfully challenged, on the grounds that it was made by councillors who had been elected as local representatives and who must be presumed to have knowledge of local conditions.[6] In modern times, however, judges have been generally less deferential to local democracy. In a 1995 judgment declaring unlawful the decision of Somerset County Council to prevent deer hunting on land controlled by it, Laws J specifically rejected the council's argument that its statutory powers to manage land should be given a wider interpretation because elected council members were entitled to reflect local feelings on the issue.[7] Nor have councillors been allowed to use popular endorsement of their local manifesto policies by electoral success as cover for otherwise unlawful decisions:[8] to do so would in effect allow them to enlarge their own powers by making reckless electoral promises. On the other hand, the courts have been sensitive to local democracy in preventing councils from suing for defamation on the grounds that to do so would inhibit free discussion and public accountability.[9] Taken together these decisions tend to show the judiciary recognizing the value of local democracy as a mechanism for accountability to local people but, somewhat paradoxically, restricting the powers that elected councillors can wield.

It would be misleading, however, to suggest that local authorities are models of representative democracy. Electoral apathy is a serious and long-standing concern. Local elections have rarely produced turn-outs of more than 40 per cent for decades,[10] unless

---

[6] *Kruse* v. *Johnson* [1898] 2 QB 91, 98–9 (Lord Russell), and 104 (Sir F. H. Jeune), Mathew J dissenting.

[7] *R* v. *Somerset CC, ex parte Fewings* [1995] 1 All ER 513, 529; the Court of Appeal affirmed the decision on slightly different grounds: [1995] 3 All ER 20.

[8] *Bromley* v. *GLC* [1983] 1 AC 768, esp. Lord Wilberforce at 814; cf. *Secretary of State for Education and Science* v. *Tameside MBC* [1977] AC 1014, holding that the council's manifesto commitment (to retain grammar schools) was relevant to the reasonableness of the minister's intervention.

[9] *Derbyshire CC* v. *Times Newspapers* [1993] AC 534.

[10] The turn-out in local government elections in May 2014 was 36%: http://www.electoralcommission.org.uk/__data/assets/pdf_file/0010/169867/EP-and-local-elections-report-May-2014.pdf.

coinciding with a general election, but when, during the 1990s, voting dropped to around 10 per cent in some parts of the country the legitimacy of local democracy was seriously called into question.

The constitutional position of local government, its powers, and democratic legitimacy are inextricably linked. Why bother to vote in local elections if councils are powerless to change anything? Equally, however, why should bodies that are ignored by the electorate be trusted with new powers by Parliament or deferred to by the courts? This conundrum explains why recent governments have attempted to reform simultaneously the powers of local government and their democratic governance in an attempt to create what has been called a 'virtuous circle' and to reverse the 'vicious circle' of decline.[11] We will examine the reforms to local powers and executive structures in turn, paying less attention to the electoral reforms.

POWERS

Much of an individual's daily contact with the state and its officials is with local authorities. Councils are responsible for services such as education, social services, roads, swimming pools and leisure centres, libraries and planning, not to mention mundane but nonetheless vital matters like refuse collection and disposal.

In recent decades, however, there has been a shift from councils acting as the primary providers of local services to coordinating and leading a range of public, private, and voluntary bodies. To some extent this had been foreshadowed in the fashionable notion of the 1980s—the 'enabling council' (i.e. enabling rather than doing)—although that was associated with an ideological bias in favour of contracting out the delivery of council services. A broader, communitarian, vision involving 'partnership' between councils, other local agencies, voluntary bodies, and the private sector was first articulated by Professor John Stewart in 1995.[12] It influenced an important report by a House of Lords Select Committee, *Rebuilding Trust*, the work of the self-styled Commission for Local Democracy, and the Labour government that took office in 1997.[13] The 1998 White Paper *Modern Local Government* endorsed this vision of local authorities as 'community leaders', describing them as 'uniquely placed' among public institutions to play this role. The 2007 Lyons Report continued in the same vein but used different terminology—speaking of the council's role in 'place-shaping'. This was described as 'the creative use of powers and influence to promote the general well-being of a community and its citizens'.[14]

---

[11] S. Bailey. and M. Elliott, 'Taking Local Government Seriously: Democracy, Autonomy and the Constitution' [2009] *Camb LJ* 436

[12] e.g. J. Stewart and G. Stoker (eds.), *Local Government in the 1990s* (1995), ch. 14.

[13] See *Report of the House of Lords Select Committee on Relations between Central and Local Government 'Rebuilding Trust'*, HL 97 (1995–6); Commission for Local Democracy, *Taking Charge: The Rebirth of Local Democracy* (1995); Labour Party, *Renewing Democracy, Rebuilding Communities* (1995).

[14] Lyons Inquiry into Local Government, *Place-shaping: A Shared Ambition for the Future of Local Government* (March 2007), para. 2.43, http://www.lyonsinquiry.org.uk/index8a20.html.

'Place-shaping' had several dimensions, including representing the local community in discussions with government and business, working with other bodies locally (such as the police, health authorities, and voluntary sector), understanding and responding to the needs and preferences of local people (rather than simply following national standards for services), and working to make the local economy more successful.

Much of this was retained in the Coalition's policy of 'localism' but with a greater emphasis on deregulation through removal of central controls and community empowerment. Alongside the new power of general competence (discussed later), the Localism Act 2011 introduced new 'community rights'. The community right to challenge is a procedure for voluntary and community groups, parish councils, or local authority staff to express an interest in running a local authority service, leading to a duty on the council to run a competitive procurement competition.[15] The community right to bid allows communities to nominate buildings and land that they consider of value to the community to be included on a local authority maintained register.[16] If any of these are later put up for sale, there is an opportunity for community expressions of interest and bids. The process is particularly useful where resources such as village shops, banks, or post offices face closure. These changes have been implemented, however, during a concentrated and prolonged period of economic austerity that has seen local authority cuts of up to one-third of their budgets over a five-year period.[17] As a result the policy of localism has been closely linked with austerity.

Successive changes have been made to the legal regime for local government which was felt to be inadequate for its changing role in being merely a collection of diverse statutory functions, powers, and duties with no indication of what the sum of the parts amounted to. Moreover, the ultra vires rule created some artificial barriers to partnership working between local authorities and other bodies. Since it prevented the unlawful delegation of power from a council to another body, the rule inhibited cooperative working with other agencies in the public, voluntary, and private sectors and the establishment of free-standing, arm's-length, enterprises (such as companies) for such joint work. All cooperative enterprises of this kind were under the shadow that the courts might find them to be unlawful if they exercised powers entrusted by Parliament to the local authority or if the council was unable to point to explicit legal authority for its participation in them.

The ultra vires rule had come to be seen as increasingly rigid. It had developed lineally from nineteenth-century legal doctrines concerning the powers of corporations, whether public or private (such as companies). Whereas in relation to companies it was applied increasingly liberally in the early twentieth century and was finally abolished by legislation, for public corporations it became an increasingly potent method of judicial control.[18]

---

[15] Localism Act 2011, Pt 5, ch. 2.   [16] Localism Act 2011, Pt 5, ch. 3.

[17] V. Lowndes and L. Pratchett, 'Local Governance under the Coalition Government: Austerity, Localism and the 'Big Society' (2012) 38(1) *Local Government Studies* 21–40.

[18] The turning point came in *Ashbury Railway Carriage Co.* v. *Riche* (1875) LR 7, HL 653 when the House of Lords rejected the argument that statutory corporations should be regarded as having the legal attributes

As Laws LJ put it in the *Fewings* decision:

> any action to be taken must be justified by positive law. A public body has no heritage of legal rights which it enjoys for its own sake; at every turn all of its dealings constitute the fulfilment of duties which it owes to others; indeed it exists for no other purpose...It is in this sense that it has no rights of its own, no axe to grind beyond its public responsibility: a responsibility which defines its purpose and justifies its existence. In law this is true of every public body. The rule is necessary in order to protect the people from arbitrary interference by those set in power over them.[19]

Central government can influence the parliamentary process to obtain wide grants of discretionary power and is only rarely subjected to detailed duties. This is not the case with local government. The legacy, then, for local authorities is that each action and decision, however minor, must be shown to rest on explicit statutory authority.[20] The courts, moreover, have compounded the situation by often interpreting narrowly even apparently widely drafted statutory powers when the actions of the council could adversely affect local taxpayers by imposing financial liability for an unsuccessful transaction[21] or where private rights or interests would be affected.[22] A particularly controversial judicial construct is the fiduciary principle, by which the courts have treated a local authority as a type of trustee of money received from local taxpayers.[23] Under the guise of this dubious doctrine some decisions involving council expenditure have been held to be unlawful in giving too little weight to taxpayers' interests.[24]

Recent attempts at statutory reform are an attempt to undo some of these negative implications of ultra vires. They have taken three main forms.[25] First, expanded discretionary powers to enter into partnership arrangements with other local bodies or agencies were introduced by the Local Government Act 2000 to remove the uncertainty over the legality of some of these cooperative ventures.[26] Secondly, a power of 'community initiative' was introduced in 2000 by the Labour government. This was hailed as enshrining in law the role of the council as 'the elected leader of their

---

of a natural person except to the extent that the statute expressly or impliedly restricted them. See M. Stokes, 'Company Law and Legal Theory' in W. Twining (ed.), *Legal Theory and Common Law* (1986); H. Rajak, 'Judicial Control: Corporations and the Decline of Ultra Vires' (1995) 26 *Cambrian Law Review* 9.

[19] *R* v. *Somerset CC, ex parte Fewings* [1995] 1 All ER 513, 524.

[20] All local authorities now enjoy their powers solely under statute: Local Government Act 1972, ss. 2(3), 14(2), and 21(2). The Act extinguished the claim that boroughs created under royal charter possessed the powers of an ordinary person and so were not subject to ultra vires; and see *Hazell* v. *Hammersmith LBC* [1992] 2 AC 1, 39–43, *per* Lord Templeman.

[21] As in *Hazell*, ibid., and *Credit Suisse* v. *Allerdale BC* [1996] 4 All ER 129, CA.

[22] e.g. *Fewings*, n. 19.

[23] M. Loughlin, *Legality and Locality: The Role of Law in Central–Local Relations* (1996), ch. 4; I. Leigh, *Law, Politics and Local Democracy* (2000), 131–9.

[24] *Roberts* v. *Hopwood* [1925] AC 578; *Prescott* v. *Birmingham Corp.* [1955] Ch 210; *Bromley LBC* v. *Greater London Council* [1983] AC 768.

[25] A fourth measure, the Local Government (Contracts) Act 1997, aimed to remedy some of the disadvantages where a contract involving a local authority was held void because it was ultra vires (as in the *Hazzell* and *Allerdale* cases), is less important here.

[26] Local Government Act 2000, ss. 2(4) and 4.

local community'.[27] It was intended as an 'overarching' or under-pinning duty, with a linked power of community initiative—a type of quasi-constitutional mission statement which would give structure and purpose to the many specific powers and duties of councils.[28] In the form in which they were ultimately introduced these proposals were diluted, however. The legal power was supplementary, rather than fundamental, and the duty was omitted. All local authorities were given power to do anything which they considered was likely to promote or improve the economic, social, or environmental well-being of their area.[29] The power could not be used by a council to override restrictions in other more detailed legislation,[30] and ministers had a wide power to exclude activities by delegated legislation.[31] The third strand was a relaxation by ministers of legal and ministerial controls over local authorities—for example, where existing legal provisions prevented councils from delivering 'best value' or from exercising their community well-being power.[32]

The coalition government has gone further than these earlier reforms by introducing a general power of competence for local government.[33] Although this idea is something of a holy grail (similar proposals have been made for more than 80 years[34]), interest in it was revived in recent years by local government reforms in Scandinavia[35] and in the Republic of Ireland.[36] In its purest form a general power of competence takes the direct obverse form to the ultra vires principle: the actions of the council are presumptively lawful if they are (in its view) for the benefit of the local area, provided they do not otherwise constitute a crime, tort, or involve a breach of contract.[37] This would radically alter the nature of legal accountability, so much so that the Widdicombe Committee argued in 1986 that such a power would be fundamentally incompatible with the current regime of statutory grants to local authorities of specific functional powers.[38]

---

[27] *Modern Local Government: In Touch With the People*, Cm 4014 (1998), para. 8.9.

[28] See the Green Paper, Department of the Environment, Transport and the Regions, *Modernising Local Government: Local Democracy and Community Leadership* (February 1998), ch. 8; and Labour Party, *Renewing Democracy, Rebuilding Communities*.

[29] Local Government Act 2000, s. 2(1).

[30] Anything subject to a 'prohibition, restriction or limitation on their powers which is contained in any enactment' is specifically excluded under s. 3(1). This applies to existing and future legislation ('whenever passed or made') and to subordinate legislation also (s. 3(6)).

[31] Local Government Act 2000, s. 3(3).   [32] Under ibid., s. 5.

[33] HM Government, *The Coalition: Our Programme for Government* (2010), 12.

[34] Leigh, *Law, Politics and Local Democracy*, 53–6.

[35] See discussions of the 'Free Local Government' initiatives: H. Kitchin, 'A Power of General Competence for Local Government' in L. Pratchett and D. Wilson (eds.), *Local Democracy and Local Government* (1996); L. Rose, 'Nordic Free-Commune Experiments: Increased Local Autonomy or Continued Central Control?' in D. King and J. Pierre (eds.), *Challenges to Local Government* (1990).

[36] Local Government Act 1991 (Republic of Ireland).

[37] As proposed by the Royal Commission on Local Government in England, Cmnd 4040 (1969), ch. 8, para. 323.

[38] The *Report of the Committee of Inquiry into the Conduct of Local Authority Business*, 9797 (1986), paras. 8.23ff.

Prior to the 2010 election a Conservative policy document described the contours of the proposed new power:

an explicit freedom to act in the best interests of their voters, unhindered by the absence of specific legislation supporting their actions.

It continued, however:

No action—except raising taxes, which requires specific parliamentary approval—will any longer be 'beyond the powers' of local government in England, unless the local authority is prevented from taking that action by the common law, specific legislation or statutory guidance.[39]

The changes introduced under the power of general competence are indeed far-reaching.[40] They confer a power 'to do anything that individuals generally may do' even if it is unlike anything that the authority or other public authorities may otherwise do.[41] In effect this takes local government powers back to the decisive fork in the road in the development of the ultra vires doctrine in the late nineteenth century. The general power includes the means to execute it 'in any way whatever' without territorial restrictions, whether as a commercial purpose or not and 'for, *or otherwise* than for, the benefit of the authority, its area or persons resident in its area' (emphasis added).[42] Councils are not, however, permitted to use the power to raise taxes or to trade in services that they are already obliged to provide. Ministers can exclude specific matters from the scope of the new power.[43] Unlike earlier liberalizing measures, the new power is not limited by the existence of overlapping statutory powers[44] nor is it subject to a specific budgetary limit.[45] Explicit limitations or restrictions on a council contained in earlier legislation cannot, however, be overridden using the power of general competence.[46] The Secretary of State has power to amend, repeal, revoke, or 'disapply' any statutory provision 'whenever passed' (therefore, including

---

[39] Conservative Party, *Control Shift: Return Power to Local Communities* (2008).

[40] The commencement of the power was brought forward to February 2012 to reverse the consequences of the judgment of Ouseley J in *R (National Secular Society)* v. *Bideford Town Council* [2012] EWHC 175 (Admin), [2012] 2 All ER 1175, holding that the saying of prayers at the beginning of the formal meetings of a town council was ultra vires s. 111 Local Government Act 1972 and there was no statutory authority for continuing the practice.

[41] Localism Act 2011, s. 1(1) and (2). And see Local Government (Northern Ireland) Act 2014, Pt 11.

[42] Localism Act 2011, s. 1(4).   [43] Localism Act 2011, s. 5(3).

[44] Localism Act 2011, s. 1(5).

[45] Contrast Local Government Act 1972, s. 137, allowing councils to 'incur expenditure which, in their opinion, is in the interests of and will bring direct benefit to, their area or any part of it or all or some of its inhabitants' subject to a specified limit. The power of general competence replaces s. 137 and also the power to promote economic well-being introduced by s. 2 of the Local Government Act 2000.

[46] Localism Act 2011, s. 2(1) and (2)(a). See *R (on the application of MK)* v. *Barking and Dagenham LB Council* [2013] EWHC 3486 (Admin) as an illustration, holding that a pre-commencement limitation under Sched. 3 of the Nationality, Immigration and Asylum Act 2002 and 17(3) of the Children Act 1989 could not be circumvented to impose a duty on an authority to house an unlawful immigrant with her family members.

later legislation) that ministers think restricts councils from exercising the general power or that overlaps with it.[47]

One thorny question concerns restrictions imposed in legislation coming after the enactment of the general competence power. This is dealt with by a provision that requires an express parliamentary statement of intention to override the general power for 'post commencement' limitations on it.[48] The apparent intention is that the courts should follow the examples of the European Communities Act 1972 and the Human Rights Act 1998 and treat this as a de facto suspension of the implied repeal rule.

Inevitably, much will depend, however, on the attitude of the courts to the new power. Despite the simple formulation of the power it is improbable that the courts will treat councils in precisely the same way as individuals and cease to apply the general public law standards of judicial review to their decision-making. Moreover, although the proposal referred to the power as one of 'first resort' it is likely that in the great majority of cases councils will continue to act under specific, detailed, and limited statutory powers. The question then will be how these specific powers and the new general competence power fit together. Attempts in the past to *liberalize* ultra vires by giving broad powers to local authorities have foundered at this stage.[49] The experience with community initiative power under the Local Government Act 2000 has been similarly mixed. Some judges gave the provision a wide and generous interpretation.[50] On the other hand, where a consortium of local authorities formed a mutual insurance company with which one of them entered into a contract of insurance (leading to an estimated 15 per cent saving in costs) the Court of Appeal found that this was ultra vires.[51] The well-being power could not be used since the economic benefit of the scheme was too generalized, being merely designed to reduce costs in general rather than achieving an identified purpose. By contrast the wording of the power of general competence seems broad enough to override most of the arguments that have prevailed in the courts against earlier apparently general powers. The economic climate in which the power was introduced during a prolonged period of cuts to local government finance has limited the scope for innovation in its early years. Nonetheless, creative examples of the use of the power of general competence can be found—for example, the establishment of a loan finance scheme in Newark for local businesses with growth potential which had been unable to secure funding from banks; the

---

[47] Localism Act 2011, s. 5(1) and (2).   [48] Localism Act 2011, s. 2(2)(b).

[49] See especially decisions in relation to Local Government Act 1972, s. 111, which allows a council to do anything 'which is calculated to facilitate, or is conducive or incidental to, the discharge of any of their functions'. As examples of restrictive interpretations of s. 111: *Hazell* v. *Hammersmith and Fulham LBC* [1991] 1 All ER 545; *McCarthy and Stone* v. *Richmond upon Thames LBC* [1991] 4 All ER 897; *Credit Suisse* v. *Allerdale BC* [1996] 4 All ER 129; *Credit Suisse* v. *Waltham Forest LBC* [1996] 4 All ER 176; *Morgan Grenfell* v. *Sutton LBC* (1996) 95 LGR 574; *Allsop* v. *North Tyneside MBC* (1992) 90 LGR 462.

[50] *R. (J)* v. *Enfield LBC* [2002] EWHC 432 (Admin), [2002] LGR 390 (potential use to give financial assistance towards rental to an asylum seeker who was specifically barred under other legislation from being offered accommodation); and see *R (Khan)* v. *Oxfordshire County Council* [2004] EWCA Civ 309, [2004] LGR 257.

[51] *Brent LBC v Risk Management Partners Limited* [2009] EWCA Civ 490.

introduction of a school improvement support programme in Oxford in conjunction with local universities, an education consultancy, and local schools; and Harrogate Borough Council's hosting of a stage of the Tour de France cycling race in 2014.[52]

Although still largely untested in litigation, the power of general competence is nonetheless a constitutionally significant measure that marks a striking departure from more than a century of local government legislation and judicial practice.

From reform of powers we turn now to the reform of local government executive structures.

NEW FORMS OF DEMOCRATIC GOVERNANCE

THE PROBLEM

The elected nature of local government inevitably gives rise to the influence of party politics: in most local authorities there are caucuses of councillors grouped according to party affiliation in imitation of the arrangements at Westminster. This is a long-standing feature of local government, although it appears that party politics at the local level became more intense during the 1970s and 1980s.[53]

Traditionally, councils have organized themselves quite differently, however, from the central state. Legally speaking, the whole council (all the councillors, of whatever political affiliation) was responsible for the authority's decisions. In practice, most decisions were delegated to committees of elected members with smaller areas of responsibility or, in the case of purely administrative matters, to council employees, the officers. The officers, however, served the council as a whole, rather than the majority group of councillors.

The mismatch between these two features—the political nature of local government and the legal responsibility of the whole council—became acute in a number of local authorities during the 1980s. The Widdicombe Committee found in 1986 that 85 per cent of local authorities were organized on political lines with party groups meeting outside the council's structure to determine political strategy.[54] These party groups, however, had no formal place within the decision-making process. Attempts to regularize the position by giving the majority party group an official decision-making power were held to be unlawful in depriving opposition councillors of access to information.[55] On the other hand, unless they were guaranteed a secure environment

---

[52] Local Government Association, *The General Power of Competence: Empowering Councils to Make a Difference* (2013), http://www.local.gov.uk/c/document_library/get_file?uuid=83fe251c-d96e-44e0-ab41-224bb0cdcf0e&groupId=10180.

[53] J. Gyford, S. Leach, and C. Game, *The Changing Politics of Local Government* (1989); K. Young, 'Party Politics in Local Government: An Historical Perspective' in *Aspects of Local Democracy, Research, IV: Report of the Committee of Inquiry into the Conduct of Local Authority Business* (1986), 81–105.

[54] *The Conduct of Local Authority Business*, Cmnd 9797 (1986), paras. 2.37–2.40. See also the follow-up study: K. Young and M. Davies, *The Politics of Local Government Since Widdicombe* (1990).

[55] *R v. Sheffield City Council, ex parte Chadwick* (1985) 84 LGR 563.

in which to reach policy decisions there was no incentive for a controlling majority of councillors to bring policy formulation out of closed party group meetings and into the council as such.

Consequently, the legal constitution of local government was founded on a bizarre and unhealthy silence about its most visible attribute—party politics. Decisions would be reached behind closed doors in the group meeting of the majority party, to be rubber-stamped in public council meetings.[56] Furthermore, the legal framework still clung doggedly to the fiction that all councillors were of equal importance, regardless of political affiliations. In many local authorities, however, the chairmen of committees had assumed a role that paralleled at the local level the function of a Secretary of State, with political direction and control of an area of the council's work. This too was of dubious legality.[57]

An obvious solution to these problems would have been to acknowledge the political realities by allowing for the legal creation of a political executive with effective balancing mechanisms. Instead, in its Local Government and Housing Act 1989, the Conservative government focused on outlawing political abuses—a duty that all council committees must reflect the political balance of the parties was introduced.[58]

REFORM

More radical proposals for reform came about because of dissatisfaction with the system of decision-making by committees that operated in local authorities and because of the need to reinvigorate local politics in the light of dwindling participation rates in local elections. These have taken three main forms: experiments in the use of 'direct' or 'deliberative' (rather than 'representative') democratic devices such as local referendums, citizens' juries, service user panels, questionnaires, and focus groups; minor reforms to electoral procedure; and changes to the democratic governance of councils.

The Localism Act 2011, contains several initiatives to promote direct democracy under the coalition's 'Big Society' agenda.[59] This programme was built around the strands of social action, public sector reform, and community empowerment and is to be achieved, *inter alia*, by decentralization, direct government financial assistance to

---

[56] In *R* v. *Amber Valley DC, ex parte Jackson* [1984] 3 All ER 501 it was held that the mere fact that a planning application had been discussed in a prior party group meeting of the majority group did not mean that the council could not later determine it fairly. In *R* v. *Waltham Forest Borough Council, ex parte Baxter* [1988] 2 WLR 257 there was an unsuccessful attack on a decision reached after councillors, who had voted against the policy in closed group meeting, but lost, later followed the party whip and supported it in a council meeting; on the facts the Court of Appeal found that their discretion not been fettered.

[57] The Local Government Act 1972 did not permit a council to delegate functions to an individual councillor, and where an officer acted under the instruction of a committee chairman this might be held unlawful: *R* v. *Port Talbot BC, ex parte Jones* [1988] 2 All ER 207.

[58] Local Government and Housing Act 1989, s. 15; the Local Government (Committees and Political Groups) Regulations 1990 (SI 1553/1990).

[59] See Cabinet Office, *Building the Big Society* (May 2010), https://www.gov.uk/government/publications/building-the-big-society.

charities and voluntary groups by-passing public bodies, and removing the obstacles currently preventing implementation of local initiatives.

Under the Localism Act residents of a local authority area are given the power to instigate local referendums on any local issue (subject to collecting signatures from 5 per cent of the electorate in a six-month period), to be held at the same time as other elections.[60] Local referendums are not entirely new and some local authorities have been experimenting with them as an exercise in direct democracy for more than a decade. Earlier legislation introduced referendums for local authorities about the adoption of directly elected mayors[61] and in Scotland and Wales older legislation allowed for local polls on Sunday opening of shops and public houses.[62] Under the Local Government Act 2003 councils have a general power to conduct a local poll on a wide range of matters.[63] These provisions are different, however, in that the initiative will lie with local residents rather than the council.

Under the council tax referendum provisions any council that sets its council tax increase above a set ceiling, approved annually by Parliament, triggers an automatic referendum of all registered electors in their area.[64] The referendum gives a choice between the council's proposed council tax rise and a shadow budget, which the council is required to prepare within the defined limit. The referendum outcome is determined by a simple majority of those voting, with no minimum requirement for voter turn-out. In the event of a 'No' vote in the referendum the council is required to refund council taxpayers or to give a tax credit at the end of the year.

This provision is linked to the abolition of central government powers of capping of council tax rates,[65] and has considerable democratic advantages.[66] A long-standing objection to capping,[67] which was first introduced during the bitter central–local disputes of the 1980s,[68] was that it amounts to the overruling by central government of budgetary decisions taken by locally elected and accountable politicians. The referendum provision returns the power of veto to the local electorate, thus restoring the direct link between local residents and the spending decisions of the local authorities

---

[60] Localism Act 2011, Sched. 2, ch. 4.

[61] The Local Authorities (Conduct of Referendums) (England) Regulations 2007 (SI 2007/2089).

[62] Under the Licensing (Scotland) Act 1959 and Licensing Act 1961 (provisions now repealed) respectively.

[63] A local authority may conduct a poll to ascertain the views of those polled about any matter relating to services provided in pursuance of the authority's functions, the authority's expenditure on such services, or any other matter relating to the authority's power to promote well-being of its area. It is for the local authority concerned to decide who is to be polled, and how the poll is to be conducted: Local Government Act 2003, s. 116.

[64] Localism At 2011, Part 5, ch. 1, and Sched. 5.

[65] Localism Act 2011, Sched. 6 (capping powers have been retained in Wales).

[66] Some critics have argued, however, that local referendums should not supplant local elections: G. Jones and J. Stewart, 'Council Tax Referendums Are Damaging', *Local Government Chronicle*, 5 August 2010, 9.

[67] Introduced by the Rates Act 1984. Capping involves imposing a legal limit on the rate of council tax that can be set by a local authority.

[68] e.g. *Nottinghamshire CC* v. *Secretary of State for the Environment* [1986] AC 240; *Hammersmith and Fulham* v. *Secretary of State for the Environment* [1990] 3 All ER 589. See generally Loughlin, *Legality and Locality*.

to whom they pay their council tax. Critics have nonetheless pointed out that it is central government that sets the parameters for the referendums by stipulating annually the amount of council tax increase deemed to be excessive (in 2013–14 it was set at 2 per cent). In practice all local authorities in England have set council tax increases within these bands since the power was introduced and to date no referendums have been held.

Apart from these moves towards direct democracy, experimental attempts have also been introduced to tackle low levels of voter turn-out more directly. Legislation permits councils to apply for permission to use alternative electoral arrangements to the traditional single-day voting in person at polling station.[69] These schemes have included the use of postal ballots, rather than polling stations, electronic voting, and the use of non-conventional polling stations such as supermarkets and doctors' surgeries. At the same time many councils moved to a cycle of more frequent elections—a third of councillors stand for re-election in three years out of a four-year cycle in an attempt to make councils more responsive to the local electorate. There is little evidence, however, that a largely uninterested electorate has an increased appetite for more frequent local elections and the 2011 Act contains provisions to make it easier for authorities to return to a four-yearly cycle of elections of the whole council.[70] More radical reform, such as the introduction of proportional representation for local elections, has been rejected—for England and Wales. In Scotland, however, following the report of the MacIntosh Committee,[71] proportional representation was introduced in local government by the Local Government (Scotland) Act 2004.

So far as the system of decision-making is concerned, the problem with the traditional local government model was its lack of separation of policy formulation, implementation, and scrutiny—the council as a whole was responsible for all of these functions. Consequently, the decision-making processes were confusing and lacked transparency. Instead of focusing on their representation and scrutiny roles, councillors were involved in close management of tasks better left to officers.[72]

A consultation paper from the Department of Environment, published in 1993, argued for recognition of political executives on several grounds: 'they provide clear political direction for the authority; make clear where accountability lies; provide a more efficient, quicker and coordinated decision-making process; and provide a confidential forum for the ruling group to test the range of policy options with its official advisers'.[73] Moreover, the change would enable councillors who were not members of the executive to take on stronger scrutiny and constituency roles. The proposal that the government should allow experimentation with different forms of political

---

[69] Representation of the People Act 2000, s. 10.   [70] Localism Act 2011, s. 24.
      [71] The Final Report of the Commission on Local Government and the Scottish Parliament, *Moving Forward Local Government and the Scottish Parliament* (June 1999).
      [72] e.g. Commission for Local Democracy, *Taking Charge: The Rebirth of Local Democracy* (1995), chs. 3 and 4.
      [73] *Community Leadership and Representation: Unlocking the Potential* (1993), para. 5.22.

executive did not appeal to the ministers at that time. However, the concept of a political executive became an accepted feature of later reform models[74] and, ultimately, part of the Labour government's programme in the Local Government Act 2000.

Initially, the legislation required councils to review their administrative arrangements and to adopt one of three forms (the status quo was not a permitted option): a leader and Cabinet system, an elected mayor and Cabinet, or an elected mayor and council manager (a powerful officer). Not surprisingly, most councils opted for the leader and Cabinet, since it represented 'the formalisation of already existing group-dominated political processes'.[75] A much smaller number adopted the elected mayor and Cabinet model. In 2007 these models were narrowed and refined by enhancing the position of the leader (compelling those councils that took this route to follow the so-called 'strong leader' model) and eliminating the (little used) mayor and council manager option. All councils were required to consult the public on a choice between a strong leader and Cabinet model and a directly elected mayor and Cabinet.[76] The Localism Act 2011 permits councils to return to the committee system where they consider this to be preferable.[77]

Under the leader and cabinet model[78] the leader is chosen by councillors[79] and is removable by them without reference to the electorate. Except in 'hung' authorities (those where no party has overall control), where the election of the leader may become a semi-transparent process, normally the leadership and membership of the Cabinet will be decided in the group meeting of the majority party and then presented to the Council meeting for endorsement. The leader decides on the size and responsibilities of the Cabinet and has power to dismiss other members of the Cabinet. The leader is elected for a four-year fixed term but can be removed by a vote of councillors.

The political executive is balanced by overview and scrutiny committees.[80] The purpose of these committees is, first, to scrutinize the discharge of executive functions and, secondly, to provide a policy role in reporting and making recommendations to the authority or the executive about the discharge of their functions and on matters which affect the authority's area or inhabitants.[81]

Overview and scrutiny committees have the power to require members of the executive and officers to attend and answer questions (and there will be a corresponding duty on them to do so) and to invite other people.[82]

---

[74] *Modernising Local Government: Local Democracy and Community Leadership* (1998), ch. 5; *Modern Local Government* (see n. 27), ch. 3.

[75] C. Copus, 'The Party Group: A Barrier to Democratic Renewal' (1999) 25(4) *Local Govt Studs* 76, 89–90.

[76] Local Government and Public Involvement in Health Act 2007, Pt 3; and see the White Paper, *Strong and Prosperous Communities* (2006), ch. 3.

[77] Localism Act 2011, ss. 21 and 22 and Scheds. 2 and 3.

[78] S. Leach, 'Introducing Cabinets into British Local Government' (1999) 52(1) *Parliamentary Affairs* 77.

[79] Local Government Act 2000, s. 10(3)(a).

[80] A council opting for a mayor and cabinet model (see later) is required to have overview and scrutiny arrangements also.

[81] Local Government Act 2000, s. 15(1).   [82] Ibid., s. 15(3) and (4).

The division between executive and scrutiny councillors is based on a parliamentary select committee model. Separation from the executive is enforced by a provision preventing oversight and scrutiny committees from including members of the executive.[83] However, as with parliamentary select committees, there is a majority of councillors who are from the same party as the executive. Critics argued that unless the reforms addressed the hidden influence of the party group they would prove ineffective.[84] Studies suggested that there may be a reluctance among councillors on scrutiny committees to criticize party colleagues[85] and that it might have been preferable to require scrutiny committees to be chaired by an opposition councillor, an omission from the legislation. There are indications that in some councils 'backbench' councillors have struggled since these reforms to find a worthwhile role, since they have been formally excluded from the policy process.[86] In an attempt to counteract this trend the possibility of single member constituencies was introduced in 2007, allowing for an enhanced role for individual backbench councillors (so-called 'Democratic Champions').[87] At the same time powers of oversight and scrutiny committees were strengthened by requiring councils to consider and publicly respond to their recommendations and by giving them powers to question and influence other public service providers in the locality.[88]

ELECTED MAYORS

The more innovative model is the directly elected mayor. This is an imported office: mayors are common in local government overseas, especially in the cities of the USA, France, Italy, and Germany.[89]

In the UK the idea was first championed by Michael Heseltine as Secretary of State for the Environment, and then taken up by the Campaign for Local Democracy in 1995.[90] It was first officially proposed as an option for the proposed new London Authority.[91] The idea was approved in a referendum held in Greater London in May

---

[83] Ibid., s. 15(2).   [84] Copus, 'The Party Group', 88–9.

[85] M. Cole, 'Local Government Modernisation: The Executive and Scrutiny Model' (2001) 72(2) Pol Q 239; R. Ashworth, 'Toothless Tiger? Councillor Perceptions of the New Scrutiny Arrangements in Welsh Local Government' (2003) 29 Local Govt Studs 1.

[86] Cole, 'Local Government Modernisation', 241–2.

[87] Local Government and Public Involvement in Health Act 2007, s. 55: see Strong and Prosperous Communities (see n. 76), ch. 3.

[88] Local Government and Public Involvement in Health Act 2007, ss. 119–28.

[89] See H. Elcock, 'Leading People: Some Issues of Local Government Leadership in Britain and America' (1995) 21(4) Local Govt Studs 546; G. Stoker, 'The Reform of the Institutions of Local Representative Democracy: Is There a Role for the Mayor–Council Model?', CLD Research Report No. 18 (1996); G. Stoker and H. Wolman, 'Drawing Lessons from US Experience: An Elected Mayor For British Local Government' (1992) 70(2) Public Admin 241.

[90] Commission for Local Democracy, Taking Charge: the Rebirth of Local Democracy (1995), ch. 4.

[91] A Mayor and Assembly for London, Cm 3897 (1998).

1998 and the Greater London Authority Act 1999 gave effect to these proposals, with the first elected mayor, Ken Livingstone, returned in May 2000.

In the case of councils outside London, a 1999 White Paper proposed that councils should be placed under a duty to consult local people about the form of government they wished to see, with an elected mayor as one of the options. Fearing resistance from councillors to the idea, the government proposed that there would be a possibility of a referendum being triggered to put the elected mayor option to the electorate, even where this was not the council's preferred choice.[92]

Advocates of the idea of a directly elected mayor hoped that it would bring about functional separation in the council between the executive (comprising a directly elected mayor or leader and the council's staff) and the elected assembly of councillors. Moreover, with an elected mayor, instead of the political leadership of council being determined by the party group, it is a matter directly for the electorate. The idea was to bring about a working tension which might increase public knowledge about local government and weaken party dominance. This has been partially successful: several of the mayors elected to date are independent and in other cases the mayorship and the majority on the council are in the hands of different parties.

Low turn-out rates however (typically between 11 and 42 per cent of the electorate) suggest that generally the experiment has failed to revive significant public interest in local democracy The significant exceptions have been the campaigns to elect a mayor for London held every four years since 2000 which have attracted extensive press attention and the entry of candidates with a high public profile from Westminster politics. Apart from the Greater London Authority there are currently 16 councils where the elected mayor and Cabinet system is in use.[93] By 2013 only 51 referendums had been held; in 16 instances the result was in favour of an elected mayor.[94] After a flurry of interest in 2001 and 2002, only a handful of referendums has been held. The failure of other major cities to follow London's lead is disappointing, especially since one aspiration was that elected mayors would be figureheads who would represent their communities nationally and in Europe.

Despite this low uptake, the Coalition government appears as enthusiastic as its predecessor about the potential of elected mayors. At the 2010 general election the Conservative Party argued that mayors would provide strong, conspicuous, individual leadership of councils and boost democratic engagement.[95] Implementing this policy under the Coalition, referendums were held in the 12 biggest English cities in May 2013, with 9 out of the 12 voting to reject an elected mayor system.

[92] *Local Leadership, Local Choice*, Cm 4298 (1999), ch. 2.

[93] Bedford, Bristol, Copeland, Doncaster, Leicester, Liverpool, Mansfield, Middlesbrough, North Tyneside, Salford, Torbay, and Watford, and in the London Boroughs of Hackney, Lewisham, Newham, and Tower Hamlets. See House of Commons Library Research Note SN/PC/5000, Directly Elected Mayors (2013); N. Rao, 'Options for Change: Mayors, Cabinets or Status Quo?' (2003) *Local Govt Studs* 1.

[94] See further Electoral Commission, *Factsheet: Directly Elected Mayors* (October 2010).

[95] Conservative Party, *Control Shift: Returning Power to Local Communities* (2008), para. 3.1.

LONDON

The creation of a mayor and a new strategic authority for London in the Greater London Authority Act 1999[96] can be counted a success in raising the profile of issues affecting London as a whole. The Authority comprises two elected institutions with complementary roles, the mayor and the London Assembly. Elections are held for both simultaneously every four years.[97] The mayor is elected under the supplementary vote system. This, if there are three or more candidates, allows voters to express a first and second preference among the candidates. At the counting stage unsuccessful candidates are eliminated and second preferences are redistributed if no candidate achieves more than 50 per cent of first preferences. (If there are fewer than three candidates, the 'first past the post' voting system is applied.) Ken Livingstone, who served as the first mayor, following his election in May 2000, as an Independent, and his re-election as a Labour candidate in 2004, and Boris Johnson, his Conservative successor since 2008, became recognizable figure-heads for the metropolis both nationally and internationally.

There are 25 Assembly members, chosen by a mix of electoral methods: 14 represent constituencies and 11 are chosen for London-wide seats, according to the Additional Member system reflecting the electoral strengths of the respective political parties.

The mayor is the most visible face of the new Authority and is the main source of initiatives in policy affecting London as a whole, as well as being responsible for coordinating other agencies and bodies across the capital. As well as running new transport and economic development bodies, the mayor works closely with (and makes appointments to) the new Metropolitan Police Authority and London Fire and Emergency Planning Authority, and is responsible for setting the overall framework for the development of London, within which borough councils deal with planning and housing strategy. He also has a coordinating role to improve the environment and air quality in London, in other environmental issues such as waste and noise, and encouraging local initiatives. The mayor prepares a series of strategies to deal with various matters: transport, economic development and regeneration, spatial development, biodiversity, municipal waste management, air quality, ambient noise, climate change mitigation, and culture.

The mayor and the Assembly operate clearly within the pattern of English local government and in that respect they perhaps compare unfavourably with their counterparts in major cities elsewhere in the world. Finance, for example, is derived from council tax and central grant: there is no power to raise money by local income tax. Although accountability for policing in the metropolis has been removed from the Home Secretary and a new Metropolitan Police Authority established,[98] the mayor's

---

[96] M. Supperstone and T. Pitt-Payne, 'The Greater London Authority Bill' [1999] PL 581; B. Pimlott and N. Rao, *Governing London* (2002). Some enhanced powers were added by the Greater London Authority Act 2007.

[97] Greater London Authority Act 2007, ss. 1 and 2 and Sched. 1.   [98] Ibid., Pt VI.

power is indirect and in keeping with arrangements for police authorities elsewhere in the UK,[99] compared, for example, to the more interventionist powers of a US mayor.

The mayor's most high-profile contribution to date has come in the field of transport.[100] In 2003, London became the first major conurbation in the world to introduce a system of congestion charging on the capital's roads. This is the type of bold policy initiative that perhaps could only be taken forward by a powerful mayor operating at a strategic level. Undoubtedly also the successful bid for the 2012 Olympics to come to London owed much to collaborative efforts of the mayor and national government.

The Assembly comprises paid, full-time politicians, with a scrutiny and policy remit. The Assembly keeps the mayor's exercise of statutory functions under review[101] and has power to investigate, and prepare reports about, any actions and decisions of the mayor or any of the Authority's staff, and matters in relation to which statutory functions are exercisable by the mayor. It may also investigate matters relating to the principal purposes of the Authority or any other matters which the Assembly considers to be of importance to Greater London. The Assembly may submit proposals to the mayor, to which he is required to make a formal response.[102] It can amend the mayor's overall budget and plans, although it requires a two-thirds majority to do so. It also exercises oversight over the performance of the functional bodies, for transport and economic development, the police, and fire authorities. It also has power to consider any other issues that it believes are important to Londoners.

The mayor is accountable to the Assembly through several mechanisms. A written report must be given by the mayor to the Assembly at least three clear working days prior to each of its monthly meetings, dealing with the significant decisions taken, with reasons, and responses to any formal proposals made by the Assembly.[103] The mayor attends the Assembly's meetings to answer questions but is not obliged to disclose advice received from the staff of the Authority or from functional bodies or their staff.[104] The Assembly has powers to summon such people, but, in the same way, they are not obliged to disclose advice given to the mayor. This is a move towards treating such officers more in the mould of civil servants than has been customary with local government officers (similar restrictions apply to Civil Service evidence to parliamentary select committees) and follows, perhaps inevitably, from the formal recognition of a distinct political executive. The Assembly meetings, the mayor's reports, the text of questions and answers, and the minutes of the meetings are open or available to the public.[105] The mayor is required to prepare an annual report assessing progress on implementing strategies, including the achievement of any targets and give any information which the Assembly has asked to be included before the

---

[99] Police Act 1996, Pt 1.   [100] Pimlott and Rao, *Governing London*, ch. 7.
[101] Greater London Authority Act 2007, s. 59.   [102] Ibid., s. 60.   [103] Ibid., s. 45.
[104] See ibid., ss. 61–5 for the attendance of witnesses at Assembly meetings and production of documents to it.
[105] Subject to the exceptions for confidential and other exempt material set out in Local Government Act 1972, Pt VA.

beginning of the relevant year. The report is followed by an annual State of London debate.[106] In addition, a 'People's Question Time' must be held twice yearly.[107] A more radical proposal for accountability—that the Assembly be able to impeach the mayor—was, however, rejected.

The overall scheme of the Act carries through the objective of creating a strong mayor's office—most power vests in the mayor and there are few formal restraints. Nevertheless, cooperation between the mayor and the Assembly is necessary since the Assembly has strong powers to review the work of the mayor. Its powers to block initiatives or policies are weak: the necessary two-thirds veto by the Assembly is unlikely to be obtainable in practice, especially within an Assembly elected at the same time as the mayor. The mayor, therefore, is clearly in the stronger position.

As we have seen the success of the arrangements in London has stimulated interest in strong leadership models for other cities. It also raises the question of whether regional government exercising strategic powers might be appropriate for other parts of England.

FROM REGIONALISM TO DECENTRALIZATION

Unlike many other countries, in England there is no tradition of government (as opposed to administration) at the regional (rather than the local) level. During the Blair government regionalism briefly came into vogue and it seemed for a time that it could develop to challenge the position of local government. This section describes how regional government became a fashionable policy option and its subsequent decline.

The main pressures for the introduction of regional government stemmed from dissatisfaction with central, rather than local, government. The principal arguments were that regional government would allow for a sense of political identity to be recognized even where the central government at Westminster failed to reflect the political mood of the regions. Regional government might therefore counteract a feeling of political disenfranchisement. A further argument related to the lack of regional democratic accountability for central government offices dispersed regionally and regional quangos. Oversight of such bodies featured prominently in the proposals for regional government from the Constitution Unit, for example.[108] However, the subsidiary arguments for regional government related more strongly to issues about local government functions and focused on the need for strategic planning in such areas

---

[106] Greater London Authority Act 2007, s. 47.   [107] Ibid., s. 48.

[108] Constitution Unit, *Regional Government in England* (1996). For earlier proposals, see the minority dissenting memorandum to the report of the Role Commission on the Constitution, suggesting that the House of Lords be amended to include a strong provincial presence, which would give it an indirectly elected character by being drawn from regional assemblies: *Report of the Royal Commission on the Constitution 1969/73*, II: *Memorandum of Dissent*, Cmnd 5460-i (1973).

as land-use and transportation and the need for coordination at the regional level of economic development and bids for and implementation of EU funding.

The Regional Development Agencies Act 1998 established agencies for London and eight regions[109] responsible for regional economic development. These were business-led and dominated boards, although the membership also contained local authority members and representatives of other regional interests, such as the education and voluntary sectors. The government intended that one-third of members should be drawn from local councillors in the region which the agency served, to reflect the size of local authorities, the geographical spread, and political balance. The Regional Development Agencies (RDAs) replaced a number of existing quangos and became the lead agencies in coordinating bids for regional EU funding.

To address the democratic deficit in these arrangements this legislation provided for discretionary ministerial designation of Regional Chambers where the Secretary of State was satisfied that a suitable representative body existed.[110] Where a Regional Chamber was designated the RDA was under a duty to consult it. The Labour government recognized eight regional assemblies.[111] These, however, were *indirectly* elected consultative assemblies drawn mainly from members of the local authorities in the region: about two-thirds of members of the regional assemblies were councillors (some also included MPs and Members of the European Parliament). The remaining members were from local business, voluntary, charitable, educational, and religious organizations.

In comparison with the directly elected chambers in other parts of the UK, the RDAs and regional assemblies were poor relations, being subject to ministerial powers and patronage and lacking any powers over central government regional offices. The Labour government was prepared to consider *elected* regional government in parts of England which could demonstrate a demand for it[112]—this would have produced an asymmetric form of regionalism in practice.

However, the policy ran aground following the first regional referendum, held in November 2004 in which the electorate in North East England voted, by a majority of more than 3 to 1 of those voting, against an elected assembly. Since the government had anticipated that, if anywhere, demand was strongest in the North East because of proximity to Scotland, distance from London, and a strongly regional identity, effectively the outcome killed the prospects of further regional campaigns. In the aftermath, critics were divided over whether the voters were uninterested because the proposals for an assembly had been too expensive and unnecessary or because it lacked sufficient

---

[109] Regional Development Agencies Act 1998, s. 1 and Sched. 1. The regions were the East Midlands, Eastern, North East, North West South, East South West, West Midlands, and Yorkshire and Humberside.

[110] Regional Development Agencies Act 1998, s. 8(1).

[111] East of England Regional Assembly, East Midlands Regional Assembly, North East Assembly, North West Regional Assembly, South East England Regional Assembly, South West Regional Assembly, West Midlands Regional Assembly, and Yorkshire and Humber Assembly.

[112] See the White Paper, *Your Region, Your Choice*, Cm 5551 (May 2002).

powers to be worth establishing as an elected body—it lacked law-making powers or the range of executive functions of the National Assembly for Wales, for instance.

Following the referendum outcome in North East England, reflecting lack of voter interest in elected regional assemblies, the existing regional chambers were left in the position of appointed and co-opted quangos, with no direct electoral accountability. Prior to the 2010 election the Conservatives argued that regional government was distant and remote ('unelected, unaccountable and unloved') and pledged to dismantle it and return power to local government. It was claimed that this would bring considerable administrative savings.[113] Subsequently the Coalition government abolished the RDAs[114] and closed the government regional offices. RDAs were replaced with Local Enterprise Partnerships—joint business–local authority bodies to promote local economic development by reflecting the 'natural' economies of cities and regions rather than mapping the jurisdiction of the regional government offices.[115]

Interest in regionalism has not entirely died, however. As a consequence of the referendum in September 2014 on Scottish independence there has been a flurry of renewed interest in English devolution or decentralization.[116] The models under discussion are, however, less threatening to local government than the Blair government's English regionalism proposals. In part because of the successful introduction of the mayor and Assembly for London, attention has focused on possible increases in the autonomy of other major cities. The Coalition introduced the City Deal scheme by which government negotiated with councils in major cities in order to transfer powers and control of local public spending, with the objective of promoting economic growth.[117] The Communities and Local Government Committee has called for a programme of 'fiscal devolution' in England under which groups of local authorities would be given greater local control over taxation and public spending.[118] Similarly, a 2014 report of the think-tank Res Publica, argues that cities (beginning with Greater Manchester) should have an elected mayor and devolved powers and control over all public spending in the area.[119] In November 2014 it was announced that the government had reached agreement with 10 local authorities in Greater Manchester on the creation of a Combined Authority with freedom to control policies and expenditure on transport, housing, social care, and policing. The Combined Authority will be led by a directly elected Mayor who will chair a Cabinet of leaders from the region's ten local authorities. In the post-referendum climate there has much further political

---

[113] Conservative Party, *Control Shift*, 6.   [114] Implemented by the Public Bodies Act 2011.
[115] Vince Cable and Eric Pickles, 'Economy Needs Local Remedies Not Regional Prescription', *Financial Times*, 6 September 2010.
[116] IPRR North, *Decentralisation Decade: A Plan for Economic Prosperity, Public Service Transformation and Democratic Renewal in England* (2014).
[117] https://www.gov.uk/government/policies/giving-more-power-back-to-cities-through-city-deals.
[118] Communities and Local Government Select Committee, *Devolution in England: The Case for Local Government*, HC 503 (2013–14).
[119] Res Publica, *Devo-Max, Devo-Manc: Place-Based Public Services* (2014), http://www.respublica.org.uk/item/Devo-Max-Devo-Manc-Place-based-public-services.

discussion of English devolution, focusing in part on city regions. What remains unclear, however, is the extent to which decentralization engages the enthusiasm of the electorate.

CONCLUSION: 'LOCALISM' AND LOCAL GOVERNMENT

'Localism' embodies two key themes: reversing the drift to centralism and community empowerment. To some extent, however, these show a contradictory and ambivalent approach. Local government appears to be both part of the solution and part of the problem.

On the one hand the 'localism' can be seen as a development and continuation of the thinking of earlier administrations under which local government's task was to enable the delivery of local services (but not necessarily to deliver them itself) and to be a community leader in partnership with other public, private, and voluntary bodies in 'place-shaping'.[120] Thus, for example, the general power of competence can be portrayed as freeing local authorities to be more innovative, responsive to local wishes, and removing obstacles to councils working in partnership with non-governmental bodies. On the other hand, a strong theme of localism is the emphasis on the empowerment of local community groups by liberating them from bureaucracy to find more participatory ways of delivering services in response to local needs. The implication of this alternative theme is that public bodies (including elected local authorities) are insufficiently responsive and that alternatives to services run by conventional representative democratic structures need to be found. The powers for local communities to apply to take over local services currently run by councils and threatened with closure, such as libraries and parks, are an illustration.[121]

One prominent example of diversion of control and funding away from local government is in the field of education with the rise of academies and free schools. The Academies Act 2010 extends the availability of academy status (schools funded directly by central government rather than under local education authority control) so that for the first time all local authority schools are able to apply to be designated academies. If approved by the Secretary of State for Education both secondary and primary schools can become academies.[122] They then have increased freedom to control use of their budget, curriculum, school year, and teachers' pay and conditions. The legislation was controversial because it was perceived by critics as an attack on local education authorities. The 'Free Schools' programme, which came into operation in 2011, is intended to make it easier to establish new schools with academy status in response to parental demand. It simplifies the process by which charities, universities, businesses,

---

[120] Lyons Inquiry, *Place-shaping*, para. 2.43.   [121] Localism Act 2011, Pt 5, ch. 2.
[122] http://www.education.gov.uk/academies.

educational groups, teachers, and groups of parents can obtain permission to start new state-funded schools free of local authority control.

The ambivalence in the Coalition government's policies—simultaneously empowering local authorities and by-passing them—encapsulates the dilemma of modern local government. Despite all recent attempts at reform it remains a necessary but imperfectly functioning democratic institution. Constitutional recognition, coupled with decentralization, look increasingly likely to be the next chapters in the long history of local government.

FURTHER READING

ARDEN, A., MANNING, J., and COLLINS, S., *Local Government Constitutional and Administrative Law* (1999)

BAILEY, S., *Cross on Principles of Local Government Law* (3rd edn, 2004)

BAILEY, S. and ELLIOTT, M., 'Taking Local Government Seriously: Democracy, Autonomy and the Constitution' [2009] *Camb LJ* 436

COMMISSION FOR LOCAL DEMOCRACY, *Taking Charge: The Rebirth of Local Democracy* (1995)

COPUS, C., *Leading the Localities: Executive Mayors in English Local Governance* (2006)

COPUS, C., *Party Politics and Local Government* (2004)

LEIGH, I., *Law, Politics and Local Democracy* (2000)

LOUGHLIN, M., *Legality and Locality: The Role of Law in Central–Local Relations* (1996)

PIMLOTT, B. and RAO, N., *Governing London* (2002)

USEFUL WEBSITES

Commission for Local Administration (Local Government Ombudsmen): **http://www.lgo.org.uk**

Department for Communities and Local Government: **http://www.communities.gov.uk**

Greater London Authority (the Mayor of London and London Assembly): **http://www.london.gov.uk**

INLOGOV (The Institute of Local Government Studies, University of Birmingham): **http://www.birmingham.ac.uk/schools/government-society/departments/local-government-studies/index.aspx**

Local Government Information Unit: **http://www.lgiu.org.uk**

Local Government Association: **http://www.lga.gov.uk**

Lyons Inquiry into Local Government: **http://www.lyonsinquiry.org.uk**

PART III

REGULATION AND THE CONSTITUTION

Editorial note

Regulation, by hard or soft law, has become an increasingly important element in the UK's constitutional arrangements. This has been particularly the case in relation to the 'rules of the game' in politics, privatized industries, public expenditure and access to official information. Over many years much formerly political decision-making has been transferred to arm's length bodies; and a body of soft law, including conventions and a range of texts such as the *Ministerial Code*, has been developed which seeks to constrain the practice of partisan party politics in government. These are the focus of chapter 11.

Before the privatization of many industries in the 1980s and 1990s much regulation was internal to government: government itself regulated, often in an informal manner, the industries that were publicly owned. Since privatization, regulation has been formalized, statutory and external to those industries. Independent expert regulatory bodies have been created to take on these tasks. Chapter 12 examines the implications of this development.

The control of public expenditure (the focus of chapter 13) is the paradigm example of internal regulation. The treasury regulates government departments' spending in various ways. The National Audit Office and Parliament do so too. But Parliament's role is increasingly only formal.

Sunshine can be a powerful disinfectant, and the accountability of public bodies is enhanced by openness about their activities. Chapter 14 considers the impact of the Freedom of Information Act 2000, which provides for and regulates rights of access to information.

Overall the chapters in this part show that the British constitution is becoming increasingly rule-bound, regulated, and juridified.

11

REGULATING POLITICS IN GOVERNMENT

Dawn Oliver

SUMMARY

While the UK remains in many respects a 'political constitution', since the 1980s a number of processes have combined to reduce the range of issues in domestic policy over which ministers have decision-making powers, and to constrain party politics in the practice of government. Alongside processes of transfer (e.g. through privatization), depoliticization, and legal regulation (e.g. through judicial review) of ministerial powers, systems of intra-governmental 'soft law' regulation and self-regulation have built up which establish the 'rules of the game'. Constitutional conventions (e.g. ministerial responsibility to Parliament) are the best-known sources of such soft law norms. Many others are to be found in documents such as the *Ministerial Code*, the *Cabinet Handbook*, and the Cabinet Office's *Guide to Making Legislation*. One common feature of these norms is that they seek to constrain party politics and inappropriate partisanship in many areas of decision-making by politicians. Governments find themselves forced to provide justifications for their policies in terms that accord with widely accepted non-partisan principles of public life: promotion of general or public or shared interests—the well-being of citizens. While it may be difficult to determine at what level these principles are to operate as senses of national identity strengthen in Scotland and Wales, in effect a new constitutional consensus about the rules of the game of politics is emerging.

INTRODUCTION

Over the last 30 years or so opinions and orthodoxies as to what decisions and actions it is, and is not, appropriate for British ministers to take, and why, have evolved. The economic crisis of the late 1970s saw a peak in the unregulated exercise of party politics, patronage, and partisanship. Since the 1970s a number of processes have combined to constrain ministerial decision-making and to reduce the range of issues in domestic policy over which ministers have decision-making powers. Judicial review has developed strongly and provides *legal* constraints on government.[1] Parliament has legislated to remove or regulate the exercise of many ministerial powers: the exercise of what had previously been ministerial decision-making powers in relation to publicly owned industries was ended as the industries were transferred to private owners and subjected to regulation or oversight by independent, expert arm's length bodies (ALBs): 'the fourth branch of government'.[2] Government's control over statistical information, interest rates, and many public appointments has also been transferred to ALBs. European[3] procurement and competition law and requirements from the Organisation for Economic Cooperation and Development (OECD) on governance standards and regulation also limit the freedom of action of governments of nation states. More recently the Fixed-term Parliaments Act 2011 has removed the right to choose the date of a general election from the prime minister: Parliaments now run for a five-year term, subject to exceptional provision for early dissolution on a vote of no confidence.[4]

Alongside this process of transfer, depoliticization, and legal regulation, systems of intra-governmental 'soft law' regulation and self-regulation have clarified the rules of the political game since the 1970s. (In this context 'soft law' refers to norms that are widely obeyed but are not to be found in Acts of Parliament or Regulations, or in the decisions of the courts, which may be referred to as 'hard law'.) Constitutional conventions are the best-known sources of soft law norms; they are sometimes textually formulated and adopted, as with the Salisbury Addison convention restricting the exercise by the House of Lords of its powers of legislative delay (1945) and the House of Commons' and House of Lords' resolutions on ministerial responsibility (1997), discussed later. Many other soft law rules of the game are to be found in the *Ministerial Code*, the *Cabinet Handbook*, and the *Guide to Making Legislation*[5] and other intra-governmental documents. They are particularly important in relations with the devolved bodies in Scotland, Wales, and Northern Ireland,[6] and fiscal and taxation policy.[7] Such norms are widely regarded as binding and are commonly obeyed.[8] One common feature of many of these norms is that they seek to regulate or constrain the exercise of party politics and inappropriate partisanship in decision-making by politicians.

This chapter explores these developments. It is about the 'why' or motivations—the rules of the game—of politics, rather than the substance or content of government policies, many of which are implemented under Acts of Parliament and are thus subject to democratic as well as legal controls. Given the continuation of the legal doctrine of parliamentary sovereignty, discussed in chapter 2, it remains legally possible for governments to secure the passing of Acts by Parliament that are—or can be accused

---

[1] See discussion in ch. 1.

[2] See T. Ginsburg 'Written Constitutions and the Administrative State: On the Constitutional Character of Administrative Law' in S. Rose-Ackerman and P. Lindseth (ed.), *Comparative Constitutional Law* (2010). Aspects of this process are discussed in ch. 12.

[3] See ch. 4 for discussion of Britain in the EU.   [4] See discussion in chs. 6 and 7.

[5] See discussion in section 'Soft law regulation and self-regulation in government' below at p. 319.

[6] See ch. 9.   [7] See ch. 13.

[8] See discussion in section 'Soft law regulation and self-regulation in government' below at p. 319.

of being—inappropriately party political or partisan. But, even if they are legally valid, such provisions will be widely recognized outside government as being contrary to the rules of the game, even unconstitutional.[9] The Lord Chancellor's proposals in 2012 not to allow 'a *culture of Left-wing-dominated, single-issue activism* to hold back our country from investing in infrastructure and new sources of energy and from bringing down the cost of our welfare state'[10] (the italics are mine) by altering the provisions for judicial review is a striking example of inappropriately partisan policy. The overt partisanship in this approach was strongly condemned in Parliament and elsewhere (as of course was the policy itself, and the indifference to the rule of law that the reform proposals revealed[11]).

The practice of such partisanship in domestic affairs, often based on bald assertions of authority or mandate and often involving secret deal-making, patronage, and the exercise of the 'dark arts' of politics, was a strong feature of the 1960s to 1980s. It has been progressively rejected in Parliament, particularly by opposition parties in the Commons and in the relatively non-partisan House of Lords and its select committees, and by many political commentators.[12] As a result governments find themselves forced to provide justifications for their policies in terms of general or public or shared interests—the general well-being of citizens in Aristotle's phrase[13]—and not simply by reference to their majority and the authority it may be claimed to give them.

In the next section of this chapter the historical and political histories of these issues are outlined. The third section explores ways in which many decisions have been depoliticized by transfers to ALBs and the use of 'soft law' techniques to prevent what have come to be regarded as abuses of governmental power. Finally, in the last section the threads of these developments are drawn together and linked to changes in society. In effect a new constitutional consensus about the rules of the game of politics is emerging.

BACKGROUND: POLITICS IN THE POST WAR PERIOD

THE POST-SECOND WORLD WAR CONSENSUS

The Labour government that was elected after the end of the Second World War in 1945 was committed to major social reform along the lines proposed in the Beveridge Report of 1942,[14] and Keynesian economic policies.[15] A full programme of reforms

---

[9] See discussion in ch. 2.

[10] Available at http://www.dailymail.co.uk/news/article-2413135/CHRIS-GRAYLING-Judicial-review-promotional-tool-Left-wing-campaigners.html#ixzz3IUbXriTU.

[11] See discussion in chs. 1 and 8.   [12] See ch. 6.

[13] See the discussion of Aristotle's views in S. Everson (ed.), *The Politics and Constitution of Athens* (1996), xxiv–xxxii; and N. Barber *The Constitutional State* (2010), ch. 3.

[14] Sir William Beveridge, *A Report on Social Insurance and Allied Services* (December 1942). Some of the Beveridge reforms were already in place before the end of the war, for instance the War Pensions Act 1943 and the Education Act 1944.

[15] J. M. Keynes, *The General Theory of Employment, Interest and Money* (1936).

was put in place in the next ten years or so: many major heavy industries were nationalized[16] and the elements of the Welfare State were put in place: the NHS,[17] the building and provision of municipal housing,[18] a system of cash welfare benefits including pensions (originally based on contributions),[19] and provision for legal aid.[20] These policies became part of a cross-party post-war *political* consensus about the role of the state. It was broadly supported by the two main parties, Labour and Conservatives, and by the population, and it continued until the 1970s. The vision it embodied was of positive state-led progress towards a fair and prosperous society.[21] It was accompanied by a *constitutional* consensus: there was very little pressure for constitutional change in this period.

POLITICAL CONFLICT AND THE END OF CONSENSUS

However, through the later part of the 1960s and into the early 1980s the post-war cross-party and political consensus broke down. Government 'interference' in the state-owned industries prevented long-term planning and investment.[22] They were criticized for being inefficient and expensive. Industrial conflict was endemic in British politics and in due course it altered assumptions about the role of the state. The conflict was caused by, and exacerbated, high unemployment and inflation, which successive governments were unable to control. These in turn were partly due to changes in the global economy.

British domestic politics were highly party political and partisan—class-based—at this time. This reflected divisions in society. Social mobility was weak. And the classes lived largely separate lives. Politics centred round conflicts between employers—mainly public but also private—and labour over pay and conditions of work and security of employment. Trade unions were strong, especially in the public services and publicly owned industries. Their institutional[23] and financial[24] links with the Labour Party gave them special access to and influence over government when Labour was in power. This was particularly the case with coal mining, steel, some car manufacturing, the

---

[16] Coal, 1946; electricity generation, 1947; rail, 1948; gas, 1949; iron and steel, 1951.

[17] National Health Service Act 1946.

[18] Housing (Financial and Miscellaneous Provisions) Act 1946.

[19] National Insurance Act, 1946.   [20] Legal Aid Act 1949.

[21] See e.g. T. H. Marshall *Citizenship and Social Class* (1956); A. Crosland *The Future of Socialism* (1956); P. Townsend et al., *Poverty and Social Exclusion in Britain* (2000).

[22] See J. Redwood and J. Hatch, *Controlling Public Industries* (1982); National Economic Development Office, *A Study of UK Nationalised Industries* (1976).

[23] See C. Crouch 'The Peculiar Relationship: The Party and the Unions' in D. Kavanagh (ed.), *The Politics of the Labour Party* (1982); D. Oliver 'The Constitutional Implications of the Labour Party Reforms' [1981] *PL* 151. Institutional links included block votes on party policies at the annual conference, nomination rights and sponsorship of MPs, rights in the election of the Leader, and rights to participate in drafting election manifestos.

[24] See K. Ewing, *The Funding of Political Parties in Britain* (1987) and *The Conservatives, Trade Unions and Political Funding* (1983).

utilities, and the provision of services by local authorities, including education, waste disposal, street cleaning, and burials. The private sector too was hit by industrial unrest in this period, notably in the road haulage, motor manufacturing, and construction industries.

Successive governments sought formal statutory or negotiated resolution to these industrial conflicts. In 1969 the government proposed to introduce legislation for strike ballots and the enforcement of settlements of industrial disputes,[25] but the proposals were rejected by the unions. Instead the Trades Union Congress offered a deal with government, a 'solemn and binding' undertaking on wage restraint, with a view to avoiding legislation on the issues.[26] But the TUC was not able to deliver on these undertakings.

Government then resorted to other non-statutory ways of enforcing its economic policies, such as including strict wage restraint requirements in government contracts, which contractors were required to impose in turn on subcontractors; and blacklisting of bodies that breached non-statutory government pay policy and refusing them grants and other benefits.[27] (In due course European competition law reduced the scope for government to use economic and contracting power as instruments of policy in these ways.)

It was widely accepted at that time[28] that conflicts of this kind were inevitable in any society, and that politics, not resort to hard law (e.g. the passing of Acts of Parliament with provisions for coercive enforcement by the courts), was the appropriate process for resolving them. Deal-making was core to the role of politicians: their elected status and the mandate it was often asserted that it entailed were assumed to provide governments with the appropriate degrees of authority and accountability for their policies; above all, they should not be subject to control by the courts.[29]

In 1976 the British government had to resort to assistance from the International Monetary Fund (IMF) to enable it to meet its spending commitments. The IMF imposed strict requirements as to British economic policy and cuts in public expenditure. Internally these proved very difficult to achieve.

During the 1960s and 1970s politics, dominated by these conflicts, came to be beset by a 'paralysis of public choice'[30] which made it impossible for government to take decisions as to public policy if labour or capital exercised what had come to be their 'veto' powers. Beer suggested that the civic culture which had supported the system after the Second World War was weakened and came to be replaced by pluralistic stagnation and in due course group-based populism. The paralysis was partly due to the emergence of a corporate bias in a corporate state:[31] Parliament was by-passed by

---

[25] *In Place of Strife*, Cmnd 388 (1969). The proposals were rejected by the unions and were dropped.

[26] See K. Middlemas, *Power, Competition and the State*, III: *End of the Post War Era—Britain since 1974* (1991).

[27] See T. C. Daintith, 'Regulation by Contract: The New Prerogative' [1979] *Current Legal Problems* 41.

[28] See B. Crick, *In Defence of Politics* (1962; 2nd edn, 1982).

[29] J. A. G. Griffith, 'The Political Constitution' (1979) 42 *MLR* 1.

[30] S. Beer, *Britain Against Itself* (1982).

[31] See K. Middlemas, *Politics in the Industrial Society* (1979).

governments, which negotiated instead directly with labour (and, where the conflicts were not between labour and state-owned industries, with private capital) to seek to end or avoid industrial disputes about inflation, wages policy, and productivity. Richardson and Jordan argued that Britain had become a 'post-parliamentary democracy'.[32] They observed that the traditional model of Cabinet and parliamentary government was a travesty of reality: 'The reality is much more murky, far more complex. Politics in a sense has gone underground...Governments have always struck bargains with barons'.[33] However, by the end of the 1970s it was clear that the conflicts of the time could not be settled politically and within the UK by deals made between the government and economic actors.

A movement for constitutional reform emerged—the constitutional consensus too was beginning to break down. Sir Leslie Scarman in his 1975 Hamlyn Lectures entitled *English Law: The New Dimension* argued the need for a bill of rights, devolution, even a written constitution. Hailsham memorably called the system an 'Elective Dictatorship'[34] and argued for constitutional reform including a bill of rights.

During the 1974–9 Parliament the Labour government's majority was small. It vanished entirely after by-election defeats in 1978, after which a Lib–Lab pact was reached: Liberal MPs agreed not to bring down the government on certain terms, including legislation for devolution to Scotland and Wales.[35] But opinion polls suggested Labour would lose an election in due course, and so the government's own backbench MPs were subject to fierce whipping, made effective by prime ministerial threats to call a general election if the government were defeated on what it regarded as an issue of confidence: here was the 'elective dictatorship' in action. Although government backbench rebellions increased in this period[36] the government managed to escape loss of a vote of confidence.

The years 1978–9 saw a 'Winter of Discontent'[37] in which the country was plagued by industrial action, especially in public services. The government lost support in the opinion polls. Prime Minister Callaghan lost a vote of confidence in the House of Commons and called a general election.

The election of 1979 produced a change of government.[38] The voters 'resolved' the conflicts of the past decade or more by electing a different party into government: this in effect institutionalized the end of the post-war political consensus. It is ironic that, in the year in which Griffith's seminal lecture on 'The Political

[32] J. J. Richardson and A. G. Jordan, *Governing under Pressure: The Policy Process in a Post-parliamentary Democracy* (1979).

[33] Ibid., 191–2.

[34] BBC, the 1976 Dimbleby Lecture. See also Lord Hailsham, *The Dilemma of Democracy* (1978).

[35] See D. Steele, *A House Divided: The Lib-Lab Pact and the Future of British Politics* (1980).

[36] P. Norton, 'The House of Commons and the Constitution: The Challenges of the 1970s' (1981) 34 *Parliamentary Affairs* 253.

[37] See A. W. Turner, *Crisis? What Crisis?Britain in the 1970s* (2013); see also A. Beckett, *When the Lights Went Out: What Really Happened in Britain in the Seventies* (2009).

[38] A. Seldon (ed.), *New Labour, Old Labour: The Wilson and Callaghan Governments 1974–79* (2004).

Constitution'[39] was published, the politics of the constitution to which he was referring changed radically.

POLITICS AFTER THE WINTER OF DISCONTENT 1978-9

The election result produced a number of reversals, in both constitutional arrangements and government policies. Immediately after the election the House of Commons
started to fight back against the 'elective dictatorship'.[40] First, reforms to the system of
select committees were introduced:[41] the former system of subject-based select committees was replaced by a set of committees to shadow and scrutinize each government department. Careful preparatory work for these reforms had been done during
the previous Parliament. There followed reform of the parliamentary control of public
expenditure by the National Audit Act 1983, the stimulus for which came from discontent on the part of backbenchers and opposition party members at the by-passing
of Parliament in the 1974–9 Parliament. These reforms were by no means the full
answer to the 'elective dictatorship', but they were the start of a continuing process
in which Parliament has been expanding its powers to scrutinize government and its
independence from government and party political pressures.[42]

Under the leadership of Mrs Thatcher from 1979 to 1990 the Conservative government in effect dismantled the corporate state and broke the paralysis of public choice.
It no longer negotiated 'social contracts' or 'solemn and binding undertakings' with
the unions or employers; it 'won' the miners' strike of 1984–5[43] (at considerable cost
to mining communities and civil liberties[44]) and adopted policies which resulted in
the weakening of the power of organized labour: coal mines were closed or sold off,
utilities, rail services, and steel were privatized. As unemployment grew, union membership fell. The pre-1979 balance between government, Parliament, interest groups,
political parties, and the public began to change.[45] These and other highly controversial
and partisan policies (for instance, changes to local government including the abolition of the Labour-controlled Greater London Council and the metropolitan counties
in 1986, and the introduction of the community charge—poll tax—in Scotland and
then in the UK in 1988) were given effect through Acts of Parliament.[46]

For a range of reasons, conflicts between capital and labour no longer dominate
politics. Industrial disputes were commonly between labour and the state as owner.
Since privatization these disputes are mostly between private bodies, and so are not
amenable to resolution by direct negotiation with government. The conduct of industrial conflicts and their resolution have been increasingly regulated by law: the closed

---

[39] Griffith, 'The Political Constitution'.   [40] See ch. 6.
[41] See G. Drewry, *The New Select Committees* (2nd edn, 1989).   [42] See ch. 6.
[43] See Ian MacGregor, *The Enemy Within: The Story of the Miners' Strike 1984–85* (1986).
[44] See K. D. Ewing and C. A. Gearty, *Freedom Under Thatcher* (1990).
[45] See Middlemas, *Power, Competition and the State*.
[46] See generally A. W. Turner, *Rejoice, Rejoice. Britain in the 1980s* (2013).

shop has been ended;[47] secondary picketing is unlawful, and unions must hold ballots of their members before striking—a proposal first made but rejected by unions in Labour's *In Place of Strife* (1969). Many services that were formerly provided by local authorities have been outsourced or put out to competitive tendering,[48] thus undermining the monopoly power of public sector unions and transforming conflicts into disputes between private parties rather than between unions and the state. In this sense they have been depoliticized.

Public opinion was of course divided on these matters during the 1980s and after; but in due course the other main political parties came to accept the policies adopted in the 1980s. Indeed they were replicated in many European Union states. The time for these policies had become ripe. In effect the politics of the previous period came to an end, and a process of regulation of what had been unregulated political action began.[49]

The brief history of political conflict in the period of the 1960s and into the 1980s in this section of the chapter illustrates a number of points about the changing role and the regulation of politics in the UK. The loss of power by Labour in the election of 1979 brought an end to the corporatism and paralysis of public choice which had led to the by-passing of normal parliamentary accountability mechanisms. There was no more talk of a post-parliamentary democracy: governments secured the implementation of their policies through Acts of Parliament. Step by step the two Houses have insisted on their right to hold government to account,[50] aided by the Freedom of Information Act 2000.[51]

ESTABLISHING THE RULES OF THE GAME OF POLITICS

Many decisions that were formerly made by ministers have been transferred by law to ALBs over the last 20 years or so, thus immunizing them from party politics. There has also been a proliferation of 'soft law' regulation and self-regulation in politics. The processes demonstrate a progressive commitment, driven by parliamentary pressures and public opinion, to a more principled and less partisan approach to important areas of public policy and decision-making.

THE SEVEN PRINCIPLES OF PUBLIC LIFE

In the 1990s a number of scandals erupted around misbehaviour by members of Parliament, other politicians, and public bodies. The worst of these was the 'cash for

---

[47] See *Young, James and Webster* v. *UK* (1981) 4 EHRR 38.
[48] See generally D. Oliver and G. Drewry, *Public Service Reform: Issues of Accountability and Public Law* (1996).
[49] This is discussed in section 'Soft law regulation and self-regulation in government'.
[50] See ch. 7.   [51] See ch. 14.

questions' affair of 1995: a number of MPs had been taking payments from outsiders for putting down parliamentary questions seeking information from ministers—an extreme example of politicians putting their own self-interests before their duties to their constituents and to the public interest.[52] This led to the appointment of a non-statutory Committee on Standards in Public Life, the Nolan Committee. In its first report[53] the Committee set out seven principles which, it argued, ought to have general application across all areas of public life. As amended by the Committee in *Standards Matter: A Review of Best Practice in Promoting Good Behaviour in Public Life* (2013)[54] they are as follows:

Selflessness. Holders of public office should act solely in terms of the public interest.

Integrity. Holders of public office must avoid placing themselves under any obligation to people or organisations that might try inappropriately to influence them in their work. They should not act or take decisions in order to gain financial or other material benefits for themselves, their family, or their friends. They must declare and resolve any interests and relationships.

Objectivity. Holders of public office must act and take decisions impartially, fairly and on merit, using the best evidence and without discrimination or bias.

Accountability. Holders of public office are accountable to the public for their decisions and actions and must submit themselves to the scrutiny necessary to ensure this.

Openness. Holders of public office should act and take decisions in an open and transparent manner. Information should not be withheld from the public unless there are clear and lawful reasons for so doing.

Honesty. Holders of public office should be truthful.

Leadership. Holders of public office should exhibit these principles in their own behaviour. They should actively promote and robustly support the principles and be willing to challenge poor behaviour wherever it occurs.

These standards have been incorporated into the *Ministerial Code* and adopted by many public bodies, including the two Houses of Parliament and local authorities: they became features of a system that demanded and relied on self-regulation of political behaviour.

Philp comments that 'The Seven Principles are non-partisan in character, so that while the judgments politicians make are usually partisan on some dimensions, the common ethical standards that apply to any given decision need to be acknowledged'.[55] This is because, as Philp puts it, 'the legitimacy of the political system depends on a high degree of consensus on the character of the political game and the rules for contesting political office'.[56] The views of the public, and

---

[52] See O. Gay and P. Leopold (eds.), *Conduct Unbecoming: The Regulation of Parliamentary Behaviour* (2004).

[53] Cm 2850 (May 1995).

[54] Fourteenth Report of the Committee on Standards in Public Life, Cm 8519 (January 2013), 24.

[55] M. Philp, *Public Ethics and Political Judgment*, paper commissioned by the Committee on Standards in Public Life (July 2014), para. 5.3 (available on the Committee's website).

[56] Ibid., para. 3.2.

thus public culture, are influential in the development of standards and ethics in politics. But if the views of substantial sections of the public become seriously divergent from this consensus, for instance on nationalist, religious, or ideological grounds, then the legitimacy of the system will itself be called into question.

The Seven Principles are in reality constitutional in nature: governments and other public bodies should act in a spirit of public service in the general interest—Aristotle's well-being principle. This is generally taken for granted and seldom articulated or analysed by public lawyers or political commentators. But if these tenets are not respected by government and the population at large a polity cannot function effectively and legitimately. The principles reflect what the population at large is assumed to expect of its leaders. They are evident in many of the measures discussed in the next section, and they have been adopted and included in many soft law documents, some of which are discussed in that section.

It does not follow from all of this that there is universal support among politicians or the public for these principles and the constraints that they impose upon politicking: adherence to them by politicians cannot be guaranteed. Assumptions about the strength or existence of shared or common interests may be challenged. Nor does it follow that members of the population are content or convinced when government claims to act in the general interest, if its policies affect them negatively. There seems currently to be a resurgence of 'politics as normal' involving partisanship, as the Lord Chancellor's approach to judicial review noted earlier reveals. However the wide condemnation of his approach by the opposition parties and by judges and lawyers serves to confirm the importance of the public service, non-partisan principle of the rules of the political game.[57] For the time being at least these principles articulate norms that are widely respected in many sectors of UK society and across public and political life.

ALBS: THE RISE OF THE UNELECTED

The powers that ministers used to exercise over state-owned industries, and which were features of politics in the 1960s to the early 1980s, were removed by their privatization since the late 1980s.[58] They have been replaced by systems of independent regulation by ALBs,[59] put in place to promote competition and prevent abuse of

---

[57] See ch. 8.

[58] Privatization has been adopted partly to raise substantial sums of money for government, partly to divide up monopolies and expose them to competition in the market, and partly to insulate enterprises from short-term political 'interference' and thus enable investment and other decisions to be made with a view to their long-term profitability and efficiency: see C. Veljanowski, *Selling the State* (1987).

[59] See discussion of regulation in ch. 12. Utility regulators include the Office of Communications (FCOM), Office of Gas and Electricity Markets (OFGEM), and the Water Services Regulation Authority (OFWAT).

monopoly power by these enterprises, and to prevent the unregulated imposition of political pressure on ALBs by governments.[60]

But many further functions have been transferred from ministers to ALBs since the late 1970s. Some examples are outlined below:

- Under the Bank of England Act 1998 (passed shortly after the change of government in the election of 1997) the fixing of interest rates was passed from the Chancellor of the Exchequer for the time being—there being suspicions that these were fixed for party political advantages—to the independent Bank of England's Monetary Policy Committee, composed of experts in the management of inflation and the economy.

- By the Freedom of Information Act 2000 (passed as part of the reform programme of the New Labour government that was elected after 18 years in opposition in 1997) the right of ministers to determine, often on highly partisan or party political grounds, what information was disclosed to the public (all such information having been until then officially secret and its secrecy having been open to abuse for political motives) was removed and replaced by a requirement for public bodies to produce schemes for the routine publication of much information, and an Information Commissioner and Information Tribunal to deal with disputes about the non-publication of requested information.[61]

- Under the Public Appointments Order in Council 2002 as amended in 2012, the making of appointments by ministers to the boards of public bodies and to public office, which it was felt had been abused for party political purposes or as exercises of patronage in favour of 'cronies', is subject to oversight by the Commissioner for Public Appointments, tasked to regulate, monitor and report on ministerial appointments.

- The Constitutional Reform Act 2005 establishes an independent Judicial Appointments Commission (and reaffirms the constitutional principle of the rule of law and the importance of judicial independence).[62]

- By the Statistics and Registration Service Act 2007 the power to decide what statistics should be collected and which should be published—a power obviously open to political abuse—has been passed to the UK Statistics Authority, established as an independent body responsible for oversight of the National Statistical Institute (NSI) and of the Office for National Statistics (ONS), its executive office and the largest producer of official statistics in the UK (they form a non-ministerial department directly accountable to Parliament).

---

[60] On regulation see A. L. Ogus, *Regulation: Legal Form and Economic Theory* (2004); B. Morgan and K. Yeung, *An Introduction to Law and Regulation* (2007); D. Oliver, T. Prosser, and R. Rawlings (eds.), *The Regulatory State: Constitutional Implications* (2010).
[61] See ch. 14.   [62] See ch. 8.

- The power formerly exercised by the Chancellor of the Exchequer and the Treasury to decide what information to publish about the national finances has been transferred to the Office for Budget Responsibility (OBR). This body was established by the Chancellor of the Exchequer on a non-statutory basis soon after the election in May 2010 as part of the Coalition response to the financial crisis dating from 2007. By the Budget Responsibility and National Audit Act 2011 the OBR was put on a formal statutory footing, independent from government, with the remit to examine and report on the sustainability of the public finances; it produces economic and fiscal forecasts, which the government is required to adopt as the 'official forecasts' for the annual Budget.

Thus many functions that would otherwise or formerly have been exercisable as a matter of course, and often without consultation or in secret, by ministers within their departments are now performed by ALBs, the whole point of which is that they are unelected, expert, and independent and designed to comply with the Seven Principles. Most of these ALBs have been established specifically to insulate the activities for which they are responsible from short-term, 'political' or party political influence, and so to promote well-informed, expert, and politically neutral decision-making in the long-term public interest. They have often been established by newly elected governments whose members in opposition came to mistrust their predecessors' exercise of power for partisan or party political advantage.[63]

Processes of this kind have been described by Vibert as 'The Rise of the Unelected'.[64] Having discussed the pros and cons of this phenomenon, Vibert concludes that it represents a new 'separation of powers', a new branch within the system of government with a 'special responsibility for the handling and dissemination of information, the analysis of evidence and the deployment and use of most up-to-date empirical knowledge'.[65]

Vibert's explanation for this development is that 'people do not trust the information that governments provide'.[66] They do not trust governments to respect the Seven Principles. The citizenry in the UK is enabled, Vibert suggests, through the work of ALBs to reach its own judgments about public policy where reliable information is available to them, insulated from politics.[67] Those in charge of these ALBs and the responsible ministers may be examined by select committees: Parliament has the final say on the parameters within which they operate.[68]

---

[63] e.g. the Bank of England Monetary Policy Committee and the Office for Budget Responsibility, discussed earlier.

[64] F. Vibert, *The Rise of the Unelected: Democracy and the New Separation of Powers* (2007). See also M. Moran, *The British Regulatory State* (2004); R. Rawlings, 'Testing Times' in D. Oliver, T. Prosser, and R. Rawlings (eds.), *The Regulatory State: Constitutional Implications* (2010).

[65] Vibert, *The Rise of the Unelected*, 12, and chapter 11.   [66] Ibid., 13.   [67] Ibid.

[68] For discussion of parliamentary oversight of regulators see D. Oliver 'Regulation, Democracy, and Democratic Oversight in the UK' in D. Oliver, T. Prosser, and R. Rawlings (eds.), *The Regulatory State: Constitutional Implications* (2010). See chs. 6 and 12 in the present volume for discussion.

SOFT LAW REGULATION AND SELF-REGULATION IN GOVERNMENT

In parallel with the formulation and application of principles of public life and the process of transfer by law of some decision-making and regulatory functions to ALBs, discussed earlier, there has been a proliferation of regulatory and self-regulatory 'soft law'[69] in the UK's governmental and constitutional arrangements.[70] In this chapter the focus is on the operation of this soft law in government. Much more of it applies in Parliament and the devolution arrangements.

Soft law differs from 'hard law' principally because it is not, for the most part, taken notice of or enforced in the courts.[71] Soft law is however generally complied with, for reasons which are discussed later in this section. These techniques of soft law regulation and self-regulation in government have developed incrementally for well over a century, but they have increased in the last 30 years or so. Guidelines,[72] conventions,[73] resolutions of the two Houses of Parliament,[74] manuals,[75] statements of principles,[76] memorandums of understanding,[77] framework documents,[78] and charters[79] are just a few forms of soft law.[80]

Like the provisions for ALBs discussed earlier, the rules of the game that these documents and conventions express generally promote the Seven Principles of Public Life and the duty of governments (and other elected bodies such as local authorities) to work selflessly to promote the general interest and not their own interests or

---

[69] See T. C. Daintith and A. Page, *The Executive in the Constitution* (1999); A. Page 'Executive Self-regulation in the United Kingdom' in T. Daintith (ed.), *Constitutional Implications of Executive Self-Regulation: Comparative Experience* (1996); J. Q. Wilson and P. Rachal, 'Can Government Regulate Itself?' (1977) 46 *Public Interest* 3–14.

[70] On self-regulation see generally Ogus, *Regulation*, 107–11; A. Ogus, *Rethinking Self-regulation* (1995)—quoted in Morgan and Yeung, *An Introduction to Law and Regulation*; C. Harlow and R. Rawlings, *Law and Administration* (3rd edn, 2009), 323–30.

[71] Exceptions to this general rule include extra-statutory tax concessions, the publication of which may give rise to legitimate expectations on the part of taxpayers: see R. Megarry 'Administrative Quasi-legislation' (1944) 60 *LQR* 125. The departure from these published concessions may lead to the tax authorities—Her Majesty's Revenue and Customs—being held in judicial review to have exercised their discretions unlawfully: they may be held to the representations in favour of tax payers that are found in these concessions; see also discussion in Harlow and Rawlings, *Law and Administration*, ch. 5; and G. Ganz, *Quasi-legislation: Recent Developments in Secondary Legislation* (1987).

[72] *Guide to Making Legislation*, Cabinet Office website.

[73] e.g. individual ministerial responsibility, discussed in ch. 6.

[74] Resolutions on Ministerial Responsibility HC Deb, 19 Mar. 1997, cols. 1046–7; HL Deb, 20 Mar. 1997, cols. 1055–62.

[75] *Cabinet Manual* (2010), on the Cabinet Office website.

[76] Seven Principles of Public Life elaborated by the Committee on Standards in Public Life in their first report of 1995, discussed earlier.

[77] Devolution Memorandum of Understanding, 2012 is on the Cabinet Office website.

[78] These lay down the terms on which Chief Executives manage 'Next Step' agencies. See ch. 7.

[79] The Citizen's Charter and charters made under it: see Oliver and Drewry, *Public Service Reform*.

[80] See ch. 13 for examples of extensive reliance on soft law by the Treasury.

those of their associates.[81] However, the *content* of the general interest is often hotly disputed, and the very idea that such a thing exists is open to challenge. Similarly the *locus* of 'the public' whose interests are to be promoted may vary, and be controversial. This has been the nub of issues over independence or increased devolution of power to Scotland: when are the interests of the UK as a whole to be promoted by government, and when and by whom those of Scotland? The same questions may be asked in relation to Wales. Which level of government, UK or devolved, is best able to identify and promote particular public interests?[82] I suggest that public service principles are nowadays widely accepted as binding on public bodies whether at UK or devolved levels, as are the norms which have developed to promote them.

Some intra-governmental soft law rules date back to the nineteenth century: Dicey highlighted constitutional conventions of ministerial responsibility in his *Introduction to the Study of the Law of the Constitution* (1885). While these conventions govern in part relations between government and Parliament, they also provide the foundation for the *internal* conduct of government.[83] It was only by resolutions on ministerial responsibility passed by the two Houses in 1997 in the wake of the Arms to Iraq scandal[84] that it became clear that compliance with the duties of individual ministerial responsibility to Parliament is demanded *by Parliament* on behalf of the public; they are not followed merely as a matter of grace by the prime minister of the day and his ministers.

The House of Commons resolution[85] is as follows:

> That, in the opinion of this House, the following principles should govern the conduct of ministers of the Crown in relation to Parliament:
>
> (1) Ministers have a duty to Parliament to account, and be held to account, for the policies, decision and actions of their Departments and Next Steps Agencies.
>
> (2) It is of paramount importance that ministers give accurate and truthful information to Parliament, correcting any inadvertent error at the earliest opportunity. Ministers who knowingly mislead Parliament will be expected to offer their resignation to the Prime Minister.
>
> (3) Ministers should be as open as possible with Parliament, refusing to provide information only when disclosure would not be in the public interest, which should be decided in accordance with [the Freedom of Information Act].
>
> (4) Similarly, ministers should require civil servants who give evidence before Parliamentary committees on their behalf and under their directions to be as helpful

---

[81] For further discussion see D. Oliver, 'The Politics-free Dimension to the UK Constitution' in M. Qvortrup (ed.), *The British Constitution: Continuity and Change* (2013) and 'Accountability and the Foundations of British Democracy: The Public Interest and Public Service Principles' in N. Bamforth and P. Leyland (eds.), *Accountability in the Contemporary Constitution* (2013).

[82] See ch. 9.

[83] On the conventions of collective responsibility see Sir W. Anson, *The Law and Custom of the Constitution*, Part II (1982); see also *Attorney General v. Jonathan Cape* [1976] QB 752 for an example of a court taking judicial notice of the conventions.

[84] See Sir Richard Scott, *Report on the Export of Dual-use Goods to Iraq*, HC 115, 1995–6.

[85] See n. 74. The House of Lords' resolution is in similar terms.

as possible in providing accurate, truthful and full information in accordance with the duties and responsibilities of civil servants as set out in the Civil Service Code.

The texts of the resolutions were added to the *Ministerial Code*[86] that was issued by Prime Minister Tony Blair after the 1997 general election. He thus accepted, as subsequent prime ministers have done, that it is their duty to observe and promote the observation of these requirements and to dismiss ministers who do not respect them. This is not a matter, however, on which the Houses of Parliament themselves have authority to act, save for the archaic possibility of a vote to reduce a minister's salary, which has not been exercised for many years.

Other examples of long-standing soft law rules in government include the *Osmotherly Rules*,[87] dating from the 1970s, which were issued by the Office of the Leader of the House of Commons and the Cabinet Office. They set out the accountability of civil servants to their ministers and the terms on which they and their departments respond to questions from select committees and their reports.

The technique of developing soft law to deal with political difficulties became more widely used when New Public Management was adopted by governments in the 1980s, involving as it did, for instance, framework documents setting out the terms and conditions of service of Agency Chief Executives.[88] When powers were devolved to bodies in Scotland, Wales, and Northern Ireland,[89] statutory provisions were supplemented by Memorandums of Understanding between executives at each level.

Many soft law rules have been developed or adopted in documentary form by political players themselves: hence the use of the term '*self*-regulation' in the heading to this part of the chapter. They have been produced by successive prime ministers, as was case of the *Ministerial Code* (discussed further later), and by the Cabinet Office in the case of the *Guide to Making Legislation*, often in response to past problems and concerns. Periodically new clauses are added to these documents, incorporating responses to lessons recently learned.

New documents are produced from time to time, as with the *Cabinet Manual* of 2011:[90] this document was drafted by senior civil servants at the request of Prime Minister Gordon Brown in the run-up to the election in 2010, when it was widely expected that a hung Parliament would result; it provides a source of information on the laws, conventions, and rules that affect the operations and procedures of government. It is not legally binding and nor is it set in stone.

Until the mid-1990s many of these internal governmental rules were treated as 'official secrets' and were not published.[91] *Questions of Procedure for Ministers* (QPM), was

---

[86] See later for discussion of the *Ministerial Code*.

[87] UK Cabinet Office, *Giving Evidence to Select Committees: Evidence to Select Committees* (2014), para. 5. See discussion in ch. 7.

[88] See ch. 7.   [89] See ch. 9.   [90] Available on the Cabinet Office website.

[91] See ch. 14, and P. Birkinshaw, *Freedom of Information: The Law, the Practice and the Ideal* (4th edn, 2010) on the history of official secrecy.

published for the first time by the then Prime Minister John Major in 1992. Newly elected Prime Minister Tony Blair revised QPM and published it as the *Ministerial Code* in 1997. By convention each prime minister revises and republishes this *Code*: thus, as noted earlier, the Seven Principles of Public Life were incorporated in the 1997 version of the *Ministerial Code* (and in many other documents).[92]

The Cabinet Office document, *Guide to Making Legislation*, formerly known as the *Guide to Legislative Procedures*, includes guidance on, for instance, how instructions to parliamentary counsel should be prepared and what preparatory steps should be taken before bills go to the Cabinet's Parliamentary Business and Legislation Committee. This 300-page document covers, among other things, the preparation of bills before they can be introduced into Parliament, the handling of bills in Parliament, and the production of memorandums for the Delegated Powers and Regulatory Reform Committee of the House of Lords; a Regulatory Impact Assessment should be prepared at an early stage—and so forth.

EXAMPLES OF SOFT LAW SELF-REGULATION: THE *MINISTERIAL CODE* AND THE *CABINET MANUAL*

As of late 2014 the *Ministerial Code* and the *Cabinet Manual*, first published in 2010, illustrate the ways in which some fundamental constitutional principles are articulated in soft law form: these include legality and the rule of law, public service, promotion of general or public interests, openness, integrity, and non-partisanship.

The *Ministerial Code* states that the overarching duty of ministers is to comply with the law, including international law and treaty obligations, to uphold the administration of justice, and to protect the integrity of public life;[93] they must ensure that no conflict arises, or appears to arise, between their public duties and their private interests—a strong example of restrictions on how conflicts may be resolved;[94] they must not use government resources for party political purposes.[95]

Ministers must uphold the political impartiality of the Civil Service;[96] they have a duty to ensure that influence over Civil Service and public appointments is not abused for partisan purposes;[97] they are personally responsible for the management and conduct of their political advisers, and the advisers are responsible to the government as a whole.[98]

Facilities provided to ministers at government expense to enable them to carry out their official duties should not be used for party or constituency work;[99] official facilities and resources may not be used for the dissemination of material which is essentially party political.[100]

---

[92] The *Code* is divided into two parts, *Procedural Guidance for Ministers*, and *A Code of Ethics*. It is now administered by the Propriety and Ethics Group in the Cabinet Office.

[93] *Ministerial Code*, s. 1.2.   [94] Ibid., s. 1.2.f.   [95] Ibid., s. 1.2.i.   [96] Ibid., s. 1.2.j.

[97] Ibid., s. 3.1.   [98] Ibid., s. 3.3.   [99] Ibid., s. 6.1.   [100] Ibid., s. 6.3.

Where ministers have to take decisions within their departments which might have an impact on their own constituencies, they must take particular care to avoid any possible conflict of interest.[101]

On taking office, ministers should give up membership or chairmanship of a select committee or all-party parliamentary group;[102] they should arrange their affairs so as to avoid any suggestion that a union of which they are members has any undue influence.[103]

The *Cabinet Manual*, first published in 2010, reiterates some of the provisions of the *Ministerial Code* and seeks to summarize common understandings as to the operation of the Cabinet system. A draft was examined by the Justice Committee of the House of Commons before the general election of 2010. A revised version was published after the election. A number of parliamentary select committees reported on the draft and, later, the *Manual*.[104] It sets out the constraints on decision-making in government at various stages of the electoral cycle and in a whole range of circumstances, as the following examples show.

Post-election constraints: If no party has a Commons majority after a general election the Prime Minister (who continues in office until another appointment to the position is made) may allow civil servants to support the political parties in negotiations for the formation of a government, but this support should be focused and provided on an equal basis to all parties involved.[105] Thus the public interest in the formation of an effective government—rather than the interests of particular parties—is promoted.

Access to papers of a previous administration of a different political party that indicate the views of their predecessors is not normally permitted.[106] Thus personalized party political vendettas are restricted.

Pre-election constraints: Ministers must ensure that no conflict arises or appears to arise between their public duties and their private interests—in which are included party political ones.[107] At the discretion of the prime minister, however, members of Cabinet may meet to discuss party political matters in a 'political Cabinet'. Such meetings may take place in the Cabinet Room as usual, but they are not attended by officials and the conclusions of the discussion are not recorded in minutes.[108] Thus the Civil Service is supposed to be kept out of direct party politics.

Neutrality of the Civil Service: Ministers are required to uphold the political impartiality of the Civil Service and not to ask civil servants to act in any way that would

---

[101] Ibid., s. 6.4.   [102] Ibid., s. 7.14.

[103] Ibid., s. 7.15. This is particularly important given the historical links between trade unions, the Labour Party and MPs, enshrined in the Party's constitution.

[104] See Report of the Justice Committee HC 396, 2009–10; Constitution Committee, 12th report (2010–12): *The Cabinet Manual* (HL Paper 107); Public Administration Select Committee, 8th Report (2010–12): *Cabinet Manual* (HC 900); the Political and Constitutional Reform Committee, 6th Report (2010–12): *Constitutional Implications of the Cabinet Manual* (HC 73).

[105] *Cabinet Manual*, para. 2.14.   [106] Ibid., para. 11.23.

[107] Ibid., para. 3.46. See also *Ministerial Code*.   [108] Ibid., para. 4.8.

conflict with the Civil Service Code or the requirements of the Constitutional Reform and Governance Act 2010.[109] The Civil Service Code includes requirements of impartiality, including political impartiality.[110] In addition, civil servants should not be asked to engage in activities likely to call into question their political impartiality or give rise to criticism that resources paid from public funds are being used for party political purposes.[111]

Special advisers: On the face of it the employment of special advisers[112] goes against the trend of constraining party politics. The *Cabinet Manual* states that their employment adds a political dimension to the advice and assistance available to ministers, while reinforcing the political impartiality of the permanent Civil Service.[113] The House of Lords Constitution Committee, in its Report on the Accountability of Civil Servants, emphasized that ministers are responsible for the actions of their special advisers. Ministers have a duty to ensure their special advisers abide by the Code of Conduct for Special Advisers at all times.[114] And they will be responsible to Parliament for these matters.

Public appointments: Ministerial patronage has been curtailed by the arrangements for the making of public appointments, discussed earlier. Under the Coalition government's Civil Service Reform Plan of 2012,[115] ministers will have a greater role than hitherto in the appointment of Permanent Secretaries in their departments, subject to consultation over procedures for this with the Civil Service Commission: this consultation, in addition to the role of the Commissioner for Public Appointments, should limit the scope for such powers to be used for partisan or party political purposes by ministers.

Election campaign constraints: During the general election campaign and until a new government is formed, the government, though it remains in office, does so as a caretaker.[116] It is customary for ministers to observe discretion in initiating any action of a continuing or long-term character.[117] Pre-election contact by civil servants with opposition parties may be permitted by the prime minister. Meetings are confidential and ministers do not receive reports of them. Senior civil servants may ask questions about opposition parties' policy statements.[118]

WHERE DOES THE CONTENT OF SOFT LAW RULES OF THE GAME COME FROM?

Selznick notes that: 'The system depends heavily on self-restraint and thus on social mechanisms for building in appropriate values and rules of conduct.'[119]

---

[109] Ibid., para. 7.2.   [110] Ibid., para. 7.4.   [111] Ibid., para. 7.3.
[112] Ibid., paras. 7.11ff; and see the *Code of Conduct for Special Advisers*, Cabinet Office, June 2010.
[113] Ibid., para. 7.13.   [114] HL 61 (2012–13), para. 59.
[115] http://www.civilservice.gov.uk/wp-content/uploas/2012/06/civil-service-reform-plan-acc-final.pdf.
[116] *Cabinet Manual*, paras. 2.27ff.   [117] Ibid., paras. 2.29 and 2.30.   [118] Ibid., para. 2.21.
[119] P. Selznick 'The Sociology of Law' in D. Sills (ed.), *International Encyclopedia of the Social Sciences* (1968), IX, 54–5.

For Daintith and Page the articulation of explicit rules and procedures in codes, handbooks, and other documents eventually furnishes an independent source of legitimacy.[120] Such documents are not only about buttressing specific reforms, for example in New Public Management, but also about 'the restatement and reinforcement of existing *expectations* [my italics] in the face of the challenge to those expectations represented by public service reforms in the shape of the growing fragmentation of the public service, increased budgetary pressures, and new modes of delivery'.[121] They also reveal a fear that established means of professional socialization are breaking down, for instance with recruitment into the public service from the private sector: the fact that codes, handbooks, and other statements of expectations are published increases the visibility of expectations.[122] This explanation implies that these rules are generated internally, within government. To an extent this is true. But it would be surprising if the existence and content of such controls over ministers and others in government were not also responses to external pressures—expectations outside government. Grunow claims that these internal controls are heavily influenced by the external demands—for economy, for legality, and, increasingly, for effectiveness as well as responsiveness—to which the executive is subject.[123]

It is the case that breaches of soft law rules and of the principles that underlie them will normally attract adverse comment from opposition members of the House of Commons and members of the House of Lords, and from the press and sections of the public. They are in practice generated from public opinion and culture and are articulated from time to time in response to those pressures. It is commonly in anticipation of such criticisms that ministers formulate and then comply with these norms.

This tells us a lot about how public opinion and culture have developed since the period of industrial unrest and conflict in the 1960s to early 1980s and indeed since then. In effect government by deal-making with vested interests, the by-passing of Parliament, and failures to meet the standards that are now set out in the Seven Principles have been rejected by the public,[124] by successive opposition parties, and by Parliament as a whole. In response governments have accepted and articulated the duty to do their best, in good faith, to promote the general interest—whatever its content may be—in a spirit of public service (and not self-interest), and to provide acceptable justifications for their conduct of government.

It does not of course follow from all of this that politicians never act self-interestedly: they often do. But if caught they will face strong and principled criticisms and this may act as a deterrent.

---

[120] Daintith and Page, *The Executive in the Constitution*, 386.   [121] Ibid.   [122] Ibid., 387.

[123] D. Grunow 'Internal Control in Public Administration' in F.-X. Kaufmann, *Guidance, Control and Evaluation in the Public Sector* (1986), 645–62.

[124] See e.g. Committee on Standards in Public Life, *Standards Matter*, Appendix 3.

REFLECTIONS

As Vibert observed, the steady increase of regulation by ALBs that was discussed in the previous section of this chapter reflects a lack of trust on the part of the public in information and data provided by politicians. But the development of regulation to replace ministerial decision-making, and of soft law to regulate it, are not only about information. They represent a shift from a culture of authority to one of substantive justification,[125] a trend that has taken place in many liberal democracies in recent years. It is 'counter-majoritarian': the fact that a government has a majority in Parliament is not considered to be sufficient of itself to legitimize its decisions and policies in the eyes of the electorate—or of the opposition. To be considered legitimate justifications must *exclude* for instance explicit party or partisan considerations or the making of secret deals, pursuit of self-interest and the interests of cronies and kin by government. They must meet the requirements of the Seven Principles. Good government is as much about what is *not allowed* as it is about what is *required*. This, I suggest, is the basis of a developing shared consensus about the rules of the game of politics.

Reliance on soft law rather than hard law—legislation and the common law—protects the courts from having to decide highly party political, non-justiciable questions,[126] and places responsibility for compliance with norms on politicians rather than on the courts. It represents recognition by those in government and in Parliament who have produced this volume of soft law of the importance of trustworthiness and trust on the part of government and other public bodies in the good functioning of a democratic political system. The public in turn rewards trust with respect, and untrustworthiness with disrespect, which affects the authority and legitimacy of government.

In summary, the broad British public culture has come to expect, i.e. demand government and Parliament to do their best to promote general or public interests—well-being—in a spirit of public service, not, for instance, specifically in the interests of their supporters or to damage their opponents, or to avoid criticism. The expectation entails a widespread assumption that there are such things as general or public or shared interests, that it is possible to promote general well-being. It allows that there may be conflicting interests, or perceptions of conflicting interests, among the population, especially between labour and capital, the nations and regions, and ethnic and religious groups. It allows also for differences of opinion as to what the

---

[125] See E. Mureinik, 'A Bridge to Where? Introducing the Interim Bill of Rights' (1994) 10 *SA Journal of Human Rights*, at 31.

[126] The UK lacks a written constitution granting constitutional judicial review powers to the courts. If the courts were to take it upon themselves to develop judicial review over 'non-justiciable' issues or (in American terms) 'political questions' they would be exposed to political attack, lacking the protection afforded by written constitutions in other liberal democracies.

promotion of general interests requires. It allows for ideology. But it imposes a need for explicit, open public interest-based justifications from a trustworthy and trusted government for its positions on these issues.

Kellner, discussing YouGov polls, observed in 2012 that:

> It's not just the ideological divide that has melted away. So, too, to a large extent, has the culture divide that used to separate working-class from middle-class voters. The range of shared experiences is far greater than it was in the heyday of class voting.[127]

This is an important point. It may be that the beginnings of what Tönnies[128] called *'Gemeinschaft'* (community, which Tönnies compared with *'Gesellschaft'*, society[129]) has developed in the UK in recent years: broadly based groupings based on feelings of togetherness and on mutual bonds, which are felt as a goal to be kept up, their members being the means for this goal. Many experiences and interests are now shared in civil society, across and outside class membership, in ways that contrast with the position in the 1960s and 1970s. They are also shared across many regional, ethnic, and religious groups. A broad popular culture has developed which gives rise to and sustains interests in (in alphabetical order) athletics, baking and cooking, cricket, dance, DIY, football, gardening, music, tennis, wildlife, even shopping, which are often fostered by widely viewed television programmes and access to the internet.[130] This process, taken with the 'melting away' of the old ideological divide, I suggest, has contributed to the fact that many individuals have come not only to share interests and senses of community but also to demand trustworthiness, non-partisanship, and ethical standards from their government.

The trend has not been universal. Many people, especially the poor and unemployed, some minority communities, and those in regions or nations far from Westminster and Whitehall, do not feel part of the national UK community, they do not sense national UK-level togetherness and mutual bonds, they do not have many shared experiences. The weakening of class divides and conflicts does not preclude the development of other conflicts that may be reflected in politics—for instance, differences in senses of national or European identity or belonging, as were revealed in the Scottish independence referendum in September 2014, in which 45 per cent of those voting were in favour of an independent Scotland. Nor does it preclude a heightening of tensions and conflicts between different cultural traditions or religions. 'Politics as usual' still takes place. The UK's is still a political constitution. But the game is supposed to be played according to written and unwritten soft law rules. The substance of many government and opposition policies, particularly in relation to immigration, Europe, and social welfare are hotly contested. The point is that they are likely to be criticized

---

[127] See P. Kellner, 'Labour's Lost Votes' *Prospect*, November 2012, 40.
[128] See F. Tönnies, *Gemeinschaft und Gesellschaft* (1887), translated as *Community and Society* 1957, discussed by M. Weber in *Economy and Society* (1921).
[129] Note that Mrs Thatcher famously said that there was no such thing as society, only individuals.
[130] See A. W. Turner, *A Classless Society: Britain in the 1990s* (2013).

for breach of the rules of the game (as well as on other grounds such as unworkability, lack of evidence, and so on).

The general trend, though striking, is not immutable: a number of factors could come together to undermine the growth of community sentiment—*Gemeinschaft*—that underpins the emerging consensus about the practice of politics: increasing inequality among members of the population, especially in the wake of the financial crisis of 2007–8; religious radicalism; sharpened political polarization over British membership of the European Union; and the breaking of promises of more devolution to Scotland, Wales, and Northern Ireland could generate political partisanship and polarization and undermine legitimacy and the parliamentary system, unless governments take steps to promote senses of social belonging.

The rules of the political game which are articulated in the soft law documents summarized earlier and in much hard law are, in reality, *foundational* (i.e. even more fundamental than principles of democracy and human rights, though they complement them) to the proper operation of the UK constitution. They require self-restraint by governments in the practice of politics. And this is the basis of an emerging new, *constitutional* consensus between government and the governed.

FURTHER READING

DAINTITH, T. C. and PAGE, A., *The Executive in the Constitution* (1999)

GRIFFITH, J. A. G, 'The Political Constitution' (1979) 42 *MLR* 1

PAGE, A. 'Executive Self-regulation in the United Kingdom' in T. Daintith (ed.), *Constitutional Implications of Executive Self-regulation: Comparative Experience* (1996)

VIBERT, F *The Rise of the Unelected: Democracy and the New Separation of Powers* (2007)

USEFUL WEBSITES

http://www.parliament.uk

http://www.civilservice.gov.uk

https://www.gov.uk/government/organisations/cabinet-office/about

https://www.gov.uk/government/organisations/committee-on-standards-in-public-life

12

REGULATION AND LEGITIMACY

Tony Prosser

SUMMARY

Although governments have to a large degree withdrawn from ownership of the economy, debate over public regulation has increased in recent years. This chapter examines the institutions and techniques used, including regulation of the public utilities such as telecommunications, energy, water, and rail but also referring to broader areas of regulation including financial services and health and safety. It is suggested that regulation has a number of rationales, notably control of natural monopoly, creating and policing competitive markets, protecting basic rights, and promoting social solidarity through the provision of universal service. The arrangements adopted for regulating the public utilities after privatization have improved, especially as a result of reforms introduced since 2000, though the regulators' work has proved much more complex than originally thought. Other regulators have also engaged in procedural innovation. The means available for challenging regulatory decisions remain inconsistent and untidy, although the existence of the Competition Appeal Tribunal permits detailed scrutiny of competition decisions. There may also be a greater concern with matters of legal principle in regulation as a result of European developments.

INTRODUCTION

There is a widely accepted view that the 1980s and 1990s were the epoch of a withdrawal of the state in favour of the marketplace. Yet, paradoxically, there is also a perception that regulation grew enormously during this period, so much that some writers now consider us to live in a 'regulatory state'.[1] Regulation is far more visible

---

[1] See e.g. G. Majone, 'The Rise of the Regulatory State in Europe' (1994) 17 *West European Politics* 77–101; M. Moran, *The British Regulatory State: High Modernism and Hyper-innovation* (2003).

than in earlier times, its extent inspires considerable public debate, and regulatory authorities themselves have a much higher profile than when government took a greater role in delivering services. Regulation is central to economic life, for example through the role of competition law and the regulation of the public utilities of telecommunications, energy, water supply, and rail transport, and also in relation to social provision, both public and private, notably in the health and education sectors. The paradox is, however, apparent rather than real. Even where government has withdrawn from direct provision of services, markets cannot be seen simply as the products of non-intervention, for they must be actively created and policed by public authorities. A vivid illustration of this was the financial crisis of 2008–9 which has been attributed both to inadequate regulation and the failures of unregulated markets. Even where public provision retains a role, there has been a marked stress on consumer empowerment through setting standards and inspecting performance against them, and in many areas regulators still take decisions on social principles rather than facilitating markets. These roles all raise constitutional issues of the legitimacy of regulatory decisions, issues that have only recently been fully addressed in British constitutional scholarship, and which are central to this chapter.

I shall adopt an institutional approach, examining some of the key institutional forms used by public actors to replace, shape, or intervene in markets or to develop regulation based on non-market principles. This will mean the neglect of many important areas; in particular the crucial one of 'self-regulation' will not be considered.[2] Nor will it be possible to consider in detail the institutions implementing general competition policy, nor the work of advisory bodies. I hope that there will be compensation for this loss of scope through the advantages of a focus on institutional issues; after all, institutional design is one of the key concerns of constitutional lawyers.

RATIONALES FOR REGULATION

There are several different rationales for regulation; these in themselves raise constitutional issues relating to the balancing of different principles and to the best institutional arrangement for resolving conflicts between them. Some rationales for regulation are based on economic principle. The first of these seeks to prevent the profit maximization of natural monopolies from distorting the efficient distribution of goods; the second seeks to resolve the problems which arise when markets operate freely, such as so-called 'externalities' which occur when the unregulated price of a good does not fully reflect its true cost to society (for example, the cost of pollution caused in its manufacture).[3] A further rationale is that of regulating for competition,

---

[2] For good discussions of the complexity of self-regulation, see I. Ayres and J. Braithwaite, *Responsive Regulation* (1992); J. Black, 'Decentring Regulation: Understanding the Role of Regulation and Self Regulation in a "Post-Regulatory" World' (2001) 54 *Current Legal Problems* 103.

[3] See e.g. A. Ogus, *Regulation* (1994), Pt I; and R. Baldwin, M. Cave, and M. Lodge, *Understanding Regulation* (2nd edn, 2012), Pt I.

where the regulator does not limit the operation of markets but develops and encourages them. This may take the form of promoting the creation of competitive markets in previously monopolistic areas; a notable example was that of energy supply. Just as important is the policing of markets after they have come into existence. This is of course primarily a task for general competition law, implemented both by the general competition authorities and by the sectoral utility regulators. It will also include the protection of consumers, now an essential task for the regulators of the public utilities and also of great importance in financial services regulation. In addition to the economic rationales, there is a quite different tradition of what is rather unhelpfully dubbed 'public interest regulation' based upon more general social or distributive principles. Thus some types of regulation, such as that of broadcasting, may be based on the protection of citizenship rights, for example to balanced news coverage; the protection of rights of patients including informed consent and quality of provision characterizes regulation in health and social care; and some regulation can be seen as promoting social solidarity, for example in providing universal access to services and contributing to sustainable development.[4]

Some of the most important regulatory innovations of recent years have been the arrangements adopted for the privatized utilities, notably telecommunications, gas and electricity, water, and railways. In the very limited official discussion available, the original rationale seems to have been conceived as primarily economic, concentrating on the control of monopoly.[5] However, if one examines the legal sources for the regulators' powers, the privatization statutes, and the licences of the utilities in question, one finds that in every case a predominantly economic rationale focused on requiring regulators to maximize economic efficiency seemed to play only a secondary role. In contrast, broader public interest considerations loomed large, for example ensuring that services were made available to meet all reasonable demands, including potentially unprofitable services, and that special consideration was given to the needs of vulnerable groups such as pensioners and the disabled.[6]

As mentioned earlier, regulation for competition has also played an increasing role. The Utilities Act 2000 was intended to replace the untidy mix of duties on the regulators by a new single competition-based primary duty, although it was at first only applied to the energy regulator. The new primary duty was to protect the interests of consumers, wherever possible by promoting effective competition. Subsidiary duties in respect of the elderly, disabled, and chronically sick were also included, and the Secretary of State was given new powers to issue guidance on social and environmental

---

[4] See e.g. the citizenship duty applying to the Office of Communications in Communications Act 2003, s. 3(1)(a); see also T. Prosser, 'Regulation and Social Solidarity' (2006) *J of Law and Society* 364.

[5] See the two official Littlechild reports: S. Littlechild, *Regulation of British Telecommunications' Profitability* (1984), and *Economic Regulation of Privatised Water Authorities* (1986).

[6] For further details, see T. Prosser, *Law and the Regulators* (1997), 15–24, and e.g. Telecommunications Act 1984, s. 3(1)(a). See also *R (T-Mobile (UK) Ltd, Vodafone Ltd, Orange Personal Communication Services Ltd)* v. *The Competition Commission and the Director General of Telecommunications* [2003] EWHC 1566 (QBD).

objectives to which regulators were required to have regard.[7] Similar provision is made for the water regulator in the Water Act 2003, while the Communications Act 2003 recasts the duties for regulation of telecommunications and broadcasting, including duties to further the interests of both consumers and citizens.[8] In the energy field, the regulator must have regard to the need to contribute to sustainable development, and the protection of consumers has been redefined to include reduction of carbon emissions and security of supply; the regulator must also consider whether means other than competition will best protect the interests of consumers.[9] Thus even in an area where economic regulation apparently predominates, there is in fact a mix of regulatory rationales, including social ones, making it particularly important to secure legitimacy for the resolution of conflicts between the different principles involved. In other areas, such as healthcare regulation, social rationales will clearly predominate. This means that institutional design is of considerable constitutional importance.

REGULATORY INSTITUTIONS

THE UTILITY REGULATORS

After the privatizations of the 1980s and 1990s, new regulatory agencies were established in relation to the public utility industries which seemed unlikely to operate in fully competitive markets; although they were by no means the first of the major UK regulatory bodies, they provide a useful introduction to the issues raised by regulatory institutions in general. The specialist agencies were the Office of Telecommunications (Oftel), the Office of Gas Supply (Ofgas), the Office of Electricity Regulation (Offer) (these latter two were later merged into the Office of Gas and Electricity Markets or Ofgem), the Office of Water Services (Ofwat), and the Office of the Rail Regulator (ORR). Each agency was headed by a director-general in whom the powers were vested personally; in this one sees a reflection of the highly personal style of UK government through ministers, and it was a key influence on the way in which these regulators operated in their early years. However, the agencies were deliberately distanced from ministerial responsibility through the adoption of the status of 'non-ministerial government department', a notion which seems curious given the centrality of ministerial responsibility in the UK constitution, but does seek to prevent accusations of political interference which could discredit the achievement of privatization. Most agency staff were seconded from the ordinary Civil Service for periods of about three years.

These arrangements underwent a process of reform, commencing with the Utilities Act 2000.[10] This established a new regulatory commission for the energy sector in

---

[7] Utilities Act 2000, ss. 9, 10, 13, and 14.   [8] Communications Act 2003, s. 3(1).
[9] Energy Act 2008 s. 83; Energy Act 2010, ss. 16–17.
[10] The background to this legislation is the Labour government's review of utility regulation: Department of Trade and Industry, *A Fair Deal for Consumers: Modernising the Framework for Utility Regulation*, Cm 3898 (1998), and *A Fair Deal for Consumers: The Response to Consultation* (1998).

the form of the Gas and Electricity Markets Authority.[11] The telecommunications and broadcasting legislation created a new communications regulator, the Office of Communications (Ofcom) in a commission form.[12] Provision was made to convert the Office of the Rail Regulator into a commission in the Railways and Transport Safety Act 2003, and the Water Act 2003 did the same for Ofwat. The commission model for regulation has now convincingly won in comparison to the older model of giving powers to an individual director-general. More recently, all the utility regulators have adopted a private sector model of a board, including executive and non-executive members; for example, the board of Ofgem consists of a chairman and four executive members, together with six non-executive members.

Finally, the effects of European Union (EU) liberalization are now of the greatest importance. For electronic communications, the 2002 regulatory package of directives requires that national regulatory authorities be established independent of those providing electronic communications services; this did not necessarily prevent regulation by a government department, but if the government retained a presence in providing services there had to be effective structural separation of the regulator from this. This was subsequently strengthened through a further requirement that they must not seek or take instructions from any other body, including government, in relation to the exercise of their tasks under EU law.[13] Similar provisions apply in the energy sector and were also strengthened to require greater regulatory independence.[14] Because of these developments, cooperation between the various regulatory authorities in Europe has become increasingly important (including through the establishment of European supervisory agencies for electronic communications and energy regulation), and it is these EU law requirements which are the most important for the spread of independent regulatory authorities beyond the UK, and for ensuring their guaranteed future.

However, it has always been the case that the government had the key role in shaping the environment in which the privatized enterprises operate. Ministers are responsible for important matters of general policy (for example, the broad mix of different sources of electricity generation). Apart from the fact that ministers appoint the regulators, it was ministers who initially possessed the major powers of deciding on the degree of competition which the enterprises would meet, through issuing licences (called 'authorizations' in the case of gas and 'appointments' in the case of water companies) necessary for the enterprises to do business; it was the conditions of

---

[11] See Pt I and Sched. 1.   [12] Communications Act 2003, s. 1.

[13] Council Directive (EC) 2002/21 on a common regulatory framework for electronic communications networks and services [2002] OJ L108/33, Art. 3(2); Council Directive (EC) 2009/140 amending Council Directive (EC) 2002/21 [2009] OJ L337/37.

[14] Council Directive (EC) 2009/72 concerning common rules for the internal market in electricity, [2009] OJ L211/55, Art. 35(4); Council Directive (EC) 2009/73 concerning common rules for the internal market in natural gas [2009] OJ L211/94, Art. 39(4). For discussion of the concept of independence in this context, see S. Lavrijssen and A. Ottow, 'Independent Supervisory Authorities: A Fragile Concept' (2012) 39 *Legal Issues of Economic Integration* 419.

these licences that determined the fundamental constraints in which the enterprises operate. The regulatory agencies were given the function of enforcing these conditions together with a number of other tasks, which include drawing up service standards (for example, relating to failure to maintain electricity supply or to meet agreed appointments with consumers) and monitoring performance by the utilities against them.

This apparent division of labour was however made less neat by the fact that the regulatory agencies were given functions relating to the modification of the licences, normally by agreement with the enterprise itself but, if this could not be obtained, through a reference to the Competition and Markets Authority (formerly the Monopolies and Mergers Commission). The agencies thus have a role in setting the basic rules of the game as well as monitoring their implementation, and it is this which has probably aroused the greatest controversy. In addition, government continued to possess important residual powers, including in some cases a power of veto over licence modifications. In gas and electricity, however, the power to issue licences has been transferred to the regulators rather than the minister and in the case of electronic communications EU law has severely limited discretion in the licensing process through providing a general entitlement to provide electronic communications services without the need for individual licences but subject to general conditions drawn up by Ofcom.[15]

The powers of the regulators to modify licence conditions have been extremely important as these powers have enabled regulators to amend the basic rules under which regulated enterprises operate. For example, regulators periodically set new price controls that limit the amounts regulated enterprises can charge for important services. Thus, for example, in the case of British Telecom, the initial control from 1984 was of RPI-3 which meant that controlled prices could rise by a figure 3 per cent below the rise in the retail price index measuring the prices of a range of products. This was subject to threats of tightening at least three times during the first five years; in 1989 it was amended to RPI-4.5 and extended to a broader range of services. Further revisions took place in 1991, 1993, 1997, and 2002; retail price control was finally abolished in 2006, although wholesale controls on prices charged to competitors remain. Licence conditions have also been used to require enterprises to trade fairly, and to meet social objectives such as avoiding disconnection of supply.

The duty to protect the interests of consumers is an important requirement for all the public utility regulators (except in rail, where this is primarily the responsibility of the Department for Transport), although the combination of roles as consumer champion and impartial arbiter between consumer and other interests is a potentially very difficult one. Part of the Labour government's early reforms was to create new, independent consumer bodies in energy, post, and water.[16] In communications, Ofcom

---

[15] Gas Act 1995, s. 5; Utilities Act 2000, s. 30; Communications Act 2003, Pt 2; and Council Directive (EC) 2001/22 [2002] OJ L249/21.

[16] See Utilities Act 2000, s. 2 and Sched. 2; Postal Services Act 2000, s. 2 and Sched. 2; and Water Act 2003, s. 35 and Sched. 2. The new bodies adopted the titles Energy Watch, Postwatch, and CC Water.

is also obliged to establish a Consumer Panel.[17] However, the move to independent, sector-specific consumer representation was later reversed after considerable tension and adversarial relations between consumer bodies and the regulators, culminating in a judicial review claim brought by the consumer body in postal services against the regulator.[18] The specialist bodies in energy and post were replaced with ombudsman schemes; consumer representation passed to the new general body, Consumer Focus, which undertook a detailed review of the operation of the utility and other regulators.[19] However, Consumer Focus was itself abolished as part of the review of arm's length bodies, with its functions passing to Citizen's Advice Bureaux.[20] The protection of consumers is also, of course, a major rationale for the exercise of the consumer functions of the regulators, as evidenced, for example, by the reference of the retail energy markets to the Competition and Markets Authority for a full competition investigation in 2014.

The key points about the regulatory institutions are thus that, while strongly distanced from governmental intervention in their ordinary operation, they work within a framework created by governmental decisions at the time of privatization, they have responsibilities determined by the privatization of particular industries rather than by a coherent sectoral approach (except in the case of electronic communications where the initiative has come from Brussels), and the original structure of individual directors-general reflected the personalized model characteristic of British government without as yet a clear procedural code. Nevertheless, we have seen some gradual moves towards a more coherent and consistent model since 2000, with the adoption of the commission model as standard and some clarification of the regulators' statutory duties, although uncertainty remains on the most appropriate means of consumer representation.

OTHER REGULATORY BODIES

The importance of the regulators of the public utilities in providing a regulatory model should not obscure the fact that there are many other types of regulation in the UK, some of which date back further than the 1980s. They exhibit a wide variety of institutional forms and functions. Some share the concern of the utility regulators with consumer protection; an important example has been that of financial services regulation. The Financial Services Authority was established under the Financial Services and Markets Act 2000 in the form of a private company limited by guarantee. It was given four regulatory objectives of market confidence, public awareness, the

---

[17] Communications Act 2003, s. 16.

[18] *R (on the application of the Consumer Council for Postal Services) v. Postal Services Commission* [2007] EWCA Civ 167.

[19] Consumers, Estate Agents and Redress Act 2007, ss. 30 and 42–52; S. Brooker and A. Taylor, *Rating Regulators* (2008).

[20] Public Bodies Act 2011, s. 1 and Sched. 1.

protection of consumers, and the reduction of financial crime, each defined more fully in subsequent sections of the statute.[21] However, with the financial crisis of 2008–9 the Authority was criticized as having failed to supervise effectively the rapidly changing developments which had undermined financial stability. The effectiveness of regulatory supervision had been severely weakened by, among other things, the range of different regulatory functions given to the same body, inadequate coordination due to complex and confused institutional relationships with the Treasury and the Bank of England, the limited role of national regulators in international markets, and the adoption of a 'light touch' approach to regulation.

A new system of financial services regulation was introduced under the Financial Services Act 2012 which created three regulatory bodies in order to achieve an increased emphasis on systemic financial stability rather than concentrating on individual actions or decisions within the markets. The first is the new Financial Policy Committee of the Bank of England, responsible for macro-prudential regulation; the second the Prudential Regulation Authority, a subsidiary of the Bank of England responsible for the prudential regulation of firms, and the third the Financial Conduct Authority responsible for consumer protection and markets regulation. The last adopted the existing legal corporate entity of the Financial Services Authority but has revised statutory objectives, with a strategic objective of securing that markets function well and three operational objectives including consumer protection and promoting effective competition in the interests of consumers.[22] The Authority will also be expected to take a more issues-based and forward-looking approach than its predecessor, and to be more prepared to take early preventative action to protect consumers.

In other areas of public policy, both regulatory form and regulatory functions vary dramatically. For example, some regulators such as the Food Standards Agency take the form of non-ministerial government departments; others, like the Care Quality Commission, are bodies corporate; many (like the latter Commission) do not have Crown status, whilst some do perform their functions on behalf of the Crown, notably the Food Standards Agency and the Health and Safety Executive. Some perform licensing functions through which they can regulate the performance of potentially controversial activities; a major example is that of the Human Fertilisation and Embryology Authority. This is responsible for licensing and inspecting clinics carrying out IVF and donor insemination treatment and establishments undertaking human embryo research. Others are more in the nature of inspectorates applying standards drawn up by government departments, notably the Care Quality Commission which is responsible for monitoring and enforcing registration requirements set out in regulations made by the Secretary of State. The Health and Safety Executive also has as one of its major roles enforcing regulations made by the Secretary

---

[21] Financial Services and Markets Act 2000, ss. 2(2) and 3–6.
[22] Financial Services Act 2012, s. 6, inserting a new s. 1B-L into the Financial Services and Markets Act 2000.

of State after a proposal from the Executive or after consulting it; the Executive also has a substantial policy role of its own.

It is thus very difficult to classify this wide range of regulatory bodies clearly by form or function. One common element is that the members of the regulatory bodies are appointed by ministers. However, even this conceals considerable variation; thus the Health and Safety Executive has a tripartite model in which employers, trade unions, and government are represented, and arrangements for security of tenure also vary widely, though in most cases dismissal of a board member during the contracted term of service is only possible for misconduct or incapacity rather than because of policy disagreement with the minister.[23]

Similarly, relations with government may be extremely diverse, although it is fair to say that no regulator is entirely independent of ministers in all its activities. For example, the primary duty of the Environment Agency is to make a contribution towards attaining the objective of sustainable development; however, what this means is defined by ministerial guidance and the duty only comes into operation when the guidance has been issued.[24] As mentioned earlier, some important regulatory bodies apply standards laid down by ministers through regulations; in many cases standards are also pervasively set by EU law. Thus it was estimated that by 2005 over 95 per cent of the legislation handled by the food standards agency originated from the EU, whilst in the fields of health and safety at work and environmental protection most standards are also EU-based.[25] As a result it does not make sense to assess any regulatory body in isolation; what is much more important is to examine the network of institutions in which it operates and which must be held accountable as a whole. This is particularly the case where there is a major EU role in regulation, for example in electronic communications and financial services markets, and where a number of regulatory institutions interact, notably in the new arrangements for financial services regulation. Nevertheless, something can be said about the accountability of regulators themselves, and it is to this that I shall now turn.

REGULATORY ACCOUNTABILITY

It is evident then that regulation involves difficult judgements based on a variety of factors, both social and economic. What are the procedures by which these judgements are made? The regulators are not elected nor are they subject to ministerial responsibility to Parliament. They therefore lack direct democratic legitimacy. Nor do they apply a coherent body of rules which have parliamentary approval; as we

---

[23] For more detailed coverage of a number of different regulatory bodies of this kind, see T. Prosser, *The Regulatory Enterprise* (2010).

[24] Environment Act 1995, s. 4; Department for Environment, Food and Rural Affairs, *The Environment Agency's Objectives and Contributions to Sustainable Development: Statutory Guidance* (2002).

[25] See B. Dean, *2005 Review of the Food Standards Agency* (2005), paras. 2.4.2 and 6.9.1.

saw earlier their statutory duties are vague, often contradictory, and remain difficult to interpret even after attempts to simplify them through stipulating new primary duties. Even where they apply standards developed through EU or ministerial processes, these typically leave considerable scope for autonomy in how they are applied by regulatory bodies themselves. Issues of regulatory accountability are thus of great constitutional importance.[26]

One way to achieve accountability may be, while accepting the inevitability of discretionary decisions, to design accountable decision-making procedures, as has been attempted in the USA.[27] It is argued that the legitimacy of the regulators' decisions would be increased through the requirement of open hearings involving the participation of affected interests, the giving of detailed reasons for decisions, and the availability of judicial review as a form of check on decision-making. The underlying rationale is a kind of pluralist one; the truth (if indeed such a thing exists) best emerges through the open testing of as many different conceptions of it as possible.[28]

The US practice was not however taken seriously in the design of the British regulators; it is fair to say that it was seen as a threat which would straitjacket regulators in legal complexities. Yet, the other extreme, which was adopted, of a near-total absence of mandatory structured procedures in regulation, faced considerable criticism. A couple of caveats need to be made here. First, the creation of the regulators of the public utilities resulted in considerably greater openness than was the case under nationalization, through imposing a form of external supervision which did not exist previously. Secondly, individual regulators have been, by the standards of British public bodies, exceptionally open in reaching their decisions. Moreover, taking regulatory bodies as a whole, considerable progress has been made in developing innovative regulatory techniques.[29]

A particularly interesting example of the evolution of regulatory procedures was that of Oftel, Ofcom's predecessor in regulating telecommunications. From the outset, the first Director General of Telecommunications promised an open approach, although he was criticized for failure to give proper reasons for fear of legal challenge.[30] During the directorship of Don Cruikshank during the mid-1990s further important steps were taken to ensure openness. An operating plan and work programme were published annually and the most important innovations concerned consultation procedures. It was already the practice to publish frequent consultation documents and to invite representations, but from March 1995 it was announced that all responses to consultations would be made public unless clearly marked confidential; the latter type

[26] For a particularly useful analysis of the accountability issues, see the House of Lords Constitution Committee, *The Regulatory State: Ensuring its Accountability*, HL 68 (2003–4).

[27] See e.g. Prosser, *Law and the Regulators*, 277–86; S. Breyer and R. Stewart, *Administrative Law and Regulatory Policy* (7th edn, 2011); G. Palast et al., *Democracy and Regulation* (2003).

[28] For a detailed discussion of this argument, see R. Stewart, 'The Reformation of American Administrative Law' (1975) 88 *Harvard Law Review* 1669.

[29] See Prosser, *The Regulatory Enterprise*, 233–4.

[30] See Oftel, *Annual Report 1985*, HC 461 (1985–6), para. 1.27.

of response might be given lesser weight by the regulator. Consultation would also incorporate a second stage; after representations had been received the director-general would be prepared to receive further comments on them for a period of 14 days, thus permitting review of submissions by others. Full explanations would be given for decisions, including references to the arguments of the parties consulted and a summary of views submitted.[31] In addition, public hearings would be employed as part of the consultative process. All these procedural innovations were used in decisions relating to price control, fair trading, and universal service. Regulation of telecommunications passed to Ofcom from the end of 2003; it also made a commitment to consult widely before reaching decisions, and is subject to various procedural duties under the Communications Act 2003, for example to review regulatory burdens, to carry out impact assessments, to publish promptness standards, and to establish, and consult, a Consumer Panel.[32] It has consulted extensively on major issues including public service broadcasting and telecommunications markets.

The other utility regulators also did much to open up their procedures, although it is fair to say that none went so far or developed such consistent procedures as Oftel.[33] More consistent arrangements were developed in the Utilities Act 2000 and in the later utilities statutes. Thus, for example, the energy regulator is required to develop a forward work programme annually after consultation and to give reasons for a wide range of decisions, including revocation and modification of licences and for enforcement action.[34] It is also under a duty to have regard to best regulatory practice, including accountability and proportionality.[35] Though divergencies are to some degree inevitable in substantive decisions made within any system of regulation which includes discretion, this is not necessarily the case in relation to procedures, where US experience shows that it is possible to adopt a reasonably standardized set through the Administrative Procedure Act.[36]

A key point is that the US legislation adopts different approaches to rule-making and adjudication. Relatively formal procedures, normally involving hearings with cross-examination, are prescribed for adjudication. Rule-making, while less formally prescribed, is also, however, subject to a number of structured procedural requirements, including as a minimum giving notice of the proposed rule and receiving comments on it, a minimum which has been supplemented in a variety of ways by agencies and courts.[37] In the UK, the Oftel model went a considerable way towards the US approach to rule-making; another model was adopted for financial services, where the Financial Conduct Authority is required to consult when it makes rules, including publishing cost–benefit analyses and its response to representations.[38] In relation to

---

[31] Oftel, *Consultation Procedures and Transparency* (1995).

[32] Communications Act 2003, ss. 6–8, 12, and 16.

[33] For details, see Prosser, *Law and the Regulators*, 83–6, 113–15, 144–7, 177–8, and 198–9.

[34] Utilities Act 2000, ss. 4, 42, and 87.   [35] Energy Act 2004, s. 178.

[36] See I. Harden and N. Lewis, *The Noble Lie* (1986), 302–10.

[37] See ibid., and for an example of rule-making on universal service under the US Telecommunications Act 1996, see Prosser, *Law and the Regulators*, 281–6.

[38] Financial Services and Markets Act 2000, s. 138(1).

more individualized decisions, legislation has also imposed duties to give reasons on the regulators in determining a number of types of individual disputes.[39] Moreover, many of the general administrative reforms of recent years will apply to the utility regulators; thus, as non-ministerial government departments they fall within the scope of the Freedom of Information Act 2000 and the jurisdiction of the Parliamentary Ombudsman; their exercise of administrative justice functions fell under the general review powers of the Administrative Justice and Tribunals Council, though this was abolished under the Coalition's review of arm's length bodies.

We do appear to be moving towards a more coherent procedural regime for decisions by the utility regulators, although it has to be said that the abolition of Consumer Focus and of the Administrative Justice and Tribunals Council have removed key parts of this regime without adequate replacement. The position is more complex for other regulatory bodies. Here a wide range of different procedures has been adopted. An important one is the holding of the meetings of regulatory boards in public; this is the practice of a number of regulators, notably the Food Standards Agency, the Environment Agency, and the Health and Safety Executive, and has met with considerable success. In most cases private meetings will have to be held as well to deal with confidential matters, but the important point is that policy-making takes place in public. In many cases open meetings are also required on the part of advisory committees, which are extensively used by some regulatory bodies. The tripartite nature of the board of the Health and Safety Executive, within which employers, the workforce and local and devolved governments are represented, means that affected interests are directly made part of the policy-making process. This also applies to the Executive's complex network of advisory committees. For example, detailed consultations take place in the preparation for the making of regulations; new construction regulations in 2007 went through a process of consideration by two working groups and a formal advisory committee before submission to ministers, and in all of these industry and workforce interests were represented. A discussion paper and consultation document were also published as part of the process. There was also a parliamentary debate on the new regulations.[40]

A further example of procedural innovation was the establishment by the Food Standards Agency of a permanent Advisory Committee on Consumer Engagement to review its processes. Such is the diversity of practice outside the utility regulators that it would be difficult to rationalize it into a common model, although better means could be created for comparing different procedural innovations and learning best practice from them.

Finally, parliamentary scrutiny has played a more important role than was initially envisaged, especially in relation to the utility regulators.[41] Thus their work on

[39] See e.g. Competition and Service (Utilities) Act 1992, ss. 17, 23, 34, and 36.

[40] They became the Construction (Design and Management) Regulations 2007 (SI 2007/320).

[41] See D. Oliver, 'Regulation, Democracy and Democratic Oversight in the UK' in D. Oliver, T. Prosser, and R. Rawlings (eds.), *The Regulatory State: Constitutional Implications* (2010).

particular subjects has been frequently examined by select committees; perhaps most importantly, the House of Lords Select Committee on the Constitution published a major report in 2004 on *The Regulatory State: Ensuring its Accountability*, followed three years later by an examination of *UK Economic Regulators* by a newly established Committee on the Regulators.[42] Detailed work on the regulators is also carried out by the National Audit Office and the Public Accounts Committee, examining both the work of individual regulators and the utility regulators as a group.[43] Alongside this is the extensive process of regulatory reform, through which regulatory bodies are subject to detailed review to minimize regulatory burdens and increase regulatory responsiveness.[44] A further initiative was been joint examination by the National Audit Office and the Better Regulation Executive of a number of regulators to assess to what extent they had implemented better regulation principles.

APPEALS AND JUDICIAL REVIEW

A further important element of accountability is the existence of opportunities to check the decisions of the regulators through appeal or judicial review; this is an area where there is considerable inconsistency at present.[45] In the case of some older regulators, enforcement was undertaken through use of the courts; this remains the case for the Health and Safety Executive, the Environment Agency, and some other regulators. Here of course the normal appeal mechanisms in the judicial system will be available. However, there has been a growing trend to give direct enforcement powers to regulators themselves without the need to go to court; moreover, many decisions other than those involving direct enforcement of regulatory requirements will have important implications for those regulated and for others.

In the case of the utility regulators, one form of appeal is the role of the Competition and Markets Authority, through an appeal or reference to the Authority against a modification of a licence condition.[46] In a different form involving a reference by the regulator, a similar procedure has existed since the establishment of the utilities regulators, and this older model is retained in the case of water. The main role of this procedure was in practice to put pressure on companies to agree to modifications so as to avoid such a reference and the resulting delay and heavy commitment of management time. There were a number of high-profile references; indeed, such a reference was crucial in preparing the ground for the opening up of the gas market to competition. The threat of referral had great advantages as a sanction for

---

[42] HL 68 (2003–4); HL 1889 (2007–8).

[43] e.g. National Audit Office, *Pipes and Wires*, HC 723 (2001–2); Public Accounts Committee, *Pipes and Wires*, HC 831 (2002–3). For discussion, see E. Humpherson, 'Auditing Regulatory Reform' in D. Oliver, T. Prosser, and R. Rawlings (eds.), *The Regulatory State: Constitutional Implications* (2010).

[44] For a summary, see Prosser, *The Regulatory Enterprise*, ch. 10.

[45] For a detailed analysis, see T. Prosser, 'The Place of Appeals in Regulation: Continuity and Change' in Centre for the Study of Regulated Industries, *Regulatory Review 2004/5* (2005).

[46] Gas Act 1986, s. 23B–23G; Electricity Act 1989, s. 11C–11H; Water Industry Act 1991, ss. 14–16.

the regulator. The current energy procedures, introduced as a result of the EU Third
Energy Package of reforms, appear much closer to an ordinary appeal, although they
go to the Authority not to the Competition Appeal Tribunal. Energy appeals may be
made not only by the company directly affected but by competitors, trade associa-
tions, or Citizens Advice.

Even considering only the utility regulators, a 'mish-mash' of different arrangements exists in relation to other decisions. The most important development has been
in the case of electronic communications licensing, where a right of appeal on the
merits to the Competition Appeal Tribunal is provided by the Communications Act
2003 for any person affected by the decision; considerable use of this right has been
made by regulated companies.[47] This full appeal is due to the special requirements of
EU law in relation to the liberalization of telecommunications.[48] There is a further
appeal on a point of law for a party or anyone else with a sufficient interest to the Court
of Appeal.[49] Where the regulators exercise their concurrent powers with the Office of
Fair Trading to apply the Competition Act 1998, there is a right of appeal on the merits
to the Competition Appeal Tribunal and then on a point of law to the Court of Appeal;
provision is also made for third-party appeals by a person with a sufficient interest.[50]
Such appeals have played an important role. Thus in one third-party appeal, the Court
of Appeal noted the breadth of the appeal right to the tribunal, permitting the latter,
where it differs from the regulator on questions of law, fact or evidence, to remit a
decision or substitute its own decision; it did not however have the power to instruct
the regulator how to proceed if the case was remitted. The Tribunal and the Court of
Appeal in this case also considered arguments based on the European Convention on
Human Rights (ECHR), arguments which are likely to be increasingly important in
relation to regulatory decisions.[51] In a number of cases, the Tribunal has had to consider in detail complex matters involving economic analysis.[52] Yet another different
model applies where financial penalties are imposed by a utility regulator; here there is
a right of appeal to the High Court against the penalties and their amount on grounds
similar to judicial review.[53] Certain decisions of the energy regulator in relation to
the organization of the wholesale markets may be appealed to the Competition and
Markets Authority on specified grounds.[54]

---

[47] Communications Act 2003, s. 192. Such an appeal also applies in competition-based broadcasting
decisions: s. 317.

[48] Council Directive (EC) 2002/21 on a common regulatory framework for electronic communications
networks and services [2002] OJ L108/33, Art. 4(1).

[49] Communications Act 2003, s. 196.

[50] Competition Act 1998, ss. 46–9, as amended by Enterprise Act 2002, s. 17.

[51] *Office of Communications* v. *Floe Telecom Ltd* [2006] EWCA Civ 768. On the scope of the Tribunal's
powers, see also *Vodafone Ltd* v. *British Telecommunications plc* [2010] EWCA Civ 391.

[52] For a rehearing involving such detailed economic analysis, see *Albion Water Ltd* v. *Water Services
Regulation Authority* [2006] CAT 23.

[53] Utilities Act 2000, ss. 59 and 95; Postal Services Act 2000, ss. 30–7; Transport Act 2000, s. 225; Water
Act 2003, s. 48.

[54] Energy Act 2004, ss. 173–7.

A further development may be of considerable importance in this context. The Macrory review of regulatory penalties recommended that regulatory bodies should be able to impose 'monetary administrative penalties' as an alternative to criminal prosecution; appeals would be heard by a Regulatory Tribunal rather than by the courts.[55] Implementation has taken place through the Regulatory Enforcement and Sanctions Act 2008 empowering ministers to authorize regulators to employ such sanctions; appeal lies to the First-tier Tribunal created by the Tribunals, Courts and Enforcement Act 2007.[56] The power to impose such penalties has not been made widely available to regulators, though the Environment Agency has been given some such powers, but the existence of the General Regulatory Chamber of the Tribunal may provide the impetus for a more rational system of administrative appeals.

In other cases judicial review will be the only remedy against regulatory decisions, for example after a licence modification has been made.[57] Once more, the US experience has in the UK been seen as offering lessons as to what should be avoided, and so there has been a reluctance to accept that the courts should play a central role in establishing principles for the operation of the regulatory bodies. Experience so far suggests that there will not be automatic resort to judicial review by those disappointed by regulatory decisions, despite the willingness of the courts to accept such challenges not only by judicial review but, in certain cases where contracts are involved, by private law action.[58] This has not resulted in a flood of cases from those regulated despite initial fears that it might do so.

In the USA, over-enthusiastic judicial review of issues of substance rather than of procedure has been identified as a major cause of the 'ossification' of the rule-making process.[59] The UK courts have in general intervened in matters of procedure while not double-guessing regulators on matters of substance. In the first case of judicial review of a utility regulator, judicial review was sought of a refusal by the Director General of Gas Supply to order reconnection of gas to the applicant's home after allegations of meter tampering.[60] The application was successful on the ground of procedural impropriety because the applicants had been given no opportunity to comment on evidence obtained by the director general from a meter reader, although all grounds alleging substantive illegality were rejected. The court stressed the broad discretion conferred on the director general and his autonomy as regards questions of fact. A similar stress on the breadth of the substantive discretion of the regulator appeared in later cases

---

[55] R. Macrory, *Regulatory Justice: Making Sanctions Effective—Final Report* (2006).

[56] Regulatory Enforcement and Sanctions Act 2008, Pt III.

[57] For a comprehensive account of the courts and related bodies here, see R. Rawlings, 'Changed Conditions, Old Truths: Judicial Review in a Regulatory Laboratory' in D. Oliver, T. Prosser, and R. Rawlings (eds.), *The Regulatory State: Constitutional Implications* (2010).

[58] *Mercury Communications* v. *Director General of Telecommunications* [1996] 1 All ER 575 (HL); see also A. McHarg, 'Regulation as a Private Law Function?' [1995] *PL* 539.

[59] T. McGarity, 'Some Thoughts on "Deossifying" the Rulemaking Process' (1992) 41 *Duke LJ* 1385, 1400, 1410–28.

[60] *R* v. *Director General of Gas Supply, ex parte Smith*, CRO/1398/88 (QBD), 31 July 1989.

attempting to challenge substantive decisions.[61] Thus, in the frequent situation of a conflict between different statutory duties of the regulator, 'he is given the choice how that conflict is to be resolved, and to decide priorities, and so long as he bears in mind the entirety of his duties, has a predisposition to fulfil all the duties so far as this is practicable and with those duties in mind makes a decision which promotes one or other of the objectives specified (and is rational), his decision stands and is not open to challenge'.[62] In the context of rail, making a decision which had particularly important implications for the role of competition in the industry, the Administrative Court emphasized that given the regulator's expertise in a highly technical field, it would be 'very slow indeed' to impugn the regulatory decision, and that it was no part of the Court's function to substitute its own view on matters of economic judgement.[63] This approach is not limited to the utility regulators; for example, the House of Lords emphasized the width of discretion of the Human Fertilisation and Embryology Authority in a challenge to the grant of a licence to permit the creation and use of embryos for diagnosis in the context of saving a sibling child. Thus '[t]he Authority was specifically created to make ethical distinctions and, if Parliament should consider it to be failing in that task, it has in reserve its regulatory powers'.[64]

In other cases the courts have taken a more interventionist approach, for example in a decision relating to the different treatment of two electricity licence holders.[65] Although it has correctly been criticized as misunderstanding the role of the (then) Monopolies and Mergers Commission in the licence-modification process, the decision does at least appeal to a principle of equal treatment rather than simply reassessing the substantive merits of the regulatory decision.[66] A decision that the use of prepayment devices in water was unlawful is also best understood as preventing the by-passing of the rigorous procedural safeguards applying to the disconnection of water supply.[67] Thus these decisions are not simply examples of over-detailed judicial intervention in the substance of regulatory discretion. Indeed, it is the establishment of expert regulators with discretionary powers which has done most to prevent such 'ossification' of decision-making.[68]

[61] R v. Director General of Telecommunications, ex parte British Telecommunications plc, CO/3596/96 (QBD), noted by C. Scott in (1997) 8 Utilities LR 120; R v. Director General of Telecommunications, ex parte Cellcom Ltd [1999] ECC 314; R (T-Mobile (UK) Ltd, Vodafone Ltd, Orange Personal Communication Services Ltd) v. Competition Commission and Director General of Telecommunications [2003] EWHC 1566 (QBD).

[62] Ex parte Cellcom, at [25], per Lightman J.

[63] Great North Eastern Railway Ltd v. the Office of Rail Regulation [2006] EWHC 1942.

[64] R (on the Application of Quintavalle) v. Human Fertilisation and Embryology Authority [2005] UKHL 28, [2005] 2 AC 561, at [28], per Lord Hoffmann. The concluding reference is to the minister's power to make regulations on the subject of the litigation in question.

[65] R v. Director General of Electricity Supply, ex parte Scottish Power, noted at (1997) 8 Utilities LR 126. See also A. McHarg, 'A Duty to be Consistent? R. v. Director General of Electricity Supply, ex parte Scottish Power' (1998) 61 MLR 93.

[66] See McHarg, 'A Duty to be Consistent?'

[67] R v. Director of Water Services, ex parte Lancashire County Council and others, The Times, 6 March 1998, noted by D. Legge, sub nom R v. Director of Water Services, ex parte Oldham Metropolitan Borough Council [1998] 9 Utilities LR 123.

[68] For a grossly inappropriate judicial role in the substance of economic regulation in the absence of a regulator in New Zealand, see the decision of the Privy Council in Telecom Corporation of New Zealand

Increasing liberalization and the move towards competition law prohibitions more susceptible to judicial enforcement are, of course, likely to lead to increased litigation; however, this is largely to be conducted through appeal to the Competition Appeal Tribunal rather than through the use of judicial review. Similarly, rights under the ECHR may increasingly be claimed as a means of challenging regulatory decisions. For example, in *Marcic* a claim was brought against a sewage provider in nuisance and under the Human Rights Act 1998, claiming repeated foul flooding of the claimant's property breached both ECHR, Art. 8 providing the right to respect for one's home, and Art. 1 of the First Protocol, providing for the peaceful enjoyment of possessions.[69] The claim was rejected in the House of Lords on the ground that there was a statutory scheme of regulation which was the appropriate vehicle for prioritizing work taking account of the balance between the rights in question and the acceptable qualifications to them, in particular the interests of the community as a whole. The statutory scheme set an appropriate balance between Convention rights and interests limiting them; moreover the regulator 'is a public authority within the meaning of the 1998 Act and has a duty to act in accordance with convention rights'.[70] The implication is clearly that a regulator has a central role in deciding on the application of Convention rights and in balancing qualified rights in the environmental field against competing public interests. This should open up considerable scope for rights-based arguments addressed to the regulatory body itself, and for judicial review of the resulting decisions.

A further area which may prove to be of great importance is that of the recovery of damages for infringement of Convention rights. The availability of damages for administrative illegality is restricted in UK law, nor are damages automatically recoverable for infringement of a right under the ECHR. However, in the *Ingenis* case where the energy regulator was held to have made an error of law which had deprived a company of a financial benefit to which it was legally entitled, the Court of Appeal was prepared to award substantial damages based on an infringement of Art. 1 of the First Protocol.[71] The case concerned an error of law rather than an exercise of discretion by the regulator, but it may have considerable potential for encouraging future litigation.

Other Convention rights may also found challenges; in the regulation of communications, the Art. 10 right to freedom of expression is of particular importance. In considering a challenge to a finding by Ofcom that generally accepted standards had not been complied with by the broadcaster of a radio interview, which had degenerated into a shouting match and contained highly offensive language, the High Court emphasized that the Court itself had to decide whether there was a disproportionate infringement of the right to freedom of expression. Although the

---

v. *Clear Communications Ltd* [1995] 1 NZLR 385; cf. *Albion Water Ltd* v. *Water Services Regulation Authority* [2006] CAT 23 before the Competition Appeal Tribunal.

[69] *Marcic* v. *Thames Water Utilities Ltd* [2003] UKHL 66, [2004] 2 AC 42.
[70] Ibid., at [71], *per* Lord Hoffmann.
[71] *Gas and Electricity Markets Authority* v. *Infinis plc* [2013] EWCA Civ 70.

political nature of the programme justified a high degree of protection of the right, the gratuitously offensive and abusive nature of the broadcast meant that Ofcom's finding was justified.[72]

A further issue of importance is the question of whether, in those areas where judicial review is the only remedy available against regulators, this is sufficient to comply with the ECHR, given that Art. 6 protects the right to a determination of civil rights by an independent and impartial tribunal established by law. The attitude of the UK courts so far is that the current law, as developed after the Human Rights Act 1998 to permit more searching review, does comply with the requirements of Art. 6. However, the cases in which this has been determined may be distinguished either as concerning matters of policy where there is a legitimate role for a minister accountable to Parliament, or as not involving the determination of a free-standing Convention right.[73] By contrast, regulatory decisions do not necessarily involve matters of policy in this sense. Furthermore, the right to peaceful enjoyment of possessions under Art. 1 of the First Protocol may be at issue, for example where a regulatory decision affects freedom of an enterprise to trade. We are likely to see some interesting attempts to challenge regulatory decisions in the courts over the next few years; moreover, the background of a Convention right is likely to result in more searching review, notably on the basis of proportionality.[74] Meanwhile, the mess of different types of procedures for challenging decisions by the regulators needs urgently to be cleared up. A general appeal right to the Competition Appeal Tribunal from the economic regulators, with appeal to the General Regulatory Chamber of the First-tier Tribunal in other cases, is one solution which would avoid the possibility of successful challenge for breach of Art. 6. A similar appeal right was in fact proposed by the House of Lords Constitution Committee, but was one of its few recommendations to be rejected by the government.[75]

Another possibility is the use of private law actions, for example in misfeasance in public office, against regulators. Such a case was brought against the Bank of England in its former regulatory role in relation to the banking system, where statute explicitly provided immunity for anything done by the Bank in its regulatory role in the absence of bad faith. The case was discontinued on the direction of the court part way through with no liability being found on the part of the Bank; the hearing had by then run for 255 days, with opening speeches by counsel of 90 and 119 days, at a cost of £100 million (not including earlier hearings on points of law, which had resulted in

---

[72] *Gaunt* v. *Ofcom* [2010] EWHC 1756 (QB).

[73] *R. (on the application of Alconbury Developments Ltd)* v. *Secretary of State for the Environment, Transport and the Regions* [2001] UKHL 23; *Runa Begum* v. *Tower Hamlets London Borough Council* [2003] UKHL 5.

[74] See *Belfast City Council* v. *Miss Behavin' Ltd* [2007] UKHL 19; cf. *R (on the application of Pro-Life Alliance)* v. *BBC* [2003] UKHL 23.

[75] House of Lords Constitution Committee, *The Regulatory State: Ensuring its Accountability*, paras. 219–32; *The Regulatory State: Ensuring its Accountability: The Government's Response*, HL 150 (2003–4), paras. 60–73.

the litigation overall lasting for a period of 12 years).[76] The heavy criticism by the judge of the conduct of the case may well deter such actions in the future.

CONCLUSIONS

Many of the problems described earlier result from the difficulty of fitting bodies such as regulators into the constitutional structure; accountability has tradition-ally been based almost exclusively on ministerial responsibility to Parliament and, despite the long history of regulatory boards not headed by ministers, other means for accountability have not been developed with any degree of sophistication. What was particularly striking on the establishment of the utility regulators was the personal-ized nature of regulation; the assumption seemed to be that appointing an acceptable personality as regulator would ensure a high-quality result. This in turn reflected the traditionally highly personalized traditions of constitutional government in the UK, once more based around ministerial responsibility rather than any stronger concept of the state and of administrative law.[77] The reforms undertaken since 2000 have moved away from the personalized model to regulatory boards and towards a more coherent system of procedural requirements for the regulatory process. However, as we have seen with the procedures for challenging regulatory decisions, considerable inconsist-ency remains, especially in relation to appeal rights. The absence of normative prin-ciple reflects a more general problem of constitutional thought in the UK,[78] and the absence of clearly applicable constitutional norms of due process has encouraged the highly pragmatic approach described, though again there are signs of a more coherent approach since 2000.

Any attempt to reform regulation more widely in order to create a more coherent system must recognize the sheer breadth of different types of regulation going beyond the economic sphere. Although the coalition government elected in 2010 took steps to cut the number of regulatory bodies, this amounted more to reorganization and merg-ers rather than wholesale abolition. More important is the taking of general powers for ministers to abolish, merge, or modify by order a number of arm's length bodies, though they do not include the regulators discussed here.[79] This was based on the belief that accountability was best secured by policy and discretionary decisions being taken within core government subject to ministerial responsibility to Parliament.

However, a rule-based system of regulation with only limited regulatory discre-tion, or the wholesale lifting of regulatory burdens, are unlikely to be effective given

---

[76] *Three Rivers District Council* v. *The Governor and Company of the Bank of England* [2006] EWHC 816 (Comm).

[77] See K. Dyson, *The State Tradition in Western Europe* (1980).

[78] See T. Daintith, 'Political Programmes and the Content of the Constitution' in W. Finnie, C. Himsworth, and N. Walker (eds.), *Edinburgh Essays in Public Law* (1991), 41.

[79] Public Bodies Act 2011, Part 1 and Sched. 1.

the impossibility of reducing the range of regulatory principles to a limited number of determinate rules. This would also have the effect of limiting severely the ability of regulators to respond to the rapidly changing environments in which they operate. Similarly, requiring that the decisions of regulators be based as far as possible on economic rather than social criteria does not reflect the range of different regulatory objectives and functions as defined by statute; if anything there has been a tendency for even the utility regulators to move towards accepting a greater role for social considerations in their decisions rather than the reverse, and this is recognized both in the reforms since 2000 and in broader European developments. A further uncertainty is in relation to legal challenges in the courts and the role of the Human Rights Act 1998; although private law actions are less likely after the failure of the case brought against the Bank of England over BCCI, it is possible that the use of judicial review will increase and that the Act will both encourage more searching judicial scrutiny and require further procedural development by the regulators themselves.

What is needed can perhaps be summarized as a greater concern with procedural and substantive principle. I have stressed that initially it was at the level of procedure that the regulatory arrangements seemed at their weakest as a matter of law, but here reforms since 2000, building on best practice of the regulators themselves, were the beginning of moves towards a more principled system. Indeed, there has been increased concern within government itself about regulatory procedure and there have been attempts to develop more coherent procedural systems across regulation in general through the regulatory reform initiatives which have been of growing importance; one theme within them is to increase regulatory responsiveness.[80] The time is ripe for incorporating the lessons learned into a more general Regulatory Reform Act setting out standardized procedures for regulation, especially for consultation and for challenge of decisions.[81]

Secondly, we need to develop further substantive principles of regulation in place of the highly empirical approach taken so far. Unresolved questions include: What is regulation for? What is the relationship between economic and social goals? What rights to services are implied by constitutional requirements and particular statutory arrangements? Impetus to this approach may be given by the increasing amount of regulatory intervention in these areas at the European level, which may lead to a less pragmatic and more litigious approach to regulation in the future and so may force these issues to be more effectively confronted than has been the case in UK domestic law. Already utility liberalization has been accompanied by a clearer definition of concepts of universal service, notably in telecommunications but also in postal services where, for the first time, UK law needed to provide such a definition. Indeed, it can

---

[80] See Prosser, *The Regulatory Enterprise*, 214–18.

[81] Despite its title, the Legislative and Regulatory Reform Act 2006 performs the quite different function of facilitating the ministerial lifting of regulatory burdens, whilst also requiring some regulators to have regard to minimal principles of better regulation. Nor does the Enterprise and Regulatory Reform Act 2013 make any attempt to standardize regulatory procedures.

be argued that this is the source of a growing body of public service law reflecting both Continental traditions of public service and the necessary conditions to make market liberalization politically and socially legitimate.[82] It is also striking that it is through the implementation of European obligations that a more satisfactory appeal process was provided in electronic communications. Similarly, European developments have led to a rationalization of the historically highly pragmatic arrangements for the policing of competition in the UK, and have also resulted in the creation of a specialist court in the form of the Competition Appeal Tribunal. As a result of these developments, we now have the foundations for undertaking a discussion of regulation in terms of constitutional principle, something not characteristic of previous UK debate. It is certainly much needed; the financial crisis may indeed have had the effect that '[t]hose who think the global market economy can be run without regulation or with self regulation or light-touch regulation have been entirely routed'.[83] However, the debates on the constitutional contribution to types of regulation which avoid the problems shown up in the crisis are only beginning.

FURTHER READING

BALDWIN, R., CAVE, M., and LODGE, M., *Understanding Regulation* (2nd edn, 2012)

HOUSE OF LORDS SELECT COMMITTEE ON THE CONSTITUTION, *The Regulatory State: Ensuring its Accountability*, HL 68 (2003–4)

MORGAN, B. and YEUNG, D., *An Introduction to Law and Regulation* (2007).

OLIVER, D., PROSSER, T., and RAWLINGS, R., *The Regulatory State: Constitutional Implications* (2010)

PROSSER, T., *Law and the Regulators* (1997)

PROSSER, T., *The Regulatory Enterprise* (2010)

USEFUL WEBSITES

Financial Conduct Authority: **http://www.fca.org.uk**

Health and Safety Executive: **http://www.hse.gov.uk**

Human Fertilisation and Embryology Authority: **http://www.hfea.gov.uk**

Ofcom: **http://www.ofcom.org.uk**

Ofgem: **http://www.ofgem.gov.uk**

Ofwat: **http://www.ofwat.gov.uk**

Office of Rail Regulation: **http://www.rail-reg.gov.uk**

---

[82] See T. Prosser, 'Public Service Law; Privatization's Unexpected Offspring' (2000) 63 *Law and Contemporary Problems* 63–82.

[83] Ed Balls, MP, quoted in 'Ministers Accused of Regulatory Amnesia', *The Financial Times*, 23 September 2008.

13

PUBLIC EXPENDITURE AND THE CONTROL OF PUBLIC FINANCE

John McEldowney

SUMMARY

Political and economic pressures for the reduction of the budget deficit continue to require major cuts in public expenditure. This has had simultaneous effects on the delivery of many public services across most sectors of the economy. The financial crisis and political influences dominate the technical rules of financial reporting and control, with significant constitutional ramifications and potential for tensions between party political controls and parliamentary accountability. The former are used by the government to pass the budget and undertake public spending; the latter allows Parliament to hold the government to account. Too often party political controls tend to dominate parliamentary systems and procedures, allowing the government to secure its spending plans. Treasury influence in policy matters related to the economy and in controlling budgets has intensified. The government's economic forecasts are subject to evaluation by the Office of Budget Responsibility, created after the 2010 election, which is itself audited by the National Audit Office (NAO) and is answerable to Parliament through the Treasury Select Committee. The Bank of England has been given pre-eminent responsibility over banking regulation, a restoration of its historic role, with the abolition of the Financial Services Authority (FSA) in 2010. The NAO is increasingly called on to consider the implications of government policy under governance reforms through a newly created Board. The Local Audit and Accountability Act 2014 provides for the abolition of the Audit Commission and the transfer of audit responsibility over local government to local auditors operating under a new Code of Audit Practice and the supervision of the National Audit Office from 2015. Current and future Public Finance Initiative (PFI) projects are under intensive review with a likely shift to simple public procurement as an alternative. More generally the question is how to reconcile the provision of financial information to Parliament, including the systems of audit and accountability, with the Coalition government's overarching policy of reducing the budget deficit and public borrowing. The use of public expenditure controls for such unprecedented budget cuts is likely to have a lasting impact on the systems of financial audit and control that are subject to political policy and in reducing effective parliamentary oversight. In the final analysis parliamentary procedures are overshadowed by powerful executive influences.

INTRODUCTION

The main focus of this chapter is on the management and control of central government funds available for the government's own use or for that of other parts of the public sector. For reasons of space the implications of devolution, regional policies, and local government for public expenditure are not covered in this chapter.

Controlling public expenditure involves: surveying public expenditure as a whole in relation to resources; improving management of the public sector through strict financial controls; and providing the opportunity for parliamentary control through improved financial information.[1] The unprecedented growth in public spending of the 2000s, the financial crisis[2] and support for the main clearing banks since 2008, aggressive use of quantitative easing that currently stands at over £375 billion (about 14 per cent of annual nominal GDP) all necessitated[3] the Treasury's Spending Review 2010. This involves a planned overall 40 per cent cut across public spending that is set to continue after the election in 2015 and beyond to 2018, when it is hoped the economy will begin to make a surplus. Quantitative easing has continued and is a sign of the vulnerability of economic growth and volatility of financial markets.[4] Uncertainties about the UK's continued EU membership and the outcome of further financial powers to devolved administrations are also likely to overshadow the functioning of public expenditure controls for the foreseeable future, and may raise doubts over the reduction of the financial deficit.[5] There is not however the space to go into these issues here.

The management and control of central government expenditure is best understood on the basis of the chronology of budgetary operations.[6] This involves a

---

[1] House of Commons Library Research Papers, *Government Borrowing, Debt and Debt Interest Payments, Historical Statistics and Forecasts*, SN/EP/5745 (23 July 2014).

[2] A budget deficit of 11.1% of GDP set tough challenges for effective public expenditure controls. Public sector net borrowing of around £60 billion is set to remain at 7.05% of GDP with a forecasted reduction of borrowing not expected until 2018/19 depending on favourable economic conditions and on a broadly optimistic assessment public sector net debt is projected to be 76% of national income.

[3] Michael A. S. Joyce and Marco Spaltro, *Quantitative Easing and Bank Lending: A Panel Data Approach*, Bank of England, Working Paper No. 504 (August, 2014); Julia Black, *Managing the Financial Crisis: The Constitutional Dimension*, LSE Working Papers (12/2010) and 'The Credit Crisis and the Constitution' in D. Oliver, T. Prosser and R. Rawlings (eds.), *The Regulatory State: Constitutional Implications* (2010). J. F. McEldowney, 'Debt Limits in German Constitutional Law: A UK Perspective' in Wolf-Georg Ringe and Peter M. Huber (eds.), *Legal Challenges in the Global Financial Crisis* (2014), 63–78.

[4] John Wanna, Lotte Jensen, and Jouke de Vries, *Controlling Public Expenditure* (2003); Alex Brazier and Vidya Ram, *The Fiscal Maze* (2006).

[5] R. Bacon and C. Hope, *Conundrum: Why Every Government Gets Things Wrong—and What We Can Do About It* (2013).

[6] House of Commons Library Research Paper, *Budget 2014: Background Briefing* SNEP- 06828 (14 March 2014) contains details of the 2014 budget and economic forecasts for the economy.

planning phase before expenditure is undertaken and an accountability phase thereafter. The planning phase is undertaken by the Treasury's Annual Public Expenditure Survey (PES) through Treasury-appointed departmental Accounting Officers. In the case of trading funds[7] the Treasury appoints the chief executive as the Accounting Officer. The accountability phase is carried out through the audit of public funds under the NAO. The Treasury's financial data and economic forecasts are subject to regular review by the recently created Office for Budget Responsibility.

This chapter is structured as follows. First of all, the institutions relevant to the control of public expenditure and their roles in the process are surveyed. Secondly, attention is given to the processes of planning public expenditure. Thirdly, the accountability phase through the audit of public expenditure is assessed. Finally, some conclusions are offered as to the adequacy of financial control in the context of the planned reductions in public expenditure amidst uncertainties about devolution and regional policy and EU membership.

GOVERNMENTAL INSTITUTIONS

Central government is the amalgam of departments, ministers, and civil servants found at the heart of policy-making and the delivery of public services. The creation of various agencies falls under the responsibility of central government if they are in receipt of public funding which is authorized through a government department.

ACCOUNTING OFFICERS

Each government department has an Accounting Officer[8] appointed by the Treasury under the Government Resources and Accounts Act 2000, and directly responsible to the House of Commons for the authorization and control of departmental expenditure. If the permanent head of a department is appointed as an Accounting Officer, he is known as the Principal Accounting Officer and in large departments is supported by a Principal Finance Officer and the Principal Establishment Officer. Chief executives of agencies established under the Next Steps initiative may be designated Agency Accounting Officers. Accounting Officers appointed by the Treasury may be assigned to distinct revenue and expenditure arrangements involving public funds. Accounting Officers are obliged to undertake two functions: to ensure that resources in their department deliver departmental objectives 'in the most economic, efficient and effective way' taking account of regularity and propriety; and to ensure that there is adequate internal audit conforming to the *Government Internal Audit Manual* and

---

[7] Trading Funds are established under Treasury supervision and might include executive agencies or related bodies. See HM Treasury, *A Guide to Set Up Trading Funds* (2006).

[8] See the Treasury guidance, *Managing Public Money* (updated annually), ch. 3.

under the current version of *Managing Public Money*, ch. 3 (a guidance manual for public accounting).[9]

Ministers may be held to account in matters of public expenditure by the departmental Accounting Officer[10] who is answerable in turn to Parliament through various Committees of the House of Commons. Specifically, Accounting Officers may be asked to defend the performance of their wider responsibilities for the economy, efficiency, and effectiveness of departmental expenditure before the Public Accounts Committee (PAC).[11] There is a presumption that the Accounting Officer will maintain, even in the face of ministerial resistance, the standards of strict financial propriety and regularity as well as 'prudent and economical administration, efficiency and effectiveness'.

In the *Pergau Dam*[12] affair of 1995 the minister overruled the Permanent Secretary of the Overseas Development Administration acting as Accounting Officer, who had reservations about the economy and efficiency of the grant in aid to Malaysia for the construction of a dam. Guidance for resolving such disputes is contained in *Managing Public Money*, as is the 'template' for the use of what are termed 'Dear Accounting Officer Letters'[13]. The affair demonstrated weakness in Treasury procedures: ministers may, under certain circumstance, override the decisions of Accounting Officers. Ultimately the expenditure was held to be ultra vires, but was paid for out of a Reserve Fund.[14] As far as is known, however, the *Pergau Dam* case is a rare exception to the normal expectation that reservations expressed by Accounting Officers should be acted upon.

Reliance on the Treasury to oversee financial controls is gaining in importance. Increases in Treasury statutory powers under the Banking Act 2009, ss. 74 and 75, which enabled the Treasury to make regulations relating to the fiscal consequences of any banking stabilization powers, led to expressions of concern by the House of Lords Delegated Powers and Regulatory Reform Committee that the Treasury's powers lacked sufficient parliamentary scrutiny.[15] The retrospective nature of the powers was also criticized by the House of Lords Constitution Committee.[16] Despite the concerns the Treasury's powers remained in the Banking Act 2009.

---

[9] There are a variety of documents available from the Treasury on the work of the Accounting Officer, including Cabinet Office, *Best Practice Handbook*.

[10] See HM Treasury, *Managing Public Money*, October 2007, foreword and para. iii,

[11] See e.g. Department for Education, NAO, *Communications with Component Auditors*, August, 2014

[12] R v. *Secretary of State for Foreign Affairs, ex parte World Development Movement Ltd* [1995] 1 All ER 611 (*Pergau Dam*). See F. White, I. Harden, and K. Donnelly, 'Audit, Accounting Officers and Accountability: The Pergau Dam Affair' [1994] *PL* 526–34. This affair is discussed further later.

[13] HMT, *Dear Accounting Officer(DAO) Letters*, HM Treasury, 26 June 2014.

[14] See further discussion later.

[15] House of Lords, *Delegated Powers and Regulatory Reform Committee Session 2008–09*, HL 12, paras. 3–4.

[16] House of Lords, *Select Committee on the Constitution Banking Bill*, Third Report Session 2008–9, HL 19, and 11th report, HL 97.

THE TREASURY AND THE CHANCELLOR OF THE EXCHEQUER

The Treasury fulfils a dual function in being a government department and also holding government departments to account through a system of internal controls over public expenditure. These functions are combined through the requirement of Treasury authority for lawful expenditure, and Treasury supervision of expenditure undertaken by departments.[17]

The development of resource accounting and resource budgeting under the Government Resources and Accounts Act 2000, fully operational since 2003–4, is intended to gauge public expenditure more accurately than previously. Whole Government Accounts include accounts of bodies within central government,[18] trading funds, and public corporations including NHS Trusts and Foundation Trusts.

The Green Paper, *The Governance of Britain*[19] in July 2007 set the steps to simplify financial reporting to Parliament. The aim was to align the different bases on which financial information was reported to Parliament and ensure continuity between different formats. This builds on the principles laid before Parliament since 1998 in the Treasury's Code for Fiscal Stability, comprising transparency, stability, responsibility, and fairness and efficiency in the formulation of fiscal policy.[20] The Alignment (Clear Line of Sight Project) undertaken by the Treasury engages with the aims of greater transparency.

The Fiscal Responsibility Act 2010 strengthened the Code. It has since been repealed and replaced by the Budget Responsibility and National Audit Act 2011. This Act created the new Office for Budget Responsibility and also modernized the governance arrangements for the National Audit Office. Under s. 1 of the 2011 Act, there is the *Charter for Budget Responsibility* (HM Treasury, 2011). This is a detailed formulation and implementation of fiscal policy and policy for the management of the national debt. Financial control is supported by the document, HM Treasury, *Improving Spending Control* (April 2012). There is an annual Financial Statement and Budget Report containing the details of the government's policy. The Coalition government has adopted two fiscal rules to constrain government spending and borrowing as follows:

- Fiscal mandate: the structural current budget must be forecast to be in balance or in surplus at the end of the five-year Parliament.

- The supplementary target states that public sector net debt as a share of national income should be falling by a fixed date of 2015/16.

---

[17] See the Treasury Committee, *Evidence on the Role of the Treasury*, HC 73 I–II (2000–1).

[18] This also includes local authority accounts that are linked to trading funds and central government accounts.

[19] Green Paper, *The Governance of Britain*, Cm 7170 (July 2007), also see the earlier White Paper, *Modernising Government*, Cm 4310 (March 1999).

[20] HM Treasury, *Improving Spending Control* (April 2012).

It is also expected that the Treasury should make regular progress reports to Parliament to ensure that the strategy to provide reductions in borrowing and for sound finances in the relevant Economic and Fiscal Strategy Reports and Pre-Budget reports is observed.

The Act provides Parliament with the power to vote on the government's medium-term fiscal plans including proposed borrowing and debt totals. The Coalition government formed in 2010 is expected to meet the borrowing expectations in the Act.[21] The Office for Budgetary Responsibility (OBR)[22] was set up when the Coalition government took office after the election in May 2010. The Budget Responsibility and National Audit Act 2011 provides that the OBR's role is to make independent budget forecasts for public finances and the economy. It is unclear how far the OBR can rely on departmental and Treasury information while retaining its independence. The nature of any parliamentary scrutiny is also uncertain if the Coalition government succeeds in its ambition to continue fixed-term five-year Parliaments for the future. This is likely to require organizational changes in the conduct of the business of the House related to the length of the Parliament.[23]

The Chancellor of the Exchequer presents the annual budget, containing a financial statement and review of taxation levels, to the House of Commons in the spring of each year. For a brief period from 1993 to 1996, the government adopted a 'unified budget' covering both the government's tax plans[24] for the coming year *and* the government's spending plans for the next three years. In July 1997 the Labour government reverted to spring budgets with a Pre-Budget Report announced in the autumn of each year. In May 2010 there was an emergency budget after the Coalition government took office, accompanied by a detailed breakdown of departmental spending.

The timetable for the financial year from April to March coincides with the announcements of taxation and spending plans. In addition to the oral budget statement to the House of Commons the Financial Statement and Budget Report contains an analysis of financial strategy and proposed plans and developments.[25] Treasury control of the purse will be at its most intense with the implementation of the Spending Review 2010 under the system of Whole Government Accounts.

The Treasury[26] was the central department responsible for regulating financial institutions as part of a Tripartite Agreement between the Treasury, the Bank

---

[21] House of Commons Library Research Papers: *Budget 2014: Background Briefing*, SNEP-06828 (14 March 2014).

[22] See House of Commons, *Government Borrowing, Debt and Debt Interest Payments: Historical Statistics and Forecasts*, Standard Note SN/EP/5745 (23 July 2014); HM Treasury, *Consolidated Budgeting Guidance from 2012–13* (March 2012).

[23] House of Commons Library Research Papers, *The Office for Budget Responsibility*, SN/EP/5657 (24 June 2014).

[24] Tax Law Review Committee, *Making Tax Law*, TLRC Discussion Paper No. 3 (2003) advocating simplification of the tax system and reviewing parliamentary scrutiny of tax legislation.

[25] House of Commons Library Research Papers, *The Budget and the Annual Finance Bill*, SNB13 (5 December 2013). Also see House of Commons Library Research Papers, *LIBOR, Public Inquiries and FCA Disciplinary Powers*, SN/BT/6376 (29 July 2014).

[26] The Treasury has considerable powers to freeze assets of individuals under the Crime and Security Act 2001.

of England, and the Financial Services Authority under the revised Memorandum of Understanding 2002. The Tripartite arrangements ended in April 2013 when the Bank of England received new responsibilities as supervisor of the United Kingdom's financial infrastructure under the Financial Services (Banking Reform) Act 2013.[27]

THE BANK OF ENGLAND

The Bank of England, the UK's central bank, acts as a banker to the government, and with the other major banks is a member of the clearing system. Since 1997[28] the Bank of England has had operational responsibility for the setting of interest rates to meet the government's inflation target. The Bank of England Act 1998 provides a statutory framework for the Bank's role. There is a requirement, under s. 4, of annual reports to the Chancellor of the Exchequer which must be laid before Parliament. There is a Monetary Policy Committee of the Bank that meets on a monthly basis and sets interest rates. This removed interest rates from the political objectives of the government of the day. Membership of the Monetary Policy Committee is subject to confirmation hearings by the Treasury Select Committee who may question the proposed appointee.[29] The Treasury Select Committee holds regular sessions on policy with the Bank of England including regular hearings with the Monetary Policy Committee and the newly created Financial Policy Committee, with statutory responsibility for maintaining financial stability of the UK economy. The Chancellor of the Exchequer provides broad policy parameters for the Bank. The UK's decision not to enter the euro in 1998 is one example[30] of the powerful influence of Gordon Brown when Chancellor under Tony Blair's premiership.[31] Accountability for the new arrangements is through a report to the Treasury Committee and to the House of Commons. The Bank issues a Quarterly Inflation Report, a Quarterly Bulletin containing research and analysis, and an Annual Report and Accounts of its activities. The Bank also publishes the Financial Stability Report containing informed debate about financial stability. In extreme economic circumstances the government retains the right to override the Bank, but subject to ratification by the House of Commons.

The Bank of England's *Framework for Monetary Policy*[32] has twin objectives: to deliver price stability through the government's inflation target and to support the

---

[27] See Bank of England, Prudential Regulation Authority, 'Consultation Paper Strengthening Accountability in Banking: A New Regulatory Framework for Individuals', July 2014 FCA CACP14/13/PRACP14/14.

[28] Hansard, HC, col. 508 (20 May 1997).

[29] Hansard, HC 520 (1999–2000). The Treasury Committee's views are not binding on the Treasury, and only in one instance was the nominee challenged by the committee.

[30] R. Ware, *EMU: The Constitutional Implications*, House of Commons Research Paper 98/78 (27 July 1998).

[31] For a full account, see A. Rawnsley, *The End of the Party* (2010), 188–97.

[32] The accounts held in the Bank of England on the government's behalf are the Consolidated Fund and the National Loans Fund. Also held are the accounts of the Inland Revenue and Customs and Excise (the Revenue Departments), the National Debt Commissioners, and the Paymaster General. There are detailed

government's economic policy. The Bank's performance over the past years has been subject to public debate[33] especially since the banking crisis.[34] The setting of interest rates by the Bank and removal from overt political manipulation by the government of the day resulted in economic stability and low inflation prior to the financial crisis from 2008.[35] The UK economy is also scrutinized by external organizations such as the International Monetary Fund (IMF) and the Organisation for Economic Co-operation and Development (OECD),[36] providing the Bank with comparative analysis in making decisions about the UK economy.[37] The Bank's performance is regularly monitored by what was the House of Lords Select Committee on the Monetary Policy Committee of the Bank of England, now the House of Lords Economic Affairs Committee. The financial crisis led to substantial criticism[38] of the Tripartite arrangements of banking regulation. Banking failures led to the whole or partial nationalization of four major banks and two building societies and the injection of capital sums into the banking sector amounting to nearly £117 billion by the end of December 2009. After the formation of the Coalition government in May 2010 there followed the unexpected abolition of the FSA, and the return of financial regulatory powers to the Bank of England. The transfer of many of the functions of the FSA to the Bank of England has resulted in a new system of financial regulation under the Financial Services Act 2012 comprising the following: the Financial Policy Committee, responsible for macro-prudential regulation and testing the resilience of the financial system of the UK economy; the Prudential Regulation Authority, an independent subsidiary of the Bank of England responsible for micro-prudential regulation of financial institutions and assessing balance sheet risk and the regulation of around 1,700 financial firms;[39] the Financial

internal rules for the various financial transactions carried out by central government departments including the use of credit cards, debit cards, and the handling of receipts and payments. The Monetary Policy Committee comprises four external members appointed by the government, the Governor of the Bank of England, two Deputy Governors, and two other senior officials of the Bank. Meetings are attended by a non-voting Treasury representative. The decision is frequently made by majority vote: see Bank of England Act 1998, Pt I and *Framework for Monetary Policy* (21 October 1999).

[33] HM Treasury, *Reforming Britain's Economic and Financial Policy: Towards Greater Economic Stability*, ed. E. Balls and G. O'Donnell (2002).

[34] John F. McEldowney, 'Managing Financial Risk: The Precautionary Principle and Protecting the Public Interest in the UK' in J. R. Labrosse, R. Olivares-Caminal, and D. Singh (eds.), *Risk and the Banking Crisis* (2011). J. F. McEldowney, 'Defining the Public Interest: Public Law Perspectives on Regulating the Financial Crisis' in J. R. Labrosse, R. Olivares-Caminal, and D. Singh (eds.), *Financial Crisis Management and Bank Resolution* (2009), 103–32.

[35] Members of the eurozone are subject to the Resolution of the European Council on the Stability and Growth Pact [1997] OJ C236/1.

[36] OECD, *OECD Economic Surveys: United Kingdom* (2005). There are also IMF country reports.

[37] The Bank has a useful working paper series that provides authoritative analysis of the economy.

[38] FSA, *The Turner Review: A Regulatory Response to the Global Banking Crisis* (March 2009).

[39] The Prudential Regulation Authority is required to promote the safety and soundness of firms and also to ensure that policyholders are protected. See House of Commons Library Research Papers, *The Independent Commission on Banking: The Vickers Report*, SNBT 6171, 30 December 2013. House of Commons Library Research Papers, *Banking Executives' Remuneration in the UK*, SNBT-6204 (13 January 2013), HL Paper 27-II (19 June 2013).

Conduct Authority responsible for the conduct of business and markets regulation. The latter will supervise firms in the UK providing financial products and services in the UK and international customers.[40] The new arrangements give a pivotal role to the Bank of England and seek to adopt a preventative stance to avoid and prevent another financial crisis.

PARLIAMENT

'Parliamentary control of the purse' is a basic principle of the constitution that has evolved since before the Bill of Rights 1689.[41] The authority of the Commons over these matters is based on its powers over expenditure and taxation.[42] *Managing Public Money*, the Treasury's code of expenditure rules, stipulates the protection afforded by the constitutional principle of the requirement of statutory authorization for the expenditure of public funds and for the raising of finance through taxation. The nature of the protection rests on three principles, namely that propriety and regularity require parliamentary approval for departmental activities and services; that the Treasury may exercise delegated approval for departmental expenditure subject to ultimate parliamentary authority; and finally, that parliamentary authority, while at times dependent on Treasury support for much of its control mechanisms, is nevertheless paramount.

The requirement of statutory authority instituted by Gladstone in the mid-nineteenth century created a 'circle of control' based on an annual cycle of revenue and expenditure. The management of public revenue is carried out by the Crown. Strong party controls over the members of the House of Commons and the general influence of ministers where the government has a majority in the House of Commons reduce the House of Commons' powers of control in practice to the right to criticize.

The Constitutional Reform and Governance Act 2010, introduced by the previous government, takes forward the Line of Sight (Alignment) Project, instituted since 1997, to bring transparency to financial reporting to Parliament.[43] The inclusion of the public spending element of non-departmental bodies into financial reporting is an aid to transparency. The enhancement potential for Parliament is dependent on MPs being willing to include public finance in their scrutiny functions.

[40] See House of Commons Library Research Papers, *LIBOR, Public Inquiries and FCA Disciplinary Powers*, SN/BT/6376 (29 July 2014).

[41] Bill of Rights 1689, Art. 4 requires parliamentary authority for the raising of taxation. See G. Reid, *The Politics of Financial Control* (1966); M. Wright, *Treasury Control of the Civil Service 1854–1874* (1969); D. W. Limon and W. R. McKay (eds.), *Erskine May: Parliamentary Practice* (22nd edn, 1997), 732 (23rd edn, 2004, ed. W. R. McKay).

[42] See Parliament Acts 1911 and 1949.

[43] Since 1997 this is subject to the NAO auditing the forecasts to ensure that Treasury assumptions are made transparent, though the system of making forecasts is not open to such scrutiny. See Fabrizio Balassone and Daniele Franco, 'Public Investment, the Stability Pact and the "Golden Rule"' (2000) 21(2) *Fiscal Studies* 207–9.

The centrality of government rather than backbench control over expenditure deci-sions is evidenced in Standing Orders of the House of Commons Nos. 46 and 47, which provide the Crown with the initiative and sole responsibility for expenditure. Private members, including the opposition, are unable to propose increased charges on public funds or to initiate legislation involving expenditure out of public funds without a financial resolution. The initiative is with the government as the Commons may not impose conditions on the grants authorized or the resources applied for without the demand by the government.

An Appropriation Act satisfies the requirement for statutory authority through the supply procedure of the House of Commons on an annual basis by means of the Consolidated Fund Acts and by an Appropriation Act. Revenue collection is largely undertaken through HM Revenue and Customs, and as part of the Budget and Public Finance Directorate of the Treasury.

SUPPLY PROCEDURE AND THE CONSOLIDATED FUND

The supply procedures required to enable the House of Commons to vote supply and provide the government with funds from the Consolidated Fund held at the Bank of England are technical and formal.[44] Little substantial scrutiny[45] is involved in such procedures. The policy objectives on which the money is spent are not determined by the Commons but by the government of the day. Policy objectives, however, under-line the constitutional authority of Parliament and the internal controls exercised by the Treasury. It must be emphasized that presentation of the main estimates to Parliament does not provide sufficient authority for expenditure. Statutory author-ity in the Appropriation Act is required. The system is complicated by the fact that in any one parliamentary session Parliament is asked to authorize not only estimates for the current year but also Votes on Account for future years and any excesses from the previous year.

Supply estimates provide the House of Commons with the information needed to provide the government with funds from the Consolidated Fund. Votes on Account and the Consolidated Fund Act must be approved by the date of the budget. Estimates of departmental expenditure are drawn up and must be approved by resolutions of the Commons for the necessary release of funds from the Consolidated Fund. The Treasury publishes a single volume entitled *Central Government Main Estimates* con-taining one estimate for each department. The estimates provide the major part—over 70 per cent—of annual public expenditure. The Treasury persuaded Parliament in 2001 to replace cash-based Appropriation Accounts with Simplified Estimates and Departmental Resource Accounts.[46]

---

[44] House of Commons Library Research Papers, *House of Commons Budget Debates and Finance Bills Parliamentary Information List*, SN/PC/02271 (10 July 2014).

[45] William McKay and Charles W. Johnson, *Parliament and Congress* (2010), 254–61.

[46] HM Treasury, *Central Government Supply Estimates 2002–3 for the Year Ending 31st March 2003: Main Supply Estimates*, HC 795 (2001–2).

An annual Appropriation Act, which is normally not subject to any debate, is enacted by July/August each year, authorizing the Bank of England to make payments to government from the Consolidated Fund. The Appropriation Act gives statutory authority for the distribution of money between votes, but this often follows the spending of some of the money, which needs only the Consolidated Fund Act (giving a total figure) for approval. The estimates must conform to Treasury format and approval and must not be altered unless Treasury authority has been granted.[47] There are two Appropriation Acts in each parliamentary session, one in March for the previous financial year, the other in July for the current main estimates.[48] The audit carried out by the Comptroller and Auditor General (C&AG) discussed later is focused on the estimates which, when divided into heads of expenditure, appear as 'votes'.

Departments work on the supply estimates in the summer or early autumn of each financial year. On or about the time of the budget each year, the estimates are published. If a department's needs exceed the estimates, then a 'supplementary' may be passed subject to Treasury and parliamentary approval. The Standing Orders of the Commons provide the government with three opportunities to introduce supplementary estimates, with the benefit of a guillotine procedure ensuring their speedy passage. Supplementaries may be presented in June, in November, and in February. At other times of the year estimates may be submitted but without the benefit of the 'accelerated' guillotine' procedure. In 2004 the government introduced a change that gives select committees up to 14 days to consider supplementary estimates.

The Treasury takes very seriously the requirement for statutory authority for authorization of public expenditure which 'must be and can only be given year by year by means of votes and the Appropriation Act'.[49] A minister 'when exercising functions which may involve the expenditure of money may only do what he does if Parliament votes him the money'.[50] Since 1982, there have been three specific days to consider the estimates. The Commons may only reduce the estimates, but even this is unlikely if the

---

[47] See HM Treasury, *Managing Resources—Full Implementation of Resources Accounting and Budgeting* (April 2001).

[48] The reform was the result of the work of the Liaison Committee, the PAC, the Treasury Committee, and the Procedure Committee. See Procedure Committee, *Estimates and Appropriation Procedure*, HC 393 (2003–4).

[49] Details of the rules relating to supply may be found in *Supply Procedure, Government Accounting* (2000, rev.) The Appropriation Act begins life as the Consolidated Fund (Appropriation) Bill. Estimate day debates may take place in July and at the time of the Appropriation Act; in November–December for the winter supplementary estimates followed by any debates and a Consolidated Fund Act; and in February–March for the spring supplementary estimates, followed by any debates on the Consolidated Fund Act. HM Treasury, *Supply and other Financial Procedure of the House of Commons* (1977), paras. 47–9, now largely updated by *Supply Procedure, Government Accounting*. The PAC considered in 1932 the question whether the Appropriation Act is sufficient authority for the expenditure, whether there is or is not specific statutory authority for the service concerned. The Treasury accepted that, provided the government of the day undertakes to ask Parliament for authorization, services under the Appropriation Act would come within the PAC Concordat. However, in the first instance, it is preferable to seek specific statutory authority. The estimates indicate where proposed expenditure is to be met by the Appropriation Act as the sole authority.

[50] HM Treasury, *Supply and other Financial Procedure of the House of Commons*, paras. 47–9.

government of the day has an overall majority. In modern times the Commons has not rejected an estimate and the scrutiny function appears a limited one.

Over the years the presentation of the estimates has become more readable. Today they contain economic information and are cross-referenced to the Departmental Report. Since an agreement in March 1995 between the PAC, the government, and the Treasury Committee to introduce a simplified format of the estimates with effect from 1996–7, the estimates are published in a single volume divided into three parts and linked to overall government planning. There is a new requirement on departments to produce an Estimate Memorandum to their parliamentary select committee at the same time as main or supplementary estimates are presented. Improvements in the presentation of financial reporting have been in place since 2009. Amendments to the Provisional Collection of Taxes Act 1968, that allow the government to collect taxes, have resulted in a resolution being given the same statutory effect since the budget report in 2011. This change in procedure is partly as a result of the introduction of fixed term Parliaments in 2011 of five years to allow for the carry-over of business at the end of the session. There are limits to the duration of the resolution of seven months to allow time for the relevant Finance Bill to be given legal effect. The experience in 2012 and 2013 has been subject to criticism[51] as not giving sufficient time for scrutiny especially when Finance Bills are over 600 pages long and only allotted two days for debate and there are delays between stages of the bill's passage through Parliament.

THE CONTINGENCIES FUND

An example of a lacuna in Commons control over expenditure is the Contingencies Fund which may be used to finance urgent expenditure. The fund is a reserve fund intended to meet unforeseen items of expenditure and where advances that are made are regarded as 'exceptional'. In technical terms it is used 'to meet payments for urgent services in anticipation of parliamentary provisions for those services becoming available'. Total advances outstanding from the fund should not exceed 2 per cent of the previous year's total estimates provision.[52] Money withdrawn from the Fund must be repaid. The Treasury may authorize payment out of the Fund subject to the limit of 2 per cent set under the Contingencies Fund Act 1974. The instructions contained in *Managing Public Money* and *Supply Estimates: A Guidance Manual* provide that the criterion is not convenience, but urgency in the public interest. If the amount of money involved, or the potentially contentious nature of the proposal is such as to create difficulty in justifying anticipation of parliamentary approval, it may be necessary to present a Supplementary Estimate, outside the normal timetable, to be followed by a special Consolidated Fund Bill.

---

[51] Treasury Committee Budget 2013, HC 1063 of 2012 (20 April 2013); Treasury Committee Fourth Special Report of Session 2012–13, HC 1076 (26 March 2013).

[52] See *The Contingencies Fund Account 2009–10*, HC 373 (22 July 2010).

The Contingencies Fund is unusual in that the main scrutiny of the government's use of the Fund largely depends on effective Treasury rather than parliamentary control. Legislation giving authority for the expenditure involved must be introduced at the earliest possible time and ought never to be postponed. Guidance issued in 1992 makes clear that the government of the day must be prepared 'to take the responsibility of assuming that legislation being considered by parliament will pass into law'.[53]

The Contingencies Fund has been used for a variety of purposes and recently for the funding of the London Olympics in 2012.[54] Historically, this includes relief of national disasters, the manufacture of the first atomic bomb, victory celebrations, and, in time of war, for financing urgent supplies. It funded the Pergau Dam project following the decision of the divisional court declaring the aid to be ultra vires.[55] In 2008–9 advances from the Fund to the Department of Transport amounted to £1.5 billion plus £0.6 billion to the Ministry of Defence for normal departmental spending. Significantly, the Contingencies Fund was used to support the making of payments in the banking crisis through the use of a Supplementary Estimate of over £42 billion for the banks' recapitalization.[56] No amendment or debate occurred in the grant of this request though generally the financial crisis was the occasion for many questions and debates more generally. Concern about the use of the Contingencies Fund is focused on the question of parliamentary accountability. The total expenditure from the Fund is considerable, but there are no clear statutory conditions for expenditure from the Fund. Reliance is placed on the system of internal Treasury control and audit[57] by the C&AG. No select committee directly monitors the use of the Fund and there are no satisfactory means to inquire into the policy behind the government's use of the Fund prior to the Fund being used. Any *ex post facto* inquiry faces a corresponding difficulty as the money has already been spent. The fact that the money is to be repaid seems hardly an adequate safeguard when questions arise about the purpose for which the Fund has been used.

Doubts about the legality of the existence of the Fund in the past have given way to greater risk analysis of the use of the Fund and tighter Treasury oversight. Parliament has, in effect, through inactivity allowed an exception in the form of the Contingencies Fund to the principle that Parliament should vote money before expenditure is incurred. There is also tacit acceptance that Treasury control may be more effective in this instance than parliamentary scrutiny, especially as such internal controls include robust systems of risk assessment.

---

[53] See J. McEldowney 'The Contingencies Fund and the Parliamentary Scrutiny of Public Finance' [1988] *PL* 232–45.

[54] NAO, *London 2012 Olympic Games and Paralympic Games: Post Games Review*, HC 794 Session 2012–13 (2 December 2012).

[55] See discussion later.   [56] Hansard, HC, vol. 482, col. 952 (2007–8).

[57] See *Contingencies Fund 2004–05*, HC 755 (3 March 2006).

THE COURTS

The courts have, since the sixteenth century, accepted Parliament's role in the matter of financial control. There is limited opportunity for judicial oversight in matters of expenditure. Public finance issues that arise before the courts involve issues of taxation—the supply side. Central government cases include *Auckland Harbour Board v. The King*,[58] in which Viscount Haldane noted that payments out of the Consolidated Fund without parliamentary authority were illegal. In *Woolwich Building Society v. Inland Revenue Commissioner (No. 2)*[59] the House of Lords articulated the general principle that money paid to a public body pursuant to an ultra vires demand for tax should be repayable as of right. The *Woolwich* case arose out of an Inland Revenue demand for tax from the Woolwich Building Society. The demand was later declared by the courts to have no legal basis. It was accepted that although the money paid to the Revenue was not paid under any mistake of law on the part of the taxpayer, the Woolwich Building Society had no express statutory right to repayment of the money. The House of Lords held that money paid pursuant to an ultra vires demand was prima facie repayable as a common law right of the subject. In the *Woolwich* case the payment of tax amounted to almost £57 million with interest and dividends, an illustration of the role of the courts in revenue matters which can have a substantial indirect effect on expenditure totals. The government has estimated that the total cost of repaying composite rate tax to all building societies which had overpaid amounted to £250 million. There is also the prospect of challenges due to the Human Rights Act 1998.[60] A challenge from 'tax-paying pacifists'[61] seeking to adopt the jurisprudence of the European Court of Human Rights on European Convention on Human Rights (ECHR), Art. 9 (freedom of thought and conscience) to challenge the use of taxation for military purposes was rejected by the Court of Appeal. This does not rule out the use of ECHR, Art. 9 arguments in the future, depending on how far the Strasbourg court is willing to develop its jurisprudence on human rights into this area.[62]

---

[58]   [1925] AC 318, 326.

[59]   [1992] 3 All ER 737, 764 D–E (see also Lord Slynn at 783E–G). J. Beatson, 'Restitution of Taxes, Levies and Other Imposts: Defining the Extent of the Woolwich Principle' [1993] 109 *LQR* 401. *Pepper v. Hart* [1993] 1 All ER 86 on the taxation of benefits in kind which may lead to £30 million in refundable taxes.

In *Metzger and others v. Department of Health and Social Security* [1977] 3 All ER 444 the duty of the Secretary of State for Social Services to carry out reviews of the rates of pension payable under the Social Security Act 1975 was considered and the cost of uprating pension benefits ascertained. The impact on public expenditure would have been large if the court had decided to grant a declaration. In the event it refused to do so.

[60]   *R (Wilkinson) v. IRC* [2005] UKHL 30, and *R (Morgan Grenfell) v. Special Commissioner* [2002] STC 786.

[61]   *R (on the application of) Boughton v. Her Majesty's Treasury (The Peace Tax Seven Case)* [2005] EWHC 1914 (Admin), and [2006] EWCA Civ 504.

[62]   See *R (Wilkinson) v. IRC* [2005] UKHL 30.

It is accepted that the role of the courts generally in decisions on taxation and public expenditure[63] has been slight, but there is scope for future development, especially in expenditure related to health care and social service delivery. In *R(W)* v. *Birmingham City Council*[64] a restriction by the Health Authority only to fund social care for critical needs was declared illegal.[65] However, the Supreme Court in *McDonald*[66] was reluctant to interfere with policy decisions on how best to allocate funds for the care of a patient with severe mobility problems who claimed for a night-time care assistant rather than the use of incontinence pads, the cheaper option. The case is illustrative of the dilemma and challenges facing public authorities under austerity budgeting and is indicative of the Supreme Court's reluctance to overturn policy-based public expenditure decisions.[67] In *Pergau Dam*[68] (see earlier), the applicant, an international pressure group, challenged the legality of aid granted by the Secretary of State for Foreign Affairs to fund the construction of the Pergau Dam in Malaysia. The pressure group relied on information obtained through an NAO Report and information gleaned from debates and evidence taken by the PAC and the Foreign Affairs Committee. The NAO and the PAC assumed the legality of the aid but criticized aspects of its value for money. However, it was revealed in various correspondences that the Accounting Officer had serious reservations about the project.

Despite such Accounting Officer reservations written ministerial instructions were given to proceed with the financial aid. The Pergau project was funded, purportedly under Overseas Development and Co-operation Act 1980, s. 1. The Divisional Court held that the provision of aid was ultra vires the 1980 Act. As a result of this decision, the C&AG qualified his opinion of the aid on the basis of irregularity. Despite this

---

[63] In 1975, in *Congreve* v. *Home Office* [1976] QB 629, the Court of Appeal held that it was unlawful for the Home Office to make use of its revocation powers under the Wireless Telegraphy Act 1949 to revoke TV licences so as to prevent licence holders benefiting from an overlapping licence purchased to avoid an increase in the licence fee. Congreve and about 20,000 other licence holders had purchased a second licence, while their existing licence was still valid in anticipation of an increase in the licence fee. Lord Denning claimed that the Bill of Rights 1689 had been infringed as a there had been a levying of money without grant of Parliament. There is some doubt on this interpretation as Congreve had sought avoidance of a tax through the purchase of a second licence, clearly not intended by the Wireless Telegraphy Act 1949. However, the case illustrates how the judges will use statutory interpretation to uphold the principle of authorization. In *Bowles* v. *Bank of England* [1913] 1 Ch 57, Bowles was successful in suing the Bank of England for declarations that income tax could not be deducted by virtue of a budget resolution alone, and until such tax had been imposed by Act of Parliament he was not required to pay it. The case provided the background for what is now the Provisional Collection of Taxes Act 1968 which gives statutory force for a limited time to resolutions of the House of Commons varying taxation levels pending the enactment in the Finance Act.

[64] [2011] EWHC 1147.

[65] The High Court, in *R(D)* v. *Worcestershire County Council* [2013] EWHC 2490 (Admin Court), rejected a claim for disability payment in the context of severe cuts in the local authority budget. See 'Harsh but Fair?', *New Law Journal* (29 November 2013).

[66] *R (McDonald)* v *Royal Borough of Kensington and Chelsea* [2011] UKSC 33.

[67] *R (KM)* v. *Cambridgeshire County Council* [2012] UKSC 23 adopted a similar approach in the scrutiny of local authority powers but a reluctance to overturn policy based expenditure decisions.

[68] See n. 7. See I. Harden, F. White, and K. Hollingsworth, 'Value for Money and Administrative Law' [1996] *PL* 661, 674.

finding and the decision of the Divisional Court, the government found the necessary additional aid required to finance the dam from a repayable charge on the Contingency Fund. Eventually the money was found from the Reserve Fund. Questions of legality may also be raised when value for money is questioned or the use of public funds is thought not to be proportionate.

PLANNING AND CONTROLLING PUBLIC EXPENDITURE

THE TREASURY'S ANNUAL PUBLIC EXPENDITURE SURVEY

The Treasury's annual PES[69] is the central factor in planning and controlling public expenditure. Inside the Treasury the Budget and Public Finances Directorate sets the agenda between different departmental demands for money. The Central Expenditure Policy group referees the bids between spending departments and reports through the Chief Secretary to the Treasury to the Cabinet in July on the likely outcome in expenditure totals. Between the end of the PES round in October and the autumn statement in November, winners and losers in the expenditure debate have to be settled. The Code for Fiscal Stability since 1998 (referred to earlier) provided an emphasis on principles of fiscal management such as transparency, stability, responsibility, fairness, and efficiency.

In September 1992, after the UK's withdrawal from the Exchange Rate Mechanism,[70] the government's Autumn Statement introduced changes to the system of public expenditure control through the introduction of a New Control Total. This replaced the planning total and excludes the main elements of cyclical social security expenditure and any privatization proceeds. It includes local authority self-financed expenditure. Totals for the control of public expenditure include both local and central government expenditure. Refinements have been made, such as, in 1998, the introduction of Total Managed Expenditure (TME) comprising the total of public-sector current expenditure and public sector net investment. All expenditure under TME facilitates better management under Treasury scrutiny. In 1998 the introduction of a Comprehensive Spending Review (CSR) allowed departments to take a more radical look at across-the-board expenditure and resist the temptation to see expenditure planning only in terms of an annual review. It also allowed comparison between Departmental Expenditure Limits which set firm three-year spending limits (the limits for departmental spending within the public expenditure total) and Actually

---

[69] It is over 40 years since the Plowden Report recommended that decisions on public expenditure should be taken 'in the light of surveys of public expenditure as a whole over a period of years, and in relation to prospective resources'.

[70] The Exchange Rate Mechanism was established to prepare the way for the introduction of the single European currency (euro) and revised in 1999 to take account of the setting up of the euro.

Managed Expenditure which covers items which are reviewed and set on an annual basis (the actual expenditure undertaken by the department).

PES continues to provide a politically expedient outcome which achieves consensus from ministers. PES underlines the Treasury's pre-eminence and the role of the Chief Secretary in the development of ministerial policy. PES supported by the CSR and the *Code of Fiscal Stability* has the potential to transform the setting of public expenditure totals through greater transparency and openness in the planning process.

THE TREASURY AND DEPARTMENTAL CONTROLS OVER PUBLIC EXPENDITURE

The various rules that set out controls on the discretion of the Treasury and Chancellor, such as fiscal rules that determine the amount of borrowing relative to the size of the economy, are in fact Treasury-made. The Treasury is effectively empowered to self-regulate,[71] and through improvements in the economic instruments to manage the economy.

The pre-eminence afforded to the Treasury through PES is complementary to the overall role of the Treasury in managing and controlling public expenditure. Under the Banking Act 2009, the Treasury may make regulations over the use of stabilization powers for the banking sector.[72] It exercises internal and less visible systems of control as well as external and more visible techniques. Treasury control is much improved through the adoption of a variety of *a priori* techniques. It prepares, monitors, audits, and authorizes under parliamentary scrutiny according to set rules and procedures. The relevant conventions, practices, and statutory arrangements are codified in various manuals. The most detailed is *Managing Public Money*. Dating back to 1934, with a revision in 1977, there is also a *Treasury Handbook: Supply and other Financial Procedures of the House of Commons*. The *Code of Fiscal Stability* is important because of its statutory authority and amendments are made through affirmation by the House of Commons. In addition, the Treasury has a *Handbook on Regularity and Propriety*. The *Financial Reporting Manual 2009–10* sets out all the technical accounting and disclosure requirements for the annual report and accounts.

In preparing legislation, departments are required to keep the Treasury informed of any proposal with a financial implication. Consultation is expected at an early stage and the amendments to bills should be included if they affect the financial arrangements. This represents a major influence over how departments consider spending public money. Since the late 1990s the Treasury has adopted a more strategic role

---

[71] There is also the quality of the Civil Service and a list of distinguished outsiders including in the recent past Shriti Vadera from UBS, Nick Stern from the World Bank, and John Kingman from BP. Currently, Edward Leigh MP and John Pugh MP have been asked to advise on accountability mechanisms.

[72] See House of Commons Research Paper 05/92, *The Centre of Government—No. 10, The Cabinet and HM Treasury* (21 December 2005); C. Thain 'Treasury Rules OK? The Further Evolution of a British Institution' (2004) 6(1) *British Journal of Politics and International Relations* 123.

with reorganization and regular contact with spending departments through annual spending reviews and targets setting inputs and outputs.

Treasury control may be exercised within government departments through the Accounting Officer (discussed earlier) appointed by the Treasury, whose responsibilities are contained in detailed Memoranda. Accounting Officers are in effect expected to combine their task of ensuring a high standard of financial management in their departments with their duty to serve their ministers. The Accounting Officer is given responsibility for signing accounts, and ensuring Treasury sanction is obtained for expenditure authorized by Parliament and appearing as the principal witness on behalf of the department before the PAC.

There is a specialized manual for government internal audit. This contains the basic standards for the Treasury's internal audit representing good practice. An internal audit is an independent appraisal within a department as a service to management in measuring and evaluating standards within the department. Through the system of internal audit the Accounting Officer may be assisted in his task. Internal audit is not however seen as a substitute for line management; it is a means to ensure that appraisal within a department is properly carried out. It is usual practice to carry out such appraisal by the appointment of a unit charged with responsibility to the Accounting Officer. As the Accounting Officer is usually the permanent head of the department this 'reflects the view that finance and policy cannot be considered separately'. Thus good management is the key to his function. He must ensure compliance with parliamentary requirements in the control of public expenditure. In his role he is to avoid waste and extravagance and to seek economy, efficiency, and effectiveness in the use of all the resources made available to the department. However the Accounting Officer is also expressly concerned with *policy*. He has responsibility to advise ministers on all 'matters of financial propriety and regularity', more broadly as to all 'considerations of prudent and economical administration, efficiency and effectiveness' and to ensure that departmental expenditure is justified to the PAC. In matters where a minister may disagree he is free to set out his own advice and the overruling of it by the minister. He is free to point out to ministers the possibility of potential criticism by the PAC of ministerial decisions.[73]

This in effect was the procedure followed in the *Pergau Dam* affair, discussed earlier. Procedures exist for an Accounting Officer to notify the C&AG should his advice be overruled.

The adoption of resource accounting under the Government Resources and Accounts Act 2000 is consistent with a more managerial approach to budgeting to match more closely resources used to meet departmental objectives[74] and the introduction of Whole of Government Accounts consistent within the UK. Generally the

---

[73] *Supply Procedure, Government Accounting*, and amendment 4/05, s. 4.1.2, para. 15.

[74] The Government Resources and Accounts Act 2000 amends the Exchequer and Audit Departments Acts 1866 and 1921.

Accepted Practice regime[75] is to provide a more complete financial analysis alongside the Alignment ('Clear Line of Sight') Project to ensure effective financial reporting.

AUDIT TECHNIQUES IN THE CONTROL OF PUBLIC EXPENDITURE

The adoption of audit strategies for the public sector infiltrates almost every form of decision-making in a wide variety of institutions.

PARLIAMENT'S ROLE: THE PUBLIC ACCOUNTS COMMITTEE, THE NEW SELECT COMMITTEES, AND THE COMPTROLLER AND AUDITOR GENERAL

Once expenditure is settled the question of scrutiny and audit arises. Since 1861 the PAC acts on behalf of Parliament to examine and report on accounts and the regularity and propriety of expenditure, which are matters usually covered by the C&AG's certification audit. In more recent times value for money audit (VFM) examinations have become a major part of the work of the PAC. In that regard the PAC works with the assistance of the C&AG. The PAC has proposed changes to Standing Order No. 148 which will enable it to appoint specialist advisers, a facility available to other Committees. The constitutional importance of the PAC is beyond question and linked to efficiency in government. There is a case for a systematic rather than random follow up by the PAC of how its recommendations have been treated by the government. The PAC produces about 50 reports a year. Its twelfth report in 2010 on *Maintaining Financial Stability across the United Kingdom's Banking System*[76] provided an analysis of the banking crisis. It has undertaken reviews into the Her Majesty's Revenue and Customs (HMRC) and the way in which tax disputes with large corporations have been resolved and the closeness of the relationship between accountancy firms and HMRC.[77] It has raised concerns about the adoption of smart meters to ensure consumers obtain cost savings.[78] The PAC has become more effective by linking its work into the work of other committees in a more coordinated way than in the past and drawing general lessons from its inquiries.[79] Evidence to the PAC is usually from

---

[75] D. A. Heald and G. Georgiou, 'Consolidation Principles and Practices for the UK Government Sector' (2000) 30 *Accounting and Business Research* 153. HM Treasury, 'Whole of Government Accounts Progress to December 2000', Memorandum to the Committee of Public Accounts and the Treasury Select Committee (unpublished).

[76] PAC Reports, *12th Report on Maintaining Financial Stability across the United Kingdom's Banking System*, HC 190 (9 February 2010).

[77] PAC, *HM Revenue and Customs 2010-11 Tax Disputes*, HC 138 (2010–12); *Tax avoidance: The Role of large Accountancy Firms* HC 870 (2012–13). Generally see Bacon and Hope, *Conundrums: Why Every Government Gets Things Wrong*.

[78] PAC, *Preparation for the Roll-out of Smart Meters*, 63rd Report (2014).

[79] See PAC Reports, *63rd Report on Delivering High Quality Services for All*, HC 1530 (2006).

senior civil servants and officials leaving ministerial policy-making largely unchecked and raising sensitivities amongst civil servants that the manner of PAC questioning is directed to holding officials, rather than ministers, to account.[80]

The PAC's authority and remit[81] differ from those of other select committees in two ways. First is the non-party political approach it adopts to its task and the fact that it is chaired by a senior opposition MP and has no more than 15 members. Secondly, its inquiries are almost all audit-based and it receives expert assistance from the C&AG through the work of the NAO. In the case of VFM examinations, its reports to Parliament carry considerable weight. In November 2009 the PAC was critical of the Treasury's indemnity of £28 billion to the Bank of England and a further emergency liquidity assurance of £60 billion to the Royal Bank of Scotland and the Halifax Bank of Scotland (HBOS).[82] Parliament had not received any prior notification before the indemnity had been agreed by the Treasury. Recent concerns about the use of long-term contracts for public services involving public money beyond the lifetime of the current Parliament have been raised.

Select committees generally exercise *ex post facto* control over public expenditure. The Treasury Committee has been particularly active in developing strategies to obtain more information on public expenditure and its more effective control. In the recent financial crisis involving banking regulation, the Treasury Committee led the way. It undertook 41 evidence sessions and published nine reports relating to the crisis between 2007 and 2009 and has remained active in scrutiny.[83] It is accepted that much of the work of Committees is by its nature retrospective review.

The Scrutiny Unit established in November 2002 in the Committee Office of the House of Commons provides select committees of the House of Commons and joint committees of the two Houses with advice on expenditure matters but also on the impact of draft bills. The Scrutiny Unit undertakes research as well as policy impact assessments. It also publishes a Review of Departmental Annual Reports, and provides training and support on impact assessments. It assists in the Treasury's Alignment Project set up in July 2007 to ensure that financial reporting and accounts are consistent and transparent.[84]

This provides a detailed and in-depth overview of how departments are performing in terms of Treasury guidance and output measurements. The primary function of the C&AG since the Exchequer and Audit Act 1866 has been the requirement to examine

[80] See PAC Reports, *The Dismantled National Programme for IT in the NHS* HC 294 (2013–14); *High Speed 2: A Review of the Early Programme Preparation* HC 478 (2013–14); *The National Offender Management Information System* HC 292 (2008–9); *Tax Avoidance—Google*, HC 112 (2013–14). One of the more controversial is House of Commons Public Accounts Committee, *High Speed 2: A Review of Early Programmes Preparation*, HC 478 (2013–14).

[81] See PAC Reports on the poor quality of higher education, HC 283 (2000–1), and on the C&AG's Reports, *The Millennium Dome*, HC 936 (1999–2000), and HC 989-I (2000–1).

[82] PAC Report, *Maintaining Financial Stability across the UK Banking System*, 12th Report, HC 190 (2001–10), para. 11.

[83] Black, *Managing the Financial Crisis*, 31.

[84] See HM Treasury, *Alignment (Clear Line of Sight) Second Parliamentary Memorandum* (2009–10).

accounts on behalf of the House of Commons. The National Audit Act 1983 recognized the constitutional implications of this requirement, made the C&AG an Officer of the House of Commons, and provided for his appointment. As head of the NAO, which was created under the 1983 Act and replaced the Exchequer and Audit Department, the C&AG is independent from both politics and political influence of the government of the day. This independence allows the C&AG to qualify financial accounts when he is not satisfied with the financial arrangements. In November 2002 this occurred over the Strategic Rail Authority sponsored by the Department of Transport[85] until it was agreed that Network Rail should be consolidated. The NAO's activities[86] cover benchmarking, quality control, developing efficient and effective monitoring systems, and engaging in annual reporting functions over departmental spending involving the audit of more than 600 accounts covering over £800 billion of public expenditure.[87] It is unable to comment on policy. Its annual net working resources are approximately £76 million with outsourcing costs of nearly 20 per cent and employing 900 staff. The remit of the NAO was established under the 1983 Act, which has been criticized for failing to give the C&AG the right to trace 'all public money'. The NAO has also undertaken a significant monitoring of the financial management of the European Union.[88] Excluded from the jurisdiction of the NAO in National Audit Act 1983, Sched. 4, is the audit of the remaining nationalized industries and other public authorities. Local authorities are separately audited by the (about to be abolished) Audit Commission which is itself subject to audit by the NAO. Increasingly, the NAO is called upon by the executive as an 'accountability adviser of choice' especially in areas of government policy implementation including through regulatory bodies.[89] Julia Black[90] detects a sense of confusion as to who the NAO acts for and to whom it is accountable, especially when used by the Cabinet Office and Treasury. Greater clarity about the NAO might be needed to ensure that there is no further blurring of the lines of responsibility.[91] More welcome is the use of the NAO by Committees of both Houses of Parliament.

The NAO is funded out of moneys provided by Parliament but one-fifth of the NAO's budget comes from audit fees, including international clients. The NAO acts on behalf of Parliament and is subject to oversight by the Parliamentary Public Accounts

[85] 11th Report of the Public Accounts Commission, Session 2001–2, HC 1251 (2002).

[86] There is a Public Audit Forum providing a discussion for the audit agencies; the NAO, the Northern Ireland Audit Office, the Audit Commission for Local Authorities, and the National Health Service in England and Wales and Audit Scotland.

[87] NAO, *Corporate Plan 2003–4 to 2005–6* (2005) contains details of the bodies audited.

[88] See Report by the Comptroller and Auditor General, *Financial Management of the European Union: A Progress Report*, HC 529 (2003–4).

[89] NAO, *Reorganising Central Government*, HC 452, Session 2009–10 (2010); also see NAO *Ofcom: The Effectiveness of Converged Regulation* HC 490, Session 2010–11 (2010).

[90] Julia Black, 'Calling Regulators to Account: Challenges, Capacities and Prospects' in N. Bamforth and P. Leyland (eds.), *Accountability in the Contemporary Constitution* (2013), 381.

[91] NAO, *Performance of Ofgem: NAO, A Review of Economic Regulators' Regulatory Impact Statements for the House of Lords Select Committee on Regulators* (2007), cited by Black, 'Calling Regulators to Account', as an example of confusion over role and function.

Commission. The Budget Responsibility and National Audit Act 2011 separated the C&AG as an independent officer of Parliament from the NAO, with the NAO receiving a new corporate status, providing resources to the C&AG who will be its chief executive but under an independent board.[92]

Significantly, following the Gershon Review in 2004, the NAO has undertaken regular reviews of efficiency savings across government. Its current strategy is estimated to help make savings of £35 billion planned over the coming year in terms of the administrative costs of running government departments.[93]

CERTIFICATION AUDIT

The NAO[94] undertakes two forms of auditing, certification audit and value for money audit. In the case of certification audit, the C&AG carries out on behalf of the House of Commons the audit and certification of all government departments and a wide range of public sector bodies. These include appropriation accounts of departments. The C&AG provides an audit certificate which states his opinion as to whether either: (a) the 'account properly presents' the expenditure and receipts of the vote and payments of the organization; or (b) the account presents a 'true and fair view' where accounts are prepared on an income-and-expenditure basis.

This form of audit is 'departmental-led'—that is, focused on departments. Increasingly, the style of the audit seeks to ensure 'regularity and propriety' with the addition that the custodians of public money have stewardship responsibilities. The link between the Treasury and the NAO is through the Departmental Accounting Officer and is one of partnership but based on independent actors with specific responsibilities. The C&AG may seek an explanation from the department concerned if he is dissatisfied with any aspect of the accounts and may qualify his certificate with his reservations. The primary focus of such an audit is to assess whether accounts are accurate or whether they may mislead someone relying on them. They must present a 'true and fair view', must be 'properly presented', and in the case of agencies must follow the format of Treasury accounts. In particular, if there is expenditure which requires Treasury authority which has not been given, the matter is reported through a draft report in the first instance to the Accounting Officer and then to the PAC and Parliament.

Normally, the audit work involved in certification audit is confined to the proper presentation of receipts and expenditure. In common with most of the auditing work of the NAO it is scrutiny *ex post facto* with the implication that any past errors may

---

[92] Remuneration, terms of conditions of the C&AG, and limitations on powers to require efficiency and cost-effectiveness in the exercise of his responsibilities. There are similar powers for Wales.

[93] PAC, *Progress with Value for Money Savings and Lessons for Cost Reduction Programes*, HC 439-I (11 September 2010).

[94] Tom Ling, 'The NAO and Parliamentary Scrutiny: A New Audit for New Times', CfPs Policy Paper Series (2005).

provide lessons for the future. This is open to the criticism that an *a priori* examination might offer a means of avoiding mistakes and therefore save public money.[95] The NAO has claimed that in 2005–6, its work resulted in £555 million in savings as a result of auditing over 500 accounts covering £800 billion in expenditure.

VALUE FOR MONEY EXAMINATIONS

VFM examinations are potentially more far-reaching as a means of audit. The National Audit Act 1983, s. 6 provides a statutory basis for VFM examinations at the discretion of the C&AG. Included within this jurisdiction are government departments and other public bodies where the C&AG has statutory rights of inspection or where he is the statutory auditor. VFM audit is not extended to any of the nationalized industries.[96] The 1983 Act placed VFM examinations on a statutory basis and over 60 reports are produced on an annual basis. However, the Act makes an important proviso that VFM examination shall not be construed as entitling the C&AG to question the merits of the policy objectives of the department or body concerned.[97]

Evaluating efficiency and effectiveness has been a common theme in recent years in the development of government policy objectives.[98] The NAO is ambitious in developing VFM examinations through their efforts to identify and prevent waste. It has become commonplace that government borrows techniques, methods, and objectives from business or commerce. How to measure efficiency and effectiveness is the key issue, and evaluation may be as difficult as setting the objectives in the first place.

In 1981 the Treasury and Civil Service Committee in its *Report on Efficiency and Effectiveness*[99] set out some criteria for evaluating efficiency and effectiveness. The criteria include clarifying the intention of the programme, setting *objectives* which are quantified as targets. Objectives can be assessed in terms of *output*. An *efficient* programme is one where the target is achieved with the least use of resources and instruments for change. An *effective* programme is one where the intention of the programme is being achieved. This means that the intention is contained in operational objectives that are set as defined targets. Thus the output of the programme is equal to the target set. In this way an effective and efficient programme may be evaluated.

The NAO has developed VFM strategies[100] that emphasize the avoidance of waste, the setting of clearly defined policy objectives, and obtaining good value for the

---

[95] PAC, *Managing Risks to Improve Public Services*, HC 444 (2004–5).

[96] *Government Accounting* (1989), para. 7.1.20, revised in 2003.

[97] See C. Beauchamp, 'National Audit Office: Its Role in Privatization' (1990) *Public Money and Management* 55–8, 57. For examples, see NAO, *The Work of the Directors of Telecommunications, Gas Supply, Water Service and Electricity Supply*, Session 1995–6, HC 645. Compare the approach to the early comments made to the Fourth Report of the Public Accounts Committee (4 November 1988).

[98] See a critical analysis by the NAO over selling the National Air Traffic Control System, HC 1096 (2001–2).

[99] Treasury and Civil Service Committee, *Efficiency and Effectiveness in the Civil Service*, HC 236. See also Cabinet Office Efficiency Unit, *Helping Managers Manage* (1984).

[100] NAO, *Helping the Nation Spend Wisely Annual Report* (1999), 13. See NAO, *A Framework for Value for Money Audits*, Cmnd 9755; Treasury Minute on the First Four Reports from the Committee of Public

taxpayer. There is a duty on government departments to consider the NAO's reports and the PAC recommendations, and to provide replies to the House of Commons on matters raised in the reports. There is a strong parliamentary link with the PAC following up the recommendations made by the NAO.[101] This is consistent with the Gershon Review that argued strongly for making efficiency savings to redistribute funds for better use. The government's claim was that £4.7 billion savings might be so identified[102] but there is a considerable risk that a reduction in the quality of services might result if over-ambitious targets have to be met. There is the need for a cost–benefit analysis to be used to assess the amount of savings as against the quality of services.

VFM examinations seem to be a blend of conventional auditing skills with management consulting techniques. In the former they benefit from a degree of independence and objectivity and the ascertaining of facts through the skills of an auditor. The latter draws on the analytical skills of the management consultant. In comparison with ordinary certification auditing, VFM takes the opportunity to understand the effects of policy and whether those effects relate to the intention behind the policy. The NAO's experience of VFM studies has been growing since 1983.[103] In 2005–6 the NAO provided Parliament with 61 major reports on VFM, representing a substantial part of the NAO's work.[104] In 2009–10 the NAO undertook 90 reports on VFM.

Particularly difficult is the distinction between the implementation of policy, a legitimate concern of VFM, and the merits of policy, which we have already noted are outside the jurisdiction of the NAO. A criticism levelled at all public sector VFM examinations is that the emphasis on economic criteria does not take account of political choices and policy-making or whether the merits of the policy, outside the remit of the NAO, impacted on the efficiency of decision-making. Given its present remit, it is clearly impossible for the NAO to move to assess the merits of policy even where this may be indicated by their examination. The *ex post facto* nature of VFM has the benefit of hindsight but this may make it difficult to evaluate all the pressures experienced by a sponsoring department.[105] The NAO published a critical analysis of the banking crisis and the problems caused by the failure of Northern Rock.[106]

Accounts Session 1985/86 (Cmnd 9846, 9859, 9917, 9924), paras. 21–3; A. Hopwood, 'Accounting and the Pursuit of Efficiency' in A. Hopwood and C. Tomkins, *Issues in Public Sector Accounting* (1984); J. Sizer, *An Insight into Management Accounting* (1989).

[101] PAC, *Achieving Value for Money in the Delivery of Public Services*, HC 742 (2005–6).

[102] NAO, *Progress in Improving Government Efficiency*, HC 802 (2005–6).

[103] See J. McEldowney, 'Audit Cultures and Risk Aversion in Public Authorities: An Agenda for Public Lawyers' in R. Baldwin (ed.), *Law and Uncertainty Risks and Legal Processes* (1997), 185–210.

[104] NAO, *Annual Report 2006*.

[105] F. White and K. Hollingsworth, *Audit, Accountability and Government* (1999).

[106] NAO, *The Financial Services Authority: A Review under Section 12 of the Financial Services and Markets Act 2000*, Session 2006–7, HC 500 (27 April 2007), 49 noted that from 2001–2 there were an average of 200 cases each year dealing with money laundering and other breaches of the financial standards. There were 17 cases involving financial penalties, totalling £17.4 million, £14 million of which was for one market protection case and £505,000 related specifically to financial crime (ibid., para. 4.63).

Perversely, the very transparency encouraged by audit systems may inhibit initiative and creative risk-taking in favour of a cautious approach over-reliant on audit advice. Placing trust in the audit process itself may be a worthy goal and achieves better control over expenditure but it may encourage heavy reliance on monitoring techniques instead of a more fundamental assessment of priorities. The political agenda may also become heavily dependent on the audit trail to provide legitimacy and public confidence for policies. This may obscure the setting of priorities and lead to the adoption of short-term as opposed to long-term goals.

The independent status of the C&AG means that heavy reliance is placed on cooperation between the departments, their Accounting Officers, and the NAO.[107] This is indicative of the delicate balance between gaining access to information through cooperation and maintaining independence.[108] Although the NAO has achieved international status as a public sector audit office of high reputation and quality, criticisms remain of its capacity to operate proactive or preventative strategies to ensure effective public spending.

CONCLUSION

The aftermath of the financial crisis of 2008 continues to have a major effect on the systems and techniques for the control of public expenditure. The independence referendum in Scotland in September 2014 and related debate on devolution is likely to create taxation and expenditure planning in devolved administrations, and further autonomy is likely to be given to regional institutions of government. Constitutional, economic, and political issues also arise in the case of any modification of the UK's membership of the European Union, or its outright withdrawal. This has already raised debates over any cost–benefit analysis of EU membership and of withdrawal,[109] and has given rise to economic uncertainties and doubts over central government's ability to cut the budget deficit. The spending plans of the devolved administrations and any further tax-raising powers will complicate matters further and make controlling overall public expenditure more difficult for central government.

These changes have uncharted consequences for the UK's system of centralized expenditure controls and may require a rethink of the relationship between the UK Parliament and the devolved institutions and potentially English regional bodies.

The financial crisis and the balance of influence between parliamentary control and government spending have shifted markedly to the government's advantage. This

---

[107] See the proposals contained in the Budget Responsibility and 2010 National Audit Bill (HL) to modernize the work of the NAO and its governance arrangements.

[108] Memorandum from Michael Power, Professor of Accounting, London School of Economics, HM Treasury Select Committee Evidence 173, 174.

[109] House of Commons Library, *In Brief: UK–EU Economic Relations—Key Statistics* SN06091 (15 October 2014); House of Commons Library, *The European Union*, LLN 2014/15 (25 April 2014).

is partly because of the need for rapid public spending cuts and partly because the systems of accountability are the main means of delivering and controlling public spending.

The government's expenditure objectives are more visible and transparent than before but, being driven by large fiscal deficits, parliamentary accountability is likely to be weak. Evaluation of the case for cuts and the proportion of savings and the role of accountability systems, has given rise to a government-centred agenda for change that prioritizes spending, leaving little room for parliamentary control.

Strengthening parliamentary scrutiny largely depends on the House of Commons in general or on individual MPs regarding financial control as relevant in their overall role in the scrutiny of government. The Public Accounts Committee has been notable in adopting a robust questioning of value for money in public expenditure, mainly driven by the approach of the current chair.

The financial crisis has also revealed the limited extent of *ex post* select committee scrutiny; despite the fact that the crisis had a major impact on institutions that control and regulate public finance, little could be done at the time. An unfortunate aspect of the Banking Act 2009 was the restricted role it gives to Parliament: the Bank of England was given real powers to implement stabilization options that were not subject to parliamentary control[110] and the Treasury was granted even wider regulatory powers without the need for prior parliamentary approval. The work of the Treasury Select Committee, however, in actively reporting on aspects of the financial crisis[111] has proved important and the Lords Select Committee on the Constitution has also been vigilant.[112]

Constitutional lawyers have accepted that controls over public expenditure lie at the heart of Parliament's control over government. The plethora of controls such as internal Treasury rules and procedures, audit systems, parliamentary reports, and management systems are fashioned to serve the dual purpose of the economic needs of the government of the day, and the interests of Parliament. Inside the system of financial control the internal workings of government can be detected, often less visible and transparent than the workings of the external systems of parliamentary accountability in select committees and the role of the courts. Financial control systems share many characteristics familiar in the development of the common law—continuity and certainty in developing rules with the potential for incremental

---

[110] See Banking Act 2009, ss. 5, 10, and 74. Section 74 gave the Treasury Henry VIII-type powers to make regulations to cover stabilization measures.

[111] HC Treasury Select Committee, *Too Important to Fail—Too Important to Ignore*, Ninth Report Session 2009–10, HC 261-1, Summary, 3. HC Treasury Select Committee, *Banking Crisis: Dealing with the Failure of UK Banks*, Session 2008–9, HC 416, paras. 203–29. House of Commons Library Research Papers, *Big Society Bank/Big Society Capital*, SN/BT/5876 (13 June 2014). Treasury Select Committee, *Reporting Contingent Liabilities to Parliament*, Session 2009–10, HC 181. Treasury and Civil Service Committee, *The Regulation of Financial Services in the UK*, Sixth Report, HC 332-I (1994–5).

[112] HL Select Committee on the Constitution Banking Bill, Session 2008–9, HL 19, and HL 97. Also see Jack Simson Caird, Robert Hazell, and dawn Oliver, *The Constitutional Standards of the House of Lords Select Committee on the Constitution*, UCL Constitution Unit (January 2014).

change. But, equally incrementally, financial controls appear to have developed many of the qualities of a codified system—written manuals containing fundamental principles that have been improved, updated, and strengthened containing many years' experience. It is possible to see financial controls as a model of what can be achieved with systemic change over 40 years through the appropriate combination of external expertise in the form of the NAO and the internal scrutiny performed by select committees. Treasury dominance in its influence over public expenditure is most marked especially in borrowing and debt arrangements. There is a systemic weakness at the heart of public expenditure control, namely that gaps left by parliamentary inertia are readily filled by executive controls driven by Treasury influence. The government's pre-eminence in the rules of procedure that allows it the initiative in public expenditure severely weakens the ability of individual MPs to play a role in financial matters. A modest reform that permits modest expenditure increases (within the remit of offsetting costs elsewhere) to MPs would make a substantial change. It would allow a greater emphasis to be given in parliamentary debate to the policies and decisions that inform, manage, and control public expenditure. At a time when audit systems are strengthened, Parliament's relevance faces further decline. The weaknesses and inertia in parliamentary control appear to reflect a decline in the standard and quality of our democracy today.[113] The influential *Institute for Fiscal Studies* concluded that public sector net debt is likely to dominate and constrain future government policy for planned public expenditure for future generations.[114] This fact alone should encourage MPs to take a greater interest in ensuring that public money is well spent.

FURTHER READING

BACON, R., and HOPE, C., *Conudrum: Why Every Government Gets Things Wrong: And What We Can Do About It* (2013)

BALLS, E. and O'DONNELL, G. (eds.), *Reforming Britain's Economic and Financial Policy: Towards Greater Economic Stability* (2002)

BRAZIER, A. and RAM, V., *The Fiscal Maze* (2006)

GAY, O. and WINETROBE, B., *Parliamentary Audit: The Audit Committee in Comparative Context, Report to the Audit Committee of the Scottish Parliament* (2003)

HANSARD SOCIETY, Commission on Parliamentary Scrutiny, *The Challenge for Parliament: Making Government Accountable* (2001)

HEALD, D. and McLEOD, A., *Public Expenditure: The Laws of Scotland: Stair Memorial Encyclopaedia* (2002)

McKAY, W. R. (ed.), *Erskine May: Parliamentary Practice* (23rd edn, 2004)

McKAY, WILLIAM and JOHNSON, CHARLES W., *Parliament and Congress* (2010)

---

[113] O. Gay and B. Winetrobe, *Parliamentary Audit: The Audit Committee in Comparative Context* (2003).
[114] IFS, *The IFS Green Budget 2014* (2014), 22.

SHARMAN OF REDLYNCH, LORD, *Holding to Account: The Review of Audit and Accountability for Central Government* (2001)

THAIN, C. and WRIGHT, M., *The Treasury and Whitehall: The Planning and Control of Public Expenditure 1976–1993* (1995)

USEFUL WEBSITES

Audit Commission: **http://www.audit-commission.gov.uk**
HM Treasury: **http://www.hm-treasury.gov.uk**
National Audit Office: **http://www.nao.gov.uk**
Public Audit Forum: **http://www.public-audit-forum.gov.uk**
UK National Statistics: **http://www.statistics.gov.uk**
UK Parliament: **http://www.parliament.uk**

14

REGULATING INFORMATION

Patrick Birkinshaw

'The future will be open' (*Open Data*, Cm 8353, 6 (2012))

SUMMARY

This chapter briefly examines the arguments for and against greater access to government information, openness, and transparency. The traditions of secrecy in British government have given way to 'reform' of official secrecy legislation and legislation for the secret services since the 1980s, most recently in 2013. Before the Freedom of Information Act 2000 (FOIA), the courts granted rights to disclosure and inspection of government documents to litigants. The 2013 reforms have placed limits on disclosures of intelligence information. The FOIA places positive duties on public authorities covered by the Act to disclose information they hold upon request, though subject to exemptions. The Act amounts to the most important provision on access to government information, and thus on increased openness. Since 2010, official policy has promoted non-statutory disclosure of information most recently set out in the White Paper *Open Data* (2012).

The state has become a massive repository of information concerning identifiable individuals. This raises alarms about the security of its data banks and the protection of personal privacy. Revelations of indiscriminate trawling of international data communications by intelligence bodies have raised concerns about the global dimension of, and lack of control over, surveillance. The Data Protection Act 1998 (DPA) provides some protection, and the European Union (EU) laws on which the DPA is based are being modified. A lacuna, however, exists.

Overall, the FOIA 2000 and DPA 1998 represent important steps in the right direction by giving public access to official information and protecting individuals against abuse of personal information. The system is not perfect and areas for reform are identified.

INTRODUCTION

There is nothing new about an information state. The state, or officialdom, has acquired information since responsibility was assumed for defence, security, taxation, census taking, or whatever. While the emphasis in the UK in the nineteenth and twentieth centuries was on protecting the information that the state had acquired, most famously by the use of Official Secrets legislation commencing in 1889, slowly, but inevitably, pressure mounted for disclosure to the public of information held by the state and public bodies. Today the emphasis has moved towards proactive access to information from the state, and towards the state and state institutions operating transparently and openly.[1] Transparency is much broader than access. It means opening up the processes of governance to scrutiny, investigation, monitoring, and explanation, and that where people wish to participate meaningful opportunities should be provided. Open government means opening up the processes of government and government meetings to public view and scrutiny. This development has been accompanied by growing awareness of the need to secure information about individuals and to protect their privacy by more effective regulation.

The arguments in favour of openness, transparency, and access to information have been well rehearsed.[2] They include the desirability of giving information about the operation of public authorities exercising public power to those who are primarily affected by that power—the public. Openness concerns the right to know what government is doing, or not doing, on our behalf and under our sufferance and in our name. It concerns widespread democratic involvement in the exercise of power, accountability, explanation, and the sharing of knowledge. It involves a vision of governance in which citizens are treated as responsible individuals and not simply as subjects or *les administrés*—there to be told what to do but not to know why they should do it or upon what basis they should act. A wider ranging objective of openness involves establishing a context in which people are better able to understand how government works and to allow them to participate more effectively in governance—to make them feel, in other words, like stakeholders and not that 'nanny knows best'.

In the UK, until 2000, provision of information directly to the public of state-held information did not sit easily with the custom and conventions of constitutional practice and representative democracy. The primary recipient of official information was Parliament by way of ministers responding to parliamentary questions in fulfilment of their ministerial responsibility to Parliament. These practices of governance had been developed over centuries. To provide information directly to the public would undermine the authority and position of Parliament, it was constantly reiterated. Provision of information, it was argued, would lead to unnecessary expense, could undermine public security, individual privacy, and confidentiality. It could produce captiousness and querulousness. Removal of the mystery surrounding governance would undermine the trust in government. Enforced secrecy, however, did not enhance that trust.[3]

---

[1] See Constitutional Reform and Governance Act 2010, s. 28; Pt 5 Protection of Freedoms Act 2012; and *Open Data*, Cm 8353 (2012). See Transparency of Lobbying etc Act 2015.

[2] See Public Administration Select Committee, *Your Right to Know: The Government's Proposals for a Freedom of Information Act*, Third Report, HC 398 (1997–8) vol. I. See also n. 44 herein.

[3] Franks Report, *Departmental Committee on Section 2 of the Official Secrets Act 1911*, Cmnd 5104, Vol. 1 (1972); and P. Birkinshaw, *Freedom of Information: The Law, the Practice and the Ideal* (4th edn, 2010), chs. 2, 3, and 9.

Official enquiries, official papers, and reports, including from the late 1960s those of the Parliamentary Ombudsman, and Hansard, all provided invaluable information to researchers, scholars, press, and media. Vital information might be published to assist those intent on social or political reform. But publication of much of this information was under the *control* of government and on its terms. There was no legal concept of a right to official information. Freedom of information (FOI), as will be shown, means access to publicly held information as a presumptive right subject to exemptions: it does not mean complete *freedom* of information.

The Public Records Acts 1958 and 1967 opened up public records to the public after initially 50 years, reduced to 30, and now to 20 years under the Constitutional Reform and Governance Act 2010.[4] These provisions cover papers transferred to the National Archives. Scotland and Northern Ireland have their own arrangements. Those not transferred are not so covered.[5] Some may be 'closed' and not published. The FOIA 2000, as amended, now governs the position on rights of access to such material. Closure may only be in accordance with a relevant exemption under the FOIA 2000 (see later under 'Exemptions').

OFFICIAL SECRECY

Traditional methods for regulating or censoring information fell into desuetude in the 1980s given the increasing access to information data banks at the press of a button. Before cyberspace, an indication of the limits on court orders enforcing confidentiality or official secrecy in globalized connections came with the *Spycatcher* saga in the 1980s, when the jurisdictional limits of criminal law and the Official Secrets Acts led the government to invoke the civil law of confidence to protect government information. It became apparent that it was impossible to prevent press reports of a book written by a former and disgruntled member of MI5 of what had become publicly available.[6] The book contained information about the author's account of security and intelligence operations. The porous quality of the digitized globe was exposed dramatically at the end of 2010 when the first tranches of 250,000 US diplomatic and security despatches were released without authorization by WikiLeaks. In 2013, Edward Snowden, a former US National Security Agency contractor, released details of global surveillance and other information about the activities of US and UK intelligence-gathering which allegedly lacked legal authorization.[7]

---

[4] s. 104 of the Protection of Freedoms Act 2012 extended reforms to Northern Ireland.

[5] Public Records Act 1958, s. 3(4).

[6] *AG* v. *Guardian Newspapers Ltd (No. 2)* [1988] 3 All ER 545. *Spycatcher* had been written by a former MI5 agent who could not be indicted under the 1911 Act because he was outside the UK jurisdiction. The book had been published overseas but copies had become freely available in the UK. The courts basically ruled that the law of confidentiality could not be used to suppress publication of information that had become widely available. An injunction would only be awarded where there was a danger to the public interest in publication. See *Observer and Guardian* v. *UK* [1991] 14 EHRR 153.

[7] See text at n. 13. The allegation is that UK services have exploited legislative limitations brought about by technological advances. Sir Iain Lobban Director of GCHQ gave a guarantee that the services 'operate

The first significant concession by central government towards relaxation of official secrets laws came with the Official Secrets Act 1989. The measure was described by the Home Secretary as an 'essay in openness'. Reform had been mooted for 17 years. This Act repealed Official Secrets Act 1911, s. 2, a notoriously broad blunderbuss covering by the criminal law every unauthorized disclosure of official information—or so it was widely reported. Whatever the position, s. 2 was a disreputable and hopelessly broad piece of legislation. The government's hand was forced by the sensational acquittal by a jury of Clive Ponting, a senior civil servant. Ponting had been prosecuted for leaking defence documents to the chair of the Commons Defence Committee, revealing that the government had been misrepresenting the circumstances leading to the sinking by HM Navy of the Argentinian battleship *General Belgrano* during hostilities leading to the retaking of the Falklands in 1982.[8] Presumably the jury placed a higher premium on openness than compliance with the judge's direction on the law.

Under the Official Secrets Act 1989, information was to be protected against unauthorized disclosure by the criminal law only when it fell within one of six protected classes of information, covering security and intelligence, defence, international relations, prevention of crime, disclosure of information relating to special investigations by the security and intelligence services, and interceptions of communications.

The Act included provisions about unauthorized disclosure (see s. 7) by three groups of persons. First, those who are security and intelligence officials or 'notified persons'. Disclosure by them of security and intelligence information is prohibited. Although the prohibition is virtually 'absolute', offences in Official Secrets Act 1989, ss. 1(1) and 4(3) (see later), are subject to a very limited defence. In *Shayler*, the Law Lords ruled that offences under ss. 1(1) and 4 did not breach European Convention on Human Rights (ECHR), Art. 10 protecting freedom of speech.[9] The Act provides no public interest defence.

The second group is other Crown servants and government contractors who make 'damaging' disclosures of information under ss. 1–3, or who disclose information under s. 4, knowing that it is protected under ss. 1–4.

The third group is others (for example editors, journalists) who make damaging disclosures of information communicated in breach of the Act knowing, or having reasonable cause to believe, the disclosure would be damaging. Disclosure of information under s. 4(3) about special investigation powers conducted by the security and intelligence services or of interception material (phone taps, email, and communications interception) does not require proof of such knowledge. Knowledge of the protected status under ss. 1–4 has to be established.

---

within the law': https://docs.google.com/viewer?a=v&pid=sites&srcid=aW5kZXBlbmRlbnQuQuZ292LnVrfG lzY3xneDoyYjM3NWU1NDQ5NTg0OTQ0.

[8] *R v. Ponting* [1985] *Crim LR* 318; C. Ponting, *The Right to Know* (1985).

[9] *R v. Shayler* [2002] UKHL 11.

In 2005, there were 336 specific statutory prohibitions on disclosure of information, breaches of many of which are punishable by criminal sanctions.[10] Furthermore, there are disciplinary offences of disclosure of information which are punishable in administrative proceedings against civil servants and police, as set out in Civil Service/police codes. It is to be noted that internal classification of documents in UK law has no legal effect—unlike EU law. Such classification is an instruction as to the manner in which information should be treated and kept—that is say, do not read on trains/planes/buses or remove from the office or disclose to a person without necessary security clearance.[11] The system of classification was revised in 2014.[12]

Throughout the public sector generally, breach of confidentiality would be regarded as a serious matter justifying disciplinary action and possibly dismissal. The Public Interest Disclosure Act 1998 amended the contractual employment relationship to allow qualifying disclosures—'whistleblowing'—in the public interest, but the thrust of the Act is that disclosure should be made to higher administrative echelons or named and official recipients, namely internal reporting. Under very exacting conditions outside disclosures may be made. The Public Interest Disclosure Act 1998 does not apply to the secret services or where breaches of the Official Secrets Act occur. The Employment and Regulatory Reform Act 2013, s. 17 emphasized the *public* interest test in qualifying disclosures. A disclosure not made in 'good faith' may lead to a reduction in compensation (ibid., s. 18).

THE SECRET SERVICES

The Official Secrets Act 1989 was introduced contemporaneously with the Security Service Act 1989, which placed the security service MI5 on a statutory basis instead of allowing MI5 to operate totally under the medieval obscurity of the royal prerogative. Under the ECHR, a statutory framework was necessary for the exercise by the service of its special investigatory powers. Provision was made for the authorization of interference with property (trespass) to obtain information under ministerial warrant. A commissioner (senior judge) was established to oversee the exercise of powers under warrant and a tribunal could hear complaints by those who were 'surveilled'. Subsequently, the Intelligence Services Act 1994 introduced limited forms of parliamentary oversight over the security and intelligence services by the Intelligence and Security Committee. Its members are 'notified persons' under Official Secrets Act 1989, s. 1 and are covered by that section (see earlier). Statutory regulation involving oversight of, and provision for dealing with, complaints about the intelligence service's

---

[10] Department for Constitutional Affairs, *Review of Statutory Prohibitions on Disclosure* (2005). Although some have been removed, others have been added: P. Birkinshaw and M. Varney, *Government and Information: The Law Relating to Access, Disclosure and Regulation* (4th edn, 2011), 935–44.

[11] Official Secrets Act 1989, s. 1(4)(b) provides disclosure of classes of documents to be considered 'damaging' under s. 1(3).

[12] *Government Security Classifications*, April 2014: https://www.gov.uk/government/uploads/system/uploads/attachment_data/file/251480/Government-Security-Classifications-April-2014.pdf.

(MI6) investigations and General Communications Headquarters (GCHQ) was introduced. Interception of communications had been placed onto a statutory basis in 1985. The statutory regulation of interception, surveillance, and the special powers of the services were either repealed or overhauled by the Regulation of Investigatory Powers Act 2000 (amended in July 2014 by emergency legislation). The revelations by Snowden (see earlier) brought home in a startling manner the shortcomings in the 2000 Act because of its alleged failure to keep abreast with the advances in technology allowing security and intelligence services to claim that global eavesdropping was not regulated by the terms of the 2000 Act. The Investigatory Powers Tribunal sat largely in public in July and October 2014 in the Royal Courts of Justice to hear arguments on the legality of security surveillance practices under Arts. 8 and 10 ECHR. The Tribunal was tasked with a review of the legality of surveillance practices of GCHQ under existing legislation and, assuming that the alleged surveillance had taken place, it found there had been no breaches of Arts. 8 or 10 ECHR in relation to the legislative framework. Specific facts and the proportionality of the surveillance in individual cases were to be subject to further examination in closed hearings. In the subsequent ruling on the system of surveillance existing prior to the date of the ruling above, as modified by the ruling on 6 February 2015, the tribunal found that the 'regime for soliciting, receiving, storing and transmitting by UK authorities of private communications of individuals located in the UK' and which had been obtained from the USA under Prism and Upstream surveillance contravened Arts 8 or 10 ECHR because the regime had not been in accordance with the law ie it had not been given adequate publicity. The two rulings above rendered the practices compliant through their disclosures.[13]

The so-called 'war on terror', as the Americans describe it, brought a new prominence to MI5 and MI6 and GCHQ, raising troubling questions about the secrecy surrounding their operations. Problems emerged in relation to secrecy in judicial proceedings, discussed later. Questions were raised about the ability of the Intelligence and Security Committee to conduct meaningful investigations into the activities of the secret services when it was revealed in litigation that important documents relevant to its enquiries had not been disclosed to the committee.[14] The committee has complained about not getting the information it requires.

The Justice and Security Act 2013, following a Green Paper (Cm 8194 (2011)), introduced some reforms to the committee and the way it operates. Part 1 of the Act creates a new Intelligence and Security Committee of Parliament (the ISC), to replace the Intelligence and Security Committee created by the Intelligence Services Act 1994. The new title emphasizes that it is a committee of Parliament and it continues to have

---

[13] *Liberty et al.* v. *General Communications HQ et al.* [2014] UKIPTrib 13-77-H, http://www.ipt-uk.com/docs/IPT_13_168-173_H.pdf. The government neither confirmed nor denied the truth of the allegations. The tribunal considered hitherto secret documents. For the further ruling see *Liberty et al v The Secretary of State for Foreign and Commonwealth Affairs etc* [2015] UKIPTrib 13 77-H at http://www.ipt-uk.com/docs/Liberty_Ors_Judgment_6Feb15.pdf (6/02/2015). Also http://www.thebureauinvestigates.com/2014/09/14/a-summary-of-the-bureaus-application-to-the-european-court-of-human-rights/.

[14] *Binyam Mohamed* v. *Secretary of State* [2009] EWHC 152 (Admin).

members from both houses. The statutory remit of the ISC is expanded to cover operations including (i) a role in overseeing the wider government intelligence community
(beyond the three security and intelligence agencies (the 'Agencies')) and (ii) retrospective oversight of the operational activities of the Agencies on matters of significant
national interest. The ISC is given powers to require information from the Agencies
subject only to a veto by the Secretary of State rather than, as was the case under the
Intelligence Services Act 1994, Agency heads. Parliament is given a more substantial
role in ISC appointments although members are nominated by the prime minister
after consulting the leader of the opposition.

ISC reports are subject to prime ministerial vetting before publication after consulting the committee. The ISC may report only to the prime minister. It appoints its
own chair although there is no specific provision for a member of the opposition to
hold this position which has been seen as a weakness. The Commissioner's functions
are also increased from those under the 2000 Act to keep under review other aspects
of the functions of the Agencies or any part of Her Majesty's forces or the Ministry of
Defence engaged in intelligence activities. The services are excluded from the FOIA
and information held by public authorities from the services or relating to them is
given an absolute exemption from that Act (see later). Public appearances before select
committees of Agency chiefs have increased and in November 2013 the Agency heads
appearance before ISC was televised (see n. 7).

COURTS, SECRECY, AND OPENNESS

The special demands of justice before courts have required inroads into government
secrecy. Long before the UK Parliament passed the FOIA 2000, the judges had increasingly recognized that the demands of justice might necessitate access to documents
in the possession of government (or government contractors) by litigants, although
they realized that it was not for the courts to create an FOI Act. Such a right, however,
had to meet a competing public interest claim from government. This was originally
expressed as Crown Privilege originating from the immunity of the Crown from suit
in its own courts.[15] Although the Crown Proceedings Act 1947 subjected the Crown
to legal suit in defined circumstances, the Crown could still resist disclosure of documents to a litigant either where the *existence* of the document should not be disclosed
or where, although the existence of the documents was acknowledged, inspection of
their class or contents would be contrary to the public interest. Public interest immunity as it came to be known often set a dramatic scene in which the competing public
interests of state security or protection of informers and investigatory methods on one
part, and the doing of justice on the other, have to be balanced by courts, if necessary
after judicial inspection of the documents.

---

[15] *Duncan* v. *Cammell Laird Co. Ltd* [1942] AC 624 originally accepted the decision of the minister as final
but *Conway* v. *Rimmer* [1968] AC 910 paved the way for the modern law.

The immunity became a matter of media and public debate in the trial of British businessmen for criminal offences involving breaches of export regulations when they exported dual-use equipment to Iraq in the 1990s. The *Matrix Churchill* trial collapsed after it was disclosed by a minister giving evidence that the government had known about the export of the equipment (one of the defendants had been assisting MI6) and that the export regulations had been changed without informing Parliament. This led to the Scott report on *The Export of Defence Equipment and Dual Use Goods to Iraq*.[16] What was of importance was that the dual-use trial had seen the reliance by the government on public interest immunity (PII) certificates in a criminal trial, and this put the defendants at risk of wrongful conviction. (The judge ruled against the certificates in several claims.) Their use in criminal trials, although predating *Matrix Churchill*, was to become more widespread in criminal trials involving terrorists and serious crime and where the prosecution was anxious to protect information about techniques, methods, and informers.[17] Eventually, a procedure was devised in cases involving suspected terrorists before the Special Immigration Appeals Commission challenging their detention before deportation on the grounds of national security and in judicial proceedings challenging control orders involving suspected terrorists. The procedure involved the use of special advocates who would meet the suspected terrorist before 'closed material' was disclosed to the special advocate, but who could not thereafter meet the suspect. This latter aspect was subject to a qualification (SI 2003/1034 r. 36(4) and (5) and CPR Pt 80(4) and (5)). The suspect would not see or hear the closed evidence and proceedings were conducted in camera for closed evidence and judgments involving closed material were not published. Closed material procedures (CMP) were extended to the statutory replacement for control orders—Terrorism Prevention and Investigation Measures.[18]

The shortcomings involved in using special advocates were well known to the courts.[19] Furthermore, the European Court of Human Rights found breaches of Art. 6 ECHR in the way the procedures operated, a judgment which had a constraining impact on the judgments of the House of Lords under domestic law.[20] The UK Supreme Court also refused to allow the extension of the CMP to common law actions.[21]

Following litigation concerning torture claims in which US intelligence information was disclosed in open judgment (after its disclosure in US litigation)[22] the prime

---

[16] HC 115 (1995–6).

[17] *R v. H* [2004] UKHL 3. See Criminal Justice Act 2003, Pt 5 and related codes and guidelines. After the Scott Report, the government undertook to make public interest immunity claims only on a contents and not a class basis.

[18] See https://www.gov.uk/government/uploads/system/uploads/attachment_data/file/298487/Un_Act_Independent_Review_print_ready.pdf.

[19] *Abu Rideh* [2008] EWHC 1993 (Admin).

[20] A v. *United Kingdom* [2009] ECHR 301 (CHR); *Secretary of State for the Home Department* v. *AF* [2009] UKHL 28. See *Bank Mellat* v. *HM Treasury* [2014] EWHC 3631 (Admin).

[21] *Al Rawi* v. *Security Service* [2011] UKSC 34. In *Bank Mellat No. 1* [2013] UKSC 38, a majority ruled in favour of the Supreme Court hearing an appeal under a CMP; see *Browning* v. *IC* [2014] EWCA Civ 1050.

[22] *R (Mohamed)* v. *Secretary of State* [2010] EWCA Civ 158.

minister announced a judicial inquiry by the Secret Services Commissioner into the allegations of torture, in which intelligence would be dealt with in private session. Prime Minister Cameron indicated that proposals would likely be made to restrict disclosure of intelligence information by courts in the future.[23]

The new regime was introduced in the Justice and Security Act 2013, Part II. Controversial proposals in the Green Paper were modified so that the court, under s. 6, now has control over the decision to allow a CMP after an application by a party to the litigation or of its own motion and which involves 'sensitive information'—that is to say, disclosure of which would be damaging to the interests of national security. It covers *all* civil litigation in the higher courts. Applications may be made for a CMP and the judge has to be satisfied that an application for a PII certificate has been considered but the requirements of fairness and justice require a CMP process. Two conditions have to be met before a declaration for a CMP is given: the proceedings would involve disclosure of sensitive information and a declaration is in the interests of fair and effective administration of justice (s. 6 (4) and (5)). The application may be supported by intercept evidence. A declaration may be revoked by the judge (s. 7) and s. 8 provides details on procedure. Under s. 12 an annual report must be made by the Secretary of State on CMPs to Parliament and s. 13 provides for a review of relevant provisions of Part 2. Decisions made must be Art. 6 compliant (s. 14(2)).

Provision is also made to amend the *Norwich Pharmacal*[24] ruling so that the court may not order disclosure under that ruling of information or 'alleged information' that is held by or for, or obtained from, an 'intelligence service' (as defined in sub-s. (6)), or which is derived from such information or relates to an intelligence service. A certificate preventing disclosure may additionally be issued if the Secretary of State considers it would be contrary to the interests of national security or the international relations of the United Kingdom to disclose the information, whether the information exists, or whether the person said to hold the information is in fact in possession of the information.

More generally, courts have developed tests for giving cogent and reliable reasons for decision-making.[25] In a striking case in 2007, the High Court ruled that the government announcement of a nuclear new-build policy was unlawful because of inadequate consultation and inadequate information on economics and nuclear waste. The government did not appeal.[26] The courts also became more conscious of the need to protect information relating to personal privacy by the application of ECHR, Art. 8

[23] Hansard, HC, cols. 175–90 (6 July 2010). The inquiry, conducted by Sir Peter Gibson, reported in December 2013, http://www.detaineeinquiry.org.uk/wp-content/uploads/2013/12/35100_Trafalgar-Text-accessible.pdf. In December 2014, the US Senate Select Committee on Intelligence issued a report of over 500 pages on Central Intelligence Agency practice on torture. Much of the report is still redacted (secret), http://www.intelligence.senate.gov/study2014/sscistudy1.pdf.

[24] *Norwich Pharmacal* v. *Customs and Excise Commissioners* [1974] AC 133.

[25] *R* v. *Secretary of State for the Home Department, ex parte Doody* [1994] AC 531; *Stefan* v. *GMC* [1999] 1 WLR 1293 (PC); *Uprichard* v. *Scottish Ministers* [2013] UKSC 21 on 'reasonableness'.

[26] *R (Greenpeace)* v. *Secretary of State for Trade and Industry* [2007] EWHC 311 (Admin).

to the law of confidentiality. The emphasis moved from protection of commercial confidences to protection of personal information.[27] But commercial organizations and celebrities were not slow to realize that they too had a right to privacy protection which might involve use of measures to stop publicity of any information about their involvement in litigation or of the litigation itself by use of 'super injunctions'.[28] Media abuse of privacy and infamous episodes forced the government to appoint an inquiry under Lord Justice Leveson to examine the *Culture, Practices and Ethics of the Press*, which included relations with the government and police.[29] Leveson's recommendation concerning statutory recognition of self-regulation of the press in a manner that maintained freedom of speech was not acted upon: the contest was between press self-regulation and regulation under a Royal Charter.

The courts have also emphasized the 'open justice' principle as a creature of the common law independently of the ECHR.[30] The demands of 'open justice' also have to cede ground to national security so even a criminal trial, or parts of a trial, may be held in camera although 'accredited members' of the press may be entitled to attend the trial on terms of confidentiality.[31]

EU REQUIREMENTS

Our international commitments brought about by membership of the Council of Europe and the European Union pressured the UK government to introduce reforms allowing individuals access to personal information or data held by what are known as data controllers. The law is now the DPA 1998, implementing Directive (EC) 95/46. The EU law is in the process of amendment based on a new regulation and directive.[32]

The DPA is one of a number of information provisions accompanying the FOIA and subsequent legislation. The legislation includes the Environmental Information Regulations 2004 (EIR 2004)[33] and the Reuse of Public Sector Information Regulations 2005. Government sits on a vast bank of information. Some of it needs to be protected for reasons of security, international relations, prevention of crime, protection of privacy. But much of it has the capacity to generate creation of wealth and development in the hands of those with the necessary skills. This was the objective behind the Reuse Directives.

---

[27] *Campbell* v. *MGN Ltd* [2002] UKHL 22. ECHR, Art. 8 protects private and family life.

[28] See the Committee of the Master of the Rolls (2011) http://www.judiciary.gov.uk/publications/committee-reports-super-injunctions/.

[29] http://webarchive.nationalarchives.gov.uk/20140122145147/http://www.official-documents.gov.uk/document/hc1213/hc07/0780/0780.asp.

[30] *Guardian News and Media* [2012] EWCA Civ 420, esp. para. 88; *Kennedy* v. *Charity Commission* [2014] UKSC 20; *A* v. *BBC* [2014] UKSC 25.

[31] *Guardian News and Media Ltd* v. *AB, CD* [2014] EWCA Crim B 1. Notes could be taken but would be 'securely stored' until the trial's conclusion.

[32] http://ec.europa.eu/justice/newsroom/data-protection/news/120125_en.htm.

[33] Implementing Directive (EC) 2003/4. The directive was based on the United Nations Aarhus Convention on Access to Information etc. (25 June 1998), http://www.unece.org/env/pp/welcome.html.

The European Court of Justice has also produced judgments in the areas of data protection with profound implications for this discussion. In *Digital Rights Ireland* the Grand Chamber of the Court of Justice ruled that the EU Electronic Communications Directive 2006/24 EC allowing indiscriminate retention of electronic data communications breached Arts. 7 and 8 of the EU Charter of Fundamental Rights (CFR). It was a disproportionate interference with privacy and there was a lack of 'clear and precise rules' governing the extent of interference with fundamental rights. The directive was invalid.[34] Domestic measures were based on this directive and emergency legislation was introduced to circumvent the ECJ's decision through legislation that was not based on the directive.[35] Existing powers to combat terrorism and serious crime were claimed by the Home Secretary to be 'inadequate'. The bill was criticized by privacy campaigners for being a 'snooper's charter'. The Home Secretary stated under the Human Rights Act that in her view the bill was compatible with the ECHR. Retention is required for *up to* 12 months. Section 1 provides that the Secretary of State may by notice require a public telecommunications operator to retain relevant communications data (identities, times, locations, and duration) if the Secretary of State considers that the requirement is necessary and proportionate for one or more specified purposes. The Act has extraterritorial effect. It also amends intercept (content) provisions.

Under the emergency legislation a review is to be conducted on investigatory powers and a report is to be completed by 1 May 2015 and will be presented to Parliament although items prejudicial to national security may be excluded (s. 7). The independent reviewer of terrorism legislation established under the Terrorism Act 2006 must consider current and future threats to the United Kingdom; capabilities needed to combat such threats; privacy safeguards; challenges faced by changing technologies; transparency and oversight; and the effectiveness of existing legislation and whether there is a case for new or amending legislation. The Interception of Communications Commissioner has oversight of the process of access to data and will now make half-yearly reports under s. 58 of the Regulation of Investigatory Powers Act 2000. The Information Commissioner (see later) monitors the security of stored data.

In *Google Spain* the Grand Chamber ruled that the service provided by Google Spain's search engines and access to third-party data links was subject to the EU Data Protection Directive on processing of personal data. In particular, the subject of the data should be allowed to require removal of their names and that data about them should no longer be available—a 'right to be forgotten'. It seemingly gives the data

---

[34] [2014] EUECJ C-293/12 (8 April 2014).

[35] Data Retention and Investigatory Powers Act 2014; see SI 2014/2042. See Counter-Terrorism and Security Act 2015, s. 21. Challenges under the EU Charter of Fundamental Rights based on arguments that the domestic measures are within the province of EU law are likely to be made. See the Director of MI5's speech on interception and retention capabilities, https://www.mi5.gov.uk/home/about-us/who-we-are/staff-and-management/director-general/speeches-by-the-director-general/director-generals-speech-on-terrorism-technology-and-accountability.html

subject a right to censorship. However, the court stated that such would not be the case 'if it appeared, for particular reasons, such as the role played by the data subject in public life, that the interference with fundamental rights is justified by the preponderant interest of the general public having...access to the information'.[36]

'OPENING UP' GOVERNMENT INFORMATION AND IT

The world has long been networked by the internet. To no surprise, governments have become prime users of networked information. In digitized government the launch of www.data.gov.uk (GOV.UK) in 2010 and the White Paper *Open Data* (Cm 8353, 2012) outline developments on information technology (IT) public service, openness, and use of government data by the private sector. *Open Data* proudly proclaimed 'The UK Government...one of the most open in the world' (p. 31). Transparency will lead to 'personalised, 21st century democracy' (p. 6). Data will be more freely available and over 9,000 datasets[37] have been released on www.data.gov.uk covering education, transport, crime, and justice. Local crime statistics, sentencing rates, school results, hospital infection rates, and GP outcomes will be published (pp. 5–6).

As well as publication schemes (see later) all 'departments' have published their first ever Open Data Strategies including commitments to publish more data. There have emerged Open Government Partnership UK, the Open Data Institute, the Public Sector Transparency Board, the Open Data User Group, and the Advisory Panel on Public Sector Information.[38] There are many policy statements on consultation[39] and numerous provisions concerning the wider public sector and regulated (formerly nationalized) industries and publication of information.

Many public bodies have responsibilities in relation to official information. The National Archives (NA—formerly Public Records Office) is responsible for national archives. It has already been noted that Scotland, Northern Ireland, and Wales have their own arrangements. The Office of Public Sector Information (OPSI) was brought within the NA and that body is at the heart of information policy, setting standards, delivering access, and encouraging the reuse of public sector information.[40] The NA's '21st-century role is to collect and secure the future of the government record, both digital and physical, to preserve it for generations to come, and to make it as accessible and available as possible'.[41] The Office for National Statistics operates under the independent UK Statistics Authority which reports to Parliament directly.

---

[36] *Google Spain AEPD* [2014] EUECJ C-131/12 (13 May 2014). See paras. 81 and 97.
[37] Protection of Freedoms Act 2012, s. 102(2)(c).
[38] See 'Transparency' and 'Open Data' on GOV.UK.
[39] https://www.gov.uk/government/publications/consultation-principles-guidance.
[40] See e.g. http://www.nationalarchives.gov.uk/information-management/re-using-public-sector-information/.
[41] http://www.nationalarchives.gov.uk/about/who-we-are.htm.

TOWARDS FREEDOM OF INFORMATION
LEGISLATION

Although the UK government was a late convert to FOI, efforts had been made to introduce greater openness into government operations involving Crown and non-Crown bodies. In local government an access to information statute was enacted in 1985: local authorities are under duties to allow the public to attend and film meetings of the authority and executive and, subject to exemptions, to disclose information.[42] Some other authorities are covered by open meetings laws, but this is not pervasive in the UK.

For the Crown, various non-legislative devices were introduced before the FOIA 2000, including John Major's 1994 Code on Openness. This imposed a non-statutory obligation on bodies covered by the Code (essentially those under the jurisdiction of the Parliamentary Ombudsman) to disclose information to requesters subject to exemptions. The Code was operational until 31 December 2004.

The Freedom of Information Bill was published in 1999. The bill was preceded by a White Paper,[43] pre-legislative consultation, and scrutiny by a House of Commons select committee as well as a special committee of the House of Lords.[44] The White Paper claimed that experience revealed the importance of changing culture by a requirement of 'active' disclosure, so that public authorities would get used to making information publicly available in the normal course of their activities.[45] It was one of several bills to be introduced by the Blair government as part of a package on constitutional reform. The bill and the eventual Act were less open than the White Paper's proposals. The bill received Royal Assent in November 2000. Rights of access came into effect on 1 January 2005. Over four years were spent preparing for a change in the culture of secrecy.

FOI was accompanied by grand claims. 'It is part of bringing our politics up to date, of letting politics catch up with the aspirations of people and delivering not just more open government but more effective, more efficient, government for the future.' It would signal a new relationship between government and governed, one which sees 'the public as legitimate stakeholders in the running of the country and sees election to serve the public as being given on trust'.[46] However, in his autobiography, Blair wrote of the FOIA as 'so utterly undermining of sensible government'.[47]

---

[42] Local Government (Access etc.) Act 1985; SIs 2012/2089, 2014/2095, 2014/2060, and 2014/2680. Statutes concerning the admission of the press to meetings of local authorities go back to 1908.

[43] *Your Right to Know: Freedom of Information*, Cm 3818 (1997).

[44] HC 398 I and II (1997–8), HC 570 I and II (1998–9), and HL 97 (1998–9).

[45] Cm 3818 (1997) paras 2.17–2.18.

[46] Tony Blair, *Speech to the Campaign for FOI Awards Ceremony*, 25 March 1996.

[47] T. Blair, *A Journey* (2010), 516.

In May 2010, the Coalition government immediately announced a new emphasis on extra-statutory transparency.[48] An initially non-statutory Independent Office for Budget Responsibility would report on public financial forecasting forming the basis of the Budget. The announcements included financial details of all government expenditure and contracts of government and details of senior officials' salaries. Publication would help to give people the information they really required rather than that which government wanted them to see. The government accepted this material was complex new data rather than easily usable comparative data. The Public Sector Transparency Board would be established in the Cabinet Office applying public data transparency principles.[49] Other proposals were outlined in *Open Data* (see earlier).

Any implicit criticism of FOI, and the fact that the FOIA 2000 was supposed to give the public the information they wanted, was overborne by the fact that extensions to the legislation were announced in the Coalition agreement in May 2010.[50] These are in the Protection of Freedoms Act 2012 and included publication of datasets. Nonetheless, in 2012 David Cameron stated 'the discovery process' under FOIA was 'furring up the arteries' of government.[51]

THE LEGAL FRAMEWORK

The main driving force behind greater official openness has been the FOIA 2000.[52] Under FOIA the body responsible for overseeing, promoting, and enforcing the Act is the Office of the Information Commissioner (IC). That office is responsible for a variety of additional information rights covered by the DPA 1998, the DP Monetary Penalty Regulations 2010, the EIR 2004, the Privacy and Electronic Communications (EC Directive) Regulations 2003, and the Information on Spacial Data in Europe Regulations. The Commissioner upholds information rights through education, empowering individuals, enabling improvement and continual engagement, as well as by enforcement. The annual reports set out the mission, vision, and goals of the Information Commissioner.

The FOIA seeks to give presumptive rights of individual access to information held by public authorities in the UK, subject to exemptions. The Information Tribunal, which may hear appeals against the Information Commissioner's decision, has stated that FOIA s. 1 creates a 'new fundamental right to information'.[53] The Act also seeks

---

[48] *The Coalition: Our Programme for Government—Government Transparency*, http://www.cabinetoffice.gov.uk/news/coalition-documents. For the development of policy on transparency, see http://transparency.number10.gov.uk.

[49] http://data.gov.uk/blog/new-public-sector-transparency-board.

[50] http://www.conservatives.com/News/News_stories/2010/05/Coalition_Agreement_published.aspx, see under 10 on civil liberties, and *The Coalition; Our Programme for Government* (2010).

[51] Commons Liaison Committee 6 March 2012 Qs 438–9, http://www.publications.parliament.uk/pa/cm201012/cmselect/cmliaisn/uc608-v/uc60801.htm.

[52] The sponsor department for FOIA is the Ministry of Justice. The Department for Environment, Food and Rural Affairs is the government sponsor for the EIR 2004 offering advice on the EIR and the environment.

[53] *DfES* v. *IC and Evening Standard (AP)*, EA/2006/0006, para. 61.

to make information available proactively through publication schemes. These were revised in 2009 and reviewed in 2012[54] together with guidance on such schemes by the Information Commissioner. The objective is that such schemes will cover more and more information, thus reducing the necessity of making a request for information. Basically schemes have to publish information about:

- what they spend and how they spend it
- who they are and what they do
- what their priorities are and how they are doing
- how they make decisions
- their policies and procedures
- lists and registers
- the services they offer.

Authorities have to specify what additional information they are to publish including financial reports, means of access and charges. The Commissioner has to approve such schemes but cannot control content.

ACCESS RIGHTS

The right of access under FOIA 2000 is to information held by a public authority.[55] On an application, an authority must confirm or deny whether it holds the information. Authorities bound by the Act are listed in FOIA, Sched. 1. If not listed—for example, the Queen, royal family, secret services—the body is *excluded* from the FOIA 2000. Estimates of bodies covered by FOIA vary between 100,000 and 115,000. It famously includes Parliament because FOIA led to disclosure of MPs abuse of expenses. Some bodies are partly under the FOIA but are excluded for some items: the Bank of England and BBC are examples here. The latter has featured in a large body of litigation on its exclusion from the FOIA for the purposes of information held relating to 'art, journalism or literature'.[56]

The Secretary of State for Justice has the power to designate private bodies as public authorities for FOIA purposes. Three bodies were designated in 2011[57]—all three had a notable quality of officialdom about them. The Secretary of State may designate as a public authority a body that is performing functions of a public authority under contract, or

---

[54] http://ico.org.uk/news/latest_news/2012/~/media/documents/library/Freedom_of_Information/Research_and_reports/publication_scheme_plan_for_2012-13.ashx.

[55] Guidance is provided on 'held', see generally https://www.justice.gov.uk/information-access-rights, https://www.justice.gov.uk/information-access-rights/foi-guidance-for-practitioners, and http://www.ico.gov.uk/what_we_cover/freedom_of_information.aspx.

[56] Birkinshaw, *Freedom of Information*, 6 and 142. See *Sugar* v. *BBC* [2012] UKSC 4.

[57] SI 2598/2011 which lists the functions covered by FOIA. The Association of Chief Police Officers was included.

performing functions of a public nature. In contracts, the FOIA will cover the authority. Guidance exists on how authorities should deal with requests for information about the contract.[58] The request is made to the authority not the private contractor. Private utilities are not covered by FOIA but the regulators are—so a request may be made for information held by them. Utilities are under duties to provide information under their governing statutes such as the Utilities Act 2000. Network Rail and Northern Rock following nationalization were identified as possible candidates for designation by the Conservatives in April 2010 and a draft order designating Network Rail was published in early 2015.

The EIR 2004 cover a wider range of bodies because of the way the regulations are phrased including those performing *functions* of *public administration* and bodies *controlled* by an authority.[59] A decision of the ECJ gave a wider interpretation to 'control' than had English case law and when a public authority covered by Art. 2(2)(a) or (b) of the directive is in a position to exert decisive influence on a body's action in the environmental field thereby removing a body's autonomy.[60] All authorities have to determine under which legal regime the information requested falls. It is not the responsibility of the requester.

The DPA 1998 covers holders of 'personal data' whether in the public or private sector. In the case of public authorities, they are covered by DPA protection in a broader range of 'unstructured' data, but these data are not regulated under the DPA as is the case with 'personal data' in electronic or 'structured filing systems'. These terms have been subject to a narrow interpretation by the Court of Appeal[61] which has been criticized by the EU Article 29 Data Protection Working Party. Personal data should be given a 'wide and flexible' interpretation.[62] In DPA cases the Commissioner can assess a data controller's processing of data at the request of a data subject to see whether there is compliance with the data protection principles which set out the standards of data protection.[63]

The FOIA 2000 covers UK bodies, Welsh and Northern Irish bodies, and English bodies as specified. Scotland has its own FOI Act, the Freedom of Information (Scotland) Act 2002 for Scottish authorities.[64] The Scottish act is based largely on the UK measure but with some crucial differences. *Anyone*, irrespective of motive, may

---

[58] http://ico.org.uk/for_organisations/guidance_index/~/media/documents/library/Freedom_of_Information/Detailed_specialist_guides/AWARENESS_GUIDANNCE_5_ANNEXE_V3_07_03_08.ashx.

[59] See *Network Rail Ltd* v. *IC and NRI Ltd, FoE etc*, EA/2006/0061-62; *Port of London Authority* v. *IC and another*, EA/2006/0083; and *Smartsource* v. *IC* [2010] UKUT 415 (AAC).

[60] *Fish Legal* v. *Information Commissioner* [2013] EUECJ C-279/12 (19 December 2013).

[61] *Durant* v. *FSA* [2003] EWCA Civ 1746. The court held that data should have a 'biographical' focus to be personal data.

[62] See the ICO, http://ico.org.uk/for_organisations/data_protection/the_guide/~/media/documents/library/Data_Protection/Detailed_specialist_guides/PERSONAL_DATA_FLOWCHART_V1_WITH_PREFACE001.ashx.

[63] DPA 1998, s. 42. The IC does not issue decision notices under the DPA; he issues figures annually on DPA 'complaint casework' and enforcement.

[64] http://www.england-legislation.hmso.gov.uk/legislation/scotland/acts2002/asp_20020013_en_1.

make a written request under the FOIA for information. The right covers 'recorded' information in whatever form. No interest or *locus* has to be established. Where the rights of others are involved, the provision of safeguards is contained in a code under FOIA, s. 45. This sets out good practice in relation to consultation with third parties. A third party has no rights of appeal under the Act and would have to commence a judicial review or private action preventing disclosure under the FOIA. After disclosure, injuries to a third party would have to be compensable under private actions. Breaches of the FOIA itself create no rights of action, but negligence and confidentiality are common law actions, not breaches of the Act. FOI disclosures are privileged unless malice is present.

Under the FOIA, authorities have 20 working days to respond to a request. This period may be extended where an authority is relying upon a public interest not to disclose (see later). A further 20 working days should suffice, the IC has suggested. Some cases have gone on for more than two years. Delays occur because of complexity or lack of personnel (in either an authority or the IC's Office).

The FOI right is a right to 'information' but records and files, subject to exemption, may be inspected *in situ*. A summary may be requested. The requester may state a preference and 'so far as possible' an authority shall respect that preference. Documents may be requested.[65] The requester has to supply a name for correspondence and an address (including email). Fees may be requested. The requester may be asked to clarify a request and for further information to assist the authority. An authority must provide advice and assistance.

If it is anticipated that the fees involved will exceed the fees limit the requester may be asked to make payment of the estimated amount. Fees are waived up to £600 in the case of central government, armed forces, and Parliament, and £450 in the case of all other authorities. Labour is costed at £25 per hour. Requests involving fees in excess of these amounts may be refused or complied with if the requester agrees to pay the required amount. Fees for copying and postage (disbursements) may be charged.

An authority refusing a request must state under FOIA, s. 17 which exemption applies and the reasons why it applies (if not apparent) and, if relying on a public interest, must state the reasons why the public interest applies. The Commissioner and Tribunal have given rulings on the giving of reasons. A mere reiteration of statutory words is not enough. The reasons must properly explain the basis of the decision without compromising properly exempt information. Notice also has to be given in the statement of the rights of internal review and of appeal to the Commissioner.

If information is refused, a requester may ask for an internal review. The justification for the administrative review was to keep the process cheap and accessible. This was also the reason for introducing the Commissioner and Tribunal. The Commissioner and Tribunal do not charge fees and each party bears their own costs before the Tribunal—unless they behave vexatiously. The Tribunal is meant to operate

---

[65] See *IPSA* v. *IC*, EA/2012/0242 and [2014] UKUT 33 (AAC).

informally so legal representation would not be required. Legal representation is, however, becoming increasingly common.

THE POWERS OF THE INFORMATION COMMISSIONER AND INFORMATION TRIBUNAL

If the Commissioner believes the authority is failing in its duties, he may issue an enforcement notice which the authority may appeal (FOIA, s. 52). When the Commissioner determines whether access should be given or denied, he issues a decision notice. In addition, the Commissioner has power to issue information notices. Failing to comply with notices by not providing the information may be treated as a contempt which is punishable by fine or (rarely) imprisonment.

False statements and alteration of documents (for example in response to a request), except where properly authorized *before* a request, are criminal offences.[66] The Commissioner may issue a practice recommendation under FOIA, s. 48 in relation to practices which do not meet the standards set out in the Code of Guidance under ss. 45 or 46 (on management of public records). The Commissioner has full powers of entry and inspection after obtaining a judicial warrant. These are considerable powers.

The Commissioner's office is on an FOI budget of £4 million (£5.5 million (2009–10)) plus fees for DPA notification of data controllers. The future of these fees may be placed in doubt with EU DP reforms. The office has been subject to a five-yearly decrease of £250,000 per annum in its grant. The main area of uncertainty for 2015–16 and beyond lay in income and expenditure.[67]

EXEMPTIONS

FOI regimes are invariably accompanied by exemptions. Most exemptions under the FOIA are qualified and subject to a public interest test which is measured first of all by the authority receiving a request. Published guidance and case law explain the approaches that authorities should adopt.[68] It is then subject to the judgement of the Commissioner and on appeal covering fact, law, or merits to the Tribunal. The onus of establishing an exemption, or public interest in non-disclosure, lies on the authority, not the requester. Decisions on the public interest ordering disclosure are subject to a ministerial veto (see later). Whether information is intended for future publication, whether requests are repetitive or vexatious,[69] whether information is available elsewhere—all grounds for denying access—are all appealable. The Upper Tribunal and Court of Appeal can only hear appeals on a point of law from the Tribunal, i.e.

---

[66] The Justice Committee reported in 2012 that there had been no prosecutions under s. 77 FOIA (see later under 'Justice Review Committee').

[67] *Justice Committee Review 2013–14*, HC 515 (2014–15). See Justice Committee HC 962 (2012–13) and *The ICO Plan 2013–16* (2013).

[68] See n. 55.   [69] See *Dr Yeong Ah Soh* v. *IC*, EA/2013/0054, on 'vexatious'.

not on the merits, so they cannot intervene in a judgement call unless it involves a legal error. To maintain secrecy, the balance in favour of secrecy has to outweigh that in favour of disclosure. Where the interests are equal in weight, disclosure prevails (FOIA, s. 2(1)(b) and (2)(b)).

Some exemptions under the Act are 'absolute', meaning there is no public interest override favouring disclosure.

Some FOIA exemptions are class exemptions—that is, if information falls within that class it is exempt. In other cases, the majority, exemptions are only allowed where damage or harm would be caused, or would be likely to be caused, by disclosure. Unless the exemption is absolute, a public interest test applies (see earlier). Some authorities have tried to argue that intellectual property rights are a de facto FOIA exemption. They are not: they have to fall within an existing exemption, for example commercial interests, trade secrets, confidentiality.[70]

The exemptions are set out in FOIA, ss. 21–44. An addition, introduced in the Intellectual Property Act 2014, s. 20, covers research and this is subject to the public interest test. These sections define the protected interests. In the case of national security (s. 24), and also the secret services (s. 23), a minister may enter a certificate to this effect which the Upper Tribunal may review but in a very limited way. Otherwise the exemption is reviewable by the Commissioner—that is to say, the Commissioner may establish whether the exemption is made out or not. If established, then the Commissioner determines the public interest in disclosure or non-disclosure where the authority has decided not to disclose.

The exemptions are too numerous to list fully but include: information intended for future publication; research; information supplied by, or relating to, bodies dealing with security matters (absolute); national security (see earlier); defence; international relations; relations within the UK; the economy; law enforcement; court records (absolute); audit functions; formulation of government policy, etc.; prejudice to effective conduct of public affairs (absolute in relation to Parliament); communications with the sovereign, etc.; and honours. Section 37 was amended by Constitutional Reform and Governance Act 2010, s. 46 and Sched. 7 so that communications by authorities with the sovereign and heir and second in line of succession to the throne are absolutely exempt as are communications with those who subsequently become sovereign, etc. Exemptions cover information provided in confidence, commercial secrets, and legal professional privilege. Personal and environmental information are covered by their own regimes. In the case of all absolute exemptions, apart from s. 23 and the new additions to s. 37, the exemption is absolute because there are other regimes dealing with access or there are legal prohibitions on disclosure which are binding on the authority. Superficially, it appears that there are 24 exemptions. In fact, there are more than this because some sections

---

[70] Under the EIR 2004, see *R (Ofcom)* v. *IC* [2009] EWCA Civ 90. See ICO guidance, *Intellectual Property Rights and Disclosures under the FOIA.*

confer multiple exemptions. The wide number of exemptions has led to a great deal of criticism.

THE VETO

The FOIA allows a Cabinet minister (or Attorney General) to issue a veto which overrides the decision of the Commissioner or Tribunal to allow disclosure or where those bodies rule that the Neither Confirm Nor Deny provision (NCND) is not applicable (FOIA, s. 53). NCDC applies to most exemptions and allows an authority to override the duty to confirm or deny whether it holds documents upon request where such confirmation or denial would involve the disclosure of exempt information. The veto is final, subject to a judicial review.

There have been seven vetoes to date (the most recent in January 2014). The first two vetoes concerned disclosure of Cabinet minutes involving discussion of the Attorney General's legal advice on invading Iraq, and on devolution.[71] In both cases the Justice Secretary emphasized the overriding need for collective responsibility and confidentiality of Cabinet discussions. In the first case the veto was issued after the Tribunal upheld the Commissioner's decision notice ordering disclosure. In the second case the veto was issued after the Commissioner's decision to order disclosure. Although legally the decision on a veto is that of the Justice Secretary, an undertaking was given in 2004 that Cabinet colleagues would be consulted. In the case of the Iraq veto, it was widely felt that the veto was issued not to protect sensitive information but to prevent the public seeing how little meaningful discussion on such a fateful decision took place.

In October 2012 a veto was issued by the Attorney General in relation to disclosure of correspondence between departments and Prince Charles. This was after the Commissioner had ruled against the requester on public interest grounds. The case involved both FOIA and EIRs. In an exceptionally detailed and comprehensive judgment the Upper Tribunal ruled in the requester's favour on an appeal from the Commissioner's decision.[72] Essentially, the Upper Tribunal ruled that 'it will generally be in the public interest for there to be transparency as to how and when Prince Charles seeks to influence government' (para. 4). This was advocacy by the Prince. It was to be distinguished from 'education' in governance in preparation for his role as monarch.

The veto was then issued. The Attorney General stated he had on reasonable grounds formed the opinion that there was no failure to comply with the relevant provisions of the FOIA or the EIR.

The veto was judicially reviewed by the Divisional Court which ruled in the Attorney General's favour.[73]

---

[71] See O. Gay and E. Potton, *FOI and Ministerial Vetoes*, SN/PC/05007 (March 2014).

[72] *Rob Evans* v. *IC etc* [2012] UKUT 313 (AAC).

[73] *R (Evans)* v. *HM Attorney General* [2013] EWHC 1960 (Admin).

However, the Divisional Court was itself overruled by the Court of Appeal.[74] In relation to the FOIA, the Master of the Rolls ruled that 'reasonable' depends upon context and facts. Here the context was a judgment of 'meticulous detail' by the Upper Tribunal with which the Attorney General disagreed and on which he did not have any 'additional material' and which did not reveal an error of law or fact (para. 37). It is not reasonable for a person to issue a s. 53 certificate merely because he disagrees with the decision. The reasoning has specifically to address the content and detail of the decision that is vetoed.

Of greater potential was the manner with which the court dealt with the appeal under the EIRs which also covered some of the information. The court found breaches of Art. 47 CFR (an effective remedy) and Art. 6(2) and (3) of the Aarhus Directive which the EIRs implement. The veto denied access to justice by the requester. The veto was an executive act terminating the legal process. Judicial review was only against the Attorney General who issued the veto not against the public authority making the original decision. In these circumstances a judicial review of the veto misses the real target—the merits of the original decision of the public authority. This bold judgment may end to the use of the veto under EIRs. The Justice Committee in its review of the FOIA reported that the veto was a necessary device to protect policy development at the highest of levels. However, on 26 March 2015, the Supreme Court dismissed the appeal against the Court of Appeal's judgment: see *Late News*, at p. vii.

POLICY-MAKING AND INTERNAL PROCESSES OF DECISION-MAKING: SOME EXAMPLES

It is not possible to examine all the FOIA exemptions here, but particularly important issues have arisen in relation to policy-making, internal processes of decision-making, and privacy protection.

FOIA, s. 35 protects among other things: government policy-making processes, collective responsibility of government, and advice of the law officers; and s. 36 the effective working of government and other authorities. They are both very broadly drafted. Provision is made under s. 35 for the release of statistical and factual information once a decision is taken and under s. 36 for statistical information. Section 35 is class-based; s. 36 is contents-based—where the reasonable opinion of a qualified person believes that prejudice or inhibition would be caused by disclosure.

DfES v. IC and Evening Standard (AP)[75] saw s. 35(1)(a) invoked. Information about setting of school budgets in England was requested; in particular the minutes of a policy committee. The formulation and development of policy had to be distinguished from implementation of policy and its analysis, the Tribunal reasoned. The Tribunal identified the dangers of 'sofa government' by use of specialist advisers. The words 'relates to formulation and development of policy' in s. 35 are to be construed broadly.

---

[74] *R (Evans) v. HM Attorney General* [2014] EWCA Civ 254.
[75] *DfES v. IC and Evening Standard (AP)*, EA/2006/0006.

There was no need to prevent disclosure of officials' identities. The status of 'minutes' does not automatically exempt documents even though they apply to the 'most senior of officials'. 'To treat such status as automatically conferring exemption would be tantamount to inventing within s. 35(1) a class of absolutely exempt information for which the subsection gives no warrant . . . '.[76] The case set out the arguments in favour of disclosure and the application of the public interest test under s. 35(1).

The guiding principles are as follows. The content of particular information is relevant. No status is automatically exempt. The protection is against compromise or unjust public opprobrium of civil servants *not* ministers. Timing of a request is paramount. What is highly relevant in June 2012 may carry little weight by January 2015. A parliamentary statement announcing the policy 'will normally mark the end of the process of policy formulation'. Facts must be viewed carefully, however, and a public interest in exemption may not disappear on announcement. Fortitude and neutrality are expected of civil servants. But there may be good reason to withhold the names of more junior civil servants.

The Tribunal proceeded on the basis that ministers will behave fairly and responsibly to civil servants who may be associated with unpopular advice. There must be a *specific reason* justifying non-disclosure of a civil servant's identity—a blanket policy cannot be justified. There is a general public interest in transparency and better understanding of how the government tackles important policy problems. The 'funding crisis' in schools was of great public concern. The information may not prove to be significant in any public debate but the public interest favoured disclosure.

R (Evans) v. *IC and MoD*[77] concerned meetings of a minister and an arms lobbying company. Sections 36(2)(b)(i) and 35(1) were invoked. The case ruled that the public interest is that at the time of a request. That interest was not advanced by disclosing informal 'notes' of the meeting. As a general rule the public interest in maintaining an exemption diminishes over time. The witnesses were not able to show evidence of inhibitory effects of disclosure of formal notes. Where the information is in a raw unconsidered form the public interest in maintaining the exemption is likely to diminish more slowly than where the information is in a finished considered form.[78] A fear of the inhibiting effect of disclosure on lobbyists was overstated. In relation to *notes* of meetings and telephone conversations the exemptions were maintained on public interest grounds because these were unfinished and incomplete. In relation to 'finished' background notes there was no such inhibition and the public interest favoured disclosure. In a subsequent ruling the Tribunal decided that s. 40 (personal data) protected the information (see later).

The Commissioner and Tribunal have made some important decisions and have not been easily impressed by official pleas of damage to Civil Service impartiality,

---

[76] At [69].

[77] *R (Evans)* v. *IC and MoD*, EA/2006/0064. See *Home Office* v. *IC*, EA/2011/0265, 66, 67 on s. 27 balance of public interest in favour of non-disclosure.

[78] *Evans*, at [41].

neutrality, or effectiveness in using the public interest override to disclose advice to ministers. Civil Service neutrality is a core feature in the UK constitution because the Civil Service is 'permanent' serving different governments independently and disinterestedly. Disclosure was nonetheless ordered and the alleged danger of a 'chilling effect' has not materialized. Where policy remains unresolved information has not been released.

The Commissioner and Tribunal have stated that there is an assumption built into the FOIA that disclosure of information by public authorities in response to a request is in the public interest in order to promote *transparency* and *accountability* in relation to the activities of public authorities. 'The public interest factors in favour of disclosure…can take into account the general public interests in the promotion of *transparency, accountability, public understanding* and *involvement* in the democratic process'.[79] Such factors will have to be balanced against inhibition on discussion, the recent status of a decision, and comprehensiveness of information used in decision-making.[80]

The Tribunal has noted the 'default setting' of the Act favours disclosure; there are generic 'good governance' arguments for transparency; the specific content and circumstances must be established on a case-by-case basis and the lapse of time of request is paramount—is the issue still live?[81]

PERSONAL INFORMATION

One interesting development has been the FOIA/DPA interface. Data protection was widely invoked to attempt to prevent access to documents which contained the names of individuals, usually officials but sometimes lobbyists and government interlocutors. There was a fear that a coach and horses would be driven through the FOIA. In numerous cases the Commissioner and Tribunal have ruled that under DPA, Sched. 2, para. 6, the legitimate interests of the requester may allow disclosure depending on the facts.[82] Disclosure under FOIA of personal data is disclosure to the whole world.[83] There has been a willingness to protect the identity of junior officials. Furthermore, FOIA, s. 41 exempts information protected by confidentiality and it is an absolute exemption. The law of confidentiality itself provides a defence against actions for breaches of confidentiality if disclosures are made in the public interest. There is no confidence in an iniquity. Unlike the FOIA and establishing the public interest in qualified exemptions, the onus on proving the public interest under confidentiality lies upon the requester. The development of protection of personal information by the application of ECHR, Art. 8 to the common law of confidentiality has

---

[79] *Dr John Pugh MP* v. *IC*, EA/2007/0055 (emphasis added).

[80] FS50126011, Freedom of Information Act 2000 (Section 50) Decision Notice (5 August 2008).

[81] EA 2007/0070 (8 August 2008), paras. 76–7. See also *FCO* v. *IC & Plowden* [2013] UKUT 275 (AAC) and *Cabinet Office* v. *IC*, EA/2013/0119.

[82] See n. 85.   [83] *M Cubells* v. *IC & GMC*, EA/2013/0038.

been noted. Documents may be redacted to allow non-confidential/private items to be disclosed.

The DPA 1998 and s. 40 FOIA do not constitute a complete privacy protection law. But protection of personal information traverses both statutes and a high degree of privacy protection is required.[84] By virtue of FOIA, s. 40, access to one's own data is provided for by the DPA. Access to data involving another is made under the FOIA but subject to the Data Protection Principles. In essence, in most cases, contravention of these principles makes access to another's personal data an absolute exemption.

The Commissioner and Tribunal have made important decisions allowing access to documents with the names of persons on them where the requester has a legitimate interest in knowing that data. The Commissioner has applied DPA, Sched. 2(6) to allow access where he believed that there was a necessary legitimate interest in ensuring openness, transparency, and accountability, and that disclosure would impose no unwarranted interference with privacy.[85] Distinguishing between 'private' and 'professional' capacities does not deprive personal data of its quality as such but in the latter case the status may assist an argument in terms of legitimate interest in accessing data.[86]

THE FOIA 2000 IN ACTION: SOME EXAMPLES

- The most high-profile case concerned the MPs' expenses saga where MPs had abused the system for claiming accommodation and other expenses (EA/2007/0061, 0122-23, 0131). The High Court judgment resulted in wider disclosure than the Commissioner had originally ordered.[87] Two ministers resigned and the Speaker of the House of Commons resigned because of severe criticism— the first time this had occurred since 1695. The expenses system was subject to a statutory overhaul under the Parliamentary Standards Act 2009.

- There was disclosure on negotiated terms of the Attorney General's advice on the legality of the war in Iraq after leaks. However, details of a telephone conversation between Prime Minister Blair and President Bush before the Iraq invasion were not disclosed.[88]

- There were disclosures over a period of four years relating to the Iraq weapons of mass destruction dossier.[89]

---

[84] *Common Services Agency* v. *Scottish Information Commissioner (Scotland)* [2008] UKHL 47. See *Google Spain*, n. 36.

[85] See FS50088016 (27 November 2008) and FS50508076 (5 June 2014); EA/2014/0023; and cf. Cases C-92/09 and 93/09 *Volker and Markus* (ECJ). See *S Lanarkshire Council* v. *IC* [2013] UKSC 55.

[86] See Case C-28/08 P, *Bavarian Lager*, 29 June 2010 (ECJ).

[87] *Corporate Officer of the HC* v. *IC* [2008] EWHC 1084 (Admin).

[88] *S Plowden/FCO* v. IC EA/2011/0225 and 0228 (21 January 2014); see para. 38 on change in public interest over time.

[89] *Foreign and Commonwealth Office* v. *IC*, EA/2007/0047.

- Disclosures have been made relating to government contracts and commercial interests of bodies dealing with public authorities.[90]

- Cabinet minutes have been the subject of vetoes as explained and in several other Cabinet cases the Commissioner has ruled against disclosure.[91] In the FS50088735 Decision Notice,[92] the Commissioner ordered disclosure of the minutes of the Cabinet meeting discussing the Westland helicopter episode in 1986 when there was a major dispute in policy between Mrs Thatcher and Mr Heseltine. The government objected to disclosure but the Tribunal upheld the Commissioner's decision notice on appeal.[93]

- Refusals to disclose Prince Charles's correspondence with ministers have been upheld, vetoed and judicially reviewed as discussed earlier.[94]

- Guidance concerning consultations with the monarch and Prince Charles in relation to legislation was disclosed.[95]

- One minister and his advisers argued that private email accounts were not covered by the Act; they were when it was government business the Information Commissioner ruled.[96]

There is nothing in their record since the FOIA came into operation to suggest timidity on the part of the Commissioner or Tribunal. Many decisions on the public interest have been more robust than government would like and have incurred vetoes under s. 53. Civil servants must accept that they now operate in an FOI culture with greater openness and transparency accompanying their advice, although timing is crucial the Commissioner and Tribunal have ruled. National security and international and diplomatic relations have been respected although there have been public interest disclosures in the latter.

REVIEWS OF AND REPORTS ON FREEDOM OF INFORMATION

Major objectives associated with FOI have been identified from official publications by Hazell and colleagues.[97] The study found that while openness and transparency in government had increased, other objectives such as improving decision-making, public understanding of government and its decision-making, and increasing trust and

---

[90] See *Derry City Council* v. *IC*, EA/2006/0014; and *Office of Government Commerce* v. *IC*, EA/2006/0068 and 0080 and [2008] EWHC 737 (Admin).

[91] *D. Bowden* v. *IC*, EA/2008/0090. 　　[92] FS50088735, Decision Notice (22 December 2009).

[93] *Cabinet Office* v. *IC*, EA/2010/0031.

[94] On refusals to disclose the prince's correspondence to public authorities, see http://www.ico.gov.uk/global/search.aspx?collection=ico&keywords=Correspondence+from+Prince+Charles.

[95] FS50425063, Decision Notice, 21 August 2012.

[96] FS50422276, Decision Notice, 1 March 2012. 　　[97] R. Hazell et al., *Does FOI Work?* (2010).

participation in government had not increased, or not significantly. The claims by the promoters of the law were exaggerated, the authors found. Claims by government for one of its reforms are always likely to be subject to exaggeration. Furthermore, a study based on four and a half years of operation of a major reform is working on limited data. Cultures take years to change. Hundreds of years of non-encouragement of wide public involvement in government will not be overcome in a short space of time. At the root of the FOIA 2000 is a basic principle: information affecting us and our welfare is not the preserve of government.

The Information Commissioner's Office produces annual reports and other reports on all their work.[98] The Commissioner[99] received 5,151 FOI and EIR complaints in 2013–14 (3,734 complaints in 2009–10); 55.8% were closed in 30 days or less (49% in 2009–10); 65.9% were closed in 90 days or less (66%); 0.2% took longer than a year to complete—a dramatic decrease (24%). Of closed cases in 2013–14, 39% were made too early (no internal review), a decision notice was served in 24% of cases, 16% were resolved informally, 20% were ineligible, and 2% were not progressed. A total of 1,261 decision notices were served (2009–10, 628), of which 25% upheld the complainant, 61% did not uphold the complainant, and 14% partially upheld the complainant. There are figures on DPA complaints of which 14,738 were received in 2013-14—a 7.1% increase on 2012–13. The report contains information on facts about other information rights, on enforcement notices, civil monetary penalties and on advice and assistance.

The report strikes up a note of warning. '[I]n order to be an effective partner in delivering modern and innovative services, the ICO needs stronger powers, a more sustainable system, and a clearer guarantee of independence' (p. 8).

THE JUSTICE COMMITTEE REVIEW

The House of Commons Justice Committee reported favourably on the Act saying the FOIA has been a 'significant enhancement of our democracy' (p. 3).[100] Overall the Act was working well. The Act has achieved its three principal objectives of greater openness, transparency, and accountability of the public sector, 'but its secondary objective of enhancing public confidence in Government has not been achieved, and was unlikely to be achieved' (p. 3). It emphasized that the right to access public sector information is an important constitutional right, 'a fact that can get lost in complaints about the operation of the freedom of information regime' (p. 3). 'We do not believe that there has been any general harmful effect at all on the ability to conduct business in the public service, and in our view the additional burdens are outweighed by the benefits' (p. 3).

---

[98] http://ico.org.uk/about_us/performance/annual_reports.

[99] ICO, *Annual Report and Financial Statements 2013–14*. The 2009–10 figures are from ICO, *Annual Report 2009–10*, HC 220 (2010–11).

[100] HC 96 I-III (2012–13), http://www.publications.parliament.uk/pa/cm201213/cmselect/cmjust/96/9602.htm. The Government Reply is Cm 8505 (November, 2012).

The Committee heard considerable evidence from *eminences grises* of the harmful effect on policy- and decision-making in central government and that a 'safe space' had been removed. It reminded critics that s. 35 FOIA had been devised to protect high-level policy-making and that government retained the veto power. The veto has been invoked by the Coalition government on five occasions in two years.

The Committee suggested various reforms on time limits and other matters and noted the criticism of the FOIA costs—the 'Achilles' Heel'. Evidence was heard of greater complexity in requests (p 29). 'However, the cost to public authorities must be weighed against the greater accountability the right to access information brings. In addition, there is evidence of both direct cost savings, where a freedom of information request has revealed erroneous public spending, and an indirect impact whereby public authorities know that they will be exposed to scrutiny as a result of the Act and use resources accordingly.' It recommended a limited reduction in the amount of time an authority has to spend on a request. All public authorities covered by the Act should publish details on compliance times (p. 44).

Some of the most fascinating pages from the report concern FOI and contracted-out government and the application of transparency to outsourcing delivery of public services. Privatization must not entail secrecy. The Justice Committee seemed to prefer clauses in contracts between authorities and private service providers rather than formal designation under the Act: 'the right to access information is crucial to ensuring accountability and transparency for the spending of taxpayers' money, and that contracts for private or voluntary sector provision of public services should always contain clear and enforceable obligations which enable the commissioning authority to meet FOI requirements' (para. 239). The Committee was anxious to preserve a level playing field between public and private competitors in research and service provision although it regarded universities as public institutions who were rightly within the FOIA's jurisdiction (para. 232). Overall, the surveys show increased support for FOI by the press and public and increased popularity of the measure. Press and media have come to have a high regard for the FOIA. One may surmise that a *volte face* on the FOIA 2000 would be disastrous public relations for government.

THE DATA PROTECTION ACT 1998, SURVEILLANCE, AND PRIVACY

The movement to greater collection, disclosure, and access to information was accompanied by growing demands for privacy protection. In 2006 the Commissioner described how we are sleep-walking into a surveillance society in which privacy is inadequately protected.[101] The Snowden revelations gave renewed support to those

---

[101] http://news.bbc.co.uk/1/shared/bsp/hi/pdfs/02_11_06_surveillance.pdf, and Surveillance Studies Network, *A Report on the Surveillance Society* (2006). It was the IC who originally identified practices that led to the Leveson inquiry.

claims. The capacity of the state as well as social media and Google to harness IT to store and disclose personal information is well known.[102] CCTV cameras are everywhere. The Regulation of Investigatory Powers Act provisions on surveillance are notoriously broad and now anachronistic and some are used to cover relatively innocuous activities. National and international data banks exist for numerous subject areas and the DPA has shown itself to be inadequate to guarantee data security. A national government communications data bank was ruled out by the Home Secretary in 2009. The government dropped plans to introduce regulations on data communications extending the scope to real-time communications but the position has been thrown into some doubt through the decision of the ECJ on *Digital Rights*[103] The government reaction by way of emergency legislation subject to a review within a year was noted earlier. The Criminal Justice and Immigration Act 2008 introduced custodial sentences for unlawful obtaining, buying, and selling of personal data and provided powers for the Commissioner to impose monetary penalties for serious breaches of the Data Protection Principles which occur 'knowingly' or 'recklessly'.[104] The custodial powers have not yet been implemented by regulations although the Fraud Act has been used as a basis to prosecute obtaining data by deception. In addition, the Coroners and Justice Act 2009, Pt 8 empowers the Commissioner to inspect the processing of personal information. However, this only covers government departments and NHS health bodies not the public sector generally or the private sector unless designated. The Commissioner must also prepare a code of practice on assessments and a code which contains practical guidance in relation to the sharing of personal data in accordance with the requirements of the DPA. This is subject to consultation with the Secretary of State and laying before Parliament.[105]

There have been a number of controversial DPA cases. The Court of Appeal in 2009 overruled the Commissioner and Tribunal, both of which had decided that minor convictions committed by young persons many years previously should be erased from the data held by police forces. Convictions may become 'spent' but there are numerous exceptions to this where information is required for specific purposes including employment. In the cases in question, the Court ruled that keeping the data for a period of 25 years was not overlong or excessive and would therefore be subject to disclosure provisions in relation to the Criminal Records Bureau (see later) and prospective employers. A conviction or reprimand for common assault or minor acts of shop-lifting by a teenager could jeopardize employment prospects for life where information is retained and disclosable for very long periods.[106] This decision must

---

[102] See *Google Spain* (n. 36) and *Delphi As* v. *Estonia*, App. No. 64569/09 CHR First Section (10 October 2013) referred to Grand Chamber.

[103] See n. 34. Council Directive (EC) 2006/24 was the basis of the previous regime authorizing data retention. Germany and several other EU member state constitutional courts ruled domestic implementing measures unconstitutional: http://www.bverfg.de/pressemitteilungen/bvg10-011en.html.

[104] SI 2010/31 and SI 2010/910.

[105] See also Law Commission, *Data Sharing*, HC 505 (2014–15).

[106] *Humberside Chief Constable of Police etc.* v. *Information Commissioner* [2009] EWCA Civ 1079.

now be seen in the light of *T and another* where the Supreme Court ruled that legislation which requires the *indiscriminate* disclosure by the state of personal data which it has collected and stored does not contain adequate safeguards against arbitrary interferences with Art. 8 rights.[107] Such disclosures were not in accordance with the law and were not necessary or proportionate it was held in a judgment heavily reliant on ECHR jurisprudence.

In 2008 the UK was found to be in breach of ECHR, Art. 8 in relation to the indefinite retention of DNA data by the police including that of unconvicted suspects.[108] In response the Crime and Security Act 2010 was passed and provided a statutory framework for the retention and destruction of biometric materials, including DNA samples, DNA profiles, and fingerprints that have been taken from an individual as part of the investigation of a recordable offence.[109] The Coalition government's Protection of Freedoms Act of 2012 removed or reduced most of the periods of retention in the 2010 measure. A Commissioner for retention and use of biometric material was established to review police retention and use of DNA samples, profiles, and fingerprints. The Act also established the Disclosure and Barring Service which replaced the Criminal Records Bureau and Independent Standards Authority.

REFLECTIONS AND CONCLUSION

The FOIA 2000 assists in meeting its identified objectives—openness, transparency, accountability, and access to information—but other procedures and opportunities need to be developed. Participation requires vehicles of participation and our open-meeting laws are of limited application. We still have a long way to go in this respect. The White Paper on *Open Government* (see earlier) sets out a framework for utilization of electronic communications to enhance 'personalized democracy', 'crowd sourcing', and so on. In terms of access, we have travelled far. The ministerial veto under FOIA, s. 53 is a problem and it has been used five times in the period 2012–14, and twice in the years from 2005–9. Many systems have vetoes or something similar to give government the last word on sensitive issues.[110]

In some aspects, the UK does not do well on some internationally agreed criteria for an FOI regime[111]—the virtually absolute nature of some offences under the OSA, the existence of the FOIA veto, and absolute exemptions and the breadth of some of those exemptions. On the other hand, I would add that the enforcement machinery,

---

[107] *R (T and another)* v. *Secretary of State for the Home Department Ministry of Justice* [2014] UKSC 35, para. 113, *per* Lord Reed. See, however, *R (Catt)* v. *Commissioner of Police of the Metropolis* [2015] UKSC 9.

[108] *S and Marper* v. *United Kingdom* [2008] ECHR 1581, CHR.

[109] See *Keeping the Right People on the DNA Database* (May 2009).

[110] Cf. Freedom of Information (Removal of Conclusive Certificates etc) Act 2009 (Australia).

[111] Atlanta Declaration, http://www.cartercenter.org/documents/Atlanta%20Declaration%20and%20 Plan%20of%20Action.pdf.

cost-free provision, coverage, and effectiveness of the legislation together with the existence of an independent champion make the UK leaders in world practice.

Resources to fund FOI are, and will continue to be, a problem. FOI is not likely to be considered a front-line service and has to bear the cuts falling more widely on the public sector. The Commissioner has spelt out the implications in his 2013–14 report (p. 39). For 2015–16 and beyond income and expenditure are the 'main area of uncertainty'. Despite this the Commissioner has stated that his office is 'effective, efficient and busier than ever' in his annual report subtitle for 2013–14.

As far as the future of FOI is concerned, three points are particularly prominent. First, the exclusion and absolute exemption covering the security and intelligence services and GCHQ and the National Crime Agency: is there a case for making the absolute exemption a qualified one? Section 37 also seems to give unmerited protection to royal intervention in the policy and legislative process.

The second relates to the extension of FOI to cover the private sector where private organizations are acting on behalf of the state or undertaking delivery of public service. The Coalition government in 2010 expressed a desire to extend the reach of FOI. Additions were minimal (see earlier). Privatization of public service will increase pressure for FOI extension. The possibilities for changes, mainly in relation to costs, were spelt out by the government in its reply to the Justice Committee Report.[112] Intriguingly, the government set out possibilities for extension of the Act to private bodies but its position on government contracting seemed set on voluntary arrangements.

The third point concerns elevation of FOI to the lexicon of human rights. Slowly, but gradually, this is being brought to fruition.[113] International analogues of ECHR, Art. 10 (freedom of speech) have been interpreted as providing a right to information as well as free speech.[114] The European Court of Human Rights in recent rulings has advanced beyond the denial of Art. 10 as a free-standing FOI provision,[115] so that where access to state-held information is necessary to realize the Art. 10 right, a right to information was thereby entailed.[116] The cases seemed to be travelling in one direction. In one of its most interesting judgments under the common law of fundamental rights, *Kennedy* v. *Charity Commission*, the Supreme Court refused to read down s. 32 FOIA, regarding information from a statutory inquiry held by a public authority to comply with recent ECHR rulings.[117] The majority ruled that a definitive ruling from

---

[112] See n. 100.

[113] P. Birkinshaw, 'Freedom of Information and Openness: Fundamental Human Rights?' (2006) 58 *Administrative LR* 177.

[114] *Reyes* v. *Chile* (2006) IACHR 19; American Human Rights Convention, Art. 13; and *Lund* v. *Brazil* (2010) IACHR 24.

[115] Art. 8 has been interpreted as providing a right to information as have Arts. 2, 6, and 3.

[116] *Tarsasag etc* v. *Hungary*, Application No. 37374/05 (2009); *Jihoceske Matky* v. *Czech Republic*, Application No. 19101/03, 10 July 2006. For recent case law of the CHR and the ECJ see Lord Mance in *Kennedy* (see n. 30), paras. 61–96. For international instruments see paras. 97–9. See *A* v. *Independent News Media Ltd* [2010] EWCA Civ 343 and *R (Guardian News and Media Ltd)* v. *City of Westminster Magistrates' Court* [2012] EWCA Civ 420 on the 'open justice' principle.

[117] See n. 30. 'Open justice' featured prominently in *Kennedy*.

the General Chamber was lacking. Previous Strasbourg judgments did not interpret Art. 10 is such a manner.[118] Despite the absolute nature of the exemption, the decision by the Charity Commissioners was subject to a searching judicial review with sight of the relevant materials if required by the court to make judgment de novo on disclosure, the majority ruled. The common law, said Lord Toulson, had not become an 'ossuary'! Two powerful dissenting judgments cast doubt on this approach. Would a similar common law approach to the majority be taken in the case of other absolute exemptions such as ss. 23 and 37? One can anticipate claims of context specificity. A valuable addition to a bill of rights would be a fundamental right of access to information.

Although FOIA has its critics,[119] my belief is that FOI has become an unremovable part of the constitution. As Lord Sumption expressed the point, FOIA is a landmark statute of 'great constitutional significance'.[120] Of the 90 or so countries that have such laws, none to my knowledge has repealed its FOI Act. There have been amendments making legislation less or more open; in Australia reforms have led to a removal of the veto and a strengthening of the law.[121] A secrecy bill in South Africa has met with considerable criticism. Government plans for 'personalizing democracy' through open data seem concentrated on commercial exploitation rather than enhancing participatory democracy, which was one of the objectives of FOIA. Where will citizens stand in this scheme of things? The efforts to promote transparency through non legal means must in time undermine FOI laws although many laws have an EU provenance.

In relation to data protection, many problems have emerged about information security and information privacy and effective protection for individuals. Scandals about sale of data to blacklist prospective employees, gross invasions of privacy, long-term retention of data, wide exemptions, security of holding data, and now global eaves-dropping all raise the spectre of 'Big Brother' gone amok. Despite the Protection of Freedoms Act 2012, in relation to data protection and surveillance, the whole area should be reviewed in the light of numerous studies and reviews with a view to bringing forward legislation to make the law comprehensible, workable, and effective in its balance of security and liberty. A statutory requirement of review of emergency legislation by the independent reviewer of terrorism legislation by May 2015—legislation enacted to evade an ECJ *Digital Rights* judgment—is not an appropriate response![122] The legislation will have to be revisited after the 2015 general election and is scheduled to be repealed on 31 December 2016. In March 2015 the Intelligence and Security Committee of Parliament published *Privacy and Security: a Modern and Transparent Legal Framework* HC 1075 (2014–15) arguing for a new legal surveillance framework

---

[118] *Leander v. Sweden* [1987] 9 EHRR 433.

[119] C. Hood and D. Heald (eds.), *Transparency: The Key to Better Governance* (2006).

[120] *Kennedy*, para. 153.   [121] See n. 110.

[122] The IC is not referred to in the Act in the review. See the Director of MI5's speech at n. 35 herein. See s. 46 Counter-Terrorism and Security Act 2015 and the creation of the Privacy and Civil Liberties Board.

bringing 'much greater openness and transparency regarding the Agencies' work' (109). http://isc.independent.gov.uk/committee-reports/special-reports

One thing is certain: holding, disclosing, and regulating information have been transformed in the UK in little over a decade and a half. Much of this regulation has a direct bearing on government and government–individual relationships. Information and its regulation are a dramatic illustration of the changing constitution.

FURTHER READING

BIRKINSHAW, P., *Freedom of Information: The Law, the Practice and the Ideal* (4th edn, 2010)

BIRKINSHAW, P. and VARNEY, M. *Government and Information: The Law Relating to Access, Disclosure and their Regulation* (4th edn, 2011)

COPPELL, P., *Information Rights: Law and Practice* (4th edn, 2014)

HAZELL, R., WORTHY, B., and GLOVER, M., *The Impact of the Freedom of Information Act on Central Government in the UK: Does FOI Work?* (2010)

USEFUL WEBSITES

Information Commissioner's Office: **http://www.ico.gov.uk**

The website of the Information Commissioner's Office has detailed information on the FOIA 2000 and DPA 1998, case law, guidance, etc.

Ministry of Justice, Freedom of Information policy: **https://www.justice.gov.uk/ information-access-rights**

INDEX